KEYS TO ECONOMIC PROSPERITY

These keys to the economic prosperity of a nation are highlighted throughout the text.

1. **Human Ingenuity.** Economic goods are the result of human ingenuity and action; thus, the size of the economic pie is variable, not fixed. [Chapter 2]

2. **Private Ownership.** Private ownership provides people with a strong incentive to take care of things and develop resources in ways that are highly valued by others. [Chapter 2]

3. **Gains from Trade.** Trade makes it possible for individuals to generate more output through specialization and division of labor, large-scale production processes, and the dissemination of improved products and production methods. [Chapter 2]

4. **Invisible Hand Principle.** Market prices coordinate the actions of self-interested individuals and direct them toward activities that promote the general welfare. [Chapter 3]

5. **Profits and Losses.** Profits direct producers toward activities that increase the value of resources; losses impose a penalty on those who reduce the value of resources. [Chapter 3]

6. **Price Stability.** Maintenance of price stability is the essence of sound monetary policy; price stability provides the foundation for both economic stability and the efficient operation of markets. [Chapter 14]

7. **International Trade.** When people are permitted to engage freely in international trade, they are able to achieve higher income levels and living standards than would otherwise be possible. [Chapter 18]

8. **Role of Government.** Governments promote economic progress when they protect individuals and their property, enforce contracts impartially, provide access to money of stable value, avoid high taxes and excessive regulation, and foster competitive markets and free international trade. [Chapter 16]

MACROECONOMICS
PRIVATE AND PUBLIC CHOICE

17E

JAMES D. GWARTNEY

Florida State University

RICHARD L. STROUP

Professor Emeritus of Economics at Montana State University

RUSSELL S. SOBEL

The Citadel

DAVID A. MACPHERSON

Trinity University, San Antonio TX

With Assistance of Jane Shaw Stroup

CENGAGE
Learning™

Australia • Brazil • Mexico • Singapore • United Kingdom • United States

CENGAGE
Learning™

Macroeconomics: Private and Public Choice, 17e

James D. Gwartney
Richard L. Stroup
Russell S. Sobel
David A. Mcpherson

Senior Vice President, Higher Education & Skills Product: Erin Joyner

Product Director: Joe Sabatino

Product Manager: Chris Rader

Senior Content Manager: Colleen A. Farmer

Product Assistant: Matt Schiesl

Executive Marketing Manager: John Carey

Intellectual Property Analyst: Ashley Maynard

Intellectual Property Project Manager: Carly Belcher and Nick Barrow

Production Service: Cenveo Publisher Services

Art Director: Bethany Bourgeois

Text and Cover Designer: Beth Bourgeois

Cover Image: iStockPhoto.com/MmeEmil

For product information and technology assistance, contact us at
Cengage Customer & Sales Support, 1-800-354-9706 or support.cengage.com.

For permission to use material from this text or product,
submit all requests online at www.cengage.com/permissions.

Library of Congress Control Number: 2020949571

ISBN: 978-0-357-13400-9

Cengage
200 Pier 4 Boulevard
Boston, MA 02210
USA

Cengage is a leading provider of customized learning solutions with employees residing in nearly 40 different countries and sales in more than 125 countries around the world. Find your local representative at **www.cengage.com.**

To learn more about Cengage platforms and services, register or access your online learning solution, or purchase materials for your course, visit **www.cengage.com.**

Printed in the United States of America
Print Number: 01   Print Year: 2020

BRIEF CONTENTS

CONTENTS

Chapter 17 The Economics of Development — 335

Part 4   International Economics — 355

Chapter 18 Gaining from International Trade — 356

RELATIONSHIP BETWEEN MAIN EDITION AND THE MACRO/MICRO EDITIONS

In addition to the full length text, Microeconomic and Macroeconomic splits of this text are also available. The chapters and special topics covered by the micro and macro split versions are indicated in this table.

Chapters

ECONOMICS	MICROECONOMICS	MACROECONOMICS	
1	1	1	The Economic Approach
2	2	2	Some Tools of the Economist
3	3	3	Demand, Supply, and the Market Process
4	4	4	Demand and Supply: Applications and Extensions
5	5	5	Difficult Cases for the Market, and the Role of Government
6	6	6	The Economics of Political Action
7		7	Taking the Nation's Economic Pulse
8		8	Economic Fluctuations, Unemployment, and Inflation
9		9	An Introduction to Basic Macroeconomic Markets
10		10	Dynamic Change, Economic Fluctuations, and the *AD–AS* Model
11		11	Fiscal Policy: The Keynesian View and the Historical Development of Macroeconomics
12		12	Fiscal Policy, Incentives, and Secondary Effects
13		13	Money and the Banking System
14		14	Modern Macroeconomics and Monetary Policy
15		15	Macroeconomic Policy, Economic Stability, and the Federal Debt
16		16	Creating an Environment for Growth and Prosperity
17		17	The Economics of Development
18	16	18	Gaining from International Trade
19		19	International Finance and the Foreign Exchange Market
20	7		Consumer Choice and Elasticity
21	8		Costs and the Supply of Goods
22	9		Price Takers and the Competitive Process
23	10		Price-Searcher Markets with Low Entry Barriers
24	11		Price-Searcher Markets with High Entry Barriers
25	12		The Supply of and Demand for Productive Resources
26	13		Earnings, Productivity, and the Job Market
27	14		Investment, the Capital Market, and the Wealth of Nations
28	15		Income Inequality and Poverty

SPECIAL TOPICS

Economics	Microeconomics	Macroeconomics	Topic Title
1	1	1	Government Spending and Taxation
2	2	2	The Economics of Social Security
3	3	3	The Stock Market: Its Function, Performance, and Potential as an Investment Opportunity
4	4	4	Keynes and Hayek: Contrasting Views on Sound Economics and the Role of Government
5	5	5	The 2020 COVID-19 Recession: Cause, Response, and Implications for the Future
6	6	6	The Great Recession of 2008–2009: Causes and Response
7	7	7	Lessons from the Great Depression
8	8		The Economics of Health Care
9	9		Earnings Differences between Men and Women
10	10		Do Labor Unions Increase the Wages of Workers?
11	11		The Question of Resource Exhaustion
12	12		Difficult Environmental Cases and the Role of Government

These are interesting times. Our lives have been shaken by a once-in-a-century worldwide pandemic, unemployment rates not seen since the Great Depression, racial unrest, and political uncertainty. Moreover, technology is altering how we communicate, learn, and interact with each other. Students are struggling to understand recent changes and their impact on their lives. Beginning with the first edition 45 years ago, our goal has been to use the tools of economics to explain how the real world works and to do so in a clear and understandable manner. This goal was at the forefront of our minds as we worked on this edition.

We have always used the tools of economics to analyze the operation of both the market and political processes. Both are central to the understanding of today's rapidly changing world. More than any other principles text, we highlight the roles of entrepreneurship, dynamic competition, and public choice analysis. Entrepreneurship is the key to understanding how markets work and the vast improvement in our living standards. Public choice is the key to understanding the structure of incentives confronted by voters, politicians, and bureaucrats and how this impacts political outcomes. This text examines both markets and political decision-making and indicates conditions under which each works well and alternative conditions that cause each to work poorly.

The micro chapters provide extensive coverage of entrepreneurship, innovation, and dynamic competition in the operation of markets. The macro chapters analyze the major alternative theories of both fiscal and monetary policy and provide up-to-date coverage of recent changes in Federal Reserve policy, government debt, and other factors impacting the macroeconomy. The "Beyond the Basics" Special Topics section includes features on micro topics such as the stock market, health care, and environmental economics as well as macro topics like the Great Depression, the Great Recession of 2008-2009, and the 2020 COVID-19 Recession.

ORGANIZATION AND INSTRUCTOR FLEXIBILITY

The organization of *Economics: Private and Public Choice* is designed to provide instructors with maximum flexibility. Those using the full-length text for a two-semester course can cover either microeconomics or macroeconomics first. As in recent editions, the text is divided into core chapters and a concluding special topics section. The 28 core chapters cover all of the material taught in most principles courses, and they are presented in the usual manner. Examples and data from the real world are used to reinforce the analysis. In addition, the "Beyond the Basics" Special Topics section includes 12 relatively short special topic applications covering both micro and macro topics. Features in this section address questions such as these: "How will the 2020 COVID-19 Recession impact our future?," "What caused the Great Depression?," "Is discrimination responsible for the earnings differences between men and women?," and "Are we running out of resources?" These features will grab the interest of students and are short enough to cover during a single class period. If you have not integrated the special topic materials into your course, please consider doing so. They will enrich your course and help students better understand the political economy debates that dominate the daily news of our world.

Instructors integrating public choice throughout their course will probably want to cover Chapters 5 and 6 before moving to the core micro or macro material. Others teaching a microeconomics course may want to jump from Chapter 4 directly to the core micro chapters. Correspondingly, some macroeconomics instructors will want to move directly from Chapter 3 or 4 to the core macro material. The chapters have been written so that any of these options will work.

NEW MATERIAL IN THIS EDITION

New material designed to enliven economics and illustrate its relevance has been integrated into just about every chapter. The following are several of these additions:

The coverage of entrepreneurship and its importance as a source of new goods, services, and production methods that enrich our lives has been expanded in several chapters, including 2, 3, 16, and 17. In addition, a new series, "Entrepreneurs Who Have Changed Our Lives," is integrated into about 10 chapters. This series highlights both the contributions and interesting personal attributes of key entrepreneurs. While students will recognize several of the entrepreneurs in the series, others are relatively unknown. Jeff Bezos, Kendra Scott, Steve Jobs, Malcom McLean, Sergey Brin, and Larry Page are among the entrepreneurs featured in the series. This feature will enhance the knowledge of students about how their lives are impacted by entrepreneurs.

Chapter 2 includes a new feature on "Are Scandinavian Countries Socialist?" The empirical evidence on this question is examined.

In Chapter 4, the analysis of the minimum wage, including the effect of recent increases in city and state minimums, has been updated and expanded.

Chapter 13 has been modified to reflect the recent changes in the operating procedures of the Federal Reserve, including the elimination of reserve requirements and substitution of interest payments to banks as the primary mechanism used to control bank reserves. The recent dramatic changes in the relationships between (a) bank reserves and checkable deposits, and (b) the monetary base and the money supply are also examined.

Chapter 14 examines the low interest rates of recent years and factors underlying those rates; it also analyzes their impact on both the economy and the conduct of monetary policy.

Chapter 15 examines the expanding federal debt, explains why it is so difficult to control, and analyzes the potential consequences of high levels of debt.

Chapters 16 and 17 on economic growth and development were revised extensively. These chapters highlight the fundamental causes of economic growth and provide analysis of the importance of economic institutions, climate and geography, history, demography, technology, investment, and changes in transportation and communication costs on the pattern of growth and development during the past 1000 years. Factors underlying the remarkable economic progress of developing countries during the past half-century are examined in detail. More than any other principles text, this edition reflects the modern view of economic growth and development.

The new Special Topic 5 on the 2020 COVID-19 Recession examines the factors underlying the huge increase in unemployment and the severe economic downturn. The causes of the economic crisis, the policy response, and examination of how this recession differs from earlier ones are all discussed. This feature provides the foundation for future analysis of an economic event that is sure to attract student interest in the years immediately ahead.

ADDITIONAL TEXT FEATURES

Economics: Private and Public Choice retains several features that make the presentation of economics both more interesting and understandable.

- Keys to Economic Prosperity. Students often fail to appreciate the organizational and institutional factors that are the foundation for economic progress. To help remedy this situation, we have incorporated a "Keys to Economic Prosperity" feature that highlights the importance of factors like gains from trade, secure property rights, competition, and free trade as sources of economic prosperity. In all, 12 key factors that underlie modern economic prosperity are highlighted at appropriate places throughout the text; they also are listed inside the front cover.

- Applications in Economics. "Applications in Economics" boxes apply economic theory to real-world issues and controversies. These features illustrate the importance and power of the principles covered in the text.
- Outstanding Economists. Boxes throughout the text highlight the lives of major economists and focus on how their work has contributed to the development of economics.
- Entrepreneurs Who Have Changed Our Lives. This new series highlights both the economic contribution and personal attributes of key entrepreneurs. It will help students better understand the role of entrepreneurs and how their actions have contributed to the development of various goods and services that are often taken for granted.
- Key Point Summaries. At the end of each chapter, the Key Points section provides students with a concise statement of the material covered in the chapter (the chapter learning objectives).
- Critical Analysis Questions. Each chapter concludes with a set of analysis and discussion questions designed to test students' ability to analyze economic issues and to apply economic theory to real-world events. Appendix B at the end of the text contains suggested answers for approximately a third of these questions.

SUPPLEMENTARY MATERIALS

The text is accompanied by a robust set of online learning tools designed to support your classroom work. MindTap includes real-time, interactive tutorials; online experiments; Graph Builder; A+ Test Prep; Graphing at a Glance; ConceptClips; Audio Cases with assessments; Concept & Application Videos; automatically graded quizzes; and automatically graded problem sets. Likewise, the book's dynamic PowerPoint presentation has been further enhanced to facilitate your teaching.

FOR THE STUDENT

MindTap MindTap is a fully online, highly personalized learning experience built via Cengage Learning content that combines student learning tools—readings, multimedia, activities, and assessments—into a singular Learning Path that guides students through their course.

FOR THE INSTRUCTOR

We are sure that many of the features incorporated with this textbook will help you become a better teacher and make your classes more interesting to students. Personally, we have incorporated the Keys to Economic Prosperity series, economics video clips, homework assignments, and online quiz questions into our own classes with great success. The full set of supplements that can accompany the book include the following:

MindTap MindTap is a fully online, highly personalized learning experience built via Cengage Learning content that combines student learning tools—readings, multimedia, activities, and assessments—into a singular Learning Path that guides students through their course. Instructors personalize the experience by customizing authoritative Cengage Learning content and learning tools, including the ability to add their own content in the Learning Path via apps that integrate into the MindTap framework seamlessly with Learning Management Systems.

Interactive eBook In addition to interactive teaching and learning tools, Economic MindTap includes an interactive eBook. Students can take notes, highlight, search, and interact with embedded media specific to their book. Use it as a supplement to the printed text or as a substitute—with MindTap, the choice is up to your students.

Test Banks The test banks for the 17th edition were prepared by the author team with the assistance of Shannon Aucoin and other members of Cengage's excellent team of subject matter experts. The authors have worked hard to update and improve the test banks for this edition. Joe Calhoun of Florida State University, was the primary author of the test bank for the last edition and the current version is reflective of this excellent work. The test bank contains approximately 6,000 questions—multiple choice and short answer. Within each chapter, the questions are tied to the major heads and specific topics within the chapter. Instructors who want to motivate their students to study will find online practice quizzes on MindTap that can easily be incorporated into their quizzes and exams. The cloud-based test banks for this edition have been enhanced significantly. Cognero contains all of the questions in the test bank so that you can create and customize tests in minutes. You can easily edit and import your own questions and graphics and edit and maneuver existing questions.

PowerPoint We believe our PowerPoint presentation, prepared by Joseph Connors of Florida Southern University, is the best you will find in the principles market. The presentation includes chapter-by-chapter lecture notes and hyperlinked slides of the exhibits included in the text. To facilitate classroom discussion and interaction, questions are strategically interspersed throughout the PowerPoint slides to help students develop the economic way of thinking. Instructions explaining how professors can easily add, delete, and modify slides in order to tailor the presentation to their liking are included. If instructors want to make the PowerPoint presentation available to students, they can place it on their website (or the site for their course).

Instructor's Manual Information on how to use and modify the PowerPoint material is contained in the front of the Instructor's Manual. The manual is divided by chapters, and each chapter begins with a detailed chapter outline in lecture-note form. It is designed to help instructors organize their notes to match the 17th edition of the book. Then there are focus questions which cover all the concepts in the chapter. Then the context of each chapter is given followed by important points and teaching suggestions. Each chapter also provides in-class economic games and experiments. Contributed in part by Professor Charles Stull of Kalamazoo College, the games are popular with many instructors. We hope you will try them.

The book companion Web site contains the key supplements designed to aid instructors, including the content from the Instructor's Manual, test banks, and PowerPoint lecture and exhibit slides

A NOTE TO INSTRUCTORS

As we try to improve the book from one edition to the next, we rely heavily on our experiences as teachers. But our experience using the book is minuscule compared to that of the hundreds of instructors who use it nationwide. If you encounter problems or have suggestions for improving the book, we urge you to let us know by writing to us in care of Cengage Learning, 5191 Natorp Blvd., Mason, OH 45040.

A NOTE TO STUDENTS

This textbook contains several features we think will help you maximize (a good economic term) the returns of your study efforts. Here are some of the things that will help you and a few tips for making the most of them.

- Each chapter begins with an opening page that indicates the central issues of the chapter. Before you read the chapter, briefly think about the questions the chapter will examine and how they relate to the material of prior chapters.

- The textbook is organized in the form of an outline. The headings within the text (in red) are the major points of the outline. Minor headings are subpoints under the major headings. In addition, important subpoints within sections are often set off and numbered. **_Bold italicized_** type is used to highlight material that is particularly important. Sometimes "thumbnail sketches" are included to recap material and help you keep the important points mentally organized.
- A "Key Points" summary appears at the end of each chapter. Use the summary as a checklist to determine whether you understand the major points of the chapter.
- A review of the exhibits and illustrative pictures will also provide you with a summary of the key points of each chapter. The accompanying captions briefly describe the economic phenomena illustrated by the exhibits.
- The key terms introduced in each chapter are defined in the margins. As you study the chapter, review the marginal definition of each key term as it is introduced. Later, you also may find it useful to review the marginal definitions. If you have forgotten the meaning of a term introduced earlier, consult the glossary at the end of the book.
- The critical analysis questions at the end of each chapter are intended to test your understanding of the economic way of thinking. Answering these questions and solving the problems will greatly enhance your knowledge of the material. Answers to approximately a third of these questions are provided in Appendix B.

If you need more practice, ask your professor about MindTap.

ACKNOWLEDGMENTS

A project of this magnitude is a team effort. Through the years, numerous people have assisted us in various ways. Jane Shaw Stroup deserves special recognition for her contribution to this edition. She researched and prepared the initial draft of the material on the "Entrepreneurs Who Have Changed Our Lives" series and assisted the author team with research and proofing. As a result, we listed her name on the title page. Reagan Sobel provided valuable assistance in updating examples, data, and content in many chapters. Signè Thomas, Joe Connors, Robert Lawson, Joe Calhoun, Hugo Moises Montesinos Yufa and Amy Gwartney assisted us with preparation of exhibits and proofing of the manuscript. The text still bears an imprint of the contributions of Woody Studenmund of Occidental College and Gary Galles of Pepperdine University, who assisted us in numerous ways with past editions.

We are also very much indebted to the excellent team of professionals at Cengage Learning, including Chris Rader, Product Manager; Sarah Keeling, Learning Designer; Colleen Farmer, Senior Content Project Manager; Ashley Maynard, Intellectual Property Analyst; John Carey, Marketing Manager; and Shannon Aucoin, Ethan Crist, Eugenia Belova, Brian Rodriguez, and Kasie Jean, the inhouse subject matter experts.

We have often revised material in light of suggestions made by reviewers, users, friends, and even a few competitors. In this regard, we would like to express our appreciation to the following people for their reviews and helpful suggestions for recent editions:

Pete Calcagno, College of Charleston; Joseph Calhoun, Florida State University; Cathy Carey, Bowling Green University; Lee Coppock, University of Virginia; Hugo Faría, University of Miami; Tawni Ferrarini, Northern Michigan University; Burton Folsom, Hillsdale College; Seth Gershenson, Michigan State University; Monica Greer, Bellarmine University; Michael Hammock, Florida State University; Robert Higgs, Independent Institute; John Hilston, Eastern Florida State College; Randall Holcombe, Florida State University; Aaron Lowen, Grand Valley State University; Lynn MacDonald, St. Cloud State University; Thomas McCaleb, Florida State University; Barbara Moore, University of Central Florida; Mark Perry, University of Michigan–Flint; Ivan Pongracic, Hillsdale College; Gerry Simons, Grand Valley State University; and Carol Sweeney, Florida Gulf Coast University.

Through the years, many other instructors have provided us with insightful comments and constructive suggestions. We would like to express our appreciation to the following:

Steve Abid, Grand Rapids Community College; Douglas Agbetsiafa, Indiana University, South Bend; James C. W. Ahiakpor, California State University, Hayward; Ali T. Akarca, University of Illinois at Chicago; Ryan C. Amacher, University of Texas at Arlington; Stephen A. Baker, Capital University; Bharati Basu, Central Michigan University; Don Bellante, University of South Florida; Jennis Biser, Austin Peay State University; Donald Boudreaux, George Mason University; George Bowling, St. Charles Community College; Robert Brittingham, Christian Brothers University; Byron Brown, Michigan State University; James Bryan, Manhattanville College; Kathy Clark, Florida Southwestern State College; Mike Cohick, Collin County Community College; David S. Collins, Virginia Highlands Community College; Steven R. Cunningham, University of Connecticut; Jeff Edwards, Lone Star College–CyFair; Ann Eike, University of Kentucky; Christina Esquivel, McLennan Community College; Robert C. Eyler, Sonoma State University; James R. Fain, Oklahoma State University; Andrew W. Foshee, McNeese State University; Mark Funk, University of Arkansas at Little Rock; Gary Galles, Pepperdine University;

Marsha Goldfarb, University of Maryland Baltimore County; Richard Gosselin, Houston Community College; Darrin Gulla, University of Kentucky; Barry Haworth, University of Louisville; Ronald Helgens, Golden Gate University; Robert E. Herman, Nassau Community College/SUNY; William D. Hermann, Golden Gate University, San Francisco; Rey Hernandez, Metropolitan State College of Denver; Brad Hobbs, Clemson University; Jim Hubert, Seattle Central Community College; Katherine Huger, Charleston Southern University; Woodrow W. Hughes, Jr., Converse College; Jeffrey Rogers Hummel, San Jose State University; Tom Jeitschko, Michigan State University; Rob H. Kamery, Christian Brothers University; Derek Kellenberg, University of Montana; Robert Kling, Colorado State University; Frederic R. Kolb, University of Wisconsin–Eau Claire; Barbara Kouskoulas, Lawrence Technological University; Cory Krupp, Duke University; Jean Kujawa, Lourdes University; Randy W. LaHote, Washtenaw Community College; John Larrivee, Mount St. Mary's University; Robert Lawson, Southern Methodist University; Don R. Leet, California State University, Fresno; Joe LeVesque, Northwood University; Andrew T. Light, Liberty University; Edward J. López, Western Carolina University; Dale Matcheck, Northwood University; G. Dirk Mateer, University of Texas; John McArthur, Wofford College; David M. Mitchell, Missouri State University; Hadley Mitchell, Taylor University; Glen A. Moots, Northwood University; Debasri Mukherjee, Western Michigan University; Todd Myers, Grossmont College; Jennifer Pate, Loyola Marymount University; Lloyd Orr, Indiana University, Bloomington; Judd W. Patton, Bellevue University; James Payne, University of New Orleans; Dennis Pearson, Austin Peay State University; Claudiney Pereira, Arizona State University; Jack Phelan, University of New Haven; Jennifer Platania, Elon University; Robert C. Rencher, Jr., Liberty University; Dan Rickman, Oklahoma State University; Karin L. Russell, Keiser University; Allen Sanderson, University of Chicago; Thomas W. Secrest, USC Coastal Carolina; Tim Shaugnessey, Louisiana State University–Shreveport; Gerald Simons, Grand Valley State University; Charles D. Skipton, University of New Haven; Marcia Snyder, College of Charleston; John Solow, University of Iowa; Ken Somppi, Southern Union State Community College; John Sophocleus, Auburn; Joe Stevano, Coker College; Edward Stringham, Trinity College; David Switzer, St. Cloud State University; Alex Tokarev, Northwood University; Richard D.C. Trainer, Warsaw School of Economics; Bich Tran, San Jacinto College; Scott Ward, Trevecca Nazarene University; Christopher Westley, Florida Gulf Coast University; David Wharton, Washington College; Mark Wheeler, Western Michigan University; Edward Wolpert, University of Central Florida; and Janice Yee, Worcester State University.

James D. Gwartney is Professor of Economics at Florida State University, where he holds the Gus A. Stavros Eminent Scholar Chair of Economic Education. He is a co-author of *Common SenseEconomics: What Everyone Should Know About Wealth And Prosperity* (St. Martin's Press, 2016), a primer on economics and personal finance. He is also the co-author of the annual report *Economic Freedom of the World*, which provides information on the consistency of institutions and policies with economic freedom for more than 160 countries. His publications have appeared in scholarly journals, including the *American Economic Review*, *Journal of Political Economy*, *Journal of Economic Education*, *Southern Economic Journal*, and *Journal of Institutional and Theoretical Economics*. During 1999–2000, he served as Chief Economist of the Joint Economic Committee of the U. S. Congress. He is a past president of the Southern Economic Association and the Association of Private Enterprise Education. His Ph.D. in economics is from the University of Washington.

Richard L. Stroup is Professor Emeritus of economics at Montana State University and Professor Emeritus of economics at North Carolina State University. His Ph.D. is from the University of Washington. From 1982–1984, he served as Director of the Office of Policy Analysis at the U.S. Department of the Interior. Stroup has published and spoken on global warming, land use regulation, archaeology, and needed environmental policy improvements. His research helped to develop the approach known as free market environmentalism. His book *Eco-nomics: What Everyone Should Know About Economics and the Environment* (Washington: Cato Institute, 2003), was sponsored by the Property and Environment Research Center, of which he is a cofounder.

Russell S. Sobel is Professor of Economics and Entrepreneurship in the Baker School of Business at The Citadel in his hometown of Charleston, South Carolina. He is co-editor of the *Southern Economic Journal* and editorial board member for the *Journal of Entrepreneurship & Public Policy* and *Public Choice*. He has received numerous awards for both his teaching and research including the Kenneth G. Elzinga Distinguished Teaching Award from the Southern Economic Association, the Georgescu-Roegen Prize for Best Article of the Year in the *Southern Economic Journal*, the Association of Private Enterprise Education Distinguished Scholar Award, and the Sir Antony Fisher International Memorial Award. He is the author or coauthor of over 250 books and articles including *Growth and Variability in State Tax Revenue: An Anatomy of State Fiscal Crises*, *The Rule of Law*, *Unleashing Capitalism*, and *The Essential Joseph Schumpeter*. His scholarly publications have appeared in journals such as the *Journal of Political Economy*, *Journal of Law and Economics*, *Public Choice*, *Journal of Business Venturing*, *Small Business Economics*, and *Economic Inquiry*. His current research focuses on the intersection of entrepreneurship and economic policy. His Ph.D. in economics is from Florida State University.

David A. Macpherson is the E.M. Stevens Professor of Economics and Economics Department Chair at Trinity University. Previously, he was Director of the Pepper Institute on Aging and Public Policy and the Rod and Hope Brim Eminent Scholar of Economics at Florida State University, where he received two university-wide awards for teaching excellence. His teaching areas include principles of microeconomics, money and banking, econometrics, and labor economics. Dr. Macpherson is an applied economist whose research focuses on real estate, pensions, discrimination, industry deregulation, labor unions, and the minimum wage. He has published more than 60 articles in leading economics and real estate journals, including *Review of Economics and Statistics*, *Journal of Labor*

Economics, *Journal of Human Resources*, *Industrial and Labor Relations Review*, and *Journal of Real Estate Economics and Finance*. His research has been funded by a variety of entities including the National Science Foundation, Florida Legislature, and the National Association of Realtors. He is co-author of the undergraduate labor economics text, *Contemporary Labor Economics, 12e*. He is included in *Who's Who in Economics, 4e*, which includes the 1,200 most frequently cited economists. Dr. Macpherson received his undergraduate degree and Ph.D. from Pennsylvania State University.

PART 1

The Economic Way of Thinking

Life is a series of choices

Economics is about how people choose. The choices we make influence our lives and those of others. Your future will be influenced by the choices you make with regard to education, job opportunities, savings, and investment. Furthermore, changes in technology, demographics, communications, and transportation are constantly altering the attractiveness of various options and the opportunities available to us. The economic way of thinking is all about how incentives alter the choices people make. It can help you make better choices and enhance your understanding of our dynamic world.

CHAPTER 1

The Economic Approach

Economist, n.–A scoundrel whose faulty vision sees things as they really are, not as they ought to be. —**Daniel K. Benjamin, after Ambrose Bierce**

Welcome to the world of economics. In recent years, economics has often been front-page news, and it affects all of our lives. Soaring unemployment as the result of the stay-at-home orders accompanying the 2020 COVID-19 pandemic, the rise of online work and school, the growth of the sharing economy, concern about robots eliminating jobs, tariffs on international trade, the rising cost of a college education, income inequality, and climate change—all of these have been in the news and have exerted a major impact on the lives of almost everyone around the world. Economics will enhance your understanding of all of these topics and many more. You will soon see that economics is about much more than just financial markets and economic policy. In fact, a field trip to the fruits and vegetables section at your local grocery store could well be filled with more economics lessons than a trip to the New York Stock Exchange.

In a nutshell, economics is the study of human behavior, with a particular focus on human decision-making. It will introduce you to a new and powerful way of thinking that will both help you make better decisions and enhance your understanding of how the world works.

You may have heard some of the following statements: The soaring federal debt is mortgaging the future of our children, and it will bankrupt the country if we do not get it under control. Foreign immigrants are stealing our jobs and paralyzing our economy. A move toward socialism would improve outcomes in the United States. A higher minimum wage will help the poor. Making college tuition free for all will promote economic growth and lead to higher earnings. Are these statements true? This course will provide you with knowledge that will enhance your understanding of issues like these and numerous others. It may even alter the way you think about them.

The origins of economics date back to Adam Smith, a Scottish moral philosopher, who expressed the first economic ideas in his breakthrough book, *An Inquiry into the Nature and Causes of the Wealth of Nations*, published in 1776. As the title of his book suggests, Smith sought to explain why people in some nations were wealthier than those in others. This very question is still a central issue in economics. It is so important that throughout this book we will use a special "Keys to Economic Prosperity" symbol in the margin to highlight sections that focus on this topic.

A listing of the major keys to prosperity is presented inside the front cover of the book. These keys and accompanying discussions will help you understand what factors enable economies, and their citizens, to grow wealthier and prosper.

As you read this chapter, look for answers to the following questions:

- What is scarcity? Why does scarcity necessitate rationing and cause competition?

- What is the economic way of thinking? What is the basic postulate of economics, and why is it so important?

- What is the difference between positive and normative economics?

©Bettmann/CORBIS

Outstanding Economist: The Importance of Adam Smith, the Father of Economic Science

Economics is a relatively young science. The foundation of economics was laid in 1776, when Adam Smith (1723–1790) published *An Inquiry into the Nature and Causes of the Wealth of Nations.*

Smith was a lecturer at the University of Glasgow, in his native Scotland. Before economics, morals and ethics were actually his concern. His first book was *The Theory of Moral Sentiments.* For Smith, self-interest and sympathy for others were complementary. However, he did not believe that charity alone would provide the essentials for a good life.

Smith stressed that free exchange and competitive markets would harness self-interest as a creative force. He believed that individuals *pursuing their own interests* would be directed by the "invisible hand" of market prices toward the production of those goods that were most advantageous to society. He argued that the wealth of a nation does not lie in gold and silver, but rather in the goods and services produced and consumed by people. According to Smith, competitive markets would lead to coordination, order, and efficiency without the direction of a central authority.

These were revolutionary ideas at the time, but they had consequences. Smith's ideas greatly influenced not only Europeans but also those who developed the political economy structure of the United States. Further, Smith's notion of the "invisible hand" of the market continues to enhance our understanding of why some nations prosper while others stagnate.[1]

[1]For an excellent biographical sketch of Adam Smith, see David Henderson, ed., *The Fortune Encyclopedia of Economics* (New York: Warner Books, 1993), 836–38. The entire text of this useful encyclopedia is now available online, free of charge, at https://oll.libertyfund.org/titles/1064.

1-1 WHAT IS ECONOMICS ABOUT?

Economics is about scarcity and the choices we have to make because our desire for goods and services is far greater than their availability from nature. Would you like some new clothes, a nicer car, and a larger apartment? How about better grades and more time to watch television, go skiing, and travel? Do you dream of driving your brand-new Porsche into the driveway of your oceanfront house? As individuals, we have a desire for goods that is virtually unlimited. We may want all of these things. Unfortunately, both as individuals and as a society we face a constraint called **scarcity** that prevents us from being able to completely fulfill our desires.

Scarcity is present whenever there is less of a good or resource freely available than people would like. There are some things that are not scarce—seawater comes to mind; nature has provided as much of it as people want. But almost everything else you can think of—even your time—is scarce. In economics, the word *scarce* has a very specific meaning that differs slightly from the way it is commonly used. Even if large amounts of a good have been produced, it is still scarce as long as there is not as much of it *freely available* as we would all like. For example, even though goods like apples and automobiles are

Scarcity
Fundamental concept of economics that indicates that there is less of a good freely available than people would like.

relatively abundant in the United States, they are still scarce because we would like to have more of them than nature has freely provided. In economics, we generally wish to determine only if a good is scarce or not, and refrain from using the term to refer to the relative availability or abundance of a good or resource.

Because of scarcity, we have to make choices. Should I spend the next hour studying or watching TV? Should I spend my last $20 on a new cell phone case or on a shirt? Should this factory be used to produce clothing or furniture? **Choice**, the act of selecting among alternatives, is the logical consequence of scarcity. When we make choices, we constantly face trade-offs between meeting one desire or another. To meet one need, we must let another go unmet. The basic ideas of *scarcity* and *choice*, along with the *trade-offs* we face, provide the foundation for economic analysis.

Resources are the ingredients, or inputs, that people use to produce goods and services. Our ability to produce goods and services is limited precisely because of the limited nature of our resources.

Exhibit 1 lists a number of scarce goods and the limited resources that might be used to produce them. There are three general categories of resources. First, there are *human resources*—the productive knowledge, skill, and strength of human beings. Second, there are *physical resources*—things like tools, machines, and buildings that enhance our ability to produce goods. Economists often use the term **capital** when referring to these human-made resources. Third, there are *natural resources*—things like land, mineral deposits, oceans, and rivers. The ingenuity of humans is often required to make these natural resources useful in production. For example, until recently, the yew tree was considered a "trash tree," having no economic value. Then, scientists discovered that the tree produces taxol, a substance that could be used to fight cancer. Human knowledge and ingenuity made yew trees a valuable resource. As you can see, natural resources are important, but knowing how to use them productively is just as important. This knowledge is something that is discovered as a result of the competitive market process.

As economist Thomas Sowell points out, cavemen had the same natural resources at their disposal that we do today. The huge difference between their standard of living and ours reflects the difference in the knowledge they could bring to bear on those resources versus what we can.[1] Over time, human ingenuity, discovery, improved knowledge, and better technology have enabled us to produce more goods and services from the available resources. Nonetheless, our desire for goods and services is still far greater than our ability to produce them. Thus, scarcity is a fact of life today, and in the foreseeable future. As a result, we confront trade-offs and have to make choices. This is what economics is about.

Choice
The act of selecting among alternatives.

Resource
An input used to produce economic goods. Land, labor, skills, natural resources, and human-made tools and equipment provide examples. Throughout history, people have struggled to transform available, but limited, resources into things they would like to have—economic goods.

Capital
Human-made resources (such as tools, equipment, and structures) used to produce other goods and services. They enhance our ability to produce in the future.

EXHIBIT 1

A General Listing of Scarce Goods and Limited Resources

History is a record of our struggle to transform available, but limited, resources into goods that we would like to have.

SCARCE GOODS	LIMITED RESOURCES
Food (bread, milk, meat, eggs, vegetables, coffee, etc.)	Land (various degrees of fertility)
Clothing (shirts, pants, blouses, shoes, socks, coats, sweaters, etc.)	Natural resources (rivers, trees, minerals, oceans, etc.)
Household goods (tables, chairs, rugs, beds, dressers, televisions, etc.)	Machines and other human-made physical resources
Education	Nonhuman animal resources
National defense	Technology (physical and scientific "recipes" of history)
Leisure time	Human resources (the knowledge, skill, and talent of individual human beings)
Entertainment	
Clean air	
Pleasant environment (trees, lakes, rivers, open spaces, etc.)	
Pleasant working conditions	

---

[1] Thomas Sowell, *Knowledge and Decisions* (New York: Basic Books, 1980), 47.

1-1a SCARCITY AND POVERTY ARE NOT THE SAME

Think for a moment about what life was like in 1750. People all over the world struggled 50, 60, and 70 hours a week to obtain the basic necessities of life—food, clothing, and shelter. Manual labor was the major source of income. Animals provided the means of transportation. Tools and machines were primitive by today's standards. As the English philosopher Thomas Hobbes stated in the seventeenth century, life was "solitary, poor, nasty, brutish, and short."[2]

Throughout much of South America, Africa, and Asia, economic conditions today continue to make life difficult. In North America, Western Europe, Oceania, and some parts of Asia, however, economic progress has substantially reduced physical hardship and human drudgery. In these regions, the typical family is more likely to worry about financing its summer vacation than about obtaining food and shelter. As anyone who has watched the TV reality show *Survivor* knows, we take for granted many of the items that modern technological advances have allowed us to produce at unbelievably low prices. Contestants on *Survivor* struggle with even basic things like starting a fire, finding shelter, and catching fish. They are thrilled when they win ordinary items like shampoo, rice, and toilet paper. During one episode, a contestant eagerly paid over $125 for a small chocolate bar and spoonful of peanut butter at an auction—and she considered it a great bargain!

It is important to note that scarcity and poverty are not the same thing. Scarcity is an **objective** concept that describes a factual situation in which the limited nature of our resources keeps us from being able to completely fulfill our desires for goods and services. In contrast, poverty is a **subjective** concept that refers to a personal opinion of whether someone meets an arbitrarily defined level of income. This distinction is made even clearer when you realize that different people have vastly different ideas of what it means to be poor. The average family in the United States that meets the federal government's definition of being "in poverty" would be considered wealthy in most any country in Africa. A family in the United States in the 1950s would have been considered fairly wealthy if it had air conditioning, an automatic dishwasher or clothes dryer, or a television. Today, the majority of U.S. families officially classified as poor have many items that would have been viewed as symbols of great wealth just 70 years ago.

People always want more and better goods for themselves and others about whom they care. Scarcity is the constraint that prevents us from having as much of *all* goods as we would like, but it is not the same as poverty. Even if every individual were rich, scarcity would still be present.

Objective
A fact based on observable phenomena that is not influenced by differences in personal opinion.

Subjective
An opinion based on personal preferences and value judgments.

Monty Brinton/CBS Photo Archive/Getty Images

The degree to which modern technology and knowledge allow us to fulfill our desires and ease the grip of scarcity is often taken for granted—as the castaways on the CBS reality series Survivor quickly find out when they have to struggle to meet even basic needs, such as food, shelter, and cleaning their bodies and clothes.

[2]Thomas Hobbes, *Leviathan* (1651), Part I, Chapter 13.

1-1b SCARCITY NECESSITATES RATIONING

Rationing
Allocating a limited supply of a good or resource among people who would like to have more of it. When price performs the rationing function, the good or resource is allocated to those willing to give up the most "other things" in order to get it.

Scarcity makes **rationing** a necessity. When a good or resource is scarce, some criterion must be used to determine who will receive it and who will go without. The choice of which method is used will, however, have an influence on human behavior. When rationing is done through the government sector, a person's political status and ability to manipulate the political process are the key factors. Powerful interest groups and those in good favor with influential politicians will be the ones who obtain goods and resources. When this method of rationing is used, people will devote time and resources to lobbying and favor seeking with those who have political power, rather than to productive activities.

When the criterion is first-come, first-served, goods are allocated to those who are fastest at getting in line or willing to spend the longest time waiting in line or searching at many different sellers or locations. Many colleges use this method to ration tickets to sporting events, and the result is students waiting in long lines. Sometimes, as at Duke University during basketball season, they even camp out for multiple nights to get good tickets! Imagine how the behavior of students would change if tickets were instead given out to the students with the highest grade point average.

In a market economy, price is generally used to ration goods and resources only to those who are willing and able to pay the prevailing market price. Because only those goods that are scarce require rationing, in a market economy one easy way to determine whether a good or resource is scarce is to ask if it sells for a price. If you have to pay for something, it is scarce.

1-1c THE METHOD OF RATIONING INFLUENCES THE NATURE OF COMPETITION

Competition is a natural outgrowth of scarcity and the desire of human beings to improve their conditions. Competition exists in every economy and every society. But the criteria used to ration scarce goods and resources will influence the competitive techniques employed. When the rationing criterion is price, individuals will engage in income-generating activities that enhance their ability to pay the price needed to buy the goods and services they want. Thus, one benefit of using price as a rationing mechanism is that it encourages individuals to engage in the production of goods and services to generate income. In contrast, rationing on the basis of first-come, first-served encourages individuals to waste a substantial amount of time waiting in line or searching, while rationing through the political process encourages individuals to waste time and other resources in competing with others to influence the political process.

Within a market setting, the competition that results from scarcity is an important ingredient in economic progress. Competition among business firms for customers results in newer, better, and less expensive goods and services. Competition between employers for workers results in higher wages, benefits, and better working conditions. Further, competition encourages discovery and innovation, two important sources of growth and higher living standards.

It [economics] is a method rather than a doctrine, an apparatus of the mind, a technique of thinking which helps its possessor to draw correct conclusions.

—John Maynard Keynes[3]

1-2 THE ECONOMIC WAY OF THINKING

One does not have to spend much time around economists to recognize that there is an "economic way of thinking." Admittedly, economists, like others, differ widely in their ideological views. A news commentator once remarked that "any half-dozen economists will normally come up with about six different policy prescriptions." Yet, in spite of their philosophical differences, the approaches of economists reflect common ground.

---

[3]John Maynard Keynes (1883–1946) was an English economist whose writings during the 1920s and 1930s exerted an enormous impact on both economic theory and policy. Keynes established the terminology and the economic framework that are still widely used when economists study problems of unemployment and inflation.

That common ground is **economic theory**, developed from basic principles of human behavior. Economic researchers are constantly involved in testing and seeking to verify their theories. When the evidence from the testing is consistent with a theory, eventually that theory will become widely accepted among economists. Economic theory, like a road map or a guidebook, establishes reference points indicating what to look for and how economic issues are interrelated. To a large degree, the basic economic principles are merely common sense. When applied consistently, however, these commonsense concepts can provide powerful and sometimes surprising insights.

Economic theory
A set of definitions, postulates, and principles assembled in a manner that makes clear the "cause-and-effect" relationships.

1-2a EIGHT GUIDEPOSTS TO ECONOMIC THINKING

The economic way of thinking requires incorporating certain guidelines—some would say the building blocks of basic economic theory—into your own thought process. Once you incorporate these guidelines, economics can be a relatively easy subject to master. Students who have difficulty with economics have almost always failed to assimilate one or more of these principles. The following are eight principles that characterize the economic way of thinking. We will discuss each of these principles in more depth throughout the book so that you will be sure to understand how and when to apply them.

1. The use of scarce resources is costly, so decision-makers must make trade-offs. Economists sometimes refer to this as the "there is no such thing as a free lunch" principle. Because resources are scarce, the use of resources to produce one good diverts those resources from the production of other goods. A parcel of undeveloped land could be used for a new hospital or a parking lot, or it could simply be left undeveloped. No option is free of cost—there is always a trade-off. A decision to pursue any one of these options means that the decision-maker must sacrifice the others. The highest valued alternative that is sacrificed is the **opportunity cost** of the option chosen. For example, if you use one hour of your scarce time to study economics, you will have one hour less time to watch television, spend on social media, sleep, work at a job, or study other subjects. Whichever one of these options you would have chosen had you *not* spent the hour studying economics is your highest valued option forgone. If you would have slept, then the opportunity cost of this hour spent studying economics is a forgone hour of sleep. In economics, the opportunity cost of an action is the highest valued option given up when a choice is made.

Opportunity cost
The highest valued alternative that must be sacrificed as a result of choosing an option.

It is important to recognize that the use of scarce resources to produce a good is always costly, regardless of who pays for the good or service produced. In many countries, various kinds of schooling are provided free of charge *to students*. However, provision of the schooling is not free *to the community as a whole*. The scarce resources used to produce the schooling—to construct the building, hire teachers, buy equipment, and so on—could have been used instead to produce more recreation, entertainment, housing, medical care, or other goods. The opportunity cost of the schooling is the highest valued option that must now be given up because the required resources were used to produce the schooling.

By now, the central point should be obvious. As we make choices, we always face trade-offs. Using resources to do one thing leaves fewer resources to do another.

When a scarce resource is used to meet one need, other competing needs must be sacrificed. The forgone shoe store is an example of the opportunity cost of building the new drugstore.

Consider one final example. Mandatory air bags in automobiles save an estimated 400 lives each year. Economic thinking, however, forces us to ask ourselves if the $50 billion spent on air bags could have been used in a better way—perhaps say, for cancer research that could have saved *more* than 400 lives per year. Most people don't like to think of air bags and cancer research as an "either/or" proposition. It's more convenient to ignore these trade-offs. But if we want to get the most out of our resources, we have to consider all of our alternatives. In this case, the appropriate analysis is not simply the lives saved with air bags versus dollars spent on them, but also the number of lives that could have been saved (or other things that could have been accomplished) if the $50 billion had been used differently. A candid consideration of hard trade-offs like this is essential to using our resources wisely.

2. Individuals choose purposefully—they try to get the most from their limited resources.

Economizing behavior
Choosing the option that offers the greatest benefit at the least possible cost.

People try not to squander their valuable resources deliberately. Instead, they try to choose the options that best advance their personal desires and goals at the least possible cost. This is called **economizing behavior**. Economizing behavior is the result of purposeful, or rational, decision-making. When choosing among things of equal benefit, an economizer will select the cheapest option. For example, if a pizza, a lobster dinner, and a sirloin steak are expected to yield identical benefits for Mary (including the enjoyment of eating them), economizing behavior implies that Mary will select the cheapest of the three alternatives, probably the pizza. Similarly, when choosing among alternatives of equal cost, economizing decision-makers will select the option that yields the greatest benefit. If the prices of several dinner specials are equal, for example, economizers will choose the one they like the best. Because of economizing behavior, the desires or preferences of individuals are revealed by the choices they make.

Utility
The subjective benefit or satisfaction a person expects from a choice or course of action.

Purposeful choosing implies that decision-makers have some basis for their evaluation of alternatives. Economists refer to this evaluation as **utility**—the benefit or satisfaction that an individual expects from the choice of a specific alternative. Utility is highly subjective, often differing widely from person to person. The steak dinner that delights one person may be repulsive to another (a vegetarian, for example).

The idea that people behave rationally to get the greatest benefit at the least possible cost is a powerful tool. It can help us understand their choices. However, we need to realize that a rational choice is not the same thing as a "right" choice. If we want to understand people's choices, we need to understand their own subjective evaluations of their options *as they see them*. As we have said, different people have different preferences. If Joan prefers $10 worth of chocolate to $10 worth of vegetables, buying the chocolate would be the rational choice for her, even though some outside observer might say that Joan is making a "bad" decision. Similarly, some motorcycle riders choose to ride without a helmet because they believe the enjoyment they get from riding without one is greater than the cost (the risk of injury). When people weigh the benefits they receive from an activity against its cost, they are making a rational choice—even though it might not be the choice you or I would make in the same situation.

Because consumers respond to incentives, store owners know they can sell off excess inventory by reducing prices.

3. Incentives matter—changes in incentives influence human choices in a predictable way. Both monetary and nonmonetary incentives matter.

If the personal cost of an option increases, people will be less likely to choose it. Correspondingly, when an option becomes more attractive, people will be more likely to choose it. This vitally important guidepost, sometimes called the basic postulate of economics, is a powerful tool because it applies to almost everything that we do.

Think about the implications of this proposition. When late for an appointment, a person will be less likely to take time to stop and visit with a friend. Fewer people will go picnicking on a cold and rainy day. Higher prices will reduce the number of units consumers will want to purchase. Attendance in college classes will be below normal the day before spring break. During the 2020 COVID-19 pandemic, persons over the age of 70 were far less likely than the young to go out to grocery stores and practiced greater social distancing,

effects are unintended. Changes in government policy often alter incentives, indirectly affecting how much people work, earn, invest, consume, and conserve for the future. When a change alters incentives, *unintended consequences* that are quite different from the intended consequences may occur.

Let's consider a couple of examples that illustrate the potential importance of unintended consequences. In an effort to help the environment, many jurisdictions, including San Francisco County, have banned plastic grocery bags. However, reusable grocery bags tend to gather harmful bacteria, such as E. coli, with repeated use. A study published by the University of Pennsylvania found that emergency room visits and deaths related to these bacteria have risen by 25 percent in areas banning plastic bags. Once you consider the harmful secondary effects on human health, these regulations are significantly less beneficial than they might first appear.

Trade restrictions between nations have important secondary effects as well. The proponents of tariffs and quotas on foreign goods almost always ignore the secondary effects of their policies. Import quotas restricting the sale of foreign-produced sugar in the U.S. market, for example, have resulted in domestic sugar prices that have often been two or three times the price in the rest of the world. The proponents of this policy—primarily sugar producers—argue that the quotas "save jobs" and increase employment. No doubt, the employment of sugar growers in the United States is higher than it otherwise would be. But what about the secondary effects? The higher sugar prices mean it's more expensive for U.S. firms to produce candy and other products that use a lot of sugar. As a result, many candy producers, including the makers of Life Savers, Jaw Breakers, Red Hots, and most candy canes, have moved to countries like Canada and Mexico, where sugar can be purchased at its true market price. Thus, employment among sugar-using firms in the United States is reduced. Further, because foreigners sell less sugar in the United States, they have less purchasing power with which to buy products we export to them. This, too, reduces U.S. employment.

Once the secondary effects of trade restrictions like tariffs on imported goods are taken into consideration, we have no reason to expect that U.S. employment will increase as a result. There may be more jobs in favored industries, but there will be less employment in others. Trade restrictions reshuffle employment rather than increase it. But those who unwittingly fail to consider the secondary effects will miss this point. Clearly, consideration of the secondary effects is an important ingredient of the economic way of thinking.

7. The value of a good or service is subjective.
Preferences differ, sometimes dramatically, between individuals. How much is a ticket to see a performance of the Bolshoi Ballet worth? Some people would be willing to pay a very high price, while others might prefer to stay home, even if tickets were free! Circumstances can change from day to day, even for a given individual. Alice, a ballet fan who usually would value the ticket at more than its price of $100, is invited to a party and suddenly becomes uninterested in attending the ballet. Now what is the ticket worth? If she knows a friend who would give her $40 for the ticket, it is worth at least that much. If she advertises the ticket on StubHub and gets $60 for it, a higher value is created. But if someone who doesn't know of the ticket would have been willing to pay even more, then a potential trade creating even more value is missed. If that particular performance is sold out, perhaps someone in town would be willing to pay $120. One thing is certain: The value of the ticket depends on several things, including who uses it and under what circumstances.

Economics recognizes that people can and do value goods differently. Mike may prefer to have a grass field rather than a parking lot next to his workplace and be willing to bear the cost of walking farther from his car each day. Kim, on the other hand, may prefer the parking lot and the shorter walk. As a science, economics does not place any inherent

THE FAMILY CIRCUS®   **By Bil Keane**

3-25

Copyright 1988
Cowles Syndicate, Inc

"Everybody wants to be sick.
I'm using M&M's for pills."

Bil Keane, Inc. King Features Syndicate

Sometimes actions change the incentives people face and they respond accordingly, creating secondary effects that were not intended.

moral judgment or value on one person's preferences over another's—in economics, all individuals' preferences are counted equally. Because the subjective preferences of individuals differ, it is difficult for one person to know how much another will value an item.

Think about how hard it is to know what would make a good gift for even a close friend or family member. Thus, arranging trades, or otherwise moving items to higher valued users and uses, is not a simple task. The entrepreneurial individual, who knows how to locate the right buyers and arranges for goods to flow to their highest valued use, can sometimes create huge increases in value from existing resources. In fact, moving goods toward those who value them most and combining resources into goods that individuals value more highly are primary sources of economic progress.

Scientific thinking
Developing a theory from basic principles and testing it against events in the real world. Good theories are consistent with and help explain real-world events. Theories that are inconsistent with the real world are invalid and must be rejected.

8. The test of a theory is its ability to predict. Economic thinking is **scientific thinking.** The proof of the pudding is in the eating. How useful an economic theory is depends on how well it predicts the future consequences of economic action. Economists develop economic theories using scientific thinking based on basic principles. The idea is to predict how incentives will affect decision makers and compare the predictions against real-world events. If the events in the real world are consistent with a theory, we say that the theory has *predictive value* and is therefore valid.

If it is impossible to test the theoretical relationships of a discipline, the discipline does not qualify as a science. Because economics deals with human beings who can think and respond in a variety of ways, can economic theories really be tested? The answer to this question is yes, if, on average, human beings respond in predictable and consistent ways to changes in economic conditions. The economist believes that this is the case, even though not all individuals will respond in the specified manner. Economists usually do not try to predict the behavior of a specific individual; instead, they focus on the general behavior of a large number of individuals.

In the 1950s, economists began to do laboratory experiments to test economic theories. Individuals were brought into laboratories to see how they would act in buying and selling situations, under differing rules. For example, cash rewards were given to individuals who, when an auction was conducted, were able to sell at high prices and buy at low prices, thus approximating real-world market incentives. These experiments have verified many of the important propositions of economic theory.

Laboratory experiments, however, cannot duplicate all real economic interactions. How can we test economic theory when controlled experiments are not feasible? This is a problem, but economics is no different from astronomy in this respect. Astronomers can use theories tested in physics laboratories, but they must also deal with the world as it is. They cannot change the course of the stars or planets to see what impact the change would have on the gravitational pull of Earth. Similarly, economists cannot arbitrarily change the prices of cars or unskilled-labor services in real markets just to observe the effects on quantities purchased or levels of employment. However, economic conditions (for example, prices, production costs, technology, and transportation costs), like the location of the planets, do change from time to time. As actual conditions change, an economic theory can be tested by comparing its predictions with real-world outcomes. Just as the universe is the main laboratory of the astronomer, the real-world economy is the primary laboratory of the economist.

1-3 POSITIVE AND NORMATIVE ECONOMICS

As a social science, economics is concerned with predicting or determining the impact of changes in economic variables on the actions of human beings. Scientific economics, commonly referred to as **positive economics**, attempts to determine "what is." Positive economic statements involve potentially verifiable or refutable propositions. For example, "If the price of gasoline rises, people will buy less gasoline." We can statistically investigate (and estimate) the relationship between gasoline prices and gallons sold. We can analyze the facts to determine the correctness of a positive economic statement. Remember, a positive economic statement need not be correct; it simply must be testable.

Positive economics
The scientific study of "what is" among economic relationships.

In contrast, **normative economics** is about "what ought to be," given the preferences and philosophical views of the advocate. Value judgments often result in disagreement about normative economic matters. Two people may differ on a policy matter because one is from one political party and the other is from another, or because one wants cheaper food while the other favors organic farming (which is more expensive), and so on. They may even agree about the expected outcome of altering an economic variable (that is, the positive economics of an issue), but disagree as to whether that outcome is desirable.

Unlike positive economic statements, normative economic statements can neither be confirmed nor proven false by scientific testing. "Business firms should not be concerned with profits." "We should have fewer parking lots and more green space on campus." "The price of gasoline is too high." These normative statements cannot be scientifically tested because their validity rests on value judgments.

Normative economic views can sometimes influence our attitude toward positive economic analysis, however. When we agree with the objectives of a policy, it's easy to overlook the warnings of positive economics. Although positive economics does not tell us which policy is best, it can provide evidence about the likely effects of a policy. Sometimes proponents unknowingly support policies that are actually in conflict with their own goals and objectives. Positive economics, based on sound economic logic, can help overcome this potential problem.

Economics can expand our knowledge of how the real world operates, in both the private and the public (government) sectors. However, it is not always easy to isolate the impact of economic changes. Let's now consider some pitfalls to avoid in economic thinking.

> **Normative economics**
> Judgments about "what ought to be" in economic matters. Normative economic views cannot be proved false because they are based on value judgments.

1-4 PITFALLS TO AVOID IN ECONOMIC THINKING

1-4a VIOLATION OF THE *CETERIS PARIBUS* CONDITION CAN LEAD ONE TO DRAW THE WRONG CONCLUSION

Economists often qualify their statements with the words ***ceteris paribus***. *Ceteris paribus* is a Latin term meaning "other things constant." An example of a *ceteris paribus* statement would be the following: "*Ceteris paribus*, an increase in the price of housing will cause buyers to reduce their purchases of housing." However, we live in a dynamic world, so things seldom remain constant. For example, as the price of housing rises, the income of consumers might also increase for unrelated reasons. Each of these factors—higher housing prices and increasing consumer income—will have an impact on housing purchases. In fact, we would generally expect them to have opposite effects: Higher prices are likely to reduce housing purchases, whereas higher consumer incomes are likely to increase them. We point out this pitfall because sometimes statistical data (or casual observations) appear inconsistent with economic theories. In most of these cases, the apparent contradictions reflect the effects of changes in other factors (violations of the *ceteris paribus* conditions). The observed effects are the result of the combination of the changes.

The task of sorting out the effects of two or more variables that change at the same time is difficult. However, with a strong grip on economic theory, some ingenuity, and enough data, it can usually be done. This is, in fact, precisely the day-to-day work of many professional economists.

> **Ceteris paribus**
> A Latin term meaning "other things constant" that is used when the effect of one change is being described, recognizing that if other things changed, they also could affect the result. Economists often describe the effects of one change, knowing that in the real world, other things might change and also exert an effect.

1-4b GOOD INTENTIONS DO NOT GUARANTEE DESIRABLE OUTCOMES

There is a tendency to believe that if the proponents of a policy have good intentions, their proposals must be sound. This is not necessarily the case. Proponents may be unaware of some of the adverse secondary effects of their proposals, particularly when they are indirect and observable only over time. Even if their policies would be largely ineffective, politicians may still find it advantageous to call attention to the severity of a problem and propose a program to deal with it. In other cases, proponents of a policy may actually be seeking a goal other than the one they espouse. They may tie their arguments to objectives that are widely supported by the general populace. Thus, the fact that an advocate says a program will help the economy, expand employment, help the poor, increase wages, improve health care, or achieve some other highly desirable objective does not necessarily make it so.

Let's begin with a couple of straightforward examples. Federal legislation has been introduced that would require all children, including those under age two, to be fastened in a child safety seat when traveling by air. Proponents argue the legislation will increase the survival rate of children in the case of an airline crash and thereby save lives. Certainly, saving lives is a highly desirable objective, but will this really be the case? *Some* lives will probably be saved. But what about the secondary effects? The legislation would mean that a parent traveling with a small child would have to purchase an additional ticket, which will make it more expensive to fly. As a result, many families will choose to travel by auto rather than by air. Because the likelihood of a serious accident per mile traveled in an automobile is several times higher than for air travel, more automobile travel will result in more injuries and fatalities. In fact, studies indicate that the increase in injuries and fatalities from additional auto travel will exceed the number of lives saved by airline safety seats.[4] Thus, even though the intentions of the proponents may well be lofty, there is reason to believe that the net impact of their proposal will be more fatalities and injuries than would be the case in the absence of the legislation.

The stated objective of the Endangered Species Act is to protect various species that are on the verge of extinction. Certainly, this is an admirable objective, but there is nonetheless reason to question the effectiveness of the act itself. The Endangered Species Act allows the government to regulate the use of individual private property if an endangered species is found present on *or* near an individual's land. To avoid losing control of their property, many landowners have taken steps to make their land less attractive as a natural habitat for these endangered species. For example, the endangered red-cockaded woodpecker nests primarily in old trees within southern pine ecosystems. Landowners have responded by cutting down trees the woodpeckers like to nest in to avoid having one nest on their land, which would result in the owner losing control of this part of their property. The end result is that the habitat for these birds has actually been disappearing more rapidly.

As you can see, good intentions are not enough. An unsound proposal will lead to undesirable outcomes, even if it is supported by proponents with good intentions. Sound economic reasoning can help us better anticipate the secondary effects of policy changes and avoid the pitfall of thinking that good intentions are enough.

1-4c ASSOCIATION IS NOT CAUSATION

In economics, identifying cause-and-effect relationships is very important. But statistical association alone cannot establish this causation. Perhaps an extreme example will illustrate the point. Suppose that each November, a witch doctor performs a voodoo dance designed to summon the gods of winter, and that soon after the dance is performed, the weather in fact begins to turn cold. The witch doctor's dance is associated with the arrival of winter, meaning that the two events appear to have happened in conjunction with one another. But is this really evidence that the witch doctor's dance actually caused the arrival of winter? Most of us would answer no, even though the two events seemed to happen in conjunction with one another.

Those who argue that a causal relationship exists simply because of the presence of statistical association are committing a logical fallacy known as the *post hoc propter ergo hoc* fallacy. Sound economics warns against this potential source of error.

---

[4]For a detailed analysis of this subject, see Thomas B. Newman, Brian D. Johnston, and David C. Grossman, "Effects and Costs of Requiring Child-Restraint Systems for Young Children Traveling on Commercial Airplanes," *Archives of Pediatrics and Adolescent Medicine* 157 (October 2003): 969–74.

1-4d THE FALLACY OF COMPOSITION: WHAT'S TRUE FOR ONE MIGHT NOT BE TRUE FOR ALL

What is true for the individual (or subcomponent) may not be true for the group (or the whole). If you stand up for an exciting play during a football game, you will be better able to see. But what happens if everyone stands up at the same time? Will everyone be better able to see? The answer is, of course, no. Thus, what is true for a single individual does not necessarily apply to the group as a whole. When everyone stands up, the view for individual spectators fails to improve; in fact, it may even become worse.

People who mistakenly argue that what is true for the part is also true for the whole are said to be committing the **fallacy of composition**. What is true for the individual can be misleading and is often fallacious when applied to the entire economy. The fallacy of composition highlights the importance of considering both a micro view and a macro view in the study of economics. **Microeconomics** focuses on the decision-making of consumers, producers, and resource suppliers operating in a narrowly defined market, such as that for a specific good or resource. Because individual decision-makers are the moving force behind all economic action, the foundations of economics are clearly rooted in a micro view.

As we have seen, however, what is true for a small unit may not be true in the aggregate. **Macroeconomics** focuses on how the aggregation of individual micro-units affects our analysis. Like microeconomics, it is concerned with incentives, prices, and output. Macroeconomics, however, aggregates markets, lumping together all 128 million households in this country. Macroeconomics involves topics like total consumption spending, saving, and employment, in the economy as a whole. Similarly, the nation's 32 million business firms are lumped together in "the business sector." What factors determine the level of aggregate output, the rate of inflation, the amount of unemployment, and interest rates? These are macroeconomic questions. In short, macroeconomics examines the forest rather than the individual trees. As we move from the microcomponents to a macro view of the whole, it is important that we beware of the fallacy of composition.

Fallacy of composition
Erroneous view that what is true for the individual (or the part) will also be true for the group (or the whole).

Microeconomics
The branch of economics that focuses on how human behavior affects the conduct of affairs within narrowly defined units, such as individual households or business firms.

Macroeconomics
The branch of economics that focuses on how human behavior affects outcomes in highly aggregated markets, such as the markets for labor or consumer products.

KEY POINTS

- Scarcity and choice are the two essential ingredients of economic analysis. A good is scarce when the human desire for it exceeds the amount freely available. As a result of scarcity, both individuals and societies must choose among the available alternatives. Every choice entails a trade-off.

- Every society will have to devise some method of rationing scarce resources among competing uses. Markets generally use price as the rationing device. Competition is a natural outgrowth of the need to ration scarce goods.

- Scarcity and poverty are not the same thing. Absence of poverty implies that some basic level of need has been met. An absence of scarcity implies that our desires for goods are fully satisfied. We may someday eliminate poverty, but scarcity will always be with us.

- Economics is a way of thinking that emphasizes eight points:
  1. The use of scarce resources to produce a good always has an opportunity cost.
  2. Individuals make decisions purposefully, always seeking to choose the option they expect to be most consistent with their personal goals.
  3. Incentives matter. The likelihood of people choosing an option increases as personal benefits rise and personal costs decline.

  4. Economic reasoning focuses on the impact of marginal changes because it is the marginal benefits and marginal costs that influence choices.
  5. Because information is scarce, uncertainty is a fact of life.
  6. In addition to their direct impact, economic changes often generate secondary effects.
  7. The value of a good or service is subjective and varies with individual preferences and circumstances.
  8. The test of an economic theory is its ability to predict and explain events in the real world.

- Economic science is positive; it attempts to explain the actual consequences of economic actions or "what is." Normative economics goes further, applying value judgments to make suggestions about what "ought to be."

- Microeconomics focuses on narrowly defined units, while macroeconomics is concerned with highly aggregated units. When shifting focus from micro to macro, one must beware of the fallacy of composition: What's good for the individual may not be good for the group as a whole.

- The origin of economics as a science dates to the publication of *An Inquiry into the Nature and Causes of the Wealth of Nations* by Adam Smith in 1776. Smith believed a market economy would generally bring individual self-interest and the public interest into harmony.

CRITICAL ANALYSIS QUESTIONS

1. Indicate how each of the following changes would influence the incentive of a decision-maker to undertake the action described.

   a. A reduction in the temperature from 80° to 50° on one's decision to go swimming

   b. A change in the meeting time of the introductory economics course from 11:00 A.M. to 7:30 A.M. on one's decision to attend the lectures

   c. A reduction in the number of exam questions that relate directly to the text on the student's decision to read the text

   d. An increase in the price of beef on one's decision to buy steak

   e. An increase in the rental rates of apartments on one's decision to build additional rental housing units

2. "The government should provide such goods as health care, education, and highways because it can provide them for free." Is this statement true or false? Explain your answer.

3. a. What method is used to ration goods in a market economy? How does this rationing method influence the incentive of individuals to supply goods, services, and resources to others?

   b. How are grades rationed in your economics class? How does this rationing method influence student behavior? Suppose the highest grades were rationed to those whom the teacher liked best. How would this method of rationing influence student behavior?

4. *In recent years, the child tax credit has been increased in the United States. According to the basic principles of economics, how will the birthrate be affected by policies that reduce the taxes imposed on those with children?

5. *"The economic way of thinking stresses that good intentions lead to sound policy." Is this statement true or false? Explain your answer.

6. Self-interest is a powerful motivator. Does this necessarily imply that people are selfish and greedy? Do self-interest and selfishness mean the same thing?

7. A restaurant offers an "all you can eat" lunch buffet for $10. Shawn has already eaten three servings, and is trying to decide whether to go back for a fourth. Describe how Shawn can use marginal analysis to make his decision.

8. *"Individuals who economize are missing the point of life. Money is not so important that it should rule the way we live." Evaluate this statement.

9. *"Positive economics cannot tell us which agricultural policy is better, so it is useless to policy makers." Evaluate this statement.

10. *"I examined the statistics for our basketball team's wins last year and found that, when the third team played more, the winning margin increased. If the coach played the third team more, we would win by a bigger margin." Evaluate this statement.

11. Which of the following are positive economic statements and which are normative?

    a. The speed limit should be lowered to 55 miles per hour on interstate highways.

    b. Higher gasoline prices cause the quantity of gasoline that consumers buy to decrease.

    c. A comparison of costs and benefits should not be used to assess environmental regulations.

    d. Higher taxes on alcohol result in less drinking and driving.

12. Why can't we consume as much of each good or service as we would like? If we become richer in the future, do you think we will eventually be able to consume as much of everything as we would like? Why or why not?

13. Suppose that in an effort to help low-skill workers the government raises the legal minimum wage to $25 per hour. Can you think of any unintended secondary effects that will result from this action? Will all low-skill workers be helped by the minimum wage law?

14. Should the United States attempt to reduce air and water pollution to zero? Why or why not?

*Asterisk denotes questions for which answers are given in Appendix B.

CHAPTER 2

Some Tools of the Economist

The key insight of Adam Smith's Wealth of Nations *is misleadingly simple: if an exchange between two parties is voluntary, it will not take place unless both believe they will benefit from it. Most economic fallacies derive from the neglect of this simple insight, from the tendency to assume that there is a fixed pie, that one party can gain only at the expense of another.* **—Milton and Rose Friedman**[1]

In the preceding chapter, you were introduced to the economic way of thinking. We will now begin to apply that approach. This chapter focuses on five topics: opportunity cost, trade, property rights, the potential output level of an economy, and the creation of wealth. These seemingly diverse topics are in fact highly interrelated. For example, the opportunity cost of goods determines which ones an individual or a nation should produce and which should be acquired through trade. In turn, the ways in which trade and property rights are structured influence the amount of output and wealth an economy can create. These tools of economics are important for answering the basic economic questions: what to produce, how to produce it, and for whom it will be produced.

As you read this chapter, look for answers to the following questions:

- What is opportunity cost? Why do economists place so much emphasis on it?

- How does private ownership affect the use of resources? Will private owners pay any attention to the desires of others?

- What does a production possibilities curve demonstrate?

- What are the sources of gains from trade? How does trade influence our modern living standards?

- What are the two major methods of economic organization? How do they differ?

---

[1]Milton Friedman and Rose Friedman, *Free to Choose* (Harcourt Brace, 1990), 13.

2-1 WHAT SHALL WE GIVE UP?

Because of scarcity, we can't have everything we want. As a result, we constantly face choices that involve trade-offs between our competing desires. Most of us would like to have more time for leisure, recreation, vacations, hobbies, education, and skill development. We would also like to have more wealth, a larger savings account, and more consumable goods. However, all these things are scarce, in the sense that they are limited. Our efforts to get more of one will conflict with our efforts to get more of others.

2-1a OPPORTUNITY COST

The choice to do one thing is, at the same time, a choice *not* to do something else. Your choice to spend time reading this book is a choice not to spend the time watching Netflix, posting on social media, or hanging out with friends. These things must be given up because you decided to read this book instead. As we indicated in Chapter 1, the highest valued alternative sacrificed in order to choose an option is called the *opportunity cost* of that choice.

Opportunity costs are subjective; they depend on the value the decision-maker places on alternative options. Because of this, opportunity cost can never be directly measured by someone other than the decision-maker. Only the person choosing can know the value of what is given up.[2] This makes it difficult for someone other than the decision-maker—including experts and elected officials—to make choices on that person's behalf. Moreover, not only do people differ in the trade-offs they prefer to make, but their preferences also change with time and circumstances. Thus, the decision-maker is the only person who can properly evaluate the options and decide which is the best, given his or her preferences and current circumstances.

Monetary costs reflect opportunities foregone, and they can be measured objectively in terms of dollars and cents. If you spend $20 on a new cell phone case, you must now forgo the other items you could have purchased with the $20—a new shirt, for example. However, it is important to recognize that monetary costs do not represent the total opportunity cost of an option. The total cost of attending a football game, for example, is the highest valued opportunity lost as a result of both the time you spend at the game and the amount of money you pay for your ticket. In cases like buying and downloading a game from an app store, for which there is minimal outlay of time, effort, and other resources to make the purchase, the monetary cost will approximate the total cost. Contrast this with a decision to sit on your sofa and play your new game on your cell phone, which involves little or no monetary cost, but has a clear opportunity cost of your time. In this second case, the monetary cost is a poor measure of the total cost.

LeBron James understands opportunity cost. As a high school player, James was already one of the best basketball players in the nation. He had received numerous scholarship offers. However, after high school graduation, LeBron decided to go directly into the NBA because the opportunity cost of college was simply too high. He was selected as the first pick in the 2003 NBA draft, signing a three-year contract worth almost $13 million, with an option for a fourth year at $5.8 million. Would you have skipped college if your opportunity cost was $19 million?

Joe Camporeale/Cal Sport Media/Alamy

2-1b OPPORTUNITY COST AND THE REAL WORLD

Is real-world decision making influenced by opportunity costs? Consider your own decision to attend college. Your opportunity cost of going to college is the value of the next best alternative, which could be measured as the salary you would earn if you had chosen to go directly into full-time work instead. Every year you stay in college, you give up what you could have earned by

---

[2]See James M. Buchanan, *Cost and Choice* (Chicago: Markham, 1969), for a classic work on the relationship between cost and choice.

Outstanding Economist: Thomas Sowell (1930–)

Thomas Sowell, a long-time senior fellow at the Hoover Institution at Stanford University, recognizes the critical importance of the institutions—the "rules of the game"—that shape human interactions. His book *Knowledge and Decisions* stresses the role of knowledge in the economy and how different institutional arrangements compare at using scarce information. Sowell is the author of many books and journal articles and for 25 years wrote a nationally syndicated column that appeared in more than 150 newspapers. His writings address subjects ranging from race preferences and cultural differences to the origins and ideology of political conflict.

working that year. Typically, students incur opportunity costs of $100,000 or more in forgone income during their stay in college.

But what if the opportunity cost of attending college changes? How will it affect your decision? Suppose, for example, that you received a job offer today for $250,000 per year as an athlete or an entertainer, but the job would require so much travel that school would be impossible. Would this change in the opportunity cost of going to college affect your choice as to whether to continue in school? It likely would. Going to college would mean you would have to say good-bye to the huge salary you've been offered. (See the accompanying illustration on LeBron James for a good example.) You can clearly tell from this example that the monetary cost of college (tuition, books, and so forth) isn't the only factor influencing your decision. Your opportunity cost plays a part, too.

Consider another decision made by college students—whether to attend a particular class lecture. The monetary cost of attending class (bus fare, parking, gasoline costs, and so on) remains fairly constant from day to day. Why then do students choose to attend class on some days and not on others? Even though the monetary cost of attending class is fairly constant, a student's opportunity cost can change dramatically from day to day. Some days, the next best alternative to attending class may be sleeping in or streaming a movie. Other days, the opportunity cost may be substantially larger, perhaps the value of attending a big football game, getting an early start on spring break, or having additional study time for a crucial exam in another class. As options like these increase the cost of attending class, more students will decide not to attend.

Failure to consider opportunity cost often leads to unwise decision-making. Suppose that your community builds a beautiful new civic center. The mayor, speaking at the dedication ceremony, tells the world that the center will improve the quality of life in your community. People who understand the concept of opportunity cost may question this view. If the center had not been built, the resources might have funded construction of a new hospital, improvements to the educational system, or housing for low-income families. Will the civic center contribute more to the well-being of people in your community than would these other facilities? If so, it was a wise investment. If not, your community will be worse off than it would have been if decision-makers had chosen a higher valued project.

2-2 TRADE CREATES VALUE

Why do individuals trade with each other, and what is the significance of this exchange? We have learned that value is subjective. It is wrong to assume that a particular good or service has a fixed objective value just because it exists.[3] The value of goods and services generally depends on who uses them, and on circumstances, such as when and where they are used, as well as on the physical characteristics. Some people love onions, whereas others dislike them. Thus, when we speak of the "value of an onion," this makes sense only within the context of its value to a specific person. Similarly, to most people an umbrella is more valuable on a rainy day than on a sunny one.

---

[3]An illuminating discussion of this subject, termed the "physical fallacy," is found in Thomas Sowell, *Knowledge and Decisions* (New York: Basic Books, 1980), 67–72.

Consider the case of Janet, who loves tomatoes but hates onions, and Brad, who loves onions but hates tomatoes. They go out to dinner together and the waiter brings their salads. Brad turns to Janet and says, "I'll trade you the tomatoes on my salad for the onions on yours." Janet gladly agrees to the exchange. This simple example will help us illustrate two important aspects of voluntary exchange.

1. When individuals engage in a voluntary exchange, both parties are made better off. In the previous example, Janet has the option of accepting or declining Brad's offer of a trade. If she accepts his offer, she does so *voluntarily*. Janet would agree to this exchange only if she expects to be better off as a result. Because she likes tomatoes better than onions, Janet's enjoyment of her salad will be greater with this trade than without it. On the other side, Brad has voluntarily made this offer of an exchange to Janet because Brad believes he will also be better off as a result of the exchange.

People tend to think of making, building, and creating things as productive activities. Agriculture, software development, and manufacturing are like this. On the one hand, they create something genuinely new, something that was not there before. On the other hand, trade—the mere exchange of one thing for another—does not create new material items. It is tempting to think that if nothing new is created, the action cannot generate gain. But this is a fallacy, and the motivation for trade illustrates why. An exchange will not occur unless both parties agree to it and they will not do so unless the exchange makes them better off. As the chapter-opening quotation of Milton and Rose Friedman illustrates, many errors in economic reasoning happen when we forget that voluntary trades, like the one between Janet and Brad, make both parties better off.

2. By channeling goods and resources to those who value them most, trade creates value and increases the wealth created by a society's resources. Because preferences differ among individuals, the value of an item can vary greatly from one person to another. Therefore, trade can create value by moving goods from those who value them less to those who value them more. The simple exchange between Janet and Brad also illustrates this point. Imagine for a moment that Brad and Janet had never met and instead were both eating their salads alone. Without the ability to engage in this exchange, both would have eaten their salads but would not have had as much enjoyment from them. When goods are moved to individuals who value them more, the total value created by a society's limited resources is increased. The same two salads create more value when the trade occurs than when it doesn't.

It is easy to think of material things as wealth, but material things are not wealth until they are in the hands of someone who values them. A highly technical medical reference book that is of no value to an art collector may be worth several hundred dollars to a doctor. Similarly, a painting that is unappreciated by a doctor may be of great value to an art collector. Therefore, a voluntary exchange that moves the medical reference book to the doctor and the painting to the art collector will increase the value of both goods. By channeling goods and resources toward those who value them most, trade creates wealth for both the trading partners and for the nation.

2-2a TRANSACTION COSTS—A BARRIER TO TRADE

Have you ever been sitting at home late at night, hungry, wishing you could have some food from your favorite restaurant, but felt it wasn't worth the time and effort to get dressed and make the drive? Have you ever seen an item you wanted on a great Black Friday sale but didn't feel like dealing with the lines and crowds just to get the lower price? The costs of the time, effort, and other resources necessary to search out, negotiate, and conclude an exchange are called **transaction costs**. High transaction costs can be a barrier to potentially productive exchange.

Transaction costs
The time, effort, and other resources needed to search out, negotiate, and complete an exchange.

Transaction costs are sometimes high because of physical obstacles, such as oceans, rivers, and mountains, that make it difficult to get products to customers. Investment in roads and improvements in transportation and communications can reduce these transaction costs. In other instances, transaction costs may be high because of the lack of information. For example, you may want a new coat in a particular style, color, and size but don't know which store has it at an attractive price. The time and energy you spend gathering this information are part of your transaction costs. In still other cases, transaction costs are high because of political obstacles, such as taxes, licensing requirements, government regulations, price controls, tariffs, or quotas. Regardless of whether the roadblocks are physical, informational, or political, high transaction costs reduce the potential gains from trade.

Because of transaction costs, we should not expect all potentially valuable trades to take place, any more than we expect all useful knowledge to be learned, all safety measures to be taken, or all potential "A" grades to be earned. The cost of information, transportation, and other elements of transaction costs will sometimes be so great that potential gains from trade will go unrealized.

Reductions in transaction costs will increase the gains from trade. In recent years, technology has reduced the transactions costs of numerous exchanges. With just a few swipes on a touch screen, buyers can now acquire information about potential sellers and virtually any product. Phone apps are routinely used to shop, book travel, obtain event tickets, order food, or even get a ride home. These reductions in transaction costs have increased the volume of trade and have enhanced living standards.

Moreover, reductions in transaction costs can be profitable, and they can even make it possible for us to achieve more value from our existing assets. Examples abound. Uber and Lyft have grown rapidly by reducing the transaction costs of arranging for ground transportation. Airbnb has become a sizable business by reducing the transaction costs between apartment and housing owners and those seeking short-term living quarters. In turn, these reductions in transaction costs have increased the value generated by our cars, houses, and apartments.

Are items less costly during Black Friday sales once you factor in the transaction costs of dealing with the lines and crowds? To some people, it isn't and they find it cheaper to simply pay full price on a different day.

Philip Pacheco/Getty Images

2-2b THE MIDDLEMAN AS A COST REDUCER

Because it is costly for buyers and sellers to find each other and to negotiate the exchange, an entrepreneurial opportunity exists for people to become **middlemen**. Middlemen provide buyers and sellers information at a lower cost and arrange trades between them. Many people think middlemen just add to the buyer's expense without performing a useful function. However, because of transaction costs, without middlemen, many trades would never happen (nor would the gains from them be realized). Services like Uber Eats and Postmates are middlemen that, for a fee, are willing to solve the problem of getting food from your favorite restaurant to you when you don't feel like making the drive.

Grocers are also middlemen. Each of us could deal with farmers directly to buy our food—probably at a lower monetary cost. But that would have a high opportunity cost. Finding and dealing with different farmers for every product we wanted to buy would take a lot of time. Stockbrokers, realtors, publishers, and merchants of all sorts are other kinds of middlemen. For a fee, they reduce transaction costs for both buyers and sellers. By making exchanges cheaper and more convenient, middlemen expand the number of trades. In so doing, they themselves create value.

Middlemen
People who buy and sell goods or services or arrange trades. A middleman reduces transaction costs.

2-3 THE IMPORTANCE OF PROPERTY RIGHTS

Property rights
The rights to use, control, and obtain the benefits from a good or resource.

Private property rights
Property rights that are exclusively held by an owner and protected against invasion by others. Private property can be transferred, sold, leased, or mortgaged at the owner's discretion.

The buyer of an orange, a laptop, a television, or an automobile generally takes the item home. The buyer of a cargo ship, satellite, or an office building, though, may never touch it. When exchange occurs, it's really the **property rights** of the item that change hands.

Private property rights involve three things:

1. the right to exclusive use of the property and to the income or benefits it produces (that is, the owner has sole possession, control, and use of the property, including the right to exclude others);
2. legal protection against invasion from other individuals who would seek to use or abuse the property without the owner's permission; and
3. the right to transfer, sell, exchange, rent, lease, or mortgage the property.

Private owners can do anything they want with their property as long as they do not use it in a manner that invades or infringes on the rights of another. For example, I cannot throw the hammer that I own through the television that you own. If I did, I would be violating your property right to your television. The same is true if I operate a factory spewing out pollution harming you or your land.[4] Because an owner has the right to control the use of property, the owner also must accept responsibility for the outcomes of that control. Private property rights represent a bundle of legal rights that are often separable, as an owner may lease the usage rights to another individual.

In contrast to private ownership, common-property ownership occurs when multiple people simultaneously have or claim ownership rights to a good or resource. If the resource is open to all, none of the common owners can prevent the others from using or damaging the property. Most beaches, rivers, and roads are examples of commonly owned property. The distinction between private- and common-property ownership is important because common ownership does not create the same powerful incentives for conservation and efficient use as private ownership. Economists are fond of saying that when everybody owns something, nobody owns it.

KEYS TO ECONOMIC PROSPERITY

Private Ownership

Private ownership provides people with a strong incentive to take care of things and develop resources in ways that are highly valued by others.

Clearly defined and enforced private property rights are a key to economic progress because of the powerful incentive effects that private ownership generates. The following four incentives are particularly important:

1. Private owners can gain by employing their resources in ways that are beneficial to others, and they bear the opportunity cost of ignoring the wishes of others. Realtors often advise homeowners to use neutral colors for countertops and walls in their house because they will improve the resale value of the home. As a private owner, you could install bright green fixtures and paint your walls deep purple, but you will bear the cost (in terms of a lower selling price) of ignoring the wishes of others who might want to buy your house later. Conversely, by fixing up a house and doing things to it that others find beneficial, you can reap the benefit of a higher selling price.

---

[4]For a detailed explanation of how property rights protect the environment, with several real-world examples, see Roger E. Meiners and Bruce Yandle, *The Common Law: How It Protects the Environment* (Bozeman, MT: PERC, 1998), available online at www.perc.org.

Similarly, you could spray paint orange designs all over the outside of your brand-new car, but private ownership gives you an incentive not to do so because the resale value of the car depends on the value that *others* place on it.

Consider a parcel of undeveloped, privately owned land near a university. The private owner of the land can do many things with it. For example, she could leave it undeveloped, turn it into a metered parking lot, erect a restaurant, or build rental housing. Will the wishes and desires of the nearby students be reflected in her choice, even though they are not the owners of the property? Yes. Whichever use is more highly valued by potential customers will earn her the highest investment return. If housing is relatively hard to find but there are plenty of other restaurants, the profitability of using her land for housing will be higher than the profitability of using it for a restaurant. Private ownership gives her a strong incentive to use her property in a way that will also fulfill the wishes of others. If she decides to leave the property undeveloped instead of erecting housing that would benefit the students, she will bear the opportunity cost of forgone rental income from the property.

Consider a second example: the incentive structure confronted by the owner of an apartment complex near your campus. The owner may not care much for swimming pools, workout facilities, study desks, washers and dryers, or green areas. Nonetheless, private ownership provides the owner with a strong incentive to provide these items if students and other potential customers value them more than the costs of their provision. Why? Because tenants will be willing to pay higher rents to live in a complex with amenities that they value. The owners of rental property can profit by providing an additional amenity that tenants value as long as the tenants are willing to pay enough additional rent to cover their cost.

"Their house looks so nice. They must be getting ready to sell it."

A private owner has a strong incentive to do things with his or her property that increase its value to others.

2. Private owners have a strong incentive to care for and properly manage what they own.

Will Ed regularly change the oil in his car? Will he see to it that the seats don't get torn? Probably so, because being careless about these things would reduce the car's value, both to him and to any future owner. The car and its value—the sale price if he sells it—belong just to Ed, so he would bear the burden of a decline in the car's value if the oil ran low and ruined the engine, or if the seats were torn. Similarly, he would capture the value of an expenditure that improved the car, like a new paint job. As the owner, Ed has both the authority and the incentive to protect the car against harm or neglect and even to enhance its value. Private property rights give owners a strong incentive for good stewardship.

Do you take equally good care not to damage an apartment you rent as you would your own house? If you share an apartment with several roommates, are the common areas of the apartment (such as the kitchen and living room) as neatly kept as the bedrooms? Based on economic theory, we guess that the answer to both of these questions is probably "No."

3. Private owners have an incentive to conserve for the future—particularly if the property is expected to increase in value.

People have a much stronger incentive to conserve privately owned property than they do commonly owned property. For example, when Steven was in college, the general rule among his

When apartments and other investment properties are owned privately, the owner has a strong incentive to provide amenities that others value highly relative to their cost.

roommates was that any food or drink in the house was common property—open game for the hungry or thirsty mouth of anyone who stumbled across it. There was never a reason for Steven to conserve food or drinks in the house because it would be quickly consumed by a roommate coming in later that night. When Steven first started living alone, he noticed a dramatic change in his behavior. When he ordered a pizza, he would save some for the next day's lunch rather than eating it all that night. Steven began counting his drinks before he had one to make sure there were enough left for the next day. When Steven was the sole owner, he began delaying his current consumption to conserve for the future because he was the one, not his roommates, who reaped the benefit from his conservation.

Similarly, when more than one individual has the right to drill oil from an underground pool of oil, each has an incentive to extract as much as possible, as quickly as possible. Any oil conserved for the future will probably be taken by someone else. In contrast, when only one owner has the right to drill, the oil will be extracted more slowly. The same applies to the common-property problems involved in overfishing of the sea compared with fisheries that use privately owned ponds.

Someone who owns land, a house, or a factory has a strong incentive to bear costs now, if necessary, to preserve the asset's value for the future. The owner's wealth is tied up in the value of the property, which reflects nothing more than the net benefits that will be available to a future owner. Thus, the wealth of private owners is dependent upon their willingness and ability to look ahead, maintain, and conserve those things that will be more highly valued in the future. This is why private ownership is particularly important for the optimal conservation of natural resources.

4. Private owners have an incentive to lower the chance that their property will cause damage to the property of others. Private ownership links responsibility with the right of control. Private owners can be held accountable for damage done to others through the misuse of their property. A car owner has a right to drive his car, but will be held accountable if the brakes aren't maintained and the car damages someone else's property. Similarly, a chemical company has control over its products, but, exactly for that reason, it is legally liable for damages if it mishandles the chemicals. Courts of law recognize and enforce the authority granted by ownership, but they also enforce the responsibility that goes with that authority. Because private property owners can be held accountable for damages they cause, they have an incentive to use their property responsibly and take steps to reduce the likelihood of harm to others. A property owner, for example, has an incentive to cut down a dying tree before it falls into a neighbor's house and to leash or restrain his or her dog if it's likely to bite others.

2-3a PRIVATE OWNERSHIP AND MARKETS

Private ownership and competitive markets provide the foundation for cooperative behavior among individuals. When private property rights are protected and enforced, the permission of the owner must be sought before anyone else can use the property. Put another way, if you want to use a good or resource, you must either buy or lease it from the owner. This means that each of us must face the cost of using scarce resources. Furthermore, market prices give private owners a strong incentive to consider the desires of others and use their resources in ways others value highly relative to cost.

Friedrich Hayek, a Nobel Prize winner in economics, used the expression "the extended order" to refer to the tendency for markets to lead perfect strangers from different backgrounds around the world to cooperate with one another. Let's go back to the example of the property owner who has the choice of leaving her land idle or building housing to benefit students. The landowner might not know any students in her town nor particularly care about providing them housing. However, because she is motivated by market prices, she might build an apartment complex and eventually do business with a lot of students she never intended to get to know. In the process, she will purchase materials, goods, and services produced by other strangers.

APPLICATIONS IN ECONOMICS

Protecting Endangered Species with Private Property Rights and Trade

PicturesWild/Shutterstock.com

Have you ever wondered why the wild tiger is endangered in much of the world but most domestic cats are thriving? Or why the northern spotted owl is threatened in the West but chickens are not? Why have elephant and rhinoceros populations declined in number but not cattle or hogs? The incentives accompanying private ownership and freedom to trade provide the answer.

To understand why many wild animals are scarce, consider what happens with animals that provide food, most of which are privately owned. Suppose that people decided to eat more beef. Beef prices would rise, and the incentive for individuals to dedicate land and other resources to raise cattle would increase so they could sell more. The result would be more cows. Because cattle are privately owned, the market demand for beef *creates* the incentive for suppliers to maintain herds of cattle and to protect them under a system of private ownership.

In some ways, the rhinoceros is similar to a cow. A rhino, like a large bull in a cattle herd, may charge if disturbed. At 3,000 pounds, a charging rhino can be very dangerous to humans. Also like cattle, rhinos can be valuable to people—a single horn from a black rhino, used for artistic carvings and medicines, can sell for many thousands of dollars.

But the rhino is endangered because trade is not allowed. Even though rhino horn can be harvested without killing the animal, the Convention on International Trade in Endangered Species (CITES) forbids selling the horn as part of its overall policy of banning trade in products of endangered species. People who want black rhino horn—and demand for it has been rising—cannot obtain it legally. When hunting rhinos and selling their horns are illegal, trade goes underground. Rhinos become a favorite target of poachers, who are sometimes even assisted by local people eager to reap some value from the horn. To stem poaching, many nations outlaw rhino hunting and forbid the sale of rhino parts. Sadly, this has not reduced the number of rhino killings.[1] After the government banned domestic trade in rhino horns in South Africa in 2009, the number of illegal killings went up. Today, over 1,000 rhinos are killed annually in South Africa, compared to less than 100 prior to the ban. In 2017, 21 government officials were even arrested for poaching-related crimes. Most of the poaching occurs in the country's famed Krueger National Park.[2]

Some parts of Africa, however, have been able to increase the numbers of wild animals such as elephants, lions, and white rhinos, by giving private owners and local communities control of them. Namibia, for example, gave ownership rights to private landholders in the 1960s and extended them to communal lands in the mid-1990s. With this policy change, tribal communities began to hold ownership rights over the wildlife in their areas and were able to keep all revenues from wildlife. This transformed the incentives in Namibia.

Namibian communities have been receiving nearly $10 million a year from wildlife, says Fred Nelson, a wildlife expert who spent 11 years in Africa developing wildlife management partnerships. Since the revenues come primarily from trophy hunting and tourism ventures, local communities had a strong incentive to protect the animals and their habitat.[3] These new incentives led to a natural resurgence in wildlife numbers. Even the number of black rhinos in Namibia rose from 707 in 1997 to 1,134 in 2004. Clearly, property rights to ownership or use and freedom to trade are among the keys to conservation. These incentives can spur protection, care, and increased numbers, just as they do with cattle. Indeed, after litigation by private rhino holders, a judge in South Africa lifted the ban on domestic trade in rhino horn. Trade will give those farmers and communities that own rhinos an incentive to protect them. But where ownership and trade are prohibited, the protection will be missing and poaching will probably continue.

[1]See Michael De Alessi, *Private Conservation and Black Rhinos in Zimbabwe: The Savé Valley and Bubiana Conservancies*, available online at www.cei.org/gencon/025,01687.cfm.

[2]See Rachael Bale, "More Than 1,000 Rhinos Killed by Poachers in South Africa Last Year," *National Geographic*, January 25, 2018, at news.nationalgeographic.com/2018/01/wildlife-watch-rhino-poaching-crisis-continues-south-africa/ and "Rhino Poaching in South Africa at Record Levels Following 18% Rise in Killings," *The Guardian*, May 15, 2015, at www.theguardian.com/world/2015/may/11/rhino-poaching-in-south-africa-at-record-levels-following-18-rise-in-killings.

[3]Fred Nelson, "Conservation Can Work: Southern Africa Shows Its Neighbours How," *Swara* (East African Wildlife Society) 32, no. 2 (2009): 36–37.

Things are different in countries that don't recognize private-ownership rights or enforce them. In his book *The Mystery of Capital*, economist Hernando de Soto argues that the lack of well-defined and enforced property rights explains why some underdeveloped countries (despite being market based) have made little economic progress. He points out that in many of these nations, generations of people have squatted on the land without any legal deed giving them formal ownership. These squatters cannot borrow against the land or the homes they built on it to generate capital because they don't have a deed to it, nor can they prevent someone else from arbitrarily taking the land away from them. Private ownership and markets can also play an important role in environmental protection and natural-resource conservation. Ocean fishing rights, tradable rights to pollute, and private ownership of endangered species are just some examples. The accompanying Applications in Economics feature, "Protecting Endangered Species with Private Property Rights and Trade," explores some of these issues.

2-4 PRODUCTION POSSIBILITIES CURVE

Production possibilities curve
A curve that outlines all possible combinations of total output that could be produced, assuming (1) a fixed amount of productive resources, (2) a given amount of technical knowledge, and (3) full and efficient use of those resources. The slope of the curve indicates the amount of one product that must be given up to produce more of the other.

People try to get the most from their limited resources by making purposeful choices and engaging in economizing behavior. This can be illustrated using a conceptual tool called the **production possibilities curve**. The production possibilities curve shows the maximum amount of any two products that can be produced from a fixed set of resources, and the possible trade-offs in production between them. The real economy obviously produces more than just two products, but this concept can help us understand a number of important economic ideas.

Exhibit 1 illustrates the production possibilities curve for Susan, an intelligent economics major. This curve indicates the combinations of English and economics grades that she thinks she can earn if she spends a total of ten hours per week studying for the two subjects. Currently, she is choosing to study the material in each course that she expects will help her grade the most for the time spent, and she is allocating five hours of study time to each course. She expects that this amount of time, carefully spent on each course, will allow her to earn a B grade in both, indicated at point *T*. But if she were to take some time away from studying one of the two subjects and spend it studying the other, she could raise her grade in the course receiving more study time. However, it would come at the cost of a lower grade in the course. If she were to move to point *S* by spending more hours on economics and fewer on English, for example, her expected

EXHIBIT 1

Production Possibilities Curve for Susan's Grades in English and Economics

The production possibilities for Susan, in terms of grades, are illustrated for ten hours of total study time. If Susan studied ten hours per week in these two classes, she could attain a D in English and an A in economics (point *S*), a B in English and a B in economics (point *T*), or an A in English and a D in economics (point *U*).

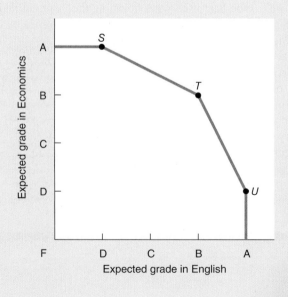

economics grade would rise, while her expected English grade would fall. This illustrates an important point: the idea of trade-offs in the use of scarce resources. Whenever more of one thing is produced, there is an opportunity cost in terms of something else that now must be forgone.

You might notice that Susan's production possibilities curve indicates that the additional study time required to raise her economics grade by one letter, from a B to an A (moving from point *T* to point *S*), would require giving up two letter grades in her English class, not just one, reducing her English grade from a B to a D. If, alternatively, Susan were to move from point *T* to point *U*, the opposite would be true—she would improve her English grade by one letter at the expense of two letter grades in economics. You can understand this by thinking about your own studying behavior. When you have only a limited amount of time to study a subject, you begin by studying the most important (grade-increasing) material first. As you spend additional time on that subject, you begin studying topics that are of decreasing importance for your grade. Thus, adding an hour of study time to the subject Susan studies least will have a larger impact on her grade than will taking away an hour from the subject on which she currently spends more time.

This idea of increasing opportunity cost is reflected in the slope of the production possibilities curve. The curve is flatter to the left of point *T*, and steeper to the right, showing that, as Susan takes more and more of her resources (time, in this case) from one course and puts it into the other, she must give up greater and greater amounts of productivity in the course getting fewer resources.

Of course, Susan could study more economics *without* giving up her English study time, if she gave up some leisure, or study time for other courses, or her part-time job in the campus bookstore. If she gave up leisure or her job and added those hours to the ten hours of study time for economics and English, the entire curve in Exhibit 1 would shift outward. She could get better grades in both classes by having more time to study.

Can the production possibilities concept be applied to the entire economy? Yes. We can grow more soybeans if we grow less corn, because both can be grown on the same land. Beefing up the nation's military would mean we would have to produce fewer nonmilitary goods than we could otherwise. When scarce resources are being used efficiently, getting more of one requires that we sacrifice others.

Exhibit 2 shows a hypothetical production possibilities curve for an economy with a limited amount of resources that produces only two goods: food and clothing. The points

EXHIBIT 2

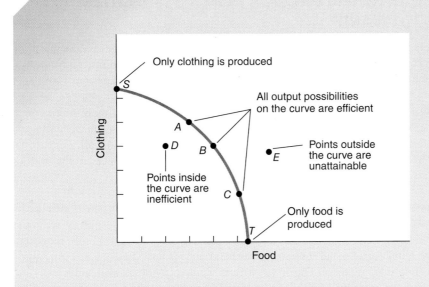

Concept of Production Possibilities Curve for an Economy

When an economy is using its limited resources efficiently, production of more clothing requires that the economy give up some other goods—such as food in this example. In time, improved technology, more resources, or improvement in its economic organization could make it possible to produce more of both goods by shifting the production possibilities curve outward.

along the curve represent all possible combinations of food and clothing that could be produced with the current level of resources and technology in the economy (assuming the resources are being used efficiently). A point outside the production possibilities curve (such as point *E*) would be considered unattainable at the present time. A point inside the production possibilities curve (such as point *D*) is attainable, but producing that amount would mean that the economy is not making maximum use of its resources (some resources are being underutilized). Thus, point *D* is considered inefficient.

More specifically, the production possibilities curve shows all of the maximum combinations of two goods that an economy will be able to produce: (1) given a fixed quantity of resources, (2) holding the level of technology constant, and (3) assuming that all resources are used efficiently.

When these three conditions are met, the economy will be at the edge of its production possibilities frontier (where points *A*, *B*, and *C* lie), and producing more of one good will necessitate producing less of others. If condition 3 above is not met, and resources are being used inefficiently, an economy would be operating inside its production possibilities curve. If the quantity of resources increases or the level of technology improves (conditions 1 and 2), this will result in an outward shift in the production possibilities curve. We will return to these factors that can shift the production possibilities curve in a moment.

Notice that the production possibilities curve is concave (or bowed out) to the origin, just as Susan's was in Exhibit 1 because of the concept of increasing opportunity cost. Here, the curved shape reflects the fact that an economy's resources are not equally well suited to produce food and clothing. If an economy were using all its resources to produce clothing (point *S*), transferring those resources least suited for producing clothing toward food production would reduce clothing output a little but increase food output a lot. Because the resources transferred would be those better suited for producing food and less suited for producing clothing, the opportunity cost of producing additional food (in terms of clothing forgone) is low near point *S*. However, as more and more resources are devoted to food production and successively larger amounts of food are produced (moving the economy from *S* to *A* to *B* and so on), the opportunity cost of food will rise. This is because, as more and more food is produced, additional food output can be achieved only by using resources that are less and less suitable for the production of food relative to clothing. Thus, as food output is expanded, successively larger amounts of clothing must be forgone per unit of additional food. This is similar to what happened to Susan when she diverted study hours from one course to another. Only this time, we are talking about an entire economy.

2-4a SHIFTING THE PRODUCTION POSSIBILITIES CURVE OUTWARD

What restricts an economy—once its resources are fully utilized—from producing more of everything? Why can't we get more of something produced without having to give up the production of something else? The same constraint that kept Susan from simultaneously making a higher grade in both English and economics: a lack of resources. As long as all current resources are being used efficiently, the only way to get more of one good is to sacrifice some of the other. Over time, however, it is possible for a country's production possibilities curve to shift outward, making it possible for more of all goods to be produced. There are four factors that could potentially shift the production possibilities curve outward.

Investment
The purchase, construction, or development of resources, including physical assets, such as plants and machinery, and human assets, such as better education. Investment expands an economy's resources. The process of investment is sometimes called capital formation.

1. An increase in the economy's resource base would expand our ability to produce goods and services.   If we had more or better resources, we could produce a greater amount of all goods. Resources such as machinery, buildings, tools, and education are human-made, and thus we can expand our resource base by devoting some of our efforts to producing them. This **investment** would provide us with better tools and skills and increase our ability to produce goods and services in the future. However, like with the production of other goods, devoting effort and resources toward producing these

long-lasting physical assets means fewer resources are available to produce other things, in this case goods for current consumption. Thus, the choice between using resources to produce goods for current consumption and using them to produce investment goods for the future can also be illustrated within the production possibilities framework. The two economies illustrated in Exhibit 3 begin with identical production possibilities curves (RS). Notice that Economy A dedicates more of its output to investment (shown by I_A) than does Economy B (shown by I_B). Economy B, on the other hand, consumes more than Economy A. Because Economy A allocates more of its resources to investment and less to consumption, A's production possibilities curve shifts outward over time by a greater amount than B's. In other words, the growth rate of Economy A—the expansion of its ability to produce goods—is enhanced by this investment. But more investment in machines and human skills requires a reduction in current consumption.

2. Advancements in technology can expand the economy's production possibilities.

Technology determines the maximum amount of output an economy can produce given the resources it has. New and better technology makes it possible for us to get more output from our resources. An important form of technological change is **invention**—the use of science and engineering to create new products or processes. In recent years, for example, inventions have allowed us to download music faster and more cheaply, process data more rapidly, get more oil and natural gas from existing fields, and send information instantly and cheaply by satellite. Such technological advances increase our production possibilities, shifting our economy's entire production possibilities curve outward.

The production possibilities of an economy can also be expanded by technological change through **innovation**—the practical and effective adoption of new techniques. Such innovation is commonly carried out by an **entrepreneur**—a person who decides what resources will be used, how they will be combined, and what goods and services they will be utilized to produce. In order to succeed, entrepreneurs must produce goods and services that increase the value of resources. Sometimes this can be achieved by introducing new products, new technologies, and lower cost production methods. When an entrepreneur produces goods that are highly valued relative to cost, their actions will both generate personal success and expand the economy's production possibilities. Take, for example, Henry Ford,

Technology
The technological knowledge available in an economy at any given time. The level of technology determines the amount of output we can generate with our limited resources.

Invention
The creation of a new product or process, often facilitated by the knowledge of engineering and science.

Innovation
The successful introduction and adoption of a new product or process; the economic application of inventions and marketing techniques.

Entrepreneur
A person who decides what resources will be used, how they will be combined, and what goods and services they will be utilized to produce. Typically, entrepreneurs will undertake these activities within a business enterprise. A successful entrepreneur's actions will increase the value of resources and expand the size of the economic pie.

EXHIBIT 3

Investment and Production Possibilities in the Future

Here we illustrate two economies (A and B) that initially confront identical production possibilities curves (RS). Economy A allocates a larger share of its output to investment (I_A, compared to I_B for Economy B). As a result, the production possibilities curve of the high-investment economy (Economy A) will tend to shift outward by a larger amount over time than the low-investment economy's will.

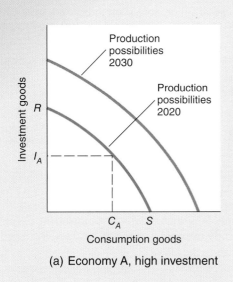

(a) Economy A, high investment

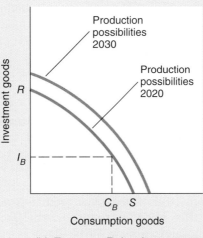

(b) Economy B, low investment

an entrepreneur who changed how cars were made by pioneering the assembly line. With the same amount of labor and materials, Ford made more cars more cheaply. Entrepreneurs like Bill Gates and Steve Jobs helped develop the personal computer and software programs that dramatically increased their usefulness to businesses and households. More recently, entrepreneurs such as Jeff Bezos (Amazon), Jack Dorsey (Twitter), and Mark Zuckerberg (Facebook) have enhanced our ability to transact, interact, and communicate online.

Creative destruction
The replacement of old products and production methods by innovative new ones that consumers judge to be superior. The process generates economic growth and higher living standards.

Through entrepreneurial discovery and innovation, new products and methods of production are continuously replacing old ones. The great Harvard economist Joseph Schumpeter called this process **creative destruction**. Digital music has largely replaced CDs, while the automobile caused the demise of the horse and buggy industry. A modern cell phone can replace more than $1,200 worth of products from the past that would fill a small room, including a portable music player, alarm clock, watch, camera, flashlight, calendar, address book, car GPS system, pedometer, level, ruler, calculator, dictionary, guitar tuner, and many more. Although this process destroys some businesses or industries, it creates new and more valuable ones in their place. Creative destruction is a powerful force leading to economic growth and prosperity.

3. An improvement in the rules under which the economy functions can also increase output.

The legal system of a country influences the ability of people to cooperate with one another and produce goods. Changes in legal institutions that promote social cooperation and motivate people to produce what others want will also push the production possibilities curve outward. Since the collapse of the Soviet Union in 1991, many countries around the world have reformed their economies in ways that have expanded the use of private ownership and markets, for example. However, poor institutions can reduce both the level of resources used (shifting the curve inward) and how efficiently they are used (causing the economy to operate inside its production possibilities curve).

Historically, legal innovations have been an important source of economic progress. During the eighteenth century, a system of patents was established in Europe and North America, giving inventors private property rights to their ideas. At about the same time, laws were passed allowing businesses to establish themselves legally as corporations, reducing the cost of forming large firms that were often required for the mass production of manufactured goods. Both of these legal changes allowed improved forms of economic organization and accelerated the growth of output by shifting the production possibilities curve outward more rapidly.

Sometimes governments, perhaps because of ignorance or prejudice, adopt legal institutions that reduce production possibilities. Laws that restrict or prohibit trade are one example. For almost a hundred years following the American Civil War, the laws of several southern states prohibited hiring African Americans for certain jobs and restricted other economic exchanges based on race. The legislation not only was harmful to African Americans; it also slowed economic progress and reduced the production possibilities of these states.

4. By working harder and giving up current leisure, we could increase our production of goods and services.

Hypothetically, the production possibilities curve would shift outward if everyone worked more hours and took less leisure time. Strictly speaking, however, leisure is also a good, so we would simply be giving up leisure to have more of other things. If we were to construct a production possibilities curve for leisure versus other goods, this would be shown as simply a movement along the curve. However, if we restrict our model to only material goods and services, a change in the amount we work would be shown as a shift in the curve.

How much people work depends not only on their personal preferences but also on public policy. For example, high tax rates on personal income may cause people to work less. This is because high tax rates reduce the payoff from working. When this happens, people spend more time doing other, untaxed activities—like leisure activities. This will

Entrepreneurs Who Have Changed Our Lives

New products and better ways of doing things do not just happen; they must be discovered. This is the function of the entrepreneur. Successful entrepreneurs exert an impact—often a huge impact—on our lives. However, their contributions are often either overlooked or misunderstood. Everyone knows that highly successful entrepreneurs make a lot of money. But their innovative ideas and product improvements enhance the lives of others. If they did not, people would not buy their products and services. Various chapters of this text will include a feature, "Entrepreneurs Who Have Changed Our Lives." Although you will recognize several of the entrepreneurs in this series, others are relatively unknown. As the series will illustrate, successful entrepreneurs come from diverse backgrounds. Some are ordinary individuals who developed and acted on a great idea. Others are truly unique. Many experienced failure prior to their success. These elements are all part of entrepreneurship.

Jeff Bezos

Jeff Bezos, founder of Amazon, dreamed of harnessing the Internet to transform retailing and expand the value of his company to more than a billion dollars. Instead, he has turned Amazon into something close to a trillion-dollar company, while becoming perhaps the world's richest person.

Amazon, which started with the sale of books in 1995, has revolutionized buying and selling products online. More than 100 million people subscribe to its Prime service, which lets them obtain quicker delivery on millions of products, online music, and videos. Often, they can receive their product within a day or two.

Amazon has drastically reduced retail transaction costs. Buyers no longer have to trudge from store to store to find the right book, gadget, or even food item; they can order it with the click of a button after seeing it on the Internet and reading reviews by previous purchasers. Amazon delivers products without the complex transaction cost of sending them to retail stores, where they might linger for months or never be bought at all.

Bezos was born in Albuquerque, New Mexico, but moved around the country; his father was a petroleum engineer. He was always interested in how things worked. When he was very young, he didn't like sleeping in a baby crib, so he took it apart with a screwdriver. When he was older, he devised a buzzer on his bedroom door to warn him if his little brother or sister was about to enter. In high school, he was an outstanding student and popular with classmates, becoming both valedictorian and president of his class.

At Princeton he tried physics, but switched to computer science. (He thought the students in physics were smarter and he wouldn't do well in that field.) After graduation he had a series of Wall Street jobs in which he created or managed computer systems. But once he learned how fast the Internet was growing, he recognized its potential for retailing. His entrepreneurial talents built a great company, but they also improved the lives of millions of consumers throughout the world.

Sources: Josepha Sherman, *Jeff Bezos: King of Amazon* (Brookfield, CT: Twenty-First Century Books, 2001).
Karen Weise, "Amazon's Profit Falls Sharply as Company Buys Growth," *New York Times*, October 24, 2019.
G. Bruce Knecht, "Wall Street Whiz Finds Niche Selling Books on the Internet," *Wall Street Journal*, May 16, 1996.

Kristoffer Tripplaar/Alamy

move the production possibilities curve for material goods inward because the economy can't produce as much when people work less.

2-4b PRODUCTION POSSIBILITIES AND ECONOMIC GROWTH

Within the production possibilities framework, economic growth is simply an outward shift in the curve through time. The more rapidly the curve shifts outward, the more rapid is economic growth. There are other economic models that are used to analyze economic growth; however, they all share the production possibilities curve as a foundation. Economic growth is one of the most important topics in modern economics for good reason. On the one hand, an economic growth rate of 3 percent per year will result in living standards doubling approximately every 23 years. On the other hand, in a country experiencing an economic growth rate of only 1 percent, it will take approximately seventy years for living standards to double.

2-5 TRADE, OUTPUT, AND LIVING STANDARDS

KEYS TO ECONOMIC PROSPERITY

Gains from Trade

Trade makes it possible for people to generate more output through specialization and division of labor, large-scale production processes, and the dissemination of improved products and production methods.

Division of labor
A method that breaks down the production of a product into a series of specific tasks, each performed by a different worker.

As we previously discussed, trade creates value by moving goods from people who value them less to people who value them more. However, this is only part of the story. Trade also makes it possible for people to expand their output through specialization and **division of labor**, large-scale production, and the dissemination of better products and production methods.

2-5a GAINS FROM SPECIALIZATION AND DIVISION OF LABOR

Businesses can achieve higher output levels and greater productivity from their workers through specialization and division of labor. Almost 250 years ago, Adam Smith noted the importance of this factor. Observing the operation of a pin manufacturer, Smith noted that when each worker specialized in a separate function needed to make pins, 10 workers together were able to produce 48,000 pins per day, or 4,800 pins per worker. Smith doubted an individual worker could produce even 20 pins per day working alone from start to finish on each pin.[5]

The division of labor separates production tasks into a series of related operations. Each worker performs one or a few of perhaps hundreds of tasks necessary to produce something. This process makes it possible to assign different tasks to those individuals who are able to accomplish them most efficiently (that is, at the lowest cost). Furthermore, a worker who specializes in just one narrow area becomes more experienced and more skilled in that task over time.

Law of comparative advantage
A principle that states that individuals, firms, regions, or nations can gain by specializing in the production of goods that they produce cheaply (at a low opportunity cost) and exchanging them for goods they cannot produce cheaply (at a high opportunity cost).

Trading partners can also benefit from specialization and the division of labor. The **law of comparative advantage**, developed in the early 1800s by the great English economist David Ricardo, explains why this is true. *The law of comparative advantage states that the total output of a group of individuals, an entire economy, or a group of nations will be greatest when the output of each good is produced by the person (or firm) with the lowest opportunity cost for that good.*

Comparative advantage applies to trade among individuals, business firms, regions, and even nations. When trading partners are able to use more of their time and resources to produce the things each is best at, they will be able to produce more together than would otherwise have been possible. In turn, the mutual gains they get from trading will result in higher levels of income for each. It's a win–win situation for both.

---

[5]See Adam Smith, *An Inquiry into the Nature and Causes of the Wealth of Nations* (1776; Cannan's ed., Chicago: University of Chicago Press, 1976), 7–16, for additional detail on the importance of the division of labor.

If a good or service can be obtained more economically through trade, it makes sense to get it that way rather than producing it for yourself. When you think about it, the law of comparative advantage is common sense. If someone else is willing to supply you with a good at a lower cost than you can produce it yourself, doesn't it make sense to trade for it and use your time and resources to produce more of the things you can produce most efficiently? Consider the situation of Andrea, an attorney who earns $300 per hour providing legal services. She has several documents that need to be typed, and she is thinking about hiring a typist earning $25 per hour to do it. Andrea is an excellent typist, much faster than the prospective employee. She could do the job in 20 hours, whereas the typist would take 40 hours.

Trade channels goods to those who value them most. Trade also helps disseminate ideas for improved products and makes production methods such as specialization, the division of labor, and mass production more feasible. Over the years, trade has enabled us to produce more with our limited resources, dramatically improving our living standards.

Because of her greater typing speed, some might think Andrea should handle the job herself. This is not the case. If she types the documents, the job will cost her $6,000—the opportunity cost of 20 hours of practicing law at $300 per hour. Alternatively, the cost of having the documents typed by the typist is only $1,000 (40 hours at $25 per hour). Andrea's comparative advantage lies in practicing law. By hiring the typist, she will increase her own productivity for clients and will make more money.

The implications of the law of comparative advantage are universal. Any group will be able to produce more output from its available resources when each good or service is produced by the person with the lowest opportunity cost. This insight is particularly important in understanding the way a market economy works. Buyers will try to get the most for their money. They will not knowingly choose a high-cost option when a lower-cost alternative of the same value is available. This places low-cost suppliers at a competitive advantage. Thus, low-cost producers will generally survive and prosper in a market economy. As a result, the production of goods and resources will naturally tend to be allocated according to comparative advantage.

Most people recognize that Americans benefit from trade among the nation's 50 states. For example, the residents of Nebraska and Florida are able to produce a larger joint output and achieve higher income levels when Nebraskans specialize in producing corn and other grain products and Floridians specialize in producing oranges and other citrus products. The same is true for trade among nations. Like Nebraskans and Floridians, people in different nations will be better off if they specialize in the goods and services they can produce at a low cost and trade them for goods they produce at a high cost. See the addendum to this chapter for additional evidence on this point.

2-5b GAINS FROM MASS PRODUCTION METHODS

Trade also promotes economic progress by making it possible for firms to lower their per-unit costs with mass production. Suppose a nation isolated itself and refused to trade with other countries. In an economy like this, self-sufficiency and small-scale production would be the norm. If trade were allowed, however, the nation's firms could sell their products to customers around the world. This would make it feasible for the firms to adopt more efficient, large-scale production processes. Mass production often leads to labor and machinery efficiencies that increase output per worker. But without trade, these gains could not be achieved.

2-5c GAINS FROM INNOVATION

Trade also makes it possible to realize gains from the discovery and dissemination of innovative products and production processes. Economic growth involves brain power, innovation, and the application of technology. Without trade, however, the gains derived from the discovery of better ways of doing things would be stifled. Furthermore, observing and interacting with other people using different and better technologies often encourage others to copy successful approaches. People also modify the technology they observe, adapting it for their own purposes. This sometimes results in new, and even better, technologies. Again, gains from these sources would be far more limited in a world without trade.

The importance of trade in our modern world can hardly be exaggerated. Trade makes it possible for most of us to consume a bundle of goods and services far beyond what we would be able to produce for ourselves.

Can you imagine the difficulty involved in producing your own housing, clothing, and food, to say nothing of computers, televisions, dishwashers, automobiles, and cell phones? Yet, most families in North America, Western Europe, Japan, and Australia enjoy all these conveniences. They are able to do so largely because their economies are organized in such a way that individuals can cooperate, specialize, and trade, thereby reaping the benefits of the enormous increases in output—in both quantity and diversity—that can be generated. In contrast, countries that impose obstacles that restrict exchange—either domestic or international—hinder their citizens from achieving these gains and more prosperous lives.

2-6 HUMAN INGENUITY, ENTREPRENEURSHIP, AND THE CREATION OF WEALTH

KEYS TO ECONOMIC PROSPERITY

Human Ingenuity

Economic goods are the result of human ingenuity and action; thus, the size of the "economic pie" is variable, not fixed.

The size of a country's "economic pie" is most easily thought of as the total dollar value of all goods and services produced during some period of time. This economic pie is the grand total of the wealth (or value) created by each member of the society. It is not some fixed total waiting to be divided up among people. On the contrary, the size of the economic pie reflects the physical effort and ingenuity of human beings. It is not an endowment from nature.

Economic output expands as entrepreneurs discover new and better ways of doing things. So over time, it is human knowledge and ingenuity—perhaps more than anything else—that limit our economic progress. If Jim, a local farmer who normally produces $30,000 worth of corn each year, finds a better growing method enabling him to produce $40,000 of corn per year, he has created additional wealth. But Jim has actually created more than the $10,000 in extra wealth. The $10,000 is only his share of the gains from the additional trades made possible by the extra corn he grew. Exchange makes both buyer and seller better off, so the total wealth created by Jim includes not only his $10,000 but also the gains of all of the buyers who purchased his additional output of corn.

This highlights an important point: in a market economy, a larger income for one person does not mean a smaller income for a trading partner. In fact, it is just the opposite. When a person earns income, he or she expands the economic pie by more than the amount of the slice that he or she gets, making it possible for the rest of us to have a bigger slice, too. When an entrepreneur, such as Chuck Hull, the inventor of the 3D printer, earns income through voluntary exchanges in the marketplace, he has enlarged the economic pie by an even larger amount. Here's why: Suppose that Linda, a freelance graphic artist, pays $2,000 for a new 3D printer developed by Chuck Hull. As a result, she can do twice as much work in the same amount of time. Because she's more productive, Linda can earn more than enough additional income with the printer to justify her purchase. In addition, the businesses she serves are also better off because the printer makes it possible for her to give them quicker service and a lower price. More is produced in total. Thus, while Chuck Hull gained, so, too, did Linda and her customers.

The same is true for other successful entrepreneurs such as Jeff Bezos or Mark Zuckerberg. Amazon and Facebook have expanded the size of the entire economic pie by enhancing the ability of businesses to market and sell products to willing consumers. Even a successful writer such as J.K. Rowling enriches the lives of millions through her novels. When income is acquired through voluntary exchange, people who earn income also help others earn more income and live better, too.

2-7 ECONOMIC ORGANIZATION

Every economy faces three basic questions: (1) What will be produced? (2) How will it be produced? and (3) For whom will it be produced? These questions are highly interrelated. Throughout the book, we will consider how different types of economies solve them. There are two broad ways that an economy can be organized: markets or government (political) planning. Let us briefly consider each.

2-7a MARKET ORGANIZATION

Private ownership of productive assets, voluntary exchange, and market prices are the distinguishing features of **market organization**. Under market organization, private parties are permitted to buy and sell ownership rights of their assets at mutually acceptable prices. The government plays the limited role of rule maker and referee. It develops the rules, or the legal structure, that recognizes, defines, and protects private ownership rights. It helps individuals enforce contracts and protects people from violence and fraud. But in this role, the government is not an active player in the economy. Ideally, it avoids modifying market outcomes in an attempt to favor some people at the expense of others. For example, it doesn't prevent sellers from slashing prices or improving the quality of their products to attract customers from other competitors. Nor does it prevent buyers from outbidding others for products and productive resources. No legal restraints limit potential buyers or sellers from producing, selling, or buying in the marketplace.

The term **capitalism** is often used to refer to an economic system based on market organization.[6] However, the term is also widely used to describe the economic systems of countries that make extensive use of regulations, trade restrictions, taxes and subsidies, and price controls to alter the operation of markets as long as property is generally privately owned and operated for profit. Therefore, economists generally prefer using market organization instead of capitalism because of the ambiguity of the latter.

Under market organization, no single individual or group of individuals guides the economy. There is no central planning authority, only individual planning. The three basic questions are solved independently in the marketplace by individual buyers and sellers making their own decentralized decisions. Buyers and sellers decide on their own what to produce, how to produce it, and whom to trade it to, based on the prices they themselves decide to charge.

Market organization
A method of organization in which private parties make their own plans and decisions with the guidance of unregulated market prices. The basic economic questions of consumption, production, and distribution are answered through these decentralized decisions.

Capitalism
An economic system in which productive resources are owned privately and goods and resources are allocated through market prices.

[6]*Capitalism* is a term coined by Karl Marx.

APPLICATIONS IN ECONOMICS

Are Scandinavian Countries Socialist?

Venezuela, Cuba, North Korea, and the former Soviet Union provide examples of socialist economies. These countries are characterized by low living standards and authoritarian political regimes. Are there any socialist success stories? During his 2016 and 2020 presidential campaigns, Bernie Sanders, a self-proclaimed democratic socialist, pointed to Scandinavian countries like Denmark and Sweden as socialist countries he would like the United States to emulate.

Are the Scandinavian countries really socialist? Scandinavian countries do have a high level of government expenditures, including large income transfer programs. But socialism involves government ownership of enterprises in major industries and allocation of resources via government planning rather than markets. Market economies are characterized by legal protection of private property, unbiased enforcement of contracts, free trade, and minimal business regulation. On the other hand, socialist economies are characterized by government ownership, trade restrictions, and imposition of mandates and regulations on the activities of business. In socialist countries, the means of production, including factories, banks, and agricultural land, are generally owned or controlled by the government.

Let's examine the institutions and policies of Scandinavian countries in order to determine where they stand on the market versus socialism spectrum. The annual *Economic Freedom of the World* report published by the Fraser Institute provides data for 162 countries on legal protection of property rights, freedom of exchange, and regulation of business.[1] These data can be used to determine whether the institutions and policies of Scandinavian countries are market oriented or predominately socialist. Higher rankings indicate more market-oriented policies and institutions.

Examination of the Fraser data for legal protection of private property rights and enforcement of contracts indicates that the Scandinavian countries rank quite high compared to predominantly market economies such as the United States and United Kingdom. Among the 162 countries examined in 2017, Finland ranked 1st, Norway 3rd, Denmark 9th, and Sweden 15th in this area, compared to 14th for the United Kingdom and 18th for the United States. Thus, the protection of private property and contracting in Scandinavian countries is highly reflective of market institutions.

In free trade and international exchange, the Scandinavian countries also compare quite favorably with predominantly market economies. In the free trade area, Denmark ranked 9th, Finland 23rd, and Sweden 28th, compared to 10th for the United Kingdom, 55th for the United States, and 63rd for Norway in 2017.

Socialist countries are known for their mandates and regulations imposed on business. However, again, the imposition of business regulations in Scandinavian countries is similar to that of market economies. In the area of business regulation, the Fraser Institute data ranked Finland 4th, Norway 13th, Sweden 24th, and Denmark 25th, compared to 12th for the United States and 26th for the United Kingdom.

The World Bank's *Doing Business* report covering 190 countries provides additional data on the regulation of business.[2] This measure examines how the regulatory environment impacts the ease of entry into markets, cost of regulatory compliance, and regulations that make it difficult to operate a business. Free market economies rank high on this list, whereas heavily regulated, government-directed economies earn lower ratings. Again, the summary rankings of Scandinavian countries are similar to those of predominately market economies. In 2020, Denmark ranked 4th, Norway 9th, Sweden 10th, and Finland 20th, compared to 6th for the United States and 8th for the United Kingdom. By way of comparison, two other high-income market-directed economies—Belgium and Italy—ranked 46th and 58th, respectively, whereas socialist Venezuela placed 188th among the 190 countries rated. (Note: Neither Cuba nor North Korea is included because of insufficient data.)

In summary, the economic institutions of Scandinavian countries are those of a market economy. The protection of private property rights, openness of markets, and regulation of business in Scandinavian countries are similar to those of market-oriented economies. Thus, it should not be surprising that Danish Prime Minister Lars Løkke Rasmussen in a 2015 speech at Harvard stated, "Denmark is far from a socialist planned economy. Denmark is a market economy. The Nordic model is an expanded welfare state which provides a high level of security for its citizens, but it is also a successful market economy with much freedom to pursue your dreams and live your life as you wish."[3]

[1] James Gwartney, Robert Lawson, Joshua Hall, and Ryan Murphy, *Economic Freedom of the World: 2019 Annual Report* (Vancouver: The Fraser Institute, 2019). See Exhibits 1.2 and 1.3.

[2] The World Bank, *Doing Business 2020*, at www.doingbusiness.org.

[3] Lars Løkke Rasmussen, "Denmark Is Not Socialist," Speech at Harvard University Kennedy School of Government, November 2015, at www.thelocal.dk/20151101/danish-pm-in-us-denmark-is-not-socialist.

2-7b POLITICAL ORGANIZATION

The major alternative to market organization is **collective decision-making**, whereby the government, through the political process, makes decisions for buyers and sellers in an attempt to solve the basic economic questions facing the economy. Sometimes, the government will maintain private ownership but uses taxes, subsidies, and regulations to resolve the basic economic questions. Alternatively, an economic system in which the government also owns the income-producing assets (machines, buildings, and land) and directly determines what goods will be produced is called **socialism**. Either way, individual planning and decisions are replaced by central planning and decisions made through the political process. These decisions can be made by a single dictator or a group of experts, or through democratic voting. Political rather than market forces direct the economy, and government officials and planning boards hand down decisions to expand or contract the output of education, medical services, automobiles, electricity, steel, consumer durables, and thousands of other commodities.

While the market and political process can be used to address the same basic economic questions, there are fundamental differences between the two. The market system relies on voluntary exchange, price signals, and freedom of entry. This results in wider variety of products, a more competitive environment, and more dynamic change. On the other hand, the democratic political process responds primarily to the votes of the majority. In varying degrees, all economies use a combination of the two main methods of economic organization. Even predominantly market economies will still use taxes, subsidies, and some government ownership to direct and control resources. Similarly, predominantly socialist economies will, to some degree, use markets to allocate certain goods and services. As examples, countries such as Venezuela, Zimbabwe, Angola, Cuba, and North Korea rely predominantly on socialism and government planning to organize economic activity. In contrast, countries such as Singapore, New Zealand, Switzerland, Canada, and Australia rely predominantly on market organization. Countries with mixed economies that have significant aspects of both systems include Portugal, Turkey, Mexico, Italy, and Greece.

As we proceed, the tools of economics will be used to analyze both the market and political sectors. We think this approach is important and that you will find it both interesting and enlightening.

Collective decision-making
The use of the political process (voting, taxes, government spending, regulation, political bargaining, lobbying, and so on) to make decisions and allocate resources. In a democratic setting, the votes of citizens and their representatives will determine the actions undertaken.

Socialism
A system of economic organization in which (1) the ownership and control of the basic means of production rest with the state and (2) resource allocation is determined by centralized planning rather than by market forces.

KEY POINTS

- The highest valued activity sacrificed when a choice is made is the opportunity cost of the choice; differences (or changes) in opportunity costs help explain human behavior.

- Mutual gain is the foundation of trade. When two parties engage in voluntary exchange, they are both made better off. Trade creates value because it channels goods and resources to those who value them the most.

- Transaction costs—the time, effort, and other resources necessary to search out, negotiate, and conclude an exchange—hinder the gains from trade in an economy. Middlemen perform a productive function by reducing transaction costs.

- Private property rights motivate owners to use their resources in ways that benefit others and avoid doing harm to them. Private ownership also motivates owners to maintain and care for items they own and conserve valuable resources for the future.

- The production possibilities curve shows the maximum combination of any two products that can be produced with a fixed quantity of resources.

- Over time, the production possibilities curve of an economy can be shifted outward by (1) investment, (2) technological advances, (3) improved institutions, and (4) greater work effort (forgoing leisure).

- The law of comparative advantage indicates that the joint output of individuals, regions, and nations will be maximized when each productive activity is undertaken by the low-opportunity-cost supplier. When a good can be acquired through trade more economically than it can be produced directly, it makes sense to trade for it.

- In addition to the gains that occur when goods are moved toward those who value them most, trade also makes it possible to expand output through specialization, division of labor, mass production processes, and innovation. These improved production techniques have contributed greatly to our modern living standards.

- The size of the economic pie is variable, not fixed. Human ingenuity can expand output by discovering lower cost methods of production and new products that are highly valued relative to cost.

- Economies can either be organized by decentralized markets or they can be centrally planned by government through political decision-making. In varying degrees, all economies use a combination or mixture of these two methods.

CRITICAL ANALYSIS QUESTIONS

1. "If Jones trades a used car to Smith for $5,000, nothing new is created. Thus, there is no way the transaction can improve the welfare of people." Is this statement true? Why or why not?

2. *Why do people engage in trade? If one trading partner gains, must the others involved in the transaction lose an equal amount? Why or why not?

3. What are transaction costs, and why do they reduce the number of trades? How have companies such as eBay (and the Internet more generally) lowered transaction costs?

4. "People in business get ahead by exploiting the needs of their consumers. The gains of business are at the expense of suffering imposed on their customers." Evaluate this statement.

5. What is the major function of the middleman? Would people be better off if there were no middlemen? Why or why not?

6. If you have a private-ownership right to something, what does this mean? Does private ownership give you the right to do anything you want with the things that you own? Explain. How does private ownership influence the incentive of individuals to (a) take care of things, (b) conserve resources for the future, and (c) develop and modify things in ways that are beneficial to others? Explain.

7. What is the law of comparative advantage? According to the law of comparative advantage, what should be the distinguishing characteristics of the goods a nation produces? What should be the distinguishing characteristics of the goods a nation imports? How will international trade influence people's production levels and living standards? Explain.

8. *Does a 60-year-old tree farmer have an incentive to plant and care for Douglas fir trees that will not reach optimal cutting size for another 50 years?

9. *What forms of competition does a private property, market-directed economy authorize? What forms does it prohibit?

10. Why is exchange important to a nation's prosperity? How does trade influence the quantity of output that trading partners are able to produce? In a market economy, will there be a tendency for both resources and products to be supplied by low-cost producers? Why or why not? Does this matter? Explain.

11. Chick-fil-A's "Eat Mor Chikin" advertising campaign features three cows holding signs that say things like "Save the cows, eat more chicken." If consumers began eating more chicken and less beef, would the cattle population increase or decrease? Explain.

12. *In many states, ticket scalping, or reselling tickets to entertainment events at prices above the original purchase price, is prohibited. Who is helped and who is hurt by such prohibitions? How can owners who want to sell their tickets get around the prohibition? Do you think it would be a good idea to prohibit the resale of other things—automobiles, books, works of art, or stock shares—at prices higher than the original purchase price? Why or why not?

13. Two centuries ago, there were more buffalo than cattle in the United States. Even though millions of cattle are killed for beef consumption each year, the cattle population continues to grow while the buffalo are virtually extinct. Why?

14. Consider the following questions:
    a. Do you think that your work effort is influenced by whether there is a close link between personal output and personal compensation (reward)? Explain.
    b. Suppose the grades in your class were going to be determined by a random drawing at the end of the course. How would this influence your study habits?
    c. How would your study habits be influenced if everyone in the class was going to be given an A grade? How about if grades were based entirely on examinations composed of the end of chapter questions in the textbook?
    d. Do you think the total output of a nation will be influenced by whether or not there is a close link between the productive contribution of individuals and their personal reward? Why or why not?

15. In this chapter, it was stated that a private property right also involves having the right to transfer or exchange what you own with others. However, selling your organs is a violation of federal law, a felony punishable by up to five years in prison or a $50,000 fine. In fact, eBay intervened when a person put one of his kidneys up for sale on the auction site (the bidding reached $5.7 million before the auction was halted). Does this lack of legal ability to exchange mean that individuals do not own their own organs? Explain.

16. During the last four decades, entrepreneurs like Steve Jobs, Jeff Bezos, and Elon Musk have earned billions of dollars. Do you think the average American is better or worse off as the result of the economic activities of these individuals? Explain your response.

17. *As the skill level (and therefore earnings rate) of, say, an architect, computer specialist, or chemist increases, what happens to his or her opportunity cost of doing other things? How is the time spent on leisure likely to change?

18. *This question pertains to the addendum to Chapter 2.* The following tables show the production possibilities for two hypothetical countries, Italia and Nire. Which country has the comparative advantage in producing butter? Which country has the comparative advantage in producing guns? What would be a mutually agreeable rate of exchange between the countries?

Italia		Nire	
Guns	Butter	Guns	Butter
12	0	16	0
8	2	12	1
4	4	8	2
0	6	4	3
		0	4

*Asterisk denotes questions for which answers are given in Appendix B.

ADDENDUM

Comparative Advantage, Specialization, and Gains from Trade

This addendum is for instructors who want to assign a more detailed numerical example demonstrating comparative advantage, specialization, and mutual gains from trade. Students who are uncertain about their understanding of these topics may also find this material enlightening. The international trade chapter later in the text provides still more information on trade and how it affects our lives.

We begin with hypothetical production possibilities curves for two countries, Slavia and Lebos, shown in **Exhibit A-1**. The numerical tables represent selected points from each country's production possibilities curve. To make calculations easier, we have assumed away increasing opportunity costs in production so that the production possibilities curves are linear.

Without trade, each country would be able to consume only what it can produce for itself. Let's arbitrarily assume that for survival, Slavia requires three units of food and Lebos requires six units

©iStockphoto.com/sorendls

EXHIBIT A-1

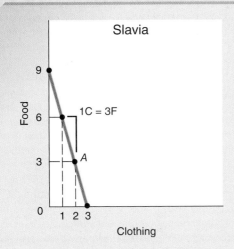

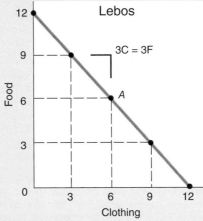

Production Possibilities for Slavia and Lebos

For Slavia, the opportunity cost of producing one unit of clothing is equal to three units of food (1C = 3F). For Lebos, the opportunity cost of producing three units of clothing is equal to three units of food (3C = 3F or 1C = 1F). The difference in the opportunity costs of production will make possible mutually beneficial trade between the countries, with each specializing in its area of comparative advantage.

SLAVIA			LEBOS	
Food	Clothing		Food	Clothing
9	0		12	0
6	1		9	3
3	2		6	6
0	3		3	9
			0	12

3F = 1C (Slavia)
3F = 3C (Lebos)

of food. As can be seen by point *A* in the exhibit, if Slavia were to produce the three units of food it requires, it would have enough resources remaining to produce two units of clothing. Similarly, if Lebos were to produce the six units of food it requires, it would have enough resources left to produce six units of clothing, again shown by point *A* in the exhibit. As we proceed, we will use this outcome as our benchmark outcome that occurs in the absence of specialization and trade between the countries.

Economic analysis suggests that both countries could gain if each were to specialize in the production of the good for which it has the comparative advantage and then trade for the other. First, let's figure out which country has a comparative advantage in the production of clothing. Doing so requires calculating the opportunity cost of producing clothing for each country. Because, in this example, the opportunity costs are constant at all points along the production possibilities curve, rather than increasing, this can be found by first selecting any two points on the production possibilities curve (or equivalently by comparing any two rows of numbers in the numerical tables given in the exhibit). For Slavia, moving from the point of producing six food units and one clothing unit to the alternative point of producing three food units and two clothing units, we see that Slavia gains one clothing unit but must give up three units of food. For simplicity, the opportunity cost for Slavia can be written as $1C = 3F$, where C stands for clothing and F for food. You might note that this same numerical trade-off is true for Slavia anywhere along its production possibilities curve (for example, beginning from nine food units and zero clothing units, it would also have to give up three food units to gain one unit of clothing).

Using a similar approach (taking any two points or two rows in the table) for Lebos shows that for every three units of clothing the country wishes to produce, it must give up three units of food $(3C = 3F)$. This can be treated as any other mathematical equation, and can be simplified by dividing both sides by three, resulting in an opportunity cost of one clothing unit equals one food unit $(1C = 1F)$. Now, compare this to the opportunity cost for Slavia $(1C = 3F)$. Slavia must give up the production of three units of food for every one unit of clothing it produces, whereas Lebos must give up only one unit of food for every one unit of clothing it produces. Thus, Lebos gives up the production of *less* food for every unit of clothing. Lebos is the low-opportunity-cost producer of clothing, and thus, it has a comparative advantage in the production of clothing.

Because comparative advantage is a relative comparison, if one country has the comparative advantage in the production of one of the products, the other country must have the comparative advantage for the other good. Thus, because Lebos has the comparative advantage in clothing, it will be true that Slavia has the comparative advantage in food. However, it is worthwhile to show this here as well. To produce one unit of food, Lebos must give up one unit of clothing (recall the $1C = 1F$ opportunity cost). To produce one unit

of food, Slavia must give up the production of only one-third of a unit of clothing (recall the $1C = 3F$ opportunity cost and rewrite the equation as $1/3 C = 1F$ by dividing both sides of the equation by 3). Thus, Slavia gives up the production of *less* clothing for every unit of food produced. Slavia is the low-opportunity-cost producer of food, and thus has a comparative advantage in the production of food.

Suppose that, according to their comparative advantages, Lebos specializes in producing clothing and Slavia in food. From the last row of the table for Lebos, you can see that it can produce twelve units of clothing (and zero food) if it specializes in producing only clothing. From the top row of the table for Slavia, you can see that it can produce nine units of food (and zero clothing) if it specializes in producing only food. Note that this joint output (nine food and twelve clothing) is greater than the benchmark joint output (nine food and eight clothing) produced and consumed without trade.

If they are to trade, the countries now must find a mutually agreeable rate of exchange. Any rate of exchange *between* the two opportunity costs of $1C = 3F$ and $3C = 3F$ would be mutually agreeable. Here we will use $2C = 3F$.

Recall that Slavia requires three units of food for survival. Now, however, they are specializing and producing nine units of food. Using this rate of exchange, Slavia would send its extra six units of food to Lebos in exchange for four units of clothing. After trade, Slavia would then have three units of food and four units of clothing. Compare this to the situation that existed before specialization and trade, in which Slavia had only three units of food and two units of clothing to consume. Specialization and trade have created two additional units of clothing for Slavia that it would not have had without trade.

With specialization, Lebos is producing twelve units of clothing. In the trade with Slavia, Lebos gave up four units of clothing to obtain six units of food. After trade, Lebos has eight units of clothing remaining and six units of food imported from Slavia. Compare this to the situation that existed before specialization and trade, in which Lebos had only six units of food and six units of clothing to consume. For Lebos, specialization and trade have also created two additional units of clothing that it would not have had without trade.

As this simple example shows, total output is greater and *both* countries are better off when they specialize in the area in which they have a comparative advantage. By doing so, each is able to consume a bundle of goods and services that exceeds what it could have achieved in the absence of trade. This concept applies equally to individuals, states, or nations. The typical worker could not begin to produce alone all of the things he or she can afford to buy with the money earned in a year by specializing and working in a single occupation. As our world has become more integrated over the past several hundred years, the gains that have occurred from specialization and trade are at the root of the significant improvements in well-being that we have experienced.

PART 2

Markets and Government

There are two primary methods of allocating scarce resources: markets and government.

Economics has a great deal to say about how both markets and governments allocate scarce resources. It gives us insight about the conditions under which each will likely work well (and each will likely work poorly). The next four chapters will focus on this topic.

MARKET ALLOCATION OF RESOURCES

Business firms purchase resources like materials, labor services, tools, and machines from households in exchange for income, bidding the resources away from their alternate uses. The firms then transform the resources into products like shoes, automobiles, food products, and medical services and sell them to households. In a market economy, businesses will continue to supply a good or service only if the revenues from the sale of the product are sufficient to cover the cost of the resources required for its production.

Entrepreneurs play an important role in the operation of markets. Their discovery of new products that are highly valued relative to cost and better (or lower cost) methods of production are a central element leading to higher income levels and living standards.

GOVERNMENT ALLOCATION OF RESOURCES

Resource allocation by the government involves a more complex, three-sided exchange. In a democratic political setting, a legislative body levies taxes on voter–citizens, and these revenues are subdivided into budgets, which are allocated to government bureaus and agencies. In turn, the bureaus and agencies use the funds from their budgets to supply goods, services, and income transfers to voter–citizens. The legislative body is like a board of directors elected by the citizens. Legislators have an incentive to take action that will attract votes. Voters have an incentive to support legislators who provide them with goods, services, and transfers that are highly valued relative to their tax payments. When decisions are made democratically, political action will require the approval of a legislative majority.

This section will first analyze the operation of markets and then turn to the political process.

CHAPTER 3

Demand, Supply, and the Market Process

I am convinced that if [the market system] were the result of deliberate human design, and if the people guided by the price changes understood that their decisions have significance far beyond their immediate aim, this mechanism would have been acclaimed as one of the greatest triumphs of the human mind. —**Friedrich Hayek, Nobel Laureate**[1]

From the point of view of physics, it is a miracle that [8 million New Yorkers are fed each day] without any control mechanism other than sheer capitalism. —**John H. Holland, scientist, Santa Fe Institute**[2]

To those who study art, the *Mona Lisa* is much more than a famous painting of a woman. Looking beyond the overall picture, they see and appreciate the brush strokes, colors, and techniques embodied in the painting. Similarly, studying economics can help you to gain an appreciation for the details behind many things in your everyday life. During your last visit to the grocery store, you probably noticed the fruit and vegetable section. Next time, take a moment to ponder how potatoes from Idaho, oranges from Florida, apples from Washington, bananas from Honduras, kiwi fruit from New Zealand, and other items from around the world got there. Literally thousands of different individuals, *working independently*, were involved in the process. Their actions were so well coordinated, in fact, that the amount of each good was just about right to fill exactly the desires of your local community. Furthermore, even the goods shipped from halfway around the world were fresh and reasonably priced.

[1]Friedrich Hayek, "The Use of Knowledge in Society," *American Economic Review* 35 (September 1945): 519–30.
[2]As quoted by Russell Ruthen in "Adapting to Complexity," *Scientific American* 268 (January 1993): 132.

How does all this happen? The short answer is that it is the result of market prices and the incentives and coordination that flow from them. To the economist, the operation of markets—including your local grocery market—is like the brush strokes underlying a beautiful painting. Reflecting on this point, Friedrich Hayek speculates that if the market system had been deliberately designed, it would be "acclaimed as one of the greatest triumphs of the human mind." Similarly, computer scientist John H. Holland argues that, from the viewpoint of physics, the feeding of millions of New Yorkers day after day with very few shortages or surpluses is a miraculous feat (see the chapter-opening quotations).

Amazingly, markets coordinate the actions of millions of individuals *without* central planning. There is no individual, political authority, or central planning committee in charge. Considering that there are more than 330 million Americans with widely varying skills and desires, and roughly 32 million businesses producing a vast array of products ranging from diamond rings to toilet paper, the coordination derived from markets is indeed an awesome achievement.

This chapter focuses on demand, supply, and the determination of market prices. For now, we will analyze the operation of competitive markets—that is, markets in which buyers and sellers are free to enter and exit. We will also assume that the property rights are well defined. Later, we will consider what happens when these conditions are absent.

The buyers' and sellers' desires and incentives determine prices and make markets work. We will begin with the demand (buyer's) side, then turn to the supply (seller's) side of the market.

The produce section of your local grocery store is a great place to see economics in action. Literally millions of individuals from around the world have been involved in the process of getting these goods to the shelves in just the right quantities. Market prices underlie this feat.

As you read this chapter, look for answers to the following questions:

- What are the laws of demand and supply?

- How do consumers decide whether to purchase a good? How do producers decide whether to supply it?

- What must a firm do in order to make a profit? What role do profits and losses play in an economy?

- How is the market price of a good determined?

- What must an entrepreneur do in order to be successful? Why are the actions of entrepreneurs important?

- What is the "invisible hand" principle?

3-1 CONSUMER CHOICE AND THE LAW OF DEMAND

Clearly, prices influence our decisions. As the price of a good increases, we have to give up more of *other* goods if we want to buy it. Thus, as the price of a good rises, its opportunity cost increases (in terms of other goods that must be forgone to purchase it). This basic principle underlies the **law of demand**. *The law of demand states that there is an inverse (or negative) relationship between the price of a good or service and the quantity of it that consumers are willing to purchase*. This inverse relationship means that price and the quantity consumers wish to purchase move in opposite directions. As the price increases, buyers purchase less—and as the price decreases, buyers purchase more.

The availability of **substitutes**—goods that help people achieve similar objectives—helps explain this inverse relationship. No single good is absolutely essential; everything can be replaced with something else. A chicken sandwich can be substituted for a cheeseburger. Wood, aluminum, bricks, and glass can take the place of steel. Going to the movies, playing tennis, watching television, and going to a football game are substitute forms of entertainment. When the price of a good increases, people cut back on their purchases of it and turn to substitute products.

Law of demand
A principle that states there is an inverse relationship between the price of a good and the quantity of it buyers are willing to purchase. As the price of a good increases, consumers will wish to purchase less of it. As the price decreases, consumers will wish to purchase more of it.

Substitutes
Products that serve similar purposes. An increase in the price of one will cause an increase in demand for the other (examples are hamburgers and tacos, butter and margarine, Chevrolets and Fords).

3-1a THE MARKET DEMAND SCHEDULE

The lower portion of **Exhibit 1** shows a hypothetical *demand schedule* for pizza delivery in a city. A demand schedule is simply a table listing the various quantities of something consumers are willing to purchase at different prices. When the price of a large pizza delivery is $35, only 4,000 people per month order pizza delivery. As the price falls to $25, the quantity of pizza deliveries demanded rises to 8,000 per month; when the price falls to $10, the quantity demanded increases to 14,000 per month.

The upper portion of Exhibit 1 shows what the demand schedule would look like if the various prices and corresponding quantities were plotted on a graph and connected by a line. This is called the *demand curve*. When representing the demand schedule graphically, economists measure price on the vertical or *y*-axis and the amount demanded on the horizontal or *x*-axis. Because of the inverse relationship between price and amount purchased, the demand curve will have a negative slope—that is, it will slope downward to the right. More of a good will be purchased as its price decreases. This is the law of demand.

Read horizontally, the demand curve shows how much of a particular good consumers are willing to buy at a given price. Read vertically, the demand curve shows how much consumers value the good. The height of the demand curve at any quantity shows the maximum price consumers are willing to pay for an additional unit. If consumers value highly an additional unit of a product, they will be willing to pay a large amount for it. Conversely, if they place a low value on the additional unit, they will be willing to pay only a small amount for it.

EXHIBIT 1

Law of Demand

As the demand schedule shown in the table indicates, the number of people ordering pizza delivery (just like the consumption of other products) is inversely related to price. The data from the table are plotted as a demand curve in the graph. The inverse relationship between price and amount demanded reflects the fact that consumers will substitute away from a good as it becomes more expensive.

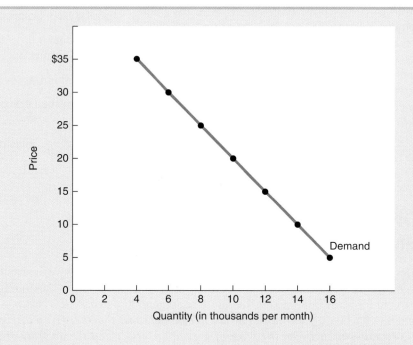

PRICE	QUANTITY (IN THOUSANDS PER MONTH)
$35	4
30	6
25	8
20	10
15	12
10	14
5	16

Because the amount a consumer is willing to pay for a good is directly related to the good's value to them, the height of the demand curve indicates the marginal benefit (or value) consumers receive from additional units. (Recall that we briefly discussed marginal benefit in Chapter 1.) When viewed in this manner, the demand curve reveals that as consumers have more and more of a good or service, they value additional units less and less.

3-1b CONSUMER SURPLUS

Previously, we indicated that voluntary exchanges make both buyers and sellers better off. The demand curve can be used to illustrate the gains to consumers. Suppose you value a particular good at $50, but you are able to purchase it for only $30. Your net gain from buying the good is the $20 difference. Economists call this net gain of buyers **consumer surplus**. Consumer surplus is simply the difference between the maximum amount consumers would be willing to pay and the amount they actually pay for a good.

Exhibit 2 shows the consumer surplus for an entire market. The height of the demand curve measures how much buyers in the market value each unit of the good. The price indicates the amount they actually pay. The difference between these two—the triangular area below the demand curve but above the price paid—is a measure of the total consumer surplus generated by all exchanges of the good. The size of the consumer surplus, or triangular area, is affected by the market price. If the market price for the good falls, more of it will be purchased, resulting in a larger surplus for consumers. Conversely, if the market price rises, less of it will be purchased, resulting in a smaller surplus (net gain) for consumers.

Because the value a consumer places on a particular unit of a good is shown by the corresponding height of the demand curve, we can use the demand curve to clarify the difference between the *marginal value* and *total value* of a good—a distinction we introduced briefly in Chapter 1. Returning to Exhibit 2, if consumers are currently purchasing Q_1 units, the marginal value of the good is indicated by the height of the demand curve at Q_1—the last unit consumed (or purchased). So at each quantity, the height of the demand curve shows the marginal value of that unit, which as you can see declines along a demand curve. The *total value* of the good, however, is equal to the combined value of all units purchased. This is the sum of the value of each unit (the heights along the demand curve) on the x-axis, out to and including unit Q_1. This total value is indicated graphically as the entire area under the demand curve out to Q_1 (the triangular area representing consumer surplus *plus* the unshaded rectangular area directly below it).

Consumer surplus
The difference between the maximum price consumers are willing to pay and the price they actually pay. It is the net gain derived by the buyers of the good.

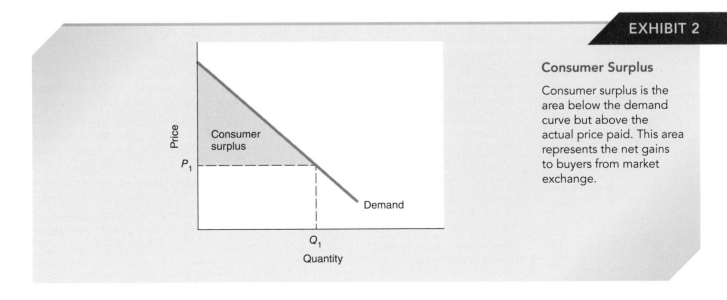

EXHIBIT 2

Consumer Surplus

Consumer surplus is the area below the demand curve but above the actual price paid. This area represents the net gains to buyers from market exchange.

You can see that the total value to consumers of a good can be far greater than the marginal value of the last unit consumed. When additional units are available at a low price, the marginal value of a good may be quite low, even though its total value to consumers is exceedingly high. This is usually the case with water. The value of the first few units of water consumed per day will be exceedingly high. The consumer surplus derived from these units will also be large when water is plentiful at a low price. As more and more units are consumed, however, the *marginal value* of even something as important as water will fall to a low level. When water is cheap, then, people will use it not only for drinking, cleaning, and cooking but also for washing cars, watering lawns, flushing toilets, and maintaining fish aquariums. Thus, although the total value of water is rather large, its marginal value is quite low.

Consumers will tend to expand their consumption of a good until its price and *marginal value* are equal (which occurs at Q_1 in Exhibit 2 at a price of P_1). Thus, the price of a good (which equals marginal value) reveals little about the *total value* derived from the consumption of it. This is the reason that the market price of diamonds (which reflects their high marginal value) is greater than the market price of water (which has a low marginal value), even though the total value of diamonds is far less than the total value of water. Think of it this way: Beginning from your current levels of consumption, if you were offered a choice between one diamond or one gallon of water right now, which would you take? You would probably take the diamond, because at the margin it has more value to you than additional water. However, if given a choice between giving up *all* of the water you use or *all* of the diamonds you have, you would probably keep the water over diamonds, because water has more total value to you.

3-1c RESPONSIVENESS OF QUANTITY DEMANDED TO PRICE CHANGES: ELASTIC AND INELASTIC DEMAND CURVES

As we previously noted, the availability of substitutes is the main reason why the demand curve for a good slopes downward. Some goods, however, are much easier than others to substitute away from. As the price of tacos rises, most consumers find hamburgers a reasonable substitute. Because of the ease of substitutability, the quantity of tacos demanded is quite sensitive to a change in their price. Economists would say that the demand for tacos is relatively *elastic* because a small price change will cause a rather large change in the amount purchased. Alternatively, goods like gasoline and electricity have fewer close substitutes. When their prices rise, it is harder for consumers to find substitutes for these products. When close substitutes are unavailable, even a large price change may not cause much of a change in the quantity demanded. In this case, an economist would say that the demand for such goods is relatively *inelastic*.

Graphically, this different degree of responsiveness is reflected in the steepness of the demand curve, as shown in **Exhibit 3**. The flatter demand curve (D_1, left frame) is for a product like tacos, for which the quantity purchased is highly responsive to a change in price. As the price increases from $2.00 to $4.00, the quantity demanded falls sharply from ten to four units. The steeper demand curve (D_2, right frame) is for a product like gasoline, for which the quantity purchased is much less responsive to a change in price. For gasoline, an increase in price from $2.00 to $4.00 results in only a small reduction in the quantity purchased (from ten to eight units). An economist would say that the flatter demand curve D_1 is "relatively elastic," whereas the steeper demand curve D_2 is "relatively inelastic." The availability of substitutes is the main determinant of a product's elasticity or inelasticity and thus how flat or steep its demand curve is.

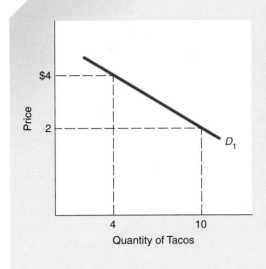

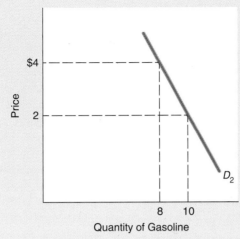

Elastic and Inelastic Demand Curves

The responsiveness of consumer purchases to a change in price is reflected in the steepness of the demand curve. The flatter demand curve (D_1) for tacos shows a higher degree of responsiveness and is called relatively elastic, while the steeper demand curve (D_2) for gasoline shows a lower degree of responsiveness and is called relatively inelastic.

3-2 CHANGES IN DEMAND VERSUS CHANGES IN QUANTITY DEMANDED

The purpose of the demand curve is to show what effect a price change will have on the quantity demanded (or purchased) of a good. Economists refer to a change in the quantity of a good purchased in response solely to a price change as a "change in *quantity demanded*." A change in quantity demanded is simply a movement along a demand curve from one point to another.

Changes in factors other than a good's price—such as consumers' income and the prices of closely related goods—will also influence the decisions of consumers to purchase a good. If one of these other factors changes, the entire demand curve will *shift* inward or outward. Economists refer to a shift in the demand curve as a "change in *demand*."

Failure to distinguish between a change in demand and a change in quantity demanded is one of the most common mistakes made by beginning economics students.[3] *A change in demand is a shift in the entire demand curve. A change in quantity demanded is a movement along the same demand curve*. The easiest way to distinguish between these two concepts is the following: If the change in consumer purchases is caused by a change in the price of the good, it is a change in quantity demanded—a movement along the demand curve; if the change in consumer purchases is due to a change in anything other than the price of the good (a change in consumer income, for example), it is a change in demand—a shift in the demand curve.

Let us now take a closer look at some of the factors that cause a "change in demand"— an inward or outward shift in the entire demand curve.

1. Changes in consumer income. An increase in consumer income makes it possible for consumers to purchase more goods. If you were to win the lottery, or if your boss were to give you a raise, you would respond by increasing your spending on many products. Alternatively, when the economy goes into a recession, falling incomes and rising unemployment cause consumers to reduce their purchases of many items. A change in consumer income will result in consumers buying more or less of a product at all possible prices. When consumer income increases, in the case of most goods, individuals will

---

[3]Questions designed to test the ability of students to make this distinction are favorites of many economics instructors. A word to the wise should be sufficient.

EXHIBIT 4

Change in Demand versus Change in Quantity Demanded

Panel (a) shows a change in quantity demanded, a movement along the demand curve D_1, in response to a change in the price of tablet computers. Panel (b) shows a change in demand, a shift of the entire curve, in this case due to an increase in consumer income.

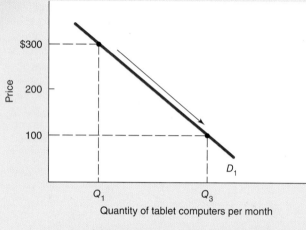

(a) Increase in quantity demanded

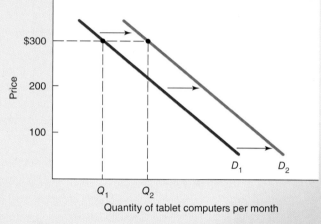

(b) Increase in demand

purchase more of the good even if the price is unchanged. This is shown by a shift to the right—an outward shift—in the demand curve. Such a shift is called an *increase in demand*. A reduction in consumer income generally causes a shift to the left—an inward shift—in the demand curve, which is called a *decrease in demand*. Note that the appropriate terminology here is an increase or a decrease in demand, not an increase or a decrease in quantity demanded.

Exhibit 4 highlights the difference between a change in demand and a change in quantity demanded. The demand curve D_1 indicates the initial demand curve for tablet computers. At a price of $300, consumers will purchase Q_1 units. If the price were to decline to $100, the *quantity demanded* would increase from Q_1 to Q_3. The arrow in panel (a) indicates the change in *quantity demanded*—a movement along the original demand curve D_1 in response to the change in price. Now, alternatively suppose there were an increase in income that caused the *demand* for tablet computers to shift from D_1 to D_2. As indicated by the arrows in panel (b), the entire demand curve would shift outward. At the higher income level, consumers would be willing to purchase more tablet computers than before. This is true at a price of $300, $200, $100, and every other price. The increase in income leads to an increase in *demand*—a shift in the entire curve.

2. Changes in the number of consumers in the market. Businesses that sell products in college towns are greatly saddened when summer arrives. As you might expect in these towns, the demand for many items—from pizza delivery to beer—falls during the summer. Exhibit 5 shows how the falling number of consumers in the market caused by students going home for the summer affects the demand for pizza delivery. With fewer customers, the demand curve shifts inward from D_1 to D_2. There is a decrease in demand; pizza stores sell fewer pizzas than before regardless of what price they originally charged. Had their original price been $20, then demand would fall from 200 pizzas per week to only 100. Alternatively, had their original price been $10, then demand would fall from 300 pizzas to 200. When autumn arrives and the students come back

the quantity supplied to the market. But last year, the price of oranges was really high and the supply of them was really low. Economists are wrong!"

13. What is the invisible hand principle? Does it indicate that self-interested behavior within markets will result in actions that are beneficial to others? What conditions are necessary for the invisible hand to work well? Why are these conditions important?

14. In a market economy, will there be a tendency for both resources and products to be supplied by low-cost producers? Why or why not? Does this matter? Explain.

15. What is the difference between substitutes and complements? Indicate two goods that are substitutes for each other. Indicate two goods that are complements.

16. Do business firms operating in competitive markets have a strong incentive to serve the interest of consumers? Are they motivated by a strong desire to help consumers? Are "good intentions" necessary if individuals are going to engage in actions that are helpful to others? Discuss.

17. What must an entrepreneur do in order to be successful? If an entrepreneur is successful, how will the lives of others be affected? Explain.

18. How has entrepreneurial activity altered the goods and services available to consumers in recent years? Provide examples.

19. What determines whether a new product will be a success or failure? Why is the profit and loss system important to guide entrepreneurial efforts in a competitive market economy?

*Asterisk denotes questions for which answers are given in Appendix B.

CHAPTER 4

Demand and Supply: Applications and Extensions

The division of labour, from which so many advantages are derived, is not originally the effect of any human wisdom, which foresees and intends that general opulence to which it gives occasion. It is the necessary, though very slow and gradual consequence of a certain propensity in human nature . . .; the propensity to truck, barter, and exchange one thing for another. —**Adam Smith**[1]

Markets are everywhere. They exist in many different forms and degrees of sophistication. In elementary schools, children trade their lunch box items; in households, individuals trade chores ("I'll clean the bathroom, if you'll clean the kitchen"); and in the stock market, individuals who have never met exchange shares of corporate stock and other financial assets worth billions of dollars each business day. Even making an activity illegal does not eliminate the market for it. Instead, the market is merely pushed underground. The exchange of illegal drugs or tickets to a big game at illegal prices illustrates this point.

As Adam Smith put it almost 250 years ago, human beings have a natural propensity "to truck, barter, and exchange one thing for another" (see the quotation at the chapter opening). We all want to improve our standard of living, and trade with others helps us achieve this goal—by allowing us to get the goods and services we really want and giving us the opportunity to earn the income necessary to buy them.

Market prices coordinate the actions of buyers and sellers, but sometimes the "price" of a good or service in a particular market is called something different. For example, in the labor market, the price is often called the "wage rate." In the loanable funds market, the price is generally referred to as the "interest rate." However, as Juliet observes in Shakespeare's Romeo and Juliet, "What's in a name? That which we call a rose by any other name would smell as sweet." The same is true for prices. When the price of something is referred to by another term, such as the wage or interest rate, it will still play the same role.

[1]Adam Smith, *An Inquiry into the Nature and Causes of the Wealth of Nations* (New York: Modern Library, 1937), 13.

Therefore, when these special terms are used, we put them along the vertical axes of supply and demand diagrams, just as we do "price"—because that's what they are.

In the previous chapter, we saw how the forces of supply and demand determine market prices and coordinate the actions of buyers and sellers in the absence of government intervention. In this chapter, we turn our attention to using the supply and demand model to understand more fully what happens when governments intervene in markets by implementing price controls, taxes, and subsidies.

As you read this chapter, look for answers to the following questions:

- How are the markets for products and resources related?

- What happens when prices are set by law above or below the market equilibrium level?

- How does a tax or subsidy affect a market? What determines the distribution of the tax burden (or subsidy benefit) between buyers and sellers?

- What is the Laffer curve? What does it indicate about the relationship between tax rates and tax revenues?

4-1 THE LINK BETWEEN RESOURCE AND PRODUCT MARKETS

Understanding the interrelationship among markets is vitally important. A change in one market will also lead to changes in other markets. This section addresses the link between the resource and product markets.

The production process generally involves (1) the purchase of resources—like raw materials, labor services, tools, and machines; (2) transformation of the resources into products (goods and services); and (3) sale of the goods and services in a product market. Production is generally undertaken by business firms. Typically, business firms will demand resources, and households will supply them. Firms demand resources *because* they contribute to the production of goods and services. In turn, households supply them in order to earn income.

Just as in product markets, the demand curve in a **resource market** is typically downward-sloping and the supply curve upward-sloping. The inverse relationship between the amount of a resource demanded and its price exists because businesses will substitute away from a resource as its price rises. In contrast, there will be a direct relationship between the amount of a resource supplied and its price because a higher price means greater rewards to those who provide more. As in product markets, prices will coordinate the choices of buyers and sellers in resource markets, bringing the quantity demanded into balance with the quantity supplied.

The labor market is a large component of the broader resource market. Actually, there is not just one market for labor, but rather there are many labor markets, one for each different skill-experience-occupational category. Let's look at the labor market for waitstaff (waiters and waitresses). **Exhibit 1** shows how resource and product markets are linked. The supply of young workers in many occupations, including waitstaff, has declined in recent years in many areas of the United States. This lower supply has caused the wages (tip-inclusive wages) of waitstaff to increase (for example, from $10 to $12 in Exhibit 1a). The higher price of this resource increases the cost of producing restaurant meals. This higher cost, in turn, reduces the supply (shifting S_1 to S_2) of restaurant meals, pushing the price upward (Exhibit 1b). When the price of a resource increases, it will lead to higher production costs, lower supply, and higher prices for the goods and services produced with the resource.

Of course, lower resource prices have the opposite effect. Lower resource prices reduce costs and expand the supply of consumer goods made with the lower-priced resources (shifting the supply curve to the right). The increase in supply will lead to a lower price in the product market. *Thus, when the price of a resource—such as labor—changes, the prices of goods and services produced with that resource will change in the same direction.*

Resource market
The market for inputs used to produce goods and services.

EXHIBIT 1

Resource Prices, Opportunity Cost, and Product Markets

When the supply of young workers falls, it pushes the wage rates of waiters and waitresses upward (a). In the product market (b), the higher wage rates will increase the opportunity costs of restaurants, reducing supply (shift from S_1 to S_2), thus leading to higher meal prices.

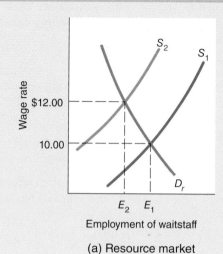

(a) Resource market

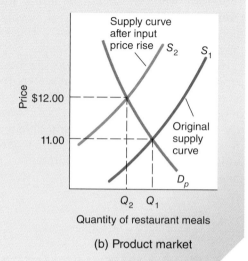

(b) Product market

Changes in product markets will also influence resource markets. There is a close relationship between the demand for products and the demand for the resources required for their production. An increase in demand for a consumer good—automobiles, for example—will lead to higher auto prices, which will increase the profitability of producing automobiles and give automakers an incentive to expand output. But the expansion in automobile output will require additional resources, causing an increase in the demand for, and prices of, the resources required for their production (steel, rubber, plastics, and the labor services of autoworkers, for example). The higher prices of these resources will cause other industries to conserve on their use, freeing them up for more automobile production.

The process will work in reverse if demand for a product falls. A decrease in demand will not only reduce the price of the product but will also reduce the demand for and prices of the resources used to produce it. ***Thus, when the demand for a product changes, the demand for (and prices of) the resources used to produce it will change in the same direction.***

4-2 THE ECONOMICS OF PRICE CONTROLS

Price controls
Government-mandated prices that are generally imposed in the form of maximum or minimum legal prices.

Buyers often complain that prices are too high, while sellers complain that they are too low. Unhappy with the prices established by market forces, various groups might try to persuade the government to intervene and impose **price controls**. Price controls force buyers or sellers to alter the prices of certain products. Price controls may be either price ceilings, which set a maximum legal price for a product, or price floors, which impose a minimum legal price. Imposing price controls may look like a simple, easy way for the government to help buyers at the expense of sellers (or vice versa). However, price controls reduce the gains from trade, and they generate secondary effects that often harm even the intended beneficiaries. Let's consider this issue in more detail.

4-2a THE IMPACT OF PRICE CEILINGS

Price ceiling
A legally established maximum price sellers can charge for a good or resource.

A **price ceiling** establishes a maximum legal price that can be charged for a good, service, or resource. Exchanges at prices above the ceiling are prohibited. Sometimes price ceilings reflect political forces wanting to keep the price of a specific item low. The rent controls adopted by some cities provide examples of this type of price ceiling. In other cases, the price ceiling is designed to prohibit temporary increases in the price of goods. Laws prohibiting price increases during an emergency such as a hurricane or spread of a contagious virus like COVID-19 illustrate this type of price ceiling. These laws against "price gouging" (as the price increases are often called) automatically go into effect once a state of emergency is declared. (The accompanying Applications in Economics box, "The Imposition of Price Ceilings after Hurricanes," provides an example.) Regardless of the reason adopted, the demand and supply model provides insight on what happens when a price ceiling forces price below the market equilibrium level.

Exhibit 2 shows the impact of imposing a price ceiling (P_1) for a product below its equilibrium level (P_0). At the lower price, the quantity supplied by producers is lower on the supply curve, at Q_S, while the quantity demanded by consumers is greater, at Q_D, on the demand curve. A **shortage** ($Q_D - Q_S$) of the good will result because the quantity demanded by consumers exceeds the quantity supplied by producers at the new controlled price. After the price ceiling is imposed, the quantity of the good exchanged declines from the equilibrium quantity to Q_S, and the gains from trade (consumer and producer surplus) fall as well.

Normally, a higher price would ration the good to the buyers most willing to pay for it and encourage consumers to conserve on their purchases. Because the price ceiling keeps this from happening, though, other means must be used to allocate the smaller quantity Q_S among consumers wanting to purchase Q_D. The situation may be worsened as consumers anticipating the shortages may hoard the item when they do find it available. Predictably, nonprice factors will become more important in the rationing process. Sellers will ration their goods and services to eager buyers on the basis of factors other than their willingness to pay. For example, sellers will be more inclined to sell their products to their friends, to buyers who do them favors, and even buyers willing to make illegal "under-the-table" payments. Time might also be used as the rationing device, with those willing to wait in line the longest being the ones able to purchase the good. Sellers may also impose quantity limits on consumer purchases. In addition, the below-equilibrium price reduces the incentive of sellers to expand the future supply of the good. At the lower price, suppliers will direct resources away from production of the good and into other, more profitable areas. As a result, the product shortage will worsen over time.

What other secondary effects can be expected? ***In the real world, there are two ways that sellers can raise prices. First, they can raise their money price, holding quality constant. Or, second, they can hold the money price constant while reducing the quality of the good.*** (The latter might also include reducing the size of the product, say, for example, a smaller candy bar or a shorter loaf of bread.) Faced with a price ceiling, sellers will use quality reductions as a way to raise their prices. Because of the government-created shortage, many consumers will buy the lower-quality good rather than do without it.

Shortage
A condition in which the amount of a good offered for sale by producers is less than the amount demanded by buyers at the existing price. An increase in price would eliminate the shortage.

EXHIBIT 2

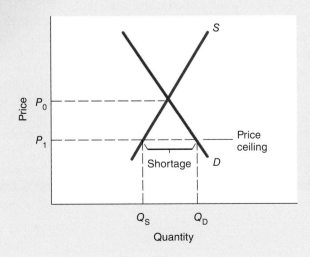

The Impact of a Price Ceiling

When a price ceiling like P_1 pushes the price of a product (rental housing, for example) below the market equilibrium, a shortage will develop. Because prices are not allowed to direct the market to equilibrium, nonprice elements will become more important in rationing the good.

APPLICATIONS IN ECONOMICS

The Imposition of Price Ceilings after Hurricanes

Major hurricanes not only cause massive property damage and widespread power outages but also dramatically increase the local demand for items such as lumber, gasoline, ice, batteries, chain saws, and gasoline-powered generators. As a result, the prices of these items rise significantly.

The higher prices play three important roles. First, they encourage suppliers to bring more of these items quickly to the disaster area. Second, they allocate the supplies to those deriving the greatest value from their use. Third, they encourage consumers to conserve on their purchases, helping to discourage hoarding of supplies. The higher prices will begin to subside as additional quantities of critically needed supplies flow into the disaster area, but it is precisely these higher prices that encourage this response.

It is a natural reaction to think that the higher prices are unfair and that price controls should be imposed to prevent "price gouging." State and local officials have often imposed price controls for precisely these reasons. While price ceilings may be motivated by a desire to help consumers by keeping prices low, they exert secondary effects that hinder both the evacuation and recovery process. At the lower mandated prices, consumer demand quickly outstrips the available supplies creating artificial shortages. The artificial shortages created by price controls in turn encourage consumers to hoard items when they do locate them. The controls also slow the flow of supplies into the area.

The price controls result in serious misallocation of resources. Electric generators provide one of the best examples.

The lack of electric power after a hurricane means that gasoline pumps, refrigerators, cash registers, ATMs, and other electrical equipment do not work. Grocery stores can't open and thousands of dollars' worth of food spoils. Although gas stations have gasoline in their underground storage tanks, it can't be pumped out. ATMs and banks can't operate without electricity, so people can't get to their money, which is critical because almost all transactions in post-hurricane environments are made with cash.

Hardware stores that sell gasoline-powered electric generators typically have only a few in stock, but after a hurricane suddenly hundreds of businesses and residents want to buy them. In the absence of price controls, the price of these generators would rise and individual homeowners would generally be outbid by businesses, which can put the generators to use operating stores, gas stations, and ATMs. It is these uses that would yield enough revenue to cover the high price of the generators because they facilitate the provision of other goods and services that people desperately want.

Market prices would allocate generators and other urgently needed supplies to those most willing to pay for them. Price ceilings keep this from happening. In the absence of price rationing people keep their generators at home, and it is commonplace for hardware store owners with a few generators on hand to take one home for their family and then sell the others to their close friends, neighbors, and relatives to run televisions and household appliances. Moreover, the incentive of people to take action and bring generators in from other areas is slowed. For example, John Shepperson of Kentucky took time away from his normal job to buy 19 generators, rent a truck, and drive it 600 miles to the Hurricane Katrina–damaged area of Mississippi. He thought he would be able to sell the generators at high enough prices to cover his cost and earn a profit. Instead his generators were confiscated, Shepperson was arrested for price gouging, held by police for four days, and the generators kept in police custody. They never made it to consumers with urgent needs who desperately wanted to buy them.

The dramatic change in conditions that often accompany a hurricane highlights the role prices play. It also illustrates how the secondary effects accompanying price controls can magnify the damage generated by hurricanes and stand in the way of evacuation efforts.

It is important to note that a shortage is not the same as scarcity. ***Scarcity is inescapable.*** Scarcity exists whenever people want more of a good than nature has provided. This means, of course, that almost everything of value is scarce. ***Shortages, on the other hand, are a result of prices being set below their equilibrium values—a situation that is avoidable if prices are permitted to rise.*** Removing the price ceiling will allow the price to rise to its equilibrium level (P_0 rather than P_1 in Exhibit 2). This will stimulate additional production, discourage consumption, and increase the incentive of entrepreneurs to search for and develop substitute goods. This combination of forces will eliminate the shortage.

4-2b RENT CONTROL: A CLOSER LOOK AT A PRICE CEILING

Rent controls are a price ceiling intended to protect residents from high housing prices. Rent controls are currently in place in 182 U.S. cities; all but two are in New Jersey, New York, and California. Most of these measures were enacted during either World War II or the 1970s, when inflation was high. Rent controls peaked in the mid-1980s. At that time, more than 200 cities, encompassing about 20 percent of the nation's population, imposed rent controls. Currently, 32 states prohibit cities within their state from enacting rental control laws.[2]

Because rent controls push the price of rental housing below the equilibrium level, the amount of rental housing demanded by consumers will exceed the amount landlords will make available. Initially, if the mandated price is only slightly below equilibrium, the impact of rent controls may be barely noticeable. Over time, however, the effects will worsen. Inevitably, rent controls that continue will lead to the following results.

1. Shortages and black markets will develop. Because the quantity of housing demanded will exceed the quantity supplied, some people who value rental housing highly will be unable to find it. Frustrated by the shortage, they will try to induce landlords to rent to them. Some will agree to prepay their rent, including a substantial damage deposit. Others might agree to rent or buy the landlord's furniture at exorbitant prices in order to get an apartment. Still others will make under-the-table (black market) payments to secure housing.

2. The future supply of rental housing will decline. The below-equilibrium price will discourage entrepreneurs from constructing new rental housing units, and private investment will flow elsewhere. A recent study of rent control in San Francisco found that the controls decreased the supply of rental units by 15 percent, primarily as the result of the sale of units to occupants and the conversion of apartment buildings to condominiums.[3] In contrast, removal of rent controls will often lead to a sharp increase in rental housing construction, as builders seek to expand the supply that lagged behind as the result of the controls. This happened in both Boston and Santa Monica following repeal of rent controls.

3. The quality of rental housing will deteriorate. When apartment owners are not allowed to raise their prices, they will use quality reductions to achieve this objective. Normal maintenance and repair service will deteriorate. Tenant parking lots will be eliminated (or rented out). Eventually, the quality of the rental housing will reflect the controlled price. Cheaper housing will be of cheaper quality.

---

[2]Prasanna Rajasekaran, Mark Treskon, and Solomon Greene, "Rent Control: What Does the Research Tell Us about the Effectiveness of Local Action?" Urban Institute *Research to Action Lab*, January 2019, at https://www.urban.org/sites/default/files/publication/99646/rent_control._what_does_the_research_tell_us_about_the_effectiveness_of_local_action_1.pdf.

[3]Rebecca Diamond, Tim McQuade, and Franklin Qian, "The Effects of Rent Control Expansion on Tenants, Landlords, and Inequality: Evidence from San Francisco," *American Economic Review* 109 (September 2019): 3365–94.

Rent controls lead to shortages, poor maintenance, and deterioration in the quality of rental housing.

4. Nonprice methods of rationing will become more important. Because price no longer rations rental housing, other forms of competition will develop. Landlords will rely more heavily on nonmonetary discriminating devices. They will favor friends, people of influence, and those whose lifestyles resemble their own. In contrast, applicants with many children or unconventional lifestyles, and perhaps racial minorities, will find fewer landlords who will rent to them. In New York City, where rent controls are in force, a magazine article suggested that "joining a church or synagogue" could help people make the connections they need to get an apartment. Can you imagine having to devote this amount of effort to finding an apartment? If your city enacts rent controls, you just might have to.

5. Inefficient use of housing space will result. The tenant in a rent-controlled apartment will think twice before moving. Why? Even though the tenant might want a larger or smaller space or an apartment closer to work, he or she will be less likely to move because it will be much more difficult to find a unit that's vacant. Turnover will be lower, and many people will find themselves in locations and in apartments not well suited to their needs.[4]

Imposing rent control laws may sound like a simple way to deal with high housing prices. However, the secondary effects are so damaging that many cities have begun repealing them. In the words of Swedish economist Assar Lindbeck: "In many cases, rent control appears to be the most efficient technique presently known to destroy a city—except for bombing."[5] Though this may overstate the case, both economics and experience show that the controls adversely impact the quantity and quality of rental housing.

4-2c THE IMPACT OF PRICE FLOORS

Price floor
A legally established minimum price buyers must pay for a good or resource.

A **price floor** establishes a minimum price that can legally be charged. The government imposes price floors on some agricultural products, for example, in an effort to artificially increase the prices that farmers receive. When a price floor is imposed above the current market equilibrium price, it will alter the market's operation. **Exhibit 3** illustrates the impact of imposing a price floor (P_1) for a product above its equilibrium level (P_0). At the higher price, the quantity supplied by producers increases along the supply curve to Q_S, while the quantity demanded by consumers decreases along the demand curve to Q_D. A **surplus** ($Q_S - Q_D$) of the good will result, as the quantity supplied by producers exceeds the quantity demanded by consumers at the new controlled price. Just like a price ceiling, a price floor reduces the quantity of the good exchanged and reduces the gains from trade.

Surplus
A condition in which the amount of a good offered for sale by producers is greater than the amount that buyers will purchase at the existing price. A decline in price would eliminate the surplus.

As in the case of the price ceiling, nonprice factors will play a larger role in the rationing process. But because there is a surplus rather than a shortage, this time buyers will be in a position to be more selective. Buyers will purchase from sellers willing to offer them nonprice favors—better service, discounts on other products, or easier credit terms, for

---

[4] Ibid.

[5] Assar Lindbeck, *The Political Economy of the New Left* (New York: Harper & Row, 1972), 39.

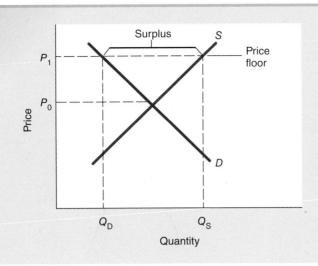

The Impact of a Price Floor

When a price floor such as P_1 keeps the price of a good or service above the market equilibrium, a surplus will result.

example. When it's difficult to alter the product's quality—in this case, improve it to make it more attractive for the price that must be charged—some producers will be unable to sell it.

It is important to note that a surplus doesn't mean the good is no longer scarce. People still want more of the good than is freely available from nature, even though they want less of it at the controlled price than sellers want to bring to the market. A decline in price would eliminate the surplus, but the item will be scarce in either case.

4-2d MINIMUM WAGE: A CLOSER LOOK AT A PRICE FLOOR

A **minimum wage** is a price floor. The federal minimum wage is currently $7.25 per hour. Because most employees in the United States earn wages in excess of the federal minimum, their employment opportunities are largely unaffected by the minimum wage law. However, low-skilled and inexperienced workers whose equilibrium wage rates are lower than the minimum wage will be affected.

Exhibit 4 shows the direct effect of a $12 per-hour minimum wage on the employment opportunities of a group of low-skilled workers. Without a minimum wage, the supply of and demand for these low-skilled workers would be in balance at some lower wage rate; here we use $7. Because the minimum wage makes low-skilled labor more expensive, employers will substitute machines and more highly skilled workers for the now more expensive low-skilled employees. Fewer low-skilled workers will be hired when the minimum wage pushes their wages up. Graphically, this is reflected in the movement up along the demand curve in Exhibit 4 from the equilibrium point to the point associated with the higher, $12 wage rate (point A). The result will be a reduction in employment of low-skilled workers from E_0 to E_1.

On the supply side of the market, as the wages of low-skilled workers are pushed above equilibrium, there will be more unskilled workers looking for jobs. Graphically, this is reflected in the movement up along the supply curve in Exhibit 4 from the equilibrium point to the point associated with the higher, $12 wage rate (point B). At the $12 wage rate, the quantity of workers searching for jobs will exceed the quantity of jobs available, causing excess supply.

In a labor market, an excess supply will take the form of an abnormally high rate of unemployment. Thus, *economic analysis indicates that minimum-wage legislation will lead to high unemployment rates among low-skilled workers*. The exceedingly high unemployment rate of teenagers in the United States (a group with limited skills because they lack work experience) is consistent with this analysis. In recent years, the unemployment

Minimum wage
Legislation requiring that workers be paid at least the stated minimum hourly rate of pay.

EXHIBIT 4

Employment and the Minimum Wage

If the market wage of a group of employees is $7 per hour, a $12 per-hour minimum wage will increase the earnings of workers able to retain their jobs, but reduce the employment opportunities of others as the number of jobs available shrinks from E_0 to E_1.

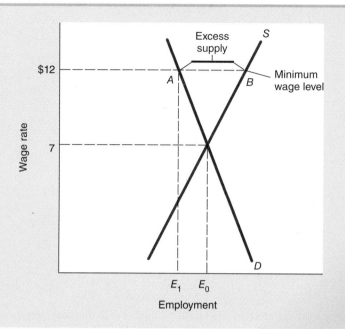

rate of teenagers has generally been about four times the rate for workers aged 25 and older. Of course, the higher unemployment rate of teenagers reflects their shifts back and forth between schooling and the labor force, but detailed studies indicate that the minimum wage is also a contributing factor.

It is important to remember that the market price—the wage rate—is only one dimension of the transaction. When a price floor pushes the wage rate above equilibrium, employers will have less incentive to offer nonwage benefits to employees because they will have no trouble hiring low-skilled workers. Predictably, a higher minimum wage will lead to a deterioration of the nonwage attributes of minimum-wage jobs, and so workers in these jobs will experience less convenient working hours, fewer training opportunities, and less continuous employment. Moreover, minimum wage legislation prohibits employers and employees from entering into agreements for mutually advantageous job opportunities that offer attractive work experiences at a wage below the minimum. As a result, employment opportunities such as internships that open doors and enhance future earnings are more difficult to arrange. In this regard, it is interesting that Congress, which utilizes hundreds of interns at a zero wage, exempts itself from minimum wage legislation.

The adverse impact of minimum wage laws on the work experience and training opportunities of youthful workers is particularly important. Low-paying, entry-level jobs often provide workers with experience that will help them move up the job ladder to higher-paying positions. Employment experience obtained at an early age, even on menial tasks, can help people acquire self-confidence, good work habits, and skills that make them more valuable to future employers. Mandated minimum wages will make it more difficult for youthful workers to acquire work experience and jobs with training opportunities.[6]

Workers who are able to maintain their employment at the higher minimum-wage rate—most likely the better qualified among those with low skill levels—gain from a minimum wage. However, some firms will respond to the higher minimum by reducing the weekly hours of the low-skill workers who remain employed. Thus, part of the increase in weekly earnings due to a higher hourly wage rate will be offset by a decrease in weekly hours worked.

---

[6]For evidence that the minimum wage limits training opportunities, see David Neumark and William Wascher, "Minimum Wages and Training Revisited," *Journal of Labor Economics* 19 (July 2001): 563–95.

Proponents of minimum wage laws argue that they help the poor. Is this really true? According to the U.S. Department of Labor, most minimum wage earners are young, part-time workers and relatively few live below the poverty line. Nearly one-half of minimum wage workers are between the ages of 16 to 24 years and approximately three-fifths hold a part-time job. Fewer than 20 percent of minimum wage workers are from families below the poverty line, and only about one out of every four is married. Only 15 percent are a sole earner providing support for a family with one or more children. Therefore, even if the adverse effects of a higher minimum wage on employment and training opportunities are small, a higher minimum wage does little to help the poor, making it a much less attractive antipoverty program than other alternatives.[7]

How does the minimum wage affect the employment of low-skilled workers? Numerous studies have been conducted on the minimum wage's impact on employment levels. It is challenging to isolate the effect of the minimum wage since other factors such as economic conditions also affect the number of workers employed. As a result, some studies find little or no effect of the minimum wage on employment levels. However, a comprehensive survey of more than 90 studies reported that 85 percent of them found that a higher minimum wage reduces employment. These studies indicate that a 10 percent increase in the minimum wage reduces the employment of low-skilled workers by 1 to 3 percent.[8] Minimum-wage supporters argue that the higher wages for low-skilled workers are worth this reduction in employment and job-training opportunities. The critics disagree, arguing that if permitted to work, the low-skill workers would gain experience and training, which would facilitate their movement up the job ladder to higher wage positions.

Cost of living and typical wage rates vary considerably across locations. As a result, the impact of the federal minimum wage differs among cities and states. During the past couple of decades, some cities and states have adopted minimum wages above the federal level. Twenty-nine states now have minimum wage rates above the federal minimum. As of January 2020, 11 states have minimum rates between $11 and $13.50.

Some cities have adopted even higher minimum rates. For example, Los Angeles, San Jose, San Francisco, Washington DC, New York City, and Seattle all have minimum wage rates of $15 or more. Because of its rapid increase in recent years, the Seattle minimum wage has been studied extensively. A team of economists from the University of Washington found that as two hikes increased the minimum rate from $9.47 in April 2015 to $13 per hour by January 2016, the percent reduction in employment was approximately equal to the percent wage increase for workers with low work experience who were impacted by the mandated hikes.[9] This means that the labor income of this group of employees was unchanged. Further, the increased minimum wage decreased the rate of new entrants into the workforce. Together, these results indicate that the minimum wage increases did not help those starting out in their careers. The employment reductions of the Seattle minimum wage hike were substantially larger than those accompanying federal and state minimum wage increases. This is not surprising. Compared to state and federal minimums, it is much easier for at least some of the employers to shift their business location away from the geographically smaller areas of cities.

[7]See David Neumark and William Wascher, "The Effects of Minimum Wages Throughout the Wage Distribution," *Journal of Human Resources* 39 (April 2004): 425–50; David Neumark and William Wascher, *Minimum Wages.* (Cambridge, MA: MIT Press, 2008); and Joseph J. Sabia and Richard V. Burkhauser, "Minimum Wages and Poverty: Will a $9.50 Federal Minimum Wage Really Help the Working Poor?" *Southern Economic Journal* 76 (January 2010): 592–623, for evidence on this point.

[8]See David Neumark and William Wascher, *Minimum Wages* (Cambridge, MA: MIT Press, 2008). Also, see David Neumark, "The Econometrics and Economics of the Employment Effects of Minimum Wages: Getting from Known Unknowns to Known Knowns," *German Economic Review* 20 (August 2019): 293–329.

[9]Ekaterina Jardim, Mark C. Long, Emma van Inwegen, Jacob Vigdor, and Hilary Wething, "Minimum Wage Increases and Individual Employment Trajectories," National Bureau of Economic Research Working Paper Number 25182, October 2018.

4-3 BLACK MARKETS AND THE IMPORTANCE OF THE LEGAL STRUCTURE

When price controls are imposed, exchanges at prices outside of the range set by the government are illegal. Governments may also make it entirely illegal to buy and sell certain products. This is the case with drugs like heroin and cocaine in the United States. Similarly, prostitution is illegal in all states except Nevada. However, controlling prices and making a good or service illegal doesn't eliminate market forces. When demand is strong and gains from trade can be had, markets will develop and exchanges will occur in spite of the restrictions. People will also engage in illegal exchanges in order to evade taxes. For example, the $5.85 per-pack cigarette tax in New York City has made cigarette smuggling into that city a thriving business.

Black market
A market that operates outside the legal system in which either illegal goods or services are sold, or legal ones are sold at illegal prices or terms.

Markets that operate outside the legal system are called **black markets**. How do black markets work? Can markets function without the protection of the law? As in other markets, supply and demand will determine prices in black markets, too. However, because black markets operate outside the official legal structure, enforcement of contracts and the dependability of quality will be less certain. Furthermore, participation in black markets involves greater risk, particularly for suppliers. Prices in these markets will have to be higher than they otherwise would be to compensate suppliers for the risks they are taking—the threat of arrest, possibility of a fine or prison sentence, and so on. Perhaps most important, in black markets there are no legal channels for the peaceful settlement of disputes. When a buyer or a seller fails to deliver, it is the other party who must try to enforce the agreement, usually through the use or threat of physical force.

Black markets like those for illegal drugs are characterized by less dependable product quality and the greater use of violence to settle disputes between buyers and sellers.

Compared with normal markets, economic analysis indicates that black markets will be characterized by a higher incidence of defective products, higher profit rates (for those who do not get caught), and more violence. The incidence of phony tickets purchased from street dealers selling them at illegal prices and deaths caused by toxic, illicit drugs are reflections of the high presence of defective goods in these markets. The expensive clothes and automobiles of many drug dealers provide evidence of the high monetary profits present in black markets. Crime statistics indicate that violence is often used to settle disputes arising from black-market transactions. In urban areas, a high percentage of the violent crimes, including murder, are associated with illegal trades gone bad and competition among dealers in the illegal drug market.

The prohibition of alcohol in the United States from 1920 to 1933 provides additional evidence that violence, deception, and fraud plague markets that operate outside the law. When the production and sale of alcohol were illegal during the Prohibition era, gangsters dominated the alcohol trade, and the murder rate soared to record highs. There were also problems with product quality (tainted or highly toxic mixtures, for example) similar to the ones present in modern-day illegal-drug markets. When Prohibition was repealed and the market for alcoholic beverages began operating once again within the legal framework, these harmful secondary effects disappeared.

The operation of black markets highlights a point often taken for granted: *A legal system that provides for secure private-property rights, contract enforcement, and access to an unbiased court system for settling disputes is vitally important for the smooth operation of markets*. Markets will exist in any environment, but they can be counted on to function efficiently only when property rights are secure and contracts are impartially enforced.

4-4 THE IMPACT OF A TAX

Tax incidence
The way the burden of a tax is distributed among economic units (consumers, producers, employees, employers, and so on). The actual tax burden does not always fall on those who are statutorily assigned to pay the tax.

How do taxes affect market exchange? When governments tax goods, who bears the burden? Economists use the term **tax incidence** to indicate how the burden of a tax is *actually* shared between buyers (who pay more for what they purchase) and sellers (who receive less for what they sell). When a tax is imposed, the government can make either the buyer or the seller legally responsible for payment of the tax. The legal assignment is called the *statutory incidence* of the tax. However, the person who writes the check to the government—that is, the person statutorily responsible for the tax—is not always the one who bears the tax burden. The *actual incidence* of a tax may lie elsewhere. If, for example, a tax is placed statutorily on a seller, the seller might simply increase the price of the product. In this case, the buyers end up bearing some, or all, of the tax burden through the higher price.

To illustrate, **Exhibit 5** shows how a $1,000 tax placed on the sale of used cars would affect the market. (To simplify this example, let's assume all used cars are identical.) Here, the tax has statutorily been placed on the seller. When a tax is imposed on the seller, it shifts the supply curve upward by exactly the amount of the tax—$1,000, in this example. To understand why, remember that the height of the supply curve at a particular quantity shows the minimum price required to cause enough sellers to offer that quantity of cars for sale. Suppose you were a potential seller, willing to sell your car for any price over $6,000, but you would keep it unless you could pocket at least $6,000 from the sale. Because you now have to pay a tax of $1,000 when you sell your car, the minimum price you will accept *from the buyer* will rise to $7,000, so that after paying the tax, you will retain $6,000. Other potential sellers will be in a similar position. The tax will push the minimum price each seller is willing to accept upward by $1,000. Thus, the after-tax supply curve will shift vertically by this amount.

Sellers would prefer to pass the entire tax on to buyers by raising prices by the full amount of the tax, rather than paying any part of it themselves. However, as sellers begin to raise prices, customers respond by purchasing fewer units. At some point, to avoid losing additional sales, some sellers will find it more profitable to accept part of the tax burden themselves (in the form of a lower price net of tax), rather than to raise the price by the full amount of the tax. This process is shown in Exhibit 5.

Before the tax was imposed, used cars sold for a price of $7,000 (at the intersection of the original supply and demand curves shown by point *A*). After the $1,000 tax is imposed, the equilibrium price of used cars will rise to $7,400 (to point *B*, the intersection of the

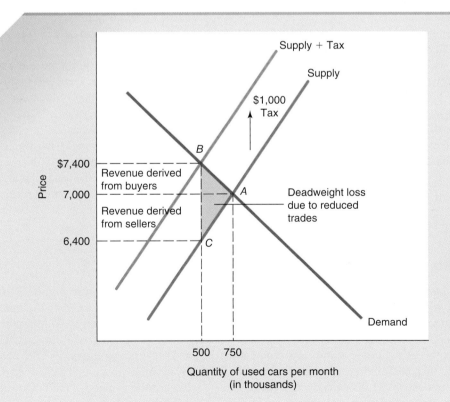

EXHIBIT 5

The Impact of a Tax Imposed on Sellers

When a $1,000 tax is imposed statutorily on the sellers of used cars, the supply curve shifts vertically upward by the amount of the tax. The price of used cars to buyers rises from $7,000 to $7,400, resulting in buyers bearing $400 of the burden of this tax. The price received by a seller falls from $7,000 to $6,400 ($7,400 minus the $1,000 tax), resulting in sellers bearing $600 of the burden.

new supply curve including the tax, and the demand curve). Thus, despite the tax being statutorily imposed on sellers, the higher price shifts some of the tax burden to buyers. Buyers will now pay $400 more for used cars. Sellers now receive $7,400 from the sale of their used cars. However, after sending $1,000 in taxes to the government, they retain only $6,400. This is exactly $600 less than the seller would have received had the tax not been imposed. Because the distance between the supply curves is exactly $1,000, this net price can be found in Exhibit 5 by following the vertical line down from the new equilibrium (point *B*) to the original supply curve (point *C*) and over to the price axis. In this case, each $1,000 of tax revenue transferred to the government imposes a burden of $400 on buyers (in the form of higher used-car prices) and a $600 burden on sellers (in the form of lower net receipts from a car sale), even though sellers are responsible for actually sending the $1,000 tax payment to the government.

The tax revenue derived from a tax is equal to the **tax base** (in this case, the number of used cars exchanged) multiplied by the **tax rate**. After the tax is imposed, the quantity exchanged will fall to 500,000 cars per month because some buyers will choose not to purchase at the $7,400 price, and some sellers will decide not to sell when they are able to net only $6,400. Given the after-tax quantity sold, the monthly revenue derived from the tax will be $500 million (500,000 cars multiplied by $1,000 tax per car).

4-4a THE DEADWEIGHT LOSS CAUSED BY TAXES

As Exhibit 5 shows, a $1,000 tax on used cars causes the number of units exchanged to fall from 750,000 to 500,000. It reduces the quantity of units exchanged by 250,000 units. Remember, trade results in mutual gains for both buyers and sellers. The loss of the mutual benefits that would have been derived from these additional 250,000 units also imposes a cost on buyers and sellers. But this cost—the loss of the gains from trade eliminated by the tax—does not generate any revenue for the government. Economists call this the **deadweight loss** of taxation. In Exhibit 5, the size of the triangle *ABC* measures the deadweight loss. The deadweight loss is a burden imposed on buyers and sellers over and above the cost of the revenue transferred to the government. Sometimes it is referred to as the **excess burden of taxation**. It is composed of losses to both buyers (the lost consumer surplus consisting of the upper part of the triangle *ABC*) and sellers (the lost producer surplus consisting of the lower part of the triangle *ABC*).

The deadweight loss to sellers includes an indirect cost imposed on the people who supply resources to that industry (such as its suppliers and employees). The 1990 luxury-boat tax provides a vivid illustration of this point. Supporters of the luxury-boat tax assumed the tax burden would fall primarily on wealthy yacht buyers. The actual effects were quite different, though. Because of the tax, luxury-boat sales fell sharply and thousands of workers lost their jobs in the yacht-manufacturing industry. The deadweight loss triangle might seem like an abstract concept, but it wasn't so abstract to the employees in the yacht industry who lost their jobs! Their losses are part of what is reflected in the triangular area. Moreover, because luxury-boat sales declined so sharply, the tax generated only a meager amount of revenue. The large deadweight loss (or excess burden) combined with meager revenue for the government eventually led to the repeal of the tax.

4-4b ACTUAL VERSUS STATUTORY INCIDENCE

Economic analysis indicates that the actual burden of a tax—or more precisely, the split of the burden between buyers and sellers—does not depend on whether the tax is statutorily placed on the buyer or the seller. To see this, we must first look at how the market responds to a tax statutorily placed on the buyer. Continuing with the auto tax example, let's suppose that the government places the $1,000 tax on the buyer of the car, rather than the seller. After making a used-car purchase, the buyer must send a check to the government for $1,000. Imposing a tax on buyers will shift the demand curve downward by the amount of the tax, as shown in **Exhibit 6**. This is because the height of the demand

Tax base
The level or quantity of an economic activity that is taxed. Higher tax rates reduce the level of the tax base because they make the activity less attractive.

Tax rate
The per-unit amount of the tax or the percentage rate at which the economic activity is taxed.

Deadweight loss
The loss of gains from trade to buyers and sellers that occurs when a tax is imposed. The deadweight loss imposes a burden on both buyers and sellers over and above the actual payment of the tax.

Excess burden of taxation
Another term for deadweight loss. It reflects losses that occur when beneficial activities are forgone because they are taxed.

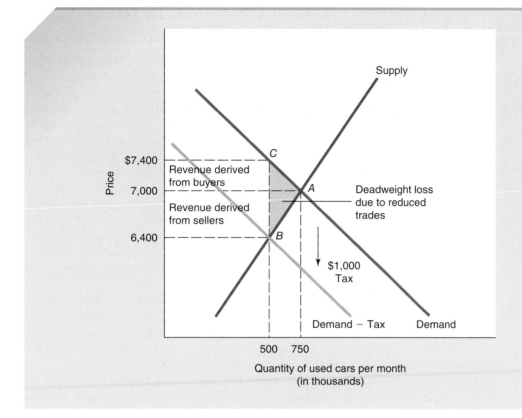

EXHIBIT 6

The Impact of a Tax Imposed on Buyers

When a $1,000 tax is imposed statutorily on the buyers of used cars, the demand curve shifts vertically downward by the amount of the tax. The price of used cars falls from $7,000 to $6,400, resulting in sellers bearing $600 of the burden. The buyer's total cost of purchasing the car rises from $7,000 to $7,400 ($6,400 plus the $1,000 tax), resulting in buyers bearing $400 of the burden of this tax. The incidence of this tax on used cars is the same regardless of whether it is statutorily imposed on buyers or sellers.

curve represents the maximum price a buyer is willing to pay for the car. If a particular buyer is willing and able to pay only $5,000 for a car, the $1,000 tax would mean that the most the buyer would be willing to pay *to the seller* would be $4,000. This is because the total cost to the buyer is now the purchase price plus the tax.

As Exhibit 6 shows, the price of used cars falls from $7,000 (point A) to $6,400 (point B) when the tax is statutorily placed on the buyer. Even though the tax is placed on buyers, the reduction in demand that results causes the price received by sellers to fall by $600. Thus, $600 of the tax is again borne by sellers, just as it was when the tax was placed statutorily on them. From the buyer's standpoint, a car now costs $7,400 ($6,400 paid to the seller plus $1,000 in tax to the government). Just as when the tax was imposed on the seller, the buyer now pays $400 more for a used car.

A comparison of Exhibits 5 and 6 makes it clear that the actual burden of the $1,000 tax is independent of its statutory incidence. In both cases, buyers pay a total price of $7,400 for the car (a $400 increase from the pretax level), and sellers receive $6,400 from the sale (a $600 decrease from the pretax level). Correspondingly, the revenue derived by the government, the number of sales eliminated by the tax, and the size of the deadweight loss are identical whether the law requires payment of the tax by the sellers or by the buyers. A similar phenomenon occurs with any tax. The 15.3 percent FICA (Social Security and Medicare) payroll tax, for example, is statutorily levied as 7.65 percent on the employee and 7.65 percent on the employer. The impact is to drive down the net pay received by employees and raise the employers' cost of hiring workers. Economic analysis tells us that the actual burden of this tax will probably differ from its legal assignment and that it will be the same regardless of how the tax is statutorily assigned. Because market prices (here, workers' gross wage) will adjust, the incidence of the tax will be identical regardless of whether the 15.3 percent is levied on employees or on employers or is divided between the two parties.

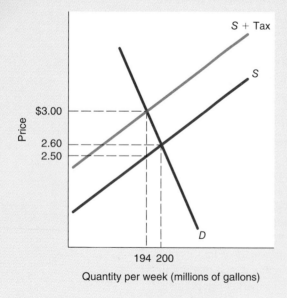

"THIS NEW TAX PLAN SOUNDS PRETTY GOOD... WE GET A 9% CUT AND BUSINESS PICKS UP THE BURDEN...."

The actual burden of a tax is independent of whether it is imposed on buyers or sellers.

4-4c ELASTICITY AND THE INCIDENCE OF A TAX

If the actual incidence of a tax is independent of its statutory assignment, then what does determine the incidence? The answer: The incidence of a tax depends on the responsiveness of buyers and of sellers to a change in price. When buyers respond to even a small increase in price by leaving the market and buying other things, they will not be willing to accept a price that is much higher than it was prior to the tax. Similarly, if sellers respond to a small reduction in what they receive by shifting their goods and resources to other markets, or by going out of business, they will not be willing to accept a much smaller payment, net of tax. The burden of a tax—its incidence—tends to fall more heavily on whichever side of the market has the least attractive options elsewhere—the side of the market that is less sensitive to price changes, in other words.

In the preceding chapter, we saw that the steepness of the supply and demand curves reflects how responsive producers and consumers are to a price change. Relatively inelastic demand or supply curves are steeper (more vertical), indicating less responsiveness to a change in price. Relatively elastic demand or supply curves are flatter (more horizontal), indicating a higher degree of responsiveness to a change in price.

Using gasoline as an example, panel (a) of **Exhibit 7** illustrates the impact of a tax when demand is relatively inelastic and supply is relatively elastic. It will not be easy for

EXHIBIT 7

How the Burden of a Tax Depends on the Elasticities of Demand and Supply

In panel (a), when demand is relatively more inelastic than supply, buyers bear a larger share of the burden of the tax. In panel (b), when supply is relatively more inelastic than demand, sellers bear a larger share of the tax burden.

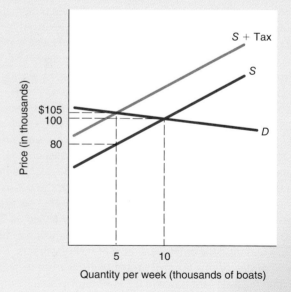

(a) Tax on gasoline

(b) Tax on luxury boats

gasoline consumers to shift—particularly in the short run—to other fuels in response to an increase in the price of gasoline. The inelastic demand curve shows this. When a 50-cent per-gallon tax is imposed on gasoline (roughly the current average of combined federal and state taxes), buyers end up paying 40 cents more per gallon ($3.00 instead of $2.60), while the net price received by sellers is only 10 cents less ($2.50 instead of $2.60). ***When demand is relatively inelastic, or supply is relatively elastic, buyers will bear the larger share of the tax burden.***

Conversely, when demand is relatively elastic and supply is inelastic, more of the tax burden will fall on sellers and resource suppliers. The luxury-boat tax illustrates this point. As we mentioned earlier, Congress imposed a tax on the sale of luxury boats in 1990. Later, the tax was repealed because of its adverse impact on sales and employment in the industry. There are many things wealthy potential yacht owners can spend their money on other than luxury boats *sold in the United States.* For one thing, they can buy a yacht someplace else, perhaps in Mexico, England, or the Bahamas. Or they can spend more time on the golf course, travel to exotic places, or purchase a nicer car or a vacation home. Because there are attractive substitutes, the demand for domestically produced luxury boats is relatively elastic compared with supply. Therefore, as panel (b) of Exhibit 7 illustrates, when a $25,000 tax is imposed on luxury boats, prices rise by only $5,000 (from $100,000 to $105,000), but output falls substantially (from 10,000 to 5,000 boats). The net price received by sellers falls by $20,000 (from $100,000 to $80,000 per boat). ***When demand is relatively elastic, or supply is relatively inelastic, sellers (including resource suppliers) will bear the larger share of the tax burden.***

4-4d ELASTICITY AND THE DEADWEIGHT LOSS

We have seen that the elasticities of supply and demand determine how the burden of a tax is distributed between buyer and seller. They also influence the size of the deadweight loss caused by the tax because they determine the total reduction in the quantity exchanged. When either demand or supply is relatively inelastic, fewer trades will be eliminated by the tax, so the deadweight loss will be smaller. From a policy perspective, the excess burden of a tax system will therefore be lower if taxes are levied on goods and services for which either demand or supply is highly inelastic.

4-5 TAX RATES, TAX REVENUES, AND THE LAFFER CURVE

It is important to distinguish between the average and marginal rates of taxation. They can be very different, and both provide important information. The average tax rate is generally used to examine how different income groups are burdened by a tax, whereas the marginal tax rate is the key to understanding the negative economic effects created by a tax. Both can be computed with simple equations. The **average tax rate (ATR)** can be expressed as follows:

$$\text{ATR} = \frac{\text{Tax liability}}{\text{Taxable income}}$$

Average tax rate (ATR)
Tax liability divided by taxable income. It is the percentage of income paid in taxes.

For example, if a person's tax liability was $3,000 on an income of $20,000, his or her average tax rate would be 15 percent ($3,000 divided by $20,000). The average tax rate is simply the percentage of income that is paid in taxes.

In the United States, the personal income tax provides the largest single source of government revenue. This tax is particularly important at the federal level. You may have heard that the federal income tax is "progressive." A **progressive tax** is defined as a tax in which the average tax rate rises with income. In other words, people with higher income pay a larger percentage of their income in taxes. Alternatively, taxes can be proportional or

Progressive tax
A tax in which the average tax rate rises with income. People with higher incomes will pay a higher percentage of their income in taxes.

Proportional tax
A tax in which the average tax rate is the same at all income levels. Everyone pays the same percentage of income in taxes.

Regressive tax
A tax in which the average tax rate falls with income. People with higher incomes will pay a lower percentage of their income in taxes.

Marginal tax rate (MTR)
The additional tax liability a person faces divided by his or her additional taxable income. It is the percentage of an extra dollar of income earned that must be paid in taxes. It is the marginal tax rate that is relevant in personal decision-making.

regressive. A **proportional tax** is defined as a tax in which the average tax rate remains the same across income levels. Under a proportional tax, everyone pays the same percentage of their income in taxes. Finally, a **regressive tax** is defined as a tax in which the average tax rate falls as income rises. If someone making $100,000 per year paid $30,000 in taxes (an ATR of 30 percent), while someone making $30,000 per year paid $15,000 in taxes (an ATR of 50 percent), the tax code would be regressive. Note that a regressive tax merely means that the percentage paid in taxes declines with income; the actual dollar amount of the tax bill might still be higher for those with larger incomes.

Although the average tax rate is useful in determining whether an income tax is progressive, proportional, or regressive, it is the marginal tax rate that is most relevant when individuals are making choices. It is the marginal tax rate that determines how much of an additional dollar of income must be paid in taxes (and thus, also, how much one gets to keep). An individual's marginal tax rate can be very different from his or her average tax rate. The **marginal tax rate (MTR)** can be expressed as follows:

$$MTR = \frac{\text{Change in tax liability}}{\text{Change in taxable income}}$$

The MTR reveals both how much of one's *additional* income must be turned over to the tax collector and how much is retained by the individual taxpayer. For example, when the MTR is 25 percent, $25 of every $100 of additional earnings must be paid in taxes. The individual is permitted to keep only $75 of his or her additional income, in other words. The marginal tax rate is vitally important because it affects the incentive to earn additional income. The higher the marginal tax rate, the less incentive individuals have to earn more income. At high marginal rates, for example, many spouses will choose to stay home rather than take a job, and others will choose not to take on second jobs or extra work. **Exhibit 8** shows the calculation of both the average and marginal tax rates within the framework of the 2019 federal income tax tables. In addition to the federal income tax, there are also state and local income taxes and payroll taxes. The taxpayer's marginal tax rate will reflect the combined impact of all taxes that reduce the take-home pay derived from additional earnings.

EXHIBIT 8

Average and Marginal Tax Rates in the Income Tax Tables

This excerpt from the 2019 federal income tax table shows that in the 22 percent federal marginal income tax bracket, each $100 of additional taxable income a single taxpayer earns ($45,000 versus $45,100, for example) causes his or her tax liability to increase by $22 (from $5,764 to $5,786). Note that the average tax rate for a single taxpayer at $45,000 is about 12.8 percent ($5,764 divided by $45,000), even though the taxpayer's marginal rate is 22 percent.

2019 Tax Table—*Continued*

If line 11b (taxable income) is–		And you are–			
At least	But less than	Single	Married filing jointly	Married filing separately	Head of a household
		Your tax is–			
45,000	45,050	5,764	5,015	5,764	5,126
45,050	45,100	5,775	5,021	5,775	5,132
45,100	45,150	5,786	5,027	5,786	5,138
45,150	45,200	5,797	5,033	5,797	5,144

$100 of additional income . . .   . . . results in $22 of additional tax liability.

Governments generally levy taxes to raise revenue. The revenue derived from a tax is equal to the tax base multiplied by the tax rate. As we previously noted, taxes will reduce the level of the activity. When an activity is taxed more heavily, people will choose to do less of it. The higher the tax rate, the greater the shift away from the activity. If taxpayers can easily escape the tax by altering their behavior (perhaps by shifting to substitutes), the tax base will shrink significantly as rates are increased. This erosion in the tax base in response to higher rates means that an increase in tax rates will generally lead to a less-than-proportional increase in tax revenue.

Economist Arthur Laffer popularized the idea that, beyond some point, higher tax rates will shrink the tax base so much that tax revenue will eventually decline as tax rates are pushed to higher and higher levels. The curve illustrating the relationship between tax rates and tax revenues is called the **Laffer curve. Exhibit 9** illustrates the concept of the Laffer curve as it applies to income taxes. Obviously, tax revenue would be zero if the income tax rate were zero. What isn't so obvious is that tax revenue would also be zero (or at least very close to zero) if the tax rate were 100 percent. Confronting a 100 percent tax rate, most individuals would go fishing or find something else to do rather than engage in taxable productive activity, since the 100 percent tax rate would eliminate all personal reward derived from earning taxable income. Why work when you have to give every penny of your earnings to the government?

As tax rates are reduced from 100 percent, the incentive to work and earn taxable income increases, income expands, and tax revenue rises. Similarly, as tax rates increase from zero, tax revenue expands. Clearly, at some rate greater than zero but less than 100 percent, tax revenue will be maximized (point *B* in Exhibit 9). This is not to imply that the tax rate that maximizes revenue is the ideal, or optimal, tax rate from the standpoint of the economy as a whole. Although it might be the tax rate that generates the most revenue for government, we must also consider the welfare reductions imposed on individuals by the deadweight loss created by the tax. As rates are increased and the maximum revenue point (*B*) is approached, relatively large tax rate increases will be necessary to expand tax revenue by even a small amount. In this range, the deadweight loss of taxation in the form of reductions in gains from trade will be exceedingly large relative to the additional tax revenue. Far from being ideal, the revenue maximizing tax rate will be highly inefficient.

Laffer curve
A curve illustrating the relationship between the tax rate and tax revenues. Tax revenues will be low at both very high and very low tax rates. When tax rates are quite high, lowering them can increase tax revenue.

EXHIBIT 9

Laffer Curve

Because taxing an activity affects the amount of it people will do, a change in tax rates will not lead to a proportional change in tax revenues. As the Laffer curve indicates, beyond some point (*B*), an increase in tax rates will cause tax revenues to fall. At high tax rates, revenue can be increased by lowering tax rates. The tax rate that maximizes tax revenue is higher than the ideal tax rate for the economy as a whole because of the large deadweight loss of taxation as tax rates increase toward point *B*.

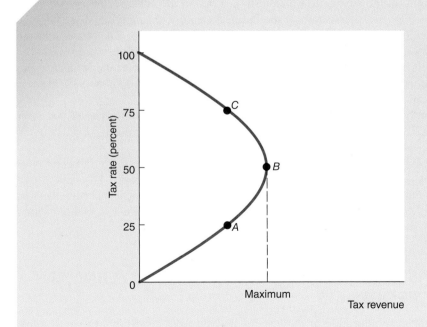

The Laffer curve shows that it is important to distinguish between changes in tax rates and changes in tax revenues. Higher rates will not always lead to more revenue for the government. Similarly, lower rates will not always lead to less revenue. ***When tax rates are already high, a rate reduction may increase tax revenues. Correspondingly, increasing high tax rates may lead to less tax revenue.***

Evidence from the sharp reduction in marginal tax rates imposed on those with high incomes during the 1980s supports the Laffer curve. The top marginal rate was reduced from 70 percent at the beginning of the decade to 33 percent by the end of the decade. Even though the top rates were cut sharply, tax revenues and the share of the personal income tax paid by high-income earners actually rose as a result. During the decade, revenue collected from the top 1 percent of earners rose a whopping 51.4 percent (after adjusting for inflation). In 1980, 19 percent of the personal income tax was collected from the top 1 percent of earners. By 1990, at the lower tax rates, the top 1 percent of earners accounted for more than 25 percent of income tax revenues. The top 10 percent of earners paid just over 49 percent of total income taxes in 1980, but by 1990 the share paid by these earners had risen to 55 percent. Thus, the reduction in the exceedingly high rates increased the revenue collected from high-income taxpayers. Additional evidence on the impact of these tax changes in the 1980s is provided in Special Topic 1.

4-6 THE IMPACT OF A SUBSIDY

Subsidy
A payment the government makes to either the buyer or the seller, usually on a per-unit basis, when a good or service is purchased or sold.

The supply and demand framework can also be used to analyze the impact of a government **subsidy**. A subsidy is a payment to either the buyer or seller of a good or service, usually on a per-unit basis. When a subsidy is granted to buyers, proponents typically argue that the subsidy will make the purchase of the good more affordable. Correspondingly, subsidies to sellers are generally thought to improve the profitability of the producers in the industry. As we have seen in other cases, however, the effect of government programs often differ substantially from the stated intentions of their proponents. Because prices change when subsidies are imposed (just as when taxes are imposed), the benefit of a subsidy can be partially, or totally, shifted from buyer to seller, or vice versa.

Suppose that the government, in an effort to make the cost of college more affordable, granted full-time students a subsidy of $4,000 per year. What impact would this subsidy have on the price and quantity in the market for a college education? **Exhibit 10** provides insight on the answer to this question. Prior to the subsidy, the market price was determined by the intersection of the initial demand and supply curves. Thus, the pre-subsidy equilibrium price for a year of college was $10,000. The subsidy to the student-buyers increases demand, causing the demand curve to shift upward by $4,000. A new equilibrium will occur at a higher price ($12,000 in our example) and larger output (Q_2 rather than Q_1). The net price to students will fall to $8,000, the $12,000 new market price minus the $4,000.

Interestingly, even though the students received an educational subsidy of $4,000, their net gain was only $2,000. The rest of the benefits went to the educational suppliers in the form of higher prices for their services.

As we previously discussed, the burden of a tax does not necessarily fall entirely or even primarily on the party writing out the check to the taxing authority. The same is true for subsidies. Parties other than the direct subsidy recipients may benefit substantially from the subsidies. Moreover, the direct recipients of the subsidy may gain less, and often substantially less, than their grant from the government.

4-6a ELASTICITY AND THE BENEFIT OF GOVERNMENT SUBSIDY PROGRAMS

What determines the allocation of the benefits derived from a subsidy? In the example of Exhibit 10, the benefit of the $4,000 subsidy granted to students was split evenly

EXHIBIT 10

The Impact of a Subsidy Granted to Buyers

Here we illustrate how a $4,000 subsidy granted to full-time college students would impact the price and quantity of a year of college education. Prior to the subsidy, the equilibrium price of a year of college was $10,000 and Q_1 students attended college. The subsidy to students would cause demand to shift vertically upward by the amount of the subsidy, pushing the equilibrium price of a year of college to $12,000. Students would gain $2,000 in the form of a lower net cost of a year of college (the new net price after the subsidy is $8,000), but the suppliers would also gain $2,000 in the form of higher prices for their services. If the supply curve was more inelastic relative to the demand curve, the gains of the students would be smaller and those of the suppliers larger.

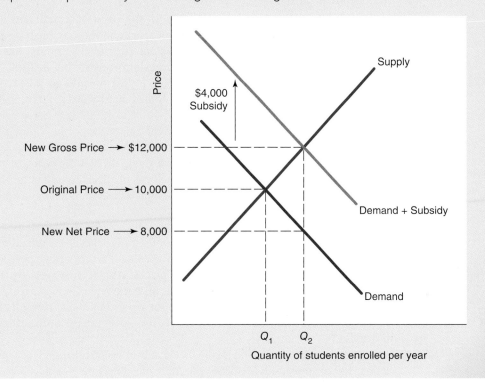

between buyers and sellers. However, the actual distribution of this benefit will depend on the elasticity of supply and demand—just as it does with a tax. Consider the case where the subsidy is granted to the buyers, causing the demand curve for the product to shift upward by the amount of the subsidy. If the supply curve is highly inelastic relative to demand, the increase in demand will lead primarily to higher prices and most of the benefits will be derived by the suppliers of the good or service. In contrast, if the supply curve is elastic and the demand curve inelastic, the increase in demand will lead to only a small increase in price and the primary beneficiaries of the subsidy will be consumers in the form of lower prices.

The greater share of the benefit of a subsidy will always be shifted toward the more inelastic side of the market. Thus, the more inelastic the supply, the larger the share of the benefit that will accrue to sellers. Conversely, the more inelastic the demand, the larger the share of the benefit that will accrue to buyers. Sometimes the subsidies will be granted to sellers rather than buyers. Nonetheless, the benefits will still flow primarily toward the more inelastic side of the market.

4-6b REAL-WORLD SUBSIDY PROGRAMS

The federal government now operates over 2,000 separate subsidy programs. Spending on these programs and the taxes that finance them are major items in the government budget.

Some subsidy programs, such as Medicare and food stamps, provide payments to buyers. Others, such as the subsidies to the arts, public broadcasting, and sports stadiums, are directed toward suppliers. As we discussed, however, the party granted the subsidy may not be the one who captures the larger share of the actual benefit from the subsidy.

Let's take a closer look at the subsidies granted to college students. There has been a substantial increase in federal and state subsidies to college students since 1990. Measured in constant 2018 dollars, federal and state grants directly to college students rose from $3,194 per full-time equivalent student in 1990–1991 to $9,431 in 2018–2019, an increase of 288 percent. Federal loans to college students increased even more rapidly. Adjusted for inflation, federal loans per full-time student more than tripled, soaring from $2,060 in 1990–1991 to $6,469 in 2018–2019.

As Exhibit 10 illustrated, subsidies in the form of grants and loans to students will increase the demand for college education and thereby push up its price. Indeed, this has been the case. Measured in constant 2017–2018 dollars, the average price of a year of college more than doubled, increasing from $5,589 in 1990–1991 to $12,615 in 2017–2018. In 1990–1991, the price of a year of college was 10.0 percent of the median household income in the United States, but by 2017–2018, the figure had risen to 20.1 percent.[10]

Most students perceive that government aid in the form of grants and low-interest loans make it more economical for them to attend college. But there is another side to this issue: The subsidies are a driving force underlying the soaring cost of a college education, and rising student loan debt. Moreover, colleges themselves are major beneficiaries of the student subsidies. Thus, it is not surprising that college administrators are at the forefront of those lobbying for additional subsidies.

Subsidies for medical care have had a similar impact. The Medicare and Medicaid programs were introduced in the mid-1960s. Since the large subsidies accompanying these programs were initiated, prices of medical services have persistently increased at twice the rate of the general level of prices. Again, this suggests that the suppliers of these services derived a substantial share of the benefits in the form of higher prices for their services. Given that the supply of most medical services is highly inelastic, this is precisely what one would expect from an increase in the subsidies granted to buyers.

Both the educational and medical care subsidies are allocated to a subset of the population. For example, the Medicare program subsidizes the healthcare purchases of senior citizens, and the Medicaid program provides subsidies to low-income households. These subsidies increase the demand for health care and drive up the prices of medical service for all consumers, including those ineligible for either program. When only some of the buyers in a market are subsidized, groups that are ineligible for the subsidies will generally be harmed because they will have to pay higher prices than would be the case in the absence of the subsidies.

Proponents of the health care and higher education subsidies argue they would make these items more affordable, but their impact has been nearly the opposite. This is not a surprising result. The prices of health care and higher education, including the cost of tuition, textbooks, and on- and off-campus housing, have increased substantially. Subsidies mean that a third party, the taxpayer, pays part of the cost. When someone else is paying for all or part of the cost, the consumer has less incentive to economize. Recognizing that consumers are less sensitive to price, producers are better able to raise their prices. Thus,

---

[10]The figures presented here are from "Trends in Student Aid 2019," The College Board, Washington, DC, 2019, Table 3; and the U.S. Department of Education, National Center for Education Statistics, *Digest of Education Statistics*, 2018, Table 330–10. For additional details on the impact of subsidies to students on the cost of college, see Robert E. Martin and Andrew Gillen, "How College Pricing Undermines Financial Aid," The Center for College Affordability and Productivity, Washington, DC, March 2011.

the price of the subsidized good will rise more rapidly than otherwise would be the case. This is precisely what has happened in the health care and higher education sectors.

Many subsidy programs are driven by political considerations—the desire of politicians to favor various groups, particularly those that are well organized, in exchange for their votes and other forms of political support. Moreover, the subsidies often generate harmful secondary effects. Subsidized firms are encouraged to spend more time lobbying politicians and less time pleasing customers. They are also encouraged to undertake wasteful projects that fail to generate revenue sufficient to cover costs. As we proceed, we will consider the nature of favoritism and its relationship to the political process in more detail.

KEY POINTS

- Resource markets and product markets are closely linked. A change in one will generally result in changes in the other.

- Legally imposed price ceilings result in shortages, and legally imposed price floors will cause surpluses. Both also cause other harmful secondary effects. Rent controls, for example, will lead to shortages, less investment, poor maintenance, and deterioration in the quality of rental housing.

- The minimum wage is a price floor for low-skilled labor. It increases the earnings of some low-skilled workers but also reduces employment and leads to fewer training opportunities and nonwage job benefits for many low-skilled workers.

- Because black markets operate outside the legal system, they are often characterized by deception, fraud, and the use of violence as a means of enforcing contracts. A legal system that provides secure private-property rights and unbiased enforcement of contracts enhances the operation of markets.

- The division of the actual tax burden between buyers and sellers is determined by the relative elasticities of demand and supply rather than on whom the tax is legally imposed.

- In addition to the cost of the tax revenue transferred to the government, taxes will reduce the level of the activity taxed, eliminate some gains from trade, and thereby impose an excess burden, or deadweight loss.

- As tax rates increase, the size of the tax base will shrink. Initially, rates and revenues will be directly related—revenues will expand as rates increase. However, as higher and higher rates are imposed, eventually an inverse relationship will develop—revenues will decline as rates are increased further. The Laffer curve illustrates this pattern.

- The division of the benefit from a subsidy is determined by the relative elasticities of demand and supply rather than to whom the subsidy is actually paid. For example, when the buyers of a good are subsidized, the subsidy will increase demand and lead to higher prices. If the supply is more inelastic than the demand, the providers of the services will derive most of the benefits even though the subsidy was granted to the purchasers.

CRITICAL ANALYSIS QUESTIONS

1. *How will a substantial increase in demand for housing affect the wages and employment of carpenters, plumbers, and electricians?

2. Suppose that college students in your town persuaded the town council to enact a law setting the maximum price for rental housing at $400 per month. Will this help or hurt college students who rent housing? In your answer, address how this price ceiling will affect (a) the quality of rental housing; (b) the amount of rental housing available; (c) the incentive of landlords to maintain their properties; (d) the amount of racial, gender, and other types of discrimination in the local rental housing market; (e) the ease with which students will be able to find housing; and, finally, (f) whether a black market for housing would develop.

3. What is the difference between a price ceiling and a price floor? If a price ceiling for a good is set below the market equilibrium, what will happen to the quality and future availability of the good? Explain.

4. *To be meaningful, a price ceiling must be below the market price. Conversely, a meaningful price floor must be above the market price. What impact will a meaningful price ceiling have on the quantity exchanged? What impact will a meaningful price floor have on the quantity exchanged? Explain.

5. The tax on cigarettes in New York City is one of the highest in the nation—$5.85 per pack. Does this tax raise a lot of revenue for New York City? Why or why not? What are some of the secondary effects of this tax?

6. Analyze the impact of an increase in the minimum wage from the current level to $25 per hour. How would the following be affected?

   a. employment of people previously earning less than $25 per hour

   b. the unemployment rate of teenagers

   c. the availability of on-the-job training for low-skilled workers

   d. the demand for high-skilled workers who are good substitutes for low-skilled workers

7. What is a black market? What are some of the main differences in how black markets operate relative to legal markets?

8. What is the Laffer curve? What are the important implications of the Laffer curve?

9. What is meant by the incidence of a tax? Explain why the statutory and actual incidence of a tax often differ.

10. What impact do government grants and loans to college students have on the cost of going to college? Are students the primary beneficiary of these subsidies? Discuss.

11. What is the nature of the deadweight loss accompanying taxes? Why is it often referred to as an "excess burden"?

12. *Suppose Congress were to pass legislation requiring that businesses employing workers with three or more children pay these employees at least $30 per hour. How would this legislation affect the employment level of low-skilled workers with three or more children? Do you think some workers with large families might attempt to conceal the fact? Why?

13. "We should impose a 20 percent luxury tax on expensive automobiles (those with a sales price of $75,000 or more) in order to collect more tax revenue from the wealthy." Will the burden of the proposed tax fall primarily on the wealthy? Why or why not?

14. *Should policy makers seek to set the tax on an economic activity at a rate that will maximize the revenue derived from the tax? Why or why not? Explain.

15. Suppose the government subsidizes the production and sale of spinach. What impact would this have on the price and output of spinach? Who would benefit and who would lose from this subsidy?

16. Several states have laws prohibiting businesses from increasing prices in response to a natural disaster such as a hurricane or during a declared state of emergency like the COVID-19 pandemic. In what ways is this legislation like a price control? Do these laws increase or decrease the quantity of needed supplies available in the affected areas? How do they affect the efficiency with which the limited supplies are allocated?

*Asterisk denotes questions for which answers are given in Appendix B.

CHAPTER 5

Difficult Cases for the Market, and the Role of Government

The principal justification for public policy intervention lies in the frequent and numerous shortcomings of market outcomes. —**Charles Wolf, Jr.**[1]

As we previously discussed, market allocation and political decision-making are the two main alternatives for the organization of economic activity. Chapters 3 and 4 introduced you to how markets work and analyzed the impact of government intervention in the form of price controls, taxes, and subsidies. We noted that when property rights are well defined, and competition present, markets will tend to direct self-interested individuals into activities that promote the general welfare. But this will not always be the case. In this chapter, we turn our attention to potential problem areas when a conflict arises between personal self-interest and getting the most out of the available resources. We will also consider the implications of these problem areas with regard to the role of government. In the following chapter, we will analyze how the political process works and will compare it more directly with markets.

As you read this chapter, look for answers to the following questions:

- What is economic efficiency and how can it be used to evaluate markets?

- What is the role of government in a market economy?

- What are externalities? What are public goods?

- Why might markets fail to allocate goods and services efficiently?

- If the market has shortcomings, does this mean that government intervention will improve things?

[1]Charles Wolf, Jr., *Markets or Government* (Cambridge, MA: MIT Press, 1988), 17.

5-1 A CLOSER LOOK AT ECONOMIC EFFICIENCY

Economic efficiency
A situation that occurs when (1) all activities generating more benefit than cost are undertaken and (2) no activities are undertaken for which the cost exceeds the benefit.

Economists use the standard of **economic efficiency** to assess the desirability of economic outcomes. We briefly introduced the concept in Chapter 3. We now want to explore it in more detail. The central idea of economic efficiency is straightforward. For any given level of cost, we want to obtain the largest possible benefit. Alternatively, we want to obtain any particular benefit for the least possible cost. Economic efficiency means getting the most value from the available resources—making the largest pie from the available set of ingredients, so to speak.

Economists acknowledge that individuals generally do not regard the efficiency of the entire economy as a primary goal for themselves. Rather, each person is interested in enlarging the size of his or her own slice. But if resources are used more efficiently, the overall size of the pie will be larger, and therefore, at least potentially, *everyone* could have a larger slice. For an outcome to be consistent with ideal economic efficiency, two conditions are necessary:

Rule 1. *Undertaking an economic action is efficient if it produces more benefits than costs.* To satisfy economic efficiency, all actions generating more benefits than costs must be undertaken. Failure to undertake all such actions implies that a potential gain has been forgone.

Rule 2. *Undertaking an economic action is inefficient if it produces more costs than benefits.* To satisfy economic efficiency, no action that generates more costs than benefits should be undertaken. When such counterproductive actions are taken, society is worse off because even better alternatives were forgone.

Economic efficiency results only when both of these conditions have been met. ***Either failure to undertake an efficient action (Rule 1) or the undertaking of an inefficient action (Rule 2) will result in economic inefficiency.*** To illustrate, consider **Exhibit 1**, which shows the benefits and costs associated with expanding the amount of any particular activity. We have avoided using a specific example here to ensure you understand the general idea of efficiency without linking it to a specific application. As we will show, the concept has wide-ranging applications, from the evaluation of government policy to how long you choose to brush your teeth in the morning.[2]

In Exhibit 1, the marginal benefit curve shows the additional benefit associated with expanding the activity. The marginal cost curve shows the cost—including any opportunity costs—of spending additional time, effort, and resources on the activity. At Q_1, the height of the marginal benefit curve exceeds the height of the marginal cost curve. Thus, at that point, the additional benefits of expanding the activity past Q_1 exceed the additional costs. According to Rule 1 of economic efficiency, we should continue to expand the activity until we reach Q_2. Beyond Q_2 (at Q_3, for example), the height of the marginal benefit curve is less than the height of the marginal cost curve. The additional benefits of expanding the activity beyond Q_2 to Q_3 are smaller than the additional costs. According to Rule 2, at Q_3, we have gone too far and should cut back on the activity. Q_2 is the only point consistent with both rules of economic efficiency.

---

[2]Note to students who may pursue advanced study in economics: Using the concept of efficiency to compare alternative policies typically requires that the analyst estimate costs and benefits that are difficult or impossible to measure. Costs and benefits are the values of opportunities forgone or accepted by individuals, *as evaluated by those individuals.* Then, these costs and benefits must be added up across all individuals and compared. But does a dollar's gain for one individual really compensate for a dollar's sacrifice by another? Some economists simply reject the validity of making such comparisons. They say that neither the estimates by the economic analyst of subjectively determined costs and benefits nor the adding up of these costs and benefits across individuals is meaningful. Their case may be valid, but most economists today nevertheless use the concept of efficiency as we present it. No other way to use economic analysis to compare policy alternatives has been found.

EXHIBIT 1

Economic Efficiency

As we use more time and resources to expand the level of an activity, the marginal benefits will generally decline and the marginal costs rise. From the viewpoint of efficiency, the activity should be expanded as long as the marginal benefits exceed the marginal costs. Therefore, quantity Q_2 is the economically efficient level of this activity.

Q_1 is inefficient because some production that could generate more benefits than costs is not undertaken. Q_3 is also inefficient because some units are produced even though their costs exceed the benefits they create. Thus, either too much or too little of an activity will result in inefficiency.

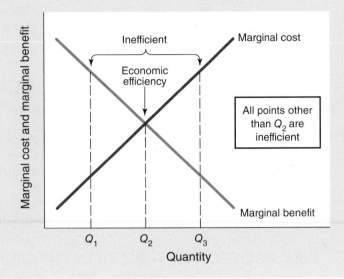

5-1a IF IT'S WORTH DOING, IT'S WORTH DOING IMPERFECTLY

Eliminating pollution. Earning straight As. Being completely organized. Cleaning your apartment until it sparkles. Making automobiles completely safe. Making airplanes fully secure against terrorist attacks. All of these are worthwhile goals, right? Well, they are until you consider the costs of actually achieving them. The heading for this section is, of course, a play on the old saying "If it's worth doing, it's worth doing to the best of your ability." Economics suggests, however, that this is not a sensible guideline. At some point, the gains from doing something even better will not be worth the cost. It will make more sense to stop short of perfection.

Exhibit 1 can also be used to illustrate this point. As more resources are dedicated to an activity, the marginal improvements (benefits) will become smaller and smaller, while the marginal costs will rise. The optimal time and effort put into the activity will be achieved at Q_2, and this will nearly always be well below one's best effort. Note that inefficiency results when either too little (for example, Q_1) or too much (for example, Q_3) time and effort are put into the activity.

Do you make decisions this way? Last time you cleaned your car or apartment, why did you decide to leave some things undone? Once the most important areas were clean, you likely began to skip over other areas (like on top of the refrigerator or under the bed), figuring that the benefits of cleaning these areas were simply not worth the cost. Very few people live in a perfectly organized and clean house, wash their hands enough to prevent all colds, brush their teeth long enough to prevent all cavities, or make their home as safe as Fort Knox. They recognize that the benefit of perfection in these, and many other areas, is simply not worth the cost.

Economics is about trade-offs; it is possible to pursue even worthy activities beyond the level that is consistent with economic efficiency. People seem to be more aware of this in their personal decision-making than when evaluating public policy. It is not uncommon to hear people say things like "We ought to eliminate all pollution" or "No price is too high to save a life."

If we want to get the most out of our resources, we need to think about both marginal benefits and marginal costs and recognize that there are alternative ways of pursuing objectives. Consequently, economists do not ask whether eliminating pollution or saving lives is worth the cost *in terms of dollars* per se, but whether it is worth the cost in terms of giving up other things that could have been done with those dollars—the opportunity cost. Spending an extra $10 billion on school safety requirements to save 50 lives isn't efficient if the funds could have been spent differently and saved the lives of 500 children. It is no more efficient for the government to pursue perfection than for individuals to do so. Regardless of sector, achievement of perfection is virtually never worth the cost.

5-2 THINKING ABOUT THE ECONOMIC ROLE OF GOVERNMENT

For centuries, philosophers, economists, and other scholars have debated the proper role of government. While the debate continues, there is substantial agreement that at least two functions of government are legitimate: (1) protecting individuals and their property against invasions by others and (2) providing goods that cannot easily be provided through private markets. These two functions correspond to what Nobel laureate James M. Buchanan conceptualizes as the protective and productive functions of government.

5-2a PROTECTIVE FUNCTION OF GOVERNMENT

The most fundamental function of government is the protection of individuals and their property against acts of aggression. As John Locke wrote more than three centuries ago, individuals are constantly threatened by "the invasions of others." Therefore, each individual "is willing to join in society with others, who are already united, or have a mind to unite, for the mutual preservation of their lives, liberties, and estates."[3] *The protective function of government involves the maintenance of a framework of security and order—an infrastructure of rules within which people can interact peacefully with one another.* Protection of person and property is crucial. It entails providing police protection and prosecuting aggressors who take things that do not belong to them. It also involves providing for a national defense designed to protect against foreign invasions. The legal enforcement of contracts and rules against fraud are also central elements of the protective function. People and businesses that write bad checks, violate contracts, or knowingly supply others with false information, for example, are therefore subject to legal prosecution.

It is easy to see the economic importance of the protective function. When it is performed well, the property of citizens is secure, freedom of exchange is present, and contracts are legally enforceable. When people are assured that they will be able to enjoy the benefits of their efforts, they will be more productive. In contrast, when property rights are insecure and contracts unenforceable, productive behavior is undermined. Plunder, fraud, and economic chaos result. Governments set and enforce the "rules of the game" that enable markets to operate smoothly.

5-2b PRODUCTIVE FUNCTION OF GOVERNMENT

The nature of some goods makes them difficult to provide through markets. Sometimes it is difficult to establish a one-to-one link between the payment and receipt of a good. If this link cannot be established, the incentive of market producers to supply these goods is

---

[3]John Locke, *Treatise of Civil Government*, 1690, ed. Charles Sherman (New York: Appleton-Century-Crofts, 1937), 82.

weak. In addition, high transaction costs—particularly, the cost of monitoring use and collecting fees—can sometimes make it difficult to supply a good through the market. When either of these conditions is present, it may be more efficient for the government to supply the good and impose taxes on its citizens to cover the cost.

One of the most important productive functions of government is providing a stable monetary and financial environment. If markets are going to work well, individuals have to know the value of what they are buying or selling. For market prices to convey this information, a stable monetary system is needed. This is especially true for the many market exchanges that involve a time dimension. Houses, cars, consumer durables, land, buildings, equipment, and many other items are often paid for over a period of months or even years. When the purchasing power of money fluctuates wildly, previously determined prices do not represent their intended values. Under these circumstances, exchanges involving long-term commitments are hampered, and the smooth operation of markets is undermined.

The government's tax, spending, and monetary policies exert a powerful influence on the stability of the overall economy. If properly conducted, these policies contribute to economic stability, full and efficient utilization of resources, and stable prices. However, improper stabilization policies can cause massive unemployment, rapidly rising prices, or both. For those pursuing a course in macroeconomics, these issues will be central to that analysis.

Bettmann/Getty Images

The English philosopher John Locke argued that people own themselves and, as a result of this self-ownership, they also own the fruits of their labor. Locke stressed that individuals are not subservient to governments. On the contrary, the role of governments is to protect the "natural rights" of individuals to their person and property. This view, also reflected in the "unalienable rights" section of the U.S. Declaration of Independence, is the basis for the protective function of government.

5-3 POTENTIAL SHORTCOMINGS OF THE MARKET

As we previously discussed, the invisible hand of market forces generally gives resource owners and business firms a strong incentive to use their resources efficiently and undertake projects that create value. Will this always be true? The answer to this question is "No." There are four major factors that can undermine the invisible hand and reduce the efficiency of markets: (1) lack of competition, (2) externalities, (3) public goods, and (4) poorly informed buyers or sellers. We will now consider each of these factors and explain why they may justify government intervention.

5-3a LACK OF COMPETITION

Competition is vital to the proper operation of the pricing mechanism. The existence of competing buyers and sellers reduces the power of both to rig or alter the market in their own favor. Although competition is beneficial from a social point of view, individually each of us would prefer to be loosened from its grip. Students do not like stiff competitors in their romantic lives, at exam time, or when they're trying to get into graduate school. Buyers in online auctions hope for few competing bidders so they can purchase the items they're bidding on at lower prices. Similarly, sellers prefer fewer competing sellers so they can sell at higher prices. This is precisely why taxi companies are quick to protest and seek bans against ride-sharing services like Uber and Lyft when they come to an area.

Exhibit 2 illustrates how sellers can gain from restricting competition. In the absence of any restrictions on competition in the market, the price P_1 and output Q_1 associated with the competitive supply curve (S_1) will prevail. Here, Q_1 is the level of output consistent with economic efficiency. If a group of sellers is able to restrict competition, perhaps by forcing some firms out of the market and preventing new firms from entering, the group would be able to gain by raising the price of the product. This is illustrated by the price P_2 and output Q_2 associated with the restricted supply (S_2). Even though the output is smaller, the total revenue (price P_2 times quantity Q_2) derived by the sellers at the restricted output level is greater than at the competitive price P_1. Clearly, the sellers gain because, at the higher price, they are being paid more to produce less.

Lack of Competition and Problems for the Market

If a group of sellers can restrict competition, the group may be able to gain by reducing supply (to S_2, for example) and raising the price (to P_2, for example) rather than charging the competitive market price of P_1. Under these circumstances, output will be less than the economically efficient level.

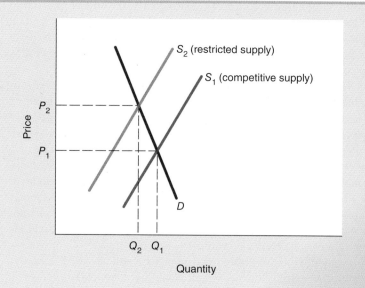

The restricted output level, however, is clearly less efficient. At the competitive output level Q_1, all units that were valued more than their cost are produced and sold. But this is not the case at Q_2. The additional units between Q_2 and Q_1 are valued more than their cost. Nonetheless, they will not be produced if suppliers are able to limit competition and restrict output. When competition is absent, there is a potential conflict between the interests of sellers and the efficient use of resources.

What can the government do to ensure that markets are competitive? The first guideline might be borrowed from the medical profession: Do no harm. A productive government will refrain from using its powers to impose licenses, discriminatory taxes, price controls, tariffs, quotas, and other entry and trade restraints that lessen the intensity of competition. In the vast majority of markets, sellers will find it difficult or impossible to limit the entry of rival firms (including rival producers from other countries). Thus, most suppliers will not be able to limit competition unless they get the government to impose various types of entry restrictions or mandates that provide them with an advantage relative to rivals. Predictably, private firms and interest groups will lobby for government action of this type. When governments succumb to these pressures and engage in actions that limit competition, however, economic inefficiency will result.

When entering a market is very costly and there are only a few existing sellers, it may be possible for these sellers by themselves to restrict competition. In an effort to deal with cases like this, the United States has enacted a series of "antitrust laws," most notably the Sherman Antitrust Act (1890) and the Clayton Act (1914), making it illegal for firms to collude or attempt to monopolize a market.

Virtually all economists favor competitive markets, but there is considerable debate about the impact of government action in this area. Many economists believe that, by and large, government policy in this area has been ineffective. Others stress that government policies have often been misused to actually limit competition, rather than promote it. Laws are often adopted that restrict entry into markets, protect existing producers from competitors, and limit price competition. For those taking a microeconomics course, noncompetitive markets and related policy alternatives will be analyzed in greater detail later.

5-3b EXTERNALITIES—A FAILURE TO ACCOUNT FOR ALL COSTS AND BENEFITS

When property rights are unclear or poorly enforced, the actions of an individual or group may "spill over" onto others and thereby affect their well-being without their consent.

These spillover effects are called **externalities**. You are probably familiar with externalities. For example, when your neighbor's loud stereo makes it hard for you to study, you are experiencing an externality firsthand. Although your neighbors do not have a right to come in to your apartment and create a disturbance, they do have a right to listen to their stereo, and if they play it loudly, this may interfere with the quietness of your apartment. Their actions impose a cost on you, and they also raise an issue of property rights. Do your neighbors have a property right to play their stereo as loudly as they please? Or do you have a property right to quietness in your own apartment? When questions like these arise, how should the boundaries of property rights be determined, and what steps should be taken to ensure adequate enforcement? Although the volume of your neighbor's stereo may not be a major economic issue, it nonetheless illustrates the nature of the problems that arise when property rights are unclear and externalities are present.

The spillover effects may either impose a cost or create a benefit for external parties—people not directly involved in the transaction, activity, or exchange. Economists use the term **external cost** to describe a situation in which the spillover effects harm external parties. If the spillover effects enhance the welfare of the external parties, an **external benefit** is present. We will analyze both external costs and external benefits and consider why both of them can lead to problems.

5-3c EXTERNAL COSTS

Economists worry about external costs because they may result in economic inefficiency. For example, resources may be used to produce goods that are valued less than their production costs, including the costs imposed on the nonconsenting parties. Consider the production of paper. The firms in the market operate mills and purchase labor, trees, and other resources to produce the paper. But they also emit pollutants into the atmosphere that impose costs on residents living around the mills. The pollutants cause paint on buildings to deteriorate more rapidly. They make it difficult for some people to breathe normally, and perhaps cause other health hazards. If the residents living near a pulp mill can prove they have been harmed, they could take the mill to court and force the paper producer to cover the cost of their damages. But it might be difficult to prove that they were harmed and that the pulp mill is responsible for the damage. As you can see, the residents' property rights to clean air may be difficult to enforce, particularly if there are many parties emitting pollutants into the air.

If the residents are unable to enforce their property rights, the production of paper will result in an external cost that will not be registered through markets. **Exhibit 3** illustrates the implications of these external costs within the supply and demand framework. As the result of the external cost, the market supply curve S_1 will understate the true cost of producing paper. It reflects only the cost actually paid by the firms, and ignores the uncompensated costs imposed on the nearby residents. Under these circumstances, the firm will expand output to Q_1 (the intersection of the demand curve D and supply curve S_1) and the market price P_1 will emerge. Is this price and output consistent with economic efficiency? The answer is clearly "No." If all of the costs of producing the paper, including those imposed on external parties, were taken into account, the supply curve S_2 would result. From an efficiency standpoint, only the smaller quantity Q_2 should be produced. The units beyond Q_2 on out to Q_1 cost more than their value to consumers. People

Externalities
Spillover effects of an activity that influence the well-being of nonconsenting parties.

External cost
Spillover effects that reduce the well-being of nonconsenting parties.

External benefit
Spillover effects that generate benefits for nonconsenting parties.

External costs resulting from poorly defined and enforced property rights underlie the problems of excessive air and water pollution.

©iStockphoto.com/rechitansorin

EXHIBIT 3

External Costs and Output That Is Greater Than the Efficient Level

When an activity such as paper production imposes external costs on nonconsenting parties, these costs will not be registered by the market supply curve (S_1). As a result, output will be beyond the economically efficient level. The units between Q_2 and Q_1 will be produced, even though their cost exceeds the value they provide to consumers.

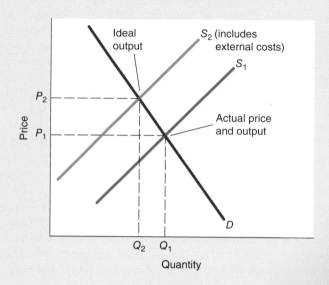

would be better off if the resources used to produce those units (beyond Q_2) were used to produce other things. Nonetheless, profit-maximizing firms will expand output into this range. Thus, when external costs are present, the market supply curve will understate production costs, and output will be expanded beyond the quantity consistent with economic efficiency. Moreover, resources for which property rights are poorly enforced will be overutilized and sometimes polluted. This is often the case with air and water when the property rights to these resources are poorly enforced.

5-3d WHAT SHOULD BE DONE ABOUT EXTERNAL COSTS?

External costs often arise because property rights are poorly defined or imperfectly enforced. Initially, therefore, it makes sense to think seriously about how property rights might be better defined and enforced. However, the nature of some goods will make the defining and enforcement of property rights extremely difficult. This will certainly be the case for resources like clean air and many fish species in the ocean. In cases that involve a relatively small number of people, the parties involved may be able to agree to rules and establish procedures that will minimize the external effects. For example, property owners around a small lake will generally be able to control access to the lake and prevent each other, as well as outsiders, from polluting or overfishing the lake.

However, in cases that involve large numbers of people, the transaction costs of arriving at an agreement will generally be prohibitively high, so it is unrealistic to expect that private contracts among the parties will handle the situation satisfactorily. For example, this will be the case when a large number of automobiles and firms emit pollutants into the atmosphere. In the case of pollution from a large number of emitters, government regulations requiring devices that limit the level of emissions may be the best option.

Sometimes creative arrangements can be devised to reduce the harmful side effects of external cost even in cases involving large numbers of people. Consider the case of ocean fisheries. Because the ocean is an open-access resource, each fisherman has an incentive to catch as many fish as possible. But their actions impose an external cost on others, because the population of many fish species will be reduced to levels that are insufficient for reproduction to sustain the species in the future. Many governments responded to this situation by shortening the fishing season. But this option was ineffective because fishermen countered with bigger boats, more advanced technology, and taking greater risk such as fishing

JOHN SOMMERS II/REUTERS/Newscom

Outstanding Economist: Elinor Ostrom (1933–2012)

In 2009, Elinor Ostrom became the first woman to earn the Nobel Prize in Economics, an award she shared with Oliver Williamson. Ostrom had a lengthy career as a distinguished professor and director of the Workshop in Political Theory and Policy Analysis at Indiana University. She was awarded the Nobel Prize for her research on the "tragedy of the commons"—the idea that when a resource is owned in common it will be overused because each person has an incentive to use it before others do. Ostrom examined numerous real-world cases and discovered that communities were often able to develop rules for the successful private management of common-pool resources. If the rules were going to work well, they must clearly define who gets what, provide for conflict resolution, and assign the duty of individuals to maintain the resource in proportion to the benefits received. Ostrom's research found that community management and rulemaking was often superior to top-down central planning by governmental authorities. Her work provides insight on how cooperative arrangements can sometime lead to efficient solutions even when a resource is owned in common.

even when weather conditions were highly unfavorable. Thus, this option was dangerous for the fishermen and did little to improve sustainability.

Recognizing the nature of the problem, fishing interests have cooperated with governments to develop a property rights system to help ensure the sustainability of the fish population. These systems provide individual fishermen with transferable quotas, representing a property right to a share of the season's total catch. A fisheries management authority determines the sustainable limit prior to each season. The quotas can be bought, sold, or leased at unregulated market prices. With the tradeable quota system, the fish population is sustainable and the race to catch fish before someone else does is eliminated. Individuals know they will be permitted to keep fishing until they catch their quota. These arrangements have now been adopted in more than 200 fishing areas throughout the world. The research of Elinor Ostrom, the 2009 Nobel laureate in economics, provides insight on both the operation and structure of effective arrangements designed to reduce the harmful side effects of common ownership and externalities in a broad range of areas. However, despite the development of innovative arrangements, failure of markets to register fully costs that are external to decision-makers is nonetheless a continuing source of economic inefficiency.

5-3e EXTERNAL BENEFITS

As we mentioned, sometimes the actions of individuals and firms generate external benefits for others. The homeowner who keeps a house in good condition and maintains a neat lawn improves the beauty of the entire community. A flood-control dam built by upstream residents for their benefit might also generate gains for those who live downstream. Scientific theories benefit their authors, but the knowledge can also help others who did not contribute to the development of them.

From the standpoint of efficiency, why might external benefits be a problem? Here, inefficiency may arise because potential producers may fail to undertake productive activities because they are unable to fully capture the benefits their actions create for others. Suppose a pharmaceutical company develops a vaccine protecting users against a contagious virus or some other communal disease. Of course, the vaccine can easily be marketed to users who will benefit directly from it. However, because of the communal nature of the virus, as more and more people take the vaccine, nonusers will also be less likely to get the virus. But it will be very difficult for the pharmaceutical companies to capture any of the benefits derived by the nonusers. As a result, too little of the vaccine may be supplied.

Exhibit 4 illustrates the impact of external benefits like those generated by the vaccine within the framework of supply and demand. The market demand curve reflects the

EXHIBIT 4

External Benefits and Output That Is Less Than the Efficient Level

A vaccine that protects users against the flu will also help nonusers by making it less likely that they will catch it. But this benefit will not be registered by the market demand curve (D_1). In cases where external benefits like this are present, output will be less than the economically efficient level. Even though the units between Q_1 and Q_2 generate more benefits than costs, they will not be supplied because sellers are unable to capture the value of these external benefits.

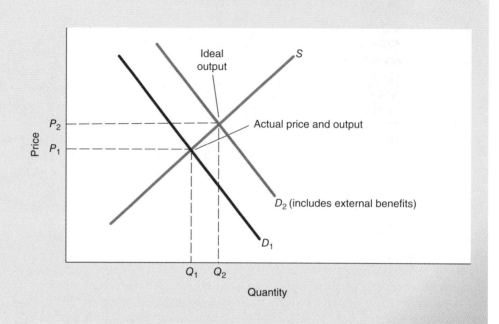

benefits derived by the users of the vaccine, while the supply curve reflects the opportunity cost of providing it. Market forces result in an equilibrium price of P_1 and output of Q_1. Is this outcome consistent with economic efficiency? Again, the answer is "No." The market demand curve D_1 will register only the benefits derived by the users. Those benefits that accrue to nonusers, who are now less likely to contract the flu, will not be taken into account by decision-makers. The producer of the vaccine makes it more likely that these people will not get sick, but it doesn't derive any benefit (sales revenue) from having done so. Thus, market demand D_1 understates the total benefits derived from the production and use of the vaccine. Demand D_2 provides a measure of these total benefits, including those that accrue to the nonusers. The units between Q_1 and Q_2 are valued more highly than what it costs to produce them. Nonetheless, they will not be supplied because the suppliers of the vaccine will be unable to capture the benefits that accrue to the nonusers. Thus, when external benefits are present, market forces may supply less than the amount consistent with economic efficiency.

5-3f EXPANDING THE SCOPE OF A PROJECT AND CAPTURING EXTERNAL BENEFITS

External benefits result in a misallocation of resources if entrepreneurs fail to undertake potentially wealth-creating projects because of their inability to fully capture the benefits of their actions. However, when entrepreneurs can figure out a way to more fully capture these benefits, some otherwise unprofitable projects can be transformed into profitable ones. Entrepreneurs have an incentive to figure out ways to do this. In some cases, they can do so by extending the scope of the project.

The development of golf courses provides an example. Because of the beauty and openness of the courses, many people find it attractive to live nearby. Thus, constructing a golf course typically generates an external benefit—an increase in the value of the nearby

HO Images/Alamy

Entrepreneurs Who Have Changed Our Lives:
Walt Disney

Although it did not open until five years after Walt Disney's death, Disney World was the culmination of a career of innovation. Disney pushed the boundaries of technology to create unusual products that appealed to the imagination and drew enormous crowds, especially families. Most of Disney's achievements were in film, particularly animated movies, as he created iconic cartoon figures such as Mickey Mouse, Donald Duck, and Goofy.

Born in Chicago in 1901, Disney was the son of a struggling businessman. His family—Walt, his parents, and three siblings—moved around the Midwest, as his father tried one business after another, and most failed. As a child, Disney loved to draw cartoons, to listen to his mother tell fairy tales, and to read the books of Charles Dickens and Mark Twain. His love of fantasy and fiction served him well over time.

Disney, along with his brother Roy and a friend, Ubbe Iwerks, began to develop animated cartoon movies in Kansas City. They moved to Los Angeles when the animated film industry was still in its early stages of development. In 1937, in the depths of the Great Depression, Disney's first full-length animated film, *Snow White and the Seven Dwarfs*, earned nearly $1.5 million at the box office and won eight Academy Awards. Animated features such as *Bambi* and *Fantasia* followed.

But he didn't stop there. As television became popular in the 1950s, Disney created such popular programs as *Zorro*, *Davy Crockett*, and *The Mickey Mouse Club*. And in 1955 he opened the most exciting amusement park of its time, Disneyland, in Anaheim, California. Disney's restless mind, supported by his brother and a friend, created joy for generations of children—and adults, too.

Sources: "Walt Disney," *Biography*, biography.com, https://www.biography.com/business-figure/walt-disney.
Marc Eliot, *Walt Disney: Hollywood's Dark Prince* (New York: HarperPaperbacks, 1993).

property. In recent years, golf course developers have figured out how to capture this benefit. Now, they typically purchase a large tract of land around the planned course *before it is built*. This lets them resell the land at a higher price after the golf course has been completed and the surrounding land has increased in value. By extending the scope of their activities to include real estate as well as golf course development, they are able to capture what would otherwise be external benefits. As a result, some wealth-creating projects are undertaken that would have otherwise gone unrealized.

The development of Florida's Walt Disney World provides another interesting case study in entrepreneurial ingenuity designed to capture external benefits more fully. When Walt Disney developed Disneyland in California, the market value of the land in the immediate area soared as a result of the increase in demand for services (food, lodging, gasoline, and so on). Because the land in the area was owned by others, the developers of Disneyland were unable to capture these external benefits. In addition, Disney felt as if some of the adult nightclubs that had opened around his existing Disneyland park were imposing external costs on him by detracting from the family image his park was trying to attain.

Because of his experience with these externalities, when Walt Disney World was developed outside of Orlando, Florida, in the mid-1960s, Walt Disney purchased far more land than was needed for the amusement park. This enabled him to capture the increased land value surrounding his development (when he resold the land for a higher price) and reduce the negative externalities imposed on him via his control of the surrounding property.

The purchases were made as secretly as possible to prevent speculators from driving up the land prices if Disney's actions were detected. Disney even created a handful of smaller companies, with names like the Latin-American Development and Managers Corporation and the Reedy Creek Ranch Corporation, to purchase the land. After his first major land purchase of 12,400 acres, Walt Disney was at a meeting at which he was offered an opportunity to purchase an additional 8,500 acres. Walt Disney's assistant was rumored to have said, "But Walt, we already own 12,000 acres, enough to build the park." Disney replied, "How would you like to own 8,000 acres around our existing Disneyland facility right now?" His assistant immediately responded, "Buy it!"

By June 1965, Disney had purchased 27,400 acres, or about 43 square miles—an area 150 times larger than his existing Disneyland park, and about twice as big as Manhattan. In October 1965, when an Orlando newspaper finally broke the story that Disney was behind the land purchases, the remaining land prices around his property jumped from $183 an acre to $1,000 an acre overnight. Just as Disney expected, the value of the land surrounding Walt Disney World soared as the demand for hotels, restaurants, and other businesses increased along with the development of the amusement park. Through the years, the resale of land near the park has been a major source of revenue for the company. To a large degree, the success of the Disney Corporation reflects Walt Disney's entrepreneurial ability to figure out how to capture external benefits by expanding the scope of the project.

5-3g PUBLIC GOODS AND WHY THEY POSE A PROBLEM FOR THE MARKET

Public goods
Goods for which rivalry among consumers is absent and exclusion of nonpaying customers is difficult.

What are public goods? **Public goods** have two distinguishing characteristics; they are (1) nonrival in consumption and (2) nonexcludable. Let's take a closer look at both of these characteristics.

Nonrivalry in consumption means that making the good available to one consumer does not reduce its availability to others. In fact, providing it to one person simultaneously makes it available to other consumers, so these goods are considered joint-in-consumption. A radio broadcast signal provides an example. The same signal can be shared by everyone within the listening range. Having additional listeners tune in does not detract from the availability of the signal. Clearly, most goods do not have this shared consumption characteristic, but are instead rival-in-consumption. For example, two individuals cannot simultaneously consume the same pair of jeans. Further, a pair of jeans purchased by one person does not make jeans more readily available to others.

The second characteristic of a public good—nonexcludability—means that it is impossible (or at least very costly) to exclude nonpaying customers from receiving the good. Suppose an antimissile system were being built around the city in which you live. How could some people in the city be protected by the system and others excluded? Most people will realize there is no way the system can protect their neighbors from incoming missiles without providing similar protection to other residents. Thus, the services of the antimissile system have the nonexcludability characteristic.

It is important to note that it is the characteristic of the good, not the sector in which it is produced, that determines whether it qualifies as a public good. There is a tendency to think that if a good is provided by the government, then it is a public good. This is not the case. Many of the goods provided by governments clearly do not have the characteristics of public goods. Medical services, education, mail delivery, trash collection, and electricity come to mind. Although these goods are often supplied by governments, they do not have either nonrivalry or nonexcludability characteristics. Thus, they are not public goods.

Free riders
People who receive the benefit of a good without paying for it. Because it is often virtually impossible to restrict the consumption of public goods to those who pay, these goods are subject to free-rider problems.

Why are public goods difficult for markets to allocate efficiently? The nonexcludability characteristic provides the answer. Because those who do not pay cannot be excluded, sellers are generally unable to establish a one-to-one link between the payment and receipt of these goods. Realizing they cannot be excluded, potential consumers have little incentive to pay for these goods. Instead, they have an incentive to become **free riders**, people who receive the benefits of the good without helping to pay for its cost. But, when a large number of people become free riders and revenues thus are low, not very much of the good is supplied. This is precisely the problem: Markets will tend to undersupply public goods, even when the population in aggregate values them highly relative to their cost.

Suppose national defense were provided entirely through the market. Would you voluntarily help to pay for it? Your contribution would have little impact on the total supply of defense available to each of us, even if you made a large personal contribution. Many citizens, even though they might value defense highly, would become free riders, and few funds would be available to finance national defense.

For most goods, it is easy to establish a link between payment and receipt. If you do not pay for a gallon of ice cream, an automobile, a laptop, and literally thousands of other items, suppliers will not provide them to you. Thus, there are very few public goods. National defense is the classic example of a public good. Radio and TV signals, software programs, flood-control projects, mosquito abatement programs, and perhaps some scientific theories also have public good characteristics. But beyond this short list, it is difficult to think of additional goods that qualify.

Just because a good is a public good does not necessarily mean that markets will fail to supply it. When the benefit of producing these goods is high, entrepreneurs will attempt to find innovative ways to gain by overcoming the free-rider problem. For example, radio and television broadcasts, which have both of the public good characteristics, are still produced well by the private sector. The free-rider problem is overcome through the use of advertising (which generates indirect revenue from listeners), rather than by directly charging listeners or viewers. Private entrepreneurs have developed things like copy limitations on digital music and movies as well as computer software, and tie-in purchases (for example, tying the inclusion of operating system software with the purchase of a computer) to overcome the free-rider problem.

In spite of the innovative efforts of entrepreneurs, however, the quantity of public goods supplied strictly through market allocation might still be smaller than the quantity consistent with economic efficiency. This creates a potential opportunity for government action to improve the efficiency of resource allocation.

5-3h POTENTIAL INFORMATION PROBLEMS

Like other goods, information is scarce. Thus, when making purchasing decisions, people are sometimes poorly informed about the price, quality, durability, and side effects of alternative products. Imperfect knowledge is not the fault of the market. In fact, the market provides consumers with a strong incentive to acquire information. If they mistakenly purchase a "lemon," they will suffer the consequences. Furthermore, sellers have a strong incentive to inform consumers about the benefits of their products, especially in comparison with competing products. However, circumstances will influence the incentive structure confronted by both buyers and sellers.

The consumer's information problem is minimal if the item is purchased regularly. Consider the purchase of soap. There is little cost associated with trying different brands. Because soap is a regularly purchased product, trial and error is an economical means of determining which brand is most suitable to one's needs. Regularly purchased items such as toothpaste, most food products, lawn service, and gasoline provide additional examples of **repeat-purchase items**. When purchasing items like these, the consumer can use past experience to acquire accurate information and make wise decisions.

Repeat-purchase items
An item purchased often by the same buyer.

Furthermore, the sellers of repeat-purchase items also have a strong incentive to supply consumers with accurate information about them because failing to do so will adversely affect future sales. Because future demand is directly related to the satisfaction level of current customers, sellers of repeat-purchase items will want to help their customers make satisfying long-run choices. This helps harmonize the interests of buyers and sellers.

But harmony will not always occur. Conflicting interests, inadequate information, and unhappy customers can arise when goods are either (1) difficult to evaluate on inspection and seldom repeatedly purchased from the same producer, or (2) potentially capable of serious and lasting harmful side effects that cannot be predicted by a typical consumer. Under these conditions, consumers might make decisions they will later regret.

When customers are unable to distinguish between high-quality and low-quality goods, business entrepreneurs have an incentive to cut costs by reducing quality. Businesses that follow this course may survive and even prosper. Consider the information problem when an automobile is purchased. Are consumers capable of properly evaluating the safety equipment? Most are not. Of course, some consumers will seek the opinion of experts, or consult the online reviews by prior customers, but this information will be costly and difficult to evaluate. In this case, it might be more efficient to have the government regulate automobile safety and require certain safety equipment.

Similar issues arise with regard to product effectiveness. Suppose a new wonder drug promises to reduce the probability a person will be stricken by cancer or heart disease. Even if the product is totally ineffective, many consumers will waste their money trying it. Verifying the effectiveness of the drug will be a complicated and lengthy process. Consequently, it may be better to have experts certify its effectiveness. The federal Food and Drug Administration was established to perform this function. However, letting the experts decide is also a less than ideal solution. The certification process is likely to be costly and lengthy. As a result, the introduction of products that are effective may be delayed for years, and they are likely to be more costly than they would be otherwise.

5-3i INFORMATION AS A PROFIT OPPORTUNITY

Consumers are willing to pay for and invest their time in acquiring information that will help them make better decisions. This presents a profit opportunity. Entrepreneurial providers of information help consumers find what they seek by offering product evaluations by experts. For example, dozens of sources provide independent expert opinions about automobiles and computers at a low cost to potential purchasers. Laboratory test results and detailed product evaluations on a wide variety of goods are provided by firms such as Consumer Reports and J.D. Power.

The online reviews written by bloggers and other customers are helping to even better overcome potential information problems than was possible prior to the widespread use of cell phones and the internet. The reviews of previous customers on eBay, Amazon, and Yelp, for example, help buyers make better informed choices. In effect, this online review process holds a seller's future sales hostage to the quality with which they satisfy even a one-time buyer, creating the same incentives present for sellers of repeat-purchase items. Failure to satisfy just a few customers can result in many other buyers not being willing to purchase from that seller. The ability of buyers and sellers to leave online reviews for others to consider in their decision process is part of the value proposition that makes these companies successful ventures.

Franchise
A right or license granted to an individual to market a company's goods or services or use its brand name. The individual firms are independently owned but must meet certain conditions to continue to use the name.

Franchises are another way entrepreneurs have responded to the need of consumers for more and better information. A **franchise** is a right or license granted to an individual to market a company's goods or services (or use their brand name). Fast-food restaurants like McDonald's and Wendy's are typically organized as franchises. The individual restaurants are independently owned, but the owner pays for the right to use the company name and must offer specific products and services in a manner specified by the franchiser. Franchises help give consumers reliable information. The tourist traveling through an area for the first time with very little time to search out alternatives may find that eating at a franchised restaurant and sleeping at a franchised motel are the cheapest ways to avoid annoying and costly mistakes that might come from patronizing an unknown local establishment.

The franchiser sets the standards for all firms in the chain and establishes procedures, including continuous inspections, designed to maintain the standards. Franchisers have a strong incentive to maintain their reputation for quality, because if it declines, their ability to sell new franchises and to collect ongoing franchise fees is adversely affected. Even though the tourist may visit a particular establishment only once, the franchise turns that visit into a "repeat purchase" because the reputation of the entire national franchise operation is at stake.

Similarly, advertising a brand name nationally puts the brand's reputation at stake each time a purchase is made. How much would the Coca-Cola Company pay to avoid the sale of a dangerous bottle of Coke? Surely, it would be a large sum. Interbrand, a branding consulting agency that evaluates and ranks the top brand names in the world, estimated that Coca-Cola's brand name was worth $63 billion in 2019. The value of that brand name is a hostage to quality control. The firm would suffer enormous damage if it failed to maintain the quality of its product. For example, in 2000 and 2001, Firestone's brand name suffered an immense reduction in value after only a few Firestone tires were suspected of being defective. More recently in 2018, amid concerns over user privacy issues, Facebook's brand value declined by 6 percent, after previously being one of the fastest growing brands.

NetPhotos/Alamy

ferdyboy/Shutterstock.com

Rose Carson/Shutterstock.com

360b/Shutterstock.com

Ingram Publishing/Newscom

Brand names (like Coca-Cola), franchises (like McDonald's or Best Western), consumer-ratings organizations (like Consumer Reports), and private-sector certification firms (like Underwriters Laboratories, Inc.) are ways the private sector helps buyers overcome potential information problems.

Creative entrepreneurs have found ways to assure buyers that products meet high standards of quality, even when the producer is small and not so well known. Consider the case of Best Western Motels.[4] Best Western owns no motels; however, building on the franchise idea, it publishes rules and standards with which motel owners must comply if they are to use the Best Western brand name and the reservation service that the company also operates. To protect its brand name, Best Western sends out inspectors to see that each Best Western Motel meets these standards. Every disappointed customer harms the reputation and reduces the value of the Best Western name, which reduces the willingness of motel owners to pay for use of the name. The standards are designed to keep customers satisfied. Even though each motel owner has only a relatively small operation, renting the Best Western name provides the small operator with the kind of international reputation formerly available only to large firms. In effect, Best Western acts as a regulator of all motels bearing its name. It profits by requiring efficient standards—those that produce maximum visitor satisfaction for every dollar spent by the motels utilizing the franchise name. As it does so, it helps eliminate problems in the market that result from imperfect information.

Underwriters Laboratories Inc. (UL) is another example of private-sector regulation aimed at overcoming potential information problems. UL is a private-sector corporation that has been testing and certifying products for more than 100 years based on its own set of quality standards. You have probably seen the UL mark on many of your household appliances. Sellers pay a fee to have UL evaluate their products for possible certification. The value of the UL brand depends on its careful evaluation of every product it certifies. If UL allows defective products to carry its mark, its brand value will diminish.

Information published by reliable sources, franchising, and brand names can help consumers make better-informed decisions. Although these options are effective, they will not always provide an ideal solution. Government regulation may sometimes be able to improve the situation, but this, too, has some predictable shortcomings. As with other things, there is no general solution to imperfect information problems.

5-4 MARKET AND GOVERNMENT FAILURE

Market failure
A situation in which the structure of incentives is such that markets will encourage individuals to undertake activities that are inconsistent with economic efficiency.

As we have shown in this chapter, a lack of competition, externalities, public goods, and information problems often pose challenges and sometimes undermine the efficient operation of markets. Economists use the term **market failure** to describe the situation where there is reason to believe that markets will fail to achieve the conditions implied by idealized economic efficiency. Private entrepreneurs can profit, however, from solving these problems so markets can sometimes overcome these potential challenges on their own.

Government failure
A situation in which the structure of incentives is such that the political process, including democratic political decision-making, will encourage individuals to undertake actions that conflict with economic efficiency.

It is tempting to jump to the conclusion that if the market fails to achieve economic efficiency, then the government can intervene and improve the situation. Indeed, even professional economists often make this error. But we must not forget that government directed by political decision-making is merely an alternative form of economic organization. It is not a corrective device that can be counted on to make choices that will promote economic efficiency. There is government failure, as well as market failure. **Government failure** is present when political choices lead to outcomes that conflict with the efficient allocation of resources. In order to evaluate the potential of political decision-making to improve on the shortcomings of the market and allocate resources efficiently, we need better knowledge about how the political process works. This will be the focal point of the next chapter.

---

[4]This section draws from Randall G. Holcombe and Lora P. Holcombe, "The Market for Regulation," *Journal of Institutional and Theoretical Economics* 142, no. 4 (1986): 684–96.

KEY POINTS

- Economists use the standard of economic efficiency to assess the desirability of economic outcomes. Efficiency requires (1) that all actions generating more benefit than cost be undertaken and (2) that no actions generating more cost than benefit be undertaken.

- Although perfection is a noble goal, it is rarely worth achieving because additional time and resources devoted to an activity generally yield smaller and smaller benefits and cost more and more. Inefficiency can result when either too little or too much effort is put into an activity.

- Governments can enhance economic well-being by performing both protective and productive functions. The protective function involves (1) the protection of individuals and their property against aggression and (2) the provision of a legal system for the enforcement of contracts and settlement of disputes. The productive function of government can help people obtain goods that would be difficult to supply through markets.

- When markets fail to meet the conditions for ideal economic efficiency, the problem can generally be traced to one of four sources: absence of competition, externalities, public goods, or poor information.

- Externalities generally reflect a lack of fully defined and enforced property rights. When external costs are present, output may be too large—units are produced even though their costs exceed the benefits they generate. In contrast, external benefits may lead to an output that is too small—some units are not produced even though the benefits of doing so would exceed the cost.

- Public goods are goods for which (1) rivalry in consumption is absent and (2) it is difficult to exclude those who do not pay. Because of the difficulties involved in establishing a one-to-one link between payment and receipt of such goods, the market supply of public goods will often be less than the economically efficient quantity.

- Entrepreneurs in markets have an incentive to find solutions to each market problem, and new solutions are constantly being discovered. But problems remain that can potentially be improved through government action.

- Both markets and government can have problems in achieving the efficient allocation of resources. The term *market failure* describes the situation where markets will fail to achieve the conditions implied by idealized economic efficiency. But political action may also result in outcomes that are inefficient, a situation known as *government failure*.

CRITICAL ANALYSIS QUESTIONS

1. *Why is it important for producers to be able to prevent non-paying customers from receiving a good?

2. In response to the terrorist attacks of September 11, 2001, airline security screening increased dramatically. As a result, the travel time of airline passengers has increased substantially. Would it make economic sense to devote enough resources to completely prevent any such future attacks? Why or why not?

3. What are the distinguishing characteristics of "public goods"? Give two examples of a public good. Why are public goods difficult for markets to allocate efficiently?

4. Which of the following are public goods? Explain, using the definition of a public good.
   a. an antimissile system surrounding Washington, D.C.
   b. a fire department
   c. tennis courts
   d. Yellowstone National Park
   e. elementary schools

5. Explain in your own words what is meant by external costs and external benefits. Why may market outcomes be less than ideal when externalities are present?

6. English philosopher John Locke argued that the protection of each individual's person and property (acquired without the use of violence, theft, or fraud) was the primary function of government. Why is this protection important to the efficient operation of an economy?

7. "If it's worth doing, it's worth doing to the best of your ability." What is the economic explanation for why this statement is frequently said but rarely followed in practice? Explain.

8. "Unless quality and price are regulated by government, travelers would have no chance for a fair deal. Local people would be treated well, but the traveler would have no way to know, for example, who offers a good night's lodging at a fair price." Is this true or false? Explain.

9. *If sellers of toasters were able to organize themselves, reduce their output, and raise their prices, how would economic efficiency be affected? Explain.

10. What are external costs? When are they most likely to be present? When external costs are present, what is likely to be the relationship between the market output of a good and the output consistent with ideal economic efficiency?

11. *"Elementary education is obviously a public good. After all, it is provided by the government." Evaluate this statement.

12. What are the necessary conditions for economic efficiency? In what four situations might a market fail to achieve ideal economic efficiency?

13. What is market failure? If market failure is present, does this imply that government intervention will lead to a more efficient allocation of resources? Why or why not?

14. Apply the economic efficiency criterion to the role of government. When would a government intervention be considered economically efficient? When would a government intervention be considered economically inefficient?

*Asterisk denotes questions for which answers are given in Appendix B.

CHAPTER 6

The Economics of Political Action

[Public choice] analyzes the motives and activities of politicians, civil servants and government officials as people with personal interests that may or may not coincide with the interest of the general public they are supposed to serve. It is an analysis of how people behave in the world as it is. —**Arthur Seldon**[1]

As we have previously discussed, the protection of property rights, evenhanded enforcement of contracts, and provision of a stable monetary environment are vital for the smooth and efficient operation of markets. Governments that perform these functions well will help their citizens prosper and achieve higher levels of income. Governments may also help allocate goods difficult for markets to handle. However, it is crucially important to recognize that government is simply an alternative form of economic organization. In most industrialized nations, the activities of governments are directed by the democratic political process. In this chapter, we will use the tools of economics to analyze how this process works.

As you read this chapter, look for answers to the following questions:

- How large is the government sector, and what are the main activities undertaken by governments?

- What are the similarities and differences between political and market allocation of goods?

- What insights can economics provide about the behavior of voters, politicians, and bureaucrats? How will their actions affect political outcomes?

- When is democratic political decision-making most likely to allocate resources efficiently? When is it most likely to lead to economic inefficiency?

- What is crony capitalism, and is it an increasing problem in the United States?

[1]Preface to Gordon Tullock, *The Vote Motive* (London: Institute of Economic Affairs, 1976), x.

6-1 THE SIZE AND GROWTH OF THE U.S. GOVERNMENT

What exactly does government do? Has its role in the economy shrunk or grown over time? Data on government spending shed light on these questions. As **Exhibit 1** illustrates, total government expenditures (federal, state, and local combined) were only 9.9 percent of the U.S. economy in 1930. (*Note:* GDP, or Gross Domestic Product, is generally how economists measure the size of the economy. The term will be explained more fully in a macroeconomics course.) In that year, federal government spending by itself was only about 3 percent of the economy. At the time, this made the federal government about half the size of all state and local governments combined.

Between 1930 and 1980, the size of government grew very rapidly. By 1980, government expenditures had risen to 33.7 percent of the economy, *more than three times* the level of 1930. Moreover, the federal government grew to about twice the size of all state and local governments combined, despite the fact that they were growing rapidly, too. After remaining fairly constant between 1980 and 2000, the size of government increased substantially to 40 percent by 2010. While government spending declined slightly to 36 percent of the economy in 2019, this was prior to the government spending undertaken

EXHIBIT 1

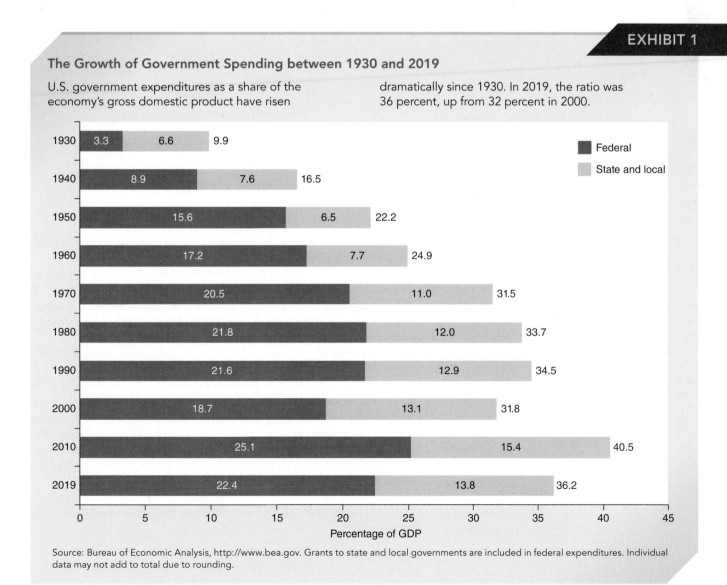

The Growth of Government Spending between 1930 and 2019

U.S. government expenditures as a share of the economy's gross domestic product have risen dramatically since 1930. In 2019, the ratio was 36 percent, up from 32 percent in 2000.

Year	Federal	State and local	Total
1930	3.3	6.6	9.9
1940	8.9	7.6	16.5
1950	15.6	6.5	22.2
1960	17.2	7.7	24.9
1970	20.5	11.0	31.5
1980	21.8	12.0	33.7
1990	21.6	12.9	34.5
2000	18.7	13.1	31.8
2010	25.1	15.4	40.5
2019	22.4	13.8	36.2

Percentage of GDP

Source: Bureau of Economic Analysis, http://www.bea.gov. Grants to state and local governments are included in federal expenditures. Individual data may not add to total due to rounding.

EXHIBIT 2

Government Spending by Category

The major categories of federal government spending are health care, Social Security, national defense, and income security (welfare transfers). The major categories of state and local government spending are education, health and welfare programs, and administration.

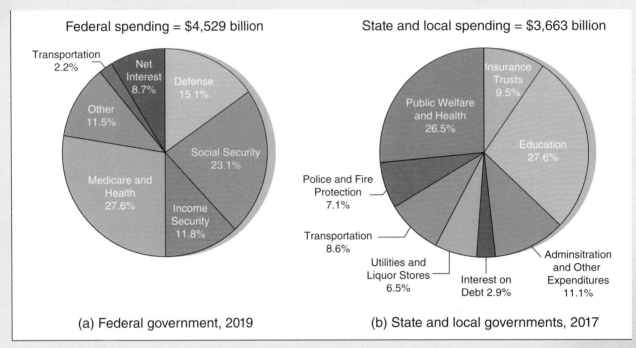

Federal spending = $4,529 billion

- Transportation 2.2%
- Net Interest 8.7%
- Defense 15.1%
- Other 11.5%
- Social Security 23.1%
- Medicare and Health 27.6%
- Income Security 11.8%

State and local spending = $3,663 billion

- Insurance Trusts 9.5%
- Public Welfare and Health 26.5%
- Education 27.6%
- Police and Fire Protection 7.1%
- Transportation 8.6%
- Utilities and Liquor Stores 6.5%
- Interest on Debt 2.9%
- Adminsitration and Other Expenditures 11.1%

(a) Federal government, 2019

(b) State and local governments, 2017

Source: Office of Management and Budget, www.omb.gov and U.S. Census Bureau, State and Local Government Finances, 2017.

to combat the COVID-19 pandemic and the associated recession which will have large effects on 2020 federal and state budgets, and perhaps budgets for years to come.

Exhibit 2 shows the major categories of government spending for both the federal government and state and local governments. The major categories of federal spending are health care, Social Security, national defense, and other income transfers. Education, administration, and public welfare and health constitute the largest areas of spending for state and local governments.

Transfer payments
Payments to individuals or institutions that are not linked to the current supply of a good or service by the recipient.

Transfer payments are transfers of income from some individuals (who pay taxes) to others (who receive government payments). Social Security, unemployment benefits, and welfare are examples of transfer payments. Direct income transfers now account for almost half of the total spending of the government. As Exhibit 3 illustrates, federal, state, and local government spending on income transfers has grown rapidly. In 1930, income transfers summed to only 1.1 percent of total income. By 1970, the figure had jumped to 8.2 percent; by 2010, it had risen to 18.5 percent of national income. In 2019 the figure had fallen slightly to 17.6 percent from its peak in 2010. Obviously, the government has become much more involved in tax-transfer activities during the past nine decades.

Given the size and growth of government, understanding how the political process works and how it is likely to affect the economy is vitally important. The remainder of this chapter will address this issue.

EXHIBIT 3

The Growth of Government Transfer Payments

The government takes almost 20 percent of national income away from some people and transfers it to others. Means-tested income transfers—those directed toward the poor—account for only about one-sixth of all income transfers. Government income-transfer activities have grown substantially since 1930.

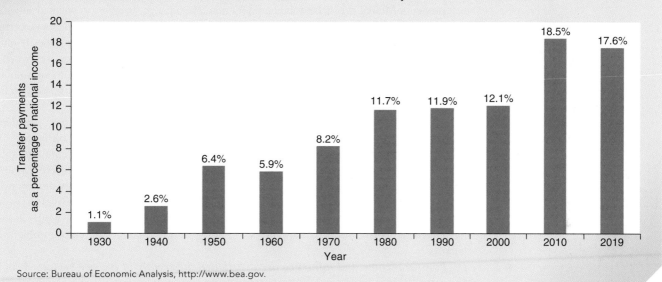

Source: Bureau of Economic Analysis, http://www.bea.gov.

6-2 SIMILARITIES AND DIFFERENCES BETWEEN POLITICAL AND MARKET ALLOCATION

Let's begin our analysis of how the political process works by considering some of the major similarities and differences between the two sectors. Competition is present in the government sector, just as it is in the market sector. The nature of the competition and criteria for success differ, but intense competition is present in both. In the government sector, politicians compete for elective office. Bureau chiefs and agency heads compete for larger budgets. Government employees compete for promotions and higher pay rates. Perhaps most importantly, business, labor, and other special interest groups compete for program funding, favorable bureaucratic rulings, and other political favors that serve their narrow interests.

Scarcity and the opportunity cost of resource use are present in both sectors. If the government uses resources to achieve one goal, those resources are unavailable to achieve others. Thus, just as in the market sector, provision of goods through government is costly, and this is true even if the good is provided free of charge to certain consumers.

But there are also important differences between market and political allocation, and these differences shed light on how the two processes allocate resources. Let's consider four of the key differences.

First, public sector organization can break the linkage between payment and consumption of a good. In the market sector, goods are allocated to those who are willing to pay the price: there is a one-to-one relationship between a person's payment and receipt of a good. This is often not the case when decisions are made politically. Sometimes goods are allocated to people even if they have paid little or nothing to cover their cost. In other instances, however, individuals are required to pay dearly for a government program even though they derive few, if any, benefits from it.

Second, private-sector action is based on mutual agreement; public-sector action is based on majority rule. In the market sector, when two parties engage in trade, their actions are voluntary and motivated by the expectation of mutual gain. Corporations like Exxon and Microsoft, no matter how large or powerful, cannot take income from you or force you to buy their products. Mutual gain is the foundation for market exchange. In contrast, political action is based on majority rule, either through direct voting or through legislative procedures involving elected representatives. If a legislative majority decides on a particular policy, the minority must accept the policy and help pay for it, even if they strongly object. Political action, even when it is democratic, creates "losers" as well as "winners." Further, as we will explain, there is no assurance that the gains the winners derive from a project will exceed the losses imposed on the losers.

Third, when choices are made politically, voters face a "bundle purchase" problem. They must choose among candidates who represent a bundle of positions on issues. On election day, the voter cannot choose the views of one politician on healthcare and agricultural subsidies for example, and simultaneously choose the views of a different politician on social security reform and national defense. This greatly limits the voter's power to make his or her preferences count on specific issues. The situation in markets is quite different. A buyer can purchase some groceries or clothing from one store, while choosing related items from different suppliers. There is seldom a bundle-purchase problem in markets.

Fourth, income and influence are distributed differently in the two sectors. People who supply more highly valued resources in the marketplace have larger incomes. The number of these dollar "votes" earned by a person in the marketplace will reflect his or her abilities, ambitions, skills, past savings, inheritance, good fortune, and willingness to produce for others, among other things. In contrast, in a democratic setting, one citizen, one vote is the rule. But there are ways other than voting to influence political outcomes. People can donate their money and time to help a campaign. They can also try to influence friends and neighbors, write letters to legislators, and speak in public on behalf of a candidate or cause. The greatest rewards of the political process go to those best able and most willing to use their time, persuasive skills, organizational abilities, and financial contributions to help politicians get votes. People who have more money and skills of this sort—and are willing to spend them in the political arena—can expect to benefit themselves and their favorite causes more handsomely. Thus, while the sources of success and influence differ between sectors, the allocation of income and influence is unequal in both.

6-3 POLITICAL DECISION-MAKING: AN OVERVIEW

Public-choice analysis
The study of decision-making as it affects the formation and operation of collective organizations, like governments. In general, the principles and methodology of economics are applied to political science topics.

When political decisions are made democratically, or in a representative democracy, as we assume in this chapter, the choices of individuals will influence outcomes in the government sector, just as they do in the market sector. **Public-choice analysis** is a branch of economics that applies the principles and methodology of economics to the operation of the political process. Public-choice analysis links the theory of *individual* behavior to political action, analyzes the implications of the theory, and tests them against events in the real world. Over the past 60 years, research in this area has greatly enhanced our understanding of how the political process works and the structure of the outcomes it generates.[2] Just as economists use self-interest and the structure of incentives to analyze markets, public-choice

---

[2]The contributions of Kenneth Arrow, James Buchanan, Duncan Black, Anthony Downs, William Niskanen, Mancur Olson, Robert Tollison, and Gordon Tullock have been particularly important. Public choice is something of a cross between economics and political science. Thus, advanced courses are generally offered in both departments.

economists use them to analyze political choices and the operation of government. After all, the same people make decisions in both sectors. If self-interest and the structure of incentives influence market choices, there is good reason to expect that they will also influence choices in a political setting.

The collective decision-making process can be thought of as a complex interaction among voters, legislators, and bureaucrats. Voters elect a legislature, which levies taxes and allocates budgets and regulatory authority to various government agencies and bureaus. The bureaucrats in charge of these agencies utilize the funds to supply government services and income transfers, and to exercise regulatory authority as well. In a representative democracy, voter support determines who is elected to the legislature. A majority vote of the legislature is generally required for the passage of taxes, budget allocations, and regulatory legislation. Let's take a closer look at the incentive structure confronting the three primary political players—voters, legislators, and bureaucrats—and consider how they affect the operation of the political process.

6-3a INCENTIVES CONFRONTED BY THE VOTER

How do voters decide whom to support? Self-interest dictates that voters, like market consumers, will ask, "What can you do for me and my goals, and how much will it cost me?" The greater the voter's perceived net personal gain from a particular candidate's election, the more likely it is that the voter will favor that candidate. In contrast, the greater the perceived net economic cost imposed on the voter by the positions of a candidate, the less inclined the voter will be to support the candidate. Other things being equal, voters will tend to support those candidates who they believe will provide the most government services and transfer benefits to them and their favorite causes, net of costs.

How well will voters be informed about political issues and candidates? When decisions are made collectively, the choices of a single person will not be decisive. The probability that an individual vote will decide a city, state, or national election is virtually zero. Realizing that their votes will not affect the outcome, individual voters have little incentive to spend much effort seeking the information needed to cast an informed ballot. Economists refer to this lack of incentive as the **rational ignorance effect**.

As the result of the rational ignorance effect, most voters simply rely on information supplied to them freely by candidates (via political advertising) and the mass media, as well as conversations with friends and coworkers. Surveys, in fact, indicate that huge numbers of voters are unable even to identify their own congressional representatives, much less know where they stand on issues like Social Security reform, tariffs, and agricultural price supports. Given that voters gain little from casting a more informed vote, their meager knowledge of political candidates and issues is not surprising.

Rational ignorance effect
Because it is highly unlikely that an individual vote will decide the outcome of an election, a rational individual has little or no incentive to search for and acquire the information needed to cast an informed vote.

Outstanding Economist: James Buchanan (1919–2013)

The 1986 winner of the Nobel Prize in Economics, James Buchanan might properly be called the "father of public choice economics." Rather than assuming that voters, elected political officials, and bureaucrats are "saints" seeking to promote the common good, Buchanan assumed that the key political players responded to the structure of incentives. His work illustrated that, like the market, the political process has deficiencies that often result in counterproductive government actions and misallocation of resources. As he put it, public-choice analysis is "government without the romance." Buchanan's most famous work, *The Calculus of Consent* (1962), coauthored with Gordon Tullock, argues that unless constitutional rules are structured in a manner that will bring the self-interests of the political players into harmony with the wise use of resources, government action will often be counterproductive.[1] Given the continued growth of government, Buchanan's work is now perhaps more relevant than at any time in American history.

[1]J. M. Buchanan and G. Tullock, *The Calculus of Consent* (Ann Arbor: University of Michigan Press, 1962).

Wally McNamee/Corbis Historical/Getty Images

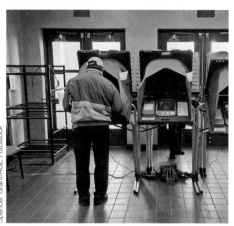

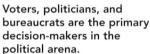

Voters, politicians, and bureaucrats are the primary decision-makers in the political arena.

When people can put information to good use in serving their own goals, they will put forth more effort to acquire it. Consider the incentive of auto purchasers to make well-informed choices. They often shop at several dealerships, take different models for test drives, review consumer publications, and consult with various car experts as they make their purchasing decisions. Most important, if an auto buyer makes a bad choice, he or she will personally bear the consequences. In contrast, voters gain little or nothing if they cast a more informed vote. It is a virtual certainty that their vote will not decide the outcome of an election, and therefore there will be no adverse consequences of casting a poorly informed vote. Thus, it is actually *reasonable* to expect people to be far better informed when choosing a car than a senatorial, congressional, or other political candidate.

The fact that citizens recognize that their individual vote will not sway the outcome also helps explain why many do not vote. Even in a presidential election, only about half of all voting-age Americans take the time to register and vote. The turnout for state and local elections is generally still lower. Given the low probability that one's vote will be decisive, low voter turnout is an expected result.

6-3b INCENTIVES CONFRONTED BY THE POLITICIAN

What motivates political candidates and officeholders? Economics indicates that their actions and political positions will be heavily affected by the pursuit of votes. No doubt, many of them genuinely care about the "public interest" and the quality of government, but they need to be elected to achieve their objectives, whatever they may be. Clearly, politicians have a strong incentive to give voters a reason to support their candidacy. One way of doing so is to convince voters that they will provide valuable goods either free of charge or at a very low cost. Predictably, politicians will exaggerate the benefits their programs will provide to voters, while understating and concealing the cost. As Stanford economist Thomas Sowell puts it:

The first lesson of economics is scarcity: there is never enough of anything to fully satisfy all those who want it. The first lesson of politics is to disregard the first lesson of economics.[3]

Moreover, if a candidate is going to be successful, their positive attributes must be brought to the attention of rationally ignorant voters focused on their families, jobs, various civic activities, and local sports teams (which are probably more entertaining). The successful candidate needs an expert staff, sophisticated polling techniques to uncover popular issues and positions, and high-quality advertising to shape his or her image favorably. This, of course, will be costly. It is not unusual for an incumbent candidate for the U.S. Senate to

---

[3]Thomas Sowell, *Is Reality Optional? And Other Essays* (Stanford, CA: Hoover Institution Press, 1993), 131.

spend $15 million or more seeking to win an election. In other words, votes are the necessary objective of politicians, but money helps them get those votes. Predictably, the pursuit of campaign contributions then shapes the actions of politicians, too.

Are we implying that politicians are selfish, caring only for their pocketbooks and re-election chances? The answer is "No." Factors other than personal political gain, narrowly defined, may well influence their actions. Sometimes an elected official may feel so strongly about an issue that he or she will knowingly take a position that is politically unpopular and damaging to his or her future electoral prospects. None of this is inconsistent with the economic view of the political process. Over time, however, the politicians most likely to remain in office are the ones who focus on how their actions will influence their reelection prospects. Just as profits are the lifeblood of the market entrepreneur, votes are the lifeblood of the politician.

Politicians face competition for elected office from other candidates. Like market suppliers, political suppliers have an incentive to find ways to gain an advantage over their competitors. Catering to the strongly held views of voters and contributors is one way of doing that. Enacting rules that put potential challengers at a disadvantage is another. When geographic political districts are redrawn, for example, politicians frequently manipulate the process to increase their chances (and those of their party) of winning elections—a process known as "gerrymandering." Incumbents can also attempt to use government resources for their reelection campaigns, an advantage challengers do not have. Campaign finance "reforms" that make it more difficult for a challenger to raise funds may also provide incumbents with an additional advantage.

6-3c INCENTIVES CONFRONTED BY THE GOVERNMENT BUREAUCRAT

Like other people, bureaucrats who staff government agencies, especially those who rise to senior decision-making levels, have narrowly focused interests. They usually want to see their own agency's goals furthered. Doing so, however, requires larger budgets or greater authority to regulate or both. In turn, larger budgets and more authority lead to more satisfaction, prestige, and career opportunities for the bureaucrats. Economic analysis suggests there is a strong tendency for government bureaucrats and employees to want to expand their budgets and their authority well beyond what would be economically efficient. Indeed, analysts recognize that bigger programs often have strong, organized political backing. In contrast "efficiency has no political constituency."

Legislative bodies are in charge of overseeing these bureaus, but the individual legislators themselves generally know little about the true costs of agency decisions, especially the costs to those regulated. This makes it even more likely that bureaucrats will be able to get funding and authority beyond what's economically efficient.

In summary, the political process, which begins with voter-driven elections and proceeds to legislative decisions and bureaucratic actions, brings about results that please some voters and displease others. The goals of the three major categories of participants—voters, politicians, and bureaucrats—frequently conflict with one another. Each group wants more of the government's limited supply of resources. Coalitions form and the members of each

Just as the general does not want his Camp Swampy budget cut, most heads of agencies want expanded budgets to help them do more and do it more comfortably.

coalition hope to enhance their ability to get the government to do what they want. Sometimes this results in productive activities on the part of the government, and sometimes it does not.

6-4 WHEN THE POLITICAL PROCESS WORKS WELL

Under what conditions are voting and representative government most likely to result in productive actions? People have a tendency to believe that support by a majority makes a political action productive. However, if a project is truly productive, it will always be possible to allocate its costs such that *all* voters gain. This would mean that, even if voting rules required unanimity or near unanimity, all truly productive government projects would pass if the costs were allocated in the right manner. **Exhibit 4** helps illustrate this point. Column 1 presents hypothetical data on the distribution of benefits from a government road construction project. These benefits sum to $40, which exceeds the $25 cost of the road, so the project is productive. But if the project's $25 cost were allocated equally among the voters (plan A), Adams and Chan gain substantially, but Green, Lee, and Diaz lose. If the fate of the project is decided by majority vote, the project will be defeated by the "no" votes of Green, Lee, and Diaz. This productive government project fails to obtain a majority vote in this case because of the way that the costs have been allocated.

Because the project is indeed productive, there is an alternative way to allocate its costs so that Adams, Chan, Green, Lee, and Diaz all benefit. This can be accomplished by allocating the cost of the project among voters in proportion to the benefits that they receive (plan B). Under this arrangement, Adams would pay half ($12.50) of the $25 cost, because he receives half ($20) of the total benefits ($40). The other voters would all pay in proportion to the benefits they receive. Under this plan, all voters would gain from the proposal. Even though the proposal could not secure a majority when the costs were allocated equally among voters, it will be favored by all five voters when they are taxed in proportion to the benefits they receive (plan B).

EXHIBIT 4

The Benefits Derived by Voters from a Hypothetical Road Construction Project

When taxes are levied in proportion to benefits received (tax plan B), any efficient project can pass unanimously (and any inefficient project will fail unanimously). When taxes are not levied in accordance with benefits received (tax plan A), efficient projects can fail to win a majority vote (or inefficient projects can pass in a majority vote).

| | | TAX PAYMENT | |
| | BENEFITS RECEIVED | PLAN A | PLAN B |
VOTER	(1)	(2)	(3)
Adams	$20	$5	$12.50
Chan	12	5	7.50
Green	4	5	2.50
Lee	2	5	1.25
Diaz	2	5	1.25
Total	$40	$25	$25.00

This simple illustration highlights an extremely important point about voting and the efficiency of government action. ***When voters pay in proportion to benefits received, all voters will gain if the government action is productive, and all will lose if it is unproductive.*[4]** ***When the benefits and costs derived by individual voters are closely related, the voting process will enact efficient projects while rejecting inefficient ones. When voters pay in proportion to the benefits they receive, there will tend to be harmony between good politics and sound economics.***

How might the cost of a government service be linked to the benefits received? **User charges**, which require people who use a service more to pay a larger share of the cost, provide one way. User charges are most likely to be levied at the local level. Local services such as electricity, water, and garbage collection are generally financed with user charges. Sometimes the intensity of the use of a service and the amount paid for it can be linked by specifying that the revenue from a specific tax be used for a designated purpose. For example, many states finance road construction and maintenance with the revenue collected from taxes on gasoline and other motor fuels. The more an individual drives—getting more benefits from the roads—the more that individual pays.

Exhibit 5 provides a useful way to look at the possible linkage between the benefits and costs of government programs. The benefits from a government action may be either widespread among the general public or concentrated among a small subgroup

User charges
Payments users (consumers) are required to make if they want to receive certain services provided by the government.

EXHIBIT 5

Distribution of Benefits and Costs among Voters

It is useful to visualize four possible combinations for the distribution of benefits and costs among voters to consider how the alternative distributions affect the operation of representative governments. When the distribution of benefits and costs is both widespread among voters (type 1) or both concentrated among voters (type 3), representative government will tend to undertake projects that are productive and reject those that are unproductive. In contrast, when the benefits are concentrated and the costs are widespread (type 2), representative government is biased toward the adoption of inefficient projects. Finally, when benefits are widespread but the costs concentrated (type 4), the political process may reject projects that are productive.

	Distribution of benefits among voters	
	Widespread	Concentrated
Widespread	Type 1	Type 2
Concentrated	Type 4	Type 3

Distribution of costs among voters

---

[4]The principle that productive projects generate the potential for political unanimity was initially articulated by Swedish economist Knut Wicksell in 1896. See Wicksell, "A New Principle of Just Taxation," in *Public Choice and Constitutional Economics*, James Gwartney and Richard Wagner (Greenwich, CT: JAI Press, Inc., 1988). Nobel laureate James Buchanan stated that Wicksell's work provided him with the insights that led to his large role in the development of modern public-choice theory.

(for example, farmers, students, business interests, senior citizens, or members of a labor union). Similarly, the costs may be either widespread or highly concentrated among voters. Thus, as the exhibit shows, there are four possible patterns of voter benefits and costs: (1) widespread benefits and widespread costs, (2) concentrated benefits and widespread costs, (3) concentrated benefits and concentrated costs, and (4) widespread benefits and concentrated costs.

When both the benefits and costs are widespread among voters (type 1 issue), essentially everyone benefits and everyone pays. Although the costs of type 1 measures may not be precisely proportional to the benefits individuals receive, there will be a rough relationship. When type 1 measures are productive, almost everyone gains more than they pay. There will be little opposition, and political representatives have a strong incentive to support such proposals. In contrast, when type 1 proposals generate costs in excess of benefits, almost everyone loses, and representatives will face pressure to oppose such issues. Thus, for type 1 projects, the political process works pretty well. Productive projects will tend to be accepted and unproductive ones rejected.

Similarly, there is reason to believe that the political process will work fairly well for type 3 measures—those for which both benefits and costs are concentrated on one or more small subgroups. In some cases, the concentrated beneficiaries may be the same group of people paying for the government to provide them a service. In other cases, the subgroup of beneficiaries may differ from the subgroup footing the bill. Even in this case, however, when the benefits exceed the costs, the concentrated group of beneficiaries will have an incentive to expend more resources lobbying for the measure than those harmed by it will expend opposing it. Thus, when the benefits and costs are both concentrated, there will be a tendency for productive projects to be adopted and unproductive ones to be rejected.

6-5 WHEN THE POLITICAL PROCESS WORKS POORLY

Although the political process yields reasonable results when there is a close relationship between the receipt of benefits and the payment of costs, the harmony between good politics and sound economics breaks down when the beneficiaries differ from those bearing the costs (type 2 and type 4 projects). Inefficiency may also arise from other sources when governments undertake economic activities. In this section, we consider four major reasons why the political allocation of resources will often result in inefficiency.

6-5a SPECIAL-INTEREST EFFECT

Trade restrictions that limit the import of steel and lumber from abroad; subsidies for sports stadiums, the arts, and various agricultural products; federal spending on an indoor rain forest in Iowa; special tax breaks for NASCAR track owners and Hollywood movie studios; and special grants and loans to a business producing expensive electric sports cars: These seemingly diverse programs funded by tax dollars from the federal government have one thing in common—they reflect the attractiveness of special-interest issues to vote-seeking politicians. A **special-interest issue** is one that generates substantial personal benefits for a small number of constituents while the costs are spread widely across the bulk of citizens (type 2 projects). Individually, a few people gain a great deal, but many others lose a small amount. In aggregate, the losses may exceed the benefits.

How will a vote-seeking politician respond to special-interest issues? Because their personal stake is large, members of the interest group (and lobbyists representing their interests) will feel strongly about such issues. Many of the special-interest voters will vote for or against candidates strictly on the basis of whether they are supportive of their positions. In addition, interest groups are generally an attractive source of campaign resources, including financial contributions. In contrast, most of the other, largely rationally ignorant, voters will either not know or will care little about special-interest issues. Even if voters know

Special-interest issue
An issue that generates substantial individual benefits to a small minority while imposing a small individual cost on many other citizens. In total, the net cost to the majority might either exceed or fall short of the net benefits to the special-interest group.

about some of these programs, it will be difficult for them to punish their legislators because each politician represents a bundle of positions on many different issues. While politicians would gain little from support of the rationally ignorant and unorganized majority, organized interest groups are eager to provide cooperative politicians with vocal supporters, campaign workers, and, most important, financial contributions.

As a result, politicians have a strong incentive to support legislation that provides concentrated benefits to special-interest groups at the expense of disorganized groups (like the bulk of taxpayers and consumers). Consider the cotton subsidy program. This program, which dates back to the New Deal era, has provided cotton farmers with subsidies averaging more than $1.5 billion per year since 2000. Moreover, because the subsidies are linked to production, the overwhelming bulk of these transfers go to well-off large farmers. Five percent of the recipients collect about two-thirds of the subsidies, and more than 80 percent of this federal largess is bestowed on the largest 10 percent of growers. The top 1 percent of cotton farmers received an average subsidy of about $150,000 per year. What explains the political popularity of this program? The special interest effect provides the answer. The subsidy recipients feel strongly about the program and congressional supporters can count on them for political contributions. In contrast, the taxpayers and consumers of cotton products are almost totally unaware of the cost the program imposes on them. Thus, there is a strong incentive for congressional representatives to support the interests of the cotton farmers even though the program promotes inefficient use of resources and redistributes income from the less well-off to those with higher incomes.

The sugar subsidy program has the same general structure as that of the cotton program. For many years, the price of sugar in the United States has been 50 to 100 percent higher than the world price. Why? Because the federal government's price support program and highly restrictive quotas limiting the import of sugar keep the domestic price of sugar high. As a result, the roughly 20,000 sugar growers in the United States gain about $1.7 billion, or approximately $85,000 per grower! In contrast, sugar consumers pay between $3.4 billion and $4.0 billion, or a little more than $25 per household, in the form of higher prices each year.[5]

The artificially high sugar prices have resulted in a steady stream of candy manufacturers exiting the United States for countries such as Canada and Mexico, where sugar can be purchased at the lower, world market price. It is estimated that three jobs are lost in candy manufacturing for every job saved in the sugar production sector. Some heavy users of sugar have shifted to substitutes. The producers of Coca-Cola and Pepsi now use corn syrup rather than the more expensive sugar in their products. As the result of the sugar program, consumers living in the country where Coca-Cola was invented drink a modified version. If Americans want to enjoy a coke the way it was initially invented, they have to import it from abroad. Many are doing just that. In recent years, there has been a surge in imports of Coca-Cola bottled in Mexico.

The cotton and sugar programs are not unusual. Numerous government programs reflect this same pattern of incentives. These programs provide politicians with an opportunity to support policies favored by special interests, solicit those parties for political contributions, and use the funds to attract the support of other voters. Even when these programs are counterproductive, they may be still a political winner.

The power of special interests is further strengthened by logrolling and pork-barrel legislation. **Logrolling** involves the practice of vote trading by politicians in order to get the necessary support to pass desired legislation. **Pork-barrel legislation** is the term used to describe the bundling of unrelated projects benefiting many interests into a single bill. Both logrolling and pork-barrel legislation will often make it possible for special-interest projects to gain legislative approval, even though each project is counterproductive and individually could not muster the needed votes.

Logrolling
The exchange between politicians of political support on one issue for political support on another.

Pork-barrel legislation
A package of spending projects bundled into a single bill. It is often used as a device to obtain funding for a group of projects intensely desired by regional or interest groups that would be unlikely to pass if voted on separately.

---

[5]See Jared Meyer and Preston Cooper, "Sugar Subsidies Are a Bitter Deal for American Consumers," *Economic Policies for the 21st Century at the Manhattan Institute*, Manhattan Institute (June 23, 2014); and John Beghin and Amani Elobeid, "Analysis of the US Sugar Program," American Enterprise Institute, November 2017, p. 1, http://www.aei.org/wp-content/uploads/2017/11/Analysis-of-the-US-Sugar-Program.pdf.

Trading Votes and Passing Counterproductive Legislation

All three projects are inefficient and would not pass majority vote individually. However, representatives from districts A, B, and C could trade votes (logrolling) or put together pork-barrel legislation that would result in all three projects passing.

	NET BENEFITS (+) OR COSTS (−) TO VOTERS IN DISTRICT			
VOTERS OF DISTRICT[a]	**CONSTRUCTION OF POST OFFICE IN A**	**DREDGING HARBOR IN B**	**CONSTRUCTION OF STADIUM IN C**	**TOTAL**
A	+$10	−$ 3	−$ 3	+$4
B	− 3	+ 10	− 3	+ 4
C	− 3	− 3	+ 10	+ 4
D	− 3	− 3	− 3	− 9
E	− 3	− 3	− 3	− 9
Total	−$ 2	−$ 2	−$ 2	−$6

[a]We assume the districts are of equal size.

Exhibit 6 provides a numeric illustration of the forces underlying logrolling and pork-barrel legislation. Here we analyze the operation of a five-member legislature considering three projects: construction of a post office in district A, dredging of a harbor in district B, and spending on a stadium in district C. For each district, the net benefit or cost is shown—that is, the benefit to the district minus the tax cost imposed on it. The total cost of each of the three projects exceeds the benefits (as shown by the negative number in the total row at the bottom of the table); therefore, each is counterproductive. If the projects were voted on separately, each would lose by a 4-to-1 vote because only one district would gain, and the other four would lose. However, when the projects are bundled together through either logrolling (representatives A, B, and C could agree to trade votes) or pork-barrel legislation (all three programs put on the same bill), they can all pass, despite the fact that all are inefficient.[6] This can be seen by noting that the total combined net benefit is positive for representatives A, B, and C.

The political incentive to support special interest projects, including those that are counterproductive, is even stronger than the simple numeric example of Exhibit 6 implies. As the result of the rational ignorance effect, those harmed by pork-barrel and other special-interest policies will often be unaware of the adverse impact the projects exert on their welfare. Moreover, the incentive to cater to special interests often deters entry of innovative firms and weakens the competitive process. Older, more established businesses have built a stronger record of political contributions, have more knowledge of lobbying techniques, and have developed a closer relationship with powerful political figures. Predictably, the more mature firms generally have more political clout than newer upstarts and will use it to deter innovative rivals.

Consider the experience of Uber, which uses technology to bring willing drivers together with potential ground transportation passengers. Consumers searching for ground transportation request cars via their smartphones, and the Uber app immediately gives them a wait time. Uber also provides feedback about drivers to potential passengers and vice versa. The technology reduces transaction costs, and the process is often faster and cheaper than traditional taxi service. As Uber has sought to enter markets in large cities throughout the world, the traditional taxi industry has fought for and often achieved legislation prohibiting the use of the technology employed by Uber and similar firms seeking to enter this market.[7] As a result, the gains from the innovative technology and expansion in the volume of exchange have been slowed.

---

[6]Logrolling and pork-barrel policies can sometimes lead to the adoption of productive measures. However, if a project is productive, there would always be a pattern of finance that would lead to its adoption even if logrolling and pork-barrel policies were absent. Thus, the tendency for logrolling and pork-barrel policies to result in the adoption of inefficient projects is the more significant point.

[7]See Holman W. Jenkins Jr., "How Uber Won the Big Apple," *Wall Street Journal*, July 24, 2015. http://www.wsj.com/articles/how-uber-won-the-big-apple-1437778176.

The experience of Tesla, an electric car manufacturer, provides another example of existing producers using the political process to deter the entry of a newcomer. Tesla's business model is based on the sale of its autos directly to consumers. But a well-organized interest group, the established auto dealers, has lobbied state legislatures demanding passage of laws making it illegal for an auto manufacturer to sell cars directly to consumers. Nearly 20 states have adopted such legislation. These laws have made it more difficult for Tesla to enter the automobile market successfully.

Why don't representatives oppose measures that force their constituents to pay for projects that benefit others? There is some incentive to do so, but the constituents of any one elected representative would capture only a tiny portion of the benefits of tax savings from improved efficiency. The savings, after all, would be spread nationwide among all taxpayers. We would not expect the president of a corporation to devote any significant amount of the firm's resources toward projects that chiefly benefit other firms. Neither should we expect an elected representative to devote political resources to projects like defeating pork-barrel programs when the bulk of the benefits derived from spending reductions and tax savings will accrue to constituents in other districts. Instead, representatives have a strong incentive to fight for more spending for their constituents and not worry much about the spending pushed by other members of Congress.

When the benefits of a governmental action are spread far and wide among the unorganized, and the costs are highly concentrated (type 4 of Exhibit 5), special-interest groups—those who stand to bear the cost—are likely to oppose and lobby strongly against even an efficient project. Most other voters will be largely uninformed and uninterested. Once again, politicians will have an incentive to respond to the views of the concentrated interests. A proposal to reduce or eliminate a tariff (tax) on an imported good would be an example of this type of legislation. Although many thousands of consumers would benefit from the lower prices that result, the domestic firms that compete with the imported good would devote substantial resources toward lobbying to keep the tariff in place. Projects of this type will tend to be rejected even when they are productive, that is, when they would generate larger benefits than costs.

There is a tendency to believe that if a project or program can muster a political majority, it will be good for the society. ***However, the special-interest effect indicates this is not necessarily the case***. The special-interest effect helps explain the presence of numerous government programs that increase the size of government but reduce the overall size of the economic pie. As we discuss diverse topics throughout this text, counterproductive political action that has its foundation in the special-interest effect will arise again and again.

6-5b SHORTSIGHTEDNESS EFFECT

Current economic conditions will have a major impact on the choices of voters on election day. As a result, incumbent politicians will want to institute programs that will provide visible results prior to the next major election. Thus, legislators have a strong incentive to favor projects that yield highly visible current benefits at the expense of costs that will be difficult to identify and mostly observable in the future. In contrast, politicians will find projects unattractive when they generate visible costs now with the expectation of future gain. Economists refer to this bias inherent in the political process as the **shortsightedness effect**.

As the result of the shortsightedness effect, elected political officials will have a strong incentive to spend on programs designed to provide highly visible benefits before the next election, but they will be reluctant to levy the taxes for their finance. Borrowing provides politicians with an alternative to current taxes: it makes it possible for them to spend now and push the visible taxes into the future. Thus, the political process is biased toward debt finance. The experience of the United States during the past six decades illustrates this bias. During the past 60 years, the federal government of the United States has run 55 budget deficits but only five surpluses. The federal debt as a share of the economy has now grown to levels not seen since World War II. Moreover, the experience of Greece and several other

Shortsightedness effect
The misallocation of resources that results because public-sector action is biased (1) in favor of proposals yielding clearly defined current benefits in exchange for difficult-to-identify future costs and (2) against proposals with clearly identifiable current costs that yield less concrete and less obvious future benefits.

European countries indicates that elected political officials will sometimes continue with a borrow-and-spend political strategy until they drive their country into virtual economic collapse.

The shortsightedness effect also explains why vote-seeking politicians find it attractive to promise future benefits without levying the taxes that are sufficient for their finance. This has been the case with both the Social Security and Medicare programs. The unfunded liabilities of these two programs are now about *four times* the size of the outstanding federal debt held by the public. By the time the higher taxes (or benefit cuts) for these programs are confronted, the politicians who gained votes from the promised benefits will be long gone.

6-5c RENT-SEEKING

There are two ways individuals can acquire wealth: production and plunder. When individuals produce goods or services and exchange them for income, they not only enrich themselves, but they also enhance the wealth of the society. Sometimes the rules—or lack of rule enforcement—also allow people to get ahead by taking, or plundering, from others. This method not only fails to generate additional income—the gain of one is a loss to another—but it also consumes resources and thereby reduces the wealth of the society.

Rent-seeking is the term economists use to describe actions taken by individuals and groups seeking to use the political process to take the wealth of others.[8] Perhaps "favor seeking" would be a more descriptive term for this type of activity, which generally involves "investing" resources in lobbying and other activities designed to gain favors from the government. The incentive for individuals to spend time and effort in rent-seeking will be determined by how rewarding it is. Rent-seeking will be unattractive when constitutional constraints prevent politicians from taking the property of some and transferring it to others (or forcing some to pay for things desired by others).

However, when the government becomes heavily involved in income transfer activities and the granting of favors to some at the expense of others (instead of simply acting as a neutral force protecting property rights and enforcing contracts), people will spend more time rent-seeking and less time producing. Rather than competing by offering consumers more for their money, rent-seekers compete by using resources to obtain more funds from taxpayers. Rent-seeking is a natural outgrowth of government activism. When the government is heavily involved in the granting of contracts, subsidies, tax credits, low-interest loans, regulatory favors, and other forms of government intervention, then business firms, labor organizations, and other well-organized interests will compete for the government favors. The result will be a shift of resources away from productive activities and into rent-seeking. Economic efficiency will decrease and output and income levels will fall below their potential.

Rent-seeking
Actions by individuals and groups designed to restructure public policy in a manner that will either directly or indirectly redistribute more income to themselves or the projects they promote.

To get elected (or reelected), politicians have a strong incentive to provide spending programs to important interest groups to secure their support.

---

[8]See the classic work of Charles K. Rowley, Robert D. Tollison, and Gordon Tullock, *The Political Economy of Rent-Seeking* (Boston: Kluwer Academic Publishers, 1988) for additional details on rent-seeking.

6-5d INEFFICIENCY OF GOVERNMENT OPERATIONS

Will government enterprises and agencies be operated efficiently? The incentive to keep costs low and provide customers with highly valued goods and services differs substantially between the market and government sectors. In the market sector, there is a strong incentive to produce efficiently because lower costs mean higher profits. The profit motive also provides private firms with a strong incentive to supply goods and services that are highly valued relative to their cost. Bankruptcy weeds out private sector firms that have high costs and serve their customers poorly.

In the public sector, the structure of incentives is much different. There is nothing like profit and loss that might be used to evaluate the performance of agencies, enterprises, and managers. Neither is there a mechanism like bankruptcy that can be counted on to eventually bring inefficient public sector operations to a halt. In fact, failure to achieve a targeted objective (for example, a lower crime rate or improvement in student achievement scores) is often used as an argument for *increased* public-sector funding of an agency or its programs. Furthermore, public-sector managers are seldom in a position to gain personally from measures that reduce costs. The opposite is often true, in fact. If an agency fails to spend its entire budget for a given year, not only does it have to return the extra money, but its budget for the next year is likely to be cut. Because of this, government agencies typically go on a spending spree near the end of a budget period if they discover they have failed to spend all the current year's allocated funds.

It is important to note that the argument of internal inefficiency is not based on the assumption that employees of a bureaucratic government are lazy or less capable. Many agency managers are highly capable, diligent, and focused strongly on their mission within the agency. Rather, the inefficiency stems from the incentives and opportunities that such managers and workers face. Government enterprises do not have owners that are risking their wealth on the future success of the firm. No decision-maker in the firm can reap substantial economic gain if the firm produces more efficiently or incorporates a new product or service highly valued relative to its costs. In the public sector, there is no test like profit and loss that might be used to measure inefficiency, much less eliminate it. Given this incentive structure, inefficient use of resources is the predicted result.

The empirical evidence is consistent with this view. Economies dominated by government control, like those of the former Soviet bloc, Indonesia, Venezuela, and Nigeria (and many other African countries), have performed poorly. The level of output per unit of resource input in countries dominated by government agencies and enterprises is low. Similarly, when private firms are compared with government enterprises providing the same goods or services (like garbage collection, hospitals, electric and water utilities, weather forecasting, and public transportation), studies indicate that private firms generally provide the services more economically.

6-6 POLITICAL FAVORITISM, CRONY CAPITALISM, AND GOVERNMENT FAILURE

Public-choice analysis indicates that as government spending, subsidies, income transfers, loan guarantees, financial bailouts, targeted tax credits, and regulatory favors grow, businesses and other well-organized groups have a greater incentive to expend resources seeking to obtain the government favors. As a result, crony capitalism tends to expand relative to market allocation. **Crony capitalism** is the situation where the allocation of resources, and winners and losers in business, are determined by political favors rather than by consumer preferences translated through the market profit-and-loss system. Under crony capitalism, rather than providing equal treatment of individuals and businesses under the law, government uses spending, subsidies, and regulations to favor those most willing to provide political decision-makers with campaign contributions and other forms of political support. In essence, crony capitalism reflects the intermingling of government and business. The politicians use the favoritism to obtain political resources (e.g. contributions,

Crony capitalism
A situation where the institutions of markets are maintained, but to a large degree the allocation of resources, and the profit and loss of businesses, are determined by political decision-making rather than consumer purchases and market forces. Many of the business firms will use contributions and other forms of political support to compete for government favors.

6-7 THE ECONOMIC WAY OF THINKING ABOUT MARKETS AND GOVERNMENT

When analyzing the operation of markets and government, it is vitally important to keep two points in mind. First, the government's protective role provides the foundation for the smooth operation of markets. A government that protects private property, enforces contracts evenhandedly, maintains monetary stability, and refrains from regulations that restrict voluntary exchange and entry into markets is central to the efficient operation of markets.

Second, both the market and the political process have shortcomings. As explained in Chapter 5, economic analysis indicates that there are cases where markets will fail to allocate resources efficiently. However, as the analysis of this chapter indicates, there are also reasons the political process will lead to the inefficient allocation of resources. There is government failure as well as market failure. As in the case of market failure, government failure reflects the situation where the structure of incentives encourages individuals to engage in counterproductive rather than productive use of resources. The accompanying **Thumbnail Sketch** lists the major sources of both market failure and government failure.

There is a tendency to idealize democratic governance—to focus on the stated objectives of political officials rather than the actual effects of their policies. Public-choice analysis warns against this naïve view. It focuses on how the political process really works, even if that is not how we might like for it to work. Public-choice analysis also indicates that the presence of government failure will grow as government becomes larger and more intrusive. A larger government will mean more grants, contracts, subsidies, and regulatory favors. This will create more special interest spending, rent-seeking, and crony capitalism. Public choice also highlights the importance of institutions, constitutional rules, and procedures that encourage productive political actions and restrain those that are counterproductive. Higher income levels *and* living standards can be achieved if institutions more consistent with economic progress are adopted. This will be a recurring theme throughout this book.

Thumbnail Sketch
Market Failure and Government Failure

Major sources of market failure:

1. lack of competition
2. externalities
3. public goods
4. poor information

Major sources of government failure:

1. the special-interest effect
2. the shortsightedness effect
3. rent-seeking
4. weak incentives for operational efficiency

KEY POINTS

- In recent years, government spending has increased, and in 2019 it was 36 percent of the U.S. economy. As the budgetary implications of the COVID-19 pandemic and associated recession unfold, this figure will increase significantly.

- There are both similarities and differences between market and political allocation. Competition is present in both, but its nature differs between the two sectors. While the government can use its taxing power to break the link between payment and receipt of a good for an individual, it cannot do so for the economy as a whole. In the public sector, voters face a "bundle" purchase problem; they are unable to vote for some policies favored by one candidate and other policies favored by the candidate's opponent. Power and income are unequal in both sectors, but the factors influencing their distribution differ between the two.

- In a representative democracy, government is controlled by voters who elect politicians to set policy and hire bureaucrats to run government agencies. The incentives faced by all three classes of participants influence political outcomes.

- Voters have a strong incentive to support the candidate who offers them the greatest gain relative to their personal costs. Because collective decisions break the link between the choice of the individual and the outcome of the issue, voters are likely to be poorly informed on most political matters.

- Politicians have a strong incentive to follow a strategy that will enhance their chances of getting elected (and reelected). Political competition more or less forces them to focus on how their actions influence their support among voters and potential contributors.

- The distribution of the benefits and costs among voters influences how the political process works. When voters pay in proportion to the benefits they receive from a public-sector project, productive projects tend to be approved and counterproductive ones rejected. When the costs of a policy are distributed among voters differently than are the benefits, democratic decision-making will tend to be less efficient.

- Government actions will often lead to economic inefficiency as the result of (1) the special-interest effect, (2) the shortsightedness effect, (3) rent-seeking, and (4) weak incentives to keep costs low within government enterprises and agencies. Thus, just as the market sometimes fails to allocate goods efficiently, so, too, will the political process.

- As the size and scope of government grows, public-choice analysis indicates that political activity involving the exchange of government favors for political support will become more widespread. More resources will be channeled into rent-seeking and inefficient government programs, particularly those favored by special interest groups.

CRITICAL ANALYSIS QUESTIONS

1. Are voters likely to be well informed on issues and the positions of candidates? Why or why not?

2. What is public-choice analysis? What are economists and others involved in public-choice analysis attempting to do?

3. What is rent-seeking? When is it likely to be widespread? How does it influence economic efficiency? Explain.

4. *"The political process sometimes leads to economic inefficiency because we elect the wrong people to political office. If the right people were elected, a democracy governed by majority rule would allocate resources efficiently." Evaluate this statement.

5. What are "bootleggers and Baptists" coalitions? Why are "bootleggers and Baptists" coalitions highly attractive to rent-seekers and politicians? How do these coalitions impact government spending, regulation, and favoritism?

6. "The average person is more likely to make a well-informed choice when purchasing a personal computer than when voting for a congressional candidate." Is this statement true? Why or why not?

7. "Government action is based on majority rule, whereas market action is based on mutual consent. The market allows for proportional representation of minorities, but minorities must

yield to the views of the majority when activities are undertaken through government." In your own words, explain the meaning of this statement. Is the statement true? Why or why not?

8. *"Voters should simply ignore political candidates who play ball with special-interest groups and vote instead for candidates who will represent all the people when they are elected. Government will work far better when this happens." Evaluate this view.

9. If a project is efficient (its total benefits exceed its total costs), would it be possible to allocate the cost of the project in a manner that would provide net benefits to each voter? Why or why not? Explain. Will efficient projects necessarily be favored by a majority of voters? Explain.

10. *"When an economic function is turned over to the government, social cooperation replaces personal self-interest." Is this statement true? Why or why not?

11. What is the shortsightedness effect? How does it influence the attractiveness of government borrowing? Explain.

12. *"Public policy is necessary to protect the average citizen from the power of vested interest groups. In the absence of government intervention, regulated industries such as

airlines, railroads, and trucking will charge excessive prices; products will be unsafe; and the rich will oppress the poor. Government curbs the power of special-interest groups." Evaluate this statement.

13. "Because government-operated firms do not have to make a profit, they can usually produce at a lower cost and charge a lower price than privately owned enterprises." Evaluate this view.

14. If a senator trades his or her vote on an issue for a $10,000 payment, would you consider this corruption? If a senator votes a certain way in "exchange" for a $10,000 contribution to his or her political campaign, would you consider this corruption? Is there a major difference between the two? Discuss.

15. The United States imposes highly restrictive sugar import quotas that result in a domestic price that is generally 50 to 100 percent higher than the world price. The quotas benefit sugar growers at the expense of consumers. Given that there are far more sugar consumers than growers, why aren't the quotas abolished? Has government action in this area improved the living standards of Americans? Why or why not?

16. The Federal Drug Administration will not approve new pharmaceutical products unless the developer can prove that its product is both safe and effective as a remedy for specified ailments. Do you think the "safe and effective" criterion would be a good one for Congress to adopt for the passage of new legislation? Why or why not? Do you think most government action would meet this criterion? Discuss.

17. "When politicians decide what is bought and sold, the first thing that will be bought and sold is politicians." What is the central point of this statement? Is it true?

*Asterisk denotes questions for which answers are given in Appendix B.

Core Macroeconomics

Growth of output is the key to a higher living standard.

Macroeconomics is about growth of the economy and fluctuations in output, employment, and the general level of prices. Growth of output is extremely important because it makes higher levels of consumption and living standards possible. Fluctuations in output and prices can inhibit growth and generate economic hardship. What causes economic fluctuations? What can economic policy do to promote more stability? Why do some countries grow and achieve high levels of income while others remain poor? Part 3 will focus on these questions and related issues.

CHAPTER 7

Taking the Nation's Economic Pulse

It has been said that figures rule the world; maybe. I am quite sure that it is figures which show us whether it is being ruled well or badly. —**Johann Wolfgang Goethe, 1830**

Measurement is the making of distinction; precise measurement is making sharp distinctions. —**Enrico Fermi**[1]

Our society likes to keep score. The sports pages supply us with the win-loss records that reveal how well the various teams are doing. We also keep score on the performance of our economy. The scoreboard for economic performance is the *national-income accounting system*. Just as a firm's accounting statement provides information on its performance, national-income accounts supply performance information for the entire economy.

Simon Kuznets, the winner of the 1971 Nobel Prize in economics, developed the basic concepts of national-income accounting during the 1920s and 1930s. Through the years, these procedures have been modified and improved. In this chapter, we will explain how the flow of an economy's output (and income) is measured. We will also explain how changes in the quantity of goods and services produced are

separated from changes that reflect merely inflation (higher prices).

As you read this chapter, look for answers to the following questions:

- What is GDP? How is GDP measured?

- When making comparisons over time, why is it important to adjust nominal GDP for the effects of changes in the price level?

- What do price indexes measure? How can they be used to estimate the rate of inflation and adjust for changes in the general level of prices?

- Is GDP a good measure of output? What are its strengths and weaknesses?

[1]As quoted by Milton Friedman in *Economic Freedom: Toward a Theory of Measurement*, ed. Walter Block (Vancouver, British Columbia, Canada: The Fraser Institute, 1991), 11.

7-1 GDP—A MEASURE OF OUTPUT

The **gross domestic product (GDP)** is the market value of final goods and services produced within a country during a specific time period, usually a year. GDP is the most widely used measure of economic performance. The GDP figures are closely watched both by policy-makers and by those in the business and financial communities. In the United States, the numbers are prepared quarterly and released a few weeks following the end of each quarter.

GDP is a "flow" concept. By analogy, a water gauge measures the amount of water that flows through a pipe each hour. Similarly, GDP measures the market value of production that "flows" through the economy's factories and shops each year (or quarter).

7-1a WHAT COUNTS TOWARD GDP?

First and foremost, GDP is a measure of output. Thus, it cannot be arrived at merely by summing the totals from the nation's cash registers during a period. The key phrases in the definition of GDP—"market value" of "final goods and services" "produced" "within a country" "during a specific time period"—reveal a great deal about what should be included in and excluded from the calculation of GDP. Let's take a closer look at this issue.

Only final goods and services count. If output is to be measured accurately, all goods and services produced during the year must be counted once and only once. Most goods go through several stages of production before they end up in the hands of their ultimate users. To avoid double-counting, one must take care to differentiate between **intermediate goods**—goods in intermediate stages of production—and **final market goods and services**—those purchased for final use rather than for resale or further processing.

Sales at intermediate stages of production are not themselves counted in GDP because the value of the intermediate goods is embodied within the final-user good. Adding the sales price of both the intermediate good and the final-user good would exaggerate GDP. For example, when a wholesale distributor sells steak to a restaurant, the final purchase price paid by the patron of the restaurant for the steak dinner will reflect the cost of the meat. Double-counting would result if we included both the sale price of the intermediate good (the steak sold by the wholesaler to the restaurant) and the final purchase price of the steak dinner.

Exhibit 1 will help clarify the accounting method for GDP. Before the final good, bread, is in the hands of the consumer, it will go through several intermediate stages of production. The farmer produces a pound of wheat and sells it to the miller for 30 cents. The miller grinds the wheat into flour and sells it to the baker for 65 cents. The miller's actions have *added* 35 cents to the value of the wheat. The baker combines the flour with other ingredients, makes a loaf of bread, and sells it to the grocer for 90 cents. The baker has *added* 25 cents to the value of the bread. The grocer stocks the bread on the grocery shelves and provides a convenient location for consumers to shop. The grocer sells the loaf of bread for $1, *adding* 10 cents to the value of the final product. Only the final market

Gross domestic product (GDP)
The market value of all final goods and services produced within a country during a specific period.

Intermediate goods
Goods purchased for resale or for use in producing another good or service.

Final market goods and services
Goods and services purchased by their ultimate user.

Outstanding Economist: Simon Kuznets (1901–1985)

Simon Kuznets provided the methodology for modern national-income accounting and developed the first reliable national-income measures for the United States. Kuznets is often referred to as the "father of national-income accounting." A native Russian, he immigrated to the United States at the age of 21 and spent his academic career teaching at the University of Pennsylvania, Johns Hopkins University, and Harvard University.

AP Images

EXHIBIT 1

GDP and the Stages of Production

Most goods go through several stages of production. This chart illustrates both the market value of a loaf of bread as it passes through the various stages of production (column 1) and the additional value added by each intermediate producer (column 2). GDP counts only the market value of the final product. Of course, the amount added by each intermediate producer (column 2) sums to the market value of the final product.

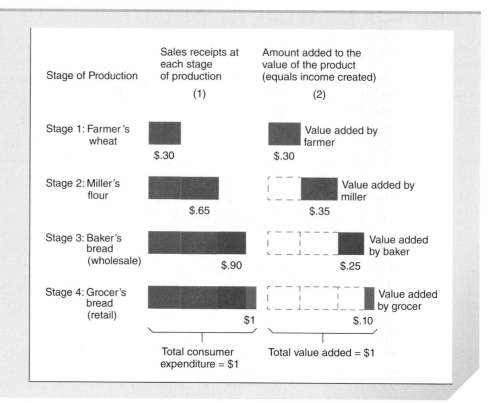

value of the product—the $1 for the loaf of bread—is included in GDP. This price reflects the value added at each stage of production. The 30 cents *added* by the farmer, the 35 cents by the miller, the 25 cents by the baker, and the 10 cents by the grocer sum to the $1 purchase price.

Only transactions involving production count. Remember, GDP is a measure of goods and services "produced." Financial transactions and income transfers are excluded because they merely move ownership from one party to another. They do not involve current production and are therefore not included in GDP. (*Note:* If a financial transaction involves a sales commission, the commission is included in GDP because it involves a service rendered during the current period.)

Thus, the purchases and sales of stocks, bonds, and U.S. securities are not included in GDP. Neither are private- and public-sector income transfers. If your aunt sends you $100 to help pay for your college expenses, your aunt has less wealth and you have more, but the transaction adds nothing to current production. Government income transfer payments, such as Social Security, welfare, and veterans payments, are also omitted. The recipients of these transfers are not producing goods in return for the transfers. Therefore, it would be inappropriate to add them to GDP.

Only production within the country is counted. GDP is a measure of "domestic product." Therefore, it counts only goods and services produced within the geographic borders of the country. When foreigners earn income within U.S. borders, it adds to the GDP of the United States. For example, the incomes of Canadian engineers and Mexican baseball players earned in the United States are included in the U.S. GDP. However, the earnings of Americans abroad—for example, an American college professor teaching in England—do not count toward the U.S. GDP because this income is not generated within the borders of the United States.

Only goods produced during the current period are counted. As the definition indicates, GDP is a measure of output "during the current period."

Transactions involving the exchange of goods or assets produced during earlier periods are omitted because they do not reflect current production. For example, the purchases of "secondhand" goods, such as a used car or a home built five years ago, are not included in this year's GDP. Production of these goods was counted at the time they were produced and initially purchased. Resale of such items produced during earlier years merely changes the ownership of the goods or assets. It does not add to current production. Thus, these transactions should not be included in current GDP. (*Note:* As in the case of financial transactions, sales commissions earned by those helping to arrange the sale of used cars, homes, or other assets are included in GDP because they reflect services provided during the current period.)

7-1b DOLLARS ARE THE COMMON DENOMINATOR FOR GDP

In elementary school, each of us was taught the difficulties of adding apples and oranges. Yet, this is precisely the nature of aggregate output. Literally millions of different commodities and services are produced each year. How can the production of apples, oranges, shoes, movies, roast beef sandwiches, automobiles, dresses, legal services, education, heart transplants, haircuts, and many other items be added together? Answer: The "market value" of each is added to GDP.

The vastly different goods and services produced in our modern world have only one thing in common: Someone pays a price for them. Therefore, when measuring output, units of each good are weighted according to their market value—the purchase price of the good or service. If a consumer pays $25,000 for a new automobile and $25 for a nice meal, production of the automobile adds 1,000 times as much to output as production of the meal. Similarly, production of a television set that is purchased for $1,000 will add 1/25 as much to output as the new automobile and 40 times the amount of the meal.

Each good produced increases output by the amount the purchaser pays for the good. The total spending on all goods and services produced during the year is then summed, in dollar terms, to obtain the annual GDP.

7-2 GDP AS A MEASURE OF BOTH OUTPUT AND INCOME

There are two ways of looking at and measuring GDP. First, *the GDP of an economy can be reached by totaling the expenditures on goods and services produced during the year.* National-income accountants refer to this method as the *expenditure approach.* Alternatively, *GDP can be calculated by summing the income payments to the resource suppliers of the things used to produce those goods and services.* Production of goods and services is costly because the resources required for their production must be bid away from their alternative uses. These costs generate incomes for resource suppliers. Thus, this method of calculating GDP is referred to as the *resource cost–income approach.*

The prices used to weight the goods and services included in GDP reflect both the market value of the output and the income generated by the resources. From an accounting viewpoint, when a good is produced and sold, the total payments to the factors of production (including the producer's profit or loss) must be equal to the sales price generated by the good.[2] For example, consider a beauty salon operator who leases a building and equipment, purchases various cosmetic products, and combines these items with labor to provide hairdressing services for which customers pay $1,000 per day. The market value of

---

[2]In the national-income accounts, the terms profit and corporate profit are used in the accounting sense. Thus, they reflect both the competitive rate of return on assets (opportunity cost of capital) and the firm's economic profit and loss, which were discussed in Chapter 3.

the output, $1,000 per day, is added to GDP. The $1,000 figure is also equal to the income resource owners receive from the provision of the service.

The link between the market value of a good and the income (including the profit or loss) earned by resource suppliers occurs for each good or service produced. This same link is also present in the aggregate economy. In accounting terms, the idea can be illustrated as follows:

The dollar flow of expenditures on final goods = The dollar flow of income
(and indirect cost) from final goods

GDP is a measure of the value of the goods and services that were purchased by households, investors, governments, and foreigners. These purchasers valued the goods and services more than the purchase price; otherwise they would not have purchased them. GDP is also a measure of aggregate income. Production of the goods involves human toil, wear and tear on machines, use of natural resources, risk, managerial responsibilities, and other of life's unpleasantries. Resource owners have to be compensated with income payments in order to induce them to supply these resources.

Thus, GDP is a measure of both (1) the market value of the output produced and (2) the income generated by those who produced the output. This highlights a very important point: Increases in output and growth of income are linked. An expansion in output—that is, the additional production of goods and services that people value— is the source of higher income levels.

Exhibit 2 summarizes the components of GDP for both the expenditure and resource cost–income approaches. Except for a few complicating elements that we will discuss in a moment, the revenues business firms derive from the sale of goods and services are paid directly to resource suppliers in the form of wages, self-employment income, rents, profits, and interest. We now turn to an examination of these components and the two alternative ways of deriving GDP.

7-2a DERIVING GDP BY THE EXPENDITURE APPROACH

When derived by the expenditure approach, GDP has four components: (1) personal consumption expenditures, (2) gross private domestic investment, (3) government consumption and gross investment, and (4) net exports to foreigners. The left side of Exhibit 3

EXHIBIT 2

Two Ways of Measuring GDP

There are two methods of calculating GDP. It can be calculated either by summing the expenditures on the "final-user" goods and services purchased by consumers, investors, governments, and foreigners (net exports) or by summing the income payments and direct cost items that accompany the production of goods and services.

EXPENDITURE APPROACH	RESOURCE COST–INCOME APPROACH
Personal consumption expenditures	Aggregate income
	Compensation of employees (wages and salaries)
+	Income of self-employed proprietors
Gross private domestic investment	Rents
	Profits
+	Interest
Government consumption and gross investment	+
	Nonincome cost items
+	Indirect business taxes
Net exports of goods and services	Depreciation
	+
=	Net income of foreigners
GDP	=
	GDP

EXHIBIT 3

EXPENDITURE APPROACH		RESOURCE COST-INCOME APPROACH	
Personal Consumption	$14,563	Employee Compensation	$11,421
Durable goods	$1,527	Proprietors' Income	$1,658
Nondurable goods	$2,978	Rents	$778
Services	$10,058	Corporate Profits	$2,075
Gross Private Investment	$3,744	Interest Income	$645
Fixed Investment	$3,676	Indirect Business Taxes	$1,579
Inventories	$68	Depreciation (Capital Consumption)[a]	$3,568
Gov. Cons. and Gross Inv.	$3,753	Net Income of Foreigners	−$296
Federal	$1,423		
State and local	$2,330		
Net Exports	−$632		
Gross Domestic Product	$21,428	Gross Domestic Product	$21,428

Two Ways of Measuring GDP— 2019 Data (billions of dollars)

The left side shows the flow of expenditures and the right side the flow of income payments and indirect costs. Both procedures yield GDP.

[a]Includes $2,274 billion for the depreciation of privately owned capital, $587 billion for the depreciation of government-owned assets, and $105 billion for statistical discrepancy.

Source: U.S. Department of Commerce. These data are also online at http://www.bea.gov.

presents the values of these four components in 2019. Later, we will discuss the right side, which deals with the resource cost–income approach.

Consumption purchases. **Personal consumption** purchases are the largest component of GDP; in 2019, they amounted to $14,563 billion. Most consumption expenditures are for nondurable goods or services. Food, clothing, recreation, medical and legal services, and fuel are included in this category. These items are used up or consumed in a relatively short time. Durable goods, such as appliances and automobiles, constitute approximately one-tenth of all consumer purchases. These products are consumed over a longer period of time, even though they are fully counted when they are purchased.

Personal consumption
Household spending on consumer goods and services during the current period. Consumption is a flow concept.

Gross private investment. The next item in the expenditure approach, **private investment**, is the production or construction of capital goods that provide a "flow" of future service. Unlike food or medical services, they are not immediately "used." Business plants and equipment are investment goods because they will help produce goods and services in the future. Similarly, a house is an investment good because it will also provide a stream of services long into the future. Increases in business inventories are also classified as investment because they will provide future consumer benefits.

Gross investment includes expenditures for both (1) the replacement of machinery, equipment, and buildings worn out during the year and (2) net additions to the stock of capital assets. Net investment is simply gross investment minus an allowance for **depreciation** and obsolescence of machinery and other physical assets during the year.

Net investment is an important indicator of the economy's future productive capability. A substantial amount of net investment indicates that the capital stock of the economy is growing, thereby enhancing the economy's future productive potential (shifting the economy's production possibilities frontier outward). In contrast, a low rate of net investment, or even worse, a negative net investment, implies a stagnating or even contracting economy. Of course, the impact of investment on future income will also be affected by the productivity of investment—whether the funds invested are channeled into wealth-creating projects. Other things being the same, however, countries with a large net investment rate will tend to grow more rapidly than those with a low (or negative) rate of net investment. In 2019, gross private investment expenditures in the United States were $3,744 billion, 17.5 percent of GDP. Of course, a large portion ($3,568 billion) of this figure was for the replacement of private assets worn out during the year. Thus, net private investment was $176 billion, only 1 percent of GDP.

Private investment
The flow of private-sector expenditures on durable assets (fixed investment) plus the addition to inventories (inventory investment) during a period. These expenditures enhance our ability to provide consumer benefits in the future.

Depreciation
The estimated amount of physical capital (for example, machines and buildings) that is worn out or used up producing goods during a period.

Inventory investment
Changes in the stock of unsold goods and raw materials held during a period.

Because GDP is designed to measure current production, allowance must be made for goods produced but not sold during the year—that is, for **inventory investment**, or changes during the year in the market value of unsold goods on shelves and in warehouses. If business firms have more goods on hand at the end of the year than they had at the beginning of the year, inventory investment will be positive. This inventory investment must be added to GDP. Conversely, a decline in inventories would indicate that the purchases of goods and services exceeded current production. In this case, inventory *disinvestment* would be a subtraction from GDP. In 2019, the United States invested $68 billion in additional inventories.

Government consumption and gross investment. In 2019, federal, state, and local government consumption and investment in the United States summed to $3,753 billion, approximately 18 percent of total GDP. The purchases of state and local governments exceeded those of the federal government by a wide margin. The government component includes both (1) expenditures on items like office supplies, law enforcement, and the operation of veterans hospitals, which are "consumed" during the current period, and (2) the purchase of long-lasting capital goods, like missiles, highways, and dams for flood control. (Remember, transfer payments are excluded from GDP because they do not involve current production.) As a result, the government's total expenditures are substantially higher than its total consumption and investment expenditures. Unlike the other components of GDP, government purchases are counted at their *cost* to taxpayers rather than their *value* to those receiving them. In cases in which the value of the item to citizens is low relative to the tax cost of providing it, the government expenditures will overstate the value derived from the item.

Net exports
Exports minus imports.

Exports
Goods and services produced domestically but sold to foreigners.

Imports
Goods and services produced by foreigners but purchased by domestic consumers, businesses, and governments.

Net exports. The final item in the expenditure approach is **net exports**, or total exports minus imports. **Exports** are domestically produced goods and services sold to foreigners. **Imports** are foreign-produced goods and services purchased domestically. Remember, GDP is a measure of domestic production—output produced within the borders of a nation. Therefore, when measuring GDP by the expenditure approach, we must (1) add exports (goods produced domestically that were sold to foreigners) and (2) subtract imports (goods produced abroad that were purchased by Americans). For national-income accounting purposes, we can combine these two factors into a single entry:

$$\text{Net exports} = \text{Total exports} - \text{Total imports}$$

Net exports may be either positive or negative. When we sell more to foreigners than we buy from them, net exports are positive. In recent years, however, net exports have been negative, indicating that we were buying more goods and services from foreigners than we were selling to them. In 2019, net exports were *minus* $632 billion.

These four major components—personal consumption, gross private investment, government consumption and investment, and net exports—sum to GDP. In 2019, this figure was equal to $21,428 billion.

7-2b DERIVING GDP BY THE RESOURCE COST–INCOME APPROACH

The right side of Exhibit 3 illustrates how, rather than summing the flow of expenditures on final goods and services, we could reach GDP by summing the flow of costs incurred and income generated. Labor services play a very important role in the production process. It is therefore not surprising that employee compensation, $11,421 billion in 2019, provides the largest source of income generated by the production of goods and services.

Self-employed proprietors undertake the risks of owning their own business and simultaneously provide their own labor services to their firm. Their earnings in 2019 contributed $1,658 billion to GDP, 7.7 percent of the total. Together, employees and self-employed proprietors accounted for slightly more than three-fifths of GDP.

Machines, buildings, land, and other physical assets also contribute to the production process. Rents, corporate profits, and interest are payments to people who provide either the physical resources or the financial resources required for the purchase of physical assets. Rents are returns to resource owners who permit others to use their assets during a time period. Corporate profits are earned by stockholders, who bear the risk of the business undertaking and provide the financial capital the firm needs to purchase resources. Interest is a payment to parties who extend loans to producers.

Not all cost components of GDP result in an income payment to a resource supplier. In order to get to GDP, we also need to account for three other factors: indirect business taxes, the cost of depreciation, and the net income of foreigners.

Indirect business taxes. Taxes imposed on the sale of a good that increase the cost of the good to consumers are called **indirect business taxes**. The sales tax is a clear example. When you make a $1.00 purchase in a state with a 5 percent sales tax, the purchase actually costs you $1.05. The $1.00 goes to the seller to pay wages, rent, interest, and managerial costs. The 5 cents goes to the government. Indirect business taxes boost the market price of goods when GDP is calculated by the expenditure approach. Similarly, when looked at from the resource cost-income viewpoint, taxes are an indirect cost of supplying the goods to the final consumers.

Indirect business taxes
Taxes that increase a business firm's costs of production and, therefore, the prices charged to consumers. Examples are sales, excise, and property taxes.

Depreciation. As machines are used to produce goods, they wear out and become less valuable. Even though this decline in the value of capital assets is a cost of producing goods during the current period, it does not involve a direct payment to a resource owner. Thus, it must be estimated. Depreciation is an estimate, based on the expected life of the asset, of the decline in the asset's value during the year. In 2019, depreciation (sometimes called *capital consumption allowance*) of private- and public-sector capital amounted to $3,568 billion, approximately 16.7 percent of GDP.

Net income of foreigners. The sum of employee compensation, proprietors' income, rents, corporate profits, and interest yields **national income**, the income of Americans, whether earned domestically or abroad. If depreciation and indirect business taxes—the two indirect cost components—are added to national income, the result will be **gross national product (GNP)**, the output of Americans, whether generated in the United States or abroad. Put another way, GNP counts the income that Americans earn abroad, but it omits the income foreigners earn in the United States.

Because GDP is a measure of domestic output, the net income earned by foreigners must be added when GDP is derived using the resource cost-income approach. The **net income of foreigners** is equal to the income foreigners earn in the United States minus the income that Americans earn abroad. If Americans earn more abroad than foreigners earn in the United States, the net income of foreigners will be negative. In recent years, this has been the case. The net income of foreigners is generally small. In 2019, it was *minus* $296 billion, less than 2 percent of GDP. As Exhibit 3 indicates, when this figure is added to the other components, GDP derived by the resource cost method summed to $21,428 billion in 2019, the same figure as for the expenditure approach.

National income
The total income earned by a country's nationals (citizens) during a period. It is the sum of employee compensation, self-employment income, rents, interest, and corporate profits.

Gross national product (GNP)
The total market value of all final goods and services produced by the citizens of a country. It is equal to GDP minus the net income of foreigners.

Net income of foreigners
The income that foreigners earn by contributing labor and capital resources to the production of goods within the borders of a country minus the income the nationals of the country earn abroad.

7-2c THE RELATIVE SIZE OF GDP COMPONENTS

Exhibit 4 shows the relative size of each of the GDP components during 2016–2019. When the expenditure approach is used, personal consumption is by far the largest component of GDP. Consumption accounted for 68 percent of GDP during 2016–2019, compared with only 16 and 18 percent for private investment and government purchases, respectively. When GDP is measured using the resource cost–income approach, compensation to employees is the dominant component (53 percent of GDP). During 2016–2019, corporate profits, interest, and rental income combined accounted for 17 percent of GDP.

EXHIBIT 4

The Major Components of GDP in the United States, 2016–2019

The relative sizes of the major components of GDP usually fluctuate within a fairly narrow range. The average proportion of each component during 2016–2019 is demonstrated here for both (a) the expenditure and (b) the resource cost–income approaches.

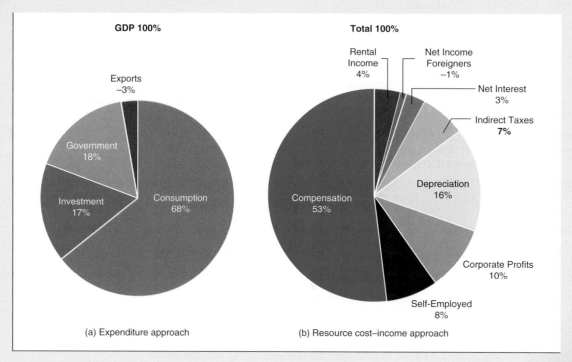

(a) Expenditure approach

(b) Resource cost–income approach

Numbers may not add up to 100 percent due to rounding.

Source: http://www.bea.gov.

7-2d THE COVID-19 PANDEMIC AND GDP

Beginning in March of 2020, federal, state, and local governments issued numerous mandates requiring most people to stay at home and the closure of many businesses in an effort to control the COVID-19 virus. Of course, the mandates exerted a huge negative impact on output. GDP declined slightly during the first quarter of 2020 and by a huge amount during the second quarter. As the mandates were gradually relaxed, there was some increase in economic activity. However, uncertainty about the future control of the virus and its long-term effects are sure to exert an impact on the economy in the years ahead. As this happens, GDP will provide valuable information on the speed and magnitude of the recovery process.

7-3 ADJUSTING FOR PRICE CHANGES AND DERIVING REAL GDP

GDP was developed to help us better assess what is happening to output (and income) over time. This is important because expansion in the production of goods and services people value is the source of higher incomes and living standards. When comparing GDP across time periods, however, we confront a problem; the nominal value of GDP may increase as the result of either (1) an expansion in the quantity of goods produced or (2) higher prices.

Because only the former will improve our living standards, it is very important to distinguish between the two.

When tracking the path of GDP and other income measures across time periods, economists use price indexes to adjust **nominal values** (or *money values*, as they are often called) for the effects of inflation—an increase in the general level of prices over time. When the term **real** accompanies GDP and income data (for example, *real GDP* or *real wages*), this means that the data have been adjusted for changes in the general level of prices across time. When comparing data at different points in time, it is nearly always the real changes that are of most interest.

What precisely is a price index, and how can it be used to adjust GDP and other figures for the effects of inflation? A price index measures the cost of purchasing a market basket (or "bundle") of goods at a point in time relative to the cost of purchasing the identical market basket during an earlier reference period. A base year (or period) is chosen and assigned a value of 100. As prices increase and the cost of purchasing the reference bundle of goods rises relative to the base year, the price index increases proportionally. Thus, a price index of 110 indicates that the general level of prices is 10 percent higher than during the base period. An index of 120 implies prices are 20 percent higher than the base period, and so on. *Note:* See the Addendum at the end of this chapter for additional details on how price indexes are constructed.

7-3a KEY PRICE INDEXES: THE CONSUMER PRICE INDEX AND THE GDP DEFLATOR

Price indexes indicate what is happening to the general level of prices. The most widely used are the consumer price index (CPI) and the GDP deflator. Because the construction of the CPI is simpler, we will begin with it.

The consumer price index (CPI) *is designed to measure the impact of price changes on the cost of the typical bundle of goods purchased by households.* A bundle of 211 item categories that constitute the "typical bundle" purchased by urban consumers during the 1982–1984 base period provides the foundation for the CPI. The quantity of each good reflects the quantity actually purchased by the typical household during the base period. Every month, the Bureau of Labor Statistics surveys thousands of retail stores, service establishments, rental units, and doctors' offices that are representative of the urban United States to derive the average price for each of the food items, consumer goods and services, housing, and property taxes included in the index. The cost of purchasing this 211-item market basket at current prices is then compared with the cost of purchasing the same market basket at base-year prices. The result is a measure of current prices compared with 1982–1984 base-period prices. In 2019, the value of the CPI was 255.7 compared with 100 during the 1982–1984 base period. This indicates that the price level in 2019 was 155.7 percent higher than the price level of 1982–1984.

There is a major deficiency of the CPI for urban households: It makes no allowance for the tendency of households to substitute away from goods and services as they become relatively more expensive. For example, if the price of beef rises, then consumers will substitute toward pork, chicken, and other meat products that are now relatively less expensive. The CPI does not account for this spending shift because it maintains the quantities of the typical bundle constant over lengthy time frames. As a result, most economists believe that the regular CPI overstates the impact of the increase in the general level of prices.

To adjust for this shortcoming, the Bureau of Labor Statistics also calculates an alternative version: the **chained consumer price index**. The chained CPI adjusts the quantities of the typical market basket each month to reflect the impact of the shifts away from the goods that have become relatively more expensive. As a result, the chained CPI is widely believed to provide a more accurate measure of changes in the general level of prices.

The GDP deflator *is a broader price index than either of the CPI measures. It is designed to measure the change in the average price of the market basket of goods*

Nominal values
Values expressed in current dollars.

Real values
Values that have been adjusted for the effects of inflation.

Consumer price index (CPI)
An indicator of the general level of prices. It attempts to compare the cost of purchasing the market basket bought by a typical consumer during a specific period with the cost of purchasing the same market basket during an earlier period.

Chained consumer price index
A measure of the consumer price index that accounts for changes in the market basket of goods bought on a monthly basis rather than on a lagged basis as done with the traditional consumer price index. This change typically reduces the annual inflation rate by 0.2 to 0.3 percentage points.

GDP deflator
A price index that reveals the cost during the current period of purchasing the items included in GDP relative to the cost during a base year (currently 2012). Unlike the consumer price index (CPI), the GDP deflator also measures the prices of capital goods and other goods and services purchased by businesses and governments.

included in GDP. In addition to consumer goods, the GDP deflator includes prices for capital goods and other goods and services purchased by businesses and governments. Therefore, in addition to consumer goods, the bundle used to construct the GDP deflator will include such items as large computers, airplanes, welding equipment, and office space. The overall bundle is intended to be representative of those items included in GDP. As in the case of the CPI, a base year (currently the year 2012) is chosen for the GDP deflator and assigned a value of 100. Values of the GDP deflator above 100 indicate that the general level of prices is higher than during the base period.

In the construction of the GDP deflator, the cost of purchasing the typical bundle of goods included in this year's GDP is always compared with the cost of purchasing that same bundle at last year's prices. Each year's percentage change in prices, based on the updated bundle, is then used to chain together the index. Like the chained CPI, the bundle of goods included in the GDP deflator is updated regularly to reflect the substitution away from goods that have become relatively more expensive. Because of this constant updating of the typical bundle, the GDP deflator is thought to yield a slightly more accurate measure of changes in the general level of prices than the regular CPI.

The annual inflation rate is simply the percentage change from one year to the next in the general level of prices. Both the CPI and the GDP deflator can be used to estimate the rate of **inflation**. When using either price index (PI),

Inflation
An increase in the general level of prices of goods and services. The purchasing power of the monetary unit, such as the dollar, declines when inflation is present.

$$\text{Inflation rate} = \frac{\text{This year's PI} - \text{Last year's PI}}{\text{Last year's PI}} \times 100$$

If the price index this year was 220, compared with 200 last year, for example, the inflation rate would equal 10 percent:

$$\frac{220 - 200}{200} \times 100 = 10$$

Exhibit 5 presents data during 2000–2015 for the CPI, chained CPI, and GDP deflator and uses each to estimate the annual rate of inflation. All three indexes were set at 100.0 in 2000 to facilitate comparability. The actual base period for each of the three indexes is 1982–1984 for the consumer price index, December 1999 for the chained CPI, and 2012 for the GDP deflator. Even though the three price indexes are based on different market baskets and procedures, their estimates for the annual rate of inflation are similar.

However, because of their more frequent updating of the typical market bundle and adjustment for the substitution away from goods with higher relative prices, the chained CPI and GDP deflator generally indicate that the annual rate of inflation is between 0.2 and 0.3 percentage points lower than the regular CPI. Over a more lengthy time frame, these relatively small annual differences add up. As Exhibit 5 indicates, between 2000 and 2019 the chained CPI and the GDP deflator price indexes rose to 141.2 and 143.9, respectively. But the regular CPI rose by a larger amount to 148.5 during this 19-year period. Despite different market baskets and procedures, their estimates for the annual rate of inflation are similar. The difference between the two alternative measures is usually only a few tenths of a percentage point.

The CPI and GDP deflator were designed for different purposes. Choosing between the two depends on what we are trying to measure. If we want to determine how rising prices affect the money income of consumers, the CPI would be most appropriate because it includes only consumer goods. However, if we want an economy-wide measure of inflation with which to adjust GDP data, the GDP deflator is clearly the appropriate index because it includes a broader set of goods and services.

Nominal GDP
GDP expressed at current prices. It is often called money GDP.

Real GDP
GDP adjusted for changes in the price level.

7-3b USING THE GDP DEFLATOR TO DERIVE REAL GDP

We can use the GDP deflator together with **nominal GDP** to measure **real GDP**, which is GDP in dollars of constant purchasing power. If prices are rising, we simply deflate the nominal GDP during the latter period to account for the effects of inflation.

EXHIBIT 5

The Consumer Price Index and GDP Deflator: 2000–2019

| YEAR | CPI | | CHAINED CPI | | GDP DEFLATOR | |
	INDEX	INFLATION RATE (%)	INDEX	INFLATION RATE (%)	INDEX	INFLATION RATE (%)
2000	100.0	-	100.0		100.0	
2001	102.8	2.8	102.3	2.3	102.2	2.2
2002	104.5	1.6	103.5	1.2	103.8	1.6
2003	106.9	2.3	105.7	2.1	105.7	1.9
2004	109.7	2.7	108.3	2.5	108.6	2.7
2005	113.4	3.4	111.5	2.9	112.0	3.1
2006	117.1	3.2	114.7	2.9	115.4	3.0
2007	120.4	2.8	117.6	2.5	118.5	2.7
2008	125.0	3.8	122.0	3.7	120.8	2.0
2009	124.6	–0.4	121.4	–0.5	121.7	0.8
2010	126.6	1.6	123.2	1.4	123.1	1.2
2011	130.6	3.2	126.9	3.1	125.7	2.1
2012	133.3	2.1	129.4	1.9	128.1	1.9
2013	135.3	1.5	131.0	1.2	130.3	1.8
2014	137.5	1.6	132.9	1.4	132.7	1.8
2015	137.6	0.1	132.7	–0.1	134.1	1.0
2016	139.4	1.3	133.9	0.9	135.5	1.0
2017	142.3	2.1	136.3	1.8	138.1	1.9
2018	145.8	2.4	139.1	2.0	141.4	2.4
2019	148.5	1.8	141.2	1.6	143.9	1.7

Each of the three indexes were set at 100.0 in 2000 in order to facilitate comparability. The actual base period for each of the three indexes is 1982–1984 for the consumer price index, December 1999 for the chained CPI, and 2012 for the GDP deflator. As we indicate in the text, a value of 100 is assigned to each of the indexes during the base year.

Exhibit 6 illustrates how real GDP is measured and why it is important to adjust for price changes. Between 2012 and 2019, the nominal GDP of the United States increased from $16,197 billion to $21,428 billion, an increase of 32.3 percent. However, a large portion of this increase in nominal GDP reflected inflation rather than an increase in real output. When making GDP comparisons across time periods, we generally do so in terms of the purchasing power of the dollar during the base year of the GDP deflator, currently 2012. The GDP deflator, the price index that measures changes in the cost of all goods included in GDP, increased from 100.0 in 2012 to 112.3 in 2019. This indicates that prices rose by

EXHIBIT 6

Changes in Prices and Real GDP in the United States, 2012–2019

YEAR	NOMINAL GDP (BILLIONS OF DOLLARS)	PRICE INDEX (GDP DEFLATOR, 2012 = 100)	REAL GDP (BILLIONS OF 2012 DOLLARS)
2012	$16,197	100.0	$16,197
2019	$21,428	112.3	$19,081
Percent Increase	32.3	12.3	17.8

Source: http://www.bea.gov

Between 2012 and 2019, nominal GDP increased by 32.3 percent. But when the 2019 GDP is deflated to account for price increases, we see that real GDP increased by only 17.8 percent.

12.3 percent between 2012 and 2019. To determine the real GDP for 2019 in terms of 2012 dollars, we deflate the 2019 nominal GDP for the rise in prices:

$$\text{Real GDP}_{2019} = \text{Nominal GDP}_{2019} \times \frac{\text{GDP Deflator}_{2012}}{\text{GDP Deflator}_{2019}}$$

Because prices were rising, the latter ratio is less than 1. Measured in terms of 2012 dollars, the real GDP in 2019 was $19,081 billion, only 17.8 percent more than in 2012. So although money GDP (nominal GDP) expanded by 32.3 percent, real GDP increased by only 17.8 percent.

Data on both money GDP and price changes are essential for meaningful output comparisons between two time periods. By itself, a change in money GDP tells us nothing about what is happening to the rate of real production. For example, not even a doubling of money GDP would lead to an increase in real output if prices more than doubled during the time period. On the other hand, money income could remain constant while real GDP increased if there were a reduction in prices. Knowledge of both nominal GDP and the general level of prices is required for real income comparisons over time.

APPLICATIONS IN ECONOMICS

Converting Prior Data to Current Dollars: The Case of Gasoline

We have explained how the GDP deflator can be used to convert nominal GDP data to real GDP (measured in terms of the dollar's purchasing power during the base year of the GDP deflator). Sometimes, however, it makes more sense to convert income or other data during prior years to the purchasing power of the dollar during the current year. A price index can also be used to accomplish this task. To convert an earlier observation to current dollars, just multiply the observation by the price index during the current period and then divide it by the price index during the earlier period. If prices have risen in recent years, this will "inflate" the data for the earlier year and thereby bring them into line with the current purchasing power of the dollar.

Let's illustrate this point and at the same time analyze the changes in gasoline prices during the last several decades. The accompanying table presents data for the nominal price (column 1) of a gallon of unleaded regular gasoline for various years since 1973. The parallel data for the consumer price

index (CPI) are presented in column 2. The nominal price of gasoline in 1973 was 39 cents. To convert this figure to the purchasing power of the dollar in January 2020, multiply the 39 cents by the ratio of the CPI in January 2020 divided by the CPI in 1973. This real price (shown in column 3), measured in terms of the 2020 price level, is equal to $2.27 (0.39 times the ratio of 258.0/44.4).

Both crude oil prices and gasoline prices rose sharply throughout the 1970s. By 1980, the nominal price of gasoline had risen to $1.25. This would make the real price of gasoline measured in 2020 dollars equal to $3.91 ($1.25 times the ratio of 258.0/82.4), more than 50 percent higher than the price in 2016. What was the real price of gasoline in 1976, 1985, 1990, 1995, and 2005? As an exercise, derive these figures to make sure that you understand how to convert data from an earlier time period into the purchasing power of the dollar during the current year

(Continued)

Price of a Gallon of Regular Unleaded Gasoline

YEAR	NOMINAL PRICE (1)	CPI (1982–1984 = 100) (2)	REAL PRICE IN JANUARY 2020 DOLLARS (3)
1973	$0.39	44.4	$2.27
1976	0.61	56.9	?
1980	1.25	82.4	3.91
1985	1.2	107.6	?
1990	1.16	130.7	?
1995	1.15	152.4	?
2000	1.51	172.2	2.26
2005	2.3	195.3	?
2010	2.79	218.1	3.30
2015	2.45	237.0	?
2020 (January)	2.57	258.0	2.57

Source: U.S. Energy Information Administration, *Monthly Energy Review*. The data for regular unleaded gasoline were unavailable prior to 1976. Thus, the 1973 observation is for regular leaded gasoline, which was slightly cheaper during that period.

7-4 PROBLEMS WITH GDP AS A MEASURING ROD

Even real GDP is an imperfect measure of current output and income. Some productive activities are omitted because their value is difficult to determine. The introduction of new products complicates the use of GDP as a measuring rod. Also, when production involves harmful side effects that are not fully registered in the market prices, GDP will fail to measure the level of output accurately. Let's take a closer look at some of the limitations of GDP.

7-4a NONMARKET PRODUCTION

GDP does not count household production because it does not involve a market transaction. As a result, the household services of millions of people are excluded. If you mow the yard, repair your car, paint your house, pick up relatives from school, or perform similar productive household activities, your efforts add nothing to GDP because no market transaction is involved. Such nonmarket productive activities are sizable—10 percent to 15 percent of total GDP.

Excluding household production results in some oddities in national-income accounting. Suppose, for example, that a woman marries her gardener, and, after the marriage, the spouse-gardener works for love rather than for money. GDP will decline because the services of the spouse-gardener no longer involve a market transaction and therefore no longer contribute to GDP. In contrast, if a family member decides to enter the labor force and hires someone to perform services previously provided by household members, there will be a double-barreled impact on GDP. It will rise as a result of (1) the market earnings of the new labor-force entrant plus (2) the amount paid to the person hired to perform the services that were previously supplied within the household.

Most important, omitting household production makes income comparisons across lengthy time periods less meaningful. Compared with the situation today, 50 years ago Americans were far more likely to produce sizable amounts of their own food and clothing. Only a small proportion of married women worked, and child care services were almost exclusively provided within the household. Today, people are also more likely to eat out at a restaurant than prepare their own food; hire a lawn service than mow their own lawn; and purchase an automatic dishwasher than do the dishes by hand. These and many other similar changes involve the substitution of a market transaction, which adds to GDP. Because the share of total production provided within the household has declined relative to production that involves market transactions, current GDP, even in real dollars, is overstated relative to the earlier period. Correspondingly, this factor causes an upward bias to the growth rate of real GDP.

7-4b UNDERGROUND ECONOMY

Underground economy
Unreported barter and cash transactions that take place outside recorded market channels. Some are otherwise legal activities undertaken to evade taxes. Others involve illegal activities, such as trafficking drugs and prostitution.

Some people attempt to conceal various economic activities in order to evade taxes or because the activities themselves are illegal. Economists call these activities, which are unreported and therefore difficult to measure, the **underground economy**.

Because cash transactions are hard for government authorities to trace, they are the lifeblood of the underground economy. This is why drug trafficking, smuggling, prostitution, and other illegal activities are generally conducted in cash. Not all underground economic activity is illegal. A large portion of the underground economy involves legal goods and services that go unreported so that people can try to evade taxes. The participants in this legal-if-reported portion of the underground economy are quite diverse. Taxicab drivers and wait staff may pocket fees and tips. Small-business owners may fail to ring up and report various cash sales. Craft and professional workers may fail to report cash income. Employees ranging from laborers to bartenders may work "off the books" and accept payment in cash in order to qualify for income-transfer benefits or evade taxes (or allow their employers to evade taxes).

Even though they are often productive, these unreported underground activities are not included in GDP. Estimates of the size of the underground economy in the United States range from 10 percent to 15 percent of total output. The available evidence indicates that the size of the underground economy is even larger in Western Europe (where tax rates are higher) and South America (where regulations often make it more costly to operate a business legally).

7-4c LEISURE AND HUMAN COSTS

GDP excludes leisure and the human cost associated with the production of goods and services. Only output matters; no allowance is made for how long or how hard people work to generate it. Simon Kuznets, the "inventor" of GDP, believed that these omissions substantially reduced the accuracy of GDP as a measure of economic well-being.

The average number of hours worked per week in the United States has declined through the years. The average nonagricultural production worker spent only 33.6 hours per week on the job in 2019, compared with more than 40 hours in 1947—a 15 percent reduction in weekly hours worked. Clearly, this reduction in the length of the workweek raised the American standard of living, even though it did not enhance GDP.

GDP also fails to take into account human costs. On average, jobs today are less physically strenuous and are generally performed in a safer, more comfortable environment than they were a generation ago.[3] To the extent that working conditions have improved through the years, GDP figures understate the growth of real income.

7-4d QUALITY VARIATION AND THE INTRODUCTION OF NEW GOODS

If GDP is going to measure accurately changes in real output, changes in the price level must be measured accurately. This is a difficult task in a dynamic world where new and improved products are constantly replacing old ones. Automobiles are now safer

---

[3]For evidence on this point, see "Have a Nice Day," *2001 Annual Report, Federal Reserve Bank of Dallas* (available online at http://www.dallasfed.org).

and get better gasoline mileage. Computers are faster and have more computing power. Refrigerators, air conditioners, and other appliances are more durable and energy-efficient. If the prices of these items rise, a portion of the price increase reflects the improvement in the quality of the product rather than inflation. Statisticians involved in the construction of price indexes attempt to make some allowance for improvements in product quality, but they are generally thought to be inadequate.

The introduction of new and dramatically different products poses an even more challenging problem. Think about the difficulty involved in determining how the price of cell phones has changed in recent years. During the past decade, a cell phone has gone from a device used primarily to make phone calls to one that also provides the user with a camera, a watch, a GPS system, a web browser, a voice recorder, a music player, a video game player, and numerous other services. The quality of today's cell phone not only is superior to that of a decade ago but also is a vastly different product that reduces the need to purchase several other products.

Most economists believe that inadequate adjustments for product quality improvement and the introduction of new products causes price indexes, including the GDP deflator, to overestimate the rate of inflation by approximately 1 percent *annually*. If so, annual changes in output are underestimated by a similar amount. Although 1 percent per year might seem small, errors of this size make a huge difference over long periods of time.

7-4e HARMFUL SIDE EFFECTS AND ECONOMIC "BADS"

GDP makes no adjustment for harmful side effects that sometimes arise from production, consumption, and the destructive acts of man and nature. If they do not involve market transactions, economic "bads" are ignored in the calculation of GDP. Yet, in a modern industrial economy, production and consumption sometimes generate side effects that either detract from current consumption or reduce our future production possibilities. When property rights are defined imperfectly, air and water pollution are sometimes side effects of economic activity. For example, an industrial plant may pollute the air or water while producing goods. Automobiles may put harmful chemicals into the atmosphere while providing us with transportation. GDP makes no allowance for these negative side effects.

Similarly, GDP makes no allowance for various acts of destruction. Consider the impact of the September 11, 2001, terrorist attacks. In addition to roughly 3,000 fatalities, property losses were estimated at approximately $20 billion, including the destruction of the World Trade Center, portions of the Pentagon, and the four commercial planes hijacked. But GDP makes no allowance for these losses. In fact, the cleanup cost, which continued for months, actually added to GDP. The same is true for destruction accompanying hurricanes, earthquakes, and other acts of nature. Even if billions of dollars of assets are destroyed, there will be no adjustment made to the GDP numbers.

7-4f GDP UNDERSTATES WELL-BEING IN THE INFORMATION AGE

In recent years, technology and the internet have substantially reduced transaction costs and expanded the availability of low-cost access to information, communications, and entertainment. Even though these changes improve our well-being substantially, they exert less impact on GDP, and sometimes lead to a reduction in GDP.

Think about how technology has reduced expenditures on classified newspaper ads, cameras, film processing, cassette tapes, CDs, watches, maps, travel agency services, encyclopedias, dictionaries, and thesauruses. Just a few years ago, Americans spent tens of billions of dollars on these items. Now services superior to that provided by these items is available through smartphones and the internet at a fraction of the cost. But the expenditures to obtain these services are now less—often substantially less. Therefore, their contribution to GDP has fallen.

Sean Gallup/Getty Images

Entrepreneurs Who Have Changed Our Lives:
Steve Jobs

Some entrepreneurs bring about changes that touch nearly everyone in the world. The late Steve Jobs, co-founder and the marketing genius of Apple Inc., was such an entrepreneur. In 1977 he and his friend Stephen Wozniak created one of the first personal computers ever made—and it was easy enough for almost anyone to use. Sales immediately took off, changing forever the way people handle information. Once-famous companies like Wang Computer and Digital Equipment Corp, which built much larger computers, soon bit the dust.

That was just the beginning. Apple invented the computer's icon and mouse and the iPhone—tools unknown a generation ago that we now take for granted. Apple also created the iPod, then iTunes, and then the iTunes store, which made it one of the nation's biggest retailers of music. Then Apple TV appeared, available on an iPhone.

Jobs, born in 1955, was the adopted son of Paul and Clara Jobs. His father was a machinist. Growing up in Cupertino, California, Jobs became interested in computers after seeing one at the age of 12. But he had other interests, too, including an appreciation of design—he even sat in on a calligraphy course after he dropped out of Reed College in Portland. He never finished college; instead he worked for a fledgling video game company and spent a year in India studying Buddhism. When he returned to the U.S., he and Wozniak started Apple in the Jobs's garage.

Jobs's career was like a roller coaster. After the Apple computer came the MacIntosh—brilliantly innovative with icons and a mouse (before that, personal computers operated only with keyboards). But the Mac didn't sell well. IBM introduced its own personal computer, and Jobs was pushed out of Apple in 1985.

Jobs tried other businesses. A spectacular success was turning a small company, Pixar, into the company that created *Toy Story*, the first feature film entirely animated by computer. That company made Jobs a billionaire. Jobs returned to Apple as CEO in 1997 as it was facing difficult times. He was a key figure in the creation of the iPhone, the revolutionary product—cellphone, camera, music player, and web browser—that turned Apple into one of the world's largest companies (often the largest in terms of market value). Further, the iPhone and the competitors who followed made communication—with friends, family, businesses, and news—part of our everyday lives.

Sources: Pilar Quezzaire, *Steve Jobs*. (Toledo, OH: Great Neck Publishing, 2011).

"Steve Jobs Biography," Encyclopedia of World Biography, https://www.notablebiographies.com/Ho-Jo/Jobs-Steve.html. Lawrence Levy, "How Steve Jobs Became a Billionaire," *Fortune*, October 19, 2016, https://fortune.com/longform/steve-jobs-pixar-apple-lawrence-levy/.

Technology is also changing the workplace. According to Bureau of Labor Statistics data, the share of workers involved in telecommuting rose from 15 percent in 2001 to 24 percent in 2018. During the 2020 COVID-19 pandemic, telecommuting made it possible for many to continue to work productively even while shut in their homes. Estimates indicate that approximately a third of the labor force worked at home during the crisis. As the technology continues to improve, the long-term upward trend in telecommuting is virtually certain to continue. Employers and employees agree to telecommuting arrangements because they improve the well-being of both. But telecommuting also reduces transportation expenditures, and this decreases GDP. Result: Advances in technology improve quality of life, but GDP shrinks.

Consider the impact of Facebook, Amazon, Netflix, and Google. During the past two decades, these high-tech firms have provided services that substantially reduced the cost of communication, exchange, entertainment, and information. The lives of tens of millions of Americans have been improved by their products and services.

Nonetheless, their contribution to both GDP and employment is modest compared to the prior options they replaced. In all of these cases, technological advancements have improved the quality of the service and breadth of the options compared to what was available just a few years ago. However, the expenditures on these new products and services are less than those for the items they replaced. Thus, they are adding less to GDP. Moreover, because the new high-tech products are different from the ones they are replacing, price indexes will fail to capture their impact. As a result, the growth of GDP tends to understate the improvement in our living standards. The magnitude of the understatement is difficult to measure with precision, but this is sure to be an exciting area of future research.[4]

7-5 DIFFERENCES IN GDP OVER TIME

Per capita GDP is simply GDP divided by population. It is a measure of income per person or the average level of income. As real per capita GDP increases, so too does the average level of real income. **Exhibit 7** presents the data for per capita real GDP (measured in 2012 dollars) for the United States for various years since 1930. In 2019, per capita GDP was more than three times the figure of 1960 and seven times the figure of 1930. What do these figures reveal? As we previously discussed, some of the measurement deficiencies of GDP will result in an overstatement of current real GDP relative to earlier periods. For example, current per capita GDP is biased upward because, compared with earlier periods, more output now takes place in the market sector and less in the household sector. Other biases, however, are in the opposite direction. Reductions in both time and physical demands of work as well as the introduction of improved products and new technologies provide examples of the latter. On balance, the direction of the overall bias is uncertain.

However, one thing is clear: GDP comparisons are less meaningful when there is a dramatic difference in the bundle of goods available. This is generally the case when comparisons are made across distant time periods. Consider the 1930s, compared with today. In the 1930s, there were no jet planes, television programs, automatic dishwashers, personal computers, or iPads. In 1930, even a millionaire could not have purchased the typical bundle consumed by the average American in 2019. When the potential goods available

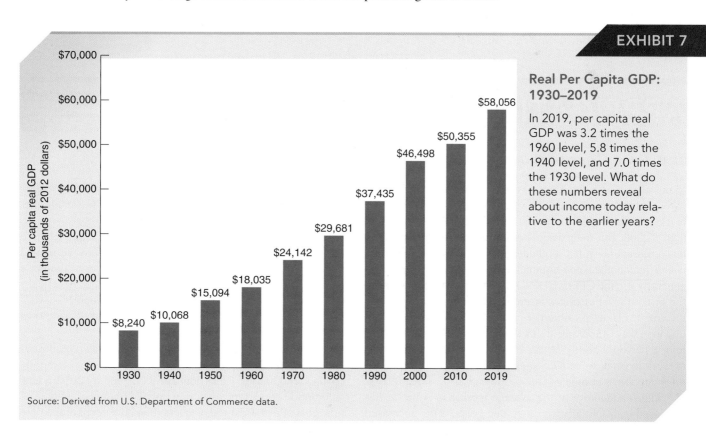

EXHIBIT 7

Real Per Capita GDP: 1930–2019

In 2019, per capita real GDP was 3.2 times the 1960 level, 5.8 times the 1940 level, and 7.0 times the 1930 level. What do these numbers reveal about income today relative to the earlier years?

Source: Derived from U.S. Department of Commerce data.

[4]The authors would like to thank Mark Perry of the American Enterprise Institute and the University of Michigan-Flint for his thoughts and helpful suggestions on this topic.

differ substantially between time periods (or countries), comparative GDP statistics lose some of their precision.

Shortcomings aside, however, there is evidence that GDP per person is a broad indicator of general living standards. As per capita GDP in the United States has increased over time, the quality of most goods has increased while the amount of work time required for their purchase has declined. In many cases, the changes have been dramatic. (See the boxed feature, "The Time Cost of Goods: Today and Yesterday.") Like per capita GDP, these data indicate that our income levels and living standards have improved. Various quality-of-life variables paint a similar picture. For example, as per capita GDP has risen in the United States and other countries, life expectancy and leisure time have gone up, whereas illiteracy and infant mortality rates have gone down. This suggests that increases in per capita GDP and improvements in living standards are closely related.

7-6 THE GREAT CONTRIBUTION OF GDP

Although GDP is a broad indicator of income levels and living standards, this is not its major purpose. ***GDP was designed to measure the value of the goods and services produced during a time period. In spite of its limitations, real GDP is a reasonably precise measure of the rate of output and the year-to-year changes in that output.***

Adjusted for changes in prices, annual and quarterly GDP data provide the information required to track the economy's performance level. These data allow us to compare the current rate of output with that of the recent past. Without this information, it would be more difficult to evaluate current performance of the economy. As we have explained, it is important to adjust nominal values for changes in the general level of prices through time. At a point in time, prices also vary considerably across geographic areas, and it is important

APPLICATIONS IN ECONOMICS

The Time Cost of Goods: Today and Yesterday

Many of you have heard stories from your parents or grandparents about how low prices were when they were young. A bottle of soda cost only a nickel, and a brand-new car was less than $2,000. But their wages were also low, typically only a few dollars per day. In this chapter, you have learned that there is a difference between nominal and real values. Economists generally use the CPI or GDP deflator to adjust for changes in the general level of prices in order to compare real wages or income levels across time periods. There is, however, an alternative way of looking at this issue: You could estimate how long a person working at the average wage rate would have to work in order to earn enough to purchase various items at different points in time.

The productivity of the average worker in America has increased substantially through the years. This increased worker productivity is the key to higher real incomes and improved living standards. When people are able to produce more per hour of work, they will be able to achieve a higher standard of living.

Using average wage rates, W. Michael Cox and Richard Alm of the Federal Reserve Bank of Dallas have computed the time of work required for the typical worker to purchase many common items. Their analysis shows that Americans today are able to acquire most goods with much less work time than was previously the case. Some examples are shown in the accompanying table.

In 1908, a new automobile cost $850, which took the average worker 4,696 hours to earn. In 1955, a new automobile costing $3,030 took 1,638 hours of work, and by 2019, a new automobile cost a typical worker only 741 hours of work. The time cost of a new car today is less than 20 percent of the time cost in 1908. Furthermore, even today's most economical

(Continued)

model is light-years away from the 1908 version with regard to power, performance, and dependability.

The prices of technology products, such as computers, calculators, and cell phones, in particular, have fallen dramatically in recent years. Cell phones and computers now cost only a small fraction of the time required for their purchase just a few years ago. In 1984, it took the average worker more than 10 weeks of work to purchase a personal computer; by 2019, the work time cost had fallen to 18 hours. In 1901, spending on food, clothing, and housing consumed 76 per-

cent of the typical worker's paycheck. Because of greater productivity and higher real earnings, today the average worker spends only 50 percent of earnings on these items.

As worker productivity grows, real incomes increase, and the time cost required to purchase products falls. This process generates higher living standards and brings goods that used to be luxuries, costing weeks' or months' worth of a worker's salary, within the reach of most Americans.

The Cost of Products to an Average-Wage Worker in Minutes or Hours of Work

ITEM	OLD COST	COST IN 2019
Eggs (1 dozen)	80 minutes in 1919	4 minutes
Sugar (5 lbs.)	72 minutes in 1919	8 minutes
Coffee (1 lb.)	55 minutes in 1919	11 minutes
Bread (1 lb.)	13 minutes in 1919	4 minutes
Mattress and box spring (twin)	161 hours in 1929	12 hours
Refrigerator	3,162 hours in 1916	25 hours
Clothes washer and dryer	256 hours in 1956	23 hours
Automobile	4,696 hours in 1908	741 hours
Coast-to-coast air flight	366 hours in 1930	11 hours
Calculator	31 hours in 1972	4 minutes
Microwave oven	97 hours in 1975	5 hours
Personal computer	435 hours in 1984	18 hours

Source: W. Michael Cox and Richard Alm, "Time Well Spent: The Declining Real Cost of Living in America," *1997 Annual Report, Federal Reserve Bank of Dallas*: 2–24. Also see Michael Cox, *Myths of Rich and Poor* (New York: Basic Books, 1999). Data updated by authors.

Is an automobile really more expensive now than it was in 1955? You might be surprised to learn that in 1955 it took a typical worker 1,638 hours of work time to purchase a car. Today, a vastly improved model can be purchased after only 741 hours of work.

to consider how these variations impact real income. Prices of goods like housing, energy, professional and repair services, health care, and even groceries often differ substantially among regions, states, and cities. In areas where prices are on average lower, the same nominal earnings will buy more goods and services than in high-price areas.

The Bureau of Economic Analysis has been tracking cost of living variations among the 50 states since 2013. The differences are substantial. For example, during 2017, the cost of purchasing the typical household consumption bundle was approximately 15 percent higher in Hawaii and New York than the average for the other 48 states. On the other hand, the general level of prices was about 15 percent lower than the national average in Mississippi, Arkansas, and Alabama. The cost-of-living also varies across cities. In general, prices tend to be higher in larger cities and lower in smaller towns and rural areas. Several different websites allow you to compare the cost of living across cities. For example, the website www.bankrate.com allows you to use data from the Cost of Living Index to compare salaries in one city versus another.

Exhibit 8 provides data on the cost of living for selected major cities. Suppose you had a job offer for $100,000 in San Francisco and another offer for $50,000 in St. Louis. If you wanted to maximize your purchasing power over goods and services, which job would you take? While your nominal earnings are twice as high in San Francisco, as Exhibit 8 indicates, the cost of living in that area is more than double that of St. Louis. Thus, your $50,000 job in St. Louis would provide you with more purchasing power than the $100,000 in San Francisco. Just as it is important to correct for changes in prices across time, it is also important to consider the impact of cost-of-living differences across locations.

EXHIBIT 8

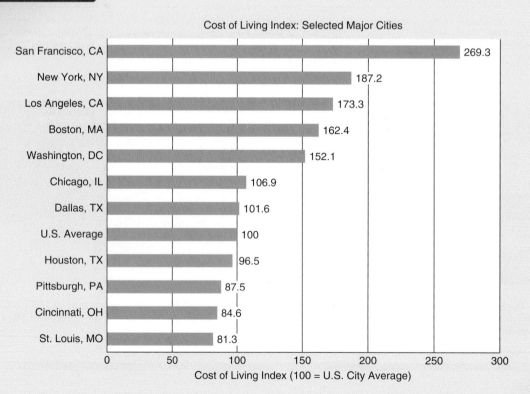

Cost of Living Index: Selected Major Cities

City	Index
San Francisco, CA	269.3
New York, NY	187.2
Los Angeles, CA	173.3
Boston, MA	162.4
Washington, DC	152.1
Chicago, IL	106.9
Dallas, TX	101.6
U.S. Average	100
Houston, TX	96.5
Pittsburgh, PA	87.5
Cincinnati, OH	84.6
St. Louis, MO	81.3

Cost of Living Index (100 = U.S. City Average)

Note: http://www.bestplaces.net is one site that provides a comparison calculator that helps individuals identify how the cost of items such as food, housing, utilities, transportation, and health in a specific location differ from the national base line of 100 and how costs vary across over 300 locations. Students interested in obtaining the most recent figures and interested in checking the cost of living in different locations are encouraged to visit the site.

KEY POINTS

- Gross domestic product (GDP) is a measure of the market value of final goods and services produced within the borders of a country during a specific time period, usually a year.

- Income transfers, purely financial transactions, and exchanges of goods and assets produced during earlier periods are not included in GDP because they do not involve current production.

- When derived by the expenditure approach, GDP has four major components: (1) personal consumption, (2) gross private investment, (3) government consumption and gross investment, and (4) net exports.

- When derived by the resource cost–income approach, GDP equals (1) the direct income components (wages and salaries, self-employment income, rents, interest, and corporate profits) plus (2) indirect business taxes, depreciation, and the net income of foreigners.

- Price indexes measure changes in the general level of prices over time. They can be used to adjust nominal values for the effects of inflation. The most widely used price indexes are the GDP deflator and the consumer price index (CPI).

- The rate of inflation is the percentage change in the general level of prices from one year to the next. It is equal to (PI_2 minus PI_1) divided by PI_1, multiplied by 100.

- In addition to the regular (or traditional) CPI, the Bureau of Labor Statistics also provides a chained CPI that adjusts the quantities of the index for movements away from goods with relative price increases. Because of their more frequent updating of the typical market bundle and adjustment for the substitution away from goods with higher relative prices, the chained CPI and GDP deflator generally provide a slightly lower estimate for the annual rate of inflation than the traditional CPI.

- The following formula can be used to convert the nominal GDP data of the current period (2) to real GDP measured in terms of the general level of prices of an earlier period (1):

$$\text{Real GDP}_2 = \text{Nominal GDP}_2 \times \frac{\text{GDP deflator}_1}{\text{GDP deflator}_2}$$

- Even real GDP is an imperfect measure of current production. It excludes household production and the underground economy, fails to take leisure and human costs into account, and adjusts imperfectly for quality changes.

- Real GDP is vitally important because it is a reasonably accurate measure of how well the economy is doing compared to the recent past. Per capita GDP is a broad indicator of income levels and living standards across time periods.

CRITICAL ANALYSIS QUESTIONS

1. *Indicate how each of the following activities will affect this year's GDP:
    a. the sale of a used economics textbook to the college bookstore
    b. Smith's $500 doctor bill for setting her son's broken arm
    c. family lawn services provided by Smith's 16-year-old child
    d. lawn services purchased by Smith from the neighbor's 16-year-old child who has a lawn-mowing business
    e. a $5,250 purchase of 100 shares of stock at $50 per share plus the sales commission of $250
    f. a multibillion-dollar discovery of natural gas in Oklahoma
    g. a hurricane that causes $10 billion of damage in Florida
    h. $60,000 of income earned by an American college professor teaching in England

2. If nominal GDP increased by 6 percent during a year, while the GDP deflator increased by 4 percent, by how much did real GDP change during the year?

3. *A large furniture retailer sells $100,000 of household furnishings from inventories built up last year. How does this sale influence GDP? How are the components of GDP affected?

4. Suppose a group of British investors finances the construction of a plant to manufacture skateboards in St. Louis, Missouri. How will the construction of the plant affect GDP? Suppose the plant generates $100,000 in corporate profits this year. Will these profits contribute to GDP? Why or why not?

5. Why might even real GDP be a misleading index of changes in output between 1950 and 2020 in the United States?

6. What are price indexes designed to measure? Outline how they are constructed. When GDP and other income figures are compared across time periods, explain why it is important to adjust for changes in the general level of prices.

7. *In 1982, the average hourly earnings of private nonagricultural production workers were $7.86 per hour. By 2019, the average hourly earnings had risen to $23.51. In 2019, the CPI was 255.7, compared with 96.5 in 1982. What were the real earnings of private nonagricultural production workers in 2019 measured in 1982 dollars?

8. The receipts and year of release of five successful movies, along with the CPI data of each year are presented below. Assuming that the receipts for each of the movies were derived during their year of release, convert the receipts for each to

real dollars for the year 2019 (2019 CPI 255.7). Which movie had the largest real box office receipts?

Movies	Box Office Receipts (millions)	Year Released	CPI in Year Released
Avatar	$760.5	2009	214.5
Titanic	600.8	1997	160.5
Star Wars	461.0	1977	60.6
Shrek 2	437.2	2004	188.9
E.T.: The Extra-Terrestrial	399.9	1982	96.5

9. *How much do each of the following contribute to GDP?

   a. Jones pays a repair shop $1,000 to rebuild the engine of her automobile.

   b. Jones spends $200 on parts and pays a mechanic $400 to rebuild the engine of her automobile.

   c. Jones spends $200 on parts and rebuilds the engine of her automobile herself.

   d. Jones sells her four-year-old automobile for $5,000 and buys Smith's two-year-old model for $10,000.

   e. Jones sells her four-year-old automobile for $5,000 and buys a new car for $20,000.

10. What is the difference between the consumer price index (CPI) and the GDP deflator? Which would be better to use if you want to measure whether your hourly earnings this year were higher than they were last year? Why?

11. *Indicate whether the following statements are true or false:

   a. "For the economy as a whole, inventory investment can never be negative."

   b. "The net investment of an economy must always be positive."

   c. "An increase in GDP indicates that the standard of living of people has risen."

12. *How do the receipts and expenditures of a state-operated lottery affect GDP?

13. GDP does not count productive services, such as child care, food preparation, cleaning, and laundry, provided within the household. Why are these things excluded? Is GDP a sexist measure? Does it understate the productive contributions of women relative to men? Discuss.

14. Indicate how each of the following will affect this year's GDP:

   a. You suffer $10,000 of damage when you wreck your automobile.

   b. You win $10,000 in a state lottery.

   c. You spend $5,100 in January for 100 shares of stock ($5,000 for the stock and $100 for the sales commission) and sell the stock in August for $8,200 ($8,000 for the stock and $200 for the sales commission).

   d. You pay $500 for this month's rental of your apartment.

   e. You are paid $300 for computer services provided to a client.

   f. You receive $300 from your parents.

   g. You get a raise from $8 to $10 per hour and simultaneously decide to reduce your hours worked from 20 to 16 per week.

   h. You earn $4,000 working in Spain as an English instructor.

15. The accompanying chart presents 2020 data from the national-income accounts of the United States.

Component	Billions of Dollars
Personal Consumption	$14,562.7
Employee Compensation	11,420.9
Rents	777.9
Gov't Consumption & Investment	3,753.0
Imports	3,136.1
Depreciation	3,568.2
Corporate Profits	2,074.6
Interest Income	644.9
Exports	2,504.3
Gross Private Investment	3,743.9
Indirect Business Taxes	1,578.6
Self-Employment Income	1,658.2
Net Income of Foreigners	−295.5

   a. Indicate the various components of GDP when it is derived by the expenditure approach. Calculate GDP using the expenditure approach.

   b. Indicate the various components of GDP when it is derived by the resource cost–income approach. Calculate GDP using the resource cost–income approach.

16. *Fill in the blanks in the following table:

Year	Nominal GDP (in Billions)	GDP Deflator (2012 = 100)	Real GDP (Billions of 2012 Dollars)
1960	542.4	16.6	a. _____
1970	1,073.3	21.7	b. _____
1980	2,857.3	c. _____	6,759.0
1990	d. _____	63.7	9,361.2
2000	10,252.3	e. _____	13,131.6
2012	16,197.0	100.0	f. _____
2019	21,427.7	112.3	g. _____

*Asterisk denotes questions for which answers are given in Appendix B

17. Can price indexes also be used to measure differences in the general level of prices between cities and geographic areas within a country? If you had a job offer paying $100,000 in San Francisco and $80,000 in Kansas City, which would provide you with the most spending power to purchase goods and services? Why? Explain using data from http://www.bestplaces.net.

ADDENDUM

The Construction of a Price Index

Price indexes are designed to measure the magnitude of changes in the general level of prices through time. The price index during the current year (PI_2) is

$$PI_2 = \frac{\text{Cost of purchasing the typical bundle this year}}{\text{Cost of purchasing the same bundle during the base year}} \times 100$$

The typical (representative) bundle might be the bundle actually chosen during the earlier base year. Alternatively, it could be the bundle chosen this year. *In either case, the quantities of the various goods do not change from year to year; only the prices change.*

Let's suppose that the bundle used to calculate the index was the quantity of each good actually chosen during the base year. This is how the consumer price index is calculated. In this case, the cost of purchasing the base-year bundle this year would be the sum of the price of each good this year (P_2) multiplied by the quantity consumed during the base year (Q_1). The cost of purchasing the *same bundle* during the base year would be the sum of the price of each good during the base year (P_1) multiplied by the quantity of each good chosen during the base year (Q_1). Therefore, the mathematical formula for the price index during the current year (PI_2) could be written:

$$PI_2 \times \frac{\Sigma\, P_2 Q_1}{\Sigma\, P_1 Q_1} \times 100$$

If prices on average are higher during the current period than they were during the base year, then this expression will be greater than 100. This indicates that it is now more costly to purchase the representative bundle than it was during the base year. Correspondingly, if the general level of prices is currently lower today than during the base period, then PI_2 would be less than 100. Thus, the current price index indicates how the current level of prices compares with the level during the base period.

Let's consider a simple example that illustrates more fully how price indexes are constructed. Suppose that your typical daily consumption bundle is two hamburgers, one order of French fries, and three Coca-Colas. Initially, the price of a hamburger was $3, French fries $1, and Coca-Cola $1. The price index during this base period is assigned a value of 100. Your expenditures on the bundle during the base period (the denominator in the previous formula) were $10 ($6 for the two hamburgers, $1 for the French fries, and $3 for the three Coca-Colas).

Now consider the implications if prices in the current period are $3.50 for a hamburger, $1.75 for French fries, and 75 cents for a Coca-Cola. Now the cost of purchasing this bundle (numerator in the previous formula) is $11 ($7 for the two hamburgers, $1.75 for the French fries, and $2.25 for the three Coca-Colas). This would yield a price index of 110 ($11 divided by $10 multiplied by 100). The price index of 110 indicates that the general level of prices for the three-good bundle is now 10 percent higher than it was during the base period.

Of course, the number of goods and the quantities included in the consumer price index (CPI) and GDP deflator are far greater than the bundle we considered in this simple illustration. Nonetheless, the general idea is the same. The cost of purchasing the typical bundle in the current period is compared with the cost of purchasing the same bundle during a base year, which is assigned a value of 100. If the cost of purchasing the bundle is now higher than it was during the base period, then the value of this year's price index will be greater than 100. As the price index changes from year to year, it indicates the magnitude of the change in the general level of prices.

CHAPTER 8

Economic Fluctuations, Unemployment, and Inflation

Prosperity is when the prices of things that you sell are rising; inflation is when the prices of things that you buy are rising. Recession is when other people are unemployed; depression is when you are unemployed. —**Anonymous**

As we have already discussed, macroeconomics is about growth of income and fluctuations in that growth. The primary objectives of macroeconomic policy are to help promote rapid and stable growth, a high level of employment, and stability in the general level of prices. Most economists are supportive of these goals, but there is considerable controversy about how they can best be achieved. Disagreements on this topic will arise again and again throughout our analysis of macroeconomics.

The performance of the economy influences our job opportunities, income levels, and quality of life. This chapter will focus on how several key economic indicators are derived and explain how changes in these measures influence our lives.

As you read this chapter, look for answers to the following questions:

- What is a business cycle? How much economic instability has the United States experienced?

- Why do economies experience unemployment? Are some types of unemployment worse than others?

- What do economists mean by full employment? How is full employment related to the natural rate of unemployment?

- How are anticipated and unanticipated inflation different? What are some of the dangers that accompany inflation?

8-1 SWINGS IN THE ECONOMIC PENDULUM

During the last hundred years, the annual growth rate of real GDP in the United States has averaged approximately 3 percent. But there have been considerable fluctuations in the year-to-year growth. During the Great Depression of the 1930s, economic growth plunged. Real GDP declined by 6 percent or more each year from 1930 to 1932. In 1933, it was more than 25 percent less than it was in 1929. The 1938 level of real GDP was virtually the same as the 1929 level. World War II was characterized by a rapid expansion of GDP, which was followed by a decline after the war. Real GDP did not reach its 1944 level again until 1951, although the output of consumer goods did increase significantly in the years immediately following the war.

Exhibit 1 presents the growth rate figures (four-quarter moving average) for real GDP for 1960–2019. Real GDP grew rapidly throughout most of the 1960s, during periods 1972–1973, 1976–1977, 1983–1988, most of the 1990s, 2002–2007, and 2010–2019. Since 1960, however, there have also been eight periods (1960, 1970, 1974–1975, 1980, 1982, 1991, 2001, and 2008–2009) of falling real GDP. Although the economic ups and downs have continued, the fluctuations have been less severe in recent decades than during the first 50 years of the twentieth century. Figures on GDP and related data can be obtained from the Bureau of Economic Analysis at http://www.bea.gov/.

8-1a A HYPOTHETICAL BUSINESS CYCLE

The United States and other industrial economies have been characterized by instability when it comes to the growth of real GDP. Inevitably, real GDP growth has been followed by economic slowdowns. Economists refer to these swings in the rate of output as the **business cycle**. The business cycle is characterized by periods of growth in real output and other aggregate measures of economic activity followed by periods of decline.

Exhibit 2 shows a hypothetical business cycle. When most businesses are operating at capacity level and real GDP is growing rapidly, a *business peak*, or boom, is present. As business conditions slow, the economy begins the *contraction*, or recessionary, phase of the cycle. During the contraction, the sales of most businesses decline, real GDP grows at a slower rate or perhaps falls, and unemployment in the labor market increases.

Business cycle
Fluctuations in the general level of economic activity as measured by variables such as the rate of unemployment and changes in real GDP.

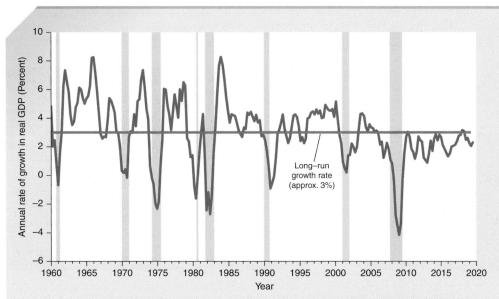

EXHIBIT 1

Instability in the Growth of Real GDP, 1960–2019

Although real GDP in the United States fluctuates substantially, periods of positive growth outweigh the periods of declining real GDP. Since 1960, the U.S. growth rate of real GDP has averaged approximately 3 percent annually. Economists refer to periods of declining real GDP as recessions. The recessionary periods are shaded.

Source: *Economic Report of the President* (Washington, DC: Government Printing Office, various issues).

EXHIBIT 2

The Business Cycle

In the past, ups and downs have often characterized aggregate business activity. Despite these fluctuations, there has been an upward trend in real GDP in the United States and other industrial nations. During economic expansions, construction and investment are increasing. In contrast, recessions are characterized by plant closings and high unemployment.

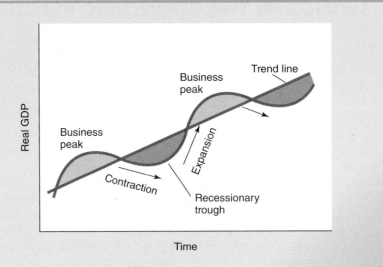

Recession

A downturn in economic activity characterized by declining real GDP and rising unemployment. In an effort to be more precise, many economists define a recession as two consecutive quarters in which there is a decline in real GDP.

Depression

A prolonged and very severe recession.

During economic expansions, construction and investment are increasing. In contrast, recessions are characterized by plant closings and high unemployment.

The bottom of the contraction phase is referred to as the *recessionary trough*. After the downturn reaches the bottom and economic conditions begin to improve, the economy enters the *expansion* phase of the cycle. Here business sales rise, GDP grows rapidly, and the rate of unemployment declines. Eventually, the expansion blossoms into another business peak. The peak, however, inevitably ends and turns into a contraction, beginning the cycle anew.

The term **recession** is widely used to describe conditions during the contraction and recessionary trough phases of the business cycle. This is a period during which real GDP declines. Often, a recession is defined as a decline in real GDP for two or more consecutive quarters.[1] When a recession is prolonged and has a sharp decline in economic activity, it is called a **depression**.

In one important respect, the term *business cycle* is misleading. The word *cycle* is often used to describe events of similar time length that occur regularly, like the seasons of the year, for example. As Exhibit 1 illustrates, this is not the case with the business cycle. The expansions and contractions last varying lengths of time, and the swings differ in terms of their magnitude. For example, the recessions of 1961, 1982, and 1990 were followed by eight years or more of uninterrupted growth of output. In contrast, the recession of 1980 was followed by an expansion that lasted only 12 months. The expansionary phase following the recessions of 1970 and 1974–1975 fell between these two extremes. Clearly, the duration of real-world expansions and contractions is varied and unpredictable.

How can we know where an economy is in the business cycle? Of course, changes in real GDP will tell us. However, these numbers are available only quarterly, and it

---

[1]See Geoffrey H. Moore, "Recessions," in *The Fortune Encyclopedia of Economics*, ed. David R. Henderson (New York: Time Warner, Inc., 1993), for additional information on recessions in the United States. This publication is also available online at http:/www.econlib.org/.

usually takes four to six weeks after the quarter is over before reliable figures are released. Various measures that are available monthly or more often can provide clues. For example, auto sales, new housing starts, new factory orders, and even the stock market will generally increase during an expansion and decline when the economy dips into a recession. As a result, these indicators are monitored carefully.

8-2 ECONOMIC FLUCTUATIONS AND THE LABOR MARKET

Fluctuations in real GDP influence the demand for labor and employment. In our modern world, people are busy with jobs, household work, school, and other activities. Each month, the Bureau of Labor Statistics contacts a sample of 55,000 households that reflects the population characteristics of the United States. **Exhibit 3** illustrates how the activities of the population are classified. The noninstitutional civilian adult population is divided into two broad categories: (1) people not in the labor force and (2) people in the labor force. There are various reasons why people aren't in the labor force. Some are retired. Others are working in their own households or attending school. Still others are not working because they are ill or disabled. Although many of these people are quite busy, their activities lie outside the market labor force.

The **civilian labor force** is the number of people aged 16 years and older who are either employed or seeking employment. People aged 16 years and older are considered employed if they (1) worked at all (even as little as 1 hour) for pay or profit during the survey week, (2) worked 15 hours or more without pay in a family- operated enterprise during the survey week, or (3) have a job at which they did not work during the survey week

Civilian labor force
The number of people 16 years of age and older who are either employed or unemployed. To be classified as unemployed, a person must be looking for a job.

EXHIBIT 3

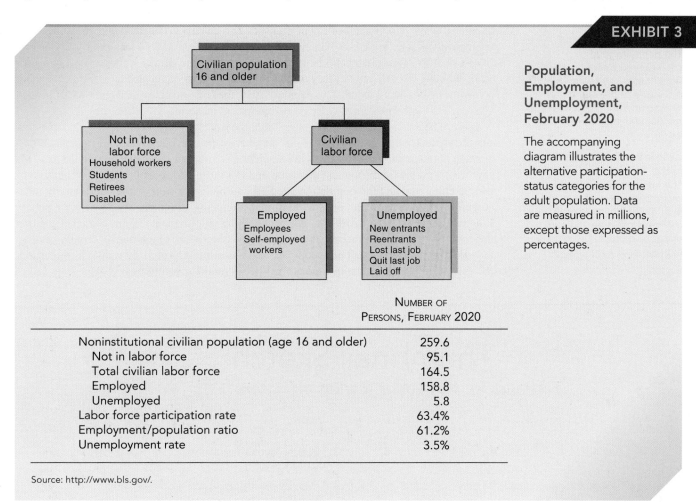

Population, Employment, and Unemployment, February 2020

The accompanying diagram illustrates the alternative participation-status categories for the adult population. Data are measured in millions, except those expressed as percentages.

	NUMBER OF PERSONS, FEBRUARY 2020
Noninstitutional civilian population (age 16 and older)	259.6
Not in labor force	95.1
Total civilian labor force	164.5
Employed	158.8
Unemployed	5.8
Labor force participation rate	63.4%
Employment/population ratio	61.2%
Unemployment rate	3.5%

Source: http://www.bls.gov/.

because of illness, vacation, industrial disputes, bad weather, time off, or personal reasons. Individuals are considered unemployed if they (1) do not have a job, (2) are available for work, and (3) have actively looked for work during the past four weeks. Looking for work involves activities such as registering at a public or private employment office, responding to an advertisement for employment, or writing letters of application. In addition, those not working are classified as unemployed if they are either waiting to start a new job within thirty days or waiting to be recalled from a layoff.

8-2a THE LABOR FORCE PARTICIPATION AND UNEMPLOYMENT RATES

Unemployed
The term used to describe a person not currently employed who is either (1) actively seeking employment or (2) waiting to begin or return to a job.

Labor force participation rate
The number of people in the civilian labor force 16 years of age or older who are either employed or actively seeking employment as a percentage of the total civilian population 16 years of age and over.

Unemployment rate
The percentage of unemployed people in the labor force. Mathematically, it is equal to the number of people unemployed divided by the number of people in the labor force.

Employment/population ratio
The number of employed civilians 16 years of age and over divided by the total civilian population 16 years of age and older. The ratio is expressed as a percentage.

As Exhibit 3 shows, **unemployed** workers who are seeking work are included in the labor force along with employed workers. The **labor force participation rate** is the number of people in the civilian labor force (including both those who are employed and those who are unemployed) as a percentage of the civilian population 16 years of age and older. In February 2020 the population (16 years of age and older) of the United States was 259.6 million, 164.5 million of whom were in the labor force. Thus, the U.S. labor force participation rate was 63.4 percent (164.5 million divided by 259.6 million).

The **unemployment rate** is a key barometer of conditions in the aggregate labor market. It is important to note that unemployment is different from not working. Part-time as well as full-time workers are counted as employed members of the labor force. The rate of unemployment is the number of people unemployed expressed as a percentage of the labor force. In February 2020, the rate of unemployment in the United States was 3.5 percent (5.8 million out of a labor force of 164.5 million).

Some argue that the unemployment rate understates the share of the labor force wanting additional work. The Bureau of Labor Statistics also calculates an alternative measure of the unemployment rate called U-6, which includes (1) part-time workers looking for full-time employment and (2) marginally attached workers (those who are neither working nor looking for work currently but indicate that they want and are available for a job and have looked for work sometime in the past 12 months). In February 2016, the U-6 unemployment rate was 9.7 percent compared to the 4.9 percent traditional unemployment measure.

In addition to the unemployment rate measures, many economists also use the **employment/population ratio**—the number of people employed expressed as a percentage of the population 16 years old and older—to monitor labor market conditions. This ratio will tend to rise during an expansion and fall during a recession. Both the number of people employed and the population aged 16 and older are well defined and readily measurable. Their measurement does not require a subjective judgment as to whether a person is actually "available for work" or "actively seeking employment." Thus, some believe that the employment/population ratio is a more objective measure of job market conditions than the rate of unemployment. The accompanying **Thumbnail Sketch** shows the formulas that are used to calculate the major indicators of labor market conditions.

Thumbnail Sketch
Formulas for Key Labor Market Indicators

1. Labor force = Employed + Unemployed
2. Labor force participation rate = Number in labor force/Population (aged 16 and older)
3. Unemployment rate = Number unemployed/Number in labor force
4. Employment/population ratio = Number employed/Population (aged 16 and older)

8-2b EMPLOYMENT FLUCTUATIONS AND TRENDS: THE HISTORICAL RECORD

Employment and output are closely linked over the business cycle. If we are going to produce more goods and services, we must either increase the number of workers or increase the output per worker. Although productivity, or output per worker, is the primary source of long-term economic growth, it changes slowly from year to year. Consequently, rapid increases in output, such as those that occur during a strong business expansion, generally require an increase in employment. As a result, output and employment tend to be positively related. Conversely, there is an inverse relationship between growth of output and the rate of unemployment.

The empirical evidence is consistent with this view. As **Exhibit 4** shows, the unemployment rate generally increases during a recession (indicated by shading) and declines during periods of expansion in output. During the recession of 1960–1961, the rate of unemployment rose to approximately 7 percent. In contrast, it declined throughout the economic boom of the 1960s, only to rise again during the recession of 1970. During the recession of 1974–1975, the unemployment rate jumped to more than 9 percent. Similarly, it soared to nearly 11 percent during the severe recession of 1982 and to 10 percent during the 2008–2009 recession. Conversely, it declined substantially during the expansions of 1983–1989, 1992–2000, 2002–2006, and 2010–2019.

Exhibit 4 also shows the huge increase in unemployment beginning during the first half of 2020. This increase in unemployment was different than that of earlier recessions because it was the result of a government-mandated shutdown designed to reduce the spread of the COVID-19 virus. Like many other governments, the federal and state

EXHIBIT 4

The Unemployment Rate, 1960–2020

Here, we illustrate the rate of unemployment during the 1960–2020 period. As expected, the unemployment rate rose rapidly during each of the eight recessions. (The shaded years indicate recessions.) In contrast, soon after each recession ended, the unemployment rate began to decline as the economy moved to an expansionary phase of the business cycle. Note, the huge upward spike in the unemployment rate accompanying the government shutdown of the economy in early 2020 in an effort to control the spread of the COVID-19 virus.

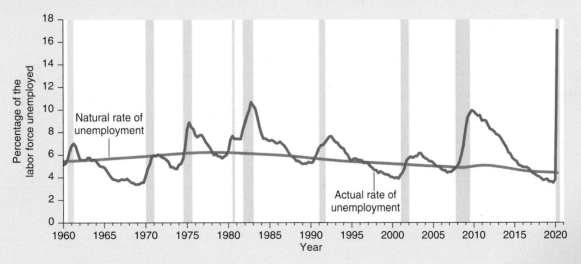

Source: https://research.stlouisfed.org/fred2/.

governments of the United States mandated that schools and businesses close, people shelter in their homes, and group meetings of more than ten people be eliminated. As a large share of the economy was shutdown, commerce was halted, businesses closed, and more than 30 million Americans lost their jobs in April of 2020. By the second quarter of 2020, the unemployment rate had soared to approximately 15 percent, substantially higher than at any time since the Great Depression of the 1930s. (Note: For additional details on this catastrophic event, see Special Topic 5, "The 2020 COVID-19 Recession.")

During the last half of the twentieth century, there was a dramatic increase in the labor force participation rate of women. **Exhibit 5** illustrates this point. In 2005, 58.6 percent of women worked outside the home, up from 32.7 percent in 1948. Married women accounted for most of this increase. More than half of all married women now are in the labor force, compared to only 20 percent immediately following World War II. Since 2005, there has been a small decline in the labor force participation rate of women. In contrast with women, the labor force participation rate of men fell. In 2019, the labor force participation rate of men was 69.2 percent, down from 83.3 percent in 1960 and 86.6 percent in 1948. Clearly, the composition of workforce participation within the family has changed substantially during the past seven decades.

Exhibit 6 tracks both the employment–population ratio and the labor force participation rate during 1980–2019. Both figures trended upward during the 1980s and 1990s. The labor force participation rate rose from 64 percent in 1980 to 67 percent in 2000. During this same period, the employment–population ratio increased from 60 percent to 64 percent. The increasing labor force participation of women boosted both of these rates during the 1980s and 1990s. Since 2000, however, the trend has reversed. By the last quarter of 2019, the labor force participation rate stood at 63.2 percent, near its lowest level in more than three decades. In the last quarter of 2019, the employment-population ratio was 61.0 percent. While most of the reductions in labor force participation and employment came during the 2008–2009 recession, both have increased only modestly since the recession ended in June 2009. Economic studies indicate a majority of the recent decline in the labor force participation rate is due to cyclical rather than demographic factors.[2]

EXHIBIT 5

Labor Force Participation Rate of Men and Women, 1948–2019

As the chart illustrates, the labor force participation rate for women rose steadily from 1948 to 2005, but there has been a modest decline since then. In contrast, the rate for men has been declining for decades.

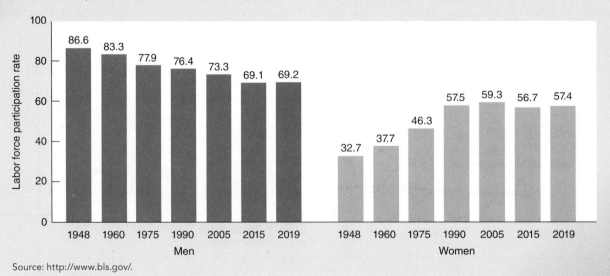

Source: http://www.bls.gov/.

[2]Willem Van Zandweghe, "Interpreting the Recent Decline in Labor Force Participation." Federal Reserve Bank of Kansas City *Economic Review* (Quarter 1, 2012): 5–34; and Daniel Aaronson, Jonathan Davis, and Loujia Hu, "Explaining the Decline in the U.S. Labor Force Participation Rate," *Chicago Fed Letter,* no. 296 (March 2012): 1–4.

EXHIBIT 6

Labor Force Participation Rate and Employment–Population Ratio, 1980–2019

Here we illustrate the path of the labor force participation rate and the employment–population ratio. Note how both ratios trended upward during 1980–2000, but they have been declining since 2000. Both fell sharply during the 2008–2009 recession, and their rebound was weak during the recovery phase of this business cycle.

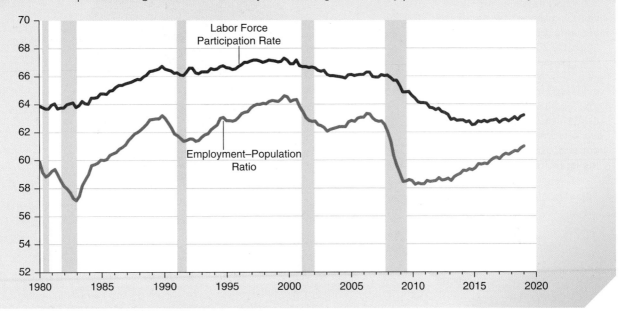

8-2c DYNAMIC CHANGE AND REASONS FOR UNEMPLOYMENT

In a dynamic world, where information is scarce and people are free to choose among jobs, some unemployment is inevitable. As new products are introduced and new technologies developed, some firms are expanding while others are contracting. Similarly, some firms will be starting operations, while others will be going out of business. This process results in the creation of new jobs and the disappearance of old ones. At the same time, some potential workers will be switching from school or other nonwork activities to the labor force, while others are retiring or taking a leave from the labor force. Furthermore, workers are mobile. At any point in time, some will voluntarily quit and search for better opportunities. Although some unemployment will always be present, there is a positive side to the unemployment–job search process: it makes it possible for individuals to better match their skills and preferences with the job requirements of employers. Better-matched employees and employers increase both productivity and earnings.

Unemployment may occur for reasons other than the loss of a job, however. For example, people often experience periods of unemployment as they enter and reenter the labor force. The Department of Labor lists five reasons why workers may experience unemployment. **Exhibit 7** shows the share of unemployed workers in each of these five categories in February 2020. Interestingly, 8.7 percent of the unemployed workers were first-time entrants into the labor force; 31.0 percent were reentering the labor force after exiting it to obtain additional schooling, do household work, or for other reasons. Therefore, 39.7 percent of the unemployed workers—two-fifths—were unemployed because they were entering or reentering the labor force. About 1 out of every 7 unemployed workers (13.4 percent) quit their job. People laid off and waiting to return to their previous positions contributed 13.8 percent to the total. Workers dismissed from their job accounted for one-third (33.1 percent) of the total number of unemployed workers.

Young workers often switch jobs and move between schooling and the labor force as they search for a career path that best fits their abilities and preferences. As the result of this

Composition of the Unemployed by Reason

This chart indicates the various reasons that people were unemployed in February 2020. One-third (33.1 percent) of the people unemployed were dismissed from their last job. Two-fifths (39.7 percent) of the unemployed workers were either new entrants or reentrants into the labor force.

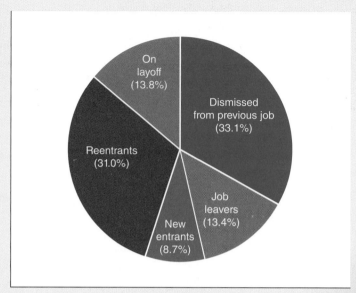

Source: http://www.bls.gov/.

The Unemployment Rate by Age and Gender, February 2020

GROUP	CIVILIAN RATE OF UNEMPLOYMENT, FEBRUARY 2020 (PERCENTAGE)
Total, all workers	3.5%
Men, Total	3.6%
Ages 16–19	11.2%
Ages 20–24	6.7%
Ages 25 and over	3.0%
Women, Total	3.4%
Ages 16–19	10.8%
Ages 20–24	6.1%
Ages 25 and over	2.8%

Source: http://www.bls.gov/.

job switching, the unemployment rate of younger workers is substantially higher than that of more established workers. As **Exhibit 8** shows, the unemployment rate of workers 20 to 24 years of age in February 2020 was about twice the rate for their counterparts aged 25 years and older. Further, the unemployment rate for teenagers was approximately four times the rate for those 25 years and older. The unemployment rates for men were higher than for women for all age groups.

8-3 THREE TYPES OF UNEMPLOYMENT

Although some unemployment is consistent with economic efficiency, this is not always the case. Abnormally high rates of unemployment generally reflect weak demand conditions for labor, counterproductive policies, and/or the inability or lack of incentive on the part of potential workers and potential employers to arrive at mutually advantageous agreements. To clarify matters, economists divide unemployment into three categories: frictional, structural, and cyclical. Let us take a closer look at each of these three classifications.

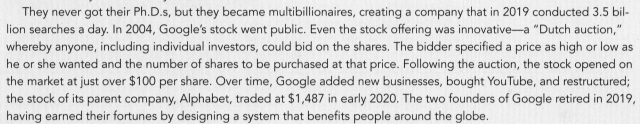

Entrepreneurs Who Have Changed Our Lives:
Sergey Brin and Larry Page

Job search is vitally important for the efficient operation of labor markets. In recent years, Google Inc., a company founded by Sergey Brin and Larry Page, has dramatically improved the search process in numerous areas, including labor markets.

Sergey Brin was born in Moscow in 1973, son of a mathematical economist who brought his family to the United States to avoid Jewish persecution. Larry Page was born the same year in East Lansing, Michigan, where his father pioneered artificial intelligence and his mother taught computer programming. Brin and Page met as graduate students at Stanford, both working on their Ph.D. in computer science. As Page tells it, he had a slew of ideas for his Ph.D. dissertation, but his adviser liked one especially: studying how information was linked on the World Wide Web. That led to the creation of Google, Inc. ("googol" is the number 1 followed by 100 zeros).

Before Google, Internet users struggled to find relevant information out of billions of bits of information scattered across the World Wide Web. Page and Brin figured they could simplify the process by creating a search engine that would rank Web pages based on popularity. Dropping out of graduate school, they used their credit cards and those of their parents and friends to launched Google in 1998 in a garage in Menlo Park, California. "Even when we started Google, we thought, 'Oh, we might fail,' and we almost didn't do it," recalls Page. "The reason we started is that Stanford said, 'You guys can come back and finish your Ph.D.s if you don't succeed.'"

They never got their Ph.D.s, but they became multibillionaires, creating a company that in 2019 conducted 3.5 billion searches a day. In 2004, Google's stock went public. Even the stock offering was innovative—a "Dutch auction," whereby anyone, including individual investors, could bid on the shares. The bidder specified a price as high or low as he or she wanted and the number of shares to be purchased at that price. Following the auction, the stock opened on the market at just over $100 per share. Over time, Google added new businesses, bought YouTube, and restructured; the stock of its parent company, Alphabet, traded at $1,487 in early 2020. The two founders of Google retired in 2019, having earned their fortunes by designing a system that benefits people around the globe.

Sources: Andy Serwer, "Larry Page on How to Change the World," *Fortune*, May 1, 2008, https://archive.fortune.com/2008/04/29/magazines/fortune/larry_page_change_the_world.fortune/index.htm.

Biography, website of A&E Television Networks.

"Google Statistics in 2020," TechJury, https://techjury.net/stats-about/google/#gref.

"The Best Advice I Ever Got: Larry Page," *Fortune*, April 30, 2008, https://archive.fortune.com/galleries/2008/fortune/0804/gallery.bestadvice.fortune/2.html.

8-3a FRICTIONAL UNEMPLOYMENT

Unemployment that is caused by constant changes in the labor market is called **frictional unemployment**. It occurs because (1) employers are not fully aware of all available workers and their job qualifications and (2) available workers are not fully aware of the jobs being offered by employers. In other words, the main cause of frictional unemployment is imperfect information.

For example, an employer looking for a new worker seldom hires the first applicant who walks into the employment office. The employer wants to find the "best available" worker to fill the opening. It is costly to hire workers who perform poorly. It is sometimes even costly to terminate their employment. So, employers search—they expend time and resources screening applicants in an effort to find the best-qualified workers who are willing to accept their wage and employment conditions.

Similarly, job seekers are searching for the employment opportunity that best fits their skills, earning capabilities, and preferences. They make telephone calls, search newspaper ads and internet sites, submit job applications, go to job interviews, use employment services, and so on. The pursuit of personal gain—landing jobs that are more attractive than the current options they face—motivates job seekers to engage in job search activities.

Frictional unemployment
Unemployment due to constant changes in the economy that prevent qualified unemployed workers from being immediately matched up with existing job openings. It results from imperfect information and search activities related to suitably matching employees with employers.

Like other types of shopping, a job search performs an important function: It helps both employees and employers make more informed choices. If the resources of an economy are going to be used effectively, the skills of workers must be matched well with the jobs of employers. Waste will result if, for example, a person with high-level computer skills ends up working as a janitor while someone else with minimal computer skills is employed as a computer programmer. Moreover, as workers try to find jobs for which their skills are well suited, they achieve higher wage rates, and the economy is able to generate a larger output.

However, as a job seeker finds out about more and more potential job opportunities, it becomes less likely that additional searching will uncover a more attractive option. Therefore, the *marginal benefit* derived from a job search declines with the time spent searching for a job because it becomes less likely that it will lead to a better position. The *marginal cost* of a job search rises as a more lengthy search leads to the discovery of more attractive job opportunities, and rejecting such options will become more and more costly.

As the marginal benefit of the job search declines and the marginal costs rise, eventually a rational job seeker will conclude that additional search is no longer worth the cost. He or she will then accept the best alternative available at that point. However, this process will take time, and during this time the job seeker is contributing to the frictional unemployment of the economy.

It is important to note that, even though frictional unemployment is a side effect, the job search process typically leads to improved economic efficiency and a higher real income for employees.

Changes that affect the costs and benefits of a job search influence the level of unemployment. The Internet has had an interesting effect on the job search process. Increasingly, both employers and employees are using Internet sites as a means of communicating with each other. Employers provide information about job openings in various skill and occupational categories, and employees supply information about their education, skills, and experience. This electronic job search process reduces information costs and makes it possible for both employers and employees to consider quickly a wide range of alternatives. This will tend to reduce both search time and frictional unemployment.

On the other hand, a change that makes it cheaper to reject available opportunities and continue searching for jobs will increase the level of unemployment. For example, an increase in unemployment benefits would make it less costly to continue looking for a preferred job. As a result, job seekers will expand the length of their search time, and the unemployment rate will rise.

8-3b STRUCTURAL UNEMPLOYMENT

Structural unemployment
Unemployment due to the structural characteristics of the economy that make it difficult for job seekers to find employment and for employers to hire workers. Although job openings are available, they generally require skills many unemployed workers do not have.

In the case of **structural unemployment**, changes in the basic characteristics of the economy prevent the "matching up" of available jobs with available workers. It is not always easy to distinguish between frictional and structural unemployment. In each case, job openings and potential workers searching for jobs are both present. The crucial difference between the two is that with frictional unemployment, workers possess the necessary skills to fill the job openings; with structural unemployment, they do not. There are many causes of structural unemployment. The introduction of new products and production technologies can substantially alter the relative demand for workers with various skills. Changes of this type can affect the job opportunities of even highly skilled workers, particularly if their skills are not easily transferable to other industries and occupations. The "computer revolution" has dramatically changed the job opportunities of many workers. The alternatives available to workers with the skills required to operate and maintain high-tech equipment have improved substantially, while the prospects of those without such skills have, in some cases, deteriorated drastically.

Shifts in public-sector priorities can also cause structural unemployment. For example, environmental regulations designed to improve air quality led to a reduction in the demand for coal during the 1990s and 2000s. As a result, many coal miners in West Virginia, Kentucky, and other coal-mining states lost their jobs. Unfortunately, the skills of many of the job losers were ill suited for employment in expanding industries. Structural unemployment was the result.

Institutional factors can also make it difficult for some workers to find jobs. For example, minimum-wage legislation may push the wages of low-skilled workers above their productivity levels and thereby reduce the job opportunities available to them. High unemployment benefits reduce the opportunity cost of unemployment and may also lead to higher levels of structural unemployment. See Applications in Economics for a suggested policy alternative that would reduce the adverse unintended consequences of the current unemployment benefit system.

8-3c CYCLICAL UNEMPLOYMENT

When there is a general downturn in business activity, **cyclical unemployment** arises. Because fewer goods are being produced, fewer workers are required to produce them. Employers lay off workers and cut back employment.

An unexpected fall in the general level of demand for goods and services will cause cyclical unemployment to rise. In a world of imperfect information, adjustments to unexpected declines in demand are often painful. When the demand for labor declines, workers will at first not know whether they are being laid off because their employer is experiencing lower demand or if the reduction in demand is widespread throughout the economy. Similarly, they will not immediately know whether their poor current employment opportunities are temporary or long term. If a reduction in demand is limited to only a few employers, the dismissed workers will generally be able to find jobs with other employers in a short period of time. The situation is different, however, when there is a general decline in demand. Many employers will lay off workers and few other employers will be hiring. Under these circumstances, workers' search efforts will be less fruitful, and the duration of their unemployment abnormally long. Unemployment of this type is referred to as cyclical unemployment. As we proceed, we will consider the causes of cyclical unemployment and analyze how it might be reduced.

Cyclical unemployment
Unemployment due to recessionary business conditions and inadequate labor demand.

APPLICATIONS IN ECONOMICS

Would Personal Savings Accounts Reduce the Rate of Unemployment?

Under the current unemployment insurance system, workers and their employers are required to pay taxes on wages and salaries, which are used to finance benefits for unemployed workers covered by the program. Typically, the benefits replace about 50 percent of a worker's prior pretax earnings for up to 26 weeks. During several recessions, Congress has extended the benefits for an additional 13 weeks. Moreover, during the recession and sluggish recovery from the 2008–2009 recession, the benefits were extended to up to 99 weeks. In many European countries, the unemployment benefits are even higher than in the United States, and people are sometimes permitted to continue drawing benefits for two or three years.

Unfortunately, unemployment programs have an unintended secondary effect: They increase the unemployment rate. The benefits make it less costly for an unemployed

worker to turn down available jobs and continue searching while receiving the payments. They also reduce the incentive of the unemployed to switch occupations or move to another location in order to find employment. As a result, workers stay unemployed longer and the overall unemployment rate is higher than it would be otherwise. In fact, empirical evidence indicates that there is a spike in the number of unemployed workers obtaining employment just prior to and immediately after their unemployment benefits are exhausted. The persistently higher unemployment rates in Europe, where the benefits are more generous, also indicate that the program pushes the unemployment rate upward, perhaps by as much as 2 or 3 percentage points.

To deal with this problem, Lawrence Brunner and Stephen Colarelli have proposed that a system of personal savings accounts be substituted for the current system.[1]

(Continued)

Instead of paying a payroll tax, employees and their employers would make equivalent payments into an unemployment personal savings account owned by the employee. Workers could then access the funds in their accounts during periods of unemployment. Upon retirement, any funds remaining in the account would be available to the worker, and, in case of death, unused funds would be passed along to the worker's heirs. Because this system would mean that workers would be using their own funds rather than the government's during periods of unemployment, the approach would eliminate the perverse incentive structure generated by the current system.

Question for Thought

1. Would the proposed reform increase the incentive to search for and accept employment rather than undergo lengthy periods of unemployment? Why or why not? Can you think of problems this system would create compared with the current system?

[1]Lawrence Brunner and Stephen M. Colarelli, "Individual Unemployment Accounts," *Independent Review* 8 (Spring 2004): 569–85.

8-4 FULL EMPLOYMENT AND THE NATURAL RATE OF UNEMPLOYMENT

Full employment
The level of employment that results from the efficient use of the labor force taking into account the normal (natural) rate of unemployment due to information costs, dynamic changes, and the structural conditions of the economy. For the United States, full employment is thought to exist when approximately 95 percent of the labor force is employed.

Natural rate of unemployment
The "normal" unemployment rate due to frictional and structural conditions in labor markets. It is the unemployment rate that occurs when the economy is operating at a sustainable rate of output. The current natural rate of unemployment in the United States is thought to be approximately 5 percent.

Full employment, a term widely used by economists and public officials alike, does not mean zero unemployment. As we have noted, in a world of imperfect information, both employees and employers will "shop" before they agree to accept a job or hire a new worker. Much of this shopping is efficient, because it leads to better matches between the skills of employees and the skills employers need. Some unemployment is therefore necessary for a dynamic labor market to operate efficiently. *Consequently, economists define full employment as the level of employment that results when the rate of unemployment is "normal," considering both frictional and structural factors.* In the United States, full employment is currently believed to be approximately 95 percent of the labor force.

Closely related to the concept of full employment is the **natural rate of unemployment**, the amount of unemployment reflected by job shopping and imperfect information. *The natural rate of unemployment is not a temporary high or low; it is a rate that is sustainable. Economists sometimes refer to it as the unemployment rate accompanying the economy's "maximum sustainable" rate of output.* When unemployment is at its natural rate, full employment is present, and the economy is achieving the highest rate of output that it can sustain.

The natural rate of unemployment, however, is not fixed. It is affected by the structure of the labor force and by changes in public policy. Over time, changes in the demographic composition of the labor force will influence the natural rate. The natural rate of unemployment increases when youthful workers expand as a proportion of the workforce. Because youthful workers change jobs and move in and out of the labor force often, they experience high rates of unemployment (see Exhibit 8). Therefore, the overall rate of unemployment is pushed upward as they become a larger share of the labor force. This is what happened during the 1960s and 1970s. In 1960, youthful workers (ages 16 to 24) constituted only 16 percent of the labor force. But as the postwar baby boom generation entered the labor market, youthful workers as a share of the labor force rose dramatically. By 1980, one out of every four workers was in the youthful-worker grouping. In contrast, prime-age workers (over age 25) declined from 84 percent of the U.S. workforce in 1960 to only 75 percent in 1980. As a result of these demographic changes, studies indicate that the natural rate of unemployment rose from approximately 5 percent in the late 1950s to more than 6 percent in the mid-1980s.

Since the late 1980s, the situation has reversed. The natural rate of unemployment has declined as the baby boomers moved into their prime working years and youthful workers shrank as a share of the labor force. Today, most researchers estimate that the natural rate is once again about 5 percent.

Public policy may also influence the natural rate of unemployment. When public policy makes it more costly to employ workers and/or less costly for people to remain unemployed, it increases the natural rate of unemployment. The economies of Spain, Italy, and France illustrate this point. During the past several decades, the labor markets of these three countries have been characterized by generous unemployment benefits, nationwide mandated wage rates, and regulations that make it expensive to dismiss workers. Regulations of this type reduce the flexibility of labor markets and make it more costly to hire and employ workers. Unsurprisingly, over the past several decades, the three European economies have persistently experienced higher unemployment rates than similar economies with freer labor markets. For example, when the unemployment rate in the United States was 3.6 percent in January 2020, the unemployment rate of Spain was 13.7 percent, Italy's was 9.8 percent, and France's was 8.2 percent. High unemployment rates over lengthy time periods are indicative of structural rather than cyclical factors.

The relationship between the *actual* unemployment rate and the *natural* unemployment rate for the United States over the last five decades can be observed in Exhibit 8. Note that the actual unemployment rate fluctuates around the natural rate in response to cyclical economic conditions. The actual rate generally rises above the natural rate during a recession and falls below the natural rate when the economy is in the midst of an economic boom. For example, the actual rate of unemployment was substantially above the natural rate during the recessions of 1974–1975, 1982, and 2008–2009. The reverse was true during the latter stages of the lengthy expansions of the 1960s, 1980s, 1990s, 2002–2007, and 2010–2019. As we proceed, we will often compare the actual and natural rates of unemployment. In a very real sense, macroeconomics studies why the actual and natural rates differ and attempts to discern the factors that cause the natural rate to change over time.

8-5 ACTUAL AND POTENTIAL GDP

If an economy is going to realize its potential, full employment is essential. When the actual rate of unemployment exceeds the natural rate, the actual output of the economy will fall below its potential. Potential output does not represent the absolute maximum level of production that could, for example, be generated in wartime or other situations during which the level of aggregate demand is abnormally high. Rather, it is the rate that would be expected under more normal circumstances.

Potential output can therefore be thought of as the maximum *sustainable* output level consistent with the full employment of resources currently available in the economy. To estimate the economy's potential output level, we need to look at three factors: the size of the labor force, the quality (productivity) of labor, and the natural rate of unemployment. Because these factors cannot be estimated with certainty, some variation exists in the estimated values of the potential rate of output.

Exhibit 9 shows the relationship between the actual and potential output of the United States since 1960. The relationship between actual and potential GDP reflects the business cycle. Note the similarity of the actual real GDP data of Exhibit 9 and the hypothetical data of an idealized business cycle of Exhibit 2. Although the actual data of Exhibit 9 are irregular compared to the hypothetical data, periods of expansion and economic boom followed by contraction and recession are clearly observable. During the boom phase, actual output expands rapidly and may temporarily exceed the economy's long-run potential. In contrast, recessions are characterized by an actual real GDP that is less than its potential. As we proceed, we will focus on how we can achieve maximum potential output while minimizing economic instability.

Potential output
The level of output that can be achieved and sustained in the future, given the size of the labor force, its expected productivity, and the natural rate of unemployment consistent with the efficient operation of the labor market. Actual output can differ from the economy's potential output.

EXHIBIT 9

The Actual and Potential GDP

Here, we illustrate both the actual and potential GDP. Note the gap between the actual and potential GDP during recessions.

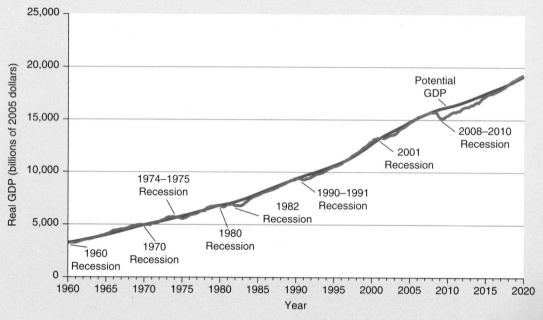

Source: http://www.bls.gov.

8-6 THE EFFECTS OF INFLATION

Inflation is a sustained increase in the general level of prices. When inflation is on the rise, it costs more to purchase a typical bundle of goods and services. Of course, even when the general level of prices is stable, some prices will be rising and others will be falling. During a period of inflation, however, the impact of the rising prices will outweigh the impact of falling prices. Because of the higher prices (on average), a dollar will purchase less than it did previously. Inflation, therefore, can also be defined as a decline in the value (the purchasing power) of money.

How do we determine whether prices are generally rising or falling? Essentially, we answered that question in the preceding chapter when we indicated how a price index is constructed. When the general level of prices is rising, the price index will also rise. In turn, the annual rate of inflation is merely the year-to-year change in an index of the general level of prices. The consumer price index (CPI) and the GDP deflator are the price indexes most widely used to measure the inflation rate in the United States. As discussed earlier, these two measures of the rate of inflation tend to follow a similar path.

It's important to note that inflation affects the prices of things we sell as well as the prices of goods we buy. Both resource and product prices are influenced by inflation. Before we become too upset about inflation "robbing us of the purchasing power of our paychecks," we need to realize that inflation influences the size of those paychecks. For example, the weekly earnings of employees would not have risen at a sharp annual rate of 7 percent during the 1970s if the rate of inflation hadn't increased rapidly during the period, too. Wages are also a price. Inflation raises both prices and wages.

How rapidly has the general level of prices risen in the United States? Using the annual rate of change in the CPI, **Exhibit 10** shows the U.S. inflation rate since the mid-1950s. During the 1950s and into the mid-1960s, the annual inflation rate was generally low. The average inflation rate during the 1956–1965 period, for example, was just 1.6 percent. Beginning in the latter half of the 1960s, however, inflation began to accelerate upward, jumping to 12 percent or more

EXHIBIT 10

The Inflation Rate, 1956–2019

Here, we present the annual rate of inflation since 1956. Between 1956 and 1965, prices increased at an annual rate of only 1.6 percent. In contrast, the inflation rate averaged 9.2 percent during the 1973–1981 era, reaching double-digit rates in several years. Since 1982, the rate of inflation has been lower (the average annual rate was 3.2 percent during 1983–1999 and 2.1 percent during 2000–2019) and more stable.

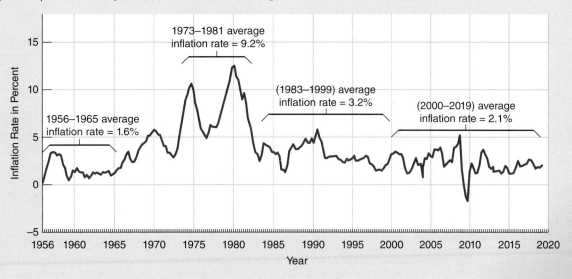

during 1974, 1979, and 1980. During the 1973–1981 period, the inflation rate averaged 9.2 percent. Price increases returned to a more level again in the mid-1980s. The annual rate of inflation averaged 3.2 percent during 1983 to 1999 and 2.1 percent during 2000 to 2019. Additional details on inflation and related measures can be obtained at http://www.bls.gov/.

8-6a UNANTICIPATED AND ANTICIPATED INFLATION

When examining the effects of inflation, it is important that we distinguish between unanticipated and anticipated inflation. **Unanticipated inflation** is an increase in the price level that comes as a surprise, at least to most individuals. For example, suppose that, based on the recent past, most people anticipate an inflation rate of 3 percent. If the actual inflation rate turns out to be 10 percent, it will catch people off guard. When the inflation rate is high and variable, it will be virtually impossible for people to anticipate it accurately. This was the case in the United States during the 1970s.

Anticipated inflation, on the other hand, is a change in the price level that is widely expected. Decision-makers are generally able to anticipate slow, steady rates of inflation with a high degree of accuracy. When the general level of prices is more stable, this will exert a positive impact on real output and the level of prosperity. During the 1983–2019 period, U.S. inflation was low and relatively stable. This 37-year period was characterized by persistent growth and only 34 months of recession.

Unanticipated inflation
An increase in the general level of prices that was not expected by most decision-makers.

Anticipated inflation
An increase in the general level of prices that was expected by most decision-makers.

8-6b WHY DOES INFLATION ADVERSELY AFFECT THE ECONOMY?

People will not be able to predict high and variable rates of inflation. There are three major reasons why such rates will adversely affect GDP and the overall health of the economy.

1. High and variable inflation reduces investment. Unanticipated inflation alters the outcomes of long-term projects, such as the purchase of a machine or an investment in a business; it will increase the risks and decrease the level of such productive activities. For example, when the price level rises 15 percent one year and 40 percent the next year and then increases again by 20 percent the following year, no one knows what to expect. Unanticipated changes of even 5 percent or 10 percent in the rate of inflation can often turn an otherwise profitable project into a personal economic disaster. Given the uncertainty that it creates, many decision makers will simply forgo capital investments and other transactions involving long-term commitments when the rate of inflation is highly variable and therefore unpredictable. As a result, mutually advantageous gains from trade will be lost and the efficiency of markets reduced.

2. Inflation distorts the information delivered by prices. Prices communicate important information concerning the relative scarcity of goods and resources. Some prices can be easily and regularly changed. But this will not be true for others, particularly those set by long-term contracts. For example, time delays will occur before the prices accompanying rental lease agreements, mortgage interest rates, and collective bargaining contracts can be changed. Because some prices will respond quickly to inflation whereas others will change more slowly, an unanticipated change in the rate of inflation will change *relative prices* as well as the *general price level*. The distorted relative prices will be a less reliable indicator of relative scarcity. As a result of these unreliable price signals, producers and resource suppliers will often make choices that they will later regret, and the allocation of resources will be less efficient than it would have been if the general level of prices had been more stable.

3. High and variable inflation results in less productive use of resources. Failing to anticipate accurately the inflation rate can have a substantial effect on one's wealth. Because of this, when the inflation rate is high, people will spend more of their time and money trying to predict and cope with the future rate of inflation. These are resources that could have been used to produce goods and services demanded by the marketplace. For example, managers will spend more time coping with frequent price changes and less time improving production methods and products. Speculative market practices will occur as people try to outguess one another about the future direction of prices. As a result, funds will flow into speculative-type investments instead of more productive ones that increase output.

8-6c WHAT CAUSES INFLATION?

We need to acquire some additional tools of analysis before we can answer in detail the question of what causes inflation. However, at this point we can list two particular causes. First, economists emphasize the link between aggregate demand and supply. If aggregate demand rises more rapidly than supply, prices will rise. Second, nearly all economists believe that a rapid expansion in a nation's money supply causes inflation. The old saying is that prices will rise because "there is too much money chasing too few goods." The hyperinflation experienced by Venezuela and Zimbabwe since 2000 has been primarily the result of monetary expansion. Once we develop additional knowledge about the operation of our economy, we will consider this issue in more detail.

KEY POINTS

- During the past century, real GDP in the United States has grown at an average annual rate of approximately 3 percent. Cyclical movements in real GDP have accompanied this growth of output.

- The four phases of the business cycle are *expansion*, *peak (or boom)*, *contraction*, and *recession*. A recession is often defined as two back-to-back quarters of declining real GDP. If a recession is quite severe, it is called a *depression*.

- Employment and output are closely linked over the business cycle. During a business expansion, employment nearly always increases and unemployment declines.

- There are three types of unemployment: (1) frictional unemployment, (2) structural unemployment, and (3) cyclical unemployment. In a world of imperfect information and dynamic change, some unemployment is inevitable. The job search process by employees and employers improves the match between the skills and preferences of workers and the job requirements of employers.

- Full employment is the employment level consistent with the economy's natural rate of unemployment. Both full employment and the natural rate of unemployment are associated with the economy's maximum sustainable rate of output.

- Potential output is the maximum *sustainable* output level consistent with the economy's resource base and current institutional arrangements.

- Inflation is an increase in the general level of prices. It is important to distinguish between anticipated and unanticipated inflation. Unanticipated changes in the rate of inflation often alter the intended terms of long-term agreements and cause people to regret choices they have previously made.

- Inflation, particularly unanticipated inflation, has harmful effects. These include (1) adverse impact on investment and other time-dimension contracts, (2) distortion of relative prices, and (3) the shift of productive resources into activities designed to prevent inflation from eroding one's wealth.

CRITICAL ANALYSIS QUESTIONS

1. List the major phases of the business cycle and indicate how real GDP, employment, and unemployment change during these phases. Are the time periods of business cycles and the duration of the various phases relatively similar and therefore highly predictable?

2. *Explain why even an efficiently functioning economic system will have some unemployed resources.

3. *Classify each of the following as employed, unemployed, or not in the labor force:

   a. Brown is not working; she applied for a job at Walmart last week and is awaiting the result of her application.
   b. Martinez is vacationing in Florida during a layoff at a General Motors plant due to a model changeover, but he expects to be recalled in a couple of weeks.
   c. Green was laid off as a carpenter when a construction project was completed. He is looking for work but has been unable to find anything except a $10-per-hour job, which he turned down.
   d. West works 70 hours per week as a homemaker for her family of nine.
   e. Carson, a 17-year-old, works six hours per week as a delivery person for the local newspaper.
   f. Chang works three hours in the mornings at a clinic and for the last two weeks has spent the afternoons looking for a full-time job.

4. What is full employment? When full employment is present, will the rate of unemployment be zero? Explain.

5. Is the natural rate of unemployment fixed? Why or why not? How are full employment and the natural rate of unemployment related? Is the actual rate of unemployment currently greater or less than the natural rate of unemployment? Why?

6. *How are the following related to one another?

   a. the actual rate of unemployment
   b. the natural rate of unemployment
   c. cyclical unemployment
   d. potential GDP

7. *Use the following data to calculate (a) the labor force participation rate, (b) unemployment rate, and (c) the employment/population ratio:

Population (aged 16 and over)	10,000
Labor force	6,000
Not currently working	4,500
Employed full-time	4,000
Employed part-time	1,500
Unemployed	500

8. How does the unemployment rate of teenagers and persons age 20 to 24 compare with the rate for older workers? Are the rate differences between the younger and older workers surprising? Why or why not? Explain.

9. How has Google impacted the job search process? How has Google impacted the ability of workers to find job opportunities consistent with their skills and preferences? Why is this important?

10. *People are classified as unemployed if they are not currently working at a job and if they made an effort to find a job during the past four weeks. Does this mean that there were no jobs available? Does it mean that there were no jobs available for which the unemployed workers were qualified? What does it mean?

11. What impact will high and variable rates of inflation have on the economy? How will they influence the risk accompanying long-term contracts and related business decisions?

12. The nominal salary paid to the president of the United States along with data for the consumer price index (CPI) are given for various years below.

Year	Presidential Salary	CPI (2000 = 100)
1920	$75,000	11.6
1940	75,000	8.1
1960	100,000	17.2
1980	200,000	47.9
2000	400,000	100.0
2019	400,000	153.5

   a. Calculate the president's real salary measured in the purchasing power of the dollar in 2000.
   b. In which year was the real presidential salary the highest? In which year was the real presidential salary the lowest?

c. The president's nominal salary was constant between 1920 and 1940. What happened to the real salary? Can you explain why?

13. "When employees are dismissed from employment for reasons other than poor performance, unemployment benefits should replace 100 percent of their prior earnings while they are searching for a new job." Do you think this proposal is a good one? Why or why not? If instituted, would the policy influence how quickly laid-off workers would find new jobs? What impact would the policy have on the unemployment rate?

14. Suppose that the consumer price index (CPI) at year end 2019 was 300 and twelve months later, at year end 2020, the CPI was 306. What was the inflation rate during 2020?

15. *"My money wage rose by 6 percent last year, but inflation completely erased these gains. How can I get ahead when inflation continues to wipe out my increases in earnings?" What's wrong with this way of thinking?

16. Data for nominal GDP and the GDP deflator (2010 = 100) in 2017 and 2018 for six major industrial countries are presented in the accompanying Table A.

a. Use the data provided to calculate the 2017 and 2018 real GDP of each country measured in 2010 prices. Place the figures in the blanks provided.

b. Use the data for the GDP deflator to calculate the inflation rate of each country. Put your answers in the blanks provided.

c. Which country had the highest growth rate of real GDP? Which had the lowest?

d. Which countries had the highest and the lowest inflation rates?

e. Which one of the countries had the most inflation during this period?

17. What is the source of frictional unemployment? Does frictional unemployment indicate that an economy is working poorly? How does the job search accompanying frictional unemployment influence the match between worker skills and performance on jobs?

*Asterisk denotes questions for which answers are given in Appendix B.

TABLE A

Country	Nominal GDP (Millions of local currency units)		GDP Deflator (2010=100)		Real GDP (in 2010 currency units)		Inflation Rate	
	2017	2018	2017	2018	2017	2018	2018	
United States	19,519.42	20,580.2	112.2	114.9	_____	_____	_____	_____
Canada	2,141.5	2,219.1	111.0	112.9	_____	_____	_____	_____
Japan	545,897.4	547,125.5	101.1	101.0	_____	_____	_____	_____
Italy	1,736.6	1,766.2	107.5	109.2	_____	_____	_____	_____
Australia	1,807.9	1,897.0	110.1	112.3	_____	_____	_____	_____
Germany	3,245.0	3,344.4	110.8	113.2	_____	_____	_____	_____

Source: International Monetary Fund, http://www.imf.org

CHAPTER 9

An Introduction to Basic Macroeconomic Markets

Macroeconomics is interesting . . . because it is challenging to reduce the complicated details of the economy to manageable essentials. Those essentials lie in the interactions among the goods, labor, and assets [loanable funds] markets of the economy. **—Rudiger Dornbusch and Stanley Fischer[1]**

Macroeconomics is primarily about economic growth and fluctuations in output, employment, and the general level of prices. As previously noted, the real GDP of the United States has grown at an average annual rate of about 3 percent during the past century. This growth has improved the living standards of Americans, but it has been uneven. In some years, the economy has grown by more than 3 percent. In others, it has grown by much less. In still other years, it has actually declined. The United States has also experienced fluctuations in employment and the rate of inflation. The experience of other countries has been similar. All countries experience short-term fluctuations in output and employment, and varying degrees of inflation.

It is one thing to describe these fluctuations and another to understand their causes. In this chapter, we will develop a simple macroeconomic model that explains the factors underlying output, employment, and the general level of prices. In subsequent chapters, we will use this model to analyze economic fluctuations and what might be done about them.

As you read this chapter, look for answers to the following questions:

- What is the circular flow of income? What are the major markets that coordinate macroeconomic activities?

- Why is an increase in the price level likely to expand output in the short run, but not in the long run?

- What determines the equilibrium level of GDP of an economy? When equilibrium is present, how will the actual rate of unemployment compare with the natural rate?

- What is the difference between the real interest rate and the money interest rate? Does inflation help borrowers relative to lenders?

- What determines the foreign exchange rate? What is the relationship between the inflow of capital and the trade deficit?

---

[1]Rudiger Dornbusch and Stanley Fischer, *Macroeconomics* (New York: McGraw-Hill, 1978).

9-1 UNDERSTANDING MACROECONOMICS: OUR GAME PLAN

A model is like a road map: It illustrates relationships. The simple model developed in this chapter will help us better understand macroeconomic relationships. It will also help us analyze the impact of macroeconomic policy.

Macroeconomic policy is usually divided into two components: fiscal policy and monetary policy. **Fiscal policy** relates to the government's taxation and spending policies to achieve macroeconomic goals. In the United States, fiscal policy is conducted by Congress and the president. It is thus a reflection of the political process. **Monetary policy** encompasses actions that alter the **money supply**—the amount of cash in our billfolds and deposits in our checking accounts. The direction of monetary policy is determined by a nation's central bank, which is the Federal Reserve System in the United States. Ideally, both monetary and fiscal policy are used to promote business stability, high employment, the growth of output, and a stable price level.

Initially, as we develop our basic macroeconomic model, we will assume that monetary and fiscal policies are unchanged—that Congress and the president aren't making fiscal policy changes and that the Federal Reserve is keeping the money supply constant. Of course, changes in government expenditures, taxes, and the money supply are potentially important. We will investigate their impact in detail in subsequent chapters.

9-2 FOUR KEY MARKETS: RESOURCES, GOODS AND SERVICES, LOANABLE FUNDS, AND FOREIGN EXCHANGE

Businesses generally purchase resources from households and use them to produce goods and services. In turn, households generally use a substantial portion of the income they earn from the sale of their productive services to purchase goods and services supplied by businesses. ***Thus, there is a circular flow of output and income between these two key sectors, businesses and households. This circular flow of income is coordinated by four key macroeconomic markets: (1) goods and services, (2) resources, (3) loanable funds, and (4) foreign exchange.***

Exhibit 1 illustrates both the circular flow of income between the household and business sectors and the interrelationships among the key macroeconomic markets. This is a very important exhibit and really much less complicated than it might first appear. It essentially depicts the macroeconomic model explained in this chapter and used to analyze the economy. It will help you see more clearly the various spending flows and interrelationships among the key markets—where the income comes from and where it goes.

The bottom loop of this circular-flow diagram depicts the **resource market**, a highly aggregated market that includes the markets for labor services, natural resources, and physical capital. In the resource market, business firms demand resources because they need them to produce goods and services. Households supply labor and other resources in exchange for income. The forces of demand and supply determine prices in the resource market. The payments made to households and the suppliers of other resources sum to national income. Some of that income is taxed and used to finance the expenditures of governments. A portion is generally saved, but most of us use the bulk of our income to buy goods and services.

The **goods and services market** constitutes the top loop of the circular-flow diagram. In this market, sometimes called the *product market*, businesses supply goods and services in exchange for sales revenue. This market counts all items in the economy's GDP. As the arrows flowing into the goods and services market (top loop) show,

---

Fiscal policy
The use of government taxation and expenditure policies for the purpose of achieving macroeconomic goals.

Monetary policy
The deliberate control of the money supply, and, in some cases, credit conditions, for the purpose of achieving macroeconomic goals.

Money supply
The supply of currency, checking account funds, and traveler's checks. These items are counted as money because they are used as the means of payment for purchases.

Resource market
A highly aggregated market encompassing all resources (labor, physical capital, land, and entrepreneurship) contributing to the production of current output. The labor market is the largest component of this market.

Goods and services market
A highly aggregated market encompassing the flow of all final-user goods and services. The market counts all items that enter into GDP. Thus, real output in this market is equal to real GDP.

deficits (shown in panel b). In the late 1970s and early 1980s, the net inflow of capital was relatively small; so too was the trade deficit. Between 1983 and 1987, the net inflow of capital soared, reaching more than 3 percent of GDP during the latter part of the period. Again, the trade deficit increased by a similar amount. Between 1988 and 1992, the net inflow of capital slowed to a trickle and the trade deficit shrank to nearly 0. During 1991–2006, however, the net inflow of capital soared once again, reaching 6 percent of GDP; the trade deficit increased hugely, too. During the last decade, the net inflow of capital has slowed, falling to approximately 2 percent of GDP in 2019. The trade deficit has followed a similar path. Clearly, these two factors are closely related; this is to be expected when a country's exchange rate is determined by market forces.

Are trade deficits bad? Trade deficits imply that a nation is borrowing financial capital from foreigners. Thus, this question is a little like asking if it is bad to borrow. The answer depends on how the funds are used. If the borrowing (inflow of capital) is channeled into productive investments, it will increase the productivity of Americans and lead to higher future income. When an economy provides an attractive investment environment, an inflow of capital and a trade deficit are likely to occur. Trade deficits arising from this source are not bad. However, if borrowing from foreigners is used unproductively or to increase current consumption, it will reduce future income. In recent years, a large portion of the capital inflow to the United States has been used to finance federal budget deficits. This borrowing has made it possible for the federal government to spend at record high levels without having to levy equivalent taxes. As a result, current consumption has been higher, and investment lower, than would otherwise have been the case. Borrowing of this type reduces the rate of capital formation and thereby slows the growth of future income. A family with financial problems cannot solve them by borrowing more in order to maintain its current level of consumption. Neither can a nation.

9-9 LONG-RUN EQUILIBRIUM

We have discussed all four basic macroeconomic markets: goods and services, resources, loanable funds, and foreign exchange. Like the legs of a chair, these four macroeconomic markets are dependent upon each other. When an economy is in long-run equilibrium, the interrelationships among these four markets will be in harmony. The relationship among resource prices, interest rates, exchange rates, and product prices will be such that, on average, firms will be just able to cover their costs of production, including a competitive return on their investment. In other words, the typical producer's return to capital must equal the interest rate, that is, the opportunity cost of capital. Higher returns would induce producers to expand output, whereas lower returns would cause them to cut back on production. These market adjustments will move an economy toward long-run equilibrium.

KEY POINTS

- The circular flow of income and expenditures shows how money flows through the four basic markets that make up the macroeconomy. Those four markets are the (a) goods and services market, (b) resource market, (c) loanable funds market, and (d) foreign exchange market.

- The aggregate demand curve shows the various quantities of domestically produced goods and services that purchasers are willing to buy at different price levels. It slopes downward to the right because the quantity purchased by consumers, investors, governments, and foreigners (net exports) will be larger at lower price levels.

- The aggregate supply (AS) curve shows the various quantities of goods and services that domestic suppliers will produce at different price levels. The short-run aggregate supply (SRAS) curve will slope upward to the right because higher product prices will improve profit margins when important cost components like long-term leases and wages set by collective bargaining agreements are temporarily fixed in the short run.

- In the long run, output is constrained by the economy's resource base, current technology, and efficiency of its existing institutions. A higher price level does not loosen these constraints. Thus, the long-run aggregate supply (LRAS) curve is vertical.

- Two conditions are necessary for long-run equilibrium in the goods and services market: (a) the quantity demanded must equal the quantity supplied, and (b) the *actual* price level must equal the price level decision-makers *anticipated* when they entered into their long-term agreements. When long-run equilibrium is present, output will be at its maximum sustainable level.

- The aggregate demand-aggregate supply model reveals the determinants of the price level and real output. In the short run, price and output will move toward the intersection of the aggregate demand (*AD*) and short-run aggregate supply (*SRAS*) curves. In the long run, price and output will gravitate to the levels represented by the intersection of the *AD*, *SRAS*, and *LRAS* curves.

- When the economy is in long-run equilibrium, potential output will be achieved and full employment will be present (the actual rate of unemployment will equal the natural rate).

- It is important to distinguish between real interest rates and money interest rates. The real interest rate reflects the real burden to borrowers and the payoff to lenders after inflation. It is equal to the money rate of interest minus the inflationary premium. The inflationary premium depends on the expected rate of inflation.

- When the exchange rate is determined by market forces, trade deficits will be closely linked with an inflow of capital. Conversely, trade surpluses will be closely linked with an outflow of capital.

- Macroeconomic equilibrium requires that equilibrium be achieved in all four key macroeconomic markets and that they be in harmony with one another.

CRITICAL ANALYSIS QUESTIONS

1. In your own words, explain why aggregate demand is inversely related to the price level. Why does the explanation for the inverse relationship between price and quantity demanded for the aggregate demand curve differ from that of a demand curve for a specific good?

2. What is the relationship between an economy's production possibilities curve and its long-run aggregate supply curve? Why is the long-run aggregate supply curve vertical?

3. Why does the short-run aggregate supply curve slope upward to the right? If the prices of both resources and goods and services increased proportionally (by the same percentage), would business firms be willing to expand output? Why or why not?

4. *If the price level in the current period is higher than buyers and sellers anticipated, what will tend to happen to real wages and the level of employment? How will the profit margins of businesses be affected? How will the actual rate of unemployment compare with the natural rate of unemployment? Will the current rate of output be sustainable in the future? Why or why not?

5. What is the current money interest rate on ten-year government bonds? Is this also the real interest rate? Why or why not?

6. *If the real interest rate in the loanable funds market increases, what will happen to the net inflow of foreign capital? Explain.

7. Explain why it's possible to temporarily achieve output levels beyond the economy's long-run potential. Why can't the high rates of output be sustained?

8. If the price level in the current period is lower than buyers and sellers anticipated, how will output and employment be affected? What is likely to happen to the rate of unemployment?

9. Suppose you purchase a $5,000 bond that pays 7 percent interest annually and matures in five years. If the inflation rate in recent years has been steady at 3 percent annually, what is the estimated real rate of interest? If the inflation rate during the next five years is 6 percent, what will happen to your real rate of return?

10. *How are the following related to each other?
    a. the long-run equilibrium rate of output
    b. the potential real GDP of the economy
    c. the output rate at which the actual and natural rates of unemployment are equal

11. Does inflation transfer wealth from lenders to borrowers? Why or why not?

12. *If a bond pays $1,000 per year in perpetuity (each year in the future), what will the market price of the bond be when the long-term interest rate is 10 percent? What would it be if the interest rate were 5 percent?

13. What determines the exchange rate? If a nation's currency appreciates in the foreign exchange market, how will this impact net exports? Explain.

14. What is a trade deficit? How is a trade deficit related to the net inflow of foreign capital? If the investments (both real and financial) of foreigners in the United States are greater than those of Americans abroad, how will this impact the trade balance? Is a trade deficit bad? Why or why not?

*Asterisk denotes questions for which answers are given in Appendix B.

CHAPTER 10

Dynamic Change, Economic Fluctuations, and the *AD–AS* Model

Not only will the [aggregate demand and aggregate supply] analysis help us interpret recent episodes in the business cycle, but it will also enable us to understand the debates on how economic policy should be conducted. —**Frederic Mishkin**[1]

In Chapter 9, we focused on the equilibrium conditions in the four basic macroeconomic markets. Equilibrium is important, but we live in a dynamic world that continually wars against it. Unexpected changes are constantly occurring. New products and technologies are developed; consumers and investors become more optimistic (or pessimistic) about the future; weather affects crop yields; international tensions disrupt or threaten to disrupt the supply of a key resource, and so on. Consequently, equilibrium is continually disrupted. Thus, if we want to understand how the real world works, we need to know how macroeconomic markets adjust to change.

We will continue to assume that the government's fiscal and monetary policies don't change. The impact of changes in these policy variables will be examined in subsequent chapters. For now, our focus is on the basic macroeconomic markets and how they respond to various disruptions.

As you read this chapter, look for answers to the following questions:

- What factors change aggregate demand? What factors change aggregate supply?

- How will an economy adjust to unanticipated changes in aggregate demand? How will it adjust to unanticipated changes in aggregate supply?

- What causes recessions and booms?

- When an economy is in a recession, will market forces help direct it back to full employment? If so, how rapidly will this adjustment process work?

- What does the *AD–AS* model reveal about the Great Recession of 2008–2009?

---

[1]Frederic S. Mishkin, *The Economics of Money, Banking, and Financial Markets*, 9th ed. (Boston: Addison-Wesley, 2010), p. 565.

10-1 ANTICIPATED AND UNANTICIPATED CHANGES

Anticipated change
A change that is foreseen by decision-makers in time for them to make adjustments.

In Chapter 8, we stated that it is important to distinguish between price-level changes that are anticipated and those that are not. This distinction is important in several areas of economics. **Anticipated changes** are foreseen by economic participants. Decision-makers have time to adjust to them before they occur. For example, suppose that, under normal weather conditions, a new drought-resistant hybrid seed is expected to expand grain production in the Midwest by 10 percent next year. As a result, buyers and sellers will plan for a larger supply of grain and lower grain prices in the future. Decision-makers will adjust their behavior accordingly.

Unanticipated change
A change that decision-makers could not reasonably foresee. The choices they made prior to the change did not take it into account.

In contrast, **unanticipated changes** catch people by surprise. New products are introduced, technological discoveries alter production costs, droughts reduce crop yields, and demand expands for some goods but contracts for others. It is impossible for decision-makers to foresee many of these changes. As we will explain in a moment, there is good reason to expect that the path of the adjustment process will be influenced by whether or not a change is anticipated.

10-2 FACTORS THAT SHIFT AGGREGATE DEMAND

The aggregate demand curve isolates the effect of the price level on the quantity demanded of goods and services. As we discussed in the previous chapter, a reduction in the price level will (1) increase the wealth of people holding a fixed quantity of money, (2) reduce the real rate of interest, and (3) make domestically produced goods cheaper than those produced abroad. All three of these factors will lead to an increase in the quantity of goods and services demanded at the lower price level.

The price level, however, is not the only factor that influences the demand for goods and services. When we constructed the aggregate demand curve, we assumed that several other factors affecting the choices of buyers in the goods and services market were constant. Changes in these "other factors" will shift the entire aggregate demand curve, altering the amount purchased at each price level. Let us take a closer look at the major factors that alter aggregate demand, causing a shift in the *AD* curve.

1. Changes in real wealth. Ownership of stocks and housing constitutes a large share of the wealth of Americans. Between December 2016 and December 2019, stock prices in the United States increased by 44 percent. During the same period, housing prices rose by 15 percent. This substantial increase in both stock and housing prices increased the wealth of Americans. In contrast, stock prices plummeted by more than 50 percent during the 16 months following October 2007, and housing prices fell by more than 30 percent between the fourth quarter of 2006 and the fourth quarter of 2008. These price declines reduced the wealth of Americans.

How will changes in the wealth of households affect the demand for goods and services? If the real wealth of households increases, perhaps as the result of higher prices in stock, housing, and/or real estate markets, people will demand more goods and services. As **Exhibit 1** illustrates, this increase in wealth will shift the entire *AD* curve to the right (from AD_0 to AD_1). More goods and services are purchased at each price level. Conversely, a reduction in wealth will reduce the demand for goods and services, shifting the *AD* curve to the left (to AD_2).

2. Changes in the real interest rate. As we discussed in Chapter 9, the major macroeconomic markets are closely related. A change in the real interest rate in

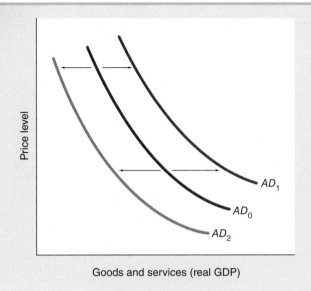

Goods and services (real GDP)

Shifts in Aggregate Demand

An increase in real wealth that would result from a stock market boom, for example, will increase aggregate demand, shifting the entire curve to the right (from AD_0 to AD_1). In contrast, a reduction in real wealth decreases the demand for goods and services, causing AD to shift to the left (from AD_0 to AD_2).

the loanable funds market will influence the choices of consumers and investors in the goods and services market. A lower real interest rate makes it cheaper for consumers to buy major appliances, automobiles, and houses now rather than in the future. Simultaneously, a lower interest rate will also stimulate business spending on capital goods (investment). If a firm must borrow, the real interest rate will contribute directly to the cost of a project. Even if the firm uses its own funds, it sacrifices interest that could have been earned by loaning the funds to someone else. Therefore, a lower interest rate reduces the opportunity cost of a project, regardless of whether it is financed with internal funds or by borrowing.

Because a fall in the real interest rate makes both consumer and investment goods cheaper, both households and investors will increase their current expenditures in response. In turn, their additional expenditures will increase aggregate demand, shifting the entire *AD* curve to the right. In contrast, a higher real interest rate makes current consumption and investment goods more expensive, which leads to a reduction in aggregate demand, shifting the *AD* curve to the left.

3. Changes in the expectations of businesses and households about the future direction of the economy.

What people think will happen in the future influences current purchasing decisions. Optimism about the future direction of the economy will stimulate current investment. Business decision-makers know that an expanding economy will mean strong sales and improved profit margins. Investment today may be necessary if business firms are going to benefit fully from these opportunities. Similarly, consumers are more likely to buy big-ticket items, such as automobiles and houses, when they expect an expanding economy to provide them with both job security and rising income in the future. Increased optimism encourages additional current expenditures by both investors and consumers, increasing aggregate demand.

Of course, pessimism about the future of the economy exerts just the opposite effect. When investors and consumers expect an economic downturn (a recession), they will cut back on their current spending to avoid overextending themselves. This pessimism leads to a decline in aggregate demand, shifting the *AD* curve to the left.

The University of Michigan conducts a monthly survey of consumers and uses the information to develop a **consumer sentiment index**. Exhibit 2 presents this index for the 1978–2019 period. An increase in the consumer sentiment index indicates that consumers are more optimistic about the future. A decline indicates increased consumer pessimism. Notice how the index fell sharply prior to and during the early stages of the

Consumer sentiment index
A measure of the optimism of consumers based on their responses to a set of questions about their current and expected future personal economic situation. Conducted by the University of Michigan, it is based on a representative sample of U.S. households.

EXHIBIT 2

Consumer Sentiment Index, 1978–2019

The consumer sentiment index developed by the University of Michigan is shown here. It is designed to measure whether consumers are becoming more optimistic or more pessimistic about the economy. Note how the index has turned down sharply prior to and during the early stages of recent recessions (shaded areas).

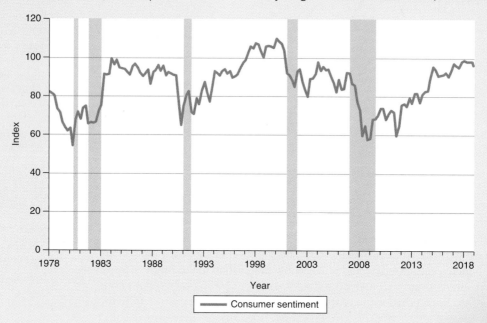

recessions that occurred in this period. The reduction was particularly sharp prior to and during the 2008–2009 recession. The index fell to 57.7 in the fourth quarter of 2008, near its all-time low. The index rebounded during 2009–2014, but remained below 90. During 2015–2019, it moved upward to the high 90s.

4. Change in the expected rate of inflation. When consumers and investors believe that the rate of inflation will go up in the future, they have an incentive to spend more during the current period. This expectation of higher inflation will stimulate current aggregate demand, shifting the *AD* curve to the right.

In contrast, if people expect inflation to decline in the future, this will discourage current spending. When prices are expected to decline (or at least increase less rapidly), people will have an incentive to wait before they buy things. This expectation of lower inflation will cause current aggregate demand to fall, shifting the *AD* curve to the left.

5. Changes in income abroad. Changes in the income of a nation's trading partners will influence the demand for its exports. If the income of a nation's trading partners increases rapidly, the demand for its exports will expand. This will stimulate its aggregate demand. For example, rapid growth of income in Europe, Canada, and Mexico increases the demand of consumers in these areas for U.S.-produced goods. This will cause U.S. exports to expand, increasing aggregate demand (shifting the *AD* curve to the right).

Conversely, when a nation's trading partners are experiencing recessionary conditions, citizens in these countries reduce their purchases, including their purchases of foreign-produced goods. Thus, a decline in the income of a nation's trading partners will reduce its exports and the aggregate demand for its products.

6. Changes in exchange rates. As we previously discussed, changes in exchange rates influence the relative price of both imports and exports. If the dollar appreciates, imported goods will be cheaper for Americans to buy, and goods exported from the United

Thumbnail Sketch
What Factors Affect Aggregate Demand?[1]

These factors *increase* aggregate demand (AD):

1. An increase in real wealth
2. A decrease in the real rate of interest
3. Optimism about future economic conditions
4. A rise in the expected rate of inflation
5. Higher real incomes abroad
6. A depreciation in the foreign exchange value of a nation's currency

These factors *decrease* aggregate demand (AD):

1. Lower real wealth
2. An increase in the real rate of interest
3. Pessimism about future economic conditions
4. A fall in the expected rate of inflation
5. Lower real incomes abroad
6. An appreciation in the foreign exchange value of a nation's currency

[1]The impact of macroeconomic policy is considered later.

States will be more expensive for foreigners to purchase. As a result, U.S. imports will rise and exports will fall. This decline in net exports (exports minus imports) will reduce aggregate demand (shifting the *AD* curve to the left).

If the dollar depreciates, the effect will be just the opposite. When the value of the dollar falls, foreign-produced goods become more expensive for U.S. consumers, whereas U.S.-produced goods become cheaper for foreigners. This is precisely what happened during the 2003–2007 period, when the dollar depreciated by about 15 percent relative to the euro and several other major currencies. When the dollar depreciates, imports will tend to fall and exports rise. In turn, this increase in net exports will stimulate aggregate demand in the United States (shifting the *AD* curve to the right).[2]

The accompanying **Thumbnail Sketch** summarizes the major factors that change aggregate demand and shift the *AD* curve. Other factors include the government's spending, taxing, and monetary policies. In subsequent chapters, we will analyze the impact of fiscal and monetary policy on aggregate demand and economic performance. We now turn to the analysis of the factors that alter aggregate supply. Then we will be in a position to consider how macroeconomic markets adjust and whether these adjustments will help keep output and employment high.

10-3 SHIFTS IN AGGREGATE SUPPLY

What factors will cause the aggregate supply curve to shift? The answer to this question will differ depending on whether the change in supply is long run and sustainable or short run and only temporary. A long-run change in aggregate supply indicates that it will be possible to achieve and sustain a larger rate of output. For example, the discovery of a lower-cost source of energy would cause a long-run change in aggregate supply. If this happened, both long-run aggregate supply (*LRAS*) and short-run aggregate supply (*SRAS*) would change.

In contrast, changes that temporarily alter the production capacity of an economy will shift the *SRAS* curve, but not the *LRAS* curve. A drought in California would be an example of such a short-run change. The drought will hurt in the short run, but it will eventually end,

---

[2]Later, when discussing international finance, we will analyze the determinants of the exchange rate and consider in more detail how changes in exchange rates affect both trade and macroeconomic markets.

and output will return to the long-run normal rate. Changes that are temporary in nature shift only the *SRAS* curve. Let's consider the factors that change long-run and short-run aggregate supply in more detail.

10-3a CHANGES IN LONG-RUN AGGREGATE SUPPLY

Productivity
The average output produced per worker during a specific time period. It is usually measured in terms of output per hour worked.

Remember, the long-run aggregate supply curve shows the maximum rate of sustainable output of an economy, given its current (1) resource base, (2) level of technology, and (3) institutional arrangements that affect its **productivity** and the efficient use of its resources. Changes in any of these three determinants of output will cause the *LRAS* curve to shift.

As panel (a) of **Exhibit 3** illustrates, changes that increase the economy's production capacity will shift the *LRAS* curve to the right. Over time, net investment will expand the supply of physical capital, natural resources, and labor (human resources). Physical capital investment expands the supply of buildings, machines, and other physical assets. Education and training improve the quality of the labor force and thereby expand the availability of human capital. Because investment in physical and human capital enhances output both now and in the future, it increases both long-run and short-run aggregate supply, causing both curves to shift to the right. However, things can work the other way around, too. Reductions in physical and human capital over time could cause the current and long-term production capacity of an economy to fall, shifting the *SRAS* and *LRAS* curves to the left.

Improvements in technology—the discovery of economical new products or less costly ways of producing goods and services—also permit us to squeeze a larger output from a given resource supply. The enormous improvement in our living standards during the last 250 years is largely the result of the discovery and adoption of technologically superior ways of transforming resources into goods and services. The development of the internal combustion engine, electricity, and nuclear power has vastly altered our energy sources (and consumption). The railroad, automobile, and airplane dramatically changed both the speed and cost of transportation. More recently, high-tech products like personal computers, checkout scanners, iPhones, and the Internet have cut the cost of doing business and expanded our production capacity. Technological improvements of this type enhance productivity and thereby shift both the *LRAS* and *SRAS* curves to the right.

Finally, institutional changes can affect productivity and efficiency and change both short- and long-run aggregate supply. Depending on how well a government's institutional or policy changes are designed, they can increase aggregate supply by enhancing economic

EXHIBIT 3

Shifts in Aggregate Supply

Factors like an increase in the stock of capital or an improvement in technology will expand the economy's potential output and shift the *LRAS* curve to the right as shown in panel (a). Factors like favorable weather or falling resource prices (say, a temporary drop in the price of a major import like oil) will shift the *SRAS* curve to the right, as shown in panel (b).

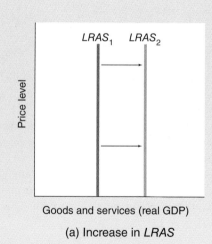

(a) Increase in *LRAS*

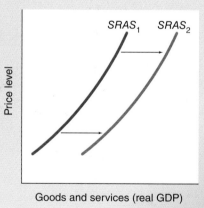

(b) Increase in *SRAS*

efficiency and productivity or decrease it by encouraging waste and making production more costly.

The long-run growth of real GDP in the United States has been about 3 percent per year. In other words, we have been able to expand our productivity steadily over the years. Hence, the *LRAS* and *SRAS* curves have gradually drifted to the right at about a 3 percent annual rate, sometimes a little faster and sometimes a little slower.

10-3b CHANGES IN SHORT-RUN AGGREGATE SUPPLY

Changes can sometimes influence current output without altering the economy's long-run capacity. When this is the case, the *SRAS* curve will shift even though the *LRAS* curve remains unchanged. What types of changes would do this?

1. Changes in resource prices. When we derived the *SRAS* curve in Chapter 9, we held resource prices constant. But a change in resource prices will alter *SRAS*, although not necessarily *LRAS*. A reduction in resource prices will lower production costs and therefore shift the *SRAS* curve to the right, as illustrated in panel (b) of Exhibit 3. However, unless the lower cost of resources reflects a long-term increase in their supply, *LRAS* won't change. Conversely, an increase in the price of resources used in production will increase firms' costs, shifting the *SRAS* curve to the left. But unless the higher prices are the result of a long-term reduction in the size of the economy's resource base, they will not reduce *LRAS*.[3]

Volina/Shutterstock.com

The price of oil declined sharply in 2014–2018. In mid-year 2014, the world price of oil was about $110 per barrel, but by year-end 2018, the price had declined to only about one-half that level. For oil importing countries, the lower oil price will reduce the costs of transportation and production, increasing short-run aggregate supply.

2. Changes in the expected rate of inflation. As we learned, a change in the expected rate of inflation will affect aggregate demand (*AD*) in the goods and services market. It will also alter short-run aggregate supply (*SRAS*).

If sellers in the goods and services market expect the future rate of inflation to increase, they will be less motivated to sell their products at lower prices in the current period. After all, goods that they do not sell today will be available for sale in the future at what they anticipate will be even higher prices because of inflation. But they will have produced them earlier at lower costs. Therefore, an increase in the expected rate of inflation will reduce the *current* supply of goods, thereby shifting the *SRAS* curve to the left. Of course, a reduction in the expected rate of inflation will have just the opposite effect. When sellers scale back their expectations of future price increases, their incentive to sell in the current period rises. Why should they wait to sell what they've produced now, if prices aren't going to go up very much in the future? Thus, a reduction in the expected rate of inflation will increase short-run aggregate supply, shifting the *SRAS* curve to the right.

3. Supply shocks. Supply shocks can also alter current output without directly affecting the productive capacity of the economy. Supply shocks are surprise occurrences that temporarily increase or decrease current output. For example, adverse weather conditions, a natural disaster, or a temporary rise in the price of imported resources (for example, oil in the case of the United States) will reduce current supply, even though they do not alter the economy's long-term production capacity. They lower short-run aggregate supply

Supply shock
An unexpected event that temporarily increases or decreases aggregate supply.

---

[3]The definition of long-run aggregate supply helps clarify why a change in resource prices will affect short-run aggregate supply but not long-run aggregate supply. When an economy is operating on its *LRAS* curve, the relationship between resource prices (costs) and product prices will reflect normal competitive market conditions. Because both profit and unemployment rates are at their normal levels, there is no tendency for resource prices to change relative to product prices when current output is equal to the economy's long-run potential. Therefore, when an economy is operating on its *LRAS* curve, any change in resource prices will be matched by a proportional change in product prices, leaving the incentive to supply resources (and output) unchanged.

Thumbnail Sketch
What Factors Affect Long-Run and Short-Run Aggregate Supply?[1]

These factors *increase* long-run aggregate supply (*LRAS*):

1. An increase in the supply of resources
2. Technology and productivity improvements
3. Institutional changes that improve the efficiency of resource use

These factors *decrease* long-run aggregate supply (*LRAS*):

1. A decrease in the supply of resources
2. Technology and productivity deteriorations
3. Institutional changes that reduce the efficiency of resource use

These factors *increase* short-run aggregate supply (*SRAS*):

1. A fall in resource prices (production costs)
2. A fall in the expected rate of inflation
3. Favorable supply shocks, such as good weather or lower prices of important imported resources

These factors *decrease* short-run aggregate supply (*SRAS*):

1. A rise in resource prices (production costs)
2. A rise in the expected rate of inflation
3. Unfavorable supply shocks, such as bad weather or higher prices of important imported resources

[1]The impact of macroeconomic policy will be considered later.

(shift the *SRAS* curve to the left) without directly affecting *LRAS*, in other words. In contrast, favorable weather conditions or a temporary fall in the world price of major resources imported by a country will expand current output, even though the economy's long-run capacity remains unchanged.

The accompanying **Thumbnail Sketch** summarizes the major factors that influence both long-run and short-run aggregate supply. Of course, macroeconomic policy can also influence aggregate supply. Like aggregate demand, we will study the impact macroeconomic policies have on aggregate supply in subsequent chapters.

10-4 STEADY ECONOMIC GROWTH AND ANTICIPATED CHANGES IN LONG-RUN AGGREGATE SUPPLY

As we've said, changes that people anticipate affect the economy differently from changes they don't. When a change takes place slowly and predictably, decision-makers will make choices based on their anticipation of the event. These changes do not generally disrupt equilibrium in markets. With time, net investment and improvements in technology and institutional efficiency will lead to increases in the sustainable rate of output and shift the economy's *LRAS* curve to the right.

Exhibit 4 illustrates the impact of economic growth on the goods and services market. Initially, the economy is in long-run equilibrium at price level P_1 and output Y_{F_1}. The growth expands the economy's potential output, shifting both the *LRAS* and *SRAS* curves to the right (to $LRAS_2$ and $SRAS_2$). Because these changes are gradual, decision-makers have time to anticipate the changing market conditions and adjust their behavior accordingly.

When economic growth expands the economy's production possibilities, a higher rate of real output can be achieved and sustained. The larger output can be attained even while unemployment remains at its natural rate. If the money supply is held constant, the increase in aggregate supply will lead to a lower price level (P_2).

During the past 60 years, real output has expanded significantly in the United States and other countries. However, contrary to the presentation of Exhibit 4, the price level has generally not declined. This is because monetary policy-makers have expanded the

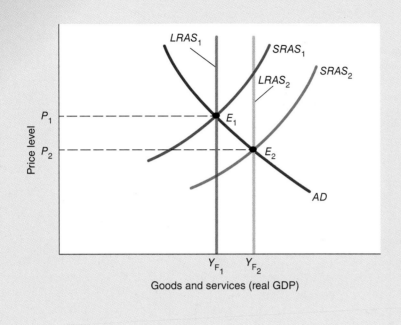

EXHIBIT 4

Growth of Aggregate Supply

Here, we illustrate the impact of economic growth due to capital formation or a technological advancement, for example. The full-employment output of the economy expands from Y_{F_1} to Y_{F_2}. Thus, both *LRAS* and *SRAS* increase (to $LRAS_2$ and $SRAS_2$). A sustainable, higher level of real output and real income is the result. If the money supply is held constant, a new long-run equilibrium will emerge at a larger output rate (Y_{F_2}) and lower price level (P_2).

supply of money. As we will see later, an increase in the money supply stimulates aggregate demand, shifting *AD* to the right and pushing the price level upward.

10-5 UNANTICIPATED CHANGES AND MARKET ADJUSTMENTS

In contrast to anticipated changes, unanticipated changes in aggregate demand and aggregate supply will disrupt long-run equilibrium in the goods and services market. If a change isn't anticipated, initially, it may be unclear to decision-makers whether the change—an increase in sales, for example—reflects a random occurrence or a real change in demand conditions. Businesses will also take some time to differentiate between temporary fluctuations and more permanent changes. Even after decision-makers are convinced that market conditions have changed, it will take some time for them to make new decisions and carry them out. Moreover, in some cases, long-term contracts will delay the adjustment process.

Equilibrium may be disrupted by unexpected changes in either aggregate demand or aggregate supply. We will begin with the analysis of unanticipated changes in aggregate demand.

10-5a UNANTICIPATED INCREASES IN AGGREGATE DEMAND

Panel (a) of **Exhibit 5** shows how an economy that is initially in long-run equilibrium will adjust to an unanticipated increase in aggregate demand. Initially, at output Y_F and price level P_{100} (point E_1), the economy is in long-run equilibrium. Aggregate demand and aggregate supply are in balance. Decision-makers have correctly anticipated the current price level, and the economy is operating at its full-employment level of output.

What would happen if this equilibrium were disrupted by an unanticipated increase in aggregate demand (a shift from AD_1 to AD_2), which might result for example from a stock market boom or the rapid growth of income abroad? An excess demand for goods

EXHIBIT 5

An Unanticipated Increase in Aggregate Demand

In response to an unanticipated increase in aggregate demand for goods and services that shifts AD_1 to AD_2 (shown in panel a), prices will rise to P_{105} in the short run and output will increase temporarily to Y_2, exceeding full-employment capacity. However, over time, prices in resource markets, including the labor market, will rise as the result of the strong demand. The higher resource prices will mean higher production costs, which will reduce aggregate supply to $SRAS_2$ (as shown in panel b). In the long run, a new equilibrium will emerge at a higher price level (P_{110}) and an output consistent with the economy's sustainable capacity. Thus, the increase in aggregate demand will expand output only temporarily.

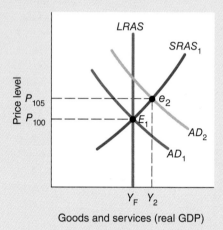

(a) Short-run effects of increase in *AD*

(b) Long-run effects of increase in *AD*

and services would result at the initial price level (P_{100}). Responding to the strong sales and excess demand, businesses would increase their prices. Their profit margins would improve (because product prices have increased relative to the cost of the resources used to make them), and they would expand output along the *SRAS* curve. As panel (a) of Exhibit 5 shows, the economy would move to a short-run equilibrium (e_2), at a larger output (Y_2) and higher price level (P_{105}). (*Note:* A short-run equilibrium is indicated with a lowercase *e*, whereas a capital *E* is used to designate a long-run equilibrium. This convention will be followed throughout the text.)

In the short run, the economy's output will deviate from full-employment capacity when prices in the goods and services market deviate from the price level people anticipated. This will happen when unusually strong demand pushes prices up more than was expected. For a time, resource prices like wage rates, interest payments, and long-term leases will remain at the initial price level (P_{100}), lagging behind the prices producers can get for their products. The higher price level will temporarily improve firms' profit margins, which will motivate them to expand both output and employment in the short run. As a result, the unemployment rate will drop below its natural rate, and the economy's output will temporarily exceed its long-run potential.

This isn't the end of the story, though. *The increase in GDP above the economy's long-run potential will last only until temporarily fixed resource prices (and interest rates) can be adjusted upward by people in light of the new stronger demand conditions.* The strong demand accompanying the high level of output (rates beyond Y_F) will put upward pressure on prices in the resource and loanable funds markets. As panel (b) of Exhibit 5 shows, eventually the rising resource prices and costs will shift the short-run aggregate supply curve to the left (to $SRAS_2$). Moreover, the strong demand for investment will push up interest rates, which will tend to dampen the increase in aggregate demand.

Given sufficient time, wages, other resource prices, and interest rates will completely adjust. When this happens, a new long-run equilibrium (E_2) will be established at a higher price level (P_{110}). Correspondingly, profit margins will return to their normal levels, output will recede to the economy's long-run potential, and unemployment will return to its natural rate.

Notice that because an increase in aggregate demand doesn't change the economy's production capacity, it cannot permanently expand output (beyond Y_F). The increase in demand temporarily expands output, but in the long term, it only increases the price level.

10-5b UNANTICIPATED REDUCTIONS IN AGGREGATE DEMAND

How would the goods and services market adjust to an unanticipated reduction in aggregate demand? For example, suppose decision-makers become more pessimistic about the future or an unexpected decline in income abroad reduces demand for their products.

Exhibit 6 will help us analyze what happens during an unanticipated reduction in aggregate demand. In panel (a) of Exhibit 6, the economy is in long-run equilibrium (E_1) at output Y_F and the price level P_{100}. The reduction in demand will shift aggregate demand from AD_1 to AD_2, disrupting the initial equilibrium. As a result of the fall in demand, businesses will be unable to sell Y_F units of output at the initial price level of P_{100}. In the short run, business firms will reduce their output (to Y_2) and cut their prices (to P_{95}) in response to the weak demand conditions. Because many business costs are temporarily fixed, profit margins will fall. Predictably, firms will cut back on output and lay off workers, causing the unemployment rate to rise. The actual rate of unemployment will rise above the economy's natural rate of unemployment. Weak demand and excess supply will be widespread in resource markets. Many firms will have excess production capacity, and the demand for investment funds will be weak. These forces will place downward pressure on both resource prices and interest rates.

An Unanticipated Reduction in Aggregate Demand

The short-run impact of an unanticipated fall in aggregate demand, shifting AD_1 to AD_2, will be a decline in output to Y_2 and a lower price level of P_{95} (as shown in panel a). Temporarily, profit margins will decline, output will fall, and unemployment will rise above its natural rate. In the long run, weak demand and excess supply in the resource market will lead to lower wages and resource prices. This will lower production costs, leading to an expansion in short-run aggregate supply, shifting it to $SRAS_2$ (as shown in panel b). However, this method of restoring equilibrium (E_2) may be both painful and quite lengthy.

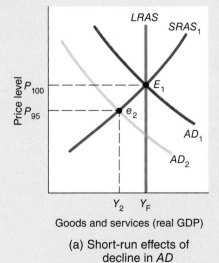

(a) Short-run effects of decline in *AD*

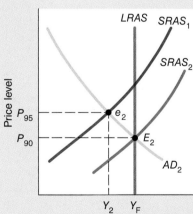

(b) Long-run effects of decline in *AD*

The United States experienced a sharp reduction in housing prices in 2007–2011. What impact did this have on aggregate demand?

If resource prices quickly adjust downward in response to weak demand, then the decline in output to Y_2 will be brief. Lower resource prices will reduce costs and increase aggregate supply, shifting the $SRAS_1$ curve to $SRAS_2$, as panel (b) shows. The result will be a new long-run equilibrium (E_2) at the economy's full-employment output rate (Y_F) and a lower price level (P_{90}). Lower interest rates will also help keep the economy on track. Given the excess production capacity of many firms, weak demand for capital goods (investment) will reduce the demand for loanable funds, which will put downward pressure on interest rates. The lower rates will stimulate current spending, which will help offset the lower demand and direct the economy back to full employment.

Resource prices and interest rates, however, may not adjust quickly. Long-term contracts and uncertainty about whether the weak demand is only temporary will slow down the adjustment process. Moreover, workers and unions may be reluctant to accept lower wages. If resource prices are downwardly inflexible, as many economists believe, the adjustment process may be lengthy and painful. Pessimism on the part of both investors and consumers may also complicate the adjustment process. This has been the case in recent recessions. As Exhibit 2 shows, consumer confidence remained at a low level for 12 to 18 months after the 1990–1991 and 2001 recessions were over and even longer in the aftermath of the 2008–2009 recession. This pessimism acted as a drag on the growth of aggregate demand, and, as a result, the initial recovery from these recessions was sluggish.

10-5c UNANTICIPATED INCREASES IN SHORT-RUN AGGREGATE SUPPLY

Supply shocks catch people by surprise. That is, in part, why they're called "shocks." What would happen if the nation's output expanded because of a favorable shock, like good weather conditions or a temporary fall in the world price of oil? **Exhibit 7** provides the

EXHIBIT 7

An Unanticipated, Temporary Increase in Aggregate Supply

Here, we show the impact of an unanticipated, but temporary, increase in aggregate supply that might result from a bumper crop caused by favorable weather, for example. The increase in aggregate supply, shifting it to $SRAS_2$, will lead to a lower price level of P_{95} and an increase in current GDP to Y_2. Because the favorable supply conditions cannot be counted on in the future, the economy's long-run aggregate supply will not increase.

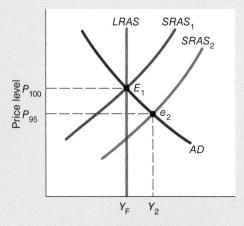

Goods and services (real GDP)

answer. Because the temporarily favorable supply conditions can't be counted on in the future, they won't change the economy's long-term production capacity. Short-run aggregate supply will increase (to *SRAS₂*), but *LRAS* will remain unchanged. Output (and income) will temporarily expand beyond the economy's full-employment constraints. This increase in current supply will put downward pressure on the price level.

Over time, however, the favorable conditions will come to an end. As this happens, the *SRAS* curve will return to its original position, and long-run equilibrium will be restored. The expansion in output will be only temporary. Knowing this, many households will save a substantial portion of the extra income they earn during the expansion for a time when things aren't so prosperous.

What would happen if the favorable conditions increasing supply reflected long-term factors? For example, suppose the discovery and development of a huge natural gas field in the United States lowered energy prices and these price reductions were expected to be long-term rather than temporary. In this instance, both the *LRAS* and the *SRAS* would increase (shift to the right). This case would parallel the analysis of Exhibit 4. A new long-run equilibrium at a higher output would result.

10-5d UNANTICIPATED REDUCTIONS IN SHORT-RUN AGGREGATE SUPPLY

The United States imports a substantial share of its domestically consumed oil. In recent decades, sharply higher world oil prices have jolted the U.S. economy. For example, in 2007–2008, the world price of crude oil jumped to more than $140 per barrel and the average nominal price of gasoline soared to more than $4 per gallon. The higher oil prices raised the transportation costs of virtually everything as well as the production costs of numerous items such as plastics, fertilizer, and asphalt.

How do unfavorable supply shocks like this affect macroeconomic markets? As Exhibit 8 (panel a) illustrates, an unfavorable supply shock, such as would result from a

---

EXHIBIT 8

The Effects of an Adverse Supply Shock

Suppose that there's an unanticipated fall in the economy's supply of resources, perhaps because of a sharp increase in the price of a major imported resource like oil or a crop failure. Resource prices will rise from P_r to P'_r as shown in panel (a). The higher resource prices will shift the *SRAS* curve to the left, as shown in panel (b). In the short run, the price level will rise to P_{110}, and output will decline to Y_2. What happens in the long run depends on whether the reduction in the supply of resources is temporary or permanent. If it is temporary, resource prices will fall in the future, permitting the economy to return to its initial equilibrium (E_1). Conversely, if it is permanent, the production capacity of the economy will shrink, shifting *LRAS* to the left, and e_2 will become the new long-run equilibrium.

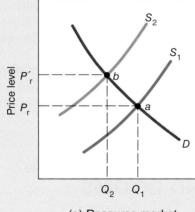

(a) Resource market

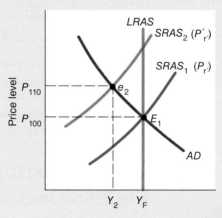

(b) Goods and services (real GDP)

sharp increase in the world price of oil, will reduce supply (from S_1 to S_2) in the domestic resource market. Resource prices will rise to P'_r. In turn, the higher resource prices will reduce short-run aggregate supply (the shift from $SRAS_1$ to $SRAS_2$ in panel b) in the goods and services market. Because supply shocks of this type are generally unanticipated, initially they will reduce output and put upward pressure on prices in the goods and services market.

If an unfavorable supply shock is expected to be temporary, as will generally be the case, long-run aggregate supply will be unaffected. For example, unfavorable weather conditions for a year or two do not represent a permanent change in the climate. As normal weather returns, supply and prices in the resource market will return to normal, and the economy will return to long-run equilibrium at output Y_F.

When an adverse supply-side factor is more permanent, the long-run supply curve will also shift to the left. For example, an oil price increase that is expected to continue for several years will reduce long-run as well as short-run aggregate supply. Under these circumstances, the economy will have to adjust to a lower level of output. When the decline in aggregate supply is permanent, other things being constant, the price level will rise. Similarly, output will decline.

10-6 THE PRICE LEVEL, INFLATION, AND THE *AD–AS* MODEL

In the basic *AD–AS* model, the level of prices is measured on the *y*-axis in both the goods and services and resource markets. This approach makes it easier to visualize relative price changes. If prices change in one of the markets, goods and services for example, this indicates that prices in that market have changed *relative* to those in other markets. It is important to note, however, that this structure implicitly incorporates the assumption that the actual and expected rates of inflation are initially zero.

As we have previously discussed, when persistent inflation is present, it will be anticipated by both buyers and sellers. Moreover, the anticipated inflation will be incorporated into the price agreements of long-term contracts, including those affecting important components of costs. When the actual and anticipated rates of inflation are equal, persistent price increases will be present in both goods and services and resource markets, even though the relative prices between the two markets are unchanged.

However, once decision-makers anticipate a given rate of inflation and build it into long-term contracts, an actual rate of inflation that is less than expected is essentially the equivalent of a reduction in the price level when price stability (zero inflation) is anticipated. For example, consider the situation in which 5 percent inflation has been present over a lengthy time period and therefore the 5 percent rate has been built into long-term contracts, including those in resource markets. If weak demand causes the inflation rate to fall to, say, 2 percent, the adjustments will be the same as those for a reduction in product prices when zero inflation is anticipated (see Exhibit 6). In both cases, prices in the goods and services market will fall relative to resource prices. In the short run, profit margins will be squeezed, and firms will cut back on output. Workers will be laid off, and the economy may well fall into a recession.

Similarly, the impact of an inflation rate that is greater than was anticipated will be like that of an increase in the price level when price stability is anticipated. Both will increase product prices relative to resource prices, which will enhance profits and thereby induce firms to expand output and employment.

10-7 UNANTICIPATED CHANGES, RECESSIONS, AND BOOMS

The *AD–AS* model indicates that unanticipated changes will disrupt macroequilibrium and result in economic instability. On the one hand, unanticipated reductions in either aggregate demand or short-run aggregate supply can throw an economy into a recession. On the other hand, unanticipated increases in aggregate demand or short-run aggregate supply can generate an unsustainable economic boom—a temporarily high level of output and employment that cannot be maintained.

However, the model also suggests that changes in resource prices and interest rates will tend to direct an economy back toward full employment following a disruption. Let's take a closer look at these two forces that underlie the self-corrective mechanism of macroeconomic markets.

1. Changes in real resource prices will help direct an economy toward equilibrium.

Price adjustments in the resource market will help keep an economy on an even keel. When an economy is in a recession and its output is less than its full-employment potential, the demand for resources will be weak. Underutilized assets and unemployment of resources will be widespread. However, the weak demand will place downward pressure on resource prices. As real resource prices fall, costs will decline, and this will help restore profit margins and strengthen the incentive of producers to expand output. Thus, the lower resource prices will help direct a recessionary economy back toward full employment.

In contrast, when a booming economy is operating beyond its full-employment capacity—when unemployment is less than the natural unemployment rate—strong demand will push up the real price of labor (wages) and other resources. In turn, the higher resource prices will increase costs and reduce profit margins. As costs increase, firms will cut back their output, directing the economy toward its full-employment potential.

2. Changes in real interest rates help stabilize aggregate demand and redirect economic fluctuations.

Real interest rates tend to reflect business conditions. During an economic downturn, businesses borrow less money for new investment projects. The demand for loanable funds is weak, and real interest rates generally fall. In turn, the lower interest rates lead to higher consumption and make investment projects cheaper, motivating businesses to undertake them. This helps offset the decline in aggregate demand and redirect output toward the full-employment level.

Conversely, during an economic boom, businesses borrow more money to invest in projects that will help them meet the stronger demand for their goods and services. The demand for loanable funds will strengthen, putting upward pressure on real interest rates. In turn, the higher interest rates will make it more expensive to purchase consumer durables and undertake investment projects. This helps restrain aggregate demand and redirect output toward the full-employment level.

Interest rate adjustments will also help offset potential economic disturbances arising from shifts in expectations about future business conditions. Suppose consumers and business operators suddenly become more pessimistic and, as a result, reduce their current level of spending. This will lower consumer spending and increase saving. Demand in the loanable funds market will be weak. Thus, the supply of loanable funds will increase relative to the demand. However, this will lead to lower real interest rates, which will help keep the economy on track by offsetting spending reductions caused by the increased pessimism.

Just the opposite will happen if consumers and businesses suddenly became more optimistic. If they suddenly decide to spend more of their current income, this will reduce the supply of loanable funds relative to the demand, causing real interest rates to rise. The higher rates will then make current spending less attractive and will help stabilize aggregate demand.[4]

---

[4] The foreign exchange market may also help stabilize the business cycle. When an economy dips into a recession, investment prospects will deteriorate, leading to a reduction in the inflow of capital from abroad. In turn, the decline in capital inflow will lead to depreciation in the foreign exchange rate, which will stimulate net exports and aggregate demand and thereby help to redirect the economy back toward full employment. Just the opposite will occur during the expansionary phase of the business cycle. However, these adjustments are not likely to be very important in countries like the United States where the international trade sector is a relatively small share of the economy. Thus, we focus on the importance of the interest rate and resource price adjustments as the primary forces that will direct a market economy toward full employment.

The implications of the *AD–AS* model with regard to economic instability might be summarized in the following manner:

Various shocks (unanticipated changes in *AD* or *AS*) can disrupt full-employment equilibrium and lead either to recessionary unemployment or to an inflationary boom. In the short run, long-term contracts and misperceptions about the current price level can lead to output levels that differ from long-run equilibrium. With time, however, changes in real resource prices and interest rates will act as a stabilizing force and direct a market economy back to its full employment potential.

But the *AD–AS* model does not indicate how quickly the market adjustment process will work. This is an area in which the views of economists often differ. Some believe that, if not undermined by harmful policies, market forces will direct the economy back to full employment within a relatively short time frame, and therefore recessions will generally last only a few quarters. Other economists argue that the self-corrective mechanism of markets works slowly, and therefore without appropriate macroeconomic policy changes, recessions will be long and painful. As we proceed, we will present each of these views in detail and examine their policy implications.

10-7a EXPANSIONS AND RECESSIONS: THE HISTORICAL RECORD

Exhibit 9 shows the time intervals of the expansions and recessions experienced by the U.S. economy since 1950. There have been ten business cycles, periods of expansion followed by a recession, during this period of seven decades. The expansions have generally been lengthier than the recessions. The ten full expansions since 1950 have averaged approximately 60 months in length, and three of those expansions have lasted seven years or more. In contrast, the average length of the recessions has been about 11 months. The recession that began in December 2007 lasted 18 months, making it the longest in more than 70 years.

10-7b USING THE *AD–AS* MODEL TO THINK ABOUT THE BUSINESS CYCLE AND THE GREAT RECESSION OF 2008–2009

The 1930s were a period of extremely high unemployment and depressed economic conditions. The unemployment rate rose to nearly 25 percent of the labor force in

EXHIBIT 9

Expansions and Recessions, 1950–2020

The accompanying table indicates the periods of both economic expansions (rising GDP) and recessions (falling GDP) since 1950. As the table indicates, the length of both varies substantially, but the expansions have clearly been longer.

PERIOD OF EXPANSION	LENGTH (IN MONTHS)	PERIOD OF RECESSION	LENGTH (IN MONTHS)
Oct '49 to July '53	44	July '53 to May '54	10
May '54 to August '57	39	August '57 to April '58	9
April '58 to April '60	24	April '60 to February '61	10
February '61 to Dec '69	105	Dec '69 to November '70	10
Nov '70 to Nov '73	36	Nov '73 to March '75	16
March '75 to January '80	58	January '80 to July '80	6
July '80 to July '81	12	July '81 to November '82	16
Nov '82 to July '90	92	July '90 to March '91	9
March '91 to March '01	120	March '01 to November '01	8
November '01 to November '07	73	December '07 to June '09	18
July '09 to February '20	128		

Source: http://www.nber.org.

1932 and 1933. Between 1931 and 1940, the rate of unemployment exceeded 14 percent during each year. These extreme conditions explain why this period is referred to as the Great Depression.

While the length and severity of the 2008–2009 downturn was not comparable to the Great Depression, it was the longest recession since the 1930s. Because of its length and severity, some refer to it as the Great Recession.

Why did the United States experience a strong expansion during 2003–2007, and why did the boom turn to a bust in 2008? The *AD–AS* model provides considerable insight on this issue. Between 2002 and mid-year 2006, there was a sharp increase in housing prices. Nationwide, the average home price increased by 89 percent during this period. At the same time, stock prices were also increasing rapidly. Just as the *AD–AS* model indicates, this huge increase in stock and housing prices increased wealth, stimulated aggregate demand, and generated an economic boom.

But the situation began to change during the second half of 2006. Housing prices reversed and began to fall. Mortgage default rates and housing foreclosures started to rise. The construction industry contracted sharply. As housing wealth fell, people became more pessimistic, causing a further reduction in aggregate demand. Then, during 2007 and the first half of 2008, the world price of crude oil soared to $140 per barrel, pushing the price of gasoline to $4 per gallon, twice the price of a year earlier. By 2008, stock prices were plummeting, further reducing wealth and aggregate demand. All of these adverse forces combined to reduce both aggregate demand and supply, and just as the *AD–AS* model indicates, they generated a sharp decline in real output and employment.

Exhibit 10 provides additional perspective on both the business cycle and the 2008–2009 recession; it shows data on the change in both real housing and stock prices during the first two years of expansions and contractions since 1969. Note how both housing and stock prices have risen during the expansionary phase of the business cycle. Prior to the 2008–2009 recession, the average real home price rose by 7 percent during the first two years of the expansionary phase. Similarly, real stock prices rose by an average of 35 percent during the expansions. These higher asset prices increase wealth and stimulate aggregate demand. This will lead to increases in output and employment during this phase of the cycle.

But just the opposite happens during the contraction. During the past seven recessions, the average real home price fell by 12 percent, and the average real stock price fell by 38 percent. When housing and stock prices fall, household wealth will decline, causing a reduction in aggregate demand. In turn, the reductions in wealth and demand will both contribute to the initial downturn and complicate the recovery process.

The rise and fall of stock prices prior to and following the 2008–2009 recession were not substantially different than for the earlier business cycles. But, this was not the case for housing prices. As Exhibit 10 shows, the increase in housing prices during the expansion prior to the 2008 recession and the subsequent decline that began more than a year before the recession were far greater than those of earlier business cycles. Housing prices fell by 35 percent during the 2008–2009 recession, nearly three times the average decline of the prior recessions. Clearly, the housing price boom and bust was a central factor underlying the 2008–2009 recession. Finally, notice what happened to housing prices during the first two years of the recovery and expansion from the 2008–2009 recession: They fell another 5 percent. This decline in housing prices during the expansionary phase is unprecedented in recent decades. No doubt, this factor contributed to the weakness of the most recent recovery. As we proceed, we will investigate this issue in more detail.

EXHIBIT 10

Changes in the Real Price of Stock Shares and Housing (Single-Family Homes) during Business Cycles since 1969

The change in stock and housing prices during the first two years of expansions and recessions are presented here. Both generally rise during expansions and fall during recessions. Note that the housing price reduction accompanying the 2008 recession was substantially greater than during earlier recessions. This was a major reason for the severity of the recession. Similarly, note how housing prices continued to decline during the recovery and expansion from the 2008 recession. This was unprecedented in recent decades and contributed to the weakness of the recovery.

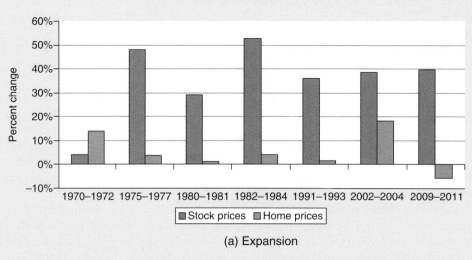

(a) Expansion

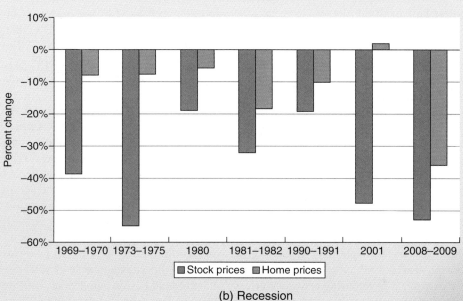

(b) Recession

Source: The stock prices are based on Standard and Poor's monthly opening prices. The housing prices prior to 1976 are based on National Association of Realtors median existing home sale prices. The sale prices for 1976 to 1986 are from the Office of Federal Housing Enterprise Oversight. The housing price data since 1987 are from the Case-Shiller quarterly housing price index. All prices were adjusted for inflation using the consumer price index (CPI).

KEY POINTS

- It is important to distinguish between changes that are anticipated and unanticipated because the impact on the economy will differ between the two.

- An increase in aggregate demand involves a shift of the entire *AD* curve to the right. Major factors causing an increase in aggregate demand (other than government policies) are (1) an increase in real wealth, (2) a lower real interest rate, (3) increased optimism on the part of businesses and consumers, (4) an increase in the expected rate of inflation, (5) higher real income abroad,

and (6) a depreciation in the exchange rate. Conversely, if these factors change in the opposite direction, a decrease in aggregate demand will result.

- It is important to distinguish between long-run and short-run aggregate supply. The following factors will increase long-run aggregate supply (*LRAS*): (1) increases in the supply of labor and capital resources, (2) improvements in technology and productivity, and (3) institutional changes improving the efficiency of resource use. Changes in resource prices, the expected rate of inflation, and supply shocks will cause shifts in short-run aggregate supply (*SRAS*).

- An increase in output due to economic growth (an increase in the economy's production capacity) will increase both short-run and long-run aggregate supply, permitting the economy to achieve and sustain a larger output level.

- Unanticipated changes in either aggregate demand or aggregate supply will disrupt long-run equilibrium and cause current output to differ from the economy's long-run potential.

- Unanticipated increases in aggregate demand and favorable supply shocks can cause economic booms that push output beyond the economy's long-run potential and unemployment below its natural rate. However, as decision-makers adjust to the strong demand, resource prices and interest rates will rise, and output will recede to long-run capacity.

- Unanticipated reductions in aggregate demand and adverse supply shocks can lead to below-capacity output and abnormally high rates of unemployment. Eventually, lower resource prices (and lower real interest rates) will direct the economy back to long-run equilibrium. This adjustment process will take time, and it may be quite lengthy if wages and prices are downwardly inflexible.

- Changes in resource prices and interest rates will help keep an economy on track. During a recession, resource prices and interest rates will decline, and this will help direct the economy back toward full employment. However, there is considerable debate about how rapidly this adjustment process works.

- During the past seven decades, economic expansions have been far lengthier than recessions. However, the depth and severity of the recession that started in December 2007 has once again placed the issue of economic instability and recovery from a recession at the forefront of macroeconomics.

CRITICAL ANALYSIS QUESTIONS

1. *Explain how and why each of the following factors would influence current aggregate demand in the United States:
   a. increased fear of recession
   b. increased fear of inflation
   c. rapid growth of real income in Canada and Western Europe
   d. a reduction in the real interest rate
   e. a higher price level (Be careful)

2. *Indicate how each of the following would influence U.S. aggregate supply in the short run:
   a. an increase in real wage rates
   b. a severe freeze that destroys half the orange trees in Florida
   c. an increase in the expected rate of inflation in the future
   d. an increase in the world price of oil, a major import
   e. abundant rainfall during the growing season in agricultural states

3. What impact would a change that shifts an economy's production possibilities curve outward have on the long-run aggregate supply curve? How have improvements in computer technology affected production possibilities and the long-run aggregate supply curve? Explain.

4. When an economy dips into a recession, consumers will often be relatively pessimistic about the future for an extended period of time. How will this pessimism affect the speed and strength of the recovery? Feel free to use the data of Exhibit 2 in your response to this question.

5. What is the difference between an anticipated and an unanticipated increase in aggregate demand? Provide an example of each. Which is more likely to result in a temporary spurt in the growth of real output?

6. Assume that both union and management representatives agree to wage increases because they expect prices to rise 10 percent during the next year. Explain why the unemployment rate will probably increase if the actual rate of inflation next year is only 3 percent.

7. During 2015, there was a substantial increase in stock prices and a reduction in the world price of crude oil. What impact would these two changes have on aggregate demand and aggregate supply in the United States? Use the *AD–AS* model to indicate the expected impact of these changes on output and the price level.

8. *When actual output exceeds an economy's full-employment output, how will the self-correcting mechanism direct the economy to long-run equilibrium? Why can't the above-normal output be maintained?

9. When an economy dips into a recession, what generally happens to interest rates? Why? How will this affect the recovery process?

10. Suppose that an unexpectedly rapid growth in real income abroad leads to a sharp increase in the demand for U.S. exports. What impact will this change have on the price level, output, and employment in the short run in the United States? In the long run?

11. Construct the *AD, SRAS,* and *LRAS* curves for an economy experiencing (a) full employment, (b) an economic boom, and (c) a recession.

12. Consider an economy with the following aggregate demand (*AD*) and aggregate supply (*AS*) schedules. These schedules reflect the fact that, prior to the period we're examining, decision makers entered into contracts and made choices anticipating that the price level would be P_{105}.

AD_{105} (IN TRILLIONS)	PRICE LEVEL	$SRAS_{105}$ (IN TRILLIONS)
$5.1	95	$3.5
4.9	100	3.8
4.7	105	4.2
4.5	110	4.5
4.3	115	4.8

a. Indicate the quantity of GDP that will be produced and the price level that will emerge during this period.
b. Is the economy in long-run equilibrium? Why or why not?
c. How will the unemployment rate during the current period compare with this economy's natural rate of unemployment?

d. What will tend to happen to resource prices in the future? How will this affect the equilibrium rate of output?
e. Will the rate of GDP produced during this period be sustainable into the future? Why or why not?

13. (a) Housing prices rose sharply between 2002 and midyear 2006. Use the *AD–AS* model to illustrate the impact of the housing price increases on output and employment. (b) During 2007 and 2008, housing prices fell sharply. Use the *AD–AS* model to illustrate the impact of these price declines on output and employment.

*Asterisk denotes questions for which answers are given in Appendix B.

CHAPTER 11

Fiscal Policy: The Keynesian View and the Historical Development of Macroeconomics

I believe myself to be writing a book on economic theory which will largely revolutionize not, I suppose, at once but in the course of the next ten years the way the world thinks about economic problems. —**John Maynard Keynes**[1]

The Great Depression exerted a huge impact on modern macroeconomics. It led to the development of a theory that provided both an explanation for the prolonged unemployment of the 1930s and a recipe for how to generate a recovery. This theory, developed by the British economist John Maynard Keynes (pronounced "canes"), dominated macroeconomics to such a large extent that the theories he developed were soon known as Keynesian economics.

This chapter presents the Keynesian view along with historical perspective on its development. The following chapter focuses on alternative theories that have arisen over the past five decades. Taken together, these two chapters provide a balanced presentation of modern views on the potential and limitations of fiscal policy as a stabilization tool.

As you read this chapter, look for answers to the following questions:

- How did the Great Depression alter views about the stability of markets? Why did it lead to the development of Keynesian Economics?

- Why do Keynesians believe economies experience economic fluctuations?

- What is the multiplier? What does it imply about the stability of a market economy?

- Is fiscal policy an effective tool with which to promote economic stability and full employment?

- Is saving good or bad for an economy? Does a high household debt to income ratio impact the effectiveness of Keynesian fiscal policy?

---

[1]Letter from John Maynard Keynes to George Bernard Shaw, New Year's Day, 1935.

11-1 THE GREAT DEPRESSION, ECONOMIC INSTABILITY, AND THE DEVELOPMENT OF KEYNESIAN ECONOMICS

The 1930s dramatically altered views about the stability of a market economy. Prior to the Great Depression, most economists thought that markets would adjust and direct an economy back to its long-run potential rather quickly. Prolonged recessionary conditions were thought to be impossible. The Great Depression changed all of that.

For those who are familiar only with the relative stability of recent decades, the depth and length of the economic decline during the 1930s are difficult to comprehend: between 1929 and 1933, real GDP in the United States fell by more than 30 percent. In 1933, nearly 25 percent—one-quarter—of the U.S. labor force was unemployed. The depressed conditions continued throughout the decade. In 1939, a decade after the plunge began, the rate of unemployment was still 17 percent, and real per capita income was approximately the same as it was in 1929. Other industrial countries experienced similar conditions during the 1930s.

11-1a THE GREAT DEPRESSION AND KEYNESIAN ECONOMICS

Keynesian economics provided a reasonable explanation for the prolonged depressed conditions of the 1930s. Keynes believed that spending motivated firms to supply goods and services. He argued that if total spending fell—as it might, for example, if consumers and investors became pessimistic about the future—then firms would respond by cutting back production. Less spending would thus lead to less output.[2]

Keynes rejected the view that lower wages and interest rates would get the economy back on track and eliminate abnormally high rates of unemployment. He argued that wages and prices are highly inflexible, particularly in a downward direction. Even when demand is weak, Keynes and his followers believed powerful trade unions and large corporations would be able to maintain their wages and prices at a high level. Further, even if wages did decline, this would reduce incomes and exert a negative impact on aggregate demand.

Keynes also rejected the potential effectiveness of interest rate cuts to get the economy back on track. He argued that when excess capacity is widespread and people are extremely pessimistic about the future, lower interest rates will fail to stimulate additional investment. Moreover, when nominal interest rates fall to extremely low levels—rates near zero, for example—significant additional reductions capable of stimulating the economy would be impossible. Keynes believed that all of these conditions were present during the Great Depression. Under these circumstances, he did not believe that market forces would direct the economy back to full employment.

The Keynesian model was an outgrowth of the Great Depression. It provided an explanation for the widespread and prolonged unemployment of the 1930s.

11-1b OUTPUT, EMPLOYMENT, AND KEYNESIAN EQUILIBRIUM

Keynes also introduced a different concept of equilibrium and a different mechanism for its achievement. In the Keynesian view, equilibrium takes place when total spending in the

---

[2]See the classic book by John Maynard Keynes, *The General Theory of Employment, Interest, and Money* (London: Macmillan, 1936), for the presentation of this theory.

economy is equal to current output. When this is the case, business firms will just be able to sell the quantity of goods and services they are currently producing. Their inventories will be neither rising nor falling, and therefore they will have no reason to either expand or contract output.

Keynesians believe that changes in output rather than changes in prices direct the economy toward equilibrium. An increase in total spending would generate expanding sales and reduce the inventories of firms. Businesses would respond with an expansion in output, and the higher level of output would be maintained as long as spending remained at the higher level.

On the other hand, a decline in total spending would lead to a reduction in sales and rising inventories. If total spending fell below the full-employment level of output, business firms would cut back on employment and reduce their output to the level of spending, and, most significantly, the lower level of output and employment would persist as long as the level of spending was unchanged. Therefore, if total spending is deficient—if it is less than full-employment output—high rates of unemployment will be present, output will continue below the economy's potential, and these conditions will persist as long as the spending on goods and services remains weak.

This is exactly what Keynes believed was happening during the 1930s. Consumers were unwilling to spend much because reductions in stock prices and the value of other assets had reduced their wealth and incomes, and they were extremely pessimistic about the future. Businesses responded to the weak demand by reducing output. Moreover, investment came to a complete standstill because underutilized resources and capacity were abundantly available.

11-1c THE MULTIPLIER AND ECONOMIC INSTABILITY

Keynes also argued that market forces could not be counted on to maintain spending levels consistent with full employment because even minor disturbances will often be amplified into major disruptions. The **multiplier principle** can be used to explain his argument. The multiplier principle ***builds on the point that one individual's expenditure becomes the income of another***. Predictably, income recipients will spend a portion of their additional earnings on consumption. In turn, their consumption expenditures will generate additional income for others who will also spend a portion of it.

Perhaps an example will illuminate the multiplier concept. Suppose an entrepreneur undertakes a $1 million investment project. The project will increase spending directly by $1 million. This is not the entire story, however. The investment project will require plumbers, carpenters, masons, lumber, cement, and many other resources. The project will generate $1 million of income for the suppliers of these resources. What will they do with this income? After setting aside (saving) a portion of it, the resource suppliers will spend a fraction of the additional income. They will buy food, clothing, recreation, medical care, and thousands of other items. How will this spending influence the incomes of those who supply these products and services? Their incomes will increase, also. These people will save a portion of it and will spend some of it on current consumption. This consumption spending will result in still more additional income generated and received by the suppliers of the additional goods and services.

The term *multiplier* is also used to indicate the number by which the initial investment would be multiplied to obtain the total increase in the economy's income. If the $1 million investment resulted in $4 million of additional income, the **expenditure multiplier** would be 4. The total increase in income would be four times the amount of the initial increase in spending. Similarly, if total income increased by $3 million, the multiplier would be 3.

Multiplier principle
The concept that an increase in spending on a project will generate income for the resource suppliers, who will then increase their consumption spending. In turn, their additional consumption will generate income for others and lead to still more consumption. As this process goes through successive rounds, total income will expand by a multiple of the initial increase in spending.

Expenditure multiplier
The ratio of the change in equilibrium output to the independent change in investment, consumption, or government spending that brings about the change. Numerically, the multiplier is equal to 1 *divided by* (1 − MPC) when the price level is constant.

The size of the multiplier depends on the proportion of the additional income that households choose to spend on consumption.[3] Keynes referred to this fraction as the **marginal propensity toconsume (MPC)**. Mathematically,

$$MPC = \frac{\text{Additional consumption}}{\text{Additional income}}$$

Marginal propensity to consume (MPC)
Additional current consumption divided by additional current disposable income.

For example, if your income increases by $100 and you increase your current consumption expenditures by $75 as a result, your marginal propensity to consume is 75/100, which is 3/4 or 0.75.

Exhibit 1 illustrates why the size of the multiplier is dependent upon the MPC. Continuing with the previous example, consider the impact of the $1 million investment project when the MPC is equal to 3/4. Initially, a $1 million investment will result in $1 million of additional income in round 1 for those undertaking the project. Because the MPC is 3/4, consumption will increase by $750,000 (the other $250,000 will flow into savings) and turn into other people's income in round 2. The recipients of the round 2 income of $750,000 will spend 3/4 of it on current consumption. Hence, their spending will increase income by $562,500 in round 3. Exhibit 1 indicates the additions to income through other rounds. In total, income will increase by $4 million, given an MPC of 3/4. The multiplier is 4.

If the MPC had been greater, income recipients would have spent a larger share of their additional income on current consumption during each round. Thus, the additional income generated in each round would have been greater, increasing the size of the multiplier. There is a precise relationship between the MPC and the multiplier, in other words. The expenditure multiplier, M, is

$$M = \frac{1}{1 - MPC}$$

EXHIBIT 1

The Multiplier Principle

Expenditure Stage	Additional Income (Dollars)		Additional Consumption (Dollars)	Marginal Propensity to Consume
Round 1	1,000,00	→	750,000	3/4
Round 2	750,000	⇄	562,500	3/4
Round 3	562,500	⇄	421,875	3/4
Round 4	421,875	⇄	316,406	3/4
Round 5	316,406	⇄	237,305	3/4
Round 6	237,305	⇄	177,979	3/4
Round 7	177,979	⇄	133,484	3/4
Round 8	133,484	⇄	100,113	3/4
Round 9	100,113	⇄	75,085	3/4
Round 10	75,085	⇄	56,314	3/4
All Others	225,253	→	168,939	3/4
Total	4,000,00		3,000,00	3/4

---

[3]For the purposes of simplicity when calculating the size of the multiplier, we will assume that all additions to income are either (1) spent on domestically produced goods or (2) saved. This assumption means that we are ignoring the impact of taxes and spending on imports as income expands via the multiplier process.

Outstanding Economist: John Maynard Keynes (1883–1946)

Keynes might properly be referred to as the "father of macroeconomics." The son of a prominent nineteenth-century economist (John Neville Keynes), he earned a degree in mathematics from King's College, Cambridge, where he would later return and spend most of his career as an economist. His *General Theory of Employment, Interest, and Money*, published in 1936, revolutionized the way that economists think about macroeconomics. This work, written in the midst of the Great Depression, provided both a plausible explanation for the massive unemployment and a strategy for ending it.

Although Keynes's work was groundbreaking, it was also controversial. Keynes argued that governments should run budget deficits during a recession to stimulate demand and direct the economy back to full employment. But this idea challenged the entrenched views of both policy-makers and economists. Nonetheless, his ideas soon triumphed and dominated the thinking of macroeconomists for three decades following his untimely death due to a heart attack in 1946. Most observers would rate Keynes as the most influential economist of the twentieth century.

The multiplier concept also works in reverse—reductions in spending will also be magnified and generate even larger reductions in income. Thus, even modest reductions in investment or consumption, perhaps due to increased pessimism about the future, might throw an economy into a recession. Keynesians argue that the multiplier concept indicates that market economies are extremely fragile and that they have a tendency to fluctuate back and forth between excessive and deficient demand.

11-1d ADDING REALISM TO THE MULTIPLIER

When considering the multiplier, it is important to understand the chain reactions that underlie the concept. The multiplier process does not occur instantaneously. The additional expenditures of each round requires time. Perhaps several months or longer will pass before the full impact of the multiplier is felt.

Even more important, the multiplier process implicitly assumes that the additional spending of each round will bring previously idle workers into the labor force. For example, the analysis implies that electricians, plumbers, masons, and others involved in the initial construction project would not have been working if the project had not been undertaken. When unemployment is exceedingly high, as it was during the Great Depression, this largely may be the case. However, during more normal times when there are fewer unemployed resources, much of the additional spending will merely bid resources away from other activities. Under these circumstances, there will be upward pressure on prices, and the additions to income will be smaller, perhaps substantially smaller, than the multiplier analysis implies.

11-1e KEYNES AND ECONOMIC INSTABILITY: A SUMMARY

The central message of Keynes can be summarized as follows: Businesses will produce only the quantity of goods and services they believe consumers, investors, governments, and foreigners will plan to buy. If these planned aggregate expenditures are less than the economy's full-employment output, output will fall short of its potential. Moreover, reductions in spending will often be amplified by the multiplier and tend to feed on themselves. Downturns will breed pessimism among both consumers and investors, which will lead to lower prices for assets such as stocks and houses, causing total spending and output to plummet downward by even larger amounts. Keynes believed when total expenditures (aggregate demand) on goods and services are deficient, market economies do not have an automatic mechanism that will return the economy to full employment. Prolonged unemployment will persist. Against the backdrop of the Great Depression, this was a compelling argument.

While the Keynesian view indicates that market economies will tend to swing back and forth between recessions caused by weak demand and economic booms generated by excessive demand, there is a positive side to Keynesian analysis. There is a remedy for the fluctuations: Fiscal policy can be used to control aggregate demand and smooth the ups and downs of the business cycle. We now turn to this topic.

11-2 THE FEDERAL BUDGET AND FISCAL POLICY

As we noted in Chapter 9, fiscal policy involves the use of the government's spending, taxing, and borrowing policies. Until now, we have assumed that the government's fiscal policy remained unchanged. We are now ready to relax this assumption and investigate the effect of fiscal policy on output, prices, and employment. We want to isolate the impact of changes in fiscal policy from changes in monetary policy. Thus, we will continue to assume that monetary policy-makers are holding the supply of money constant. We will relax this assumption and investigate the impact of monetary policy in subsequent chapters.

The federal budget is the primary tool of fiscal policy. When the supply of money is constant, government expenditures must be financed with either (1) taxes or revenues derived from other sources or (2) borrowing. If the government's revenue from taxes and other sources is equal to its total expenditure, a **balanced budget** is present. The budget need not be in balance, however. A **budget deficit** occurs when total government spending exceeds total government revenue from all sources. When this happens, the government must borrow funds to finance the excess of its spending relative to revenue. It borrows by issuing interest-bearing bonds that become part of what we call the national debt, the total amount of outstanding government bonds. Conversely, a **budget surplus** is present when the government's revenues exceed its total expenditures. The surplus allows the government to reduce its outstanding debt.

While budget conditions are often used to gauge the direction of fiscal policy, it is important to recognize that changes in the size of the deficit or surplus can originate from two different sources. ***First, changes in the size of the deficit or surplus may merely reflect the state of the economy***. During a recession, tax revenues generally fall and expenditures on transfer programs increase because of the weak economic conditions. This will shift the budget toward a deficit—even with no changes in fiscal policy. Just the opposite will happen during the expansionary phase of the business cycle. The rapid growth of income during an expansion will increase tax revenues and reduce income transfers, causing the budget to shift toward a surplus (or smaller deficit), even if there has not been any change in fiscal policy. ***Second, changes in the deficit or surplus may reflect*** **discretionary fiscal policy**. Discretionary fiscal policy requires passage of tax and/or spending legislation by Congress and the president that alter the size of the budget deficit (or surplus). When we speak of "changes in fiscal policy," we are referring to this latter type of action—a deliberate change in tax laws or government spending levels (or both) that affect the budget deficit or surplus.

11-3 FISCAL POLICY AND THE GOOD NEWS OF KEYNESIAN ECONOMICS

Keynesians argue that the federal budget should be used to promote a level of total spending (aggregate demand) consistent with the full-employment rate of output. How might policy-makers use the budget to stimulate aggregate demand? First, an increase in government purchases of goods and services will directly increase aggregate demand. As the government spends more on highways, flood-control projects, education, and national defense,

Balanced budget
A situation in which current government revenue from taxes, fees, and other sources is just equal to current government expenditures.

Budget deficit
A situation in which total government spending exceeds total government revenue during a specific time period, usually one year.

Budget surplus
A situation in which total government spending is less than total government revenue during a time period, usually a year.

Discretionary fiscal policy
A change, in laws or appropriation levels, that alters government revenues and/or expenditures.

for example, these expenditures will increase demand in the goods and services market. Second, changes in tax policy will also influence aggregate demand. For example, a reduction in personal taxes will increase the current disposable income of households. As their after-tax income rises, people will spend more on consumption. In turn, this increase in consumption will stimulate aggregate demand. Similarly, a reduction in business taxes increases after-tax profitability, which will stimulate both business investment and aggregate demand.

11-3a USING THE BUDGET TO PROMOTE STABILITY

When an economy is operating below its potential capacity, Keynesians believe the government should institute **expansionary fiscal policy**. In other words, the government should increase its purchases of goods and services, cut taxes, or both. Of course, this policy will increase the government's budget deficit. To finance the enlarged budget deficit, the government will have to borrow from either private domestic sources or foreigners.[4]

Exhibit 2 illustrates the case for expansionary fiscal policy when an economy is experiencing abnormally high unemployment caused by deficient aggregate demand. Initially, the economy is operating at e_1. Output is below potential capacity, Y_F, and unemployment exceeds its natural rate. As we discussed in Chapter 10, if there is no change in policy, abnormally high unemployment and excess supply in the resource market will

Expansionary fiscal policy
An increase in government expenditures and/or a reduction in tax rates, such that the expected size of the budget deficit expands.

EXHIBIT 2

Expansionary Fiscal Policy to Promote Full Employment

Here, we illustrate an economy operating in the short run at Y_1, below its potential capacity of Y_F. There are two routes to a long-run, full-employment equilibrium. First, policy-makers could wait for lower wages and resource prices to reduce costs, increase supply to $SRAS_3$, and

restore equilibrium at E_3. Most Keynesians believe this market-adjustment method will be slow and uncertain. Alternatively, expansionary fiscal policy could stimulate aggregate demand (shift it to AD_2) and guide the economy to E_2.

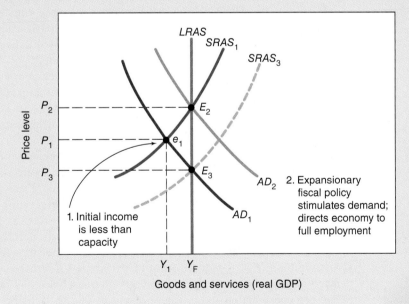

4. Alternatively, the government could borrow from its central bank—the Federal Reserve Bank in the United States. However, as we will see in the following chapter, this method of financing a budget deficit would expand the money supply. Because we want to differentiate between fiscal and monetary effects, we must hold the supply of money constant. So for now, we assume that government deficits must be financed by borrowing from private sources.

According to the Keynesian view, increases in government spending on infrastructure during a recession will stimulate aggregate demand and thereby help promote recovery.

eventually reduce real wages and other resource prices, which will lower costs and direct the economy toward a full-employment equilibrium like E_3. In addition, weak demand for investment goods will place downward pressure on interest rates, which will stimulate aggregate demand and also help to direct the economy back to full employment. However, these adjustments may work slowly.

Rather than depending on the economy's self-corrective mechanism, Keynesians favor a shift to a more expansionary fiscal policy—an increase in government spending or a reduction in taxes, or some combination of the two. In other words, they advocate a deliberate increase in the budget deficit in order to stimulate aggregate demand. Furthermore, they argue that the multiplier process will magnify the initial increase in spending.

Suppose that the government holds taxes constant and increases its spending on highways and school construction by $200 billion. The additional spending will generate $200 billion in income for those undertaking the construction projects. As these individuals use a portion of this income to buy consumer goods, the multiplier process indicates that their spending will trigger more income and spending by others. Thus, Keynesians expect that the total increase in aggregate demand will be substantially greater than the initial $200 billion increase in government purchases.

When an economy is operating below its potential capacity, the Keynesian prescription calls for expansionary fiscal policy—a deliberate change in expenditures and/or taxes that will increase the size of the government's budget deficit. An appropriate dose of expansionary fiscal policy, if timed properly, will stimulate aggregate demand (shift the curve to AD_2 in Exhibit 2) and guide the economy to full-employment equilibrium (E_2).

Moreover, Keynesians argue that economic recovery will be a struggle for market economies because the downturn will tend to feed on itself. As incomes decline during a recession, consumers will cut their spending, which will reduce the demand for goods and services and lead businesses to cut back on both output and employment. Pessimism will spread throughout the economy and output will plunge downward. But government can break the pattern by stepping in with expansionary fiscal policy. If the government increases its spending and reduces taxes, this will enhance private-sector incomes, stimulate consumption, and thereby boost aggregate demand and help keep the economy on a positive growth path.

Restrictive fiscal policy
A reduction in government expenditures and/or an increase in tax rates such that the expected size of the budget deficit declines (or the budget surplus increases).

The Keynesian view also provides a fiscal policy remedy for inflation. Suppose that an economy is experiencing an inflationary economic boom as the result of excessive aggregate demand. As **Exhibit 3** illustrates, in the absence of a change in policy, the strong demand (AD_1) will push up wages and other resource prices. In time, the higher resource prices will increase costs, reduce aggregate supply (from $SRAS_1$ to $SRAS_3$), and lead to a higher price level (P_3). Keynesians argue, however, that **restrictive fiscal policy** can be used to reduce aggregate demand (shift it to AD_2) and guide the economy to a noninflationary equilibrium (E_2). A reduced level of government purchases will diminish aggregate demand directly. Alternatively, higher taxes on households and businesses could be used to dampen consumption and private investment. The restrictive fiscal policy—a spending reduction and/or an increase in taxes—will shift the government budget toward a surplus (or smaller deficit). *Keynesians believe that a shift toward a more restrictive fiscal policy is the proper prescription with which to combat inflation generated by excessive aggregate demand.*

The Keynesian theory challenges the view that a responsible government should constrain spending within the bounds of its revenues. *Rather than balancing the budget*

EXHIBIT 3

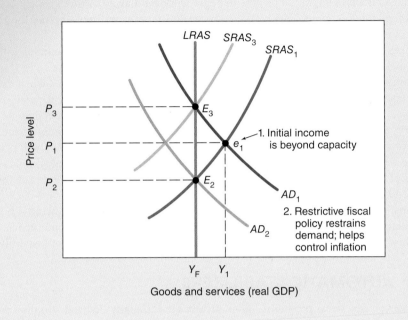

Restrictive Fiscal Policy to Combat Inflation

Strong demand such as AD_1 will temporarily lead to an output rate beyond the economy's long-run potential (Y_F). If the high level of demand persists, it will lead to a long-run equilibrium (E_3) at a higher price level. However, restrictive fiscal policy could restrain demand to AD_2 (or better still, prevent demand from expanding to AD_1 in the first place) and thereby guide the economy to a noninflationary equilibrium (E_2).

annually, Keynesians stressed the importance of countercyclical policy, *that is, policy designed to "counter" or offset fluctuations in aggregate demand.* On the one hand, when an economy is threatened by a recession, the government should shift to a more expansionary fiscal policy, increasing spending or reducing taxes in a manner that will increase the size of the budget deficit. On the other hand, fiscal policy should become more restrictive—the budget should be shifted toward a smaller deficit or larger surplus—in response to a threat of inflation. According to the Keynesian view, fluctuations in aggregate demand are the major source of economic disturbances. Moreover, wise use of fiscal policy can help stabilize and maintain demand at or near the full-employment rate of output.

Countercyclical policy
A policy that tends to move the economy in an opposite direction from the forces of the business cycle. Such a policy would stimulate demand during the contraction phase of the business cycle and restrain demand during the expansion phase.

11-3b FISCAL POLICY CHANGES AND PROBLEMS OF TIMING

In the 1960s, Keynesian economists were highly optimistic that fiscal policy could be instituted in a manner that would smooth the ups and downs of the business cycle. Over time, the earlier optimism has been tempered. If discretionary fiscal policy changes are going to reduce economic instability, they must be timed correctly. Fiscal stimulus must be felt during recessions and restraint during inflationary booms. But proper timing of fiscal policy is not an easy task. There are three major reasons why this is true.

First, a change in fiscal policy will require legislative action. But the political process moves slowly. This is particularly true in a country like the United States that has a number of checks and balances built into its political system. Congressional committees must meet, hear testimony, and draft legislation. Key legislators may choose to delay action in an attempt to amend the legislation so that it provides greater benefits to their own constituents and supporters. Passage will require the approval of the House of Representatives, the Senate, and the president. Predictably, this process will take a significant amount of time.

Second, a change in policy will not immediately impact the macroeconomy. Even after a policy change is adopted, another 6 to 12 months will generally pass before it will have much impact on the economy. If government expenditures are going to be increased, time will be required for competitive bids to be submitted and government contracts granted. Contractors might not be able to begin work right away. Although a tax cut might exert some stimulus more quickly, typically several months will pass before the primary effects of the cut are felt throughout the economy.

Third, because of these delays, if fiscal policy is going to exert a stabilizing influence, policy-makers need to know what economic conditions are going to be like 12 to 18 months in the future. However, this is a big problem because our ability to forecast when the economy is about to dip into a recession or experience an economic boom is extremely limited. Therefore, in a world of dynamic change and unpredictable events, macroeconomic policy making is a little bit like lobbing a ball at a target that often moves in unforeseen directions.

Given these time lags and forecasting limitations, policy-making errors will occur. By the time a fiscal policy change is enacted, sometimes it will end up adding stimulus during periods of strong demand, or restraint during periods of recession. Changes of this type would add to rather than reduce economic instability.

Thus, a discretionary change in fiscal policy is like a double-edged sword—it has the potential to do harm as well as good. If timed correctly, it will reduce economic instability. But, when timed incorrectly, a fiscal policy change can also be a source of instability.

11-3c AUTOMATIC STABILIZERS

Automatic stabilizers
Built-in features that tend automatically to promote a budget deficit during a recession and a budget surplus during an inflationary boom, even without a change in policy.

Fortunately, a few fiscal programs automatically tend to apply demand stimulus during a recession and demand restraint during an economic boom. Programs of this type are called **automatic stabilizers**. They are automatic in that, without any new legislative action, they tend to increase the budget deficit (or reduce the surplus) during a recession and increase the surplus (or reduce the deficit) during an economic boom.

The major advantage of automatic stabilizers is that they institute countercyclical fiscal policy without the delays associated with legislative action. They minimize the problem of proper timing, in other words. On the one hand, when unemployment is rising and business conditions are slow, these stabilizers automatically reduce tax revenues collected and increase government spending, giving the economy a boost. On the other hand, automatic stabilizers help apply the brakes to an economic boom, increasing tax revenues and decreasing government spending. Three of these built-in stabilizers deserve specific mention: unemployment compensation, the corporate profit tax, and the progressive income tax.

Unemployment compensation When an economy begins to dip into a recession, the government will pay out more money in unemployment benefits as the number of laid-off and unemployed workers expands. Simultaneously, the receipts from the employment tax that finance the unemployment compensation system will decline because fewer workers are paying into the system. Therefore, this program will automatically run a deficit during a business slowdown. In contrast, during an economic boom, the tax receipts from the program will increase because more people are now working, and the amount paid out in benefits will decline because fewer people are unemployed. Thus, the program will automatically tend to run a surplus during good times. So without any change in policy, the unemployment compensation program has the desired countercyclical effect on aggregate demand.[5]

The corporate profit tax The corporate profit tax is a highly important automatic stabilizer because corporate profits are highly sensitive to cyclical conditions. During a recession, corporate profits decline sharply, and so, too, do corporate tax payments. In turn,

---

[5]Although unemployment compensation has the desired countercyclical effect on demand, it also reduces the opportunity cost of remaining unemployed. As a result of this incentive effect, higher unemployment benefits and longer periods of eligibility will lead to more lengthy spells of unemployment and higher unemployment rates. Historically, in the United States unemployed workers have been permitted to draw benefits for 26 weeks, and this was extended to 39 weeks a few times during serious recessions, such as in 2020 due to government-mandated shutdowns because of the COVID-19 virus. However, during the 2008–2009 recession and recovery, the benefits were extended to up to 99 weeks. Research in this area indicates that these benefit extensions led to a higher unemployment rate.

the decline in tax revenues will enlarge the size of the budget deficit. In contrast, when the economy is expanding, corporate profits typically increase much more rapidly than wages, income, or consumption. This increase in corporate profits will result in a rapid increase in the "tax take" from the business sector during the expansion phase of the business cycle. Thus, corporate tax payments will go up during an expansion and fall rapidly during a contraction, even though no new legislative action has been instituted.

The progressive income tax When incomes grow rapidly, the average personal income tax liability of individuals and families increases. With rising incomes, more people will find their income above the "no tax due" cutoff. Others will jump up into higher tax brackets. Therefore, during an economic expansion, personal income tax revenues increase more rapidly than income. Other things constant, the budget moves toward a surplus (or smaller deficit), even though the economy's tax rate structure is unchanged. Conversely, when incomes decline, many individuals will be taxed at lower rates or not at all. Income tax revenues will fall more rapidly than income, automatically enlarging the size of the budget deficit during a recession.

During the 1960s, it was widely believed that discretionary fiscal policy could be instituted in a manner that would help promote economic stability. Both Keynesian and non-Keynesian economists now recognize that proper timing of fiscal policy is more difficult than was previously thought. Automatic stabilizers minimize the problem of appropriate timing and thereby exert an important stabilizing impact on the economy. However, the timing difficulties mean that the potential of discretionary fiscal policy is substantially more limited. Discretionary changes may have their greatest relevance during severe and lengthy recessions such as the one that began in December of 2007. As we proceed, we will consider the potential of fiscal stimulus to promote the recovery of a highly depressed economy in detail.

11-4 SAVING, SPENDING, DEBT, AND THE IMPACT OF FISCAL POLICY

Currently, consumption spending comprises approximately 70 percent of GDP. Household saving is merely after-tax income not spent on consumption. Historically, Keynesian economists have persistently stressed the importance of consumption spending and warned of the dangers accompanying excessive saving. Keynesians argue that when a large number of households try to increase their saving and reduce their consumption, total saving may not increase. Instead, the reduction in consumption may reduce the overall demand for goods and services, causing businesses to reduce output and lay off workers. In turn, as output and income fall, saving may decline rather than increase. This is often referred to as the **paradox of thrift**.

Within the framework of the *AD–AS* model, the increase in saving by households would increase the supply of loanable funds and reduce interest rates, which would tend to offset the reduction in consumer demand. Keynesians do not believe this will be the case. Perhaps a simple example will help to explain their concerns and the underlying logic of the paradox of thrift. Suppose a family decides to eat out less often and save an additional $200 per month. Keynesians argue that their actions will reduce the incomes of restaurants by $200 per month, and as a result of this reduction in net income, the savings of the restaurant owners will fall by this amount. Thus, the family saves $200 more per month, but the restaurant owners earn and save $200 less, so there is no net change in saving. If numerous families cut back on their consumption spending in an effort to increase their saving, the results would be the same. According to the Keynesian view, there would be no increase in saving, but consumption, aggregate demand, and output would decline.[6]

Paradox of thrift
The idea that when many households simultaneously try to increase their saving, actual saving may fail to increase because the reduction in consumption and aggregate demand will reduce income and employment.

---

[6]For additional details on both the paradox of thrift and the Keynesian perspective, see Interview with Steve Fazzari of Washington University, "On Keynesian Economics," January 12, 2009, EconTalk.org, at http://www.econtalk.org/archives/2009/01/fazzari_on_keyn.html.

Eventually, the deficient demand, excess capacity, and weak investment would place downward pressure on both interest rates and resource prices, but this might well be a painful process. Keynesians fear that this will be the case, and that is why they have persistently stressed the implications of the paradox of thrift and the potential dangers of excessive saving.

However, there is also a paradox of excessive consumption and deficient saving, which is often overlooked. You cannot have a strong, healthy economy if all or most households face financial troubles because they are spending just about everything they earn (or can borrow) on consumption. When families and individuals are heavily indebted and have little or no savings, they are in a very poor position to deal with irregular expenses like repairs, health issues, or other financial setbacks that are a part of life.

Is saving good or bad for the economy? Straight thinking on this question is important. Although an abrupt increase in saving may exert an adverse impact on the economy in the short run, saving provides the source of investment capital that allows businesses to expand production and the economy to grow. Other things remaining constant, countries that persistently save and invest more will grow more rapidly. Moreover, when households save on a regular basis, live within their means, and avoid excessive debt, they will be better able to deal with unexpected expenses, sustain a steady consumption rate, and achieve greater financial security.

There is evidence that deficient saving and excessive household debt have caused problems for the American economy. As **Exhibit 4** shows, household debt as a share of income increased significantly for more than two decades prior to the Great Recession. From 1960 to 1985, household debt fluctuated between 55 percent and 65 percent of after-tax income. However, beginning in the mid-1980s, the household debt to income ratio started to increase, soaring to a peak of almost 125 percent in 2007.

The high level of debt made it more difficult for households to deal with the 2008–2009 recession. It also reduced the effectiveness of Keynesian fiscal policy. As the recession set in during the first half of 2008, the Bush administration responded with a Keynesian tax cut. Households were sent a check for $600 for each adult and another $300

EXHIBIT 4

Household Debt as a Share of After-Tax Income: 1960–2019

The household debt to income ratio increased during 1985–2000, and it surged upward during 2000–2007. By 2007, just prior to the Great Recession, the ratio was twice the level of the 1960–1980 era. In recent years, the ratio has declined, but it is still well above the figure for the 1970s and 1980s. Heavy indebtedness makes it more difficult for households to deal with unexpected expenses and achieve financial security.

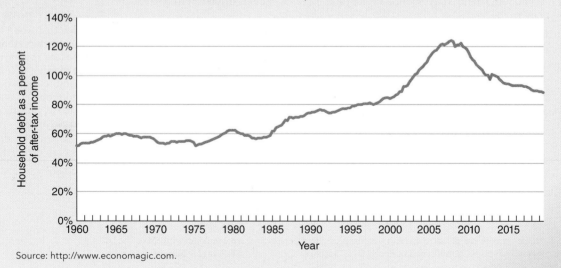

Source: http://www.economagic.com.

for each child. It was hoped that this would induce households to increase their spending and ignite economic recovery.

The Obama Administration also applied the Keynesian prescription. In February 2009, the new administration adopted an $800 billion spending package financed by borrowing. As in the case of the Bush strategy, it was hoped that the additional spending would increase household income and trigger a multiplier effect of additional consumption. The federal budget deficit, first under President Bush and then under President Obama, soared to almost 10 percent of GDP, the highest levels since World War II. According to Keynesian analysis, the large budget deficits would stimulate aggregate demand and ignite recovery. Nonetheless, the growth of real GDP was slow and the unemployment rate was still above 9 percent during the early summer of 2011.

Why weren't the Keynesian responses to the 2008–2009 recession more effective? Given their high level of indebtedness, households were in no mood to spend more and take on still additional debt. Instead, as Exhibit 4 shows, they increased their saving and reduced their indebtedness. Since the end of the Great Recession, the household debt to income ratio has fallen persistently, receding to less than 90 percent in 2019. This declining household debt to income ratio is indicative of both greater financial strength and increased sustainability of the recovery.

The high levels of household debt probably dampened the Keynesian stimulus, but there are also other explanations. The following chapter will consider several of them.

KEY POINTS

- The British economist John Maynard Keynes provided an explanation of and remedy for prolonged high rates of unemployment such as those seen during the Great Depression.

- In the Keynesian model, equilibrium occurs when the spending on consumption, investment, government purchases, and net exports is equal to total output. Firms will produce only the quantity of goods and services they believe consumers, investors, governments, and foreigners plan to buy. If this spending level is less than full-employment output, firms will not alter their production levels and the less than full-employment rate of output will persist. Keynes believed this was the situation during the Great Depression.

- According to the Keynesian view, fluctuations in total spending (aggregate demand) are the major source of economic instability. Keynesians believe that market economies have a tendency to fluctuate between economic booms driven by excessive demand and recessions resulting from insufficient demand. The multiplier concept magnifies these fluctuations.

- When an economy is in a recession, Keynesians do not believe that reductions in either resource prices or interest rates will promote recovery, and as a result, market economies are likely to experience recessions that are both severe and lengthy.

- The federal budget is the primary tool of fiscal policy. The Keynesian model highlights the use of fiscal policy as a tool with which to maintain demand at a level consistent with full employment and price stability.

- Rather than balancing the budget annually, Keynesians believe that fiscal policy should reflect business cycle conditions. During a recession, fiscal policy should become more expansionary (a larger deficit should be run). During an inflationary boom, fiscal policy should become more restrictive (shift toward a budget surplus).

- Changes in fiscal policy must be timed properly if they are going to exert a stabilizing influence on an economy. The ability of policy-makers to time fiscal policy changes in a countercyclical manner is reduced by (1) the inability of the political process to act rapidly, (2) the time lag between when a policy change is instituted and when it affects the economy, and (3) the inability to forecast accurately the future direction of the economy.

- Automatic stabilizers help promote stability because they are able to add demand stimulus during a recession and restraint during an economic boom without legislative action.

- Although an abrupt increase in saving may exert an adverse impact on the economy in the short run, saving provides the financing for investment that powers long-term growth. Moreover, a healthy economy is dependent on households saving regularly and avoiding excessive debt.

CRITICAL ANALYSIS QUESTIONS

1. What determines the equilibrium rate of output in the Keynesian model? Why did Keynes think the Great Depression lasted so long and the unemployment rate remained so high throughout the 1930s?

2. What do Keynesians think cause fluctuations in output? What must be done to maintain full-employment capacity?

3. *What is the multiplier principle? What determines the size of the multiplier? Does the multiplier make it more or less difficult to stabilize the economy? Explain.

4. What is a budget deficit? How are budget deficits financed? Why do Keynesians believe that budget deficits will increase aggregate demand?

5. From a stabilization standpoint, why is proper timing of a change in fiscal policy important? Is it easy to time fiscal policy changes properly? Why or why not?

6. *According to the Keynesian view, what fiscal policy actions should be taken if the unemployment rate is high and current GDP is well below potential output?

7. Are discretionary changes in fiscal policy likely to be instituted in a manner that will help smooth the ups and downs of the business cycle? Why or why not?

8. What are automatic stabilizers? Explain their major advantage.

9. "An increase in aggregate demand will tend to increase real output by a larger amount when unemployment is widespread than when the economy is operating at or near full employment." Is this statement true? Explain.

10. When output and employment slowed in early 2008, the Bush Administration and the Democratic Congress passed legislation sending households a check for $600 for each adult (and $300 per child). These checks were financed by borrowing. Would a Keynesian favor this action? Why or why not?

11. If uncertainty about the future causes households to increase their saving and reduce their consumption spending during a recession, how will this affect the economy? Explain. If households save little and spend most of their income on current consumption, how will this affect the economy? Explain.

12. How did Keynesian analysis change the views of economists and policy-makers with regard to the appropriateness of a balanced budget?

13. Even though the United States was in the midst of a historically long economic expansion, the federal government ran large budget deficits (more than 3 percent of GDP) during 2016–2019. Would a Keynesian economist believe this was sound policy? Why or why not?

*Asterisk denotes questions for which answers are given in Appendix B.

CHAPTER 12

Fiscal Policy, Incentives, and Secondary Effects

The main difference between Keynes and modern economics is the focus on incentives. Keynes studied the relation between macroeconomic aggregates, without any consideration for the underlying incentives that lead to the formation of these aggregates. By contrast, modern economists base all their analysis on incentives. —**Luigi Zingales**[1]

As we discussed in the previous chapter, Keynesian analysis indicates that fiscal policy provides a potential tool through which aggregate demand can be controlled and maintained at a level consistent with full employment and price stability. During the 1970s, however, the economic instability—along with high rates of both unemployment and inflation—illustrated some of the difficulties involved in the effective use of fiscal policy as a stabilization tool. Moreover, in recent decades, economists have become more aware of secondary effects that reduce the potency of fiscal policy. More attention has also been paid to the incentive effects accompanying fiscal changes. The chapter-opening quote by Luigi Zingales highlights these points. This chapter focuses on these topics and the current debate among economists about the effectiveness of

fiscal policy and its potential to improve the performance of a market economy.

As you read this chapter, look for answers to the following questions:

- How do the crowding-out and new classical models of fiscal policy modify the Keynesian analysis?

- Is discretionary fiscal policy an effective stabilization tool? Why or why not?

- Are there supply-side effects of fiscal policy?

- Will increases in government spending financed by borrowing help promote recovery from a recession?

[1]Luigi Zingales, Booth School of Business at the University of Chicago, March 10, 2009. Online debate sponsored by *The Economist*, http://www.economist.com/debate/days/view/276/print.

12-1 FISCAL POLICY, BORROWING, AND THE CROWDING-OUT EFFECT

Keynesian analysis indicates that expansionary fiscal policy will exert a powerful impact on aggregate demand, output, and employment. Other economists disagree. When the government runs a budget deficit, the funds will have to come from somewhere. If we rule out money creation (monetary policy), the government will have to finance its deficit by borrowing from either domestic or foreign lenders. But the additional government borrowing will increase the demand for loanable funds, which will push real interest rates upward. In turn, the higher real interest rates will reduce private investment and consumption, thereby dampening the stimulus effects of expansionary fiscal policy. Economists refer to this squeezing out of private spending by a deficit-induced increase in the real interest rate as the **crowding-out effect**.

Crowding-out effect
A reduction in private spending as a result of higher interest rates generated by budget deficits that are financed by borrowing in the private loanable funds market.

Suppose the government increases its spending or reduces taxes and, as a result, runs a budget deficit of $100 billion. As **Exhibit 1** shows, the government's additional borrowing will increase demand in the loanable funds market and place upward pressure on real interest rates. How will the higher interest rates influence private spending? Consumers will reduce their purchases of interest rate-sensitive goods, such as automobiles and consumer durables. A higher interest rate will also increase the opportunity cost of investment projects. Businesses will reduce spending on plant expansions, heavy equipment, and capital improvements. Residential-housing construction and sales will also be hurt. Thus, the higher real interest rates caused by the larger deficit will inhibit private spending. If it were not for the reduction in private spending, aggregate demand would increase to AD_2 (the dotted curve of panel a), but given the reduction in private spending, aggregate demand remains unchanged at AD_1.

EXHIBIT 1

The Crowding-Out Model: Higher Interest Rates Crowd Out Private Spending

The crowding-out effect indicates that budget deficits will lead to higher interest rates, which will reduce private investment and consumption, offsetting the demand stimulus of expansionary fiscal policy. If the government borrows an additional $100 billion to finance a budget deficit, the demand for loanable funds will increase by this amount (shift from D_1 to D_2 in panel b), leading to higher real interest rates. If it were not for the higher real interest rates, aggregate demand would increase to AD_2 (dotted curve of panel a). However, at the higher interest rates, private investment and consumption will decline. As a result, aggregate demand will remain unchanged at AD_1. The crowding-out effect indicates that expansionary fiscal policy will have little or no impact on aggregate demand.

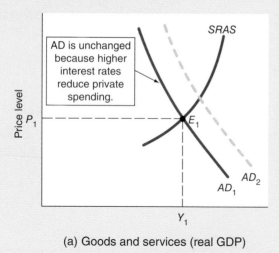

(a) Goods and services (real GDP)

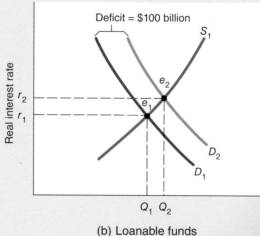

(b) Loanable funds

The crowding-out effect implies that the demand stimulus effects of budget deficits will be weak because borrowing to finance the deficits will increase interest rates and thereby crowd out private spending on investment and consumption. This reduction in private spending will partially, if not entirely, offset the additional spending financed by the deficit. Thus, the net impact of expansionary fiscal policy on aggregate demand, output, and employment will be small.

Furthermore, as private investment is crowded out by the higher interest rates, the output of capital goods will decline. As a result, the future stock of capital (for example, heavy equipment, other machines, and buildings) available to future workers will be smaller than it would have been otherwise. In other words, deficits will have an adverse effect on capital formation and tend to hinder the growth of productivity and income.

Keynesians respond that even if crowding out occurs when the economy is at or near full employment, it will be less important during a recession, particularly a serious one. During the severe recession of 2008–2009, short-term interest rates fell to nearly zero even though the federal government was running huge deficits.[2] Under circumstances like these, the immediate crowding-out effect is likely to be small, and therefore, the budget deficits will stimulate output and employment just as the Keynesian analysis implies. The proponents of crowding out counter that while this may be true during the recession, the deficits will mean more borrowing and less private spending as the economy begins to recover. As a result, the recovery will be weaker than would have been the case if government borrowing had been more restrained.

The implications of the crowding-out analysis are symmetrical. Restrictive fiscal policy will "crowd in" private spending. If the government collects greater tax revenues and/or reduces spending, the budget will shift toward a surplus (or smaller deficit). As a result, the government's demand for loanable funds will decrease, placing downward pressure on the real interest rate. The lower real interest rate will stimulate additional private investment and consumption. So the fiscal policy restraint will be partially, if not entirely, offset by an expansion in private spending. *As the result of this crowding in, restrictive fiscal policy will be largely ineffective as a weapon against inflation.*

12-1a DO GLOBAL FINANCIAL MARKETS MINIMIZE THE CROWDING-OUT EFFECT?

Today, financial capital can rapidly move in and out of countries. Suppose the budget deficit of the United States increases and additional borrowing by the U.S. Treasury pushes real interest rates upward, just as the crowding-out theory implies. Think about how investors will respond to this situation. The higher real interest yields on bonds and other financial assets will attract funds from abroad. In turn, this inflow of financial capital will increase the supply of loanable funds and thereby moderate the rise in real interest rates in the United States.[3]

At first glance, the crowding-out effect would appear to be weakened because the inflow of funds from abroad will lessen the upward pressure on domestic interest rates. Closer inspection, though, reveals that this will not be the case. Foreigners cannot buy more U.S. bonds and financial assets without "buying" more dollars in the foreign exchange market. Thus, additional bond purchases will increase the demand for U.S. dollars (and the supply of foreign currencies) in the foreign exchange market—the market that coordinates exchanges of the various national currencies. As foreigners demand more dollars to buy financial investments in the United States, this will increase the demand for the dollar, causing it to appreciate. In turn, the appreciation of the dollar will make imports cheaper for Americans. Simultaneously, it will make U.S. exports more expensive for

---

[2]Expansionary monetary policy also contributed to the low short-term interest rates of 2008–2009. The impact of monetary policy on interest rates, output, and employment will be discussed in Chapter 14.

[3]For students who are unsure about the demand for and supply of loanable funds, this would be a good time to review the topic within the framework of our basic macro model outlined by Exhibit 1 in Chapter 9. As this exhibit indicates, household saving and the inflow of financial capital from abroad supply loanable funds. In turn, private investment and borrowing by the government to finance budget deficits generate the demand for these funds.

foreigners. Predictably, the United States will import more and export less. Thus, net exports will decline (or net imports increase), causing a reduction in aggregate demand. Therefore, while the inflow of capital from abroad will moderate the increase in the interest rate and the crowding out of private domestic investment, it will also reduce net exports and thereby decrease aggregate demand. This means that the crowding-out effect still stifled what was intended to boost aggregate demand.

Exhibit 2 summarizes the crowding-out view of budget deficits in an open economy. The additional government borrowing triggered by the budget deficits will cause interest rates to rise, and this will lead to two secondary effects that will dampen the stimulus impact of the deficits. First, the higher interest rates will reduce private investment, which will directly restrain aggregate demand. Second, the higher interest returns will also attract an inflow of foreign capital, which will lessen the increase in interest rates, but it will also cause the dollar to appreciate. In turn, the appreciation of the dollar will reduce both net exports and aggregate demand. *According to the crowding-out theory, these two factors will largely, if not entirely, offset the stimulus effects of a larger budget deficit.*

12-2 FISCAL POLICY, FUTURE TAXES, AND THE NEW CLASSICAL MODEL

Thus far, we have implicitly assumed that the current consumption and saving decisions of taxpayers are unaffected by budget deficits. This may not be the case. Robert Lucas (University of Chicago), Thomas Sargent (New York University), and Robert Barro (Harvard University) have been leaders among a group of economists arguing that budget deficits imply higher future taxes and that taxpayers will reduce their current consumption just as they would have if the taxes had been collected during the current period. Because this position has its foundation in classical economics, these economists and their followers are referred to as **new classical economists**.

New classical economists
Economists who believe that there are strong forces pushing a market economy toward full-employment equilibrium and that macroeconomic policy is an ineffective tool with which to reduce economic instability.

In the Keynesian model, a tax cut financed by borrowing will increase the current income of households, and they respond by increasing their consumption. New classical economists argue that this analysis is incorrect because it ignores the impact of the higher future tax liability implied by the budget deficit and the interest payments required to

---

EXHIBIT 2

A Visual Presentation of the Crowding-Out Effect in an Open Economy

The implications of the crowding-out effect in an open economy are illustrated here. As was shown in the previous exhibit, government borrowing to finance a budget deficit will place upward pressure on real interest rates. This will reduce private investment and aggregate demand. In an open economy, the higher interest rates will also increase the inflow of capital from abroad, which will cause the dollar to appreciate and net exports to decline. Thus, in an open economy, the higher interest rates will trigger reductions in both private investment and net exports, which will weaken the expansionary impact of a budget deficit.

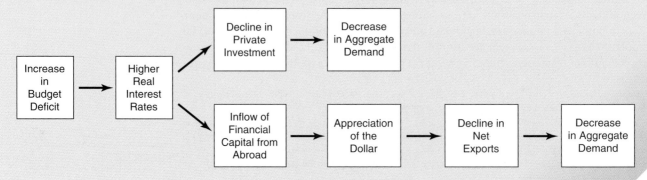

service the additional debt. Rather than increasing their consumption in response to a larger budget deficit, new classical economists believe that households will save all or most of their increase in disposable income so that they will be able to pay the higher future taxes implied by the additional government debt. Thus, new classical economists do not believe that budget deficits will stimulate additional consumption and aggregate demand.

The new classical economists stress that debt financing simply substitutes higher future taxes for lower current taxes. Thus, budget deficits affect the timing of the taxes but not their magnitude. A mere change in the timing of taxes will not alter the wealth of households. Therefore, there is no reason to believe that current consumption will change when current taxes are cut, and government debt and future taxes are increased by an equivalent amount. This view that taxes and debt financing are essentially equivalent is known as **Ricardian equivalence**, after the nineteenth-century economist, David Ricardo, who initially developed the idea.[4]

Perhaps an illustration will help explain the underlying logic of the new classical view. Suppose you knew that your taxes were going to be cut by $1,000 this year, but that next year they were going to be increased by $1,000 plus the interest on that figure. Would this year's $1,000 tax cut cause you to increase your consumption spending? New classical economists argue that it would not. They believe that most people would recognize that their wealth is unchanged and would therefore save most of this year's tax cut to be better able to pay next year's higher taxes. Correspondingly, new classical economists argue that when debt is substituted for taxes, people will recognize that the additional debt means higher future taxes and that therefore they will save more in order to pay them.

Exhibit 3 illustrates the implications of the new classical view on the potency of fiscal policy. Suppose that the fiscal authorities issue $100 billion of additional debt in

Ricardian equivalence
The view that a tax reduction financed with government debt will exert no effect on current consumption and aggregate demand because people will fully recognize the higher future taxes implied by the additional debt.

EXHIBIT 3

The New Classical View: Higher Expected Future Taxes Crowd Out Private Spending

New classical economists emphasize that budget deficits merely substitute future taxes for current taxes. If households did not anticipate the higher future taxes, aggregate demand would increase to AD_2. However, demand remains unchanged at AD_1 when households fully anticipate the future increase in taxes (panel a). Simultaneously, the additional saving to meet the higher future taxes will increase the supply of loanable funds to S_2 and allow the government to borrow the funds to finance its deficit without pushing up the real interest rate (panel b). In this model, fiscal policy exerts no effect. The real interest rate, real GDP, and level of employment all remain unchanged.

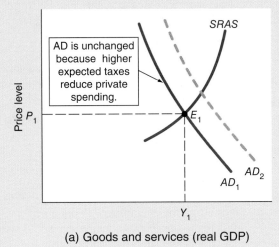

(a) Goods and services (real GDP)

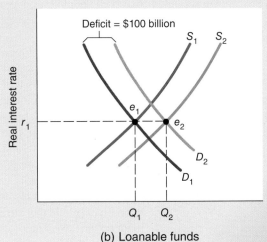

(b) Loanable funds

---

[4]For a classical statement of this view, see Robert J. Barro, "The Ricardian Approach to Budget Deficits," *Journal of Economic Perspectives* (Spring 1989): 37–44.

order to cut taxes by an equal amount. The government borrowing increases the demand for loanable funds (D_1 shifts to D_2 in panel b) by $100 billion. If taxpayers didn't think that higher future taxes would result from the debt, they would expand their consumption in response to the lower taxes and the increase in their current disposable income. Under these circumstances, aggregate demand in the goods and services market would expand to AD_2 (panel a). In the new classical model, though, this will not be the case. Realizing that the $100 billion in additional debt will mean higher future taxes, taxpayers will maintain their initial level of consumption spending and use the tax cut to increase their savings in order to generate the additional income required to pay the higher future taxes. Because consumption is unchanged, aggregate demand also remains constant (at AD_1). At the same time, the additional saving (to pay the implied increase in future taxes) allows the government to finance its deficit without an increase in the real interest rate.

According to the new classical view, changes in fiscal policy have little effect on the economy. Debt financing and larger budget deficits will not stimulate aggregate demand. Similarly, the real interest rate is unaffected by deficits because people will save more in order to pay the higher future taxes. In the new classical model, fiscal policy is completely impotent.

In Chapter 1, we indicated that failure to consider the secondary effects is one of the most common errors in economics. Once the secondary effects are considered, both the crowding-out and new classical models indicate that spending increases financed by borrowing will provide little if any net stimulus to the economy. *Put another way, both the crowding-out and new classical theories indicate that budget deficits and expansionary fiscal policy will be far less potent than the Keynesian analysis implies.*

12-2a IS JOB CREATION A GOOD REASON TO SUPPORT A GOVERNMENT SPENDING PROGRAM?

Jobs are typically used to produce goods and services that we value. But we must not forget that it is the production of goods and services that people highly value relative to cost that is important; the jobs are merely a means to that end. If people do not keep their eyes on this basic fact, they may be misled to support projects that destroy wealth rather than create it.

Politicians are fond of talking about the jobs created by their spending programs. Suppose the government spends $50 billion employing one million workers to build a high-speed train linking Los Angeles and Las Vegas. Supporters of projects like this often argue that they should be undertaken because they will create a huge number of jobs. Is this a sound argument? When thinking about the answer to this question, consider the following two points.

First, the government will have to use either taxes or borrowing to finance the project. Taxes of $50 billion will reduce consumer spending and private savings by this amount, and this will diminish employment in other sectors by a magnitude similar to the employment created by the spending on the project. Alternatively, if the project is financed by debt, the additional borrowing will lead to higher interest rates and future taxes to cover interest payments. This will also divert funds away from other projects, both private and public. Thus, the net impact will be primarily a reshuffling of jobs rather than job creation.

Second, what really matters is the value of what is produced, not jobs. If jobs were the key to high incomes, we could easily create as many as we wanted. For example, the government could pay attractive wages hiring the unemployed to dig holes one day and fill them up the next. The program would create jobs, but as a nation we would also be poorer because such jobs would not generate goods and services that people value. Job creation, either real or imagined, is not a sound reason to support a program. Instead, the proper test is opportunity cost: The value of what is produced relative to the value of what is given up. If people value the output generated by the government-spending program more than the production it crowds out, it will increase our incomes and living standards. If the opposite is the case, then the additional spending will make us worse off.

12-3 POLITICAL INCENTIVES AND THE EFFECTIVE USE OF DISCRETIONARY FISCAL POLICY

As we discussed in the last chapter, inability to forecast the future direction of the economy and the time lag between when a fiscal change is needed and when it can be instituted and begin to exert an impact on the economy make it difficult to use discretionary fiscal policy in a stabilizing manner. In addition to these practical problems, the political incentive structure also makes appropriate timing of fiscal changes less likely.

As public choice analysis stresses, politicians will be delighted to spend money on programs that benefit their constituents but reluctant to raise taxes because they impose a visible cost on voters. As a result, fiscal policy will tend to be instituted in an asymmetric manner. Rather than shifting toward deficits during periods of economic weakness and toward surpluses when the economy is strong, the political incentive structure will result in far more deficits than surpluses. The evidence is consistent with this view. During the 60 years since 1960, there have been 55 deficits and 5 surpluses. Given the political incentive structure, discretionary fiscal policy is unlikely to be instituted in a strictly countercyclical manner.

12-4 IS DISCRETIONARY FISCAL POLICY AN EFFECTIVE STABILIZATION TOOL?

In recent decades, the effectiveness of fiscal policy as a stabilization tool has been hotly debated and widely analyzed by macroeconomists. A synthesis view has emerged. Most macroeconomists—both Keynesian and non-Keynesian—are now largely in agreement on the following three issues.

1. Proper timing of discretionary fiscal policy is both difficult to achieve and crucially important. Given our limited ability to forecast ups and downs in the business cycle, the delays that inevitably accompany fiscal changes, and the structure of political incentives, the effectiveness of discretionary fiscal policy as a stabilization tool is limited. Put simply, persistent fiscal changes are unlikely to be instituted in a manner that will smooth the ups and downs of the business cycle. Therefore, most macroeconomists now place less emphasis on the use of discretionary fiscal policy as a stabilization tool.[5]

2. Automatic stabilizers reduce fluctuations in aggregate demand and help keep the economy on track. Because they are not dependent upon legislative action, automatic stabilizers are able to consistently shift the budget toward a deficit during a recession and toward a surplus during an economic boom. Thus, they add needed stimulus during a recession and act as a restraining force during an inflationary boom. Although some economists question their potency, nearly all agree that they exert a stabilizing influence.

3. Fiscal policy is much less potent than the early Keynesian view implied. Both the crowding-out and new classical models indicate that there are secondary effects of budget deficits that will substantially, if not entirely, offset their impact on aggregate demand. In the crowding-out model, higher real interest rates and a decline in net exports offset the expansionary effects of budget deficits. In the new classical model, higher future taxes lead to the same result. Both models indicate that fiscal policy will have little, if any, effect on current aggregate demand, employment, and real output during normal economic times.

---

[5]As the following statement from Keynes indicates, he did not believe that spending on government projects would be an effective countercyclical tool:

Organized public works, at home and abroad, may be the right cure for a chronic tendency to a deficiency of effective demand. But they are not capable of sufficiently rapid organization (and above all cannot be reversed or undone at a later date), to be the most serviceable instrument for the prevention of the trade cycle.

John Maynard Keynes in *Collected Works, vol. XXVII,* 122.

12-5 THE SUPPLY-SIDE EFFECTS OF FISCAL POLICY

Supply-side economists
Economists who believe that changes in marginal tax rates exert important effects on aggregate supply.

So far, we have focused on the potential impact of fiscal policy on aggregate demand. However, when fiscal changes alter tax rates, they influence the incentive of people to work, invest, and use resources efficiently. Thus, tax changes may also influence aggregate supply. Prior to 1980, macroeconomists generally ignored the supply-side effects of changes in tax rates, thinking they were of little importance. **Supply-side economists** challenged this view. The supply-side argument was central to the tax rate reductions of the 1980s, the capital gains rate reductions of 1997, and the tax legislation of 2002 and 2017.

From a supply-side viewpoint, the marginal tax rate is crucially important. As we discussed in Chapter 4, the marginal tax rate determines the breakdown of a person's additional income between tax payments on the one hand and personal income on the other. Lower marginal tax rates mean that individuals get to keep a larger share of their additional earnings. For example, reducing the marginal tax rate from 40 percent to 30 percent allows individuals to keep 70 cents of each additional dollar they earn, instead of only 60 cents. In turn, the lower tax rates and accompanying increase in take-home pay provide them with a greater incentive to earn. The same analysis applies to business taxation: a reduction in the marginal tax rate imposed on corporations and other businesses increases returns and encourages entrepreneurial activity. Supply-side economists believe that these incentive effects will bring more resources into productive activities. Most significantly, they argue that high marginal rates—for example, rates of 50 percent or more—substantially reduce the incentive of people to work, invest, and use resources productively.

The supply-side effects of a tax change are fundamentally different from the demand-side effects. On the demand side, lower taxes increase the after-tax incomes of consumers and thereby stimulate consumption and aggregate demand. *On the supply side, lower tax rates increase the incentive of people to work, supply resources, and undertake entrepreneurial activities and thereby increase aggregate supply.*

Exhibit 4 graphically depicts the impact of a supply-side tax cut, one that reduces marginal tax rates. The lower marginal tax rates increase aggregate supply because the new incentive structure encourages taxpayers to earn more and use resources more efficiently.

EXHIBIT 4

Tax Rate Effects and Supply-Side Economics

Here, we illustrate the supply-side effects of lower marginal tax rates. The lower marginal tax rates increase the incentive to earn and use resources efficiently. Because these are long-run as well as short-run effects, both *LRAS* and *SRAS* increase (shift to the right). Real output expands. In turn, the higher income levels accompanying the expansion in real output will stimulate aggregate demand (shift it to *AD₂*).

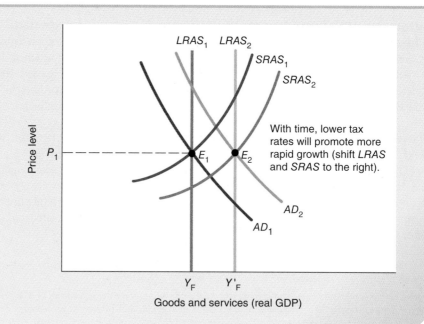

If taxpayers think the cut will be permanent, both long- and short-run aggregate supply (*LRAS* and *SRAS*) will increase. Real output and income will expand. As real income expands, aggregate demand will also increase (shift to AD_2). If the lower marginal rates are financed by a budget deficit, though, aggregate demand may increase by a larger amount than aggregate supply, putting upward pressure on the price level.

Supply-side economics should not be viewed as a short-run countercyclical tool. It will take time for people to react to the tax cuts and move their resources out of investments designed to lower their taxes and into higher-return, production-oriented activities. The full positive effects of lower marginal tax rates will not be observed until both labor and capital markets have time to adjust fully to the new incentive structure. *Supply-side economics is a long-run, growth-oriented strategy, not a short-run stabilization tool.*

12-5a WHY DO HIGH TAX RATES DECREASE OUTPUT?

There are three major reasons why high tax rates are likely to reduce the growth of output. *First, as we have explained, high marginal tax rates discourage work effort and productivity.* When marginal tax rates soar to 55 or 60 percent, people get to keep less than half of what they earn, so they tend to work less. Some (for example, those with a working spouse) will drop out of the labor force. Others will simply work fewer hours. Still others will decide to take longer vacations, forgo overtime opportunities, retire earlier, or forget about pursuing that promising but risky business venture. In some cases, high tax rates will even drive highly productive citizens to other countries where taxes are lower. In recent years, high-tax countries such as Belgium and France have experienced an outflow of highly successful professionals, business entrepreneurs, and athletes.

Second, high tax rates will adversely affect the rate of capital formation and the efficiency of its use. When tax rates are high, foreign investors will look for other places to put their money, and domestic investors will look for investment projects abroad where taxes are lower. In addition, domestic investors will direct more of their time and effort into hobby businesses (like collecting antiques, raising horses, or giving golf lessons) that may not earn much money but are enjoyable and have tax-shelter advantages. This will divert resources away from projects with higher rates of return but fewer tax-avoidance benefits. As a result, scarce capital will be wasted and resources channeled away from their most productive uses.

Third, high marginal tax rates encourage individuals and entrepreneurs to substitute less-desired tax-deductible goods for more-desired nondeductible goods. High marginal tax rates make tax-deductible expenditures cheap for people in high tax brackets. Because purchasing tax-deductible goods lowers their tax bill, people will often buy them even though they do not value them as much as it costs to produce them. Because the personal cost (but not the cost to society) is cheap, these taxpayers will spend more money on pleasurable, tax-deductible items, like plush offices, professional conferences held in favorite vacation spots, and various other fringe benefits (for example, a company-paid luxury automobile or business entertainment).

12-5b HOW IMPORTANT ARE THE SUPPLY-SIDE EFFECTS?

There is considerable debate among economists about the strength of the supply-side incentive effects. Critics of supply-side economics argue that the tax cuts of the 1980s reduced real federal tax revenues and led to large budget deficits, without having much impact on economic growth. This suggests that the supply-side effects are not very strong. Defenders of the supply-side position respond by noting that rate reductions in both the 1960s and the 1980s resulted in impressive growth and lengthy economic expansions. They also stress that the supply-side response in top income brackets—where lowering rates have the

APPLICATIONS IN ECONOMICS

Do High Marginal Tax Rates Soak the Rich?

Under a progressive rate structure, marginal tax rates rise with income level. The highest marginal tax rates are imposed on those with the largest incomes.

Since 1960, the personal income tax rate imposed on high-income earners has varied considerably. What effect have the rate changes had on the revenue collected from them? **Exhibit 5**

presents data on the share of the personal income tax collected from the top one-half percent of income recipients. When the top marginal tax rate was sliced from 91 percent to 70 percent by the Kennedy–Johnson tax cut of 1964, the share of the personal income tax paid by these high earners rose from 16 percent to 18 percent. In contrast, as inflation pushed more and more

EXHIBIT 5

How Have Changes in Marginal Tax Rates Affected the Share of Taxes Paid by the Rich?

The accompanying graph shows the share of the personal income taxes paid by the top one-half percent of earners from 1960 to 2017. During this period, there were several major reductions in marginal tax rates. First, the Kennedy–Johnson tax cut reduced the top rate from 91 percent in 1963 to 70 percent in 1965. During the Reagan years, the top rate was reduced from 70 percent in 1980 to 50 percent in 1982 and to approximately 30 percent in 1986. In 1997, the capital gains tax rate was

sliced from 28 to 20 percent. Interestingly, the share of the tax bill paid by these "super-rich" earners increased after each of these tax cuts. These findings suggest that, at least for this group of high-income earners, strong supply-side effects accompanied the rate cuts. Perhaps surprising to some, these high-income taxpayers paid a larger portion of the tax bill when the top marginal rate was less than 40 percent (1986–2017) than when it was 70 percent or more.

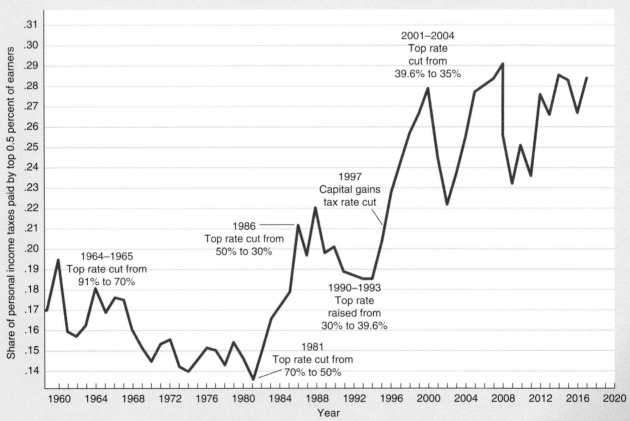

Source: http://www.irs.gov.

(Continued)

taxpayers into higher brackets during the 1970s, the share paid by the top one-half percent declined. When the tax cuts of the 1980s once again reduced the top rates, the share paid by the top one-half percent climbed to more than 20 percent of the total. When the top marginal rate was increased in 1991 and again in 1993, there was little change in the share of taxes paid by the top group. Beginning in 1997, the tax rate on income from capital gains was cut from 28 percent to 20 percent. This rate reduction was accompanied by a substantial increase in revenues derived from the capital gains taxes and personal income taxes collected from high-income taxpayers.[1]

Throughout 1986–2017, the top federal marginal personal income tax rate was less than 40 percent. In contrast, prior to 1981, the top marginal rate was 70 percent or more. Nonetheless, as Exhibit 5 illustrates, the share of federal income tax revenue collected from high earners was larger during the more recent period. Between 2006 and 2017, the share of the income tax paid by the top one-half percent of taxpayers ranged from 23 percent to 29 percent. These recent figures

are well above the 14 percent to 19 percent collected from the top one-half percent of taxpayers in the 1960s and 1970s, when much higher marginal rates were imposed on the rich.[2]

In recent years, several important politicians have argued that the top marginal income tax rates should be increased to 60 percent, 70 percent, or even higher. The proponents of this view believe that these rate increases will generate more tax revenue from high-income taxpayers. History indicates that this position should be viewed with a degree of caution.

[1] People also respond to high marginal tax rates imposed by states. A recent study estimated that in 2016 more than 1,000 people per day moved from the 25 highest-tax states to the 25 lowest-tax states. See Chris Edwards, "Tax Reform and Interstate Migration," *Cato Institute Tax & Budget Bulletin,* September 6, 2018, Number 84.

[2] For additional information on supply-side economics, see James Gwartney, "Supply-side Economics" in *The Encyclopedia of Economics,* ed. David Henderson (Indianapolis: Liberty Fund, 2007: available online). For a critical analysis of supply-side economics, see Joel B. Slemrod, ed., *Does Atlas Shrug?: The Economic Consequences of Taxing the Rich* (New York: Russell Sage Foundation, 2000).

largest incentive effects—is particularly strong.[6] See the boxed feature "Do High Marginal Tax Rates Soak the Rich?"

Supply-side critics also point out that most elasticity estimates indicate that a 10 percent change in after-tax wages increases the quantity of labor supplied by only 1 or 2 percent. This suggests that changes in tax rates exert only a modest impact on the amount of labor supplied. Supply-side advocates, however, argue that these estimates reflect only the adjustments that occur over relatively short time periods. In the long run, they claim that tax cuts increase the labor supply by much more. The research of Nobel laureate Edward Prescott of Arizona State University supports this view. Prescott used marginal tax differences between France and the United States to estimate the labor supply response in the long run. Prescott found that the elasticity of labor supply in the long run was substantially greater than in the short run. He estimates that France's higher marginal tax rates reduce the hours of labor supplied by French adults by nearly 30 percent annually compared to their American counterparts.[7]

The supply-side view has exerted considerable impact on tax policy throughout the world. Since 1980, there has been a dramatic shift away from high marginal tax rates. Sixty-two countries imposed a personal income tax with a top marginal rate of 50 percent or more in 1980, but only 14 countries levied such high rates in 2017. Almost all countries with a personal income tax have lower rates today than in the early 1980s.

----

[6] The incentive effects are greater in the upper brackets because a similar percentage rate reduction will have a greater impact on take-home pay in this area. For example, if a 70 percent marginal tax rate is cut to 50 percent, take-home pay per additional dollar of earnings will increase from 30 cents to 50 cents, a 67 percent increase in the incentive to earn. Conversely, if a 14 percent marginal rate is reduced to 10 percent, take-home pay per dollar of additional earnings will increase from 86 cents to 90 cents, only a 5 percent increase in the incentive to earn.

[7] Prescott concludes, "I find it remarkable that virtually all of the large difference in labor supply between France and the United States is due to differences in tax systems. I expected institutional constraints on the operation of labor markets and the nature of the unemployment benefit system to be more important. I was surprised that the welfare gain from reducing the intratemporal tax wedge is so large." See Edward C. Prescott, "Richard T. Ely Lecture: Prosperity and Depression," *American Economic Review,* Papers and Proceedings 92, No. 2 (May 2002): 9.

12-6 FISCAL POLICY AND RECOVERY FROM RECESSIONS

As we previously discussed, time lags, inability to forecast the future direction of the economy, and the political process all reduce the likelihood that discretionary fiscal policy will be used effectively to reduce the ups and downs of the business cycle. However, debate continues on the potential of expansionary fiscal policy to promote recovery from a serious recession like that of 2008–2009. Let's consider two of the key issues of this continuing debate.

12-6a WILL FISCAL STIMULUS SPEED RECOVERY?

Will increases in government spending financed by borrowing speed recovery from a severe recession? Keynesians clearly believe that the answer to this question is "yes." The Keynesian view stresses that private sector spending will decline during a severe recession and that the government needs to expand its spending in order to reignite the private sector. During a severe recession like that of 2008–2009, interest rates may essentially fall to zero, and even these low rates may fail to stimulate much private investment. Under these conditions, crowding out of private spending will be minimal. Moreover, unemployed and underemployed resources will be widespread, and, as a result, the additional government spending will have a substantial multiplier effect. Thus, Keynesians argue that expansionary fiscal policy will stimulate aggregate demand and help promote recovery from serious recessions.

In contrast, critics of Keynesian economics argue that the side effects of the increased spending and expanded debt will exert an adverse impact on both the recovery process and long-term growth. They raise three major points in support of their view. First, they argue that the increased borrowing, upward pressure on interest rates, inflow of capital, and appreciation of the dollar will reduce net exports and aggregate demand. Moreover, the larger outstanding debt will reduce consumption because of the anticipation of higher future taxes. This combination of factors slows long-term growth. Even if the government is able to borrow at low interest rates during a downturn, as was the case during the 2008–2009 recession, higher interest rates and higher taxes will eventually be required for the future financing and refinancing of the larger debt.

Second, government spending is driven by political rather than economic considerations. The political process does not have anything like profit and loss that will direct resources into productive projects and away from unproductive ones. Political favoritism will become more important, and efficient allocation of resources less so. Predictably, counterproductive use of resources will result.

Third, when the government is spending a lot on special projects, subsidies, grants, and income transfers, businesses and other organized groups will spend more on lobbying, political contributions, and other efforts designed to attract the government funds. Resources will be channeled toward wasteful rent-seeking and away from productive activities that provide consumers with goods and services that are more highly valued than their cost. Predictably, the result will be favoritism, cronyism, and even political corruption. Ironically, most of the wasteful rent-seeking activity will add to GDP as it is currently measured. For example, if business executives, lawyers, and even economists are spending more of their time schmoozing government officials, preparing grant proposals, designing politically attractive projects, and so on, such expenditures will enhance GDP. So, too, will inefficient government projects. As a result, GDP will overstate the value of the goods and services produced.

12-6b TAX CUTS VERSUS SPENDING INCREASES

When seeking to promote recovery from a recession, would it be better to reduce taxes or increase government spending? Keynesian economists tend to favor spending increases.

They often argue that increases in government spending will expand GDP by more than tax reductions, because 100 percent of the increase in government purchases will be pumped into the economy, whereas part of the tax reduction will be saved or spent abroad. As a result, Keynesians believe that the multiplier effect of an increase in government spending will be greater than that of a tax cut.[8]

But the rapidity of the effects is also a consideration, and tax cuts can generally begin to impact the economy more rapidly than increases in government spending. Reductions in tax rates can increase both the disposable income and the incentive to earn almost immediately. Even if a substantial portion of an increase in after-tax income is not spent quickly, there will be an immediate positive impact on the financial position of households. In contrast, government-spending projects are often a lengthy process spread over several years. For example, the Congressional Budget Office estimated that only 15 percent of the spending funded by the stimulus package passed in February 2009 occurred during the initial year, while nearly half (48 percent) was not spent until two or more years in the future.

Compared to an increase in government spending, a tax cut is less likely to change the composition of labor demand or increase structural unemployment. New government spending programs often change the structure of aggregate demand. As a result of this structural change, increases in government spending often exert an adverse transitional impact on the rate of unemployment.

When considering the impact of a tax cut, it is important to differentiate between one-time tax rebates and reductions in tax rates. An example of a tax rebate is the sending of government checks to most all households (as was done by the 2008–2009 and 2020 stimulus packages), which increases disposable income but it does not provide additional incentive for people to earn, invest, and employ others. As supply-side analysis indicates, a tax rebate of this type is unlikely to exert much impact on long-term productive activity.

Similarly, the impact of a temporary tax cut will be much weaker than a permanent one. A temporary tax cut provides a short-term windfall increase in current income, but it does not exert much impact on either long-term income or the incentive to earn. Moreover, compared to a permanent tax reduction, a temporary tax cut generates uncertainty. As a result, market participants, unsure about whether and how policies might change, often choose to cancel or delay long-term business ventures. Thus, temporary tax rebates and even rate reductions are largely ineffective as a tool for the promotion of recovery and long-term growth.

12-7 U.S. FISCAL POLICY: 1990–2019

Changes in government expenditures and shifts in the federal budget are indicative of the direction of fiscal policy. Increases in government spending financed by borrowing will shift the budget toward a deficit. This combination is indicative of a more expansionary fiscal policy. In contrast, reductions in government spending and shifts in the federal budget toward surplus are indicative of a move toward a more restrictive fiscal policy.

Exhibit 6 provides data on federal spending during 1990–2019. As Exhibit 6 (upper frame) shows, real federal spending was relatively constant during the 1990s. Measured in constant 2012 dollars, real federal spending in 2000 was $2.62 trillion, compared to $2.25 trillion in 1990. Thus, real federal spending increased by only 16 percent during the 1990s. By 2010, real federal spending had soared to $3.91 trillion, almost 50 percent higher than a decade earlier. Measured as a share of GDP, federal spending fell from 21.6 percent in 1990 to 18.7 percent in 2000 (lower frame). However, by 2010 federal

---

[8]The empirical evidence on the size of the tax and spending multipliers is mixed. Estimates of the multipliers range from approximately 1 to 3, and some have found the multiplier effects of a tax cut to be stronger than those for an increase in government spending, whereas others have found the reverse. See Valerie A. Ramey, "Identifying Government Spending Shocks: It's All in the Timing," *Quarterly Journal of Economics*, February 2011, pp. 1–50; Christina D. Romer and David H. Romer, "The Macroeconomic Effects of Tax Changes: Estimates Based on a New Measure of Fiscal Shocks," *American Economic Review*, June 2010, pp. 763–801; and John F. Cogan, Tobias Cwik, John B. Taylor, and Volker Wieland, "New Keynesian versus Old Keynesian Government Spending Multipliers," *Journal of Economic Dynamics and Control*, March 2010, pp. 281–295.

EXHIBIT 6

Federal Spending, 1990–2019

As shown in the top frame, real federal spending was relatively constant during the 1990s, but it rose steadily during 2000–2007 and sharply during 2008–2010. As the bottom frame indicates, federal spending as a share of GDP fell modestly during the 1990s, but it was relatively constant during 2001–2007 and increased substantially during 2008–2010. In 2019, federal spending was 22 percent of GDP, about 2 percentage points higher than during the past two decades.

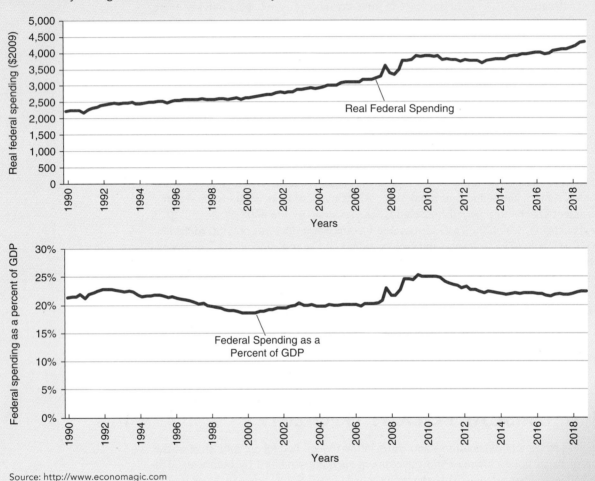

Source: http://www.economagic.com

spending had risen to 25.1 percent of GDP, substantially higher than the figure at the beginning of the decade. Thus, both real government spending and federal spending as a share of GDP grew far more rapidly during 2000–2010 than during the 1990s. The 2010 figures were elevated by the recession. Since 2010, real federal spending has increased slowly, but declined as a share of GDP. Nonetheless, federal spending as a share of GDP was 22.4 percent in 2019, well above the 18.7 figure for 2000.

As **Exhibit 7** shows, the federal budget moved from deficit to surplus during the 1990s, but it shifted in the opposite direction during 2000–2010. Measured as a share of GDP, the budget deficit was in the 3 percent to 5 percent range in the early part of the 1990s, but it fell steadily throughout the remainder of the decade. By 2000, a federal budget surplus of 2.3 percent was present. But the situation changed dramatically during the following decade. The combination of the 2001 recession and sluggish recovery, increases in defense spending, and the Bush administration's tax cut quickly moved the budget from surplus to deficit. During 2003–2007, deficits between 1.1 percent and 3.4 percent of GDP were present. As the economy dipped into a recession in 2008, the shortfall soared to 9 percent during 2009–2010. Thus, both government expenditures and the federal budget

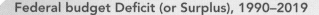

EXHIBIT 7

Federal budget Deficit (or Surplus), 1990–2019

During the 1990s, the federal budget shifted from deficit to surplus. But it moved in the opposite direction during 2002–2007, and it soared during the 2008–2009 recession.

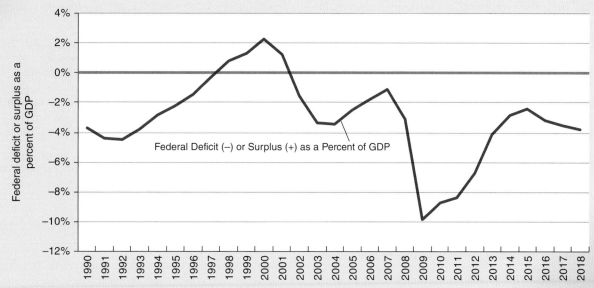

Source: http://www.economagic.com and http://www.cbo.gov (see tables e-2 and 1–1).

indicate that fiscal policy was relatively restrictive during the 1990s, but it shifted toward expansion beginning in 2001. Interestingly, the economy performed well with both the restrictive fiscal policy of the 1990s and the more expansionary fiscal policy of the early twenty-first century. As Exhibit 7 shows, the U.S. continued to run a large budget deficit during 2010–2019, even though the economy was quite strong.

Clearly, the fiscal policy response to the recession of 2008–2009 was precisely what Keynesian analysis would recommend. As Exhibits 6 and 7 show, the administrations of both Presidents Bush and Obama increased government spending and enlarged the budget deficit. Federal spending increased both in real terms and as a share of GDP during 2008–2011. The budget deficit rose to 8.4 percent of GDP during 2009–2012, and 36 percent of the federal budget was financed by borrowing during these years.

What does the experience of the recession of 2008–2009 reveal about the validity of the three major fiscal policy models? Keynesians argue that the increases in government spending and large budget deficits prevented the 2008–2009 recession from spiraling into another Great Depression. While this may be an exaggeration, the recession was followed by steady growth of output and employment. This is consistent with the view that the fiscal policy stimulus helped to keep the economy on track. The crowding-out theory indicates that the deficits will increase the demand for loanable funds, pushing interest rates upward. Even though the deficits were exceedingly large during 2008–2012, interest rates remained low. No doubt, the weak demand for investment because of the severity of the downturn and the inflow of foreign capital to finance the large deficits placed downward pressure on interest rates. All things considered, however, this episode provides little evidence for the crowding-out theory. Finally, the new classical theory indicates that people will save more as they plan for higher future taxes. There was some evidence that this was the case. Households increased their saving and reduced their debt during 2010–2019 (see Chapter 11, Exhibit 4), which helped to keep interest rates low.

In economics, it is often difficult to isolate the impact of a specific change because other factors are also changing. This may be the case with the low interest rates following the 2008–2009 recession. Other changes may have contributed to the low interest rates. As we proceed, we will examine this possibility in Chapter 14.

KEY POINTS

- The crowding-out model indicates that expansionary fiscal policy will lead to higher real interest rates and less private spending, particularly for investment. In an open economy, the higher interest rates will also lead to the following secondary effects: an inflow of capital, an appreciation of the dollar, and a reduction in net exports. The crowding-out theory implies that these secondary effects will largely offset the intended demand stimulus of expansionary fiscal policy.

- The new classical model stresses that financing government spending with debt rather than taxes changes the timing, but not the level, of taxes. According to this view, people will expect higher future taxes, which will lead to more saving and less private spending. This will tend to offset the expansionary effects of a deficit.

- Keynesian and non-Keynesian economists are now largely in agreement on the following three issues: (1) Proper timing of discretionary fiscal policy is both difficult to achieve and crucially important, (2) automatic stabilizers reduce the fluctuation of aggregate demand and help promote economic stability, and (3) fiscal policy is much less potent than early Keynesians thought.

- When fiscal policy changes marginal tax rates, it influences aggregate supply by altering the attractiveness of productive activ-

ity relative to leisure and tax avoidance. Other things constant, lower marginal tax rates will increase aggregate supply. Supply-side economics should be viewed as a long-run strategy, not a countercyclical tool.

- Keynesian economists believe that increases in government spending financed by borrowing will increase aggregate demand and help promote recovery from a serious recession like that of 2008–2009. Non-Keynesian economists argue that Keynesian policies will lead to higher future interest rates and taxes, inefficient use of resources, and wasteful rent-seeking that will both hinder recovery and slow future economic growth.

- Tax cuts can generally begin to exert an impact on the economy more rapidly than spending increases. Further, permanent rate reductions will exert a larger impact than tax rebates or temporary tax cuts.

- Slow growth of real government spending and declining budget deficits characterized the U.S. economy during the 1990s. Since 2000, both real government spending and budget deficits as a share of GDP have increased. Despite these fiscal policy differences, solid economic performance was achieved during both periods.

CRITICAL ANALYSIS QUESTIONS

1. Suppose that you are a member of the Council of Economic Advisers. The president has asked you to prepare a statement on the question, "What is the proper fiscal policy for the next twelve months?" Prepare such a statement, indicating (a) the current state of the economy (that is, the unemployment rate, growth in real income, and rate of inflation) and (b) your fiscal policy suggestions. Should the budget be in balance? Explain the reasoning behind your suggestions.

2. *What is the crowding-out effect? How does it modify the implications of the basic Keynesian model with regard to fiscal policy? How does the new classical theory of fiscal policy differ from the crowding-out model?

3. What impact will budget deficits have on the exchange rate value of the dollar? How will this impact net exports and aggregate demand? Explain.

4. Suppose that the government provides each taxpayer with a $1,000 tax rebate financed by issuing additional Treasury bonds. Outline alternative views that predict how this fiscal action will influence interest rates, aggregate demand, output, and employment.

5. Will increases in government spending financed by borrowing help promote a strong recovery from a severe recession? Why or why not?

6. Outline the supply-side view of fiscal policy. How does this view differ from the various demand-side theories? Would a

supply-side economist be more likely to favor a $1,000 rebate to all taxpayers or an equivalent reduction in marginal tax rates? Why?

7. If the government becomes more heavily involved in subsidizing some businesses and sectors of the economy while levying higher taxes on others, how will this influence the quantity of rent seeking? How will this affect long-term growth? Explain your response.

8. Does fiscal policy have a strong impact on aggregate demand? Did the shift of the federal budget from deficit to surplus during the 1990s weaken aggregate demand? Did the government spending increases and large budget deficits of 2008–2011 strengthen aggregate demand? Discuss.

9. *How do persistently large budget deficits affect capital formation and the long-run rate of economic growth? Do the proponents of the Keynesian, crowding-out, and new classical theories agree on the answer to this question? Discuss.

10. Marginal tax rates were cut substantially during the 1980s, and although rates were increased in the early 1990s, the marginal rates applicable in the highest income brackets were still well below the top rates of the 1960s and 1970s. How did the lower rates of the 1980s and 1990s affect the share of taxes paid by high-income taxpayers? Were the lower rates of the 1980s and 1990s good or bad for the economy? Discuss.

11. "In the early stages of the Keynesian revolution, macroeconomists emphasized fiscal policy as the most powerful and balanced remedy for demand management. Gradually, shortcomings of fiscal policy became apparent. The shortcomings stem from timing, politics, macroeconomic theory, and the deficit itself." What is the meaning of this statement by Nobel Laureate Paul Samuelson? Is the statement true?

12. *The American Wind Energy Association argues for additional government support because wind-generated electricity creates more employment per kilowatt-hour than the alternatives: 27 percent more jobs than coal and 66 percent more than natural gas. Is this a sound economic argument for increased use of wind power? If the jobs created pay similar wages, what does the statement imply about the cost of generating energy with wind power relative to coal and natural gas?

*Asterisk denotes questions for which answers are given in Appendix B.

CHAPTER 13

Money and the Banking System

Money is whatever is generally accepted in exchange for goods and services—accepted not as an object to be consumed but as an object that represents a temporary abode of purchasing power to be used for buying still other goods and services. **—Milton Friedman**[1]

The simple macroeconomic model we have developed so far has four major markets: (1) the goods and services market, (2) the resources market, (3) the loanable funds market, and (4) the foreign exchange market. When people make exchanges in any of these markets, they generally use money. Money is used to purchase all types of goods, services, physical assets like houses, and financial assets like stocks and bonds. This chapter focuses on the nature of money, how the banking system works, and how the central bank—the Federal Reserve System in the United States—controls the supply of money.

As you read this chapter, look for answers to the following questions:

- What is money? How is the money supply defined?

- What is a fractional reserve banking system? How does it influence the ability of banks to create money?

- What are the major tools with which the Federal Reserve controls the supply of money?

- How has the conduct of monetary policy by the Federal Reserve changed in recent years?

---

[1]Milton Friedman, *Money Mischief: Episodes in Monetary History* (New York: Harcourt Brace Jovanovich, 1992), 16.

13-1 WHAT IS MONEY?

As the chapter-opening quote from Milton Friedman indicates, money is the item commonly used to pay for goods, services, assets, and outstanding debts. Most modern money is merely paper or electronic digits indicating funds in a bank account. Paradoxically, money has little or no intrinsic value. Nonetheless, most of us would like to have more of it. Why? Because money is an asset that performs three basic functions: It serves as a medium of exchange, it provides a means of storing value for future use, and it is used as an accounting unit.

13-1a MONEY AS A MEDIUM OF EXCHANGE

Money is one of the most important inventions in human history because of its role as a **medium of exchange**. Money simplifies and reduces the costs of transactions. Think what it would be like to live in a barter economy—one without money, in which goods were traded for goods. If you wanted to buy a pair of jeans, for example, you would first have to find someone willing to trade you the jeans for your labor services or something else you were willing to supply. Without money, transaction costs would be exceedingly high and gains from trade vastly reduced. But money frees us from cumbersome barter procedures and "oils the wheels" of trade. As a result, each of us can specialize in the supply of those things that we do best and easily buy the many goods and services we want.

At various times in the past, societies have used gold, silver, beads, seashells, and other commodities as mediums of exchange. It is costly to use a valuable commodity as money. Here's why. Precious metals, like gold, would be cumbersome to carry around for use as payment. In fact, it might even be dangerous to do so. Moreover, think about how much it costs to create a hundred dollar bill: just a cent or two, perhaps. But if gold bars, for example, were used instead of bills as money, it would take a lot of resources to produce enough of them to facilitate today's current volume of trade. Further, if a precious metal were used as money, people would employ scarce resources producing "money," and as a result, fewer resources would be available to produce desired goods and services.

Medium of exchange
An asset that is used to buy and sell goods or services.

13-1b MONEY AS A STORE OF VALUE

Money is also a financial asset—a method of storing value for use in the future. Put another way, it provides readily available purchasing power for dealing with an uncertain future. Thus, most people hold some of their wealth in the form of money. Moreover, it is the most **liquid** of all assets. It can be easily and quickly transformed into other goods at a low transaction cost, usually without an appreciable loss in value.

However, there are some disadvantages of using money as a **store of value**. The value of a unit of money—a dollar, for example—is measured in terms of what it will buy. Its value, therefore, is inversely related to the price level in the economy. When inflation is present, the purchasing power of money declines—as does its usefulness as a store of value. This imposes a cost on people holding money.

Other assets, like land, houses, stocks, or bonds, also serve as a store of value, but they aren't as liquid as money. It will take time to locate an acceptable buyer for a house, a plot of land, or an office building. Stocks and bonds are quite liquid—they can usually be sold quickly for only a small commission—but they are not readily acceptable as a direct means of payment.

Liquid asset
An asset that can be easily and quickly converted to money without loss of value.

Store of value
An asset that will allow people to transfer purchasing power from one period to the next.

13-1c MONEY AS A UNIT OF ACCOUNT

Money also serves as a **unit of account**. Just as we use yards or meters to measure distance, we use units of money—the dollar in the United States—to measure the exchange value and cost of goods, services, assets, and resources. The value (and cost) of movie tickets, personal computers, labor services, automobiles, houses, and numerous other items

Unit of account
A unit of measurement used by people to post prices and keep track of revenues and costs.

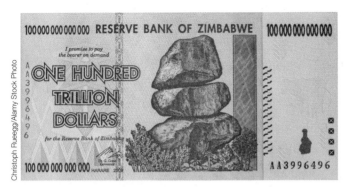

Zimbabwe's $100-trillion-dollar note is shown here. As the Zimbabwe government expanded the money supply at an exceedingly rapid rate during 2006–2008, purchasing power of the currency declined precipitously. As its function as a medium of exchange was eroded, eventually it was replaced by the U.S. dollar.

Fiat money
Money that has neither intrinsic value nor the backing of a commodity with intrinsic value; paper currency is an example.

is measured in units of money. Money serves as a common denominator for the expression of both costs and benefits. If consumers are going to spend their income wisely, they must be able to compare the costs of a vast array of goods and services. Prices measured in units of money help them make such comparisons. Similarly, sound business decisions require cost and revenue comparisons. Resource prices and accounting procedures measured in money units facilitate this task.

13-2 HOW THE SUPPLY OF MONEY AFFECTS ITS VALUE

Money in most modern nations is **fiat money**—money with no intrinsic value. Why is fiat money valuable? Governments often designate it as "legal tender," meaning it must be accepted as payment for debt. But the main thing that makes money valuable is the same thing that generates value for other commodities: demand relative to supply. People demand money because it reduces the cost of exchange and provides other valuable services. When the supply of money is limited relative to the demand, money will become more valuable. Conversely, when the supply of money expands relative to demand, it will become less valuable.

If the purchasing power of money is to remain stable over time, its supply must be limited. When the supply of money grows more rapidly than the output of goods and services, prices will rise. In layman's terms, "too much money is chasing too few goods."

When government authorities rapidly expand the supply of money, it becomes less valuable in exchange and is virtually useless as a store of value. The rapid growth in the supply of money in Germany following World War I provides a dramatic illustration of this point. During the period 1922–1923, the supply of German marks increased by 250 percent in some months. The German government was printing money almost as fast as the printing presses would run. Because money became substantially more plentiful in relation to goods and services, it quickly lost its value. As a result, an egg cost 80 billion marks and a loaf of bread 200 billion. Workers picked up their wages in suitcases. Shops closed at the lunch hour to change price tags. The value of money had eroded. More recently, several countries including Poland, Russia, Ukraine, Zimbabwe, and Venezuela, have followed this same pattern. These countries expanded the supply of money rapidly to pay for government expenditures and, as a result, experienced very high rates of inflation. Thus, while fiat money is economical to produce, this feature also makes it easier for governments to use money creation to finance expenditures, expand the money supply rapidly, and thereby erode its purchasing power.

13-3 HOW IS THE MONEY SUPPLY MEASURED?

How is the money supply defined and measured? There is not a single answer to this question. Economists and policy makers have developed several alternative measures. We will briefly describe the two most widely used measures.

13-3a THE M1 MONEY SUPPLY

M1 (money supply)
The sum of (1) currency in circulation (including coins), and (2) checkable deposits maintained in depository institutions.

Currency
Medium of exchange made of metal or paper.

Above all else, money is a medium of exchange. The narrowest definition of the money supply, **M1**, focuses on this function. Based on its role as a medium of exchange, it is clear that **currency**—coins and paper bills—falls into this definition. But currency isn't the only form of money readily used for exchange. If you want to buy something from a store, many will let you pay with either a check or debit card that will transfer funds from your bank account to theirs. Therefore, checkable bank deposits that can easily be used as a means of payment should be included in the M1 money supply measure.

There are two kinds of checkable deposits. First, there are **demand deposits**, non–interest-earning deposits with banking institutions that are available for withdrawal ("on demand") at any time without restrictions. Demand deposits are usually withdrawn either by writing a check or by using a debit card tied to your account. Second, there are **other checkable deposits** that earn interest but carry some restrictions on their transferability. Interest-earning checkable deposits generally either limit the number of checks depositors can write each month or require the depositor to maintain a substantial minimum balance ($1,000, for example).

Like currency and demand deposits, interest-earning checkable deposits are available for use as a medium of exchange. ***Thus, the M1 money supply comprises (1) currency in circulation and (2) checkable deposits (both demand deposits and interest-earning checkable deposits).***

As Exhibit 1 shows, the total M1 money supply in the United States was $4,010 billion in February 2020. Demand and other checkable deposits accounted for more than one-half of the M1 money supply. This large share reflects the fact that most of the nation's business is conducted with checks and electronic payment transfers.

13-3b THE BROADER M2 MONEY SUPPLY

In modern economies, several financial assets can be easily converted into checkable deposits or currency; therefore, the line between money and "near monies" is often blurred. Broader definitions of the money supply include various assets that can be easily converted to checking account funds and cash. The most common broad definition of the money supply is **M2**. It includes all the items included in M1 plus (1) savings deposits, (2) time deposits of less than $100,000 at all **depository institutions**, and (3) money market mutual funds.

Although the non-M1 components of the M2 money supply are not generally used as a means of making payment, they can be easily and quickly converted to currency or

Demand deposits
Non–interest-earning checking deposits that can be either withdrawn or made payable on demand to a third party. Like currency, these deposits are widely used as a means of payment.

Other checkable deposits
Interest-earning deposits that are also available for checking.

M2 (money supply)
Equal to M1 plus (1) savings deposits, (2) time deposits (accounts of less than $100,000) held in depository institutions, and (3) money market mutual fund shares.

Depository institutions
Businesses that accept checking and savings deposits and use a portion of them to extend loans and make investments. Banks, savings and loan associations, and credit unions are examples.

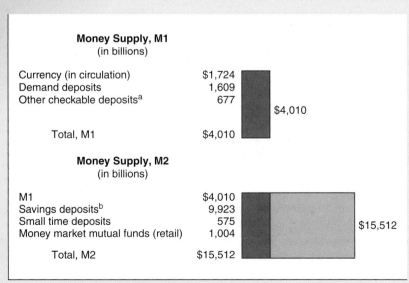

EXHIBIT 1

Money Supply, M1 (in billions)		
Currency (in circulation)	$1,724	
Demand deposits	1,609	
Other checkable deposits[a]	677	$4,010
Total, M1	$4,010	

Money Supply, M2 (in billions)		
M1	$4,010	
Savings deposits[b]	9,923	
Small time deposits	575	
Money market mutual funds (retail)	1,004	$15,512
Total, M2	$15,512	

[a]Traveler's checks are included in other checkable deposits.
[b]Including money market deposit accounts.

Source: http://www.federalreserve.gov.

The Composition of Money Supply in the United States

The size and composition (as of February 2020) of the two most widely used measures of the money supply are shown. M1, the narrowest definition of the money supply, is composed of currency and checking deposits. M2, which contains M1 plus the various savings components indicated, is approximately four times the size of M1.

©iStockphoto.com/Sinopics

checkable deposits for such use. For example, if you maintain funds in a savings account, you can easily transfer the funds to your checking account. **Money market mutual funds** are interest-earning accounts offered by banks and brokerage firms that pool depositors' funds and invest them in highly liquid short-term securities. Because these securities can be quickly converted to cash, depositors are permitted to write checks against these accounts.

Many economists—particularly those who stress the store-of-value function of money—prefer the broader M2 definition of the money supply to the narrower M1 concept. As Exhibit 1 shows, in February 2020 the M2 money supply was $15,512 billion, about four times the M1 money supply. Other definitions of the money supply have been developed for specialized purposes, but the M1 and M2 definitions are the most important and most widely used.

13-3c CREDIT CARDS VERSUS MONEY

Money market mutual funds
Interest-earning accounts that pool depositors' funds and invest them in highly liquid short-term securities. Because these securities can be quickly converted to cash, depositors are permitted to write checks (which reduce their share holdings) against their accounts.

Credit
Funds acquired by borrowing.

It is important to distinguish between money and credit. Money is a financial asset that provides the holder with future purchasing power. **Credit** is a liability acquired when one borrows funds. This distinction sheds light on a question students frequently ask: "Because credit cards are often used to make purchases, why aren't credit card expenditures part of the money supply?" In contrast with money, credit cards do not have purchasing power. They are merely a convenient way of arranging a loan. When you use your Visa or MasterCard to buy an iPad, for example, you are not really paying for the tablet. Instead, you are taking out a loan from the institution issuing your card, and that institution is paying for the iPad. You haven't paid for the iPad until you've paid your credit card bill down far enough to cover its cost. The same goes for your other credit card purchases. Thus, credit cards are not money because they don't represent purchasing power. Instead, the outstanding balance on your credit card is a liability, money you owe to the company that issued the card.

Although credit cards are not money, their use will influence the amount of money people will want to hold. Credit cards make it possible for people to buy things throughout the month and then pay for them in a single transaction at the end of the month. This makes it possible for people to conduct their regular business affairs with less money than would otherwise be needed. Thus, widespread use of credit cards will tend to reduce the average quantity of money people hold.

13-4 THE BUSINESS OF BANKING

Federal reserve system
The central bank of the United States; it carries out banking regulatory policies and is responsible for the conduct of monetary policy.

Central bank
An institution that regulates the banking system and controls the money supply.

We must understand a few things about the business of banking before we can explain the factors that influence the supply of money. The banking industry in the United States operates under the jurisdiction of the **Federal Reserve System**, the nation's **central bank**. We will discuss the Federal Reserve System in detail later in this chapter.

The banking system is an important component of the loanable funds market. Like other private businesses, banks are profit-seeking operations. Banks provide services (for example, the safekeeping of funds and checking account services) and pay interest to attract both checking and savings depositors. They help bring together people who want to save for the future and those who want to borrow in order to undertake investment projects. The primary source of revenue for banks is the income they derive from their loans and investments.

When deciding whether to extend a loan for a project, bankers have a strong incentive to take into account the project's expected profitability and the borrower's creditworthiness. If the borrowed funds are channeled into an unprofitable project, the borrower may not be able to repay the bank for the loan. This incentive structure provides the bank with a strong incentive to support projects that are expected to be profitable. The efficient allocation of investment funds by banks is an important source of economic growth. Profitable business projects increase the value of resources and promote economic growth; unprofitable projects have the opposite effect and tie up resources better used elsewhere. Thus, an efficiently operating loanable funds market is an important source of growth and prosperity, and the banking system plays a central role in the operation of this market.

In the United States, the banking system consists of **savings and loan institutions**, **credit unions**, and **commercial banks**. All of these institutions now accept both checking and savings deposits and extend a wide variety of loans to their customers. They are all under the jurisdiction of the Federal Reserve System, which applies similar regulations and offers similar services to each. ***Therefore, when we speak of the banking industry, we are referring not only to commercial banks but also to savings and loan associations and credit unions.***

The major functions of banks can be discerned by examining their balance sheets. The major liabilities of banks are transaction (checking), savings, and time deposits. *From the viewpoint of a bank*, these are liabilities because they represent an obligation of the bank to its depositors. Outstanding interest-earning loans constitute the major class of banking assets. In addition, most banks own sizable amounts of interest-earning securities—bonds issued by either governments or private corporations. Banks use the deposits of their customers to finance their loans and investments.

Typically, banks will keep some of their assets in the form of **bank reserves**—vault cash or deposits with the Federal Reserve. These reserves place the bank in a position to provide customers with their money if they want to withdraw some of their deposits. Historically, Federal Reserve regulations required banks to maintain a fraction of their assets in the form of reserves. This requirement was eliminated in March of 2020. We will return to this issue as we proceed, but before we do so, we want to explain the historical development and operation of a fractional reserve banking system.

13-4a FRACTIONAL RESERVE BANKING

Economists often draw an analogy between our current banking system and the goldsmiths of a long-ago era. In the past, gold was used as the means of making payments. It was money. People would store their money with a goldsmith for safekeeping, just as many of us open a checking account for safety reasons. Gold owners received a certificate granting them the right to withdraw their gold any time they wished. If they wanted to buy something, they would go to the goldsmith, withdraw gold, and use it as a means of making a payment. Thus, the money supply was equal to the amount of gold in circulation plus the gold deposited with goldsmiths.

It was inconvenient to make a trip to the goldsmith every time one wanted to buy something. Because the certificates were redeemable in gold, they began to circulate as a means of payment. The depositors were pleased with this arrangement because it eliminated the need for a trip to the goldsmith every time something was purchased. As long as they had confidence in the goldsmith, sellers were glad to accept the certificates as payment.

As gold certificates began to circulate, the daily withdrawals and deposits with goldsmiths declined even more. Goldsmiths earned money by lending out gold. They made nothing on the gold just sitting in their vaults. Think what would happen if the local goldsmiths kept 20 percent of the total gold deposited with them in order to meet the day-to-day requests to redeem gold certificates and loaned out the remaining 80 percent to merchants, traders, and other citizens. One hundred percent of the gold certificates would then circulate as money, along with that portion of gold that had been loaned out—80 percent of total deposits, in other words. As a result, the *total* money supply circulating in the economy—gold certificates plus actual gold—would expand to 1.8 times the amount of gold deposited

Savings and loan institutions
Financial institutions that accept deposits in exchange for shares that pay dividends. Historically, these funds were channeled into residential mortgage loans, but today they offer essentially the same services as a commercial bank.

Credit unions
Financial cooperative organizations of individuals with a common affiliation (such as an employer or a labor union). They accept deposits, including checkable deposits, pay interest (or dividends) on them out of earnings, and lend funds primarily to members.

Commercial banks
Financial institutions that offer a wide range of services (for example, checking accounts, savings accounts, and loans) to their customers. Commercial banks are owned by stockholders and seek to operate at a profit.

Bank reserves
Vault cash plus deposits of banks with Federal Reserve banks.

with the goldsmiths. By issuing loans and retaining only a fraction of the total gold in their vaults, the goldsmiths actually increased the money supply.

In principle, our modern banking system is quite similar to goldsmithing. Like the goldsmiths, banks maintain a fraction of their assets as reserves—either vault cash or deposits with the Federal Reserve. Just as the early goldsmiths did not have enough gold to pay all their depositors simultaneously, within the framework of a **fractional reserve banking** system, banks also do not have enough reserves to pay all depositors at once. To make money, the early goldsmiths loaned out some of their gold, and as they did so, their actions expanded the supply of money. Modern bankers also extend loans and undertake investments in order to generate earnings, and their actions also expand the money supply.

There are important differences between modern banking and early goldsmithing, though. Today, the actions of individual banks are regulated by a central bank. The central bank is supposed to follow policies designed to promote a healthy economy. It also acts as a lender of last resort. If the customers of a bank all attempted to withdraw their deposits simultaneously, the central bank would intervene and supply the bank with enough funds to meet the demand.

Fractional reserve banking
A system that permits banks to hold reserves of less than 100 percent against their deposits.

13-4b BANK RUNS, BANK FAILURES, AND DEPOSIT INSURANCE

Compared to other businesses, banks are more vulnerable to failure because their liabilities to depositors are current but most of their assets are illiquid. This means that if a significant share of depositors lose confidence and withdraw their funds from a bank, it will quickly lead to problems. In turn, when a bank fails, it affects not only the bank's owners and employees but its depositors as well. If many banks fail, the effects can spread and undermine the operation of an economy.

The U.S. economy has had its share of banking problems. Between 1922 and 1933, more than 10,000 banks (one-third of the total) failed. Most of these failures were the result of "bank runs"—panic withdrawals when people lost confidence in the banking system. Remember, under a fractional reserve system, banks do not have a sufficient amount of reserves to redeem the funds of all (or even most) depositors if they should seek to withdraw their funds at the same time.

The bank failures of the 1920s and 1930s led to the establishment of the **Federal Deposit Insurance Corporation (FDIC)** in 1934. The FDIC guarantees the deposits of banking customers up to some limit—currently $250,000 per account. Even if the bank should fail, depositors will be able to get their money (up to the $250,000 limit). Member banks pay an insurance premium to the FDIC for each dollar deposited with them, and the FDIC uses these premiums to reimburse depositors when a bank fails.

The FDIC protected depositors, restored confidence, and led to the virtual elimination of bank runs. But there is a down side to the system: It reduces the incentive of depositors to monitor banks and move their funds toward those with a strong portfolio of high-quality investments and loans. As a result, it is easier for banks to undertake riskier investments, which are also a source of bank failure. There are still bank failures; four failed in 2019. But bank failures are far less common now, and they are almost always the result of bad investments rather than bank runs.

Federal Deposit Insurance Corporation (FDIC)
A federally chartered corporation that insures the deposits held by commercial banks, savings and loans, and credit unions.

13-5 HOW BANKS CREATE MONEY BY EXTENDING LOANS

Let us consider a simple banking system where only currency acts as a reserve against deposits. We will also assume that all banks are required by law to maintain 20 percent or more of their deposits as cash in their vaults. This amount is called **required reserves** and the percentage of reserves that must be maintained against checkable deposits is called the **required reserve ratio**. The required reserve ratio in our example is 20 percent.

Required reserves
The minimum amount of reserves that a bank is required by law to keep on hand to back up its deposits. If reserve requirements were 15 percent, banks would be required to keep $150,000 in reserves against each $1 million of deposits.

Required reserve ratio
The ratio of reserves relative to a specified liability category (for example, checkable deposits) that banks are required to maintain.

Now suppose that you find $1,000 that your long-deceased uncle had apparently hidden in the basement of his house. You take the bills to the First National Bank and open a checking account. How much will the $1,000 in your newly opened account expand the economy's money supply? First National is now required to keep $200 of the $1,000 in vault cash—20 percent of your deposit. So after placing $200 in the bank vault, First National has $800 of **excess reserves**—reserves over and above the amount the law requires it to retain. Given its current excess reserves, First National can now extend an $800 loan. Suppose it loans $800 to a local citizen to help pay for a car. At the time the loan is extended, the money supply will increase by $800 as the bank adds the funds to the checking account of the borrower. No one else has less money. You still have your $1,000 checking account, and the borrower has $800 for the car.

When the borrower buys the car, the seller accepts a check and deposits the $800 in a bank, Citizen's State Bank. What happens when the check clears? The temporary excess reserves of the First National Bank will be eliminated when it pays $800 to the Citizen's State Bank. But when Citizen's State Bank receives $800 in currency, it will now have excess reserves. It must keep 20 percent of it, or $160, as required reserves, but the remaining $640 can be loaned out. Because Citizen's State, like other banks, wants to earn income, it will be quite happy to "extend a helping hand" to someone who wants to borrow that money. When the second bank loans out its excess reserves, the deposits of the person borrowing the money will increase by $640. Another $640 has now been added to the money supply. You still have your $1,000, the automobile seller has an additional $800, and the new borrower has just received an additional $640. Because you found the $1,000 and deposited it in the bank, the money supply has increased by $1,440 ($800 + $640).

Of course, the process can continue. Exhibit 2 shows what happens when the money creation process continues through several more stages. When the reserve requirement is 20 percent, the money supply can expand to a maximum of $5,000, the initial $1,000 plus an additional $4,000 in demand deposits that can be created by extending new loans.

The multiple by which new reserves increase the stock of money is called the **deposit expansion multiplier**. As banks use more of the newly created reserves to extend additional loans, the size of the deposit expansion multiplier will increase. In fact, if all of the additional reserves are held as bank deposits rather than currency and the banks loan out all of their excess reserves, the **potential deposit expansion multiplier** is merely the

Excess reserves
Actual reserves that exceed the legal requirement.

Deposit expansion multiplier
The multiple by which an increase in reserves will increase the money supply. It will be larger when banks loan out a larger share of the newly created reserves.

Potential deposit expansion multiplier
The maximum potential increase in the money supply as a ratio of the new reserves injected into the banking system. If the newly created reserves are all held as bank deposits rather than currency and banks loan out all of their excess reserves, it will be equal to the inverse of the required reserve ratio.

EXHIBIT 2

Creating Money from New Reserves

When banks are required to maintain 20 percent reserves against demand deposits, the creation of $1,000 of new reserves will potentially increase the supply of money by $5,000.

Bank	New Cash Deposits: Actual Reserves	New Required Reserves	Potential Demand Deposits Created by Extending New Loans
Initial deposit (Bank A)	$1,000.00	$ 200.00	$ 800.00
Second stage (Bank B)	800.00	160.00	640.00
Third stage (Bank C)	640.00	128.00	512.00
Fourth stage (Bank D)	512.00	102.40	409.60
Fifth stage (Bank E)	409.60	81.92	327.68
Sixth stage (Bank F)	327.68	65.54	262.14
Seventh stage (Bank G)	262.14	52.43	209.71
All others (other banks)	1,048.58	209.71	838.87
Total	5,000.00	1,000.00	4,000.00

reciprocal of the required reserve ratio (r). Mathematically, the potential deposit expansion multiplier is equal to $1/r$. In our example, the required reserves are 20 percent or one-fifth of the total deposits. So the potential deposit expansion multiplier is 5. If only 10 percent reserves were required, the potential deposit expansion multiplier would be 10, the reciprocal of one-tenth. *The lower the percentage of reserves required, the larger the potential expansion in the money supply generated by creation of new reserves. However, the fractional reserve requirement does place a ceiling on the expansion in the money supply resulting from the creation of new reserves.*

13-5a THE ACTUAL DEPOSIT EXPANSION MULTIPLIER

Will the introduction of new currency reserves fully expand the money supply by the amount of the multiplier? The answer is "No." The actual deposit expansion multiplier will generally be less than its potential for two reasons.[2]

First, the deposit expansion multiplier will be reduced if some people decide to hold the currency rather than deposit it in a bank. For example, suppose the person who borrowed the $800 in the preceding example spends only $700 and stashes the remaining $100 away for a possible emergency. Only $700 can then end up as a deposit in the second stage and contribute to the excess reserves that underlie the expansion of the money supply. The potential of new loans in the second stage and in all subsequent stages will be reduced proportionally. When currency remains in circulation outside of banks, it reduces the size of the deposit expansion multiplier.

Second, the actual deposit expansion multiplier will be less than its maximum potential if banks fail to use all the new excess reserves to extend loans. Banks are in business to make profit, and they will generally be able to increase their net income by extending loans and undertaking investments, rather than holding excess reserves. Prior to 2008, this was certainly the case, as banks shaved their excess reserves to minimal levels. However, in October 2008, the Federal Reserve began paying banks interest on their reserves. Like the required reserve ratio, this interest rate can be used to affect the reserve assets of banks and therefore the size of the deposit expansion multiplier. There will be an inverse relationship between the ratio of bank reserves to checkable deposits and the deposit expansion multiplier. The larger the ratio of bank reserves to checkable deposits, the smaller the deposit expansion multiplier. We now turn to an examination of the Federal Reserve and the tools it has to control the money supply of the United States.

13-6 THE FEDERAL RESERVE SYSTEM

Most countries have a central banking authority that controls the money supply and conducts monetary policy. As we previously noted, the central bank of the United States is the Federal Reserve System. The European Central Bank is the central bank for countries using the euro as their currency. In the United Kingdom, the central bank is the Bank of England; in Canada, it is the Bank of Canada; in Japan, it is the Bank of Japan. Central banks are responsible for the conduct of monetary policy.

13-6a STRUCTURE OF THE FED

The Federal Reserve (and most other central banks) is supposed to regulate the money supply and provide a monetary climate that is in the best interest of the entire economy. Congress has instructed the Federal Reserve, or the Fed, as it is often called, to conduct monetary policy in a manner that promotes both full employment and price stability. Unlike commercial banks, the Federal Reserve is not a profit-making institution. The earnings of the Fed, over and above its expenses, belong to the U.S. Treasury.

---

[2]With the Fed's elimination of a formal reserve requirement in March 2020, the potential deposit expansion multiplier now has little relevance; however, the actual deposit expansion multiplier is still relevant and influenced by the holding of reserves by banks.

EXHIBIT 3

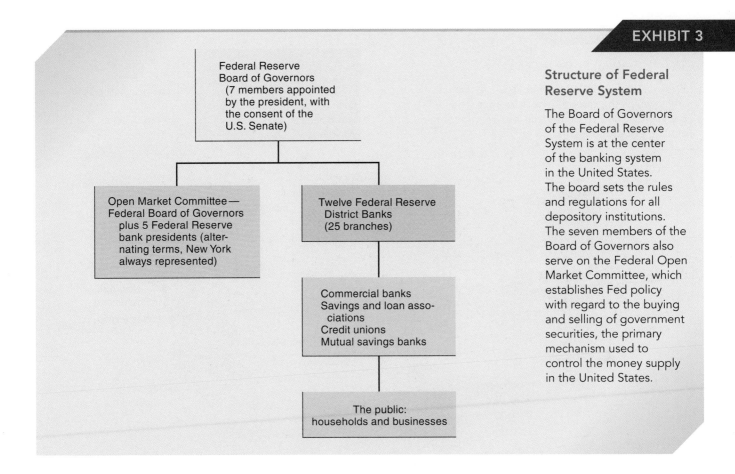

Structure of Federal Reserve System

The Board of Governors of the Federal Reserve System is at the center of the banking system in the United States. The board sets the rules and regulations for all depository institutions. The seven members of the Board of Governors also serve on the Federal Open Market Committee, which establishes Fed policy with regard to the buying and selling of government securities, the primary mechanism used to control the money supply in the United States.

Exhibit 3 illustrates the structure of the Fed. There are three major centers of decision making within the Federal Reserve: (1) the Board of Governors, (2) the district and regional banks, and (3) the Federal Open Market Committee.

The Board of Governors The Board of Governors is the decision-making hub of the Fed. This powerful board consists of seven members, each appointed to a staggered 14-year term by the nation's president with the advice and consent of the U.S. Senate. The president designates one of the seven members as chair for a four-year term. The Fed chair directs the Federal Reserve staff, presides over board meetings, and testifies frequently before Congress. Because of the importance of monetary policy and the power of the position, the Fed chair is often said to be the second most influential person—next to the president—in the United States. In 2018, Jerome Powell was appointed Fed chair, succeeding Janet Yellen, who served as chair during the previous four years.

The Board of Governors establishes the rules and regulations that apply to all depository institutions. It sets the reserve requirements and regulates the composition of the asset holdings of depository institutions. The board is the rule maker, and often the umpire, of the banking industry.

The Federal Reserve District Banks There are 12 Federal Reserve District Banks with 25 regional branches spread throughout the nation. Exhibit 4 shows the regions covered by each of the twelve district banks. These district and regional banks operate under the supervision of the Board of Governors. Federal Reserve banks are bankers' banks; they provide banking services for commercial banks. Private citizens and corporations do not bank with the Fed.

The district banks are primarily responsible for the monitoring of the commercial banks in their region. They audit the books of depository institutions regularly to ensure their compliance with reserve requirements and other regulations of the Fed. The district

The 12 Federal Reserve Districts

The map shows the 12 Federal Reserve districts and the city in which the district bank is located. These district banks monitor the commercial banks in their region and assist them with the clearing of checks.

If you look at any dollar bill, it will identify the Federal Reserve district bank that initially issued the currency. The Board of Governors of the Fed is located in Washington, D.C.

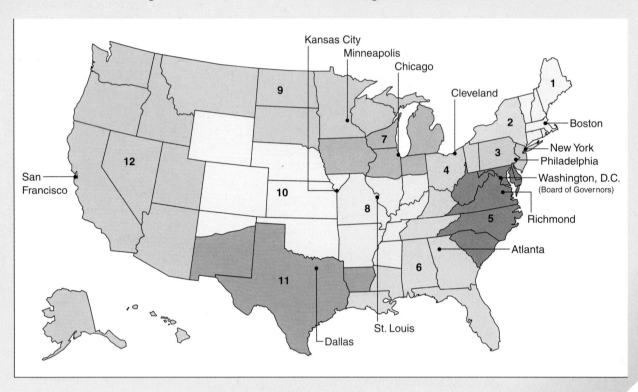

banks also play an important role in the clearing of checks throughout the banking system. Most depository institutions, regardless of their Fed membership status, maintain deposits with Federal Reserve Banks. As a result, the clearing of checks through the Federal Reserve System becomes merely an accounting transaction.

The Federal Open Market Committee The **Federal Open Market Committee (FOMC)** is a powerful committee that determines the Fed's policy with respect to the purchase and sale of government bonds and other financial assets. As we shall soon see, this is the primary tool used by the Fed to control the money supply in the United States. The seven members of the Board of Governors, plus the twelve presidents of the Federal Reserve district banks, participate in the FOMC meetings, but at any point in time, only twelve of the nineteen members will get to vote. The twelve voting members of this important policy-making arm of the Fed are (1) the seven members of the Board of Governors, (2) the president of the New York district bank, and (3) four (of the remaining eleven) additional presidents of the Fed's district banks, who rotate as voting members. The FOMC meets every four to six weeks in the huge conference room of the Federal Reserve Building in Washington, D.C.

The independence of the Fed The structure of the Federal Reserve is designed to insulate it from political pressure and enhance its ability to follow a stable, non-inflationary monetary policy. Several factors contribute to this independence. The Fed does not need to go to Congress for its funding. The Fed's earnings on its financial assets, mostly

Federal Open Market Committee (FOMC)
A committee of the Federal Reserve system that establishes Fed policy with regard to the buying and selling of government securities—the primary mechanism used to control the money supply. It is composed of the seven members of the Board of Governors and the twelve district bank presidents of the Fed.

government bonds, provide it with substantially more funding than is needed to cover its operating costs. The Fed does not even need to undergo audits from the General Accounting Office, a government agency that audits the books of most government operations. Like Supreme Court justices, Fed Governors are appointed to lengthy terms design to diminish political influence on their decision-making. The seven members of the Board of Governors are appointed to staggered fourteen-year terms. Because a Board member is appointed only every two years, even two-term presidents are well into their second term before they are able to appoint a majority of the Fed's governing board. The independence derived from the lengthy terms, however, may be more apparent than real. Fed Governors have very attractive private sector alternatives; therefore, they often resign well before the end of their term. The average tenure of members of the Board of Governors appointed during the past two decades has fallen to less than five years. This makes it easier for a President to influence the Board. For example, by the seventh year of his two terms, President Obama had appointed every member of the Fed's Board of Governors. Moreover, by the end of his third year, President Trump had already appointed a majority of the Fed Board of Governors.

Does the independence of a central bank affect policy? There is considerable variation in the independence of central banks. Like the Fed, the European Central bank and the central banks of Japan, England, and Canada also have considerable independence from the other branches of their governments. In other instances, however, central banks are directly beholden to political officials. Studies indicate that central banks that are strongly influenced by political considerations are more likely to follow inflationary policies. Politicians in countries with high budget deficits have often pressured their central banks to expand the money supply in order to finance government spending. When they do so, the result is rapid growth in the money supply and inflation.

13-6b HOW THE FED CONTROLS THE MONEY SUPPLY

The Fed has four potential tools it can use to control the money supply: (1) the establishment of reserve requirements for banks, (2) buying and selling U.S. government securities and other financial assets in the open market, (3) the extension of loans to banks and other institutions, and (4) the interest rate it pays banks on funds held as reserves. We will analyze how each of these tools can be used to regulate the amount of money in circulation.

Reserve requirements Prior to March 2020, the Federal Reserve required banks to maintain a fraction of their assets in the form of reserves—vault cash and deposits with the Fed—against their checking deposits. Historically, reserve requirements were a tool the Fed used to control the money supply. If the Fed wanted to increase the supply of money, it could reduce the reserve requirements. The lower required reserve ratio would increase the excess reserves of banks, placing them in a position to extend more loans and undertake additional investments. Because banks are in business to make money, they would generally use the newly created excess reserves to increase their outstanding loans and investments. As they did so, their actions would increase the supply of money.

In contrast, an increase in the reserve requirements would have the opposite effect. The higher reserve requirements would force banks to maintain more of their assets as vault cash and deposits with the Fed and reduce their funds available to extend loans and undertake investments. As banks cut back on their loans and investments, their actions would decrease the money supply.

In recent decades, the Fed required banks to maintain reserves of approximately 10 percent against the checkable deposits of their customers. However, changes in the reserve requirements were seldom used as a tool with which to alter the money supply. Changes in reserve requirements are a blunt instrument, and they can be disruptive to banking operations. As a result, for several decades, the Fed has generally preferred to use its other tools to control the supply of money. Further, in 2008, the Fed began paying banks interest on their reserves. This provided the Fed with an alternative tool to control the reserves of banking institutions, further diminishing the role of reserve requirements. In March of

2020, the Fed eliminated reserve requirements. Does this mean that reserve requirements will not be used as a tool of monetary policy in the future? It is too early to jump to that conclusion. The Fed has indicated that reserve requirements could be reinstituted if warranted by future conditions.

Open market operations The most common tool used by the Fed to alter the money supply is **open market operations**—the buying and selling of U.S. securities and other financial assets on the open market. As we indicated earlier, Fed policy in this area is conducted by the Federal Open Market Committee (FOMC). This committee meets every few weeks to map out the Fed's policy.

For six decades following World War II, the Fed purchased and sold only U.S. government securities in its conduct of open market operations. However, since 2008, the Fed has been buying and selling a broader range of financial assets, including corporate bonds, commercial paper, and mortgage-backed securities. If the Fed wants to expand the money supply, it simply purchases more of these financial assets. It pays for them merely by writing a check on itself. Unlike you and me, the Fed does not have to check to see if it has adequate funds in its account. ***When the Fed buys things, it injects "new money" into the economy in the form of additional currency in circulation and deposits with commercial banks. In essence, the Fed creates money out of nothing.***

Consider the following case. Suppose the Fed purchases $10,000 of U.S. securities from Maria Valdez. The Fed receives the securities, and Valdez receives a check for $10,000. If she merely cashes the check drawn on the Federal Reserve, the amount of currency in circulation would expand by $10,000, increasing the money supply by that amount. If, as is more likely to be the case, she deposits the funds in her checking account at the First National Bank, her checking account will increase by $10,000, and the bank's reserves will also increase by that amount. The additional reserves will place the bank in a position to extend more loans or undertake more investment. Suppose the bank decides to keep 10 percent of the deposit in reserves (vault cash and deposits with the Fed) and extend $9,000 of additional loans. As the deposit expansion multiplier indicates, the extension of the new loans will contribute to a further expansion in the money supply. Moreover, part of the new loans will eventually be deposited in other banks, and these banks will also be able to extend additional loans. As the process continues, the money supply expands by a multiple of the securities purchased by the Fed.

Open market operations can also be used to reduce the money supply. ***If the Fed wants to reduce the money supply, it sells some of its current holdings of government securities or other assets.*** When the Fed sells assets, a buyer like Maria Valdez will pay for them with a check drawn on a commercial bank. As the check clears, both the buyer's checkable deposits and the reserves of the bank on which the check was written will decline. Thus, the action will reduce the money supply both directly (by reducing checkable deposits) and indirectly (by reducing the quantity of reserves available to the banking system).

Extension of loans by the Fed When banking institutions borrow from the Federal Reserve, they must pay interest on the loans. Historically, member banks have borrowed from the Fed primarily to meet temporary shortages of reserves. The interest rate that banks pay on these short-term loans from the Federal Reserve is called the **discount rate**. Essentially, these loans through the discount window are for brief time periods, generally a few days or weeks. Essentially, these discount rate loans are a temporary bridge extended to banks with a short-term liquidity problem, and typically they are repaid in a matter of days or a few months at the most. Other things being constant, an increase in the discount rate will reduce borrowing from the Fed and thereby exert a restrictive impact on the money supply. Conversely, a lower discount rate will make it cheaper for banks to borrow from the Fed and exert an expansionary impact on the supply of money.

Prior to 2008, the Fed extended only short-term discount rate loans, and they were extended only to member banks. As the Fed responded to the severe downturn of 2008, there was a dramatic change in its loan extension policy. The Fed began making longer-term

Open market operations
The buying and selling of U.S. government securities and other financial assets in the open market by the Federal Reserve.

Discount rate
The interest rate the Federal Reserve charges banking institutions for short-term loans.

loans as well as loans to nonbank financial institutions such as insurance companies and brokerage firms. Like the discount rate loans, these new types of loans injected additional reserves into the banking system and thereby exerted an expansionary impact on the money supply. In 2020, the Fed again expanded the range of its loan activities, extending loans to businesses and even municipal governments experiencing financial difficulties. Of course, these loans would also expand both bank reserves and the money supply.

Interest rate the Fed pays banks on reserves Beginning in October 2008, the Fed began paying commercial banks interest on their reserves. Payment of interest on reserves places the Fed in a position to exert a major impact on the reserves of banks. The Fed can set the interest rate on these reserves at whatever rate it chooses. This provides it with a tool with which to both control the reserves of banks and conduct monetary policy.

If the Fed wants the banks to expand the money supply by extending more loans, it will set the interest rate paid on reserves at a very low level, possibly even zero. This will encourage banks to use more of their reserves to extend additional loans, and thereby expand the supply of money. On the other hand, if the Fed wants to reduce the money supply, it can increase the interest rate paid on reserves and thereby increase the incentive of banks to hold more reserves and extend fewer loans. This will reduce the deposit expansion multiplier and thereby reduce the money supply.

Since 2010, the Fed has used this tool to increase the bank holdings of reserves against checking deposits to substantially higher levels than was previously the case. In early 2020, the reserves of banks were nearly 80 percent as large as their checking deposits. This high ratio of bank reserves to checking deposits explains why it was possible for the Fed to eliminate the 10 percent reserve requirement in March 2020 without exerting a significant impact on banking operations. As we previously discussed, the deposit expansion multiplier is inversely linked to the ratio of bank reserves to checking deposits. Interestingly, because the ratio of bank reserves to checking deposits has been higher since the Fed began using interest payments rather than reserve requirements to control bank reserves, the deposit expansion multiplier has been smaller.

Controlling the money supply—a summary Exhibit 5 summarizes the monetary tools of the Federal Reserve. If the Fed wants to increase the money supply, it can decrease reserve requirements, purchase additional financial assets, extend additional loans, and/or lower the interest rate it pays banks on excess reserves. On the other hand, if the Fed wants to reduce the money supply, it can increase the reserve requirements, sell some of its asset holdings, extend fewer loans, and/or pay banks a higher interest rate on their excess reserves. Because the Fed typically seeks only small changes in the money stock (or its rate of increase), at any point in time, it typically uses only one of these tools, usually open market operations, to accomplish a desired objective.

13-6c RECENT FED POLICY, THE MONETARY BASE, AND THE MONEY SUPPLY

Federal Reserve policy changed dramatically during the financial crisis of 2008. Seeking to combat the severe economic downturn, the Fed both (1) sharply increased its asset purchases to substantially increase the reserves available to the banking system, and (2) began extending loans to troubled non-bank institutions, the collapse of which might have endangered the stability of financial markets. The Fed also began paying banks interest on their reserve deposits held with the Fed. These policy changes can be observed in the pattern and movement of several monetary aggregates.

The **monetary base** is a highly important monetary aggregate because it provides the foundation for the money supply. The monetary base is equal to the currency in circulation plus the reserves of commercial banks (vault cash and reserve deposits with the Fed). The currency in circulation contributes directly to the money supply, while the bank reserves provide the underpinnings for checking deposits.

Monetary base
The sum of currency in circulation plus bank reserves (vault cash and reserves with the Fed). It reflects the purchases of financial assets and extension of loans by the Fed.

EXHIBIT 5

Summary of Monetary Tools of the Federal Reserve

FEDERAL RESERVE POLICY	EXPANSIONARY MONETARY POLICY	RESTRICTIVE MONETARY POLICY
1. Reserve requirements[a]	*Reduce reserve requirements* because this will create additional excess reserves and induce banks to extend more loans, which will expand the money supply.	*Raise reserve requirements* because this will reduce the excess reserves of banks and induce them to make fewer loans, which will contract the money supply.
2. Open market operations	*Purchase additional U.S. securities and other assets,* which will increase the money supply and also expand the reserves available to banks.	*Sell U.S. securities and other assets,* which will decrease the money supply and also contract the reserves available to banks.
3. Extension of loans	*Extend more loans* because this will increase bank reserves, encouraging banks to make more loans and expand the money supply.	*Extend fewer loans* because this will decrease bank reserves, discourage bank loans, and reduce the money supply.
4. Interest paid on excess bank reserves	*Reduce the interest paid on excess reserves* because this will induce banks to hold less reserves and extend more loans, which will expand the money supply.	*Increase the interest paid on excess reserves* because this will induce banks to hold more reserves and extend fewer loans, which will contract the money supply.

[a]Beginning in October of 2008, the Fed began paying banks interest on their reserves held as deposits with the Fed. Since that time, this has been the primary tool used by the Fed to influence bank reserves. In March of 2020, the Fed eliminated (reduced the required reserve ratio to zero) the reserve requirement on bank deposits.

Exhibit 6 shows the path of the monetary base since 1990. Before 2008, as the Fed increased its purchases of Treasury securities, the monetary base increased, leading to an even larger increase in the M1 money supply just as the deposit expansion multiplier implies. Some of the additional reserves went into currency and some into bank reserves. In turn, banks used most of their additional reserves to extend loans and undertake investments, which further enhanced the expansion in the money supply. During this era, banks shaved their excess reserves to near zero because neither vault cash nor deposits with the Fed generated revenue for the bank. As Exhibit 6 illustrates, under these conditions, the (1) monetary base and (2) currency plus required reserves were virtually equal, and they moved up in lockstep together. Throughout this period, as the Fed injected additional reserves into the system and thereby expanded the monetary base, the M1 money supply increased by a similar proportion.

But all of this changed dramatically starting in the second half of 2008 as the Fed increased its security holdings and outstanding loans and began paying banks interest on their reserve deposits with the Fed. To combat the 2008–2009 recession, the Fed adopted a series of quantitative easing policies. The quantitative easing policies involved huge purchases of both Treasury and mortgage-back securities, as well as a large increase in loans to non-banking institutions. The Fed's huge increase in asset purchases and extension of loans during and following the 2008–2009 recession dramatically increased the monetary base. As Exhibit 6 shows, the monetary base (currency plus bank reserves) doubled between mid-year 2008 and mid-year 2009 and doubled again over the next four years. By 2016 (first quarter), the monetary base had soared to $3.8 trillion, more than four and a half times the figure of mid-year 2008.

How did this more than quadrupling of the monetary base affect the money supply? The M1 money supply expanded at an average annual rate of 7 percent during 2009–2015,

EXHIBIT 6

The Monetary Base, M1 Money Supply, and Excess Reserves, 1990–2020

The monetary base reflects the Fed's purchase of financial assets and its extension of loans. Prior to 2008, the monetary base grew gradually year after year, and excess reserves were negligible. Note, the monetary base and the sum of currency plus required reserves were virtually equal before 2008. While the M1 money supply was substantially greater than the monetary base, the two expanded together. But, since the second half of 2008, Fed asset purchases and extensions of loans have increased bank reserves by a massive amount, causing both the monetary base and excess reserves to soar. However, the M1 money supply increased far less rapidly than the monetary base, because the interest payments on reserve deposits with the Fed encouraged banks to hold more of their assets in the form of reserves.

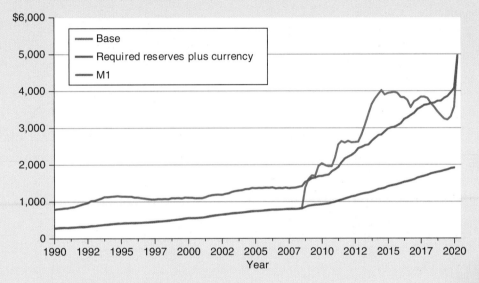

Source: http://www.economagic.com (All figures are in billions.)

while the M2 measure grew at a 6 percent annual rate during the same period. By the first quarter of 2016, the M1 and M2 money supply figures were, respectively, 117 percent and 61 percent greater than in 2008. Although these money supply increases are substantial, they are far less than the expansion in the monetary base. The smaller growth of the money supply compared to the monetary base reflects the impact of the interest payments earned by banks on their deposits with the Fed. These interest payments increase the incentive of banks to hold larger deposits with the Fed and use less of their reserves to extend loans and undertake investments. As a result, the deposit expansion multiplier has been smaller, and therefore, the money supply has not grown nearly as rapidly as the monetary base since 2008. Put another way, while the Fed has vastly increased its asset purchases and expanded the monetary base since 2008, it has used its interest payments on the deposits of banks with the Fed to induce banks to hold more reserves, which reduces the impact of the Fed's asset purchases on the money supply.

As Exhibit 6 illustrates, Fed asset purchases during the 2020 COVID-19 crisis generated another surge in the monetary base. The monetary base increased from $3.4 trillion at the beginning of 2020 to more than $7 trillion just six months later. The M1 money supply also increased rapidly from $4 trillion at the beginning of the year to $5 trillion in June, a 25 percent increase in just six months. There was also a large increase in the reserve holdings of banks during the first half of 2020. Presumably, the Fed will use the interest payments on bank deposits with the Fed in the future to encourage banks to maintain large reserve balances rather than extend loans and thereby expand the money supply by an even larger amount. This will be an interesting experiment to follow.

Exhibit 7 provides additional insight on the impact of the interest payments to banks on their deposits with the Fed. The ratio of bank reserves divided by checking deposits is

EXHIBIT 7

The Ratio of Bank Reserves to Checking Deposits and the Monetary Base to the M1 Money Supply, 1990–2020

The ratio of bank reserves to checking deposits is shown here. This ratio rose after the Fed began paying interest to banks on their deposits with the Fed in 2008 because the interest payments caused banks to hold more reserves against their checking deposits. Similarly, the ratio of the monetary base to the M1 money supply rose after the interest on deposits with the Fed was instituted in 2008 because when banks hold more reserves, increases in the monetary base will exert a smaller expansionary impact on the money supply. Thus, the ratio of the monetary base to the money supply will be higher.

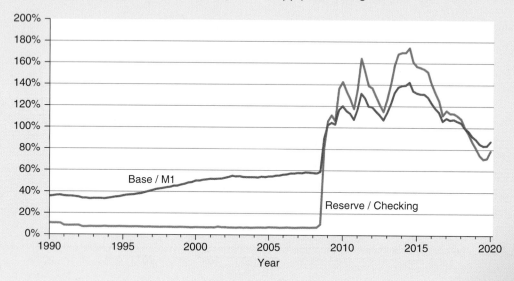

shown here for 1990 through 2020. Before 2008, the reserves were less than 10 percent of the checking deposits. However, between 2009 and the second quarter of 2018, the reserves of banks were 100 percent or more as a share of checking deposits. During the first quarter of 2020, the bank reserves were 79 percent of checking deposits, far greater than prior to 2008. The large increase in bank reserves relative to checking deposits reflects the payment of interest to banks on deposits with the Fed since October of 2008. As the result of these interest payments, banks increased their reserves, causing the reserve/checking deposit ratio to rise. The large reserves of banks relative to their checking deposits also provide insight on the Fed's March 2020 elimination of reserve requirements. Because of the interest earned on deposits with the Fed, most banks already had reserves far greater than the reserve requirement, which had been set at approximately 10 percent for many years. Thus, elimination of this requirement exerted little or no impact on either banking operations or the Fed's control of the money supply.

Exhibit 7 also illustrates the path of the ratio of the monetary base divided by the M1 money supply during 1990–2020. The ratio of the monetary base to the M1 money supply was generally in the 30 to 50 percent range during 1990–2007, but it has been much higher since 2008. In fact, the ratio exceeded 100 percent throughout 2009–2017, and it stood at 88 percent during early 2020. The Fed's payment of interest on reserves also explains why this ratio was higher in the years following 2008. The interest payments on deposits with the Fed encourage banks to hold more reserves and extend fewer loans. As a result, compared to the earlier period, the deposit expansion multiplier was smaller and this reduced the expansionary effects of increases in the monetary base on the M1 money supply. Therefore, the ratio of the monetary base divided by the M1 money supply was higher during 2008–2020 than during 1990–2007.

As Exhibits 6 and 7 highlight, the Fed's conduct of monetary policy has changed dramatically since 2008. The Fed has increased its asset purchases and bank reserves by a huge amount. But, it has used its interest payments to banks to induce them to hold most of these funds as reserves rather than extend loans or undertake investments. Thus the increase in the money supply has been relatively modest.

However, the recent changes have also altered the nature of the Fed. The vast expansion in the Fed's asset purchases provided a substantial share of the financing for the large budget deficits of the federal government. As a result, the Fed now faces more intense pressure to assist with the financing of federal deficits. The Fed's involvement with business has also changed. Beginning with the recession of 2008-2009, the Fed expanded its purchases of mortgage-backed and corporate securities and increased its loans to non-banking businesses. This places the Fed in a position to provide subsidies and other favors to a vast array of private interests. Both of these factors – the expanded role in providing financing for federal deficits and increased involvement with business interests—place additional political pressure on the Fed and detract from its central goal of providing a stable monetary environment. These factors may well exert a major impact on the future operation of the Fed.

13-6d THE FED AND THE TREASURY

Many students tend to confuse the Federal Reserve with the U.S. Treasury, probably because both sound like monetary agencies. However, the Treasury is a budgetary agency. If the federal government is running a budget deficit, the Treasury will issue U.S. securities as a method of financing the deficit. Newly issued U.S. securities are almost always sold to domestic or foreign investors (or government trust funds). Bonds issued by the Treasury to finance a budget deficit are seldom purchased directly by the Federal Reserve. In any case, the Treasury is primarily interested in obtaining funds so that it can pay Uncle Sam's bills. Except for nominal amounts, mostly coins, the Treasury does not issue money. Borrowing—the public sale of new U.S. securities—is the primary method used by the Treasury to cover any excess of expenditures in relation to revenues from taxes and other sources.

While the Treasury is concerned with how the federal government will pay its bills, the Fed is concerned primarily with the availability of money and credit for the entire economy. The Fed does not issue U.S. securities. It merely purchases and sells them as a means of controlling the economy's money supply. Unlike the Treasury, the Fed can purchase government bonds by writing a check on itself without having deposits, gold, or anything else to back it up. In doing so, the Fed creates money out of thin air. The Treasury does not have this power. The Fed does not have an obligation to meet the financial responsibilities of the U.S. government. That is the domain of the Treasury. Although the two agencies cooperate with each other, they are distinctly different institutions established for different purposes (see the accompanying **Thumbnail Sketch**).

Thumbnail Sketch
What Are the Differences between the U.S. Treasury and the Federal Reserve Banking System?

The U.S. Treasury

1. Is concerned with the finances of the federal government
2. Issues bonds and sells them to investors to finance the budget deficits of the federal government
3. Does not determine the money supply

The Federal Reserve

1. Is concerned with the monetary climate of the economy
2. Does not issue bonds
3. Controls the money supply and often uses the buying and selling of bonds issued by the U.S. Treasury to do so

Entrepreneurs Who Have Changed Our Lives:
Peter Thiel

Money reduces transaction costs and thereby promotes gains from trade. Sometimes, transfer systems can provide additional reductions in transaction cost. This is the case with PayPal, a payment system that increases the convenience and security of various types of money transfers. Most of you have probably used PayPal and thereby benefited from the entrepreneurial genius of Peter Thiel. Thiel was a cofounder of PayPal in 1998 and served as its CEO. He sold the online-payment company to eBay in 2002 for $1.5 billion (personally netting $60 million). Thiel is also a major investor in Facebook and still serves on its board of directors.

Born in Germany, Thiel moved as an infant to the United States with his family. His father was a mining engineer, and Peter lived in southern Africa as well as the United States. He was a chess champion in his youth, ranking seventh in the U.S. under-13 age bracket. As a student at Stanford, he founded *The Stanford Review* newspaper. Thiel has also authored a best-selling book on entrepreneurship, *Zero to One*.

Thiel has many and varied talents and interests, from human rights, philosophy, and technology to film. His creativity carries over to his charitable giving. In 2008, he pledged $500,000 to the new Seasteading Institute, to support its mission "to establish permanent, autonomous ocean communities to enable experimentation and innovation with diverse social, political, and legal systems." In 2010, he established the Thiel Fellowship, which awards $100,000 each year to 20 young people who promise to quit college and create their own entrepreneurial ventures.

Source: "Profile: Peter Thiel," *Forbes*, January 23, 2020.

It is important to recognize that the buying and selling of bonds by the Treasury and by the Fed have different effects on the supply of money. The key point here is that the Treasury and the Fed handle revenues collected from the selling of bonds in different ways. When the Treasury issues and sells bonds, it does so in order to generate additional funds to cover the spending of the federal government. The people who buy the bonds from the Treasury have less money, but when the federal government spends the funds, the recipients of the spending will have more money. Thus, Treasury borrowing and spending do not change the supply of money.

In contrast, when the Fed sells bonds, in effect, it takes the revenues and holds them, keeping them out of circulation. Because this money is out of circulation and can no longer be used for the purchase of goods and services, the money supply shrinks. However, if the Fed later wishes to increase the money supply, it can buy bonds, which will increase the availability of bank reserves and the money supply.

13-7 AMBIGUITIES IN THE MEANING AND MEASUREMENT OF THE MONEY SUPPLY

In the past, economists have generally used the *growth rate* of the money supply (either M1 or M2) to gauge the direction of monetary policy. A rapid growth rate of the money supply was indicative of expansionary monetary policy. Conversely, slow growth, or a decline, in the money stock implied a more restrictive monetary policy. However, financial innovations and structural changes can alter the nature of money across time. Let's consider two changes during the past several decades that have altered the nature of money and the reliability of money supply growth figures as a gauge of monetary policy.

1. Widespread use of the U.S. dollar outside of the United States. The U.S. dollar is widely used in other countries. To a degree, this has been true for a long time. However, in recent years, many countries have relaxed legal restraints that limited the domestic use of foreign currencies (and the maintenance of foreign currency bank accounts). The number of countries in which it is legal for citizens to maintain a foreign currency bank account increased from 42 in 1985 to more than 110 in 2017.[3] As noted earlier, the currency component of the M1 money supply was $1,724 billion in February 2020. According to a study by the Federal Reserve, more than one-half and perhaps as much as two-thirds of this currency is held overseas. The movement of these funds abroad (and our inability to measure them with any degree of precision) reduces the reliability of the M1 money supply figures and their growth as an indicator of monetary policy. (*Note:* There is also some impact on M2. However, because the currency component is a much smaller proportion of M2 than M1, the distortion of M2 is less severe.)

2. Substitution of electronic payments for checks and cash.
Increasingly, money is becoming electronic. More and more consumer purchases are being handled with debit cards, credit cards, and electronic transfers rather than by check or cash. Many people have their "paycheck" deposited directly into their bank account and make regular payments like those for utilities, mortgage and auto loans, and investment accounts with automatic transfers. With the touch of a few computer keys, you can also shop on the Internet and use your deposits to pay for magazines, financial advice, and numerous consumer goods. Currently, less than half of consumer purchases are paid for with either check or cash, compared to 80 percent just a decade ago. These changes in payment methods make it possible for both individuals and businesses to hold smaller money balances (cash and checkable deposits) than would otherwise be the case. They also reduce the comparability across time periods of the money supply data, particularly the M1 figures.

Because of these dynamic changes in the nature of money, economists now place less emphasis on the growth rate of the money supply figures as a monetary policy indicator. Most now rely on a combination of factors to evaluate the direction and appropriateness of monetary policy. We will follow this procedure as we consider the impact of monetary policy in subsequent chapters.

KEY POINTS

- Money is a financial asset that is widely accepted as a medium of exchange. It is a means of storing purchasing power for the future and is used as a unit of account. Without money, exchange would be both costly and tedious. Money derives its value from its scarcity (supply) relative to its usefulness (demand).

- There are two primary measures of the money supply. The narrowest definition of money supply (M1) includes only (1) currency in the hands of the public and (2) checkable deposits (both demand and interest earning) held in depository institutions. The broader M2 money supply includes M1 plus (1) savings deposits, (2) time deposits (of less than $100,000), and (3) money market mutual fund shares.

- Banking is a business. Commercial banks, savings and loan associations, and credit unions provide similar services and they are all part of the banking industry.

- Banks provide their depositors with the safekeeping of money, clearing services on checkable deposits, and interest payments on time

(and some checking) deposits. They earn most of their income by extending loans and investing in interest-earning securities.

- Under a fractional reserve banking system, banks are required to maintain only a fraction of their deposits in the form of reserves (vault cash or deposits with the Fed). Excess reserves may be invested or loaned to customers. When banks extend loans, they create additional deposits and thereby expand the money supply.

- The Federal Reserve System was established to provide a stable monetary framework for the entire economy. The Fed is a banker's bank. The structure of the Fed is designed to insulate it from political pressures so it will have greater freedom to follow policies more consistent with economic stability.

- The Fed has four major tools with which to control the money supply: (1) the establishment of reserve requirements, (2) open market operations, (3) the extension of loans, and (4) setting the interest rate paid to banks on their excess reserves. If the Fed wanted to increase the money supply, it

---

[3]See James Gwartney, Robert Lawson, Joshua Hall, and Ryan Murphy, *Economic Freedom of the World: 2019 Annual Report* (Vancouver, British Columbia: Fraser Institute, 2019).

could decrease the reserves banks are required to hold, buy government bonds and other financial assets in the open market, extend more loans, or reduce the interest rate it pays banks on their excess reserves. Open market operations—the buying or selling of bonds and other assets—have been the primary tool used by the Fed to alter the money supply.

- The monetary base provides the foundation for the money supply. Since 2008, the Fed has paid banks interest on their deposits with the Fed. These interest payments encourage banks to hold more reserves. As a result, the ratios of (a) bank reserves to checking deposits and (b) the monetary base to the M1 money supply have been higher since 2008 than was previously the case.

- The Federal Reserve and the U.S. Treasury are distinct agencies. The Fed is concerned primarily with the money supply and the establishment of a stable monetary climate, whereas the Treasury focuses on budgetary matters—tax revenues, government expenditures, and the financing of government debt.

- Historically, the rate of change of the money supply has been used to judge the direction and intensity of monetary policy. However, recent financial innovations and the widespread use of U.S. currency in other countries have blurred the meaning of money and reduced the reliability of the money growth figures as a monetary policy indicator.

CRITICAL ANALYSIS QUESTIONS

1. *What is meant by the statement "This asset is illiquid"? List some things you own and rank them from most liquid to most illiquid.

2. What determines whether a financial asset is included in the M1 money supply? Why are interest-earning checkable deposits included in M1, whereas interest-earning savings accounts and Treasury bills are not?

3. *What makes money valuable? Does money perform an economic service? Explain. Could money perform its function better if there were twice as much of it? Why or why not?

4. Describe the business of banking. How do banks generate revenue? What is their biggest liability?

5. Why are banks able to maintain reserves that are only a fraction of the demand and saving deposits of their customers? Is your money safe in a bank? Why or why not?

6. *Suppose you withdraw $100 from your checking account. How does this transaction affect (a) the supply of money, (b) the reserves of your bank, and (c) the excess reserves of your bank?

7. Currently, the excess reserves of banks are very large. If banks used these excess reserves to extend additional loans, what would happen to the money supply? Explain. If the Fed wanted to keep the banks from extending the additional loans, how could it do so?

8. *How will the following actions affect the money supply?

   a. a reduction in the discount rate
   b. an increase in the reserve requirements
   c. purchase by the Fed of $100 million in U.S. securities from a commercial bank
   d. sale by the U.S. Treasury of $100 million in newly issued bonds to a commercial bank
   e. an increase in the discount rate
   f. sale by the Fed of $200 million in U.S. securities to a private investor

9. What's wrong with this way of thinking? "When the government runs a budget deficit, it simply pays its bills by printing more money. As the newly printed money works its way through the economy, it waters down the value of paper money already in circulation. Thus, it takes more money to buy things. Budget deficits are the major cause of inflation."

10. *How has the size of the Fed's holdings of U.S. government securities and other financial assets changed since 2009? How has this change influenced the ability of the federal government to finance its budget deficits? Explain.

11. *If the Fed wants to expand the money supply, why is it more likely to do so by purchasing bonds and other financial assets rather than by lowering reserve requirements?

12. What is the monetary base? During the decade following 2010, what happened to the ratio of the monetary base divided by the M1 money supply? Why? What happened to bank reserves relative to checking deposits during this period? Why?

13. Why is the actual deposit expansion multiplier generally less than the potential deposit expansion multiplier?

14. How would the following influence M1 and M2 money supply figures?

    a. an increase in the quantity of U.S. currency held overseas
    b. a shift of funds from interest-earning checkable deposits to money market mutual funds
    c. a shift from currency to checkable deposits by the general public because debit cards have become more popular and widely accepted
    d. the shift of funds from money market mutual funds into stock and bond mutual funds because the fees to invest in the latter have declined

15. *Suppose that the Federal Reserve purchases a bond for $100,000 from Donald Truck, who deposits the proceeds in the Manufacturer's National Bank.

a. How will this transaction impact the supply of money?

b. How will the transaction impact the reserves of the Manufacturer's National Bank?

c. Could this have an additional impact on the money supply? Explain.

d. Would you expect this to happen? Why or why not? Explain.

16. Prior to their elimination in March of 2020, what impact did the approximately 10 percent reserve requirement have on the reserve holdings of banks? Why?

*Asterisk denotes questions for which answers are given in Appendix B.

CHAPTER 14

Modern Macroeconomics and Monetary Policy

The conventional wisdom once held that money doesn't matter. Now there is wide agreement that monetary policy can significantly affect real economic activity in the short run, though only price level in the long run. **—Daniel L. Thornton and David C. Wheelock[1]**

In the preceding chapter, we noted that many consider the chair of the Federal Reserve System to be the second most important person—next to the president—in the United States. Why is this so? Along with other members of the Fed's Board of Governors and Federal Open Market Committee, the Fed chairman is in charge of monetary policy. Monetary policy exerts a major impact on the economy. When conducted properly, it will provide for the smooth operation of a market economy. But if conducted improperly, it will generate uncertainty and undermine economic growth.

Until now, within the framework of the aggregate demand–aggregate supply model, we assumed that the supply of money was constant. We now relax this assumption. The previous chapter outlined the tools the Fed has to alter the supply of money. This chapter focuses on how monetary policy works—how changes in the supply of money affect the economy.

As you read this chapter, look for answers to the following questions:

- How does monetary policy affect interest rates, output, and employment?

- Can monetary policy stimulate real GDP in the short run? Can it do so in the long run?

- How does monetary policy affect economic stability? How does it affect inflation?

- Why have interest rates been so low during the past decade? Is expansionary monetary policy responsible for the low interest rates?

---

[1]Daniel L. Thornton and David C. Wheelock, "Editor's Introduction," *Federal Reserve Bank of St. Louis: Review* (May/June 1995): vii.

14-1 IMPACT OF MONETARY POLICY: A BRIEF HISTORICAL BACKGROUND

Like the modern view of fiscal policy, the modern view of monetary policy has evolved over the years. In the aftermath of the Great Depression and Keynesian revolution, there was great debate about the importance of monetary policy. During the 1950s and 1960s, many economists argued that monetary policy could be used to control inflation but that it was often ineffective as a means of stimulating aggregate demand. It was popular to draw an analogy between monetary policy and the workings of a string. Like a string, monetary policy could be used to "pull" (hold back) price increases and thereby control inflation. However, just as one cannot "push" with a string, many leading economists did not believe that monetary policy could be used to push (stimulate) aggregate demand.

Beginning in the late 1950s, this view was hotly contested by Nobel laureate Milton Friedman and other economists, who later became known as monetarists. The monetarists argued that changes in the money supply had a powerful influence on the economy's output in the short run, but in the long run, monetary policy affected only the general level of prices. Furthermore, monetarists argued that erratic monetary policy was the primary *source* of both economic instability and inflation. Milton Friedman summarized the monetarists' position in his 1967 presidential address to the American Economic Association when he stated,

> *Every major contraction in this country has been either produced by monetary disorder or greatly exacerbated by monetary disorder. Every major inflation episode has been produced by monetary expansion.*[2]

During the 1970s, monetary policy was both expansionary and erratic. This resulted in both inflation and economic instability. This strengthened the position of the monetarists regarding the potency of monetary policy. While minor disagreements remain, most economists now agree that monetary policy exerts an impact on output, employment, inflation, and economic stability.[3] We now turn to the presentation of this modern consensus view.

14-2 THE DEMAND AND SUPPLY OF MONEY

Why do individuals and businesses want to hold cash and bank deposit money rather than bonds, stocks, automobiles, buildings, and consumer durables? As you think about this question, don't confuse (1) the desire to hold money balances with (2) the desire for more wealth (or income). Of course, all of us would like to have more wealth, but we may be perfectly satisfied with our holdings of money in relation to our holdings of other goods, *given our current level of wealth*. When we say people want to hold more (or less) money, we mean that they want to restructure their wealth toward larger (smaller) money balances (holdings of currency and bank deposits).

People hold money for several reasons. At the most basic level, we hold money so that we can buy things. Households hold money balances so that they can pay for the weekly groceries, the monthly utilities and house payments, gasoline for the car, lunch for the kids, and other items purchased regularly. Businesses demand money so they can pay their workers, buy supplies, and conduct other transactions. People also hold money for unexpected expenses like an accident or a medical emergency. Economists call this the

---

[2]Milton Friedman, "The Role of Monetary Policy," *American Economic Review* (March 1968): 12.

[3]The evolution of the views of Paul Samuelson, who might properly be regarded as the father of American Keynesian economics, illustrates the change in the Keynesian view with regard to the relative importance of monetary and fiscal policy. Commenting on the twelfth edition of his classic text in 1985, Samuelson stated, "In the early editions of the book, fiscal policy was top banana. In later editions that emphasis changed to equality. In this edition we've taken a stand that monetary policy is most important."

precautionary motive for holding money. In addition, money is a means of storing value—a convenient way to set aside purchasing power for future use.

Higher interest rates make it more costly to hold money, however. Consider the cost of holding $1,000 in currency and demand deposits (which do not earn interest) rather than in interest-earning bonds, for example. If the interest rate is 10 percent, it will cost you $100 per year to hold an additional $1,000 of non-interest-earning money. In contrast, if the interest rate is 1 percent, the annual cost of holding the $1,000 money balance will be only $10. Even if you put the $1,000 in an interest-earning checking account, you could probably earn more interest if you purchased a U.S. Treasury security or some other less liquid form of savings with the funds. Thus, the opportunity cost of holding money is directly related to the nominal interest rate.

A curve that outlines the relationship between the interest rate (measured on the *y*-axis) and the quantity of money (measured on the *x*-axis) is called the **demand for money**. As panel (a) of **Exhibit 1** shows, there is an inverse relationship between the interest rate and the quantity of money demanded. This inverse relationship reflects the fact that higher interest rates make it more costly to hold money instead of interest-earning assets like savings deposits and Treasury securities. Therefore, as interest rates rise, individuals and businesses will try to manage their affairs with smaller money balances.

The demand for money balances will generally increase with the nominal value of transactions. If wages and prices increase, people will need more money in their wallets (or checking accounts) to make their regular daily, weekly, and monthly purchases. Businesses will also require more money to pay their bills. Similarly, if prices remain constant but the quantity of goods bought and sold in the economy increases, larger money balances will be needed to conduct those transactions. In other words, as nominal GDP increases, as the result of *either* higher prices or the growth of real output, the demand for money balances will also increase. When this happens, the entire demand curve for money will shift to the right. Conversely, a decline in nominal GDP will decrease the demand for money, shifting the curve to the left.

Changes in institutional factors can also affect the demand for money. For example, the greater availability and widespread use of credit and debit cards in recent years has made it easier for households to manage their affairs with less money. The increased availability of short-term loans has had a similar effect. Both of these factors have gradually reduced the demand for money (shifting the entire curve to the left).

As we discussed in the previous chapter, monetary policy is conducted by the monetary authorities—the Federal Reserve in the case of the United States. The Fed can use the extension of loans, interest paid on reserve deposits, and especially open market

Demand for money
A curve that indicates the relationship between the interest rate and the quantity of money people want to hold. Because higher interest rates increase the opportunity cost of holding money, the quantity of money demanded will be inversely related to the interest rate.

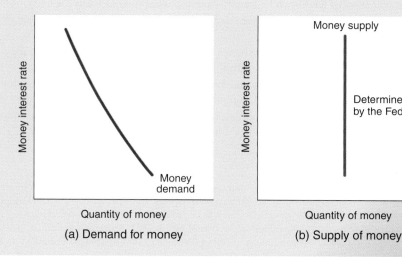

EXHIBIT 1

The Demand and Supply of Money

The demand for money is inversely related to the money interest rate (panel a). The supply of money is determined by the monetary authorities (the Fed) through their open market operations and other monetary policy tools (panel b).

Outstanding Economist: Milton Friedman (1912–2006)

Milton Friedman, the 1976 recipient of the Nobel Prize, is widely regarded as the most influential spokesman for a free market economy in the twentieth century. More than anyone else, Friedman developed the modern view of monetary policy. At a time when the role of money was largely ignored by the dominant Keynesian perspective, Friedman almost single-handedly convinced the economics profession that monetary policy exerted a strong impact on the economy. His *Monetary History of the United States* (1963) with Anna Schwartz presented powerful evidence that monetary policy not only mattered but it was also the major source of economic instability. The chapter on the Great Contraction illustrated that the Great Depression was primarily, if not exclusively, the result of a perverse monetary policy rather than a defect of market economies. Even his critics eventually concluded that, by and large, his views about the importance of monetary policy were correct.

Friedman's popular books *Capitalism and Freedom* (1962) and *Free to Choose* (1980), coauthored with his wife, Rose, are classic treatises in support of economic freedom. He had an uncanny ability to connect with both the general public and the brightest in his field. After retiring from the University of Chicago, he went on to spend nearly three decades on the faculty of Stanford University. Most economists would rate Friedman and John Maynard Keynes as the most influential economists of the twentieth century.

operations to regulate the supply of money. Changes in the interest rate do not alter the Fed's ability to determine the supply of money. Therefore, as Exhibit 1 (panel b) shows, the money supply schedule is vertical. The vertical supply curve reflects that the quantity of money is determined by Fed policy, and the Fed's ability to set the money supply is unaffected by the interest rate.

14-2a THE EQUILIBRIUM BETWEEN MONEY DEMAND AND MONEY SUPPLY

Exhibit 2 brings money demand and money supply together and shows how they determine the equilibrium rate of interest. The money interest rate will move toward i_e when the quantity of money demanded by households and businesses is just equal to the quantity supplied by the Fed. At the equilibrium interest rate, people are willing to hold the stock of money the Fed has supplied to the economy.

At a preceding equilibrium interest rate, i_2, for example, people will not want to hold as much money as the Fed has supplied. Accordingly, they will try to reduce their money

EXHIBIT 2

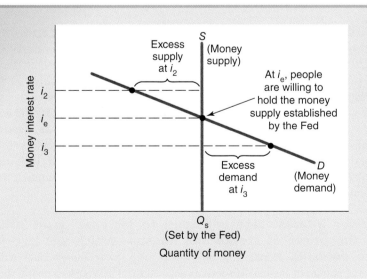

Money Supply, Money Demand, and Equilibrium

The money interest rate will tend to gravitate toward equilibrium, i_e, where the quantity of money demanded by households and businesses will equal the quantity of money supplied by the Fed.

balances. A number of people (and businesses) will do so by using some of their money balances to buy bonds. This increase in the demand for bonds will drive bond prices up and interest rates down. (*Remember:* Higher bond prices imply lower interest rates.) As a result, the money interest rate will move toward the i_e equilibrium. In contrast, at a below-equilibrium money interest rate, i_3, for example, an excess demand for money will be present. People would like to hold a larger quantity of money than the Fed has supplied. In this case, people will sell some of the bonds they own to get more money. In turn, the sale of their bonds will reduce bond prices and put upward pressure on interest rates. This will cause the interest rate to once again move toward i_e.

14-3 HOW DOES MONETARY POLICY AFFECT THE ECONOMY?

How will a change in the money supply affect the economy? As we previously discussed, the Fed typically uses open market operations to control the supply of money. If the Fed wants to shift to a more **expansionary monetary policy**, it will generally buy bonds issued by the U.S. Treasury or a financial institution. The Fed will pay for the bonds by writing a check on itself, thereby creating money out of thin air; and as the check clears, it will also make additional reserves available to the banks.

Exhibit 3 shows the impact on the economy. Let's first consider the situation in which the money interest rate (i_1 in the money balances market) is equal to the real interest rate (r_1 in the loanable funds market). This indicates that the expected rate of inflation is zero. When the Fed purchases bonds in order to increase the money supply (shifting S_1 to S_2 in panel a), it bids up bond prices and injects additional reserves into the banking system. Profit-seeking banks will generally use the additional reserves to extend more loans and increase their investments. This combination of factors—higher bond prices and additional reserves—will increase the supply of loanable funds (shift from S_1 to S_2 in panel b). In the short run, this will cause the real interest rate to fall to r_2.

How will the Fed's bond purchases, the creation of additional bank reserves, and a lower real interest rate influence the demand for goods and services? As panel (c) of Exhibit 3 shows, aggregate demand will increase (shift from AD_1 to AD_2). Economists stress the importance of three factors that contribute to this increase in aggregate demand.

1. The lower real interest rate will make current investment and consumption cheaper. At the lower interest rate, entrepreneurs will undertake some investment projects they otherwise wouldn't have. Spending by firms on structures and equipment will increase. Likewise, consumers will decide to expand their purchases of automobiles and consumer durables, which can now be bought with smaller monthly payments.

2. The lower interest rate will tend to cause financial capital to move abroad, the foreign exchange rate of the dollar to depreciate, and net exports to expand. Here's how: As domestic interest rates fall, both domestic and foreign investors will shift some of their financial investments to countries where interest rates are higher and they can get better returns on their investments. As investors shift funds abroad, they will supply dollars and demand foreign currency to purchase the new foreign assets. This will cause the dollar to depreciate in the foreign exchange market. In turn, the depreciation in the exchange-rate value of the dollar will make imports more expensive for Americans and U.S. exports cheaper for foreigners. As a result, U.S. imports will decline and exports will expand. This increase in net exports will also stimulate the nation's aggregate demand as foreigners buy more U.S. goods and services.

3. The lower interest rate will tend to increase asset prices—for example, the prices of stocks and houses—which will also increase aggregate demand. Here's how this works: The lower interest rates will increase the value of the stream of income or services derived from assets. As a result, the prices of

---

Expansionary monetary policy
A shift in monetary policy designed to stimulate aggregate demand. Injection of additional bank reserves, lower short-term interest rates, and acceleration in the growth rate of the money supply are indicators of a more expansionary monetary policy.

EXHIBIT 3

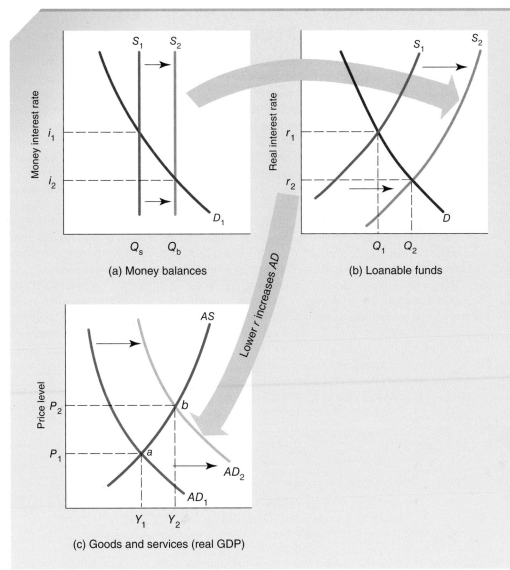

(a) Money balances

(b) Loanable funds

(c) Goods and services (real GDP)

The Transmission of Monetary Policy

When the Fed shifts to a more expansionary monetary policy, it will generally buy additional bonds. This will supply the banking system with additional reserves. Both the Fed's bond purchases and the banks' use of the additional reserves to extend new loans will increase the supply of loanable funds (shift it from S_1 to S_2, panel b) and put downward pressure on the real rate of interest. As the real interest rate falls (to r_2), aggregate demand increases (to AD_2 in panel c). Because the effects of the monetary expansion were unanticipated, the expansion in AD leads to both an increase in current output (to Y_2) and higher prices (inflation) in the short run. The increase in output, however, will only be temporary.

stocks, bonds, houses, and other assets will rise. In turn, the rising prices of these assets will increase the wealth of households, inducing them to consume more and thereby stimulate aggregate demand. Further, the higher prices of housing and other physical assets will make their production more profitable and motivate entrepreneurs to expand their investment spending on them. This, too, will add to aggregate demand.

In summary, when the Fed purchases bonds and expands the availability of bank reserves the real interest rate will decline. The lower interest rate will lead to an increase in investment and consumption, a depreciation in the foreign exchange value of the dollar, and higher asset prices. In turn, these factors will stimulate aggregate demand, output, and employment. This sequence is sometimes referred to as the interest rate transmission mechanism of monetary policy.[4]

---

[4]There is also a more direct route through which expansionary monetary policy may stimulate aggregate demand. When the Fed expands the supply of money, it will create an "excess supply of money" *at the initial money interest rate*. People may respond by directly increasing their purchases of goods and services in an effort to reduce their money balances to desired levels. Obviously, this will increase aggregate demand. This direct path is most relevant when the government expands the supply of money by paying its bills with newly created currency. Because the money supply of the United States is generally expanded via open market operations and control of short-term interest rates, we have focused on the transmission of monetary policy through the interest rate. The implications of both the direct and indirect paths are identical—both indicate that expansionary monetary policy will stimulate aggregate demand.

14-3a THE EFFECTS OF AN UNANTICIPATED EXPANSIONARY MONETARY POLICY

As we have previously discussed, modern macroeconomic analysis emphasizes whether a change is anticipated or unanticipated. If people do not anticipate the increase in aggregate demand accompanying an expansionary monetary policy, the prices of products will rise more quickly than the costs of producing them in the short run. As a result, the profit margins of businesses will improve, and they will respond by expanding their output (as the increase in real output from Y_1 to Y_2 in panel c of Exhibit 3 shows).

Exhibit 4 (panel a) shows the potential of expansionary monetary policy to direct a recessionary economy to full employment. Consider an economy initially at output Y_1, which is below full-employment capacity (Y_F). Expansionary monetary policy will lower interest rates and increase aggregate demand (to AD_2). Real output will then expand (to Y_F). In essence, the expansionary monetary policy provides an alternative to the economy's self-corrective mechanism. If demand is unchanged, reductions in real interest rates and resource prices will eventually direct the economy back to full employment, but many economists believe that expansionary monetary policy can speed up this process.

How will an expansion of the money supply by the Fed influence the price level and output if the economy is already at full employment? Although this is not a desirable strategy, it is interesting to analyze the outcome. As panel (b) of Exhibit 4 shows, an unanticipated shift to a more expansionary monetary policy will increase aggregate demand, causing the prices of products to rise relative to the costs of making them. Keep in mind that important production components, like labor, lease agreements, and insurance premiums are generally temporarily fixed by long-term contracts. When this is the case, real output will initially increase to Y_2, which is beyond the economy's long-run capacity of Y_F.

EXHIBIT 4

The Effects of Expansionary Monetary Policy

If the impact of an increase in aggregate demand accompanying an expansionary monetary policy is felt when the economy is operating below capacity, the policy will help direct the economy to a long-run full-employment equilibrium (E_2 in panel a). In this case, the increase in output from Y_1 to Y_F will be long term. In contrast, if the stimulus on aggregate demand is imposed on an economy already at full employment (panel b), it will lead to excess demand and higher product prices. Output will temporarily increase (to Y_2). However, in the long run, the strong demand will push up resource prices, shifting short-run aggregate supply to $SRAS_2$. The price level will rise to P_3, and output will recede (to Y_F) from its temporary high.

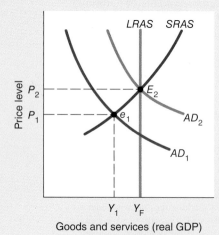

(a) Output is initially at less than full employment

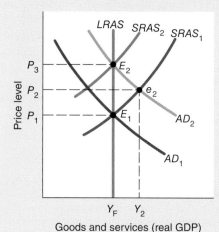

(b) Output is initially at full employment

However, the high rate of output (Y_2) will not be sustainable. Eventually, the long-term contracts based on the previously weaker demand (AD_1) will end, and the newly negotiated agreements will reflect the new stronger demand. As a result, the temporarily fixed resource prices will rise, pushing costs up, which will shift *SRAS* upward and to the left. Eventually, a new long-run equilibrium (E_2) will be established at a higher price level (P_3). Output will fall to Y_F. Thus, when an economy is already at full employment, an unexpected shift to a more expansionary monetary policy will temporarily increase output, but in the long run, it only leads to higher prices.

14-3b THE EFFECTS OF AN UNANTICIPATED RESTRICTIVE MONETARY POLICY

Suppose that the Fed moves toward a more **restrictive monetary policy** by selling bonds to the general public. The sale of bonds will reduce both the supply of money and the reserves of banks as people take money out of their accounts to buy the bonds. Exhibit 5 shows the impact of the more restrictive monetary policy on the loanable funds and goods and services markets. The Fed's sale of bonds increases their supply and pushes bond prices downward. It also drains reserves from the banking system as people buy the bonds (reducing the ability of banks to extend loans). As a result, the supply of loanable funds will fall, causing the real interest rate to rise (from r_1 to r_2 in panel a of Exhibit 5). In turn, the higher real interest rate will reduce spending on both investment goods and consumer durables because they'll be more costly to finance. The higher rate will also cause an inflow of capital from abroad and lead to the appreciation in the exchange rate of the dollar. The dollar appreciation will encourage U.S. citizens to buy imported products (which will become cheaper for them) and discourage foreigners from buying U.S. exports (because they will be more costly for them). This will then lead to lower net U.S. exports (and lower aggregate demand in the United States). The higher interest rates will also reduce housing and other asset prices, discouraging new construction and investment. All of these factors will tend to reduce aggregate demand (shift it from AD_1 to AD_2 in panel b of Exhibit 5).

Restrictive monetary policy
A shift in monetary policy designed to reduce aggregate demand and put downward pressure on the general level of prices (or the rate of inflation). A reduction in bank reserves, higher short-term interest rates, and a reduction in the growth rate of the money supply are indicators of a more restrictive monetary policy.

EXHIBIT 5

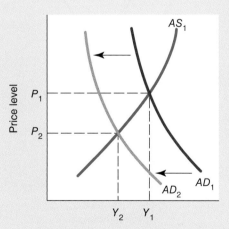
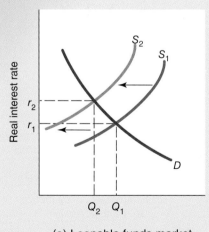
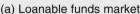

(a) Loanable funds market   (b) Goods and services (real GDP)

The Short-Run Effects of a More Restrictive Monetary Policy

When the Fed shifts to a more restrictive policy, it sells bonds, which reduces the reserves available to banks, decreases the supply of loanable funds, and puts upward pressure on interest rates (panel a). The higher interest rates decrease aggregate demand (shift it to AD_2 in panel b). When the reduction in aggregate demand is unanticipated, real output will decline (to Y_2) and downward pressure on prices will result.

The unexpected decline in the demand for goods and services will put downward pressure on prices, squeeze profit margins, and reduce output. As panel (b) of Exhibit 5 shows, the price level will decline (to P_2), and output will fall (to Y_2) as a result of the restrictive monetary policy.

The appropriateness of a restrictive policy depends on the state of the economy. Exhibit 6 illustrates this point. When there is upward pressure on prices because of strong demand, restrictive policy is an effective weapon against inflation. Suppose that, as illustrated by panel (a) of Exhibit 6, an economy is temporarily operating at e_1 and Y_1—beyond its full employment real GDP of Y_F. Strong aggregate demand is putting upward pressure on prices. In this case, a restrictive policy will help keep the price level constant and offset the inflationary forces. If a proper "dose" of a restrictive policy is administered at the right time, it will lower aggregate demand (to AD_2) and direct the economy to a noninflationary, long-run equilibrium at P_2 and Y_F (that is, E_2).

As panel (b) of Exhibit 6 shows, however, an unanticipated shift to restrictive policy will be damaging to an economy operating at full-employment equilibrium. If the output of an economy is at full employment (or worse still, at less than full employment), a restrictive policy will reduce aggregate demand (shift it to AD_2), and output will decline from Y_F to Y_2. Under these circumstances, the restrictive policy will cause output to fall below the economy's full-employment capacity and throw the economy into a recession.

14-3c SHIFTS IN MONETARY POLICY AND ECONOMIC STABILITY

As with fiscal policy, monetary policy must be properly timed if it is going to exert a stabilizing impact on the economy. Exhibits 4 and 6 highlight this point. When an economy is operating below its long-run capacity, expansionary monetary policy can increase aggregate demand and push the output of the economy to its sustainable potential

---

EXHIBIT 6

The Effects of a Restrictive Monetary Policy

The stabilization effects of restrictive monetary policy depend on the state of the economy when the policy exerts its primary impact. Restrictive monetary policy will reduce aggregate demand. If the restraint takes effect when aggregate demand is strong and the economy is overheated, it will limit or even prevent the occurrence of an inflationary boom (a). In contrast, if the restraint in aggregate demand takes effect when the economy is at full employment, it will disrupt the long-run equilibrium, reduce output, and result in a recession (b).

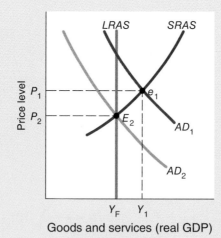

(a) Restrictive policy to control inflation

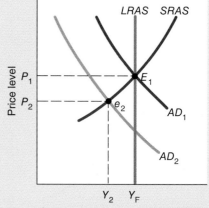

(b) Restrictive policy that causes a recession

(panel a of Exhibit 4). Similarly, if properly timed, restrictive monetary policy can help control (or prevent) inflation (panel a of Exhibit 6).

If it is timed improperly, however, monetary policy can be destabilizing. Expansionary monetary policy will cause inflation if the effects of the policy are felt when the economy is already at or beyond its capacity (panel b of Exhibit 4). Similarly, if the effects of a restrictive policy come when an economy is operating at its potential GDP, a recession is the likely outcome (panel b of Exhibit 6). Worse still, the impact of a restrictive policy can be disastrous if imposed on an economy that's already in a recession.

14-4 MONETARY POLICY IN THE LONG RUN

14-4a THE QUANTITY THEORY OF MONEY

Since the middle of the eighteenth century, economists have argued that excessive money growth leads to inflation. A century ago, Englishman Alfred Marshall and American Irving Fisher formalized the **quantity theory of money** in support of this view. ***The quantity theory of money predicts that an increase in the supply of money will cause a proportional increase in the price level.***

The quantity theory of money can be more easily understood once we recognize that there are two ways of viewing GDP. As the *AD–AS* model shows, nominal GDP is the sum of the price, *P*, times the output, *Y*, of each final-product good purchased during the period. In aggregate, *P* represents the economy's price level, while *Y* indicates real income or real GDP. There is also a second way of visualizing GDP. When the existing money stock, *M*, is multiplied by the number of times, *V*, that money is used to buy final products, this, too, yields the economy's nominal GDP. Therefore,

$$PY = GDP = MV$$

The **velocity of money** (*V*) is simply the average number of times a dollar is used to purchase a final product or service during a year. Velocity is equal to nominal GDP divided by the size of the money stock. For example, in 2019, GDP was equal to $21,428 billion, whereas the M1 money supply was $3,842 billion. Therefore, the velocity of the M1 money stock was 5.6 ($21,428 billion divided by $3,842 billion). The velocity of the M2 money stock can be derived in a similar manner. In 2019, the M2 money stock was $14,826 billion. Thus, the velocity of M2 was 1.4 ($21,428 billion divided by $14,826 billion).

The concept of velocity is closely related to the demand for money. When decision-makers conduct a specific amount of business with a smaller amount of money, their demand for money balances is reduced. Each dollar, though, is being used more often, so the velocity of the money has increased. Thus, for a given GDP level, when the demand for money declines, the velocity of money increases. Correspondingly, an increase in the demand for money is a reflection of a reduction in velocity.

When considering the behavior of prices, output, money, and velocity over time, we can write the quantity theory equation in terms of growth rates:

Rate of inflation + Growth rate of real output = Growth rate of the money supply + Growth rate of velocity

Economists call the $MV = PY$ relationship the **equation of exchange** because it reflects both the monetary and real sides of each final-product exchange. The quantity theory of money, though, assumes that *Y* and *V* are determined by factors other than the amount of money in circulation. Classical economists believed that real output, *Y*, was determined by factors like technology, the size of the economy's resource base, and the skill of its labor force. These factors were thought to be unrelated to changes in the money supply. Likewise, the velocity of money, *V*, was thought to be determined primarily by institutional factors, like the organization of banking and credit, the frequency of income payments, transportation speed, and the communication system. These factors will generally change slowly.

Quantity theory of money
A theory that hypothesizes that a change in the money supply will cause a proportional change in the price level because velocity and real output are unaffected by the quantity of money.

Velocity of money
The average number of times a dollar is used to purchase final goods and services during a year. It is equal to GDP divided by the stock of money.

Equation of exchange
$MV = PY$, where *M* is the money supply, *V* is the velocity of money, *P* is the price level, and *Y* is the output of goods and services produced in an economy.

Thus, classical economists thought that, for all practical purposes, both Y and V were constant (or changed only by small amounts) over periods of two, three, or four years. If both Y and V are constant, then the $MV = PY$ relationship indicates that an increase in the money supply (M) will lead to a proportional increase in the price level (P). Correspondingly, an increase in the growth rate of the money supply can be expected to cause a similar increase in the rate of inflation. Thus, the quantity theory of money highlights the linkage between monetary growth and inflation.

14-4b LONG-RUN IMPACT OF MONETARY POLICY: THE MODERN VIEW

Now let's consider the long-run impact of expansionary monetary policy within the framework of our basic macroeconomic model. We will begin with a simple case. Suppose real GDP is growing at a 3 percent annual rate and that the monetary authorities (the Fed in the case of the United States) are expanding the money supply by 3 percent each year. In addition, let's assume that the velocity of money is constant. This would imply that the 3 percent annual increase in output, or GDP, would lead to a 3 percent annual increase in the demand for money. In this case, the 3 percent monetary growth would be consistent with stable prices (zero inflation). Initially, we will assume that the economy's real interest rate is 4 percent. Because the inflation rate is zero, the nominal rate of interest is also equal to 4 percent. **Exhibits 7 and 8** illustrate an economy initially (period 1) characterized by these conditions.

EXHIBIT 7

The Long-Run Effects of a More Rapid Expansion in the Money Supply on the Goods and Services Market

Here, we illustrate the long-run impact of an increase in the annual growth rate of the money supply from 3 to 8 percent. Initially, prices are stable (P_{100}) when the money supply is expanding by 3 percent annually. The acceleration in the growth rate of the money supply increases aggregate demand (shifts it to AD_2). At first, real output may expand beyond the economy's potential (Y_F). However, abnormally low unemployment and strong demand

conditions will create upward pressure on wages and other resource prices, shifting aggregate supply to AS_2. Output will return to its long-run potential and the price level will increase to P_{105} (E_2). If the more rapid monetary growth continues in subsequent periods, AD and AS will continue to shift upward, leading to still higher prices (E_3 and periods beyond). The net result of the process is sustained inflation.

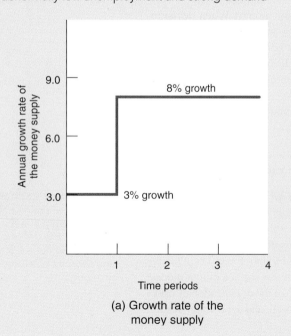

(a) Growth rate of the money supply

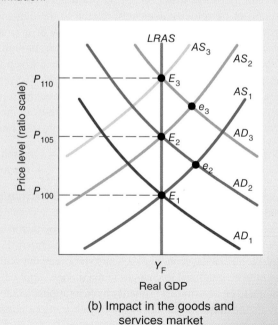

(b) Impact in the goods and services market

EXHIBIT 8

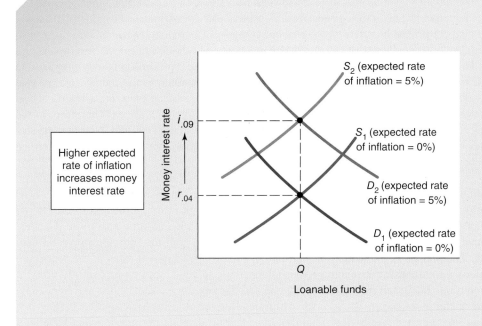

The Long-Run Effects of More Rapid Expansion in the Money Supply on the Loanable Funds Market

When prices are stable, supply and demand in the loanable funds market are in balance at a real and nominal interest rate of 4 percent. If a more rapid monetary expansion leads to a long-term 5 percent inflation rate, borrowers and lenders will build the higher inflation rate into their decision-making. As a result, the nominal interest rate (i) will rise to 9 percent—the 4 percent real rate plus a 5 percent inflationary premium.

What will happen if the monetary authorities permanently increase the growth rate of the money supply from 3 percent to 8 percent annually (see panel a of Exhibit 7, beginning in period 2)? In the short run, the expansionary monetary policy will reduce the real interest rate and stimulate aggregate demand (shift it to AD_2 in panel b of Exhibit 7), just as we previously explained (in Exhibits 3 and 4). For a time, real output will exceed the economy's potential. However, many resource suppliers will want to modify their long-term agreements as soon as they can in light of the strong demand conditions. Over time, more and more resource suppliers (including workers represented by union officials) will have the opportunity to alter their prior contracts. As this happens, wages and other resource prices will increase. As they do, costs will rise and profit margins will fall back to normal levels. The higher costs will reduce aggregate supply (shift it to AS_2). As the rapid monetary growth continues in subsequent periods (periods 3, 4, and so on), both AD and AS will shift upward. As shown in Exhibit 7(b), the price level will rise to P_{105}, P_{110}, and so on to still higher levels as the money supply continues to grow more rapidly than the monetary growth rate consistent with stable prices. The continuation of the expansionary monetary policy leads to a higher and higher price level—that is, a sustained inflation.

Suppose an inflation rate of 5 percent eventually emerges from the more rapid growth rate of the money supply (8 percent rather than 3 percent). In the long run, more and more people will make decisions based on the persistent 5 percent inflation because it will be what they come to expect. In the resource market, both buyers and sellers will eventually include the 5 percent expected inflation rate into long-term contracts like collective bargaining agreements. Once this happens, resource prices and costs will rise as rapidly as prices in the goods and services market. When the 5 percent long-run rate of inflation is fully anticipated, it will fail to either reduce real wages or improve profit margins. Output will recede to its long-run potential, and unemployment will return to its natural rate.

Exhibit 8 shows the long-run adjustments in the loanable funds market once borrowers and lenders expect the 5 percent inflation rate. When lenders expect a 5 percent annual increase in the price level, a 9 percent interest rate will be necessary to provide them with as much incentive to supply loanable funds as a 4 percent rate did *when stable prices were expected*. Thus, the supply of loanable funds will shift vertically by the 5 percent expected rate of inflation. Simultaneously, borrowers who were willing to pay 4 percent interest on their loans when stable prices were expected will be willing to pay 9 percent when they expect prices to increase by 5 percent annually. The demand for loanable funds will therefore also increase (shift vertically) by the expected inflation rate. Once borrowers and lenders anticipate the higher (5 percent) inflation rate, the equilibrium money interest rate will rise to 9 percent. Of course, the real interest rate is equal to the money interest rate (9 percent) minus the expected rate of inflation (5 percent). In the long run, a 4 percent real interest rate will emerge with inflation, just as it did with stable prices. Therefore, in the long run, expansionary monetary policy will not reduce real interest rates. Nominal interest rates will rise and reflect the higher expected rate of inflation, but real interest rates will be unchanged.

Real-world observations support the linkage between monetary expansion and high nominal interest rates. During the 1970s, the monetary policy of the United States was highly expansionary, and it led to both inflation and high nominal interest rates. On the other hand, interest rates were lower during both the 1960s and the past three decades, when monetary policy was generally less expansionary and the inflation rate relatively low. The picture is the same internationally. The highest interest rates in the world are found in countries experiencing hyperinflation due to very rapid money supply growth: Argentina and Brazil in the 1980s, Russia and Turkey during the 1990s, and Venezuela during the most recent decade, for example. Conversely, the lowest interest rates are found in countries like Switzerland that have followed monetary policies that have kept the inflation rate low.

14-4c MONEY AND INFLATION

Modern analysis highlights the difference between the short- and long-run effects of monetary policy. In the short run, shifts in monetary policy exert an impact on real output and employment. A shift to a more restrictive policy will tend to reduce real output and employment, while a shift to a more expansionary monetary policy will tend to increase them.

However, if the more expansionary policy persists, the long-run impact will be inflation and higher nominal interest rates, without any positive impact on real output and employment. The more rapid the sustained growth rate of the money supply (relative to real output), the higher the expected rate of inflation. Thus, modern analysis indicates that the long-run implications of the earlier quantity theory of money are correct: Money growth and inflation are closely linked.

14-5 MONEY, ECONOMIC STABILITY, AND PROPER MONETARY POLICY

What can be achieved with monetary policy? When thinking about this question, it is important to keep two points in mind. First, shifts in monetary policy exert an impact on output and the general level of prices with a time lag. Moreover, these time lags are of variable length, and sometimes they will be quite long. Second, expansionary monetary policy cannot promote long-term growth. Increasing the money supply will not create more output.

14-5a TIME LAGS, MONETARY SHIFTS, AND ECONOMIC STABILITY

While analyzing how monetary policy works, we glossed over a crucially important issue: the time lag between a change in monetary policy and when the change begins to exert an impact on interest rates, aggregate demand, and eventually output and the price level.

While the Fed can shift policy rapidly, it will take time for the change to impact the economy. Economists estimate that it will generally take 6 to 18 months for a shift in monetary policy to exert a major impact on aggregate demand and real output. An even longer time lag—12 to 30 months—often passes before there is a significant impact on the price level and inflation rate.

The transmission of monetary policy sheds light on why it takes time for monetary policy to work. When the Fed shifts toward monetary expansion and injects additional reserves into the banking system, short-term interest rates will fall. But this reduces the opportunity cost of holding money balances. At the lower interest rate, households and businesses are willing to hold a larger quantity of money, and therefore, the velocity of money will decline. As a result, the initial effects of the expansionary monetary policy will often be weak. For a time, total spending (aggregate demand) may not change much because the reduction in velocity is, at least partially, offsetting the increase in the supply of money. If the reduction in the interest rate is substantial and persistent, the weak impact of the monetary expansion may be lengthy. Of course, if the more expansionary monetary policy persists, it will eventually lead to increasing aggregate demand, rising interest rates, and upward pressure on the general level of prices. As this happens and 18 to 36 months may pass before it does the velocity of money will increase, amplifying the demand stimulus of the monetary expansion. It is at this point that the effects on inflation will be the strongest.

The same forces will also affect the operation of restrictive monetary policy. When the Fed shifts to a more restrictive policy and drains reserves from the banking system, the federal funds and other short-term interest rates will rise. At the higher rates, however, people will want to hold less money, and the velocity of money will increase. For a time, the increase in velocity will at least partially offset the reduction in the supply of money and weaken the initial restrictive effects of the policy. Of course, if the restrictive policy persists, higher interest rates will eventually reduce aggregate demand, but several quarters may pass before the restrictive policy exerts a strong impact on the economy.

In the long run, the impact of monetary policy will be primarily on the general level of prices. Thus, control of inflation is the responsibility of monetary policy-makers. Equally important, price stability provides the foundation for the smooth operation of a market economy. When monetary policy keeps the inflation rate at a low and therefore easily predictable rate, it lays the foundation for long-term healthy growth. In fact, price stability is so important that it is one of our 12 Keys to Prosperity.

14-5b MONETARY POLICY AND PRICE STABILITY

In the long run, the impact of monetary policy will be primarily on the general level of prices. Thus, control of inflation is the responsibility of monetary policy-makers. Equally important, price stability provides the foundation for the smooth operation of a market economy. When monetary policy keeps the inflation rate at a low and therefore easily predictable rate, it lays the foundation for long-term healthy growth. In fact, price stability is so important that it is one of our 12 Keys to Prosperity.

KEYS TO ECONOMIC PROSPERITY

Price Stability

Maintenance of price stability is the essence of sound monetary policy; price stability provides the foundation for both economic stability and the efficient operation of markets.

The high standard of living that Americans enjoy is the result of gains from exchange, specialization, and mass production processes. Price stability and the smooth operation of the pricing system will help individuals more fully realize the potential gains from these sources. In contrast, high and variable rates of inflation create uncertainty, distort relative prices, and reduce the efficiency of a market economy.

The Federal Reserve is responsible for the conduct of monetary policy. If it achieves approximate price stability, it has done all it can do to create an environment for growth and prosperity.

While shifts to a more expansionary monetary policy can promote real output and employment in the short run, they cannot do so in the long run. Moreover, constant shifts in monetary policy will result in policy errors and generate uncertainty. If investors and other business decision makers can count on monetary policy-makers to maintain price stability, a potential source of uncertainty is reduced. This will encourage investment and other business activities and thereby promote a high level of employment and strong economic growth.

How can Fed policy best achieve price stability? Some believe the Fed should establish an inflation target, between zero and 2 percent, for example, and promise to keep the rate of inflation within that range. If the rate of inflation rose above the 2 percent upper limit, the Fed would shift toward a more restrictive monetary policy. On the other hand, if the inflation rate fell below the zero limit, monetary policy would be shifted toward expansion. Others favor Fed targeting of nominal GDP growth. Suppose the Fed promised to use monetary policy to keep the annual growth rate of nominal GDP as close as possible to 5 percent. If nominal GDP growth was greater than 5 percent, the Fed would shift toward restriction. When nominal GDP growth fell below the 5 percent target, the Fed would be more expansionary. The long-term annual real growth of the U.S. economy has averaged a little more than 3 percent. Thus, 5 percent growth of nominal GDP would keep the inflation rate low—in the 2 percent range.

Those who favor either an inflation or nominal GDP target typically buttress their case with two additional points. First, the monetary authorities should focus on a long run pre-announced strategy such as the targeting of either of these variables. This would reduce uncertainty by providing people with assurance regarding the future direction of monetary policy. Second, it is a mistake for monetary policy-makers to target real variables such as real GDP, employment, or unemployment. Monetary policy cannot control real variables, at least not for long, and when it seeks to do so, it will nearly always result in more rather than less instability. When the monetary authorities persistently achieve price stability, they have done all they can do to establish the environment for long-run prosperity.

14-6 RECENT LOW INTEREST RATES AND MONETARY POLICY

As the U.S. economy plunged into recession during the first half of 2008, the Fed injected a huge quantity of reserves into the banking system. In the 12 months beginning in July

2008, the Fed doubled both its asset holdings and the monetary base. Short-term interest rates fell to near zero, and the M2 money supply expanded at an annual rate of 9 percent, well above the average of the two previous decades. During 2010–2015, the Fed continued to purchase huge quantities of Treasury securities and other financial assets, vastly expanding the reserves available to the banking system. As government mandates designed to control the spread of the COVID-19 virus in 2020 caused output to plunge, the Fed again shifted to a highly expansionary monetary policy (see Chapter 13, Exhibits 6 and 7).

During 2010–2020, both the nominal and real interest rates in the United States were exceedingly low. Exhibit 9 shows the path of the nominal and real interest rates for the 5-year Treasury bond during 1990–2020. During the 1990s, the nominal interest rate on the 5-year bond was generally between 5 percent and 7.5 percent. During the last decade, however, the nominal rate never exceeded 2.5 percent, well below the rate during the earlier decade. The pattern was the same for the real interest rate. Remember, the real interest rate is the nominal rate minus the inflationary premium. The real interest rate was generally between 2.5 percent and 3.5 percent during the 1990s. It declined to approximately 2 percent during 2002–2004 and remained below 3 percent during the rest of the decade. During 2010–2020, however, the real interest rate was generally less than 1 percent, and at various times, it even fell below zero. Thus, both the nominal and real interest rates were exceedingly low during 2010–2020.

Most people believe that the low interest rates of the past decade are the result of Fed policy. However, there is a major problem with this view. While expansionary monetary policy can reduce interest rates temporarily, it cannot do so over a lengthy time span. If the expansionary monetary policy persists, it will eventually lead to inflation and rising

EXHIBIT 9

The Nominal and Real Interest Rates in the United States, 1990–2020

The nominal and real interest rates on five-year Treasury bonds during 1990–2020 are shown here. Note, both the nominal and real interest rates were substantially lower during 2010–2020 than during the 1990s. The real interest rate was persistently below 1 percent and occasionally fell below zero during 2008–2020. This is approximately two percentage points lower than the real rate during the 1990s. It is unlikely that expansionary monetary policy would have been able to push the real interest rate downward by this magnitude for such a prolonged time period.

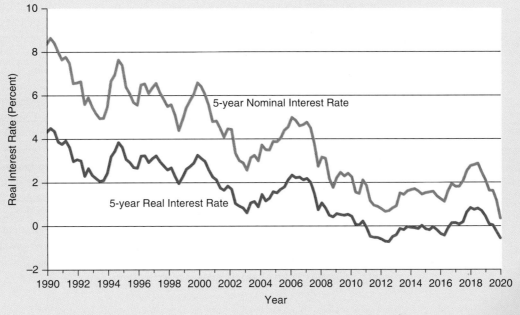

Source: https://fred.stlouisfed.org/ and https://www.clevelandfed.org/our-research/indicators-and-data/inflation-expectations.aspx

nominal interest rates. This did not happen. Even as the U.S. economy moved into the ninth year of a lengthy expansion and the unemployment rate fell to less than 4 percent in 2019, the inflation rate remained low and both nominal and real interest rates persisted at historically low levels for a non-recessionary economy. Further, the low interest rates are a worldwide phenomenon. Interest rates are also low in Japan, Canada, throughout Europe, and in several other areas of the world. This indicates that the low interest rates of 2010–2020 are the result of something other than expansionary monetary policy.

If expansionary monetary policy is not the source (at least not the primary source) of the low interest rates, how can they be explained? The real interest rate is determined in the world market for loanable funds. Abnormally low real interest rates will result if either the demand for loanable funds is weak or the supply strong. Some economists believe that, compared to earlier times, recent changes in the structure of output have reduced the demand for loanable funds. A sizeable share of production in the Information Age does not involve a tangible product that requires a large investment in physical capital. For example, important recent ventures such as Facebook, Amazon, Netflix, and Google require far less investment per unit of output than the steel, railroad, and automobile manufacturing that drove economic growth during previous eras. In turn, the reduction in physical capital and the demand for its finance results in lower real interest rates.

Increases in the supply of loanable funds relative to demand will also result in low real interest rates. Are there reasons to believe this has happened? Michael Walker of the Fraser Institute argues that the huge demographic changes in high-income developed countries in recent decades have increased the supply of loanable funds relative to demand.[5] When adults are between ages 20 and 50 years, they often borrow for the financing of housing, cars, education (both their own and that of their children), the cost of raising children, and even the start-up of businesses. During this phase of life, most people are net borrowers—they are generating a demand for loanable funds. As they grow older, somewhere around age 50, they begin to pay down outstanding debt and save more heavily for retirement. During this phase, generally between the ages of 50 and 75, most people are net lenders. Demographic changes that increase the number of people in the lending phase (approximately age 50 to 75) relative to the number in the borrowing phase (under age 50) will increase the supply of loanable funds relative to demand, leading to lower interest rates. This is precisely what Walker and other proponents of the demographic theory believe has happened.

Exhibit 10 presents the data for the ratio of the population age 50 to 75 years divided by the population under age 50 for six large high-income countries during 1970–2020 (with projections to 2030). Note the strong upward trend for each of the countries since 1990. The increasing ratio in the lending relative to the borrowing age categories has been particularly strong in Italy, Japan, and Spain. In Italy, the ratio rose from .39 in 1990 to .62 in 2020, and projections indicate it will rise to .75 by 2030. In Japan, the ratio rose from .36 in 1990 to .51 in 2000 and .62 in 2020, and it is projected to increase to .72 by 2030. In Spain, the ratio rose from .38 in 2000 to .53 in 2020, and it is projected to rise to .74 in 2030. The upward trend of the ratio is less pronounced in the United States than in Japan and Western Europe, but it is nonetheless substantial, increasing from .29 in 2000 to .45 in 2020.

The increase in the population share age 50 to 75 relative to the population share under age 50 reflects the combination of a falling birth rate and an increase in life expectancy, trends that are present in virtually all high-income countries. To the extent the low interest rates are the result of demographic factors, they are likely to continue in the years immediately ahead. Demographic changes occur slowly, and as Exhibit 10 indicates, the upward trend in the ratio of persons in the lending divided by borrowing age groups is projected to continue in the high-income countries for at least another decade. If so, the prolonged period of abnormally low interest rates is also likely to continue.

[5]Michael A. Walker, "Why Are Interest Rates So Low? A Framework for Modeling Current Global Financial Developments," Fraser Institute Report, February 2016, https://www.fraserinstitute.org/sites/default/files/why-are-interest-rates-so-low.pdf

EXHIBIT 10

Changes in the Size of Lending and Borrowing Age Categories in Various High-Income Countries, 1970–2030

The ratio of the population age 50 to 75 divided by the population under age 50 is shown here for six high-income economies. Note how the ratio has increased in each of the countries, particularly since 1990. When persons are between the ages of 50 and 75, they are generally net lenders—they are saving and repaying

debt. In contrast, people under age 50 are generally net borrowers. Thus, an increase in the share of the population age 50 to 75 relative to under age 50 will expand the supply of loanable funds relative to demand, and thereby place downward pressure on real interest rates.

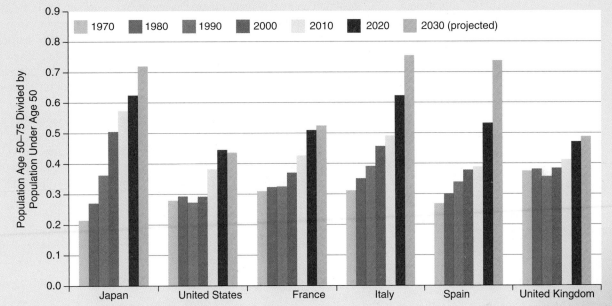

Source: United Nations, Department of Economic and Social Affairs. Population Division. World Population Prospects, the 2015 Revision: http://esa.un.org/unpd/wpp/

Of course, the demand-side and supply-side explanations for the recent prolonged low interest rates are not mutually exclusive. Both demand- and supply-side factors may be contributing to the abnormally low real interest rates of recent years.

14-7 INTEREST RATES, VELOCITY OF MONEY, AND MONETARY POLICY

When factors other than monetary policy reduce interest rates, how will this impact monetary policy? As the analysis of the demand for money indicates, there will be an inverse relationship between the nominal interest rate and the amount of money people are willing to hold (see Exhibit 1). When interest rates decline to low levels, people will hold a larger quantity of money, and the velocity of money will fall. This is precisely what happened during 2010–2020 as interest rates remained low and the short-term rates hovered near zero.

Exhibit 11, panel (a), tracks the velocity of both the M1 and M2 money supply during 1990–2020. Prior to 2007, the velocity of M1 trended upward while the velocity of M2 fluctuated within a narrow range. But look what happened when interest rates fell and remained low during 2010–2020. The velocity of both M1 and M2 plunged and continued to recede throughout the decade. When interest rates are near zero, there is little incentive for households and businesses to shift away from money balances into the loanable funds market (bonds, certificates of deposit, and similar savings instruments).

When the velocity of money declines during a period of low and declining interest rates, the potency of expansionary monetary policy will also be affected. As we have previously discussed, the Fed made huge purchases of Treasury bonds and other financial assets during and following the Great Recession of 2008–2009. Quantitative easing was the central feature of Fed policy through 2015. Many economists, particularly monetarists, expected the highly expansionary monetary policy to cause the inflation rate to accelerate. However, the impact of the policy on aggregate demand and the growth of nominal GDP was modest.

Exhibit 11, panel (b), presents data on the growth of nominal GDP since 1990. The annual growth of nominal GDP averaged 5.3 percent during 1990–2007, and it generally fluctuated within the 4 percent to 6 percent range. During the recession of 2001, the growth rate of nominal GDP dipped to 3 percent, but it soon returned to the 4 percent to 6 percent range. However, as the 2008 recession set in, nominal GDP declined in 2009. During the expansion of 2010–2020, the annual growth rate of nominal GDP averaged 3.9 percent, even a little lower than during the 1990s. Thus, even with the Fed's massive purchase of assets and accompanying substantial growth in the money supply, nominal GDP grew at a modest rate during 2010–2020.

Why didn't the Fed's highly expansionary policy in response to the Great Recession exert a larger impact on aggregate demand, output, and prices? The low and receding interest rates of the period provide the answer. Responding to the low interest rates, the velocity of money declined and, to a large degree, offset the impact of the more rapid growth rate of the money supply. As a result, the impact on aggregate demand and nominal GDP was modest.

EXHIBIT 11

The Velocity of Money and Growth of Nominal GDP, 1990–2020

Panel (a) illustrates the substantial reduction in the velocity of money for both M1 and M2 during 2010–2020 in response to the low and receding interest rates of this period. Panel (b) shows the annual growth rate of nominal GDP during 1990–2020. Even though the Fed injected large quantities of reserves into the banking system and expanded the money supply rapidly during and following

the recession of 2008–2009, nominal GDP grew only at a modest rate because the reduction in the velocity of money blunted the impact of the expansionary monetary policy. Note: The average annual growth rate of nominal GDP during 2010–2019 was 3.9 percent, down from 5.3 percent during 1990–2007 (see trend line).

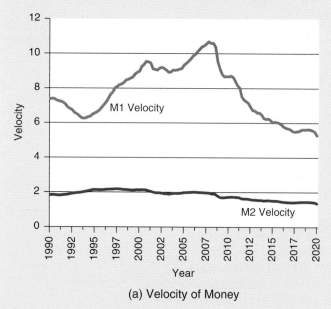

(a) Velocity of Money

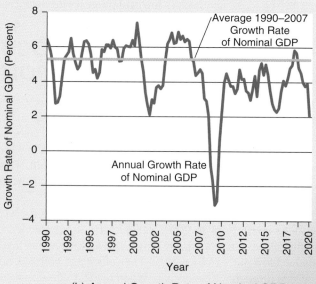

(b) Annual Growth Rate of Nominal GDP

Source: http://www.economagic.com

During the 2020 COVID-19 Recession, the Fed responded with an even larger purchase of assets than during 2008–2009. In just four months during March–June 2020, the Fed expanded its purchases of assets by $2.9 trillion, an increase of nearly 70 percent. The M1 money supply increased from $4.0 trillion to $5.1 trillion, an increase of more than 25 percent during this same time frame. The Fed is anticipating that low interest rates will further reduce the velocity of money and dampen the impact of this huge monetary expansion. This may be the case, but it is a risky strategy. If the inflation rate begins to rise and triggers higher nominal interest rates, predictably, the velocity of money will increase rather than decline, making it very difficult for the Fed to control inflation. It will be interesting to monitor this situation as it unfolds in 2021 and 2022.

Uncertainty about potential changes in velocity complicates the use of monetary policy as a stabilization tool. In addition to the variable time lags between when a policy is instituted and when it begins to exert an impact on aggregate demand, output, and prices, monetary policy-makers must also consider how a policy change will impact the velocity of money. When monetary policy affects interest rates and inflation, the velocity of money will also be impacted. Moreover, interest rates can change for reasons other than monetary policy. The interactions among changes in monetary policy, interest rates, inflation, and the velocity of money complicate the use of monetary policy as a stabilization tool.

The impact of changes in interest rates on the velocity of money also affects the linkage between the growth rate of the money supply and inflation. The quantity theory of money assumes that velocity is constant. When this is the case, if the money supply increases more rapidly than real output, the general level of prices will rise proportionally. However, if interest rates decline, as the result of demographic changes for example, the lower opportunity cost of holding money will cause the velocity of money to fall. As a result, the growth of the money supply will exert a less than proportional impact on inflation. This is precisely what happened in the United States (and other countries) during 2010–2020.

The interactions among interest rates, changes in monetary policy, and the short- and long-run effects on aggregate demand, real output, and the price level are clearly challenging. However, these challenges also add to the excitement accompanying the study of economics and the search for answers to important questions.

KEY POINTS

- The quantity of money people want to hold is inversely related to the money interest rate. Higher interest rates make it more costly to hold money instead of interest-earning assets like bonds. The supply of money is vertical because it is determined by the Fed. The money interest rate will gravitate toward the rate at which the quantity of money people want to hold is just equal to the quantity supplied by the Fed.

- The impact of a shift in monetary policy is generally transmitted through interest rates, exchange rates, and asset prices.

- When instituting a more expansionary monetary policy, the Fed generally increases the reserves available to banks and pushes interest rates downward. In the short run, an *unanticipated* shift to a more expansionary policy will stimulate aggregate demand and thereby increase output and employment.

- When instituting a more restrictive monetary policy, the Fed drains reserves from the banking system and pushes interest rates upward. In the short run, an unanticipated shift to a more restrictive monetary policy will increase real interest rates and reduce aggregate demand, output, and employment.

- The quantity theory of money postulates that the velocity of money is constant (or approximately so) and that real output is independent of monetary factors. When these assumptions hold, an increase in the stock of money will lead to a proportional increase in the price level.

- While monetary policy can influence real output in the short run, in the long run expansionary monetary policy will merely lead to inflation.

- Shifts in monetary policy exert an impact on output and employment only after time lags that are variable and sometimes lengthy. These variable time lags reduce the likelihood that monetary policy-makers will be able to make regular changes in monetary policy in a stabilizing manner. Historically, erratic monetary policy has often been a source of economic instability.

- If the monetary authorities are able to keep the inflation rate low and stable, they are providing the framework for economic stability and the smooth operation of markets. Maintenance of price stability is the essence of sound monetary policy.

15-1 ECONOMIC FLUCTUATIONS: THE PAST 100 YEARS

Wide fluctuations in the general level of business activity—income, employment, and the price level—make personal economic planning extremely difficult. Such changes can cause even well devised investment plans to go awry. The tragic stories of unemployed workers begging for food and newly impoverished investors jumping out of windows during the Great Depression vividly portray the enormous personal and social costs of economic instability and the uncertainty that it generates.

Historically, there have been substantial fluctuations in real output. **Exhibit 1** illustrates the growth record of real GDP in the United States during the past century. Prior to World War II, double-digit swings in real GDP during a single year were not uncommon. Real GDP rose by more than 10 percent annually during World War I, during an economic boom in 1922, during a mid-1930s recovery, and again during World War II. In contrast, output fell at an annual rate of 5 percent or more during the 1920–1921 recession, in the depression years of 1930–1932 and 1938, and again following World War II. Since 1950, economic ups and downs have been more moderate. Nevertheless, periods of recession and economic boom are still observable.

15-2 CAN DISCRETIONARY POLICY PROMOTE ECONOMIC STABILITY?

There is widespread agreement about the goals of macroeconomic policy. Economists of almost all persuasions favor the goals of steady growth, price stability, and full employment (unemployment at the natural rate). However, there are disagreements about how to

---

EXHIBIT 1

Economic Instability: The Record of the Past Century

Prior to the conclusion of World War II, the United States experienced double-digit increases in real GDP in 1918, 1922, 1935–1936, and 1941–1943. In contrast, real output fell by 5 percent or more in 1920–1921, 1930–1932, 1938, and 1946. However, as illustrated here, fluctuations in real GDP have been considerably more moderate since 1950. Most economists believe that more appropriate macroeconomic policy—particularly monetary policy—deserves much of the credit for the increased stability of recent decades.

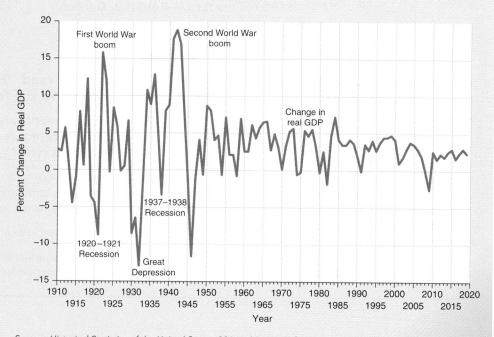

Source: *Historical Statistics of the United States*, 224 and Bureau of Economic Analysis, http://www.bea.gov

achieve these objectives. Most of these disagreements focus on the potential and limitations of discretionary macro policy as a stabilization tool.

If monetary and fiscal policies could inject stimulus during economic slowdowns and apply restraint during inflationary booms, this would help reduce the ups and downs of the business cycle. Some macroeconomists, sometimes called **activists**, believe that this is possible. The activists believe that policy-makers will be able to manage demand and respond to various disruptions and changing economic conditions in a manner that will promote economic stability. Other economists, called **nonactivists**, argue that the discretionary use of monetary and fiscal policy in response to changing economic conditions is likely to do more harm than good. The nonactivists note that erratic use of macro policy has been a major source of economic instability in the past. Thus, they believe that the economy would be more stable if policy-makers merely followed a steady course rather than constantly responding to turns in the economic road.

Both activists and nonactivists recognize that conducting macro policy in a stabilizing manner is not an easy task. Let's take a closer look at some of the complicating factors and available tools that might help improve the effectiveness of stabilization policy.

15-2a THE TIME LAG PROBLEM

If monetary and fiscal policies are going to exert a stabilizing impact, proper timing is crucially important. Three different types of time lags complicate the achievement of proper timing.

First, there is the **recognition lag**, the time period between a change in economic conditions and recognition of the change by policy-makers. It generally takes a few months to gather and tabulate reliable information on the recent performance of the economy in order to determine whether it has dipped into a recession or whether the inflation rate has accelerated, and so forth.

Second, even after the need for a policy change is recognized, there is generally an additional time period before the policy change is instituted. Economists refer to this delay as **administrative lag**. In the case of monetary policy, the administrative lag is generally quite short. The Federal Open Market Committee meets every few weeks and is in a position to institute a change in monetary policy quickly. This is a major advantage of monetary policy. For discretionary fiscal policy, the administrative lag is usually more lengthy. Congressional committees must meet. Legislation must be proposed and debated. Congress must act, and the president must consent. Each of these steps typically takes several months. These delays are a major disadvantage that limits the use of discretionary fiscal policy as a stabilization tool.

Finally, there is the **impact lag**, the time period between the implementation of a macro policy change and when the change exerts its primary impact on the economy. Although the impact of a change in tax rates is generally felt quickly, the expansionary effects of an increase in government spending are usually less rapid. It will take time for contractors to submit competitive bids and new contracts to be arranged and signed. Several months may pass before work on a new project actually begins. As we discussed in the previous chapter, the impact lag for monetary policy is variable and often lengthy. Six to eighteen months may pass before a shift in monetary policy exerts much impact on demand, output, and employment. Moreover, the time lag before there is a significant impact on the general level of prices and the rate of inflation is likely to be even longer.

15-3 FORECASTING TOOLS AND MACRO POLICY

If a shift in policy is going to exert the desired effect at the proper time, policy-makers cannot wait until a problem develops before they act. They need to know what economic conditions will be like six to fifteen months in the future. Policy-makers need to know if

Activists
Economists who believe that discretionary changes in monetary and fiscal policy can reduce the degree of instability in output and employment.

Nonactivists
Economists who believe that discretionary macro policy adjustments in response to cyclical conditions are likely to increase, rather than reduce, instability. Nonactivists favor steady and predictable policies regardless of business conditions.

Recognition lag
The time period after a policy change is needed from a stabilization standpoint but before the need is recognized by policy-makers.

Administrative lag
The time period after the need for a policy change is recognized but before the policy is actually implemented.

Impact lag
The time period after a policy change is implemented but before the change begins to exert its primary effects.

a recession or an economic boom is around the corner. How can they find out? Forecasting tools can provide them with some information. Let's consider some of the forecasting devices available to policy-makers.

15-3a INDEX OF LEADING INDICATORS

Index of leading indicators

An index of economic variables that historically has tended to turn down prior to the beginning of a recession and turn up prior to the beginning of a business expansion.

The **index of leading indicators** is the single most widely used and closely watched forecasting tool. The index is a composite statistic based on ten key variables that generally turn down prior to a recession and turn up before the beginning of a business expansion (see the Measures of Economic Activity, "The Index of Leading Indicators" below). The index is published monthly, and a decline for three consecutive months is considered a warning that the economy is about to dip into a recession.

Exhibit 2 illustrates the path of the index during the 1959–2020 period. The index has correctly forecast each of the nine recessions since 1959. On five occasions, the downturn occurred eight to ten months prior to a recession, providing policy-makers with sufficient lead time to modify policy, particularly monetary policy. In all but two instances, the downturn in the index preceded the recession by an even longer period. For example, it turned down 18 months prior to the 1990–1991 recession.

A downturn in the index, however, is not always an accurate indicator of the future. On four occasions (1962, 1966, 1984, and 1995), a decline in the index of leading indicators forecast a recession that did not materialize. This has given rise to the quip that the index has accurately forecast thirteen of the last nine recessions.

Consider the path of the index of leading indicators prior to and during the recession that started in December 2007. The index turned down eight months before the start of the recession and declined steadily until it reached a low in March 2009. The index rose three consecutive months in April, May, and June of 2009, thereby forecasting the recovery that

APPLICATIONS IN ECONOMICS

The Index of Leading Indicators

History indicates that no single indicator is able to forecast accurately the future direction of the economy. However, several economic variables do tend to reach a high or low prior to the peak of a business expansion or the trough of an economic recession. Such variables are called leading economic indicators.

To provide more reliable information on the future direction of the economy, economists have devised an index of ten such indicators:

1. Length of the average workweek in hours
2. Initial weekly claims for unemployment compensation
3. New orders placed with manufacturers
4. Percentage of companies receiving slower deliveries from suppliers
5. Contracts and orders for new plants and equipment
6. Permits for new housing starts
7. Interest rate spread, ten-year Treasury bonds less federal funds rate
8. Index of consumer expectations
9. Change in the index of stock prices (500 common stocks)
10. Change in the money supply (M2)

The variables included in the index were chosen both because of their tendency to lead (or predict) turns in the business cycle and because they are available frequently and promptly. In some cases, it is easy to see why a change in an economic indicator precedes a change in general economic activity. Consider the indicator of "new orders placed with manufacturers" (measured in constant dollars). An expansion in the volume of orders is generally followed by an expansion in manufacturing output. Similarly, manufacturers will tend to scale back their future production when a decline in new orders signals the probability of weak future demand for their products. The index of leading indicators can be found in *Business Cycle Indicators*, published by the Conference Board, a nonprofit business and research organization and online at http://www.conference-board.org.

EXHIBIT 2

Index of Leading Indicators

The shaded periods represent recessions. The index of leading indicators forecast each of the nine recessions during the 1959–2020 period. As the arrows show, however, the time lag between when the index turned down and when the economy fell into a recession varied. In addition, on four occasions (1962, 1966, 1984, and 1995), the index forecast a recession that did not occur.

[a] The arrows indicate the number of months that the downturn in the index preceded a recession. An asterisk (*) indicates a false signal of a recession.

Source: http://www.conference-board.org.

actually started in June of that year. Following the Great Recession, the index increased steadily, and by 2017, it had surpassed the previous peak level of 2006. Interestingly, the index fell during the five months following July 2019, forecasting a forthcoming recession. Of course, the economic shutdown accompanying the COVID-19 virus caused the potential recession.

15-3b COMPUTER FORECASTING MODELS

Economists have developed highly complex econometric (statistical) models to improve the accuracy of macroeconomic forecasts. In essence, these models use past data on economic interrelationships to project how currently observed changes will influence the future path of key economic variables, such as real GDP, employment, and the price level. The most elaborate models use hundreds of variables and equations to simulate the future direction of various sectors and the economy's overall output and employment. Powerful high-speed computers are employed to forecast the future direction of the economy and analyze the effects of policy alternatives.

To date, the record of computer forecasting models is mixed. When economic conditions are relatively stable (for example, when the growth of real GDP and the rate of inflation follow a steady trend), the models have generally provided accurate forecasts for both aggregate economic variables and important subcomponents of the economy. Unfortunately, however, they have generally missed the major turns in the economic road.

For example, none of the major computer models predicted the recessions of either 1990 or 2001. Neither did they forecast the severity of the downturn in 2008.

15-3c MARKET SIGNALS AS FORECASTING TOOLS

Many policy-makers have favorite indicators—such as the consumer confidence index or the number of first-time applicants for unemployment benefits—that they believe are particularly good forecasting tools. Information supplied by certain markets can also sound an early warning that a change in policy is needed. For example, because they fluctuate daily and are determined in auction markets, changes in commodity prices often foretell future changes in the general price level. An increase in a broad index of commodity prices implies that money is plentiful (relative to demand). This suggests that the Fed should shift toward a more restrictive policy in order to offset future inflation. In contrast, falling commodity prices indicate that deflation is a potential future danger, in which case the Fed might want to shift toward a more expansionary policy.

Changes in exchange rates are also a source of information about the relative scarcity of money and fear of inflation. A decline in the exchange rate value of the dollar relative to other currencies suggests a fear of higher inflation and a reluctance to hold dollars. This would signal the need to shift to a more restrictive policy. Conversely, an increase in the exchange rate value of the dollar would indicate that the Fed has some leeway to shift to a more expansionary monetary policy. Most policy-makers view market signals like commodity prices and exchange rates as supplements to, rather than substitutes for, other forecasting devices.

15-3d IS ACCURATE FORECASTING FEASIBLE?

Many economists maintain that accurate forecasts of turns in the economy are beyond the reach of economics. Two major factors underlie this view. First, turns in the economic road often reflect economic shocks and unforeseen events—for example, discovery of a new resource or technology, abnormal weather, or political upheaval in an important oil-exporting nation. There is no reason to believe that economists or anyone else will be able to predict these changes accurately and consistently. Thus, while economic theory helps to predict the implications of unforeseen events, it cannot foretell what those events will be and when they might occur. Second, the critics of forecasting models argue that the future will differ from the past because people will often make different choices as the result of what they learned from previous events. Therefore, forecasting models based on past relationships—including elaborate computer models—will never be able to generate consistently accurate predictions.

One thing is for sure: Forecasting the future direction of the economy is an imperfect science, and it is likely to remain so in the foreseeable future. But this is not the only deterrent to effective stabilization policy. Policy-makers must also deal with expectations. A policy shift may exert a very different impact, depending on whether it is widely expected or catches people by surprise. Expectations may also influence the length of time lags and potency of alternative policy measures. Given the importance of expectations, we need to analyze in more detail how they are formed.

15-4 HOW ARE EXPECTATIONS FORMED?

There are two general theories about how expectations are formed: adaptive and rational expectations.

Under the simplest theory, the **adaptive-expectations hypothesis**, it is assumed that decision-makers rely on what has happened in the recent past as the best indicator of what will happen in the future. For example, individuals would expect the price level to be stable next year if stable prices had been present during the past two or three years. Similarly, if prices had risen at an annual rate of 4 or 5 percent during the past several years,

Adaptive-expectations hypothesis
The hypothesis that economic decision-makers base their future expectations on actual outcomes observed during recent periods. For example, according to this view, the rate of inflation actually experienced during the past two or three years would be the major determinant of the rate of inflation expected for the next year.

then people would expect similar increases next year. Of course, as conditions change, people will alter their expectations. However, under the adaptive expectations theory, there will always be a time lag before people will alter their expectations in response to changing conditions.

The **rational-expectations hypothesis** is more complex. Under this theory, people form their expectations about the future on the basis of all available information, including knowledge about policy changes and how they affect the economy. According to this view, rather than merely assuming that the future will be like the immediate past, people also consider the expected effects of changes in policy. Based on their understanding of economic policy, for example, people may alter their expectations regarding the future rate of inflation when the government runs a larger deficit or expands the supply of money more rapidly.

Perhaps an example will help clarify the difference between the two theories. Suppose that prices had increased at an annual rate of 3 percent during each of the past three years. In addition, assume that decision-makers believe there is a relationship between the growth rate of the money supply and rising prices. They note that the money stock has expanded at a 12 percent annual rate during the last nine months, up from the 4 percent rate of the past several years. According to the rational-expectations hypothesis, people will integrate the shift to the more expansionary monetary policy into their forecast of the future inflation rate. For example, they might project an increase in the inflation rate, perhaps to the 6 to 10 percent range. In other words, based on the more expansionary monetary policy, people will begin to anticipate the higher rate of inflation even before it actually occurs. In contrast, under the adaptive-expectations hypothesis, the more expansionary monetary policy would exert no impact on the expectations of people, at least not until there was an increase in the rate of inflation.

The rational-expectations hypothesis does not assume that forecasts will always be correct. We live in a world of uncertainty. Even rational decision-makers will err. But they will not continue to make the same errors.

There are two major differences between the two theories: (1) how quickly people adjust to a change and (2) the likelihood of systematic forecasting errors. If the adaptive-expectations theory is correct, people will adjust more slowly. When a more expansionary policy leads to inflation, for example, there will be a significant time lag, perhaps two or three years, before people come to expect the inflation and incorporate it into their decision-making. In contrast, the rational-expectations theory implies that people will begin to anticipate more inflation as soon as they observe a move toward a more expansionary policy—perhaps even before there is an actual increase in the rate of inflation. Therefore, the time lag between a shift in policy and a change in expectations will be shorter under rational than under adaptive expectations.

Second, systematic errors will occur under adaptive but not under rational expectations. For example, with adaptive expectations, when the inflation rate is rising, decision-makers will systematically tend to underestimate the future rate of inflation. In contrast, when the rate of inflation is falling, individuals will tend systematically to overestimate its future rate. The errors will be random under rational expectations. With rational expectations, people will be as likely to overestimate as to underestimate the inflationary impact of a shift to a more expansionary policy.

Rational-expectations hypothesis
The hypothesis that economic decision-makers weigh all available evidence, including information concerning the probable effects of current and future economic policy, when they form their expectations about future economic events (such as the probable future inflation rate).

Scott Olsons/Reuters/Corbis

Outstanding Economist: Robert Lucas (1937–)

The 1995 Nobel laureate Robert Lucas is generally given credit for the introduction of the rational-expectations theory into macroeconomics. Lucas's technical work in this area has substantially altered the way economists think about macroeconomic policy. Lucas is also a major contributor to the literature on development and economic growth. He argues that the forces influencing growth are similar in both rich and poor countries. He is a longtime professor of economics at the University of Chicago.

15-5 MACRO POLICY IMPLICATIONS OF ADAPTIVE AND RATIONAL EXPECTATIONS

When it comes to setting macro policy, does it make any difference how quickly people alter their expectations and whether errors are random or systematic? The *AD–AS* model can be used to address this question. Suppose that there is a shift to a more expansionary macro policy—an increase in the money growth rate, for example. As **Exhibit 3** illustrates, the policy shift will stimulate aggregate demand and place upward pressure on the price level (or the inflation rate in the dynamic case). Under adaptive expectations (panel a), people will initially fail to anticipate the higher prices. Therefore, as we have previously discussed, output will temporarily increase to Y_2, beyond the economy's long-run potential. Correspondingly, employment will expand and unemployment will recede below the economy's natural rate. When the effects of expansionary policy are unanticipated, both output and employment increase in the short run.

However, the output rate beyond the economy's capacity will be unsustainable even with adaptive expectations. As the expansionary policies persist and the rate of inflation increases, people will eventually begin to anticipate the higher rate of inflation. Once this happens, resource prices will rise as rapidly as product prices, and output will return to its long-run potential (Y_F). As a result, the high level of output and employment will only be temporary.

Panel (b) of Exhibit 3 illustrates the impact of expansionary macroeconomic policy under rational expectations. Remember, with rational expectations, decision-makers will

---

EXHIBIT 3

Adaptive and Rational Expectations and the Short-Run Effects of Demand Stimulus

Because under adaptive expectations people do not anticipate inflation until after it occurs, a shift to a more expansionary policy will increase aggregate demand and lead to a temporary increase in real GDP from Y_F to Y_2, (panel a). In contrast, under rational expectations, people quickly anticipate the inflationary impact of demand–stimulus policies and therefore resource prices and production costs rise as rapidly as production prices. In this case, both *AD* and *SRAS* shift upward, leading to an increase in the general level of prices (inflation), but there is no change in real output, even in the short run (panel b).

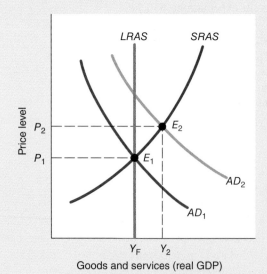

(a) Expansionary policy under adaptive expectations

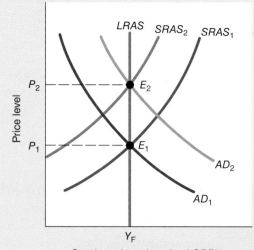

(b) Expansionary policy under rational expectations

quickly begin to anticipate the probable effects of the more expansionary policy—stronger demand and a rising rate of inflation, for example—and alter their choices accordingly. Agreements specifying future wage rates and resource prices will quickly make allowance for an expected increase in the price level. When buyers and sellers in the resource market anticipate fully and adjust rapidly to the effects of the demand–stimulus policies, wage rates and resource prices will rise as rapidly as product prices. Hence, the short-run aggregate supply curve will shift upward (to $SRAS_2$) as rapidly as the aggregate demand curve. Under these circumstances, an expansionary policy that leads to an increase in aggregate demand will generate only a higher general level of prices (the move from E_1 to E_2 in panel b of Exhibit 3). There will be no real output increase even in the short run. Thus, the rational-expectations hypothesis implies that when decision-makers quickly anticipate the inflationary side effects of an expansionary policy, the policy will fail to expand output even temporarily.

The policy implications of the two theories differ in the short run but not in the long run. In the short run, demand–stimulus policies will expand output and employment under adaptive expectations but not under rational expectations. In the long run, however, the implications of the two theories are identical. Like rational expectations, the adaptive-expectations theory indicates that decision-makers will eventually anticipate the inflationary effects of the more expansionary policy. Once this happens, output will recede to the economy's long-run potential. Therefore, both theories imply that the long-run effects of a more expansionary macro policy will be inflation rather than sustainable increases in output. Both also imply that price stability and full-employment output are complementary when considered over lengthy time frames.

15-6 THE PHILLIPS CURVE: THE VIEW OF THE 1960s VERSUS TODAY

In the late 1950s, British economist A. W. Phillips examined the historical data on the relationship between wage inflation and unemployment in the United Kingdom.[2] As a result, a curve indicating the relationship between the rate of inflation and the rate of unemployment is known as the **Phillips curve**. **Exhibit 4** uses a graphic from the 1969 *Economic Report of the President* to illustrate the idea of the Phillips curve. When the unemployment rate was plotted against the rate of inflation in the United States during 1954–1968, the points mapped out a curve indicating that there was an inverse relationship between the rate of inflation and the rate of unemployment. When inflation was high, the unemployment rate tended to be low. Correspondingly, when the inflation rate was low, the unemployment rate tended to be high.

In the 1960s, most macroeconomists ignored the potential impact of expectations. Instead, they believed that there was a direct trade-off between inflation and unemployment—that a lower rate of unemployment could be achieved if we were willing to tolerate a little more inflation. For example, Nobel prize winners Paul Samuelson and Robert Solow told the American Economic Association in 1959, *In order to achieve the nonperfectionist's goal of high enough output to give us no more than 3 percent unemployment, the price index might have to rise by as much as 4 to 5 percent per year. That much price rise [inflation] would seem to be the necessary cost of high employment and production in the years immediately ahead.*[3] The inflation–unemployment trade-off view provided the foundation for the inflationary policies of the 1970s. As John Maynard Keynes once noted, ideas have consequences, both when they are right and when they are wrong.

Beginning in the latter part of the 1960s, both monetary and fiscal policy became more expansionary. The inflation rate rose to the 3 percent to 6 percent range, but as the higher

Phillips curve
A curve that illustrates the relationship between the rate of inflation and the rate of unemployment.

[2]A. W. Phillips, "The Relationship between Unemployment and the Rate of Change of Money Wages in the United Kingdom, 1861–1957," *Economica* 25 (1958): 238–99.

[3]Paul A. Samuelson and Robert Solow, "Our Menu of Policy Changes," *American Economic Review* (May 1960).

EXHIBIT 4

Early View of the Phillips Curve

The Phillips curve shows the relationship between inflation and unemployment. The dots on this diagram from the 1969 *Economic Report of the President* represent the inflation rate and unemployment rate for each year between 1954 and 1968. Note that the chart suggests that higher rates of inflation are associated with lower rates of unemployment. Because they failed to recognize the importance of expectations, many economists and policy-makers in the 1960s and 1970s thought this relationship was stable. Thus, they believed that expansionary (inflationary) policies could permanently reduce the rate of unemployment. As the record of the 1970s shows, this view is fallacious.

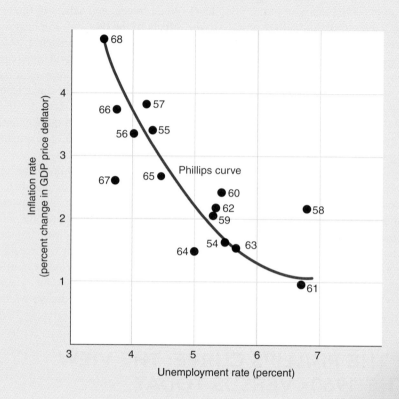

rates of inflation persisted, the unemployment rate also began to rise. As macroeconomic policy became even more expansionary, the unemployment rate dipped briefly, but it soon returned to exceedingly high levels. By the end of the 1970s, the U.S. economy was characterized by high rates of both inflation and unemployment. The inflation rate in 1979 was 11.3 percent, and in 1980 it jumped to 13.5 percent, about 10 percentage points higher than the rates of the late 1960s. But even these high rates of inflation failed to reduce the unemployment rate. In 1980, the rate of unemployment stood at 7.1 percent, well above the 4.9 percent registered during the recessionary year of 1970.

What went wrong? Given what we know today about expectations, this is now an easy question to answer. As both the adaptive- and rational-expectations theories indicate, the alleged trade-off between inflation and unemployment will dissipate once people anticipate a higher rate of inflation. Put another way, the Phillips curve is not fixed. When the inflation rate increases, people will come to anticipate the higher rate of inflation, and this will cause the Phillips curve to shift upward and to the right. The adaptive-expectations theory implies that there will be a time lag—perhaps one to three years—before people are able to anticipate and adjust fully to a higher rate of inflation. But once the higher inflation rate is anticipated, it will not lead to an expansion in either output or employment. The rational-expectations theory indicates that the adjustment period will be brief. In fact, with rational expectations, there may not be any trade-off between inflation and unemployment, even in the short run.

Integration of expectations into the Phillips curve analysis indicates that there is no sustainable trade-off between inflation and unemployment. Expectations undermine the simple Phillips curve analysis of the 1960s.[4]

15-6a EXPECTATIONS AND THE MODERN VIEW OF THE PHILLIPS CURVE

If accurately anticipated by decision-makers, even high rates of inflation—rates of 10 or 15 percent, for example—will fail to reduce unemployment below its natural rate.[5] Of course, people won't always correctly anticipate the rate of inflation, particularly if there is an abrupt change in the rate. Within the expectations framework, it is the difference between the actual and expected inflation rate that will influence output and employment. On the one hand, when inflation is greater than anticipated, profit margins will improve, output will expand, and unemployment will fall below its natural rate. On the other hand, when the actual rate of inflation is less than the expected rate, profits will be abnormally low, output will recede, and unemployment will rise above its natural rate.

Exhibit 5 recasts the Phillips curve within the expectations framework. When people underestimate the actual rate of inflation, abnormally low unemployment will occur. Conversely, when decision-makers expect a higher rate of inflation than what actually occurs—when they overestimate the inflation rate—unemployment will rise above its

EXHIBIT 5

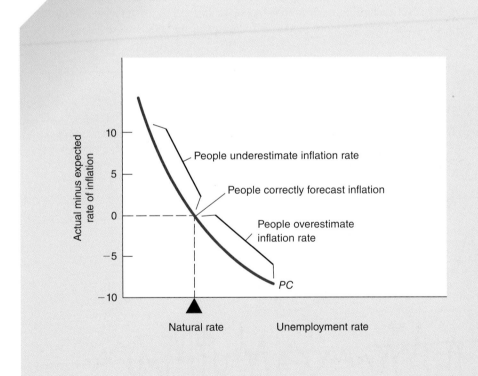

Modern Expectational Phillips Curve

It is the difference between the actual and expected rates of inflation that influences the unemployment rate, not the size of the inflation rate, as the earlier, naive Phillips curve analysis implied. When inflation is greater than anticipated (people underestimate it), unemployment will fall below the natural rate. In contrast, when inflation is less than people anticipate (people overestimate it) unemployment will rise above the natural rate. If decision-makers correctly anticipate the inflation rate, the natural rate of unemployment will result.

---

[4]Even during the 1960s, there were some critics of the inflation–unemployment trade-off view. See Edmund S. Phelps, "Phillips Curves, Expectations of Inflation and Optimal Employment over Time," *Economica* 3 (1967): 254–81; and Milton Friedman, "The Role of Monetary Policy," *American Economic Review* (May 1968): 1–17.

[5]Empirically, higher rates of inflation are generally associated with greater variability in the inflation rate. Erratic variability increases economic uncertainty. It is likely to inhibit business activity, reduce the volume of mutually advantageous exchange, and cause the level of employment to fall. Thus, higher, more variable inflation rates may well increase the rate of unemployment.

natural rate. When the actual and expected inflation rates are equal, the economy's output will be at its potential and unemployment at its natural rate.

When the inflation rate is steady, when it is neither rising nor falling, people will come to anticipate the rate accurately. The steady rate will be built into long-term contracts, like collective bargaining agreements, building leases, and bank loans. Under these conditions, profit margins will be normal, and output will move toward the economy's long-run potential. Correspondingly, the actual rate of unemployment will move toward its natural rate—its minimum sustainable rate. In fact, the natural rate of unemployment is sometimes defined as the unemployment rate present when the inflation rate is neither rising nor falling. In contrast with the early Phillips curve view, the modern view indicates that if policymakers want to keep the unemployment rate low, they should follow policies consistent with a low and steady rate of inflation—one that people will be able to forecast accurately.

Exhibit 6 presents data on the *change* in the inflation rate (the four-quarter moving average) over the past several decades. The exhibit illustrates the impact of both abrupt changes and low steady rates of inflation. When the change in the inflation rate spikes upward, it means there has been a sharp increase in the rate of inflation during the last 12 months. Conversely, a downward spike means that the inflation rate has fallen sharply. Predictably, these abrupt changes will be difficult for people to forecast accurately. Therefore, the actual rate of inflation is likely to rise above the expected rate when the inflation rate increases abruptly and fall below it when there is an abrupt downturn in the inflation rate.

Thus, one would expect the unemployment rate to fall when there is a sharp upturn in the inflation rate and rise when there is a sharp downturn. As Exhibit 6 shows, this has been the case. Notice how the substantial increases in the rate of inflation during 1973 and 1976–1978 and even the more moderate increases of the 1980s were associated with

EXHIBIT 6

Unemployment Rate and the Change in the Rate of Inflation, 1971–2019

Here, we show the relationship between changes in the inflation rate (four-quarter moving average) and the rate of unemployment. Abrupt changes in the inflation rate will be difficult for people to anticipate correctly. Notice how the sharp declines in the inflation rate during 1974, 1980–1981, and 1988–1989 preceded recessions and substantial increases in the unemployment rate. Also notice that the steadier (and lower) inflation rates during 1990–2004 and 2010–2019 were associated with lower and more stable rates of unemployment.

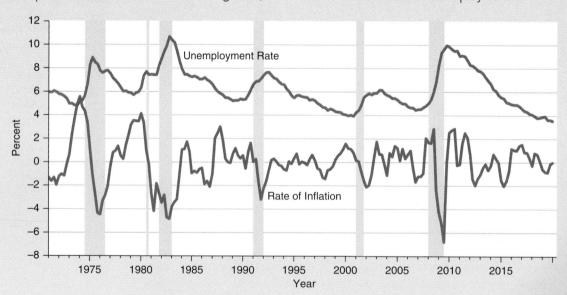

Source: http://www.economagic.com.

downturns in the rate of unemployment. In contrast, the sharp reductions in the rate of inflation during 1974, 1980–1981, and 1989 preceded substantial increases in the rate of unemployment. The economic crisis of 2008–2009 was a little different. In that case, a sharp decline in the inflation rate was associated with a substantial increase in the unemployment rate during the same time period.

Exhibit 6 also shows that when the inflation rate is steadier, the unemployment rate tends to be lower and more stable. Note how, compared to the 1970s, the inflation rate was lower and the swings in the rate were more moderate during 1990–2004 and during 2010–2019. Correspondingly, the rate of unemployment was also lower and more stable during the latter period of greater price stability.

15-7 THE GROWING FEDERAL DEBT AND ECONOMIC STABILITY

Since 2000, the federal government has run large deficits and the national debt has risen to a historically high level. How will high debt levels impact economic stability? Why is it difficult to control the growth of government debt? Are the debt levels of the United States dangerous? We now turn to an examination of these questions.

15-7a DEFICITS, SURPLUSES, AND THE NATIONAL DEBT

When federal expenditures exceed revenues, the U.S. Treasury issues bonds to cover this budget deficit. These bonds compose the **national debt**. In effect, the national debt consists of loans extended by various parties to the general fund of the U.S. Treasury. A budget deficit increases the size of the national debt by the amount of the deficit. Conversely, a budget surplus allows the federal government to pay off some of the bonds and thereby reduce the size of the national debt. In essence, the national debt represents the cumulative effect of all the prior budget deficits and surpluses.

National debt
The sum of the indebtedness of the federal government in the form of outstanding interest-earning bonds. It reflects the cumulative impact of budget deficits and surpluses.

The creditworthiness of an organization is dependent upon the size of its debt relative to its income base. Therefore, when analyzing the significance of budget deficits, surpluses, and the national debt, it makes sense to consider their size relative to the entire economy.

The defense effort of World War II was financed largely with debt, not taxes. As a result, the national debt ballooned to slightly more than 100 percent of GDP during and immediately following the war. However, during the 1950s and 1960s, the budget deficits were small, generally less than 1 percent of GDP. Because the growth rate of the economy (about 3 percent annually) was larger than the deficits as a share of GDP during 1950–1970, the national debt fell as a share of the economy.

Exhibit 7 presents data for the 1960–2020 period for both the federal budget deficit and the national debt as a percentage of GDP. Because of the small deficits and strong economic growth, the national debt continued to decline as a share of GDP until the mid-1970s. But the deficits were large during 1974–1995. As Exhibit 7, panel (a) shows, budget deficits averaged about 3.5 percent of GDP during this time frame. These large deficits pushed the national debt up from 33 percent of GDP in 1974 to 65 percent in 1995. As the economy grew rapidly in the 1990s, the budget deficits were eventually transformed into surpluses, leading to a temporary reduction in the national debt. However, the budget deficits were large during and following the severe recession of 2008–2009 and more recently during the 2020 recession. As Exhibit 7, panel (b) shows, the ratio of federal debt to GDP rose from 56 percent in 2000 to 68 percent in 2008 and then soared to 107 percent in 2019.

Even though the economy was in the midst of a lengthy economic expansion and the unemployment rate was low, the budget deficits remained large during 2015–2019. During 2020, the deficit soared because of a shutdown of the economy to slow the spread of the COVID-19 virus and a huge increase in government spending to minimize the damages of the shutdown. Emergency government spending increased by more than $2.5 trillion, and the deficit ballooned to $4 trillion. These large deficits pushed the national debt up from

EXHIBIT 7

Budget Deficits, Surpluses, and the National Debt as a Percentage of GDP

Panel (a) shows the path of the federal budget deficits and surpluses as a share of GDP from 1960–2020. Note the budget deficits were large during 1982–1993 and 2008–2020. Panel (b) shows both the national debt and the privately held debt as a share of GDP. These ratios rose during the 1980s, declined during the 1990s, and expanded to historically high levels in recent years. The national debt as a share of GDP in 2020 was higher than the year immediately after WWII.

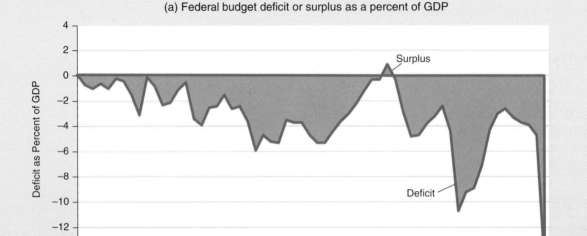

(a) Federal budget deficit or surplus as a percent of GDP

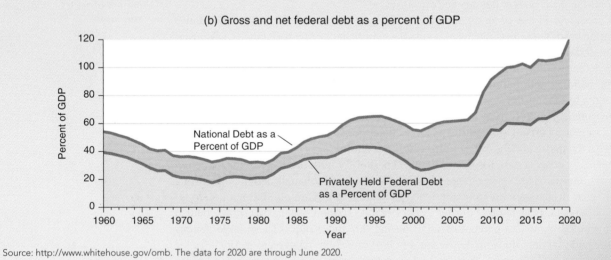

(b) Gross and net federal debt as a percent of GDP

Source: http://www.whitehouse.gov/omb. The data for 2020 are through June 2020.

$23.2 trillion to more than $26 trillion in just four months during March through June of 2020. Measured as a share of GDP, the federal debt rose to 120 percent in June of 2020, and projections indicate it will reach 130 percent of GDP by the end of the year. These are historically high levels, even greater than the debt-to-GDP ratio at the end of World War II. Further, while sharp declines in national defense spending resulted in reductions in both government expenditures and budget deficits following the war, the current federal deficits are structural and, therefore, almost certain to continue in the years immediately ahead.

Would you like to know the current level of the national debt? The debt clock will provide you with the answer: http://www.usdebtclock.org.

15-7b WHO OWNS THE NATIONAL DEBT?

Exhibit 8, panel (a), indicates the ownership of the national debt at year end 2019. More than a quarter (25.8 percent) of the national debt is held by agencies of the federal government. For example, Social Security Trust Funds were often used to purchase U.S. bonds. When the debt is owned by a government agency, it is little more than an accounting transaction indicating that one government agency (for example, the Social Security Administration) is making a loan to another government agency (the U.S. Treasury). Even the interest payments in this case represent little more than an internal government transfer.

Another 11.7 percent of the public debt is held by the Federal Reserve System. When the Fed purchases U.S. securities, it creates money. The bonds held by the Fed, therefore, are indicative of prior government expenditures that have been paid for with "printing-press" money—money created by the central bank. As in the case of the securities held by government agencies, the interest on the bonds held by the Fed is returned to the Treasury after the Fed has covered its costs of operation. The U.S. Treasury both pays and receives almost all of the interest, approximately $55 billion in 2019, on the bonds held by the Federal Reserve. Thus, the bonds held by the Fed, like those held by U.S. government agencies, do not create a net interest liability for the U.S. Treasury.

In contrast, **privately held government debt** imposes a net interest burden on the federal government. In the case of the privately held debt—that is, the bonds held by individuals, insurance companies, mutual funds, and other investors—the federal government will have to impose taxes to meet the future interest payments on these bonds. Therefore, it is important to distinguish between (1) the total national debt and (2) the privately held government debt. Only the latter imposes a net interest obligation on the federal government. As Exhibit 8, panel (b) shows, the privately held portion of the national debt at year end 2019 was $14.49 trillion, 62 percent of the $23.20 trillion national debt. Foreigners own one-half of the privately held debt, and this share has increased in recent decades.

Privately held government debt
The portion of the national debt owed to domestic and foreign investors. It does not include bonds held by agencies of the federal government or the Federal Reserve.

EXHIBIT 8

Who Owns the National Debt?, December 2019

Of the $23.20 trillion national debt, about two-fifths is held by government entities (primarily the Social Security Trust Fund) and Federal Reserve banks. Of the $14.49 trillion federal debt held privately, a little less than one-half is held by foreign Investors.

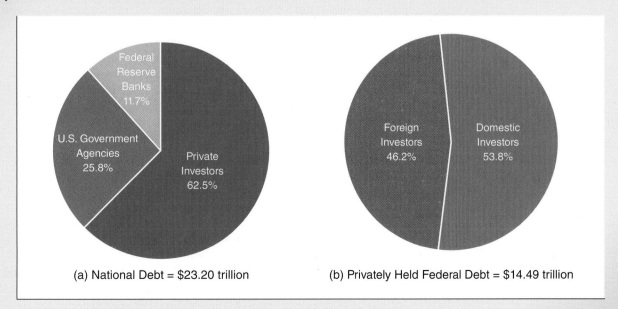

(a) National Debt = $23.20 trillion   (b) Privately Held Federal Debt = $14.49 trillion

Source: https://www.fiscal.treasury.gov/fsreports/rpt/treasBulletin/treasBulletin_home.htm

Panel (b) of Exhibit 7 presents data on the size of the privately held federal debt for the 1960–2019 period. Measured as a share of GDP, the general pattern of the privately held debt has been similar to that for the national debt as a whole. Like the total debt, the privately held debt has soared in recent years. Driven by the huge deficits of 2008–2019, the privately held debt rose from 36 percent of GDP in 2008 to 47 percent in 2009 and 69 percent in 2019.

15-7c HOW DOES DEBT FINANCING INFLUENCE FUTURE GENERATIONS?

The impact of government debt on future generations has been a hotly debated topic among economists for more than a half century. When considering this issue, it is important to keep three points in mind. First, in the case of domestically held debt, our children and grandchildren will indeed pay the taxes to service the debt, but they will also receive the interest payments. Admittedly, those paying the taxes and receiving the interest payments will not always be the same people. Some will gain, and others will lose. But both those who gain and those who lose will be members of the future generation.

Second, debt financing of a government activity cannot push the opportunity cost of the resources used by the government onto future generations. If current GDP is $25 trillion and the federal government spends $5 trillion on goods and services, then only $20 trillion will be available for consumption and investment by domestic businesses, state and local governments, and individuals. This will be true regardless of whether the federal government finances its expenditures with taxes or debt. When the government builds a highway, constructs an antimissile defense system, or provides police protection, it draws resources with alternative uses away from the private sector. This cost is incurred in the present; it cannot be avoided through debt financing.

Third, debt financing will influence future generations primarily through its impact on capital formation. If future generations inherit many factories, machines, houses, technical knowledge, and other productive assets, then their productive potential will be high. Alternatively, if the next generation inherits fewer productive assets, then its productive capability will be lower.

As Exhibit 8 shows, a little less than half of the privately held federal debt is currently financed by borrowing from foreigners. The foreign borrowing will lead to an inflow of financial capital, appreciation of the dollar, and a reduction in net exports. However, even in the case of borrowing from foreigners, future generations would not be harmed if the funds were channeled into productive investments that generated sufficient income to cover the interest payments.

But this may not be the case. Instead of allocating the borrowed funds into investment, they may be used to enlarge current consumption. To the degree that current citizens increase their consumption and future generations pay higher taxes to service the debt to foreigners, the current generation will benefit at the expense of future Americans. There is some evidence this has been the case. As the United States experienced large budget deficits during 2001–2020, consumption expenditures increased as a share of GDP, private investment was weak, and the trade deficits were large. This pattern indicates that the current generation was the primary beneficiary of these deficits.

15-7d WHY IS DEFICIT SPENDING SO DIFFICULT TO CONTROL?

The attractiveness of financing spending by debt issue to the elected politicians should be obvious. Borrowing allows spending to be made that will yield immediate political payoffs without the incurring of any immediate political cost.—James Buchanan[6]

Keynesian budget finance argues that instead of balancing the budget, the federal budget should be used to help stabilize the economy. Since the early 1960s, this view has been widely accepted by both economists and policymakers. But acceptance of the Keynesian

---

[6]James Buchanan, *The Deficit and American Democracy* (Memphis: P. K. Steidman Foundation, 1984).

view results in a secondary effect: a strong bias toward deficit spending.[7] Since 1960, there have been four budget surpluses and 56 budget deficits.

The political bias toward spending financed by borrowing rather than taxation is not surprising. It reflects what economists call the shortsightedness effect: the tendency of elected political officials to favor projects that generate immediate, highly visible benefits at the expense of costs that can be cast into the future and are difficult to identify. Legislators have an incentive to spend money on programs that benefit the voters of their district and special-interest groups that will help them win reelection. They do not like to tax because taxes impose a visible cost on voters. Debt is an alternative to current taxes; it pushes the visible cost of government into the future. Budget deficits and borrowing allow politicians to supply voters with immediate benefits without imposing higher taxes. Thus, deficits are a natural outgrowth of the political process unrestrained by a commitment to a balanced budget.

The unconstrained political process plays into the hands of well-organized interest groups and encourages politicians to increase spending to gain benefits for a few at the expense of many. For example, each member of Congress has a strong incentive to fight hard for expenditures beneficial to his or her constituents. In contrast, there is little incentive for a legislator to be a spending "watchdog" for two reasons. First, such a watchdog would incur the wrath of colleagues because the spending restraint would make it more difficult for them to deliver special programs for their districts. They would retaliate by providing little support for spending in the watchdog's district. Second, and more importantly, the benefits of spending cuts and deficit reductions that the watchdog is trying to attain (for example, lower taxes) will accrue equally to voters in the other 434 districts. Thus, even if the watchdog is successful, the constituents in his or her district will reap only a small fraction of the benefits.

The political incentive structure explains the popularity of deficit financing and why it is difficult to control the growth of debt. Further, the formal debt obligations are not the only debt-related problem. The structures of the Social Security and Medicare programs have the same bias toward debt financing. The unfunded promises of these programs also make it possible for politicians to take credit for visible benefits now without having to levy the equivalent amount of taxes.

At current tax rates, the revenues flowing into the Social Security system will cover only about 75 percent of the promised benefits. The unfunded future benefits promised to senior citizens under the Social Security and Medicare programs are another form of debt, and these obligations are more than three times the size of the privately held federal debt.[8] As the baby boomers move into the retirement phase of life between now and 2030, spending on Social Security and Medicare will outstrip the revenues for their finance, further complicating the debt liabilities of the federal government in the years immediately ahead.

15-7e HAVE FEDERAL DEBT OBLIGATIONS GROWN TO A DANGEROUS LEVEL?

What will happen if a government does not bring its finances under control? As a nation's debt gets larger and larger relative to the size of its economy, there will be repercussions in credit markets. Extending loans to the government of a country with a large ratio of debt to GDP is risky. As a result, the highly indebted government will have to pay higher interest rates. In turn, the higher interest costs will make it even more difficult for the government to restrain spending to the level of revenue and keep taxes at reasonable levels. Moreover, as tax rates are raised to a high level, the economy will slow, which will make it even more difficult for the government to obtain more revenue. Eventually, the government will be unable to raise enough revenue to meet its other obligations and make the interest payments

---

[7]See James M. Buchanan and Richard Wagner, *Democracy in Deficit: The Political Legacy of Lord Keynes* (New York: Academic Press, 1977), for a detailed account of the changes wrought by the Keynesian revolution.

[8]See *2019 Annual Report of the Boards of Trustees of the Federal Hospital Insurance and Federal Supplementary Medical Insurance Trust Fund*, https://www.cms.gov/Research-Statistics-Data-and-Systems/Statistics-Trends-and-Reports/ReportsTrustFunds/index.html.

on its debt. This recently happened in Greece. The European Union, at least for now, agreed to restructure the Greek debt in exchange for various accommodations.

When confronting a debt crisis, several governments have defaulted on their promises to bondholders. In the case of a government with a central bank, such as the United States, default is unlikely. Instead, it is far more likely that the government will resort to money creation to service the debt and meet other obligations. But if lenders even begin to sense that might happen, they will sell their bonds and other dollar-denominated assets, the foreign exchange value of the dollar will plunge, and inflation will soar. These factors will generate uncertainty, a breakdown in market exchange, and a destructive impact on the economy.

As we discussed in the previous chapter, real interest rates during the past decade have fallen to historic low levels throughout the world. The low rates have made it easier for highly indebted governments to meet their interest obligations. If the low interest rates continue, the current level of federal debt is unlikely to pose a serious problem. But there is also danger here. The low interest rates may encourage continued growth of debt. If this is the case, once interest rates reverse and move upward, the revenues required to make the interest payments will increase sharply. This will make it very difficult for a heavily indebted country to meet its obligations and make the interest payments, particularly if interest rates increase abruptly. Other countries have experienced financial crises as the result of excessive debt, and the United States is not immune to these disruptive forces. Thus, the high level of federal debt is a potential source of economic instability.

15-8 PERSPECTIVE ON RECENT MACROECONOMIC POLICY AND ECONOMIC INSTABILITY

While reflecting on the current troubles of the U.S economy, we must not forget that 1983–2019 was the most stable period in American history. During this 37-year period, there were only three downturns, and the economy experienced only 34 months of recession. As Exhibit 9 illustrates, this stability is unprecedented. From 1910 to 1959, the U.S. economy was in recession 32.8 percent of the time. From 1960 through 1982, recession was present 22.8 percent of the time. But, during 1983–2019, the economy was in recession only 7.7 percent of the time. The economic ups and downs of the past 59 years have been less severe than during earlier periods. Inspection of Exhibit 1 also illustrates this point.

EXHIBIT 9

Reduction in the Incidence of Recession

The U.S. economy was in recession 32.8 percent of the time during the 1910–1959 period and 22.8 percent of the time between 1960 and 1982, but only 7.7 percent of the time during 1983–2019.

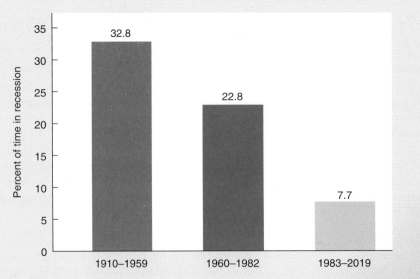

Source: R. E. Lipsey and D. Preston, Source Book of Statistics Relating to Construction (1966); and National Bureau of Economic Research, http://www.nber.org.

KEY POINTS

- Historically, the United States has experienced substantial swings in real output. Prior to World War II, year-to-year changes in real GDP of 5 to 10 percent were experienced on several occasions. In recent decades, the fluctuations in real GDP have been more moderate.

- If stimulus could be injected during periods of recession and restraint during inflationary booms, macro policy could moderate the ups and downs of the business cycle. Proper timing, however, is difficult to achieve because it takes time to recognize and institute a policy change, and the effects of the change are not immediate.

- In order to time a change properly, policy-makers need to know where the economy will be six to eighteen months in the future. Forecasting devices such as the index of leading indicators will be helpful, but forecasting is a highly imperfect science.

- There are two major theories as to how expectations are formed. According to the adaptive-expectations hypothesis, individuals form their expectations about the future on the basis of data from the recent past. The rational-expectations hypothesis assumes that people use all pertinent information, including data on the conduct of current policy, when forming their expectations about the future.

- With adaptive expectations, an unanticipated shift to a more expansionary policy will temporarily stimulate output and employment. In contrast, with rational expectations, expansionary policy may fail to increase output, and, if achieved, any increase in output will be brief. However, both expectations theories indicate that sustained expansionary policies will lead to inflation without permanently increasing output and employment.

- The Phillips curve outlines the relationship between inflation and unemployment. In the 1960s, it was widely believed that higher rates of inflation could be used to reduce the unemployment rate. This view provided the foundation for the expansionary policies of the 1970s and the inflation they generated. Integration of expectations into macro analysis makes it clear that the early view of the Phillips curve is fallacious.

- The federal debt-to-GDP ratio has increased sharply since 2000, and it is now even higher than the period immediately following World War II. There is a political bias toward deficit spending because political officials will find it attractive to spend on current programs without having to levy an equivalent amount of taxes.

- The political bias toward debt financing and upward pressure on spending for Social Security and Medicare as the baby boomers move into the retirement phase of life in the years immediately ahead will make it difficult to control the growth of federal debt. This will be particularly true if there is a substantial increase in interest rates. These conditions are a potential source of uncertainty and future instability.

CRITICAL ANALYSIS QUESTIONS

1. The chair of the Council of Economic Advisers has requested that you write a short paper explaining how economic policy can be used to stabilize the economy and achieve a high level of economic growth during the next five years. Be sure to make specific proposals. Indicate why your recommendations will work. You may submit your paper to your instructor.

2. *How does economic instability during the past sixty years compare with instability prior to World War II? Is there any evidence that stabilization policy has either increased or decreased economic stability during recent decades?

3. State in your own words the adaptive-expectations hypothesis. How does the theory of rational expectations differ from that of adaptive expectations?

4. What is the index of leading indicators? Why is it useful to macro policy-makers?

5. *How would you expect the actual rate of unemployment to compare with the natural rate of unemployment in the following cases?

   a. Prices are stable and have been stable for the last four years.

   b. The current inflation rate is 3 percent, and this rate was widely anticipated more than a year ago.

   c. Expansionary policies lead to an abrupt increase in the inflation rate from 3 to 7 percent.

   d. There is an abrupt reduction in the inflation rate from 7 to 2 percent.

6. Compare and contrast the impact of an unexpected shift to a more expansionary monetary policy under rational and adaptive expectations. Are the implications of the two theories different in the short run? Are the long-run implications different? Explain.

7. What are some of the practical problems that limit the effective use of discretionary monetary and fiscal policy as stabilization tools?

8. Will the national debt have to be paid off at some time in the future? What will happen if it is not?

9. How does debt financing influence the welfare of future generations? Does it make any difference whether the debt is financed by domestic citizens or foreigners? Explain.

10. Prior to the mid-1970s, many economists thought that inflation would lead to a lower rate of unemployment. Why? Did

the early fallacious view of the Phillips curve contribute to the inflationary policies of the 1970s? How does the modern view of the Phillips curve differ from the earlier view?

11. *Answer the following questions:

   a. What is the most important thing the Fed can do to promote economic stability?

   b. Can expansionary monetary policy reduce interest rates and stimulate a higher growth rate of real output in the long run?

   c. If monetary policy is too expansionary, how will nominal interest rates and the general level of prices be affected?

12. Why is debt financing so difficult to control? How has widespread acceptance of Keynesian macroeconomics influenced debt financing? Does the high level of the federal debt threaten the welfare of future generations? Why or why not?

13. Is the current level of the federal debt dangerously high? How would an increase in interest rates influence the dangers accompanying the federal debt? Carefully explain your answers.

14. What are unfunded government liabilities? In what respect are unfunded liabilities similar to debt financing? Are unfunded liabilities attractive to politicians? Why or why not?

*Asterisk denotes questions for which answers are given in Appendix B.

CHAPTER 16

Creating an Environment for Growth and Prosperity

Certain fundamental principles—formulating sound monetary and fiscal policies, removing domestic price controls, opening the economy to international market forces, ensuring property rights and private property, creating competition, and reforming and limiting the role of government—are essential for a healthy market economy. **—Economic Report of the President, 1991**

Robert Lucas, the 1995 Nobel laureate, has stated, "Once you start thinking about economic growth, it is hard to think about anything else."[1] Why do Lucas and many other economists place so much emphasis on economic growth? Growth of real output is necessary for the growth of real income. Without growth, higher income levels and living standards cannot be achieved.

Beginning with the publication of Adam Smith's *The Wealth of Nations* (1776), economists have sought to discover why some nations grow and prosper while others stagnate. The Keys to Prosperity series has already addressed several dimensions of this issue, but we now want to consider it more directly and in a more comprehensive manner.

As you read this chapter, look for answers to the following questions:

- How does sustained economic growth change income levels and the lives of people?

- What are the major sources of economic growth?

- What institutions and policies will promote growth and prosperity?

- What does the empirical evidence reveal with regard to the linkage between economic institutions and policies and the quality of life of people?

---

[1]Robert E. Lucas Jr., "On the Mechanics of Economic Development," *Journal of Monetary Economics* 22, no. 1 (1988): 3–42.

16-1 WHY IS ECONOMIC GROWTH IMPORTANT?

Economic growth expands the productive capacity of an economy. As **Exhibit 1** shows, an expansion in output can be illustrated within the production possibilities framework. For example, if a country experiences economic growth between 2020 and 2030, this means the country will be able to produce a larger quantity of both consumer and capital goods in 2030 than was true in 2020. This growth will shift the economy's production possibilities curve outward (from *AA* to *BB*).

Per capita GDP

Income per person. Increases in income per person are vital for the achievement of higher living standards.

When a nation's real GDP is increasing more rapidly than its population, **per capita GDP**—that is, real GDP per person—will also expand. Growth of real per capita GDP means more goods and services per person. In most cases, this will mean that the typical person has a higher standard of living—a better diet, improved health and access to medical services, and greater educational opportunities. Studies have also shown that as real per capita income increases, people place more emphasis on clean air and water and generally take more time for recreation and leisure. Thus, a higher real per capita income means not only more material goods but also better health, a cleaner environment, more leisure time, and the availability of a wider range of goods and services that enhance the quality of life.

16-1a THE IMPACT OF SUSTAINED ECONOMIC GROWTH

There is a tendency to think that a 1 or 2 percent difference in growth is of little consequence. When sustained over a lengthy period, however, seemingly small differences in growth can have a huge impact.

Rule of 70

If a variable grows at a rate of *x* percent per year, 70/*x* will approximate the number of years required for the variable to double.

The **rule of 70** provides a simple tool that can help us understand the importance of sustained growth. This rule makes it easy to figure how many years it will take for income to double at various rates of growth. If you divide 70 by a country's average growth rate, it will approximate the number of years required for the income level to double.[2] For example, at an average annual growth rate of 5 percent, it would take 14 years (70 divided by 5) for the income level to double. At a 1 percent growth rate, it would take 70 years for

EXHIBIT 1

Economic Growth and Production Possibilities

Economic growth expands the sustainable output level of an economy. This can be illustrated by an outward shift in the production possibilities curve.

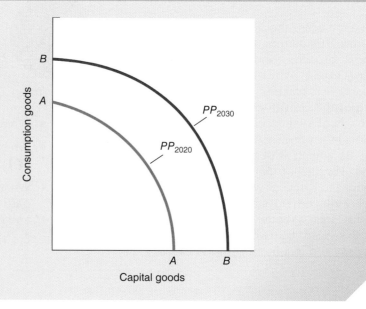

---

[2]Sometimes this rule is called the rule of 72, rather than 70. Whereas 70 yields more accurate estimates for growth rates of less than 5 percent, 72 yields slightly more accurate estimates when the annual rate of growth exceeds 5 percent.

income to double. (Note: The rule of 70 also applies to the rate of return on savings and investments. Clearly, over a long period, small differences in rates of return can make a big difference in the accumulated value of your savings or investment.)

Exhibit 2 illustrates the impact of differences in growth rates over 30 years. Consider four countries with the same initial level of per capita income, $10,000. The exhibit indicates what their incomes will be 30 years later at four different growth rates: 4 percent, 2 percent, 1 percent, and 0 percent. After 30 years, the country growing at an annual rate of 4 percent will have an income of $32,434. The income of the country growing at a 2 percent rate will be only $18,114. A country with a 1 percent rate of growth will achieve only an income of $13,478 after 30 years, while the income of the country with a 0 percent growth rate will still be $10,000. Thus, even though the four countries all had the same initial income, 30 years later the income level of the one with the 4 percent growth rate will be far greater than that of the others. Clearly, differences in sustained growth rates over a few decades will substantially alter the relative incomes of countries.

16-2 SOURCES OF ECONOMIC GROWTH AND HIGH INCOMES

Why do some countries grow and achieve high income levels, whereas others remain poor and less developed? Gains from trade, entrepreneurial discovery, and investment are the major sources of economic growth. Let's take a closer look at each.

16-2a GAINS FROM TRADE

As we have stressed throughout this textbook, trade is mutually advantageous. Trade moves goods, services, and resources from people who value them less to people who value them more. It also helps trading partners achieve larger outputs and income levels as the result of the division of labor, specialization, and adoption of methods of mass production. For example, goods ranging from pencils to automobiles to cell phones can be produced more economically when they are supplied by firms producing them in the millions to sell to the world marketplace rather than selling only thousands domestically. More than 250 years

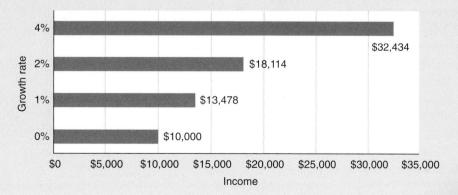

EXHIBIT 2

The Impact of Growth Rate Differences over a 30-Year Period

Here, we consider the impact of growth over a 30-year period on four economies with the same initial income level, $10,000. If a country grows 4 percent annually, 30 years later its income will be $32,434, more than 3.2 times the initial figure. In contrast, if a country grows at a 2 percent annual rate, 30 years later its income will be only a little more than half that of the economy with the 4 percent annual rate of growth. The income of a country growing at a 1 percent rate will be even lower, $13,478.

Hulton Archive/Getty Images

Mass production methods make larger outputs and lower per unit costs possible. Henry Ford developed the automobile assembly line shown here. His mass production methods cut the cost of producing automobiles by nearly two-thirds during 1912–1930. Auto prices plummeted, and the share of Americans with access to a car increased from 2 percent to 89 percent.

Archive Pics/Alamy

Entrepreneurs Who Have Changed Our Lives:
Henry Ford

The name of Henry Ford is forever connected with automobiles. He didn't invent them (that happened in Europe in the 1880s), but in 1913 he adopted a method of production that drastically reduced costs, making possible a mass market for cars. His method of production—the assembly line—changed the course of a multitude of other industries as well.

The son of a Michigan farmer, Henry Ford was more interested in gadgets than in farming. He became an engineer at Thomas Edison's Edison Illumination Company, but was fascinated by the new "horseless carriages" that were beginning to appear. As a hobby, he built an experimental car in 1896. It had a 4-horsepower engine, no reverse gear, and its top speed was 10 miles per hour; but it ran, and he sold it for $200. Soon after, he left Edison to produce cars. His first two companies failed, but the third, the Ford Motor Company, remains a success more than a century later.

Before the assembly line, cars were built by craftsmen who worked on complex tasks such as building engines and gear shifts and, once the parts were finished, took them to the automobile that was under construction. But Ford copied a technique used in Chicago's meatpacking plants. There, animals were killed, and their carcasses processed as they were moved from station to station by a conveyor belt, with each worker responsible for a single task. Ford adapted that process to cars, cutting the amount of time to build a car from 12 hours to 90 minutes.

Productivity per worker increased, and the price per car went down, from $850 to $300. Before the assembly line, Ford was already the nation's biggest car company, producing 17,000 autos per year. But after the assembly line process was installed in August 1913, output jumped to more than 300,000 just two years later. By 1923, the Ford Motor company produced 1.8 million automobiles, more than 100 times the pre–assembly line level! While Ford played only a minor role in the invention of the automobile, he figured out how to make cars more affordable, vastly altering the mobility of Americans and others throughout the world.

Sources: David L. Cohn, *Combustion on Wheels: An Informal History of the Automobile Age* (Boston: Houghton Mifflin, 1944).

David Long, *Henry Ford* (New York: Cavendish Square Publishing, 2017).

Ford Motor Company, "100 Years of the Moving Assembly Line," https://corporate.ford.com/articles/history/100-years-moving-assembly-line.htm.

ago, Adam Smith even noted that the ability of individuals to specialize was limited by the extent of the market. Thus, the ability to trade openly also allows people and resources to discover and more finely specialize in their areas of comparative advantage.

Our living standard would be meager if we could not trade with others, as we all acquire numerous goods through trade that would be costly or virtually impossible for us to produce for ourselves. When individuals and businesses are permitted to trade over a broader market area, they will be able to achieve lower per unit costs, produce larger outputs, and achieve higher living standards. Conversely, obstacles that restrict trade, either domestic or international, will reduce output, reduce income, and lower the general living standard of the populace.

16-2b ENTREPRENEURSHIP, TECHNOLOGY, AND THE DISCOVERY OF BETTER WAYS OF DOING THINGS

The discovery of new products and new production methods is a powerful force for economic growth. Sometimes these discoveries reflect **technological advancement**. In other instances, they are the result of innovation; the practical application, extension, and dissemination of new ideas, processes, and technologies. During the past two centuries, the substitution of power-driven machines for human labor; the development of miracle grains, fertilizer, and new sources of energy; and improvements in transportation and communication have vastly improved living standards. Innovations and advancements in technology continue to affect the availability of goods and services. Consider the new products introduced during the past 50 years: high-definition televisions, personal computers, electronic mail, microwave ovens, video cameras, cell phones, heart bypass surgery, knee, shoulder, and hip replacements, LASIK eye surgery, online shopping, text messaging, and so on. Think about how your life would be affected if these products had not been discovered and developed. These products and others developed in recent decades have made it possible for us to live longer, travel safer and faster, communicate with both the written and spoken word with people throughout the world, and enjoy entertainment well beyond what was available to even kings and queens of another era.

Technological advancement
The introduction of new techniques or methods that increase output per unit of input.

New and improved products have replaced older ones and often rendered them obsolete. The automobile replaced the horse and buggy; the computer word processor replaced the typewriter; the phonograph was replaced by the cassette tape player, which was later largely replaced by CDs and now by smartphones like the iPhone. Joseph Schumpeter, a great Austrian economist, referred to this discovery and replacement process as "creative destruction."

But new and improved products do not just happen. They must be discovered. This fact highlights the role of the entrepreneur, the decision-maker willing to take risks and try out new ideas.[3] Some of the new ideas will be good ones, but many will not. The majority of new businesses fail within the first few years, and relatively few turn into major successes like Microsoft, Amazon, or FedEx did.

In order to be successful, an entrepreneur must be good at discovering how to apply scientific knowledge in a practical manner. Before a new idea is tried, however, it is difficult to tell if it is a good one. From the standpoint of economic growth, it is vitally important that entrepreneurs have a strong incentive to try out new ideas, but it is also important that wasteful projects that reduce the value of resources be brought to a halt. In a market economy, profits and losses achieve these objectives. New ideas that increase the value of resources—by creating enough value to consumers to offset the opportunity cost of production—generate economic profits for the entrepreneurs who discover and

---

[3]The modern understanding of the importance of entrepreneurship as a source of economic growth is founded on the work of Joseph Schumpeter and Israel Kirzner. See Joseph A. Schumpeter, *Capitalism, Socialism, and Democracy* (New York: Harper, 1942); Israel M. Kirzner, *Competition and Entrepreneurship* (Chicago: University of Chicago Press, 1973); and Israel M. Kirzner, "Entrepreneurial Discovery and the Competitive Market Process: An Austrian Approach," *Journal of Economic Literature* 35, no. 1 (1997): 60–85.

Entrepreneurial discovery of improved products and lower-cost production methods is a driving force of economic growth. For example, when it was initially developed, the phonograph made recorded music available to millions of listeners. But it was eventually replaced by the CD player and still later by the iPhone. Economists refer to this discovery and replacement of a product by a new and superior one as "creative destruction."

undertake them. In contrast, ideas that drain resources away from other more valuable uses and turn them into something not as valuable to consumers result in losses, which will provide entrepreneurs with a strong incentive to discontinue such projects. Thus, the market process encourages actions that increase the value of resources, but penalizes those who use resources in ways that reduce their value. In this manner, the profit and loss system helps to direct (and quickly redirect) resources toward projects that promote economic growth.

16-2c INVESTMENT IN PHYSICAL AND HUMAN CAPITAL

Investment in both physical capital (machines) and human capital (knowledge and skills) can expand the productive capacity of a worker. For example, farmers working with modern tractors and plows can cultivate many more acres than could their great grandparents, who probably worked with hoes. Similarly, a cabinetmaker, skilled after years of training and experience, can build cabinets far more rapidly and efficiently than can a beginner. In turn, people who produce more goods and services valued by others will tend to have higher incomes.

Other things constant, countries using a larger share of their resources to produce tools, machines, and factories will tend to grow more rapidly. Correspondingly, the allocation of more resources to education and training will also enhance economic growth. It is important, however, to recognize that investment is not a "free lunch." When more resources are used to produce machines, factories, and schooling, fewer resources are available to produce current-consumption goods.

While investment is a source of growth, high investment rates do not guarantee rapid growth. The experiences of the centrally planned economies of the former Soviet bloc countries illustrate this point. These economies had both very high rates of capital formation and rapid improvements in schooling levels. Despite their high rates of investment, however, their performance was unimpressive. Slow growth and poor living standards eventually led to their collapse.

Exhibit 3 summarizes the three major sources of economic growth and high levels of income. It also summarizes how and why each of the three factors contributes to the growth and income of an economy.

Recognition of trade, entrepreneurial discovery, and investment as the cornerstones of economic growth and the achievement of higher income levels also sheds light on why per capita income was so low throughout most of world history. Prior to sometime around 1800, most people were involved in agricultural activities where they produced most of what they consumed. The costs of both transportation and communications were high, and there was very little trade. Moreover, the trade that did occur was generally among those residing in the same village or within close proximity. Given this limited amount of trade, the gains from specialization, economies of scale, technological improvements, innovation, and even investment were relatively small. Against this background, low and stagnating income levels are an expected result.

EXHIBIT 3

SOURCE OF GROWTH	EXPLANATION
1. Gains from trade	Specialization, division of labor, and economies of scale lead to larger outputs.
2. Entrepreneurship	Innovation, technological improvements, and discovery of better ways of doing things make larger outputs and higher income levels possible.
3. Investment in physical capital, work experience, and human capital	Machines, structures, and tools (physical capital) and education and training (human capital) make larger outputs possible.

EXHIBIT 3

Major Sources of Economic Growth and High Levels of Income

The major sources of growth and high-income levels are gains from trade, entrepreneurial discovery, and investment in physical and human capital.

16-3 WHAT INSTITUTIONS AND POLICIES WILL PROMOTE GROWTH?

Institutions and policies influence the volume of trade, entrepreneurial discovery, and investment. How important are the legal, business, political, trade, and social rules and regulations that make up a country's institutional environment? During the past several decades, considerable research has addressed this question. Building on the work of Peter Bauer and Douglass C. North, modern growth analysis stresses the importance of institutions and policies for the development and efficient use of resources. Daron Acemoglu of MIT, Robert Barro of Harvard University, and Barry Weingast of Stanford University are among the leading contributors to the recent literature in this area.[4] This institutional approach stresses that when nations foster a sound economic environment, people will trade, invest, and engage in entrepreneurial activities in a manner that will stimulate economic growth and make high levels of income possible. In many ways, the modern institutional approach to growth reflects the view of Adam Smith, who also stressed the importance of policies and institutions.

A combination of institutional factors impacts the growth process, and these factors are often interrelated. Much as the performance of an athletic team reflects the joint output of the team members, economic growth is jointly determined. Moreover, just as one or two weak players can substantially reduce overall team performance, weakness in one or two key areas can substantially harm the overall performance of an economy.

Institutions
The legal, regulatory, and social constraints that affect the security of property rights and enforcement of contracts. They exert a major impact on the incentive to engage in productive activities, innovate, and realize gains from trade, particularly when the trading partners do not know each other.

Outstanding Economist: Douglass C. North (1920–2015)

The 1993 recipient of the Nobel Prize in Economics, Douglass C. North is best known for his application of both economic theory and statistical analysis to topics in the field of economic history. A longtime professor of economics at Washington University in St. Louis and senior fellow at Stanford's Hoover Institution, North's work focused on how differences in the political, economic, and social institutions help explain why some countries grow and prosper while others remain poor. His research on the dynamics of institutional change brought rigor to this topic and provided the foundation for the modern analysis of economic growth and development. Along with fellow Nobel Laureate Ronald Coase, North played a leading role in the 1997 founding of the International Society for the New Institutional Economics.

Rolf Haid/picture alliance via Getty Images

---

[4]For background on this literature, see Peter T. Bauer, *Dissent on Development: Studies and Debates in Development Economics* (Cambridge, MA: Harvard University Press, 1972); Douglass C. North, *Institutions, Institutional Change, and Economic Performance* (Cambridge: Cambridge University Press, 1990); Robert Barro and Xavier Sala-i-Martin, *Economic Growth* (New York: McGraw-Hill, 1995); Daron Acemoglu, Simon Johnson, and James A. Robinson, "Institutions as a Fundamental Cause of Long-Run Growth," in *Handbook of Economic Growth,* vol.1, Philippe Aghion and Steven Durlauf, eds. (Amsterdam: Elsevier, 2005), 385–472; and Daron Acemoglu and James A. Robinson, *Why Nations Fail: The Origins of Power, Prosperity, and Poverty* (New York: Crown, 2012).

KEYS TO ECONOMIC PROSPERITY

Role of Government

Governments promote economic progress when they protect individuals and their property, enforce contracts impartially, foster competitive markets, provide access to money of stable value, and avoid excessive regulations, high taxes, and the imposition of barriers that restrict trade.

The role of government is vitally important for the achievement of economic growth and high levels of income. If an economy is going to achieve its full potential, institutions and policies must encourage productive activities and discourage counterproductive ones. Let's take a closer look at the role of government and six key factors that are central to the growth process.

16-3a LEGAL SYSTEM: SECURE PROPERTY RIGHTS, RULE OF LAW, AND EVEN-HANDED ENFORCEMENT OF CONTRACTS

As we discussed in Chapter 2, private ownership rights legally protect people against those who would use violence, theft, or fraud to take things that do not belong to them. The important thing about private ownership is the incentive structure that it creates. When labor services, other resources, goods, and assets are privately owned, people will have a strong incentive to engage in productive activities, actions that increase the value of resources. With well-defined and enforced private ownership rights, people get ahead by helping and cooperating with others. Employers, for example, have to provide prospective employees and other resource suppliers with at least as good a deal as they can get elsewhere. Similarly, if they are going to succeed, business owners will have to provide potential customers with goods and services that they value highly (relative to cost). Entrepreneurs will have a strong incentive to innovate and discover new and better products and production methods. Investors will have a potent incentive to search for and undertake productive projects. The bottom line: When property is owned privately and people permitted to keep what they earn, they will have a strong incentive to develop and use resources wisely, innovate and discover better ways of doing things, and invest and conserve for the future.

Throughout history, people have searched for, and established, alternatives to private ownership they thought would be more humanitarian or more productive. These experiences have ranged from unsuccessful to disastrous. To date, there is no record of an institutional arrangement that provides individuals with as much freedom and incentive to use resources productively and efficiently as does private ownership.[5]

In contrast, when private ownership rights are insecure or highly restricted, the incentive of entrepreneurs to engage in productive activity is eroded. Citizens will spend more time trying to take the property of others through political and legal plunder and less time producing and developing resources. When a citizen's or investor's assets are at risk of being taken by others because property rights are not enforced, the incentive to invest in building the productive capital assets that help to generate prosperity is diminished. As a result, growth will be retarded, and income will fall well short of its potential.

The security of property rights is often undermined by political instability, civil unrest, and war. Historically, some governments have confiscated the physical and financial assets

---

[5]For evidence that a legal system that protects property rights, enforces contracts, and relies on rule-of-law principles for the settlement of disputes among parties promotes economic growth, see Stephen Knack and Philip Keefer, "Institutions and Economic Performance: Cross-Country Tests Using Alternative Institutional Measures," *Economics and Politics* 7 (1995): 207–27.

of their citizens, imposed punitive taxes on them, and used regulations to punish those out of favor with the current political regime. Countries with a history like this will find it difficult to restore confidence and reestablish the security of property rights.

Unfortunately, the political climate of many poor, **less-developed countries** is highly unstable. In some cases, prejudice, injustice, and highly unequal wealth status create a fertile environment for political upheaval. In other instances, political corruption and a history of favoritism to a ruling class provide the seeds for unrest. In recent years, political instability has contributed to the dismal economic performance of several nations, including the Democratic Republic of the Congo, Haiti, Iraq, Syria, and Venezuela.

Less-developed countries Countries with low per capita incomes, low levels of education, widespread illiteracy, and widespread use of production methods that are largely obsolete in high-income countries. They are sometimes referred to as developing countries.

16-3b COMPETITIVE MARKETS

Freedom of entry and open competition provide the lifeblood of a market economy. The competitive process imposes discipline on both buyers and sellers. In a competitive environment, producers must provide goods at a low cost and serve the interests of consumers. Firms that develop improved products and figure out how to produce them at a low cost will succeed. Sellers that are unwilling or unable to provide consumers with quality goods at competitive prices will be driven from the market. This process leads to improved products and production methods and directs resources toward projects that create more value. Government policies that restrict these competitive forces, like business subsidies, price controls, and entry barriers and restraints, stifle competition and thus hinder economic progress.

When property rights are clearly defined and enforced, competitive markets direct entrepreneurs toward projects that both generate profits and increase the value of resources. Rising incomes and higher living standards are a natural result.

16-3c STABLE MONEY AND PRICES

A stable monetary environment provides the foundation for the efficient operation of a market economy. In contrast, monetary and price instability makes both the price level and relative prices unpredictable, generates uncertainty, and undermines the security of contractual exchanges. When prices increase 20 percent one year, 50 percent the next year, 15 percent the year after that, and so on, the ability of individuals and businesses to develop sensible long-term plans and investment decisions is undermined. If money does not have a stable and predictable value, time-dimension transactions (such as payment for a house or an automobile) will be fraught with additional uncertainty, borrowers and lenders will have difficulty finding mutually agreeable terms for a loan, and saving and investing will involve additional risks. When the value of money is unstable, many potentially beneficial exchanges will not occur and the gains from specialization, large-scale production, and social cooperation diminished.

Moreover, many investors and business decision-makers will move their activities to countries with a more stable environment. Foreigners will invest elsewhere, and citizens will often go to great lengths to get their savings (potential funds for investment) out of the country. Without monetary stability, potential gains from capital investment and other exchanges involving time commitments will be eroded, and the people of the country will fail to realize their full potential.

Further, monetary policy that shifts back and forth between expansion and restriction will generate economic instability. Persistent booms and busts will result. This pattern of monetary policy will also create uncertainty, retard private investment, and reduce the rate of economic growth.

16-3d AVOIDANCE OF REGULATIONS THAT RESTRICT TRADE AND ENTRY INTO MARKETS

Regulations that interfere with voluntary exchange and make it more difficult to enter markets will reduce the gains from trade, entrepreneurial discovery, and social cooperation.

Proponents often argue that regulations will keep the unqualified out of a market, prohibit unfair competition, raise wages, reduce prices, or restrict the layoff of workers. Unfortunately, even when regulations are motivated by good intentions, they often generate harmful unintended consequences. For example, restrictions that make it more difficult to lay off an employee will reduce the incentive of employers to hire workers. Regulations designed to keep some potential producers out of a market will limit competition and lead to higher prices. Fixing prices below the market level will lead to shortages and deterioration in the quality of a product or service, but fixing prices above market levels will lead to surpluses. The list of unintended side effects of regulations goes on and on.

Governments in many countries impose regulations that limit entry into various businesses and occupations. In those countries, if you want to start a business or provide a service, you have to acquire a license, fill out forms, get permission from different bureaus, show that you are qualified, indicate that you have sufficient financing, and meet various other regulatory tests. For example, the World Bank reports that given the regulations in place in 2019, legally opening a business would take 97 days in Haiti, 99 days in Cambodia, and 230 days in Venezuela. By way of comparison, opening this same business would take only 1.5 days in Hong Kong and Singapore and 4.2 days in the United States.[6] Moreover, regulations of this type are a major source of cronyism and political corruption. When political approval is needed to enter a market, invariably there will be government officials who are unwilling to grant the approval unless the applicant is willing to pay a bribe or contribute to their political coffers. Often times existing producers push for regulations that protect them from competition, or capture and have influence over the government agencies that do the regulating. In these cases regulations work to the advantage of incumbent producers and actually harm consumers and the economy as a whole.

Many worry that without government regulation of food, safety, and other items, people will be harmed by bad products or employers providing unsafe working conditions. However, under a legal system with sound enforcement of liability, individuals and businesses are accountable for their actions that harm others. Those harmed will be in a position to collect for damages in a court of law. Moreover, competition is the great regulator. When competition is present, business firms that offer shoddy products, fail to keep their promises, or seek to mislead consumers will soon be exposed by rivals. Unethical business practices may lead to some temporary returns, but this is not a recipe for long-term success. Regulation is a poor substitute for well-defined property rights, a sound legal system, and the natural regulatory process of competitive markets.

16-3e AVOIDANCE OF HIGH TAX RATES

High marginal tax rates take a large share of the rewards generated by productive activities, making it less attractive for people to work and undertake profitable business projects. In less-developed economies, high taxes often drive business activity into the underground economy, or black markets, where the legal structure is less certain and property rights are less secure. In developed economies, the high rates often reduce the supply of labor and other productive resources. Some potential workers will drop out of the labor force or engage in activities that are not taxed. Others will simply work fewer hours, retire earlier, or take jobs with longer vacations or a more preferred location. High tax rates may even drive some of a nation's most productive citizens abroad where taxes are lower. People who are not permitted to keep much of what they earn tend not to earn as much.

High taxes also retard capital formation. They will both repel foreign investment and cause domestic investors to search for investment projects abroad where taxes and production costs are lower. In turn, the lower level of investment will mean slower growth of worker productivity and earnings.

High marginal tax rates also encourage individuals to consume tax-deductible goods in place of nondeductible goods, even though the nondeductible goods may be more

---

[6]World Bank, *Doing Business 2020.*

desirable. The high marginal rates artificially reduce the personal cost (but not the cost to society) of items that are tax-deductible or that can be taken as a business expense. Predictably, taxpayers confronting high marginal tax rates will spend more money on tax-deductible items such as plush offices, Hawaiian business conferences, business entertainment, and a company-provided automobile. Because such tax-deductible expenditures reduce their taxes, people often will buy goods they would not buy if they were paying full cost.

The sales of the British-made luxury car Rolls-Royce in the 1970s provides a vivid illustration of this point. During this era, the marginal income tax rates in the United Kingdom were as high as 98 percent on large incomes. A business owner paying that tax rate could buy a car as a tax-deductible business expense, so why not buy an exotic, more expensive car? The purchase would reduce the owner's profit by the car's price—for example, £100,000—but the owner would have received only £2,000 of the £100,000 of additional profit anyway, because of the 98 percent marginal tax rate. In effect, the government was paying 98 percent of the car's costs. When the UK cut the top marginal tax rate to 70 percent, the sales of Rolls-Royces plummeted. After the rate reduction, the £100,000 car now cost the business owner not £2,000 but £30,000. The lower marginal rates made it much more expensive for wealthy Brits to purchase Rolls-Royces, and they responded by reducing their purchases.

To the novice, high marginal tax rates may look like an easy way to extract more revenue from the rich. But the incentive effects will cause people to alter their behavior. Given these incentive effects, waste, inefficient use of resources, and income levels below the economy's potential are by-products of high marginal tax rates.

16-3f TRADE OPENNESS

Like domestic trade, international trade is mutually beneficial. The residents of a country can gain by specializing in the production of goods and services they can produce at a relatively low cost and trade for those that would be costly to produce domestically. Thus, trade makes it possible for each country to use more of its resources producing goods and services it can supply at a low cost. Together, trading partners are able to produce more goods and services and purchase a wider variety of them at cheaper prices. **Trade openness** and the competition that flows from it will also keep domestic producers on their toes—they will be less likely to gouge consumers with high prices, for example.

In contrast, policies that restrict international trade stifle this process and retard economic progress. Obviously, tariffs (taxes on imported goods) and quotas fall into this category because they limit the ability of domestic citizens to trade with people in other countries. So, too, do trade restrictions that impede international exchanges involving financial and real assets. When a nation's financial markets are integrated with the world, the nation will be able to attract worldwide savings at the lowest possible price (or interest rate). Similarly, its citizens will have access to the most attractive investment opportunities, regardless of where those opportunities are located.

As a result, domestic businesses will be able to acquire financial capital at a lower cost, and domestic investors will be able to earn more attractive returns than would otherwise be the case. During the past several decades, transportation costs have fallen and trade barriers have declined. The reduction in trade barriers has been most pronounced in low-income countries. In 1980, it was commonplace for poor, less-developed countries to impose tariffs of 20 percent or more. Many also imposed exchange rate controls, which made it difficult for their citizens to get their hands on the foreign currency needed to purchase imports. Today, the situation is dramatically different. Beginning in the 1980s, numerous less-developed countries including China and India lowered their tariffs, relaxed exchange rate controls, and reduced other trade barriers. As a result, international trade has grown rapidly and the world's per capita income is now higher than would have been the case otherwise. The international trade section of this book will analyze the impact of trade issues in more detail.

Trade openness
Situation where the residents of a country are permitted to trade freely with foreigners. Trade restrictions such as tariffs, quotas, restrictions on the convertibility of currency, and other political roadblocks limiting international trade are largely absent.

16-4 ECONOMIC FREEDOM AS A MEASURE OF SOUND INSTITUTIONS

Economic analysis indicates that if a country protects individuals and their property from aggressors, maintains open markets, provides access to a currency of stable value, keeps taxes low, and avoids regulations that restrict trade, it will achieve higher income levels per person, grow more rapidly, and have a lower rate of poverty. Is this really true? How can this hypothesis be tested?

Economic freedom
Method of organizing economic activity characterized by (1) personal choice, (2) voluntary exchange coordinated by markets, (3) freedom to enter and compete in markets, and (4) protection of people and their property from aggression by others.

In the mid-1980s, the Fraser Institute of Vancouver, Canada, began work on a special project designed to measure the consistency of a nation's economic institutions and policies with **economic freedom**. Several leading scholars, including Nobel laureates Milton Friedman, Gary Becker, and Douglass North, participated in the endeavor. This eventually led to the development of the *Economic Freedom of the World* (EFW) index that is now published annually by a worldwide network of institutes in more than 90 countries.

To a large degree, the EFW index is designed to measure the presence or absence of the institutional and policy conditions economic analysis indicates are important for growth. In order to achieve a high EFW rating, a country must provide secure protection of privately owned property, evenhanded enforcement of contracts, and a stable monetary environment. It also must keep taxes low, refrain from creating barriers to both domestic and international trade, and rely more fully on markets rather than political decision-making to allocate goods and resources. Essentially, the economic freedom measure identified the degree to which governments throughout the world (a) provide the legal and monetary systems for the smooth operation of markets and (b) rely on market prices rather than political decision-making to allocate resources.

Economic freedom is complex and multidimensional. The Fraser Institute EFW index incorporates 43 separate components and measures their consistency with personal choice, voluntary exchange, open markets, and protection of private property. To the fullest extent possible, the components of the index are based on objective variables such as government consumption as a share of the total, the standard deviation of the inflation rate, and the average tariff rate. When it is necessary to use survey data to measure important elements of economic freedom, as is often the case in the legal and regulatory areas, data from outside sources are used in order to minimize value judgments. The data for each of the 43 components are placed on a zero to ten scale, with higher values indicating more economic freedom. The component ratings are used to derive a summary rating as well as ratings in five major areas: (1) size of government; (2) legal system and protection of property rights; (3) access to sound money; (4) freedom to trade with foreigners; and (5) regulation of credit, labor, and business.[7]

Hong Kong is a modern economic miracle. Its real income per person in 2018 was approximately ten times its 1960 level. For the past several decades, it has been the world's freest economy. Since 1997, Hong Kong has been a special zone within China. China is substantially less economically free, and many fear that Chinese interventions will undermine the economic freedom of Hong Kong in the future.

The EFW data are available for 123 countries throughout the 1995–2017 period. Exhibit 4 presents data on the average EFW rating during 1995–2017 for the ten highest- and ten lowest-rated economies, as well as the ratings of ten other large countries. In order to rank in the top group, a country would have to maintain persistently high ratings throughout the 22-year time frame. Thus, the countries in the top group might be thought of as those that persistently maintained institutions and policies supportive of economic freedom.

joyfull/Shutterstock.com

---

[7]For additional details, see James Gwartney, Robert Lawson, Joshua Hall, and Ryan Murphy, *Economic Freedom of the World: 2019 Annual Report* (Vancouver, British Columbia: Fraser Institute, 2019), and the Web site http://www.freetheworld.com.

EXHIBIT 4

The Economic Freedom Rating for the Top-, Middle-, and Lowest-Rated Countries, Average for 1995–2017

	Top-Rated Countries			Middle-Rated Countries			Lowest-Rated Countries	
Rank	Country	Rating	Rank	Country	Rating	Rank	Country	Rating
1	Hong Kong	8.9	15	Germany	7.9	114	Ukraine	5.2
2	Singapore	8.7	16	Japan	7.8	115	Syria	5.0
3	New Zealand	8.6	18	Chile	7.7	116	Central African Republic	5.0
4	Switzerland	8.5	29	France	7.4	117	Zimbabwe	4.9
5	United States	8.3	36	South Korea	7.3	118	Guinea-Bissau	4.8
6	United Kingdom	8.3	65	Mexico	6.7	119	Algeria	4.7
7	Ireland	8.2	70	Indonesia	6.6	120	Congo, Rep. of	4.7
8	Canada	8.1	73	India	6.5	121	Congo, Dem. Rep.	4.6
9	Australia	8.1	93	China	6.0	122	Myanmar	4.2
10	Denmark	7.9	96	Brazil	5.9	123	Venezuela	4.0

Note: Cuba and North Korea were not rated because the required data were unavailable.

Source: James Gwartney, Robert Lawson, Joshua Hall, and Ryan Murphy. *Economic Freedom of the World, 2019 Annual Report* (Vancouver: Fraser Institute, 2019).

As Exhibit 4 shows, Hong Kong, Singapore, New Zealand, Switzerland, and the United States headed the list of the most persistently free economies during 1995–2017. At the other end of the spectrum, Algeria, Republic of Congo, Democratic Republic of the Congo, Myanmar, and Venezuela were the least free economies. Among the large economies, Germany, Japan, Chile, and France were more toward the economically free end of the spectrum, whereas India, China, and Brazil were in the less free range.

16-5 INSTITUTIONS, POLICIES, AND ECONOMIC PERFORMANCE

The institutions and policies of countries shape the structure of incentive. As the work of the noted economist William Baumol highlights, the rules of the game make a huge difference; they determine what individuals do with their time, talents, and energy.[8] Baumol notes that the institutional environment may encourage productive, unproductive, or even destructive activities. When institutions and policies provide secure property rights, a fair and balanced judicial system, monetary stability, and effective limits on the transfer of wealth through taxation and regulation, creative individuals will generally engage in product development, investment, and other productive activities. However, if the legal and regulatory environment fails to protect property rights and is often used to favor some at the expense of others, the same individuals will instead engage in attempts to manipulate the political and legal process in order to plunder wealth from others. In this case, rent seeking, lobbying, bribes, and other forms of plunder will replace productive activities.

If institutions and policies are important, the freer economies should outperform those that are less free. Let's see if this is the case. When examining the impact of institutions, it is important to consider institutional quality over a lengthy time frame. Thus, the average economic freedom rating during 1995–2017 will be used as the measure of the quality of economic institutions. Similarly, we will focus on indicators that reflect economic

---

[8]See William Baumol, "Entrepreneurship: Productive, Unproductive and Destructive," *Journal of Political Economy* 98 (October 1990): 893–921; and William J. Baumol, *Entrepreneurship, Management, and the Structure of Payoffs* (Cambridge, MA: MIT Press, 1993).

performance over a lengthy time period, rather than short-term indicators that might well reflect the ups and downs of the business cycle. We now turn to an examination of the linkage between economic institutions and various measures of performance.

16-5a ECONOMIC FREEDOM AND PER CAPITA INCOME

Quartile
A quarter (25 percent) of a group. The quartiles are often arrayed on the basis of an indicator like income or degree of economic freedom.

Purchasing power parity (PPP) method
Method in which the relative purchasing power of each currency is determined by comparing the amount of each currency required to purchase a common bundle of goods and services in the domestic market. This information is then used to convert the GDP of each nation to a common monetary unit like the U.S. dollar.

The 123 countries with economic freedom ratings throughout 1995–2017 were divided into **quartiles**. The 31 countries with the highest average economic freedom rating over the period compose the top quartile, the 31 with the next highest average ratings make up the next quartile, and so on.

The per capita GDP for each of the 123 countries was derived in terms of a common currency, the US dollar. When comparing income levels across countries, economists use the **purchasing power parity (PPP) method**. This procedure is very similar to the use of the consumer price index (CPI) to adjust for differences in the general level of prices across time periods. The cost in the domestic currency of purchasing a specific bundle of goods and services that is typically consumed is derived. This bundle would include items like housing, food, electricity, gasoline, automobiles, and other items that are consumed in almost every country. The cost of purchasing this bundle is then used to derive the general level of prices (and the purchasing power of the domestic currency) in each country. Finally, this price index is used to convert the incomes in different countries to a common currency, the US dollar. Most economists believe that the purchasing power parity method results in real income differences across countries and time that are more accurate than alternative procedures that might be used.

Exhibit 5 presents the average 2017 per person income (measured in 2011 dollars) of countries in each of the EFW quartiles, ranging from the least free to the most free. On average, the per person income level in the freest quartile was $36,770, compared to $22,082 for the second freest quartile. The average per person income level in the least free quartile was $6,140, less than one-sixth the figure for those in the freest quartile. Clearly, the economies with institutions and policies more consistent with economic freedom had substantially higher income levels. Although the figures of Exhibit 5 do not adjust for other factors that might influence per capita income, more detailed statistical analysis indicates that the strong positive relation between persistently high levels of economic freedom and income remains after adjustment for other major factors that might influence per capita income.

EXHIBIT 5

Economic Freedom and Per Capita Income

The 2017 income per person of countries ordered by economic freedom rating is shown here by quartiles. Note the strong positive linkage. The income per person in countries in the freest quartile was $36,770, more than six times the figure for the least free quartile.

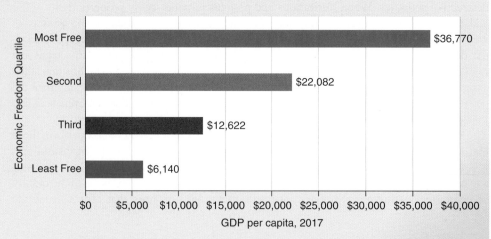

Source: James Gwartney, Robert Lawson, Joshua Hall, and Ryan Murphy, *Economic Freedom of the World, 2019 Annual Report* (Vancouver: Fraser Institute, 2019).

16-5b ECONOMIC FREEDOM AND GROWTH OF PER CAPITA INCOME

Exhibit 6 uses the quartile analysis to illustrate the relationship between economic freedom and growth. In the freest quartile of economies, per person income grew at an average annual rate of 2.38 percent during the 22 years, compared to 1.40 percent and 1.47 percent for the second and third quartiles. Countries in the least free group grew at an annual rate of only 0.90 percent. Thus, the average annual growth rate of per capita GDP of countries in the top quartile was more than twice the average rate of the countries in the bottom quartile.

The growth figures of Exhibit 6 were adjusted for initial income level and change in economic freedom during 1995–2017. The statistical analysis indicates that when the initial (1995) per capita GDP of a country was $10,000 higher, this reduced the annual growth rate of the country by 0.46 of a percentage point. This reflects that during this time frame, countries with higher initial income levels grew less rapidly than their lower income counterparts. The analysis also shows that a one-unit increase in economic freedom during 1995–2017 was associated with a 0.61 percentage point increase in the annual growth rate of per capita GDP. This illustrates that increases in economic freedom during the period enhanced the growth of per capita GDP. The analysis of Exhibit 6 was not adjusted for factors such as years of schooling, age composition of the population, climate, location relative to major markets, and access to ocean coastline. However, more comprehensive analysis indicates that even after these factors are taken into consideration, countries with more economic freedom achieve higher income levels and grow more rapidly.[9]

EXHIBIT 6

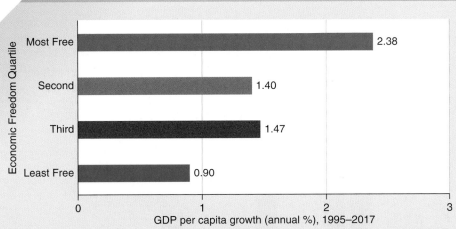

Economic Freedom and Growth of Per Capita GDP, 1995–2017

The relation between the economic freedom of a country and its growth rate during 1995–2017 is shown here. Countries in the most economically free quartile grew at an annual rate of 2.38 percent compared to 0.90 percent growth for the least free quartile.

Note: The data for growth were adjusted to control for the initial level of income (in tens of thousands of dollars) and change in economic freedom during the period. The regression equation indicated that increases in the initial per capita GDP of a country reduced the annual growth rate by 0.46 percent. An increase of one unit in the EFW rating during 1995–2017 increased the estimated annual growth rate by 0.61 percent. Both of these figures were significant at the 99 percent level of confidence.

Source: The data for the annual growth rate of per capita GDP and initial per capita GDP are from the World Bank, *World Development Indicators*. The economic freedom data are from James Gwartney, Robert Lawson, Joshua Hall, and Ryan Murphy, *Economic Freedom of the World, 2019 Annual Report* (Vancouver: Fraser Institute, 2019).

[9]For additional details on how economic freedom affects income levels and growth rates, see Niclas Berggren, "The Benefits of Economic Freedom: A Survey," *Independent Review* 8 (Fall 2003): 193–211; John W. Dawson, "Institutions, Investment, and Growth: New Cross-Country and Panel Data Evidence," *Economic Inquiry* 36 (October 1998): 603–19; and James Gwartney, "Institutions, Economic Freedom, and Cross-Country Differences in Performance," *Southern Economic Journal* 75, no. 4 (April 2009): 937–56.

16-5c ECONOMIC FREEDOM AND THE POVERTY RATE

The data of Exhibits 5 and 6 are for average per capita income and growth rate, respectively. What about the poorest segment of the population? What impact does economic freedom have on the poverty rate? The World Bank provides data on extreme and moderate poverty rates. The **extreme poverty rate** is the percentage of the population with an income of less than $1.90 per day, whereas the **moderate poverty rate** is the share of the population with an income of less than $3.20 per day (measured in 2011 international dollars).

Exhibit 7 provides data for both the extreme and moderate poverty rates in 2017 according to economic freedom quartiles arranged from lowest to highest. Clearly, the poverty rates were much lower in the freer economies. The extreme poverty rate in 2017 was 26.8 percent for the least free economies, but only 0.5 percent in those that were most free. Correspondingly, the moderate poverty rate was 46.2 for the least free quartile compared to only 0.9 percent in the most-free quartile. The two middle quartiles had both extreme and moderate poverty rates between those of the least and most free economies.

Moreover, more detailed analysis indicates that countries moving toward more economic freedom achieved larger poverty rate reductions than did those that were less free. These relationships held even after adjustments for geographic and locational factors, receipt of foreign aid, and political institutions.[10]

16-5d ECONOMIC FREEDOM AND LIFE EXPECTANCY

Exhibit 8 presents the World Bank life expectancy figures for the countries in the quartile groups. People living in countries with more economic freedom live longer. On average, the life expectancy of persons living in the most economically free quartile of countries was 79.4 years, compared to only 65.2 years for persons living in the least free quartile of

Extreme poverty rate
Share of the population with income less than $1.90 per day, measured in 2011 purchasing power parity dollars.

Moderate poverty rate
Share of the population with income less than $3.20 per day, measured in 2011 purchasing power parity dollars.

EXHIBIT 7

Economic Freedom and the Poverty Rate, 2017

The 2017 extreme and moderate poverty rates are shown here according to the economic freedom quartiles arrayed from least to most free. Clearly, both the extreme and the moderate poverty rates are substantially lower in the more free economies.

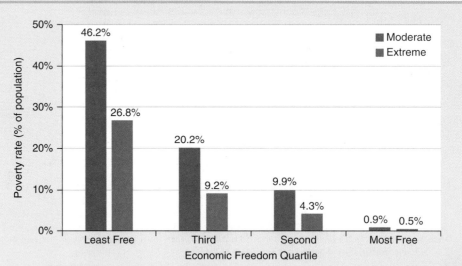

Note: The extreme and moderate poverty rates are the percentages of the population living on less than $1.90 and $3.20 per day, respectively. These numbers are measured in constant 2011 dollars and normalized across countries using the purchasing power parity method.

Source: World Bank, *World Development Indicators*, and James Gwartney, Robert Lawson, Joshua Hall, and Ryan Murphy, *Economic Freedom of the World, 2019 Annual Report* (Vancouver: Fraser Institute, 2019). The World Bank poverty rate data were used to calculate the poverty rate for each country. There were missing values for the poverty rate for some countries. Estimation procedures were used to fill in the missing values. For details, see chapter 2 addendum in Hugo Montesinos, *On Geography, Institutions, Human Capital, and Economic Development* (PhD diss., Florida State University, 2019).

---

[10]See Joseph Connors, *Global Poverty: The Role of Economic Freedom, Democracy, and Foreign Aid* (PhD diss., Florida State University, 2011).

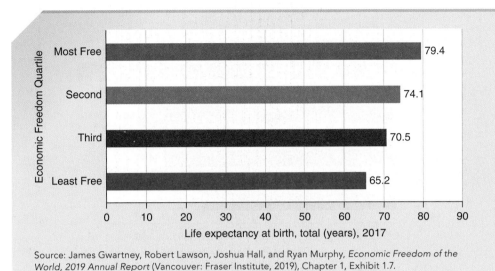

Source: James Gwartney, Robert Lawson, Joshua Hall, and Ryan Murphy, *Economic Freedom of the World, 2019 Annual Report* (Vancouver: Fraser Institute, 2019), Chapter 1, Exhibit 1.7.

EXHIBIT 8

Economic Freedom and Life Expectancy, 2017

There is a strong positive relationship between economic freedom and life expectancy. The average life expectancy in 2017 of countries in the most economically free quartile was 79.4 years, compared to only 65.2 years in the least free quartile.

countries. Thus, people living in the most free economies enjoy more than 14 additional years of life relative to those in the least free quartile.

16-5e ECONOMIC FREEDOM AND ENVIRONMENTAL QUALITY

The Yale Center for Environmental Law and Policy publishes a comprehensive Environmental Performance Index (EPI) for 180 countries. This index rates the quality and performance of countries in ten categories of environmental health and ecosystem vitality. The ten categories are: Air Quality, Water and Sanitation, Heavy Metals, Biodiversity and Habitat, Forests, Fisheries, Climate and Energy, Air Pollution, Water Resources, and Agriculture. The index ranges from zero to 100, with larger numbers indicating a higher level of environmental quality and performance.

Exhibit 9 shows the average of the EPI of countries for the economic freedom quartile groups. The average EPI for the most economically free quartile was 74.6, compared to 60.1 for the second freest quartile and 54.2 and 45.7 for the two least free groups. There is a strong positive relationship between economic freedom and the quality of the environment. To a large degree, this positive relationship reflects the impact of economic freedom on per capita income. As income levels increase, the demand for a cleaner environment also increases. Therefore, as economic freedom increases per capita GDP (see Exhibit 5), the demand for environmental quality is enhanced. Thus, the positive relationship between economic freedom and the quality of the environment is an expected result.

16-6 ECONOMIC FREEDOM AND PER CAPITA INCOME: HOW STRONG IS THE LINKAGE?

Does economic freedom guarantee that a country will be able to achieve high income levels? Can a country with little economic freedom nonetheless achieve a high per capita GDP? Examination of the economic freedom and per capita GDP of the 123 countries with EFW data during 1995–2017 sheds light on both of these questions.

EXHIBIT 9

Economic Freedom and Environmental Performance, 2018

The average Environmental Performance Index of countries is shown here according to quartiles of economic freedom. The scale of this index ranges from zero to 100, with higher figures indicative of greater environmental quality. The average Environmental Performance Index of the countries in the most economically free quartile was 74.6, compared to 45.7 for the least free quartile.

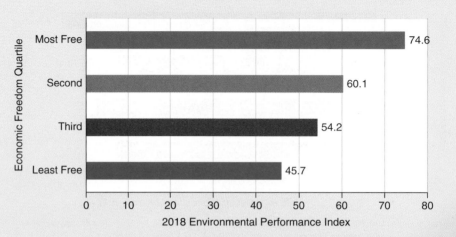

Source: Derived from the Economic Freedom data of the Fraser Institute, *Economic Freedom of the World, 2019*, and Z. A. Wendling, J. W. Emerson, D. C. Esty, M. A. Levy, A. de Sherbinin, et al., *2018 Environmental Performance Index* (New Haven, CT: Yale Center for Environmental Law & Policy, 2018), https://epi.yale.edu/.

Exhibit 10, columns one and two, provides the average EFW rating during 1995–2017 and 2017 per capita GDP for the 25 countries with the highest average EFW summary rating during 1995–2017. (Note: There are actually 27 countries in the top group because seven countries had the same EFW average rating). All 27 of these countries had an average EFW rating of 7.5 or greater during the 22-year period. This high average rating reflects that the EFW rating of these countries was persistently high throughout 1995–2017. All 27 of these countries had a 2017 per capita GDP of more than $20,000. Only four (Mauritius, Chile, Estonia, and Panama) of the 27 freest economies had a 2017 per capita GDP of less than $30,000. The four countries with a per capita GDP of less than $30,000 were relatively poor at the beginning of the period. But they are catching up rapidly; all four had impressive growth rates during the period. The annual growth rates of per capita GDP of these four countries were: Mauritius 3.66, Chile 2.78, Estonia 4.40, and Panama 3.98. Moreover, 18 of the 27 countries with the most economic freedom had a 2017 per capita GDP of more than $40,000. Only three other countries among the 123 with economic freedom data had a 2017 per capita GDP of this magnitude, and all three (Bahrain, United Arab Emirates, and Kuwait) were major oil exporters with a small population.

Columns three and four of Exhibit 10 show the average EFW rating during 1995–2017 and the 2017 per capita GDP for the 25 countries (there are actually 26 because of a tie) with the lowest average EFW rating during 1995–2017. These countries ranked 98 through 123 among the 123 countries with economic freedom data during the time frame. The low average rating of these countries reflects that their institutions and policies were inconsistent with economic freedom throughout the period. None of these countries had a 2017 per capita GDP as high as $20,000. Only four of the 26 (Gabon, Iran, Algeria, and Venezuela) had a per capita GDP greater than $10,000. All four of these countries are major oil exporters. Only one other country (Ukraine) was able to achieve a per capita GDP greater than $6,000. Thus, 21 of the 26 lowest rated countries had a per capita GDP of less than $6,000.

Summarizing, the 2017 per capita income of the 27 countries with the highest average EFW rating during 1995–2017 exceeded $20,000 and the per capita GDP of 23 of

EXHIBIT 10

The 2017 Per Capita GDP of the 25 Countries with the Highest and Lowest Average
Economic Freedom Ratings during 1995–2017

25 MOST FREE ECONOMIES				25 LEAST FREE ECONOMIES			
RANK	COUNTRY	AVE EFW 1995–2017	REAL PER CAPITA GDP, 2017	RANK	COUNTRY	AVE EFW 1995–2017	REAL PER CAPITA GDP, 2017
1	Hong Kong	8.9	$56,088	98	Pakistan	5.8	$4,771
2	Singapore	8.7	$87,760	99	Madagascar	5.8	$1,418
3	New Zealand	8.6	$36,046	100	Mali	5.8	$2,019
4	Switzerland	8.5	$57,998	101	Nigeria	5.7	$5,351
5	United States	8.3	$54,471	102	Cote d'Ivoire	5.7	$3,565
6	United Kingdom	8.3	$39,862	103	Benin	5.7	$2,069
7	Ireland	8.2	$66,132	104	Cameroon	5.7	$3,313
8	Canada	8.1	$43,871	105	Senegal	5.7	$3,232
9	Australia	8.1	$44,888	106	Togo	5.6	$1,530
10	Denmark	7.9	$47,270	107	Gabon	5.6	$16,145
11	Luxembourg	7.9	$93,102	108	Malawi	5.5	$1,154
12	Finland	7.9	$41,174	109	Iran	5.4	$19,098
13	Netherlands	7.9	$48,809	110	Sierra Leone	5.4	$1,404
14	Mauritius	7.9	$20,319	111	Chad	5.3	$1,754
15	Germany	7.9	$45,462	112	Burundi	5.3	$671
16	Japan	7.8	$38,907	113	Niger	5.3	$921
17	Austria	7.8	$45,493	114	Ukraine	5.2	$7,907
18	Chile	7.7	$22,297	115	Syria	5.0	
19	Sweden	7.7	$46,681	116	Central African Republic	5.0	$754
20	Estonia	7.7	$29,916	117	Zimbabwe	4.9	$2,568
21	Panama	7.6	$22,244	118	Guinea-Bissau	4.8	$1,577
22	Iceland	7.6	$47,840	119	Algeria	4.7	$13,876
23	Malta	7.6	$36,989	120	Congo, Rep. of	4.7	$5,103
24	Belgium	7.6	$42,781	121	Congo, Dem. Rep.	4.6	$808
25	Spain	7.6	$34,269	122	Myanmar	4.2	$5,610
26	Taiwan	7.6	$42,165	123	Venezuela	4.0	$15,219
27	Norway	7.6	$64,965				

Note: There are 27 most free countries instead of 25 because Panama, Iceland, Malta, Belgium, Spain, Taiwan, and Norway all tied for a rank of 21. There are 26 least free economies because Pakistan, Madagascar, and Mali all tied at the top of the least free list.

Source: James Gwartney, Robert Lawson, Joshua Hall, and Ryan Murphy. *Economic Freedom of the World, 2019 Annual Report* (Vancouver: Fraser Institute, 2019); and World Bank, *World Development Indicators, 2020.*

the 27 countries was greater than $30,000. In contrast, none of the 26 countries with low levels of economic freedom was able to achieve an income level as high as $20,000, and with the exception of four major oil exporters, the per capita GDP of all of the countries in the least free group was exceedingly low.

The data in Exhibit 10 indicate that, virtually without exception, countries with persistently high economic freedom ratings grow and achieve high levels of income. Conversely, except for a few of the world's leading oil exporters, no country has been able to achieve a high level of per capita income without having a high degree of economic freedom. This close linkage between economic freedom and high per capita income highlights the importance of economic institutions. However, factors other than economic institutions may also exert a strong impact on economic development, growth, and per capita GDP. The following chapter will examine other potential sources of growth and development.

KEY POINTS

- Economic growth increases the production possibilities of an economy. The growth of per capita real GDP means more goods and services per person, which typically leads to higher living standards and improvements in the quality of life.

- Even seemingly small differences in growth rates sustained over two or three decades will substantially alter relative incomes. For example, if Country A and Country B have the same initial income but the growth rate of A is 2 percentage points greater than that of B, after 35 years, the income level of Country A will be twice that of B.

- There are three major sources of economic growth: gains from trade and expansion in the size of the market, discovery of new technologies and innovative applications, and investment in physical and human capital.

- The institutional and policy environment exerts a major impact on growth and income. The following institutions and policies provide the foundation for efficient use of resources, economic growth, and the achievement of high levels of income:

  1. A legal system that protects property rights and enforces contracts in an even-handed manner
  2. Competitive markets
  3. Monetary and price stability
  4. Avoidance of regulations that restrict trade and entry into markets

  5. Avoidance of high tax rates
  6. Openness to international trade

- The Economic Freedom of the World (EFW) index is designed to measure the consistency of a nation's institutions and policies with personal choice, voluntary exchange, open markets, and protection of property rights. To a large degree, the EFW index provides a measure of the factors economic theory indicates will improve the performance of economies.

- Institutions and policies shape the structure of incentives. The institutional environment may encourage productive, unproductive, or even destructive activities. Institutions supportive of economic freedom generally encourage productive activities and discourage counterproductive actions.

- Countries with institutions and policies more consistent with economic freedom have attained higher income levels, grown more rapidly, and achieved lower poverty rates than those that are less free. People in countries with more economic freedom also live longer and enjoy a cleaner environment than those living in countries with less economic freedom.

- Countries with a high level of economic freedom almost always grow and achieve a high per capita GDP. Similarly, with the exception of a few major oil exporters, countries with low levels of economic freedom virtually always have a low per capita income.

CRITICAL ANALYSIS QUESTIONS

1. How does economic growth influence the living standards of people? Does it really make much difference whether an economy grows at 2 percent or 4 percent annually? Discuss.

2. What is the rule of 70? If the annual growth rate of a country was 5 percent, how many years would it take for income to double?

3. *What are the three major sources of economic growth? Explain why each makes it possible for the people of a nation to produce more output and achieve higher income levels.

4. What is creative destruction? Is it good or bad for economic growth? Explain.

5. Why is competition important for the efficient use of resources? What must a firm do in order to compete effectively? Competitive forces often result in firms being driven out of business. How does this "business failure" influence the growth of income?

6. In a market economy, what must an entrepreneur do in order to introduce a new innovative product? What determines whether the new product will be a success or failure? How important is innovation as a source of economic growth? Discuss.

7. What is the Economic Freedom of the World (EFW) index designed to measure? What must a country do in order to achieve a high rating on the EFW index?

8. *When examining the linkage between institutional quality and economic performance, why is it important to consider both the quality of institutions and indicators of performance such as the growth of per capita GDP over a lengthy time frame?

9. How do the income levels, growth rates, and poverty levels of countries with institutions and policies more consistent with economic freedom compare with those that are less free? Is this surprising? Why or why not?

10. *"Because government-operated firms do not have to make a profit, they can usually produce at a lower cost and charge a lower price than privately owned enterprises." Is this statement true? Why or why not?

11. Are there countries with a high degree of economic freedom that do not also have a relatively high per capita GDP? Are there countries with only a low level of economic freedom that have a high per capita GDP? Cite evidence in support of your answers.

12. *When governments restrict entry into various markets, impose price controls, and use taxes, subsidies, and regulatory favors to politically direct the allocation of goods and services, how will this influence the gains from trade? How will it influence the degree of rent-seeking by business and labor groups and the campaign contributions available to politicians? Will policies of this type enhance economic growth? Why or why not?

13. How does economic freedom influence life expectancy and the quality of the environment? Is this surprising?

14. Is economic freedom the same thing as democracy? Could a country have democratic political institutions and still have relatively little economic freedom? Could a country have a high degree of economic freedom without being a democracy? Cite examples in support of your answer.

15. Suppose that you have just been appointed to a high-level position in the economic analysis unit of the State Department. The secretary of state has asked you to prepare a memo describing the key policies and economic arrangements that less-developed countries should follow in order to achieve rapid growth and high income levels. Briefly describe your response. Be sure to indicate why each factor you mention is important if a nation is going to attain a high level of economic progress.

*Asterisk denotes questions for which answers are given in Appendix B.

ADDENDUM

The 2018 Economic Freedom of the World Country Rankings and Ratings

Institutions and policies generally change slowly, and it takes time for changes to exert much impact on income. Thus, we have generally focused on the quality of institutions and policies over a lengthy time frame such as 1995–2017. However, the recent data are also of interest. The map and the following chart provide the 2018 economic freedom ratings and rankings for the 162 countries now included in the Economic Freedom of the World Project.

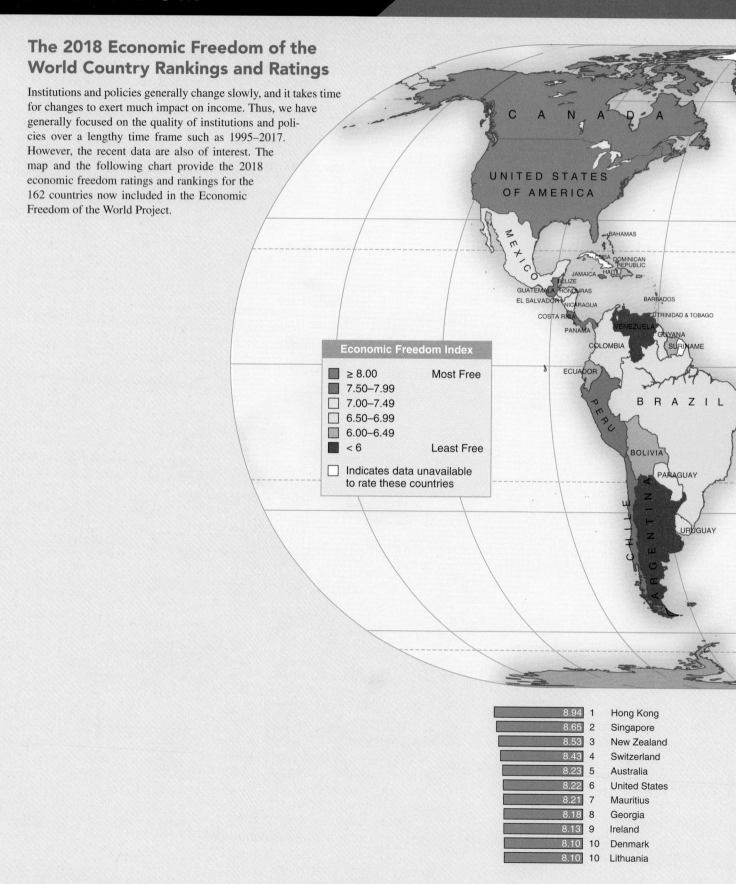

Economic Freedom Index

≥ 8.00	Most Free
7.50–7.99	
7.00–7.49	
6.50–6.99	
6.00–6.49	
< 6	Least Free
Indicates data unavailable to rate these countries	

Rating	Rank	Country
8.94	1	Hong Kong
8.65	2	Singapore
8.53	3	New Zealand
8.43	4	Switzerland
8.23	5	Australia
8.22	6	United States
8.21	7	Mauritius
8.18	8	Georgia
8.13	9	Ireland
8.10	10	Denmark
8.10	10	Lithuania

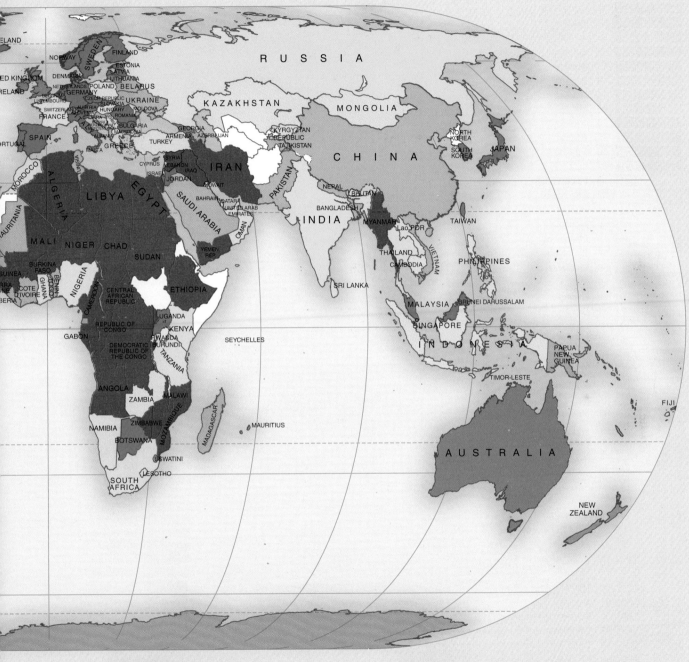

8.09	12	Canada
8.08	13	United Kingdom
7.96	14	Chile
7.96	14	Estonia
7.94	16	Malta
7.94	16	Taiwan
7.92	18	Armenia
7.89	19	Latvia
7.88	20	Japan
7.85	21	Germany
7.84	22	Cyprus
7.83	23	Romania
7.82	24	Netherlands
7.81	25	Czech Republic
7.80	26	Albania
7.80	26	Austria
7.80	26	Panama
7.76	29	Finland
7.76	29	Peru
7.75	31	Luxembourg
7.74	32	Bulgaria
7.73	33	Spain
7.71	34	Iceland

7.70	35	Guatemala
7.69	36	Jamaica
7.69	36	Korea, Rep.
7.63	38	Slovak Republic
7.62	39	Bahamas
7.62	39	Costa Rica
7.62	39	Israel
7.62	39	Jordan
7.60	43	Botswana
7.60	43	Norway
7.60	43	Portugal
7.58	46	Dominican Republic
7.58	46	Malaysia
7.58	46	Sweden
7.56	49	Belgium
7.55	50	Uganda
7.51	51	Italy
7.49	52	Cabo Verde
7.49	52	Seychelles
7.44	54	Hungary
7.43	55	Mongolia
7.43	55	Philippines
7.41	57	El Salvador
7.40	58	France
7.39	59	Indonesia
7.39	59	Rwanda
7.36	61	Croatia
7.33	62	Slovenia
7.28	63	Cambodia
7.28	63	Honduras
7.26	65	Trinidad and Tobago
7.25	66	Uruguay
7.23	67	Paraguay
7.21	68	Mexico
7.19	69	Zambia
7.16	70	Bahrain
7.15	71	North Macedonia
7.14	72	Gambia, The
7.12	73	Kazakhstan
7.05	74	Nicaragua
7.05	74	Serbia
7.05	74	United Arab Emirates
7.04	77	Poland
6.99	78	Kyrgyz Republic
6.99	78	Moldova
6.94	80	Montenegro
6.93	81	Nigeria
6.90	82	Bosnia and Herzegovina
6.88	83	Lebanon
6.88	83	Qatar
6.88	83	Sri Lanka
6.84	86	Kenya
6.79	87	Oman
6.75	88	Thailand
6.74	89	Russian Federation
6.73	90	South Africa
6.73	90	Tanzania
6.71	92	Colombia
6.71	92	Greece
6.70	94	Morocco

6.68	95	Guyana
6.65	96	Ghana
6.65	96	Lesotho
6.63	98	Bhutan
6.62	99	Lao PDR
6.62	99	Turkey
6.60	101	Belize
6.60	101	Brunei Darussalam
6.60	101	Kuwait
6.58	104	Haiti
6.56	105	Brazil
6.56	105	India
6.52	107	Namibia
6.50	108	Fiji
6.48	109	Nepal
6.46	110	Ecuador
6.39	111	Papua New Guinea
6.37	112	Azerbaijan
6.37	112	Suriname
6.35	114	Belarus
6.31	115	Saudi Arabia
6.30	116	Bolivia
6.29	117	Timor-Leste
6.28	118	Liberia
6.27	119	Eswatini
6.27	119	Senegal
6.25	121	Togo
6.22	122	Barbados
6.22	122	Mauritania
6.21	124	China
6.20	125	Benin
6.20	125	Madagascar
6.20	125	Vietnam
6.09	128	Cote d'Ivoire
6.07	129	Pakistan
6.07	129	Tunisia
6.06	131	Ukraine
6.05	132	Tajikistan
6.04	133	Bangladesh
5.94	134	Burundi
5.94	134	Mozambique
5.93	136	Mali
5.87	137	Cameroon
5.87	137	Sierra Leone
5.86	139	Gabon
5.85	140	Burkina Faso
5.85	140	Niger
5.81	142	Myanmar
5.79	143	Malawi
5.78	144	Argentina
5.71	145	Chad
5.61	146	Ethiopia
5.61	146	Iraq
5.57	148	Guinea
5.51	149	Yemen, Rep.
5.46	150	Guinea-Bissau
5.45	151	Syrian Arab Republic
5.38	152	Egypt, Arab Rep.
5.27	153	Central African Republic
5.15	154	Congo, Dem. Rep.
5.12	155	Zimbabwe
5.03	156	Congo, Rep.
4.97	157	Algeria
4.80	158	Iran, Islamic Rep.
4.75	159	Angola
4.72	160	Libya
4.21	161	Sudan
3.34	162	Venezuela, RB

CHAPTER 17

The Economics of Development

History is overwhelmingly a story of economies that failed to produce a set of economic rules of the game (with enforcement) that induce sustained economic growth. The central issue of economic history and of economic development is to account for the evolution of political and economic institutions that create an economic environment that induces increasing productivity. **—Douglass C. North, 1993 Nobel Laureate[1]**

In the last chapter, we explained why the institutions and policies of a country exert a major impact on economic growth. However, economic growth and development are multidimensional. In addition to institutions, several other factors, including climate, location, history, demography, and technology, exert an impact on economic development. Moreover, these factors change through time. This chapter will focus on how these factors have impacted human progress throughout history.

As you read this chapter, look for answers to the following questions:

- What was life like before 1800, and how did the Industrial Revolution change life throughout the world?

- How have history, geography, demography, technology, and entrepreneurship influenced both economic institutions and development?

- How did the huge reductions in transportation and communication costs of the past half-century alter economic development? How did income levels, economic growth, and poverty rates change during this era?

- How do the changes in economic growth and breadth of development of the past half-century compare with the Industrial Revolution?

[1]Douglass C. North, "Institutions," *Journal of Economic Perspectives* 5 (Winter 1991): 98.

17-1 THE ECONOMIC RECORD OF THE LAST 1000 YEARS

Developing countries
Countries with stagnating levels of GDP per capita that lagged behind the high-income countries of Western Europe, North America, Oceania, and Japan during the decades following the Industrial Revolution. They are sometimes referred to as less-developed countries.

Industrial Revolution
Development of machines and improvements in technology beginning around 1800 that propelled increases in output and rising income levels.

Before 1800, most of the world's population struggled 50, 60, and 70 hours per week to obtain enough food, shelter, and other basic necessities for survival. The child mortality rate was high, and life expectancy was short, hovering around 25 years. It was a constant struggle for survival, and many lost the battle. Moreover, this had been the case for centuries.

The late Angus Maddison, an economist for the Organization for Economic Co-operation and Development (OECD), is widely recognized as the leading authority on historical income and life expectancy data. Exhibit 1, panel (a) presents Maddison's estimates of per capita GDP (measured in 2011 purchasing power parity dollars) during the past thousand years for the 21 high-income countries of Western Europe, North America, and Oceania, along with Japan, as well as the parallel figures for **developing countries**.[2] In 1820, the per capita income of the high-income group was $1,461, slightly more than 50 percent higher than it was in 1500. The per capita GDP for the rest of the world in 1820 was $816, less than 5 percent higher than it was in 1500.

Around 1800, however, the **Industrial Revolution** began to transform the lives of the 12 to 15 percent of the world's population living in the high-income countries. Driven by capital formation, improved technology, and expansion in international trade, income

EXHIBIT 1

GDP Per Capita (in 2011 PPP dollars) for High-Income and Developing Countries, 1000–2015

The GDP per capita for the 21 long-standing high-income, developing (excluding sub-Saharan Africa), and sub-Saharan African countries are shown here. Note, per capita income changed very little between 1000 and 1820. Beginning with the Industrial Revolution of the early 1800s, the high-income countries began to experience sustained economic growth. By 1950, the per capita

GDP of the high-income countries was almost six times the level of 1820. In contrast, the per capita income of the developing countries continued to stagnate for another century and a half. However, the income level of the developing countries outside of sub-Saharan Africa has grown rapidly since 1970, and the sub-Saharan group has achieved solid growth since 2000.

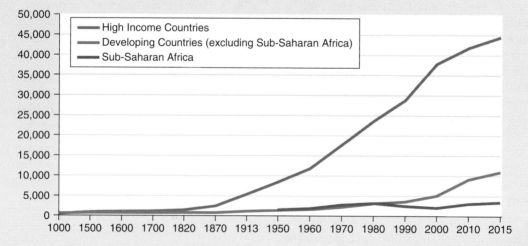

Source: J. Bolt, R. Inklaar, H. de Jong, and J. van Zanden, "Rebasing 'Maddison': New Income Comparisons and the Shape of Long-Run Economic Development," Maddison Project Working Paper No. 10, 2018. Available at www.ggdc.net/maddison; and Angus Maddison, *Contours of the World Economy, 1-2030 AD: Essays in Macro-Economic History* (Oxford: Oxford University Press, 2007).

---

[2]The 21 high-income countries are Australia, Austria, Belgium, Canada, Switzerland, Germany, Denmark, Spain, Finland, France, United Kingdom, Ireland, Iceland, Italy, Japan, Luxembourg, Netherlands, Norway, New Zealand, Sweden, and the United States.

growth began to outpace expansion in the population in these countries. As Exhibit 1 shows, per capita GDP in these areas rose from $1,461 in 1820 to $2,506 in 1870 and $5,413 in 1913. By 1950, the per capita GDP in these regions had soared to $8,464, an increase of 480 percent in 130 years.

But the change was much less transformative elsewhere. During the 130 years from 1820 to 1950, the real per capita GDP of the developing countries outside of sub-Saharan Africa rose from $816 to $1,426, an increase of only 75 percent, about a half of a percent annually. Moreover, the $1,426 real per capita GDP of these countries in 1950 was even lower than the $1,461 per capita income of the high-income countries in 1820. These figures show that while the Industrial Revolution triggered growth in Western Europe, North America, Oceania, and Japan, its impact on the 85 percent of the population living in the rest of the world was minimal. People in these countries did a little better during this period than before 1800, but not much.

Now, consider what has happened during the past half-century. Since 1970, something like a second economic revolution has occurred, and it has affected the entire world. Per person real income levels in the high-income countries have continued to rise, but for the first time in history, the rest of the world has achieved sustained economic growth and income levels well above subsistence. The rising per person real income levels occurred first in developing countries outside of sub-Saharan Africa, but more recently, sustained growth has also occurred in sub-Saharan Africa. As Exhibit 1 shows, real per capita GDP of the developing countries outside of sub-Saharan Africa rose from $1,698 in 1960 to $11,015 in 2015, a whopping increase of 549 percent. This increase in just 55 years was even larger than the increase in per capita GDP of the high-income countries during the 130 years following 1820. Moreover, there are signs of change in Africa. The per capita GDP of sub-Saharan African countries has increased from $2,104 in 2000 to $3,466 in 2015, an increase of 65 percent in 15 years.

How can the pattern of economic growth of the past two centuries be explained? After centuries of stagnation, why have the developing countries grown rapidly during the past half-century? We now turn to an examination of these questions.

17-2 THEORIES OF DEVELOPMENT

As the last chapter indicated, countries with economic institutions supportive of voluntary exchange, open markets, and protection of property rights generally grow more rapidly than countries where these elements are absent. But economic institutions are not the only factor influencing the performance of economies. Economic analysis indicates that there are other factors that will also impact economic growth and development. Some of these factors may even exert an impact on the historical development of economic institutions. This section will examine these factors and their potential importance as determinants of variations in the growth rates and income levels of countries and regions.

17-2a MALTHUSIAN THEORY OF DEVELOPMENT

Writing in 1798, the renowned English economist Thomas Malthus argued that income per person could never increase much above the subsistence level because, if it did, the higher income level would trigger a population boom that would soon drive income back to the subsistence level.[3] Malthus argued that when the income level is above subsistence, population will grow exponentially while the resources required to expand production will only grow linearly. Thus, the world is caught in a **Malthusian trap**: It will be impossible to sustain income above the subsistence level.

The theory of Malthus described the world in which he lived. As Exhibit 1 shows, per person income levels in 1800 were near the subsistence level, and they had been largely

Malthusian trap
Theory that income per person can never rise much above subsistence level, because if it does, population will grow rapidly and soon drive the income per person back to the subsistence level.

---

[3]Thomas Malthus, *An Essay on the Principle of Population* (London: J. Johnson, 1798).

unchanged for centuries. However, even as Malthus was writing, the Industrial Revolution was beginning to undermine his theory. In the West, rising income per person was achieved throughout the nineteenth century. Given the rising income levels in the West following the Industrial Revolution, it is easy to discard the Malthusian theory. However, Exhibit 1 also indicates that per capita GDP of developing countries continued to stagnate at or near subsistence levels for at least another century and a half following the Industrial Revolution. To a large degree, 85 percent of the world's population continued to live in a Malthusian world until the 1950s.

17-2b COLONIALISM, EUROPEAN SETTLEMENTS, AND INSTITUTIONS

Why do some nations have institutions supportive of growth and development, while others do not? In a classic 2001 article, Daron Acemoglu, Simon Johnson, and James Robinson argue that history during the colonial era provides a big part of the answer. Acemoglu, Johnson, and Robinson highlight the importance of incentives.[4] When Europeans migrated to other parts of the world, they had an incentive to establish protective institutions when they planned to settle permanently in a region. This long-term commitment provided the European settlers with a strong incentive to establish institutions that protected individual rights and limited the powers of government. In contrast, when an area was unfavorable for settlement as the result of conditions like a harsh climate, disease-prone environment, and the presence of a large domestic population, the Europeans had little incentive to establish sound institutions because they did not plan on a permanent settlement. As a result, extractive institutions—that is, minimal legal restraints preventing the seizure of resources by powerful interests—generally emerged in areas unfavorable for settlement.

According to this view, differences in the structure of incentives during the colonial era exerted a major impact on the evolution of institutions. Even after independence, the colonial institutional influences remained and continued to exert an impact on institutions and policies. In countries like the United States, Canada, Australia, and New Zealand, sound institutions emerged because the European colonizers planned on staying. They had long-range plans and sought to protect their investments, gains from trade, and returns on new discoveries. Conversely, protective institutions were largely absent in Africa and Latin America because the climate, diseases, and/or density of the domestic population made settlement in these regions unattractive. In these regions, extractive institutions often emerged because the European colonizers were often primarily interested in resource extraction. Thus, the structure of incentives contributed to the development of institutions more consistent with economic growth and progress in Canada, Australia, New Zealand, and the United States than was the case in Africa and Latin America.

17-2c NEOCLASSICAL PRODUCTION FUNCTION THEORY OF DEVELOPMENT

This theory focuses on the inputs of physical and human capital and technological advances as the sources of economic growth. Output is a function of three things: (1) physical capital (machines, structures, tools, etc.), (2) human capital (education and training), and (3) technology. In turn, as the inputs of physical and human capital increase and technology improves, output expands. Patterned after the pioneering research of Robert Solow of the Massachusetts Institute of Technology, the neoclassical theory dominated the growth and development literature during 1960–1995.[5]

---

[4]See Daron Acemoglu, Simon Johnson, and James A. Robinson, "The Colonial Origins of Comparative Development: An Empirical Investigation," *American Economic Review* 91 (2001): 1369–401.

[5]Robert M. Solow, "A Contribution to the Theory of Economic Growth," *Quarterly Journal of Economics* 70 (1956): 65–94.

The neoclassical theory explained the breakout of the Malthusian trap and the growth of per capita income. Malthus failed to consider the importance of capital formation and technology as sources of growth. Beginning with the Industrial Revolution, sustained increases in real per capita income were achieved because investments in physical and human capital and technological advancements expanded output more rapidly than population growth.

The neoclassical theory also suggests the ingredients for strong economic growth: large investments in physical capital and education, and rapid advancements in technology. The experiences of Japan and Germany during 1950–1990 highlight the importance of capital and technology. Both had high investment rates and strong economic growth. But, this was not the case in the Soviet bloc countries. The former centrally planned economies of the Soviet Union and Eastern Europe all had high rates of investment in both physical and human capital, but they failed to achieve and sustain high rates of economic growth. During the 1980s, income levels in these countries stagnated, and they collapsed in the early 1990s as the result of poor economic performance.

Thus, while the neoclassical model provides insights on the growth process, clearly economic growth involves more than increases in the inputs. As Douglass North and Robert Thomas put it, "The factors we have listed (innovation, economies of scale, education, capital accumulation, etc.) are not causes of growth; they *are* growth."[6] This view brings out a highly important point: Even if investment in physical and human capital and advancements in technology are closely related to growth, they are not the fundamental cause of growth. Other factors are necessary to explain why capital formation, innovation, and strong economic growth occur in some countries (and time periods), but not others. What are these other factors? Without good institutions, investment and technology will not generate economic growth. Similarly, climate, location, and even cultural factors may also impact both productivity and the incentive to expand physical and human capital.

17-2d GEOGRAPHY AND DEVELOPMENT

Jeffrey Sachs of Columbia University has been at the forefront of those arguing that geographic factors such as climate, location, and access to an ocean coastline are primary determinants of economic development and growth.[7] According to this view, people living in hot, humid climates located distant from the major markets of Europe, North America, and Asia with limited access to an ocean coastline face major economic disadvantages. Hot and humid tropical climatic conditions erode the energy level of workers and increase the risk of disabling and life-threatening diseases such as malaria and yellow fever. Locations distant from the world's major markets make trade more costly and reduce the availability of potential trading partners. Limited access to ocean shipping, particularly when landlocked, further reduces the attractiveness of a country for the conduct of business and location of productive activities.

Climate and location may also exert an impact on the quality of institutions. When a hot, humid climate remote from major markets makes a country an unattractive location for productive activities, the gains derived from a legal system that provides for secure property rights and even-handed enforcement of contracts will be small. Under these circumstances, political decision-makers will have little incentive to establish a sound legal system. Similarly, location distant from major markets will reduce the potential gains derived from the removal of trade barriers, reducing the gains derived from liberal trade policy. Thus, countries with major geographic disadvantages are also often characterized

---

[6]Douglass C. North and Robert Paul Thomas, *The Rise of the Western World: A New Economic History* (Cambridge: Cambridge University Press, 1973): 2.

[7]See Jeffrey D. Sachs, "Tropical Underdevelopment," National Bureau of Economic Research Working Paper No. 8119, 2001; and John Luke Gallup, Jeffrey D. Sachs, and Andrew D. Mellinger, "Geography and Development," National Bureau of Economic Research Working Paper No. 6849, 1998.

by economic institutions and policies inconsistent with economic growth and development. This makes it difficult to determine if the poor economic performance of these countries is the result of their geographic disadvantages or poor institutions.[8]

Which countries suffer from the largest geographic disadvantages? **Exhibit 2** shows the list of the 40 most disadvantaged countries on the basis of their (1) distance from major markets; (2) hot, humid, and disease-prone climate; and (3) proportion of the population residing within 100 kilometers of an ice-free ocean coastline. Standardized values for these three variables were derived and summed to develop a measure of geographic disadvantage for the countries of the world. Exhibit 2 shows the standardized value of the aggregated geographic disadvantage variable for the 40 most disadvantaged countries. (Note: Larger values are indicative of greater geographic disadvantages.) The five most geographically disadvantaged countries are Burkina Faso, Mali, Niger, Chad, and Central African Republic. These five countries are located far from the world's major markets, are landlocked (no access to an ocean coastline), and have climates that are hot, humid, and

EXHIBIT 2

The 40 Most Geographically Disadvantaged Countries

Rank	Country	Standardized Geographic Disadvantage	Rank	Country	Standardized Geographic Disadvantage	Rank	Country	Standardized Geographic Disadvantage
1	Burkina Faso	2.54	15	Congo	1.40	29	Kenya	1.01
2	Mali	2.44	16	Zambia	1.37	30	Madagascar	0.97
3	Niger	1.86	17	Zimbabwe	1.33	31	Argentina	0.89
4	Chad	1.85	18	Namibia	1.30	32	Senegal	0.87
5	Central African Rep.	1.78	19	Cameroon	1.29	33	Burundi	0.85
6	Nigeria	1.63	20	Lesotho	1.26	34	Angola	0.84
7	Ghana	1.57	21	Tanzania	1.23	35	South Africa	0.81
8	Botswana	1.56	22	Uganda	1.19	36	Bolivia	0.81
9	D.R. of the Congo	1.54	23	Gabon	1.17	37	Gambia	0.78
10	Guinea	1.44	24	Paraguay	1.09	38	Rwanda	0.75
11	Togo	1.44	25	Benin	1.07	39	Ethiopia	0.70
12	Côte d'Ivoire	1.43	26	Sierra Leone	1.05	40	Brazil	0.69
13	Mozambique	1.43	27	Liberia	1.03			
14	Malawi	1.42	28	Eswatini	1.02			

Source: Joseph Connors, James D. Gwartney, and Hugo M. Montesinos, "The Transportation-Communication Revolution: 50 Years of Dramatic Change in Economic Development," *Cato Journal* 40, no. 1 (2020). Table 2. Larger figures in the Standardized Geographic Disadvantage column indicate greater geographic disadvantage.

[8]The importance of geographic relative to institutional factors as an explanation for poor economic performance and absence of development is a major topic of debate among economists. See Dani Rodrik, Arvind Subramanian, and Francesco Trebbi, "Institutions Rule: The Primacy of Institutions over Geography and Integration in Economic Development," *Journal of Economic Growth* 9 (June 2004): 131–65 and Jeffrey D. Sachs, "Institutions Don't Rule: Direct Effects of Geography on Per Capita Income," National Bureau of Economic Research Working Paper no. 9490 (February 2003).

disease-prone. The standardized summary measure indicates these five countries confront unfavorable geographic conditions that are between 1.78 and 2.54 standard deviations from the world sample mean. Other countries with sizeable geographical disadvantages include Nigeria, Ghana, Democratic Republic of the Congo, Togo, Zambia, and Zimbabwe. Note that sub-Saharan African countries dominate this list of the world's most geographically disadvantaged countries. Only four (Paraguay, Argentina, Bolivia, and Brazil) of the 40 most disadvantaged countries are located outside of sub-Saharan Africa.

While geographic factors such as location, climate, and access to ocean coastline do not change through time, their impact on growth and development may change. Changes in the cost of transportation and communication may alter the adverse impact of a location distant from major markets. Changes in technology and the availability of medical products and treatments may affect the disadvantages accompanying climatic conditions. Thus, the effects of geographic disadvantages may differ across time periods.

The four theories of growth outlined here provide some insight into the historic pattern of economic development shown in Exhibit 1. Both colonization and geographic disadvantages adversely impacted the quality of economic institutions and the economic growth of sub-Saharan African countries. In turn, these disadvantages have contributed to the lagging per capita income levels of this region. The alternative theories are not mutually exclusive. Each may have impacted the growth and development of different regions and at various points throughout history. They all may help us better understand the growth process and the historic pattern of economic development.

17-3 THE TRANSPORTATION-COMMUNICATION REVOLUTION

Since the 1950s, there has been a huge reduction in transportation and communication costs, driven by improvements in technology and entrepreneurship.[9] The jet engine substantially reduced the cost of both air travel and shipment of cargo. The integrated circuit and the microprocessor have improved the quality and reduced the cost of products ranging from cell phones to airplanes. The internet has vastly reduced the cost and increased the speed of transmitting information. The standardized steel container and mechanization have dramatically reduced the cost of shipping cargo. In the United States, the cost of loading and unloading ocean freighter cargo plunged from $48 per ton in 1956 to 18 cents in 2006,[10] a reduction of 99 percent.

The timing and financial cost reductions for several forms of communication have been so dramatic they are difficult even to estimate. As recently as 1990, international telephone calls were of uncertain quality and cost several dollars per minute. Today calls involving both audio and video transmission, including conference calls, can be made over the internet at a small fraction of their cost just a few decades ago. In 1990, sending documents and written messages would have cost tens of dollars, and the delivery taken seven days or more. Today, digital documents can be delivered in seconds at a near-zero price.

Data on the shipping of cargo via ocean and air provide insight into the magnitude of the changes in shipping costs. Ocean shipping constitutes 99 percent of world trade by weight and a majority by value. Exhibit 3, panel (a) presents the data for ocean shipping costs expressed as a percent of cargo value. Two series are shown in order to track the figures over a lengthier time frame. The first is from the classic study of David Hummels based on the cost and value of all imports entering U.S. ports by ship each year during

---

[9]Our analysis of the Transportation-Communication Revolution borrows freely from Joseph Connors, James D. Gwartney, and Hugo M. Montesinos, "The Transportation-Communication Revolution: 50 Years of Dramatic Change in Economic Development," *Cato Journal* 40, no. 1 (2020). Moreover, both Connors and Montesinos provided us with helpful comments on this chapter.

[10]Both figures are in 2011 U.S. dollars; see A. Hammond, "Heroes of Progress, Pt. 17: Malcom McLean," Human Progress (May 2019). Available at https://humanprogress.org/article.php?p=1905.

EXHIBIT 3

The Dramatic Reduction in the Cost of Ocean and Air Shipping during the Past Half-Century

As panel (a) indicates, ocean shipping costs as a share of cargo value declined by more than 50 percent during 1974–2016. Air revenue per ton-kilometer (panel b) fell by 78 percent during 1970–2019 and by a whopping 94 percent during 1955–2019.

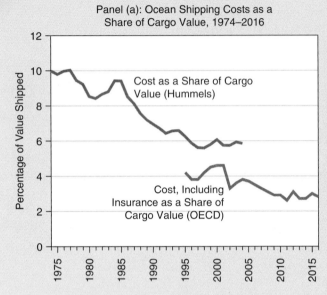

Panel (a): Ocean Shipping Costs as a Share of Cargo Value, 1974–2016

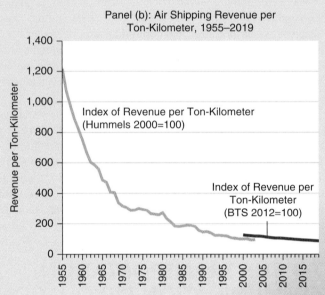

Panel (b): Air Shipping Revenue per Ton-Kilometer, 1955–2019

Source: Joseph Connors, James D. Gwartney, and Hugo M. Montesinos, "The Transportation-Communication Revolution: 50 Years of Dramatic Change in Economic Development," *Cato Journal* 40, no. 1 (2020). Figure 1.

1974–2004. The second series, derived from OECD data, covers 1995–2016. The Hummels figures indicate that ocean shipping costs fell from 10 percent of the value of the shipment in 1974 to 5.8 percent in 2004, a reduction of 42 percent over these three decades.[11] The OECD data indicate that ocean shipping costs, including insurance, declined from 4.2 percent of cargo value in 1995 to 2.8 percent in 2016, a reduction of 33 percent during the 21 years. Together, the two series imply that real ocean shipping costs declined by slightly more than 50 percent during 1974–2016.

Exhibit 3, panel (b) presents data on shipping costs via air freight. As in the case of panel (a), two series are presented. While both are based on the revenue of air carriers per ton-kilometer shipped, they cover different time spans and air carriers. The first series from Hummels is an index of the revenue per ton-kilometer shipped for all international carriers during 1955–2003. The second series, from the U.S. Bureau of Transportation Statistics (BTS), covers 2000–2019, but is only for U.S. carriers on international cargo flights. Each series is an index reflecting the real revenue earned by air carriers in U.S. dollars. Hummels's data indicate that the index of air cargo shipping revenue fell from 1,217 in 1955 to 95 in 2003, a 92 percent reduction in real cost during this time span. The BTS index of revenue per ton-kilometer fell from 126 in 2000 to 87 in 2019, a 31 percent reduction during the two decades. Using the last year in which the two series overlap, the overall percentage decline in real revenue per ton-kilometer for air transport during 1955–2019 was a whopping 94 percent. While a substantial share of the decline in the cost of air shipping occurred before 1970, the reduction during 1970–2019 was still huge—78 percent.

---

[11]David Hummels, "Transportation Costs and International Trade in the Second Era of Globalization," *Journal of Economic Perspectives* 21, no. 3 (2007): 131–54.

These huge reductions in transportation and communication costs exerted a dramatic impact on the world. For the first time in history, a substantial share of the world's population interacted with people in faraway countries and regions. Knowledge of economic activities and conditions increased by leaps and bounds. People in poor countries became vastly more aware of what life was like in wealthier regions, and vice versa. The change was so dramatic that this period, which began around 1970, might properly be thought of as the **Transportation-Communication Revolution**.

17-4 THE TRANSPORTATION-COMMUNICATION REVOLUTION AND ECONOMIC DEVELOPMENT

How did the substantial reductions in transportation and communication cost impact economic development? To address this question, data were assembled for per capita GDP, international trade, demographics, and economic institutions. There are 134 countries for which per capita GDP data can be obtained continuously since 1970 for which the Fraser Institute data on economic freedom are also available in 2015. In 2015, the population of these countries composed 94 percent of the total for the world. The 134 countries were further subdivided into three groups: (1) the 21 high-income countries of Western Europe, North America, and Oceania plus Japan; (2) the 40 most geographically disadvantaged countries of Exhibit 2; and (3) the 73 other developing countries.

There are four major reasons to expect that the substantial reductions in transportation and communication costs will exert a strong positive impact on development: (1) gains from expansion in international trade; (2) gains from increases in entrepreneurial activities and adoption of technology and successful business practices from other countries; (3) improvements in economic institutions; and (4) a **virtuous cycle of development**. Let's consider each of these factors and examine their impact on economic growth and development.

1. The reductions in transportation and communication costs will expand the volume of international trade, enlarging the gains from specialization and adoption of mass production techniques. As a result, it will be possible for the trading partners to achieve lower costs, larger outputs, and higher income levels. In a dynamic sense, these factors will enhance economic growth.

Exhibit 4, panel (a) illustrates the path of international trade (merchandise goods) as a share of GDP for the world during 1960–2017. Economic analysis indicates that lower transportation and communication costs will increase international trade. This is precisely what happened. During the 1960s, international trade as a share of GDP averaged 19 percent of world GDP. Throughout the 1980s, the ratio hovered near 30 percent. Moreover, international trade as a share of world GDP continued to rise, reaching 43 percent in 2000 and 50 percent in 2010. Since 2010, the ratio has fluctuated around 50 percent. Thus, international trade as a share of world GDP in recent years has been approximately 2.5 times the level of the 1960s.

Exhibit 4, panel (b) shows the path of international trade as a share of GDP for the 21 high-income countries, 40 most geographically disadvantaged developing countries, and the 73 other developing countries during 1960–2017. In the case of the high-income countries, the international trade/GDP ratio rose steadily, increasing from 20 percent in the 1960s to 35 percent in the late 1980s, before soaring to the 55 percent to 60 percent range during 2010–2017. The trade/GDP ratio of the less geographically disadvantaged developing countries was smaller than the ratio for the high-income countries. However, it has increased even more dramatically, expanding from the 15 percent to 25 percent range during most of 1960–1990 to the 40 percent to 50 percent range during 2003–2017. Finally, the trade/GDP ratio of the 40 most geographically disadvantaged countries was both smaller and increased by a lesser amount than the parallel figures for the other two groups.

Transportation-Communication Revolution
Large reductions in transportation and communication costs that propelled higher growth rates of GDP per capita beginning around 1970. The acceleration of economic growth in developing countries was particularly strong.

Virtuous cycle of development
The reduction in the birth rate, slower population growth, and increase in the share of population in the prime working-age categories that generally provide a boost to productivity and economic growth once per capita GDP begins to grow. This pattern is nearly always observed soon after a country begins the growth process.

International Trade as a Percent of GDP, for the World and for High-Income and Developing Countries, 1960–2017

As panel (a) shows, international trade as a percent of world GDP rose from 20 percent in 1960 to 30 percent in 1990, and then accelerated to approximately 50 percent of GDP during 2005–2017. Panel (b) indicates that international trade as a percent of GDP of the high-income countries has steadily increased since 1960. For the developing countries, international trade as a percent of GDP of the less geographically disadvantaged countries changed little during 1960–1990, but has increased sharply since 1990. In the case of the geographically disadvantaged countries, the relative size of the trade sector was largely unchanged prior to 2000 but has gradually increased since.

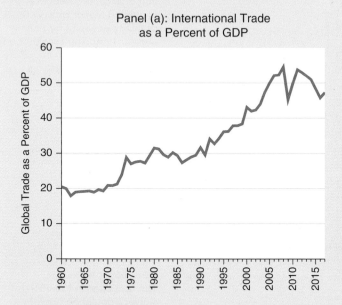

Panel (a): International Trade as a Percent of GDP

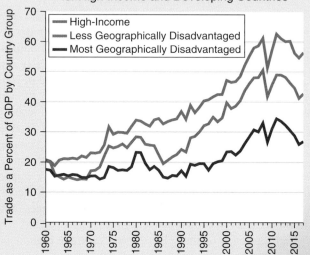

Panel (b): International Trade as a Percent of GDP for High-Income and Developing Countries

Sources: Derived from R. Feenstra, R. Inklaar, and M. Timmer, "The Next Generation of the Penn World Table," *American Economic Review* 105 (2015): 3150–82; and J. Bolt, R. Inklaar, H. de Jong, and J. van Zanden, "Rebasing 'Maddison': New Income Comparisons and the Shape of Long-Run Economic Development," Maddison Project Working Paper No. 10, 2018. Available at www.ggdc.net/maddison.

International trade as a share of GDP of the more geographically disadvantaged countries fluctuated between 15 percent and 20 percent throughout most of 1960–2000, before climbing to the 25 percent to 35 percent range during 2005–2017.

2. The lower transportation and communication costs will lead to larger gains from entrepreneurship and the adoption of advanced technologies and successful business practices employed in other countries. Entrepreneurs often derive important ideas from the successful production procedures and innovative practices of others. Entrepreneurial activities of this type also increase the speed at which improved products and technologies are disseminated throughout the world. This factor will be particularly important for developing countries. Businesses and entrepreneurs in developing countries can merely copy (or adopt at a low cost) the successful technologies and practices of the more advanced economies. However, to do so, they need to know about them. The reductions in transportation and communication costs and accompanying increased interaction among people living in high- and low-income countries will provide valuable information that will accelerate this process. So, too, will the ease of accessing and transmitting information and communicating with others throughout the world.

3. The lower transportation and communication costs will also increase the incentive to adopt economic policies more consistent with growth and development. Consider how reductions in shipping costs will impact the incentive to reduce trade barriers. When the cost of shipping goods or obtaining resources from distant locations is high, the incentive to remove trade barriers is weak, particularly in countries located distant from the world's major markets. Given the high shipping cost, little trade would occur even if the trade barriers were reduced. However, lower shipping costs will provide greater access to markets, including those in distant locations, expanding the potential gains derived from reductions in trade barriers. In turn, the larger potential gains from trade will increase the incentive of businesses and entrepreneurs to bring additional pressure for trade liberalization.

Reductions in transportation and communication costs will also influence the incentive to support a legal structure protective of property rights and enforcement of contracts. Foreign businesses and investors will be reluctant to engage in business activities when the country's legal system fails to provide for the security of property rights and enforcement of contracts. If high transportation costs make the country an unattractive place to do business, the gains derived from improvements in the legal system will be small. However, when reductions in transportation and communication costs increase the attractiveness of a country to potential businesses and investors, the gains derived from improvements in the legal system will increase, enhancing the incentive to move toward legal system improvements. Thus, in addition to their more direct impact on the volume of trade and entrepreneurship, lower transportation and communication costs will generate a positive secondary effect: enhancement of the incentive to remove trade barriers and improve the legal system.

The Economic Freedom of the World (EFW) data of the Fraser Institute can be used to track changes in institutional quality. The summary economic freedom rating of countries generally rose during 1985–2015, but the increases were greater for the developing countries. Thus, the institutional gap between the high-income and the developing groups' EFW ratings narrowed. In 1985, the mean EFW summary rating of the high-income countries was 1.4 units greater than it was for the developing countries and 2.4 units greater than for the 40 most disadvantaged developing countries. By 2015, however, this gap had fallen to 0.8 for the less geographically disadvantaged developing countries and 1.6 for those that were most geographically disadvantaged.

The Fraser Institute data can also be used to track the path of trade openness (area 4 of the Fraser index). The mean trade openness rating of the high-income countries was 7.7 in 1985, compared to only 4.5 for the less geographically disadvantaged developing countries and 3.5 for the most geographically disadvantaged group. In 2015, the trade openness mean rating of the high-income countries was 8.1, slightly higher than it was in 1985. In contrast, the mean ratings for the less geographically disadvantaged developing countries rose sharply during 1985–2015, narrowing the gap in trade openness between the developing and high-income countries from 3.2 in 1985 to only 0.9 in 2015. In the case of the most geographically disadvantaged countries, the mean trade openness gap fell from 4.2 in 1985 to 2.0 in 2015. Thus, as the incentive to adopt sound institutions and policies increased following the reduction in transportation and communication costs, the developing countries moved toward better economic institutions and more open trade.

4. Once the growth process begins, countries experience a virtuous cycle of development that will cause the growth rate of per capita GDP to accelerate. Higher income levels increase the opportunity cost of having children and increase the incentive of individuals to improve their education and skill level. As a result, the birth rate declines, leading to a reduction in the share of the population within the youngest age categories and an increase in the population share within the prime working-age group. In turn, this expansion in the share of the population within the prime working-age category propels additional growth. Moreover, the declining share of children and higher earnings both increase the incentive to invest in additional schooling and improve human capital, which eventually leads to still higher worker productivity and income levels. Thus, as reductions in transportation and communication costs, increases in gains from trade and entrepreneurship, and improvements in economic institutions ignite the growth process, increases in the share of the population in the prime working-age categories will further boost economic growth.

The Prime Working-Age (25–59) Group as a Percent of the Total Population for High-Income, Developing, and Geographically Disadvantaged Countries, 1960–2020

The share of the total population in the prime working-age category for the high-income, less geographically disadvantaged, and 40 most geographically disadvantaged countries is shown here. Increases in the prime working-age population will provide a boost to economic growth. The substantial increase in the prime working-age population percent enhanced the growth rate of the high-income countries during 1970–2000 and the less geographically disadvantaged developing countries during 1990–2010. In contrast, the decline in the prime working-age population share of the high-income countries since 2000 has slowed their rate of economic growth.

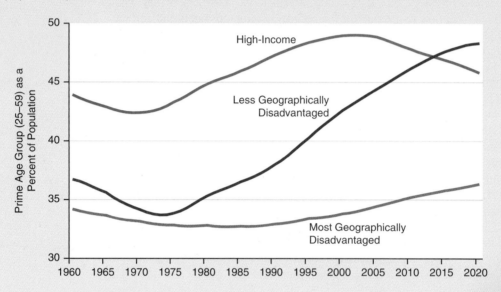

Source: Derived from World Bank, *World Development Indicators*, 2019.

Because the productivity and earnings of individuals are higher during the prime working-age phase of life (generally ages 25–59 years), changes in the share of the population in this age category exert an impact on economic growth. **Exhibit 5** shows the prime working-age population share for each of our three major groups since 1960. During the 1960s, the prime working-age share of the population trended downward across all three groups. This worldwide trend reflected the dearth of births during the economic hardship of the Great Depression and World War II and the substantial increase in the birth rate following the postwar boom. In the high-income countries, the prime working-age population share rose by approximately two percentage points per decade during 1970–2000. This enhanced the economic growth of these countries during this time frame. However, as the population in the high-income countries has aged and an increasing share of the population moved into the retirement phase of life, the prime working-age share has declined from 49 percent in 2000 to 45.8 percent in 2017. This reduction has slowed the growth of per capita GDP of the high-income countries.

The prime working-age share of the population for the 73 less geographically disadvantaged developing countries was much lower than it was for the high-income countries during the 1970s, but this situation changed dramatically over the next four decades. The prime working-age population share of the less geographically disadvantaged developing countries rose from 34 percent in 1975 to 38 percent in 1990, before soaring to 46 percent in 2010. During 1990–2010, the prime working-age share of this group's population increased by a whopping 4 percentage points per decade. By 2020, the prime working-age population share of the less disadvantaged developing countries (48.3 percent) was well above the parallel figure for the high-income group (45.8 percent).

Entrepreneurs Who Have Changed Our Lives:
Malcom McLean

You have probably never heard of Malcom McLean, but his innovative entrepreneurial activities have vastly reduced shipping costs, expanded the gains from trade, and improved the lives of millions of people throughout the world. McLean invented and pioneered the development of the standardized steel ocean shipping container, which revolutionized international trade during the last half of the twentieth century. In 1956, most ocean cargo was loaded and unloaded by hand by longshoremen. In the decades that followed, the standardized container eliminated the repeated handling of individual pieces of cargo, reducing loading and unloading cost to a tiny fraction of earlier figures.

One day in 1937, McLean was waiting for hours at a New Jersey pier as cotton bales from his truck were being loaded onto a ship, reports Martime. "Suddenly it occurred to me," he says. "Would it not be great if my trailer could simply be lifted up and placed on the ship without its contents being touched?"

By the early 1950s, he had earned enough money to do just that—to create containers that could go from truck to ship (and back) and to create ships that could carry them. Today "intermodal" shipping is the norm, but it was just an idea then. "The obstacles to McLean's concept were daunting. Suitable containers, cranes, and ships did not exist; McLean hired engineers and naval architects and set them loose to solve the problems," writes Marc Levinson in the *Smithsonian Magazine*.

McLean didn't get much help from the ocean transportation industry. He was an "outsider" to the industry leaders and a threat to dockworkers. While the savings were obvious to customers—he charged 25 percent less than competitors—the success of intermodal shipping occurred gradually. With time, as the advantages of McLean's container system became more apparent, others emulated his procedures. Shippers built bigger ships, and port facilities were redesigned with larger cranes that expedited the loading and unloading process. Through innovation, strategic thinking, and determination, Malcom McLean drastically reduced shipping costs and expanded the gains from specialization and trade that underlie our modern living standards.

Sources: A. Hammond, "Heroes of Progress, Pt. 17: Malcom McLean," *Human Progress* (May 2019), https://humanprogress.org/article.php?p=1905.

Marc Levinson, "The Now-Ubiquitous Shipping Container Was an Idea Before Its Time," *Smithsonian Magazine* (June 16, 2017), https://www.smithsonian-mag.com/innovation/shipping-container-idea-before-time-180963730/.

"The Story of Malcom McLean," *The Maritime Executive*, December 28, 2016, https://www.maritime-executive.com/article/the-story-of-malcolm-mclean.

These demographic changes exert an impact on the pattern of economic growth. The expansion in the share of the population in the high-productivity, prime working-age category of the high-income countries during 1970–2000 and the less geographically disadvantaged developing countries during 1975–2017 enhanced their economic growth. In contrast, the declining prime working-age population share of the high-income countries since 2000 has reduced their growth rate. Similarly, the low and relatively stable prime working-age share of the population in the most geographically disadvantaged countries has adversely affected their growth and development.

17-5 THE TRANSPORTATION-COMMUNICATION REVOLUTION AND THE HISTORIC ECONOMIC PROGRESS OF THE PAST 50 YEARS

What impact has the reduction in transportation and communication costs had on economic development? As expected, the sharp reductions in transportation and communication cost increased the volume of international trade and gains from specialization and large-scale production methods. But the lower transportation and communication costs will also generate indirect gains from the adoption of successful technologies and business practices of other countries, increased entrepreneurial activity, and greater incentive to institute sound policies. All of these factors will enhance the ability of poor countries, particularly those with less geographic disadvantages, to escape the Malthusian trap. As this happens, the growth rate of developing countries will be further enhanced by the virtuous cycle of development. If this analysis is correct, it should be reflected in the performance of economies. Let's examine this issue empirically.

17-5a GROWTH OF HIGH-INCOME AND DEVELOPING COUNTRIES DURING THE PAST HALF-CENTURY

What has happened to the growth rate of high-income and developing countries during the past half-century? Exhibit 6 shows the 15-year moving average of the annual growth rate of real per capita GDP for the high-income countries, less geographically disadvantaged developing countries, and 40 most geographically disadvantaged developing countries. Before the mid-1980s, the high-income countries grew more rapidly than the less geographically disadvantaged developing countries. Since the mid-1980s, however, this situation has changed dramatically. During 1985–2000, the average annual growth rate of the less geographically disadvantaged developing countries was 3.4 percent, compared to 2.1 percent for the high-income countries. By 2016, that growth advantage was even greater—5.0 percent for the developing group compared to 0.8 percent for the high-income countries. As Exhibit 5 shows, the share of the population in the prime working-age category of the less geographically disadvantaged developing countries during the more recent period was increasing, while it was declining in the high-income countries. Of course, this pattern of demographic change would tend to increase income growth in the former, but

EXHIBIT 6

Fifteen-Year Moving Average Annual Growth Rate of Real Per Capita GDP for High-Income, Developing, and Geographically Disadvantaged Countries, 1965–2016

The 15-year moving average of the high-income, less geographically disadvantaged, and the 40 most geographically disadvantaged countries is shown here. Before the mid-1980s, the high-income countries grew more rapidly than the developing countries that are less geographically disadvantaged, but the reverse has

been true in recent decades. Further, the growth gap has widened. The 15-year growth rate of per capita GDP of the less geographically disadvantaged countries in 2016 was 5 percent, compared to less than 1 percent for the high-income countries.

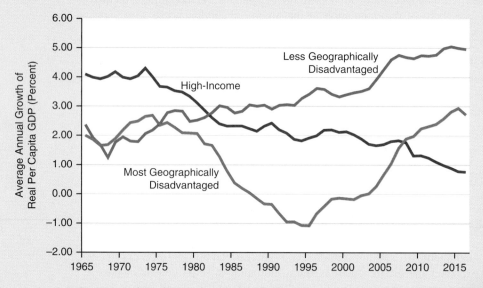

Source: Joseph Connors, James D. Gwartney, and Hugo M. Montesinos, "The Transportation-Communication Revolution: 50 Years of Dramatic Change in Economic Development," *Cato Journal* 40, no. 1 (2020). Figure 6.

reduce it in the latter. During 2001–2016, even the 40 most geographically disadvantaged developing countries achieved a solid annual growth rate (2.7 percent).

17-5b COUNTRIES WITH THE BEST AND WORST GROWTH RECORDS

Which countries are growing most rapidly? Which are falling behind? Exhibit 7 presents data on the growth of real GDP per person for (a) high-growth economies, (b) high-income developed nations, and (c) the economies with the worst growth records. The left side of Exhibit 7 indicates the ten fastest-growing countries in the world during 1990–2018. The annual growth rate of real per capita GDP of these countries ranged from 3.8 percent to 8.4 percent during this lengthy 28-year time frame. China, Myanmar, Vietnam, Laos, and India head the list of the fastest-growing economies. One-third of the world's population lives in China and India, two of the countries on the high-growth list. The populous countries of Vietnam, South Korea, and Bangladesh are also on the fast-growth list. Except for Ireland, all of the ten fastest-growing economies are developing countries. Remember, a 4 percent annual growth rate means that GDP per person doubles every generation, approximately 17.5 years. Clearly, per person incomes have increased sharply, and living standards improved dramatically since 1990 in the countries on the high-growth list.

The growth rates of the more populous high-income developed economies are also shown in Exhibit 7 (middle columns). The annual growth rates of per capita GDP of the high-income countries are substantially lower than those of countries in the rapid growth group. They are also closely clustered. The annual growth rates of Australia, Canada, the Netherlands, the United Kingdom, the United States, Germany, and Spain were all in the range between 1.4 percent and 1.6 percent. The growth rates of France, Japan, and Italy lagged behind.

Developing countries dominate not only the high-growth list but, unfortunately, they also dominate the group with the worst economic record (see the right side of Exhibit 7). The income levels of this latter group have not only failed to grow; they have regressed. The per capita incomes of these ten LDCs declined at an annual rate of 0.2 percent or more during 1990–2018. The annual growth of per capita GDP of four of these countries (Yemen, Venezuela, Burundi, and the Democratic Republic of Congo) fell at an annual rate of 1.4 percent or more during the 28 years.

EXHIBIT 7

The Growth of Real Per Capita GDP for High-Growth, High-Income, and Low-Growth Countries, 1990–2018

High Growth	Growth of Per Capita GDP	High Income	Growth of Per Capita GDP	Low Growth	Growth of Per Capita GDP
China	8.4%	Australia	1.6%	Republic of Congo	−0.2%
Myanmar	7.5%	Canada	1.5%	Madagascar	−0.5%
Vietnam	5.4%	Netherlands	1.5%	Tajikistan	−0.6%
Laos	4.8%	United Kingdom	1.5%	Gabon	−0.7%
India	4.6%	United States	1.5%	Haiti	−0.8%
Sri Lanka	4.3%	Germany	1.4%	Central African Republic	−0.9%
Ireland	4.1%	Spain	1.4%	Yemen	−1.4%
South Korea	4.1%	France	1.1%	Venezuela	−1.6%
Bangladesh	3.8%	Japan	0.9%	Burundi	−1.6%
Panama	3.8%	Italy	0.5%	Democratic Republic of Congo	−1.8%

Note: Countries with a 2000 population of less than 2 million were not included in this exhibit.
Source: World Bank, *World Development Indicators*, 2020

The pattern of the developing countries in the high-growth and low-growth groups is interesting. None of the ten countries in the fast-growth group were among the 40 most geographically disadvantaged countries of Exhibit 2. While most of the high-growth countries were not in the freest quartile of the Fraser Institute's EFW measure, neither were they in the bottom quartile. Several, including China, India, South Korea, Bangladesh, and Panama, achieved substantial increases in economic freedom during 1985–2017. In contrast, all of the ten countries with falling income levels during 1990–2018 either faced severe geographic disadvantages or had exceedingly poor economic institutions, and often both were present. Six (Republic of Congo, Madagascar, Gabon, Central African Republic, Burundi, and the Democratic Republic of Congo) of the ten countries with the worst growth records were among the 40 countries with the most severe climate and location disadvantages. With regard to economic institutions, Venezuela, Gabon, Central African Republic, and Burundi all ranked among the 20 least economically free countries in the world during 1995–2017.

Exhibit 7 highlights the importance of both institutional and geographic factors. As lower transportation and communication costs enhanced economic growth in recent decades, several developing countries achieved remarkably high growth rates. Per capita income in these countries increased far more rapidly than in high-income countries. No country with a really low economic freedom rating or major geographic disadvantage was in the high-growth group. On the other hand, all of the countries with the worst growth records either had bad economic institutions or major geographic disadvantages, and often both.

17-5c DRAMATIC REDUCTION IN THE WORLDWIDE POVERTY RATE

Some observers fear that growth propelled by freer markets and expanded international trade will leave the poor behind. This has not been the case in recent decades. **Exhibit 8** presents the extreme and moderate poverty rates of the world for various years during 1980–2017. Persons with incomes of less than $1.90 per day (measured in 2011 international dollars) are classified as extremely poor by the World Bank. As Exhibit 8 shows, the world's extreme poverty rate in 2017 was 9.2 percent, down from 27.0 percent in 2000 and 41.3 percent in 1980. Thus, the world's extreme poverty rate is now less than one-quarter of what it was in 1980.

EXHIBIT 8

The Extreme and Moderate Poverty Rates of the World, 1980–2017

The extreme poverty rate ($1.90 per day) of the world fell from 41.3 percent in 1980 to 9.2 percent in 2017. The moderate poverty rate ($3.20 per day) followed a similar pattern, falling from 58.6 percent in 1980 to 24.3 percent in 2017.

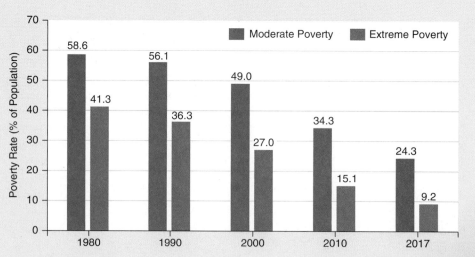

Source: World Bank, *World Development Indicators*, 2019. The World Bank poverty rate data were used to calculate the poverty rate for each country. There were missing values for the poverty rate for some countries. Estimation procedures were used to fill in the missing values. For details, see Chapter 2 addendum in Hugo Montesinos, *On Geography, Institutions, Human Capital, and Economic Development* (PhD diss., Florida State University, 2019).

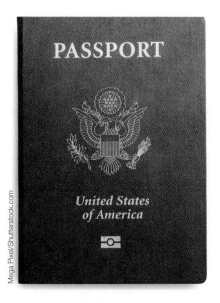

Persons with incomes of less than $3.20 per day (measured in 2011 international dollars) are classified by the World Bank as living in moderate poverty. As Exhibit 8 illustrates, nearly three-fifths (58.6 percent) of the world's population had an income level below the moderate poverty threshold in 1980. By 2000, the moderate poverty rate had fallen to 49 percent, and by 2017, the figure had declined to 24.3 percent. Thus, in the 17 years between 2000 and 2017, the world's moderate poverty rate was cut in half.

Clearly, enormous progress has been made against poverty since 1980. If the poverty rates of 1980 were present today, there would be more than 2 billion additional people experiencing both extreme and moderate poverty in the world.

17-6 THE TRANSPORTATION-COMMUNICATION REVOLUTION VERSUS THE INDUSTRIAL REVOLUTION

The past half-century has been a remarkable time period. Huge reductions in the cost of transportation and communication have led to dramatically higher rates of integration, entrepreneurial activity, and exchange of both goods and ideas among people living in high- and low-income countries. After centuries of income levels at or near subsistence, a large share of the developing world has escaped the Malthusian trap and achieved sustained high rates of economic growth. Poverty rates have declined more during the past 50 years than during the previous thousand years. Most of this progress has been in developing countries with the smallest geographic disadvantages. Since 2000, however, there is some evidence that people living in countries with more severe geographic disadvantages may also be escaping the Malthusian trap.

These changes have created something akin to a second Industrial Revolution: the Transportation-Communication Revolution. Like the Industrial Revolution, this more recent revolution has expanded opportunities and enhanced economic growth. But the two revolutions differ in three important respects.

First, the impact of the Transportation-Communication Revolution is much broader. The Industrial Revolution resulted in substantial income gains for between 12 and 15 percent of the world's population. However, as Exhibit 1 indicates, its impact on the rest of the world was minimal for nearly a century and a half. In contrast, the Transportation-Communication Revolution has already exerted a major impact on approximately 70 percent of the world's population, and its scope is still expanding.

Second, growth rates during the Transportation-Communication Revolution have been more rapid than they were during the Industrial Revolution. During 1960–2015, the real per

The reductions in the cost of transportation and communication of the past half-century have increased the gains from trade and entrepreneurship and increased the incentive to improve economic institutions and policies. As a result, developing economies, particularly those that are less geographically disadvantaged, achieved historically high growth rates.

capita GDP of developing countries outside of sub-Saharan Africa rose by 549 percent in just 55 years, an even larger increase than that of the high-income countries during the 130 years (1820–1950) following the Industrial Revolution (see Exhibit 1). Moreover, developing countries today are able to achieve growth rates beyond what was thought to be possible only a few decades ago. Prior to 1950, long-term growth rates above 2 percent were extremely rare. No country was able to achieve a decade-long annual growth rate of per capita GDP greater than 3 percent before 1950. In contrast, the 15-year moving average growth of real GDP of the less geographically disadvantaged developing countries has exceeded 3 percent since the mid-1980s (see Exhibit 6). Many developing countries have grown even more rapidly (see Exhibit 7).

Some countries were able to achieve high rates of economic growth, starting in the 1960s. The real per capita GDP of Hong Kong grew at an annual rate of 4.9 percent from 1960 to 2000. The growth rate of Singapore was even more impressive, hitting 5.7 percent during that same 40-year period. Botswana grew at an annual rate of 5.4 percent from 1965 to 2015. From 1970 to 2015, the real per capita GDP of South Korea and Indonesia grew at annual rates of 5.5 percent and 3.6 percent, respectively.

Third, while the Industrial Revolution increased income inequality, the Transportation-Communication Revolution has reduced it. Following the Industrial Revolution, income levels in the high-income countries grew, while they stagnated in the rest of the world. Thus, decade after decade, worldwide income inequality increased. In contrast, since the mid-1980s, the per capita income in developing countries, particularly those with less geographic disadvantages, has increased more rapidly than it has in high-income countries. For the first time since the rise of sustained economic growth about 200 years ago, the income inequality of the world is now declining.[12]

There is widespread recognition of the human progress that accompanied the Industrial Revolution. In many ways, the Transportation-Communication Revolution of the past half-century is even more remarkable. The impact of the former is widely recognized. It is time for the more recent economic revolution to also be acknowledged.

17-7 THE FUTURE OF ECONOMIC DEVELOPMENT

As the past two centuries illustrate, history, institutions, geography, demography, technology, and entrepreneurial discovery all exert an impact on economic development. Moreover, these factors are interrelated. Institutions and policies that support voluntary exchange, reward discovery of better ways of doing things, and protect people and their property from the harmful acts of others encourage productive activities. But institutions do not exist in a vacuum. Their development reflects history, geography, and technology, among other things. The huge reductions in transportation and communication costs of recent decades were driven by technology and entrepreneurship. But they also expanded the payoff of productive opportunities in developing countries, particularly those that were less geographically disadvantaged. Further, the lower transport and communication cost enhanced the ability of entrepreneurs to choose where to locate production facilities. These forces combined to increase the incentive of political decision-makers to adopt sound policies, including those supportive of economic freedom, investment, and importation of technology. As reductions in transportation and communication costs and improvements in institutional quality unleashed economic growth in developing countries, an additional boost was derived from favorable demographics (increase in the prime working-age share of the population). Remarkably, for the first time in history, the world experienced solid economic growth during the past three decades, while per capita income in developing countries increased more rapidly than in the high-income developed countries.

---

[12]For a comprehensive analysis of the recent decline in worldwide income inequality, see Xavier Sala-i-Martin, "The World Distribution of Income: Falling Poverty and... Convergence, Period," *Quarterly Journal of Economics* 121 (2006): 351–97; and Joseph Connors, James Gwartney, and Hugo Montesinos, "The Rise and Fall of Worldwide Income Inequality, 1820–2035," *Southern Economic Journal* (July 2020).

Can the economic progress of the past several decades be maintained? Economics indicates the types of institutions and policies that will lead to wealth creation, growth, and prosperity. However, institutions and policies are an outgrowth of the political process. Unfortunately, there is no assurance that political decision-making will lead to sound policies.

Won't **democracy** ensure that a government will undertake productive policies? Think about the difference between markets and political democracy as you ponder this question. The two are quite different. Market exchange is based on agreement and mutual gain. When markets are open and property rights are well defined, market activities will persist only when they are mutually advantageous. Most important, the agreement of the market participants provides strong evidence that the activity is productive. In contrast, the majority rule criterion of democracy generates "losers" as well as "winners." And there is no assurance that the gains of the winners will be greater than the costs imposed on the losers.

As public choice analysis indicates, several factors in democracies can lead the costs imposed on the minority to be greater than, and often substantially greater than, the benefits derived by the political majority. Predictably, voters will be poorly informed on both issues and candidates. The democratic political process is biased toward the adoption of programs that provide immediate, highly visible benefits at the expense of future costs that are difficult to identify. Furthermore, special interests exert disproportional power at the expense of the ordinary citizen. When the government becomes heavily involved in activities that provide favors to some at the expense of others, people will be encouraged to divert resources away from productive activities and toward lobbying, campaign contributions, and other forms of political favor seeking. All of these shortcomings tend to corrupt the political process and cause even democratic governments to adopt policies inconsistent with productivity and growth.

The future is further complicated by the COVID-19 pandemic and its potential impact on economic policy. To control the virus, governments throughout the world engaged in unprecedented expansion in debt and restrictions on economic activity. International travel was severely restricted, and several restraints on international trade were enacted. Protectionist sentiment appears to be on the rise in the United States and other countries. As we have shown, trade and travel have played a central role in the dramatic growth and progress of the past half-century. How will the COVID-19 crisis impact future taxes, trade policy, and other key elements of the Transportation-Communication Revolution? At this point, the answer to this question is uncertain, but the response will clearly exert an impact on future growth and prosperity.

Compared to the past, we now have better knowledge and stronger evidence about the types of economic institutions and policies that enhance human progress. However, merely because we have knowledge about what works does not mean sound institutions will be adopted. As the chapter-opening quote from Professor North indicates, history is a story about countries that failed to adopt and enforce a set of economic rules that generate sustained economic growth. Countries that adopt sound institutions and policies will grow and prosper. Those that fail to do so will stagnate and regress. The future of the United States and other countries throughout the world in the twenty-first century will be shaped by their actions in this vitally important area.

Democracy
A form of political organization in which adult citizens are free to participate in the political process (vote, lobby, and choose among candidates), elections are free and open, and majority voting, either directly or by elected representatives, decides outcomes.

KEY POINTS

- Before 1800, the world was characterized by income per person at or near the subsistence level, absence of economic growth, and short life expectancy. Starting with the Industrial Revolution around 1800, people in Western Europe, North America, Oceania, and Japan began to achieve sustained increases in income per person and higher living standards. However, economic stagnation and income near the subsistence level continued in the rest of the world for at least another 150 years.

- During 1800–1950, most of the world continued in the Malthusian trap of low income, poverty, and short life expectancy. During this era, colonialism, locational and climate disadvantages, and poor institutions undermined economic progress throughout most of the world.

- During the past half-century, there has been a huge reduction in transportation and communication costs. This resulted in a second economic revolution: the Transportation-Communication Revolution.

- The sharp reductions in transportation and communication costs led to a substantial increase in international trade, increased gains from entrepreneurial activities, and improved economic institutions, enhancing the economic performance of developing countries during 1970–2015. As many developing countries, particularly those with lesser geographic disadvantages, broke out of the Malthusian trap, expansion in the share of the population in the prime working-age category provided an additional boost to economic growth.

- Since the mid-1980s, the growth of per capita GDP of developing countries that are less geographically disadvantaged has been more rapid than that of the high-income developed countries. Since 2000, even the 40 most geographically disadvantaged developing countries have grown at an impressive rate.

- In recent decades, developing countries have dominated the list of the world's fastest-growing economies. However, developing countries also dominate the list of countries with the slowest rates of economic growth. The countries with the worst record of economic growth almost all suffer from severe geographic disadvantages and poor economic institutions.

- There have been dramatic reductions in both extreme and moderate poverty rates since 1980. If the poverty rates of 1980 were present today, there would be an additional 2 billion people experiencing both extreme and moderate poverty.

- Like the Industrial Revolution, the Transportation-Communication Revolution of the past half-century has exerted a huge impact on the world. Compared to the earlier revolution, the more recent economic revolution has exerted an impact on a larger share of the world's population, resulted in substantially more rapid growth of per capita GDP, and reduced worldwide income inequality rather than increased it.

- Economic institutions and policies reflect political choices. The future challenge is to bring political decision-making into closer harmony with economic policies and institutions supportive of human progress.

CRITICAL ANALYSIS QUESTIONS

1. Describe the general pattern of economic growth over the past 1,000 years. What was the growth rate of real per capita GDP prior to 1800? What happened to the growth rate of per capita GDP following the Industrial Revolution that occurred around 1800? How does the growth rate of per capita GDP during the past half-century compare with the rate following the Industrial Revolution?

2. Why did Thomas Malthus believe that per person income could never rise much above the subsistence level? Given the era of his writings, was Malthus's view on this topic surprising? Why or why not?

3. *What are the three geographic disadvantages that Jeffery Sachs argues have adversely affected the development process? Explain why each would tend to reduce development.

4. What is the Transportation-Communication Revolution? What impact has it had on economic development?

5. How will reductions in transportation and communication cost influence the volume of international trade? How will they influence gains from entrepreneurship? How will they impact capital investment in developing countries? Explain your response.

6. What is the virtuous cycle of development? How does it impact the growth of developing countries? What impact will it have on the poverty rate?

7. *What area of the world is most affected by geographic disadvantages? How has this impacted the development of this region?

8. How has the poverty rate of the world changed since 1980? What are the major factors underlying this change? Explain your responses.

9. *If there were no high-income developed countries like those of Western Europe, North America, and Japan, would less-developed countries like Hong Kong, South Korea, China, and India have been able to grow so rapidly in recent decades? Why or why not?

10. What happened to the relative income of people living in poor countries compared to those living in high-income countries during 1800–1980? What has happened to this income ratio since 1990?

11. Why do nations adopt sound economic institutions? How was institutional development impacted by whether Europeans planned to settle permanently in an area? Have history, geography, and technology exerted an impact on the quality of economic institutions? Discuss.

12. After centuries of stagnation, why did developing countries begin to grow during the past half-century? Explain your response.

13. *How do the growth rates of developing countries during recent decades compare with those of the United States, western Europe, and Japan during the decades following the Industrial Revolution? Is this surprising? Why or why not?

14. Why are per capita incomes so low in Africa? Have poor economic institutions contributed to the low income levels? Have geographic disadvantages contributed to the low income levels of Africa?

15. Does democracy ensure that a country will adopt sound institutions and achieve a high income level? Can you name a country with a high per person income that is not democratic? Can you name a country that is democratic that does not have a high per person income?

*Asterisk denotes questions for which answers are given in Appendix B.

PART 4

International Economics

The world is becoming a global village.

The volume of international trade has grown dramatically in recent decades. Although the same general principles apply to both domestic and international trade, the latter also involves the exchange of one currency for another. Thus, this part will analyze the impact of both international trade and the operation of the foreign exchange market.

CHAPTER 18

Gaining from International Trade

The evidence is overwhelmingly persuasive that the massive increase in world competition—a consequence of broadening trade flows—has fostered markedly higher standards of living for almost all countries who have participated in cross-border trade. I include most especially the United States.—**Alan Greenspan**[1]

We live in a shrinking world. Spurred by substantial cost reductions in transportation and communications, the volume of international trade has grown rapidly in recent decades. The breakfast of many Americans includes bananas from Honduras, coffee from Brazil, or hot chocolate made from Nigerian cocoa beans. Many Americans listen to music on iPhones assembled in China, fuel their automobiles with gasoline refined from crude oil from Mexico or Canada, and watch television on a set produced in South Korea. Similarly, many Americans work for companies that sell a substantial number of their products to foreigners. Why do people engage in international trade? The expectation of gain provides the answer. If both parties did not expect to gain, they would not agee to the exchange.

As you read this chapter, look for answers to the following questions:

- How has the volume of international trade changed in recent decades?

- Under what conditions can a nation gain from international trade?

- What effects do trade restrictions have on an economy?

- How have open economies performed relative to those that are more closed?

- What accounts for the political popularity of trade restraints?

- Do trade restrictions create jobs? Does trade with low-wage countries depress wage rates in high-wage countries like the United States?

---

[1]Alan Greenspan, speech before the Alliance for the Commonwealth Conference on International Business (Boston, Massachusetts, June 2, 1999).

18-1 THE TRADE SECTOR OF THE UNITED STATES

As **Exhibit 1** illustrates, the size of the trade sector of the United States has grown rapidly during the last several decades. In 1960, total exports of goods and services accounted for 5.0 percent of the U.S. economy, whereas imports summed to 4.2 percent. By 1980, both exports and imports were approximately 10 percent of the economy. In 2019, exports accounted for 11.7 percent of total output, while imports summed to 14.6 percent. Thus, U.S. international trade (exports + imports) in goods and services has risen by 30 percent as a share of the economy since 1980 and almost tripled since 1960.

Who are the major trading partners of Americans? **Exhibit 2** shows the share of U.S. trade (exports + imports) with each of its ten leading trading partners. These ten countries account for approximately two-thirds of the total volume of U.S. trade. China, Canada, Mexico, and Japan are the four largest trading partners of Americans. Half of all U.S. trade is with these four countries. The United States also conducts a substantial volume of trade with the nations of the European Union, particularly Germany, the United Kingdom, and France.

What are the leading imports and exports of the United States? Capital goods like automobiles, computers, semiconductors, telecommunications equipment, and industrial machines are bought and sold in worldwide markets. The United States both imports and exports substantial quantities of these goods. Civilian aircraft, electrical equipment, chemicals, and plastics are also among the leading products the United States exports. Crude oil, textiles, toys, sporting goods, and pharmaceuticals are major products it imports.

Clearly, the impact of international trade differs across industries. The majority of the television sets, diamonds, shoes, DVD players, and motorcycles consumed in the United States are imported. In contrast, a large proportion of the aircraft, power-generating equipment, scientific instruments, construction equipment, and fertilizers produced in the United States are exported to foreigners.

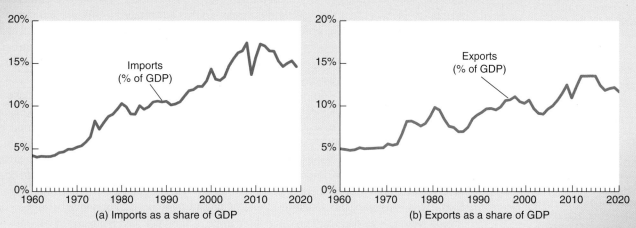

EXHIBIT 1

The Growth of the Trade Sector in the United States: 1960–2019

During the past several decades, international trade has persistently risen as a share of GDP. Imports of goods and services as a share of GDP rose from 4 percent in 1960 to 10 percent in 1980 and 15 percent in 2019. Similarly, exports increased from 5 percent of GDP in 1960 to 10 percent in 1980 and 12 percent in 2019.

(a) Imports as a share of GDP

(b) Exports as a share of GDP

Source: http://www.economagic.com. The figures are based on data for imports, exports, and GDP.

EXHIBIT 2

The 2019 Leading Trading Partners of the United States

China, Canada, Mexico, and Japan are the leading trading partners of the United States. Approximately one-half of all U.S. trade involves imports from or exports to these four countries.

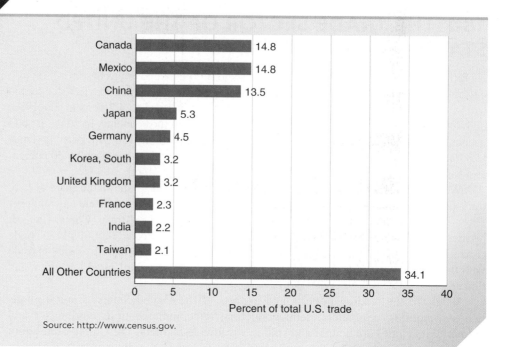

Country	Percent of total U.S. trade
Canada	14.8
Mexico	14.8
China	13.5
Japan	5.3
Germany	4.5
Korea, South	3.2
United Kingdom	3.2
France	2.3
India	2.2
Taiwan	2.1
All Other Countries	34.1

Source: http://www.census.gov.

18-2 GAINS FROM SPECIALIZATION AND TRADE

Comparative advantage
The ability to produce a good at a lower opportunity cost than others can produce it. Relative costs determine comparative advantage.

Like domestic trade, international trade promotes growth and prosperity. The law of **comparative advantage** explains why a group of individuals, regions, or nations can gain from specialization and exchange. International trade leads to mutual gains because it allows residents of different countries to (1) specialize in the production of those things they do best and (2) import goods foreign producers are willing to supply at a lower cost than domestic producers. Resources and labor-force skills differ substantially across countries, and these differences influence costs. A good that is quite costly to produce in one country might be produced at a lower cost in another. For example, the warm, moist climates of Brazil, Colombia, and Guatemala make it more economical to produce coffee. Countries with temperate climates and an abundance of fertile land, such as Canada and Australia, are able to produce products such as wheat, feed grains, and beef at a low cost. In contrast, land is scarce in Japan, a nation with a highly skilled labor force. The Japanese, therefore, specialize in manufacturing, using their comparative advantage to produce cameras, automobiles, and electronic products for export. With international trade, the residents of different countries can gain by specializing in the production of goods they can produce economically. They can then sell those goods in the world market and use the proceeds to import other goods that are expensive to produce domestically.

Because the law of comparative advantage is often misunderstood, we will take the time to illustrate the principle in some detail. To keep things simple, let's consider a case involving only two countries, the United States and Japan, and two products, food and clothing. Furthermore, let's assume that labor is the only resource used to produce these products. In addition, because we want to illustrate that gains from trade are nearly always possible, we are going to assume that Japan has an **absolute advantage**—that the Japanese workers are more efficient than the Americans—at producing both food and clothing. **Exhibit 3** illustrates this situation. Perhaps due to their prior experience or higher skill levels, Japanese workers can produce three units of food per day, compared with only two units per day for U.S. workers. Similarly, Japanese workers are able to produce nine units of clothing per day, compared with one unit of clothing per day for U.S. workers.

Absolute advantage
A situation in which a nation, as the result of its previous experience and/or natural endowments, can produce more of a good (with the same amount of resources) than another nation can.

EXHIBIT 3

Gains from Specialization and Trade

Columns 1 and 2 indicate the assumed daily output of either food or clothing of each worker in the United States and Japan. If the United States moves three workers from the clothing industry to the food industry, it can produce six more units of food and three fewer units of clothing. Similarly, if Japan moves one worker from food to clothing, clothing output will increase by nine units, while food output will decline by three units. With this reallocation of labor, the United States and Japan are able to increase their aggregate output of both food (three additional units) and clothing (six additional units).

COUNTRY	OUTPUT PER WORKER DAY		POTENTIAL CHANGE IN OUTPUT[a]	
	FOOD (1)	CLOTHING (2)	FOOD (3)	CLOTHING (4)
United States	2	1	+6	−3
Japan	3	9	−3	+9
Change in Total Output			+3	+6

[a]Change in output if the United States shifts three workers from the clothing to the food industry and if Japan shifts one worker from the food to the clothing industry.

Can two countries gain from trade if one of them can produce both goods with fewer resources? The answer is "Yes." As long as the *relative* production costs of the two goods differ between Japan and the United States, gains from trade will be possible. Consider what would happen if the United States shifted three workers from the clothing industry to the food industry. This reallocation of labor would allow the United States to expand its food output by six units (two units per worker), while clothing output would decline by three units (one unit per worker). Suppose Japan reallocates labor in the opposite direction. When Japan moves one worker from the food industry to the clothing industry, Japanese clothing production expands by nine units, while food output declines by three units. The exhibit shows that this reallocation of labor *within* the two countries has increased their joint output by three units of food and six units of clothing.

The source of this increase in output is straightforward: Aggregate output expands because the reallocation of labor permits each country to specialize more fully in the production of the goods it can produce at a *relatively* low cost. Our old friend, the opportunity-cost concept, reveals the low-cost producer of each good. If Japanese workers produce one additional unit of food, they sacrifice the production of three units of clothing. Therefore, in Japan the opportunity cost of one unit of food is three units of clothing. Conversely, one unit of food in the United States can be produced at an opportunity cost of only a half-unit of clothing. American workers are therefore the low-opportunity-cost producers of food, even though they cannot produce as much food per day as the Japanese workers. Simultaneously, Japan is the low-opportunity-cost producer of clothing. The opportunity cost of producing a unit of clothing in Japan is only a third of a unit of food, compared with two units of food in the United States. The reallocation of labor illustrated in Exhibit 3 expanded joint output because it moved resources in both countries toward areas where they had a comparative advantage.

To reiterate: As long as the relative costs of producing the two goods differ in the two countries, gains from specialization and trade will be possible. Both countries will find it cheaper to trade for goods they can produce only at a high opportunity cost. For example, both countries will gain if the United States trades food to Japan for clothing at a trading ratio greater than one unit of food to one half-unit of clothing (the U.S. opportunity cost of food) but less than one unit of food to three units of clothing (the Japanese opportunity cost of food). Any trading ratio between these two extremes will permit the United States to acquire clothing more cheaply than it could be produced within the country and simultaneously permit Japan to acquire food more cheaply than it could be produced domestically.

18-2a HOW TRADE EXPANDS CONSUMPTION POSSIBILITIES

Because trade permits nations to expand their joint output, it also allows each nation to expand its consumption possibilities. The production possibilities concept can be used to illustrate this point. Suppose that there were 200 million workers in the United States and 50 million in Japan. Given these figures and the productivity of workers indicated in Exhibit 3, **Exhibit 4** presents the production possibilities curves for the two countries. If the United States used all of its 200 million workers in the food industry, it could produce 400 million units of food per day—two units per worker—and zero units of clothing (N). Alternatively, if the United States used all its workers to produce clothing, daily output would be 200 million units of clothing and no food (M). Intermediate output combinations along the production possibilities line (MN) between these two extreme points also could be achievable. For example, the United States could produce 150 million units of clothing and 100 million units of food (US_1).

Panel (b) of Exhibit 4 illustrates the production possibilities of the 50 million Japanese workers. Japan could produce 450 million units of clothing and no food (R), 150 million units of food and no clothing (S), or various intermediate combinations, like 225 million units of clothing and 75 million units of food (J_1). The slope of the production possibilities constraint reflects the opportunity cost of food relative to clothing. Because Japan is the high-opportunity-cost producer of food, its production possibilities constraint is steeper than the constraint for the United States.

In the absence of trade, the consumption of each country is constrained by its own production possibilities. Trade, however, expands the consumption possibilities of both. As we previously said, both countries can gain from specialization if the United States trades food to Japan at a price greater than one unit of food equals one half-unit of clothing but less than one unit of food equals three units of clothing. Suppose that they agree on an intermediate price of one unit of food equals one unit of clothing. As panel (a) of **Exhibit 5** shows, when the United States specializes in the production of food (where it has a comparative

---

EXHIBIT 4

The Production Possibilities of the United States and Japan before Specialization and Trade

Here, we illustrate the daily production possibilities of a U.S. labor force with 200 million workers and a Japanese labor force with 50 million workers, given the cost of producing food and clothing presented in Exhibit 3. In the absence of trade, consumption possibilities will be restricted to points such as US_1 in the United States and J_1 in Japan along the production possibilities curve of each country.

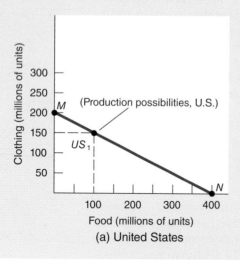

(a) United States

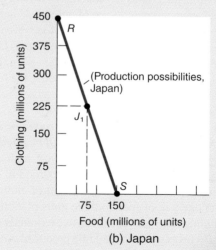

(b) Japan

EXHIBIT 5

Consumption Possibilities with Trade

The consumption possibilities of a country can be expanded with specialization and trade. If the United States can trade one unit of clothing for one unit of food, it can specialize in the production of food and consume along the ON line (rather than its original production possibilities constraint, MN). Similarly, when Japan is able to trade one unit of clothing for one unit of food, it can specialize in the production of clothing and consume any combination along the line RT. For example, with specialization and trade, the United States can increase its consumption from US_1 to US_2, gaining 50 million units of clothing and 100 million units of food. Simultaneously, Japan can increase consumption from J_1 to J_2, a gain of 125 million units of food and 25 million units of clothing.

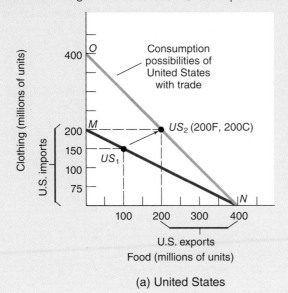

(a) United States

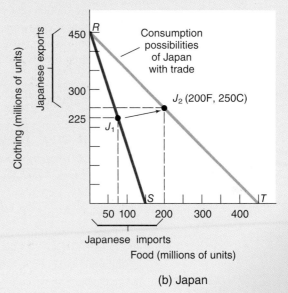

(b) Japan

advantage) and trades food for clothing (at the price ratio where one unit of food equals one unit of clothing), it can consume along the line ON. If the United States insisted on self-sufficiency, it would be restricted to consumption possibilities like US_1 (100 million units of food and 150 million units of clothing) along its production possibilities constraint of MN. With trade, however, the United States can achieve a combination like US_2 (200 million units of food and 200 million units of clothing) along the line ON. Trade permits the United States to expand its consumption of both goods.

Simultaneously, Japan is able to expand its consumption of both goods when it is able to trade clothing for food at the one-to-one price ratio. As panel (b) of Exhibit 5 illustrates, Japan can specialize in the production of clothing and consume along the constraint RT when it can trade one unit of clothing for one unit of food. Without trade, consumption in Japan would be limited to points like J_1 (75 million units of food and 225 million units of clothing) along the line RS. With trade, however, it is able to consume combinations like J_2 (200 million units of food and 250 million units of clothing) along the constraint RT.

Look what happens when Japan specializes in clothing and the United States specializes in food. Japan can produce 450 million units of clothing, export 200 million to the United States (for 200 million units of food), and still have 250 million units of clothing remaining for domestic consumption. Simultaneously, the United States can produce 400 million units of food, export 200 million to Japan (for 200 million units of clothing), and still have 200 million units of food left for domestic consumption.

The implications of the law of comparative advantage are clear: Trade between nations will lead to an expansion in total output and mutual gain for each trading partner when each country specializes in the production of goods it can produce at a relatively low cost and uses the proceeds to buy goods that it could produce only at a high cost.

18-2b SOME REAL-WORLD CONSIDERATIONS

To keep things simple, we ignored the potential importance of transportation costs, which, of course, reduce the potential gains from trade. Sometimes transportation and other transaction costs, both real and artificially imposed, exceed the potential for mutual gain. In this case, exchange does not occur.

We also assumed that the cost of producing each good was constant in each country. This is seldom the case. Beyond some level of production, the opportunity cost of producing a good will often increase as a country produces more and more of it. Rising marginal costs as the output of a good expands will limit the degree to which a country will specialize in the production of a good. This situation would be depicted by a production possibilities curve that was convex, or bowed out from the origin. In a case like this, there will still be gains from trade, but generally such a situation won't lead to one country completely specializing in the production of the good.

KEYS TO ECONOMIC PROSPERITY

International Trade

When people are permitted to engage freely in international trade, they are able to achieve higher income levels and living standards than would otherwise be possible.

Like trade within a country, trade between people living in different nations is mutually beneficial. As we just explained, the trading partners will be able to produce a larger joint output and consume a larger, more diverse bundle of goods when they each specialize in areas where they have a comparative advantage. Open markets also lead to gains from other sources. We will briefly discuss three of them.

1. More gains from large-scale production. International trade makes it possible for both domestic producers and consumers to derive larger gains from the lower per-unit costs that often accompany large-scale production, marketing, and distribution activities. When economies of scale are important in an industry, successful domestic firms will be able to produce larger outputs and achieve lower unit costs than they would if they were unable to sell their products internationally. This is particularly important for firms located in small countries. For example, textile manufacturers in Malaysia, Taiwan, and South Korea would face much higher per-unit costs if they could not sell abroad because the domestic markets of these countries are too small to support large-scale production. There simply aren't enough buyers. However, if the firms can access the world market, where there are many more buyers, they can operate on a large scale and compete quite effectively.

Domestic consumers also benefit because international trade often makes it possible for them to acquire goods at lower prices from large-scale producers in other countries. The aircraft industry vividly illustrates this point. Given the huge design and engineering costs it takes to produce a single jet, no firm would be able to produce them economically if it weren't able to sell them abroad. Because of international trade, however, consumers around the world are able to purchase planes economically from large-scale producers like Boeing, which is based in the United States.

International trade generates gains from specialization, economies of scale, and more competitive markets. As a result, trading partners are able to achieve higher living standards.

2. Gains from more competitive markets. International trade promotes competition and encourages production efficiency and innovation. Competition from abroad keeps domestic producers on their toes and gives them a strong incentive to improve the quality of their products.

International trade also allows technologies and innovative ideas developed in one country to be disseminated to others. In many cases, local entrepreneurs will emulate production procedures and products that have been successful in other places and even further improve or adapt them for local markets. Dynamic competition of this type is an important source of growth and prosperity, particularly for less-developed countries (LDCs).

3. More pressure to adopt sound institutions. Not only do firms in open economies face more intense competition, so, too, do their governments. The gains from trade and the prosperity that results from free trade motivate political officials to establish sound institutions and adopt constructive policies. If they do not, both labor and capital will move toward more favorable environments. For example, neither domestic nor foreign investors will want to put their funds in countries characterized by hostile business conditions, monetary instability, legal uncertainty, high taxes, and inferior public services. When labor and capital are free to move elsewhere, implementing government policies that penalize success and undermine productive activities becomes more costly. This aspect of free trade is generally overlooked, but it may well be one of its most beneficial attributes.[2]

18-3 SUPPLY, DEMAND, AND INTERNATIONAL TRADE

Like other things, international trade can be analyzed within the supply and demand framework. An analysis of supply and demand in international markets can show us how trade influences prices and output in domestic markets.

Consider the market for a good that U.S. producers are able to supply at a low cost. Using soybeans as an example, **Exhibit 6** illustrates the relationship between the domestic and world markets. The price of soybeans is determined by the forces of supply and demand in the world market. In an open economy, domestic producers are free to sell and domestic consumers are free to buy the product at the world market price (P_w). At this price, U.S. producers will supply Q_p, and U.S. consumers will purchase Q_c. Reflecting their low cost (comparative advantage), U.S. soybean producers will export $Q_p - Q_c$ units at the world market price.

Let's compare this open-economy outcome with the outcome that would occur in the absence of trade. If U.S. producers were not allowed to export soybeans, the domestic price would be determined by the domestic supply (S_d) and demand (D_d) only. A lower "no-trade" price (P_n) would emerge.

Who are the winners and losers as the result of free trade in soybeans? Clearly, soybean producers gain. Free trade allows domestic producers to sell a larger quantity (Q_p rather than Q_n). As a result, the net revenues of soybean producers will rise by $P_w bc P_n$. In contrast, domestic consumers of soybeans will have to pay a higher price under free trade. Soybean consumers will lose (1) because they have to pay P_w rather than P_n for the Q_c units they purchase, and (2) because they lose the consumer surplus on the $Q_n - Q_c$ units now purchased at the higher price. Thus, free trade imposes a net cost of $P_w ac P_n$ on consumers. As you can see in Exhibit 6, however, the gains of soybean producers outweigh the losses to the consumers by the triangle *abc*. In other words, free trade leads to a net welfare gain.

This exporting example makes it seem like free trade benefits producers relative to consumers, but this ignores the secondary effects: If foreigners do not sell goods to

---

[2]For evidence that trade openness helps improve the institutional quality of a country, see International Monetary Fund, "Building Institutions," *IMF World Economic Outlook* (September 2005).

EXHIBIT 6

Producer Benefits from Exports

The price of soybeans and other internationally traded commodities is determined by the forces of supply and demand in the world market (b). If U.S. soybean producers are prohibited from selling to foreigners, the domestic price will be P_n (a). Free trade permits the U.S. soybean producers to sell Q_p units at the higher world price (P_w). The quantity $Q_p - Q_c$ is the amount U.S. producers export. Compared with the no-trade situation, the producers' gain from the higher price ($P_w bcP_n$) exceeds the cost imposed on domestic consumers ($P_w acP_n$) by the triangle abc.

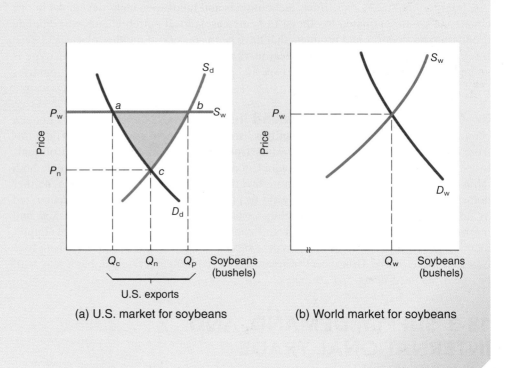

(a) U.S. market for soybeans

(b) World market for soybeans

Americans, they will not have the purchasing power necessary to purchase goods from Americans. U.S. imports—the purchase of goods from low-cost foreign producers—provide foreigners with the dollar purchasing power necessary to buy U.S. exports. In turn, the lower prices in the import-competitive markets will benefit the U.S. consumers who appeared at first glance to be harmed by the higher prices (compared with the no-trade situation) in export markets.

Using shoes as an example, **Exhibit 7** illustrates the situation when the United States is a net importer. In the absence of trade, the price of shoes in the domestic market would be P_n, the intersection of the domestic supply and demand curves. However, the world price of shoes is P_w. In an open economy, many U.S. consumers would take advantage of the low shoe prices available from foreign producers. At the lower world price, U.S. consumers would purchase Q_c units of shoes, importing $Q_c - Q_p$ from foreign producers.

Compared with the no-trade situation, free trade in shoes results in lower prices and greater domestic consumption. The lower prices lead to a net consumer gain of $P_n abP_w$. Domestic producers lose $P_n acP_w$ in the form of lower sales prices and reductions in output. However, the net gain of the shoe consumers exceeds the net loss of producers by *abc*.

International competition will direct resources toward producers who have a comparative advantage. If domestic producers have a comparative advantage in the production of a good—if they are a low opportunity cost producer, they will be able to compete effectively in the world market and profit from the export of goods to foreigners. In turn, the exports will generate the purchasing power necessary to buy goods that foreigners can supply more economically.

EXHIBIT 7

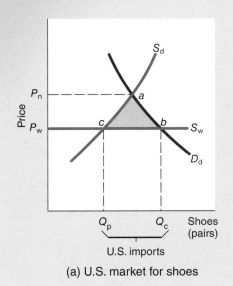

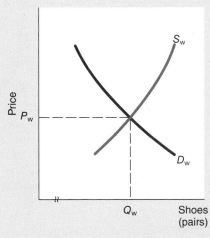

(a) U.S. market for shoes   (b) World market for shoes

Consumer Benefits from Imports

In the absence of trade, the domestic price of shoes would be P_n. Because many foreign producers have a comparative advantage in the production of shoes, international trade leads to lower prices. At the world price P_w, U.S. consumers will demand Q_c units, of which $Q_c - Q_p$ are imported. Compared with the no-trade situation, consumers gain $P_n ab P_w$, while domestic producers lose $P_n ac P_w$. A net gain of abc results.

18-4 THE ECONOMICS OF TRADE RESTRICTIONS

Despite the benefits provided by free trade, almost all nations have erected trade barriers. Tariffs, quotas, and exchange rate controls are the most commonly used trade-restricting devices. Let's consider how various types of trade restrictions affect the economy.

18-4a THE ECONOMICS OF TARIFFS

A **tariff** is a tax on imports from foreign countries. As Exhibit 8 shows, average tariff rates of between 30 percent and 50 percent of product value were often levied on products imported to the United States prior to 1945. The notorious Smoot-Hawley Tariff Act of 1930 pushed the average tariff rate upward to 60 percent. Many economists believe that this legislation contributed significantly to the length and severity of the Great Depression. During the past 80 years, however, tariff rates in the United States have declined substantially. In 2018, the average tariff rate on imported goods was only 5.7 percent.

Exhibit 9 shows the impact of a tariff on automobiles. In the absence of a tariff, the world market price of P_w would prevail in the domestic market. At that price, U.S. consumers purchase Q_1 units. Domestic producers supply Q_{d1}, while foreigners supply $Q_1 - Q_{d1}$ units to the U.S. market. When the United States levies a tariff, t, on automobiles, Americans can no longer buy cars at the world price. U.S. consumers now have to pay $P_w + t$ to purchase an automobile from foreigners. At that price, domestic consumers demand Q_2 units (Q_{d2} supplied by domestic producers and $Q_2 - Q_{d2}$ supplied by foreigners). The tariff results in a higher domestic price and lower level of domestic consumption.

The tariff benefits domestic producers and the government at the expense of consumers. Because domestic producers don't have to pay the tariff, they will expand their output in response to the higher (protected) market price. In effect, the tariff acts as a subsidy to domestic producers. Domestic producers gain the area S (Exhibit 9) in the form of additional

Tariff
A tax levied on goods imported into a country.

EXHIBIT 8

How High Are U.S. Tariffs?

Tariff rates in the United States spiked up sharply in the early 1930s, then declined during the period from 1935 to 1950. After rising slightly during the late 1950s, they have trended downward since 1960. In 2018, the average tariff rate on merchandise imports was 5.7 percent.

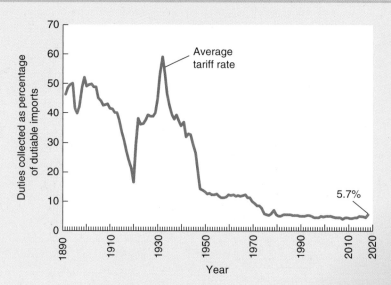

Source: https://www.usitc.gov/documents/dataweb/ave_table_1891_2018.pdf.
The average tariff rate is for those goods for which tariffs are imposed.

EXHIBIT 9

The Impact of a Tariff

Here, we illustrate the impact of a tariff on automobiles. In the absence of the tariff, the world price of automobiles is P_w. U.S. consumers purchase Q_1 units (Q_{d1} from domestic producers plus $Q_1 - Q_{d1}$ from foreign producers). The tariff makes it more costly for Americans to purchase automobiles from foreigners. Imports decline and the domestic price increases. Higher prices reduce consumer surplus by the areas $S + U + T + V$. Producers gain the *area S*, and the tariff generates T tax revenues for the government. The areas U and V are deadweight losses.

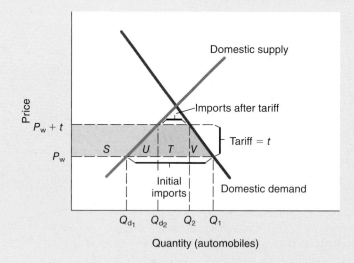

net revenues. The tariff raises revenues equal to the area T for the government. The areas U and V represent costs imposed on consumers that do not benefit the government. Simply put, U and V represent *deadweight losses*: consumer surpluses that could have been gained if the tariff hadn't been imposed.

As a result of the tariff, resources that could have been used to produce other U.S. goods more efficiently (compared with producing them abroad) are diverted to automobile production. Ultimately, we end up producing fewer products in areas where we have a comparative advantage and more products in areas where we are a high-cost producer. Because of this, potential gains from specialization and trade will go unrealized. In addition, most nations, including the United States, impose higher tariffs on some goods than others. This encourages producers in specific industries to lobby for higher tariffs on goods they produce. This diverts resources away from production and toward plunder, which also reduces the overall size of the economic pie.

18-4b THE ECONOMICS OF QUOTAS

An **import quota**, like a tariff, is designed to restrict foreign goods and protect domestic industries from foreign competition. A quota places a ceiling on the amount of a product that can be imported during a given period (typically a year). The United States imposes quotas on several products, including brooms, shoes, sugar, dairy products, and peanuts. For example, since 1953, the United States has imposed an annual peanut quota that in 2018 limited imports to 116.6 million pounds, about one-third of a pound per American.

Using peanuts as an example, **Exhibit 10** illustrates the impact of a quota. If there were no trade restraints, the domestic price of peanuts would be equal to the world market price (P_w). Under those circumstances, Americans would purchase Q_1 units. At the price P_w, domestic producers would supply Q_{d1}, and the amount $Q_1 - Q_{d1}$ would be imported from foreign producers.

Now consider what happens when a quota limits imports to $Q_2 - Q_{d2}$, a quantity well below the free-trade level of imports. Because the quota reduces the foreign supply of peanuts to the domestic market, the price of the quota-protected product increases (to P_2). At the higher price, U.S. consumers will reduce their purchases to Q_2, and domestic producers will happily expand their production to Q_{d2}. With regard to the welfare of consumers, the impact of a quota is similar to that of a tariff. Consumers lose the area $S + U + T + V$ in the

Import quota
A specific limit or maximum quantity (or value) of a good permitted to be imported into a country during a given period.

EXHIBIT 10

The Impact of a Quota

Here, we illustrate the impact of a quota, such as the one the United States imposes on peanuts. The world market price of peanuts is P_w. If there were no trade restraints, the domestic price would also be P_w, and the domestic consumption would be Q_1. Domestic producers would supply Q_{d1} units, while $Q_1 - Q_{d1}$ would be imported. A quota limiting imports to $Q_2 - Q_{d2}$ would push up the domestic price to P_2. At the higher price, the amount supplied by domestic producers increases to Q_{d2}. Consumers lose the sum of the area $S + U + T + V$, while domestic producers gain the area S. In contrast with tariffs, quotas generate no revenue for the government. The area T goes to foreign producers, who are granted permission to sell in the U.S. market.

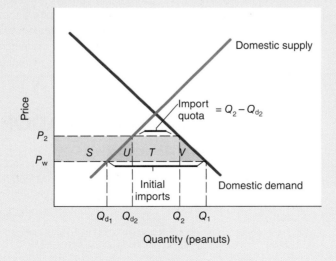

form of higher prices and the loss of consumer surplus. Similarly, domestic producers gain the area S, while the areas U and V represent deadweight losses in the form of reductions in consumer surplus, gains that buyers would have derived in the absence of the quota.

While the adverse impact of a quota on consumer welfare is similar to that of a tariff, there is a big difference with regard to the area T. Under a tariff, the U.S. government would collect revenues equal to T, representing the tariff rate multiplied by the number of units imported. With a quota, however, these revenues will go to foreign producers, who are granted licenses (quotas) to sell various amounts in the U.S. market. Clearly, this right to sell at a premium price (because the domestic price exceeds the world market price) is extremely valuable. Thus, foreign producers will compete for the permits. They will hire lobbyists, make political contributions, and engage in other rent-seeking activities in an effort to secure the right to sell at a premium price in the U.S. market.

In many ways, quotas are more harmful than tariffs. With a quota, foreign producers are prohibited from selling additional units regardless of how much lower their costs are relative to those of domestic producers. In contrast to a tariff, a quota brings in no revenue for the government. Whereas a tariff transfers revenue from U.S. consumers to the Treasury, quotas transfer these revenues to foreign producers. Rewarding domestic producers with higher prices and foreign producers with valuable import permits will create *two* interest groups with a strong incentive to lobby for a quota. As a result, lifting the quota will often be more difficult than lowering a tariff would be.

In addition to tariffs and quotas, governments sometimes use regulations and political pressure to restrain foreign competition. For example, the United States prohibits foreign airlines from competing in the domestic air travel market. Japanese regulations make it illegal for domestic automobile dealers to sell both foreign and domestically produced vehicles; this makes it more difficult for foreign manufacturers to establish the dealer networks they need to penetrate the Japanese market effectively. Like tariffs and quotas, regulatory barriers such as these reduce the supply to domestic markets and the gains from potential trades. Overall output is reduced, and domestic producers benefit at the expense of domestic consumers.

18-4c EXCHANGE RATE CONTROLS AS A TRADE RESTRICTION

Some countries fix the exchange rate value of their currency above the market rate and impose restrictions on exchange rate transactions.[3] At the official (artificially high) exchange rate, the country's export goods will be extremely expensive to foreigners. As a result, foreigners will purchase goods elsewhere, and the country's exports will be small. In turn, the low level of exports will make it extremely difficult for domestic residents to obtain the foreign currency they need to purchase imports. Exchange rate controls both reduce the volume of trade and lead to black-market currency exchanges. Indeed, a large black-market premium indicates that the country's exchange rate policy is substantially limiting the ability of its citizens to trade with foreigners. While exchange rate controls have declined in popularity, they are still an important trade barrier in countries such as Algeria, Argentina, and Venezuela.

18-5 WHY DO NATIONS ADOPT TRADE RESTRICTIONS?

As social philosopher Henry George noted over a century ago, trade restraints act like blockades. Why would political officials want to erect blockades against their own people?

Protective tariffs are as much applications of force as are blockading squadrons, and their objective is the same—to prevent trade. The difference between the two is that blockading squadrons are a means whereby nations seek to prevent their enemies from trading; protective tariffs are a means whereby nations attempt to prevent their own people from trading.
—Henry George[4]

---

[3]The most common exchange rate restriction is that individuals are required to obtain approval from the government before they engage in transactions involving foreign currency.

[4]Henry George, *Protection or Free Trade* (Washington, DC: U.S. Government Printing Office, 1886), 37.

As we consider this question, we will take a look at three arguments often raised by the proponents of trade restrictions: the national-defense, infant-industry, and antidumping arguments. Finally, we will look at the politics of trade restrictions and analyze how the nature of the restraints influences their political popularity.

18-5a THE NATIONAL-DEFENSE ARGUMENT

According to the national-defense argument, certain industries—aircraft, petroleum, and weapons, for example—are vital to a nation's defense. Therefore, these industries and their inputs should be protected from foreign competitors so that a domestic supply of necessary materials would be available in case of an international conflict. Would we want to be entirely dependent upon Arabian or Russian petroleum? Would complete dependence on French aircraft be wise? Many Americans would answer "no," even if it meant imposing trade restrictions that would lead to higher prices on products they buy.

Although the national-defense argument has some validity, it is often abused. Relatively few industries are truly vital to our national defense. If a resource is important for national defense, often it would make more sense to stockpile the resource during peacetime rather than follow protectionist policies to preserve a domestic industry. Furthermore, fostering an economy robust enough to produce the mass quantity of goods necessary to sustain a war effort in the first place is, itself, part of a strong defense.

18-5b THE INFANT-INDUSTRY ARGUMENT

Infant-industry advocates believe that new domestic industries should be protected from foreign competition for a period of time so that they will have a chance to develop. As the new industry matures, it will be able to stand on its own feet and compete effectively with foreign producers, at which time the protection can be removed.

The infant-industry argument has a long and often notorious history. Alexander Hamilton used it to argue for the protection of early U.S. manufacturing. The major problem with the argument is that the protection, once granted, will be difficult to remove. For example, a century ago, this argument was used to gain tariff protection for the newly emerging steel industry in the United States. Over time, the steel industry developed and became very powerful, both politically and economically. Despite its maturity, the tariffs remained. To this day, legislation continues to provide the steel industry with various protections that limit competition from abroad.

18-5c THE ANTIDUMPING ARGUMENT

Dumping involves the sale of goods by a foreign firm at a price below cost or below the price charged in the firm's home-base market. Dumping is illegal and if a domestic industry is harmed, current law provides relief in the form of antidumping duties (tariffs imposed against violators). Proponents of the antidumping argument argue that foreign producers will temporarily cut prices, drive domestic firms out of the market, and then use their monopoly position to gouge consumers. However, there is reason to question the effectiveness of this strategy. After all, the high prices would soon attract competitors, including other foreign suppliers.

Antidumping cases nearly always involve considerable ambiguity. The prices charged in the home market generally vary, and the production costs of the firms charged with dumping are not directly observable. This makes it difficult to tell whether a dumping violation has really occurred. Furthermore, aggressive price competition is an integral part of the competitive process. When demand is weak and inventories are large, firms will often temporarily slash prices below per unit production cost in order to reduce excessively large inventories. Domestic firms are permitted to engage in this practice, and consumers benefit from it. Why shouldn't foreign firms be allowed to do the same?

Dumping
Selling a good in a foreign country at a lower price than what it cost to produce, or at a lower price than it's sold for in the domestic market.

One thing is for sure: Antidumping legislation gives politicians another way to channel highly visible benefits to powerful business and labor interests—another open invitation for rent seeking. The dumping charges are adjudicated by political officials in the International Trade Commission and the Department of Commerce. Consequently, it's naive to believe that political considerations won't be an important element underlying the charges that are levied and how they are resolved. Unsurprisingly, the number of claimants bringing charges of dumping has increased substantially over the past few decades.

18-5d SPECIAL INTERESTS AND THE POLITICS OF TRADE RESTRICTIONS

Regardless of the arguments made by the proponents of trade restrictions, their political attractiveness is primarily the result of their special interest nature. Murray Weidenbaum, former chairman of the President's Council of Economic Advisors, put it this way: "Protectionism is a politician's delight because it delivers visible benefits to the protected parties while imposing the costs as a hidden tax on the public."[5] As we discussed in Chapter 6, special interest issues are often a source of economic inefficiency.

The politics of trade restrictions are straightforward and play out over and over again. Well-organized business and labor interests gain substantially from restrictions that limit competition from abroad. Because their personal gain is large, they will feel strongly about the issue and provide politicians with various forms of political support based on their positions on trade restrictions. Most important, the special-interest groups will be an attractive source of political contributions. When it comes to consumers, however, even if the total cost of the restrictions is quite large, it will be spread thinly among them; most consumers will be unaware that they are paying slightly higher prices for various goods because of the restrictions.

As you can see, courting special-interest groups helps politicians solicit campaign contributions and generate votes on the one hand. On the other hand, little political gain can be derived from poorly organized and largely uninformed consumers. Given this incentive structure, the adoption of trade restrictions is not surprising.

The U.S. tariff code itself is a reflection of the politics of trade restrictions. It is both lengthy (the schedule fills more than 3,000 pages) and highly complex. This makes it difficult for even a well-educated citizen to figure out how it works. High tariffs are imposed on some products (for example, apparel, tobacco, light trucks, brooms, Japanese leather products, and footwear), whereas low tariffs are imposed on others. Highly restrictive quotas limit the import of a few commodities, most notably agricultural products. Even though this complex system of targeted trade restrictions is costly to administer, it is no accident. It reflects the rent seeking of special-interest groups and the political contributions and other side payments the system generates for politicians.

Proponents of trade restrictions usually frame the issue as a conflict between American and foreign producers. But this is a misrepresentation designed to mislead. The real conflict is between American producers and American consumers. Why do Americans buy from foreigners? The answer is because they are getting more for their money. The trade restrictions help producers in the protected sectors but harm consumers, who now must pay higher prices and confront more limited options. Do we want our government to harm one group of Americans to favor another? Moreover, when a government becomes heavily involved in favoring some at the expense of others, how will this impact rent seeking, cronyism, and even corruption? In addition to their economic impact, trade barriers also influence the operation of the political process.

---

[5]Murray L. Weidenbaum, personal correspondence with the authors. Weidenbaum was a former chairman of the President's Council of Economic Advisers and former director of the Center for the Study of American Business of Washington University.

18-6 DO MORE OPEN ECONOMIES PERFORM BETTER?

Economic theory indicates that trade openness will improve the performance of an economy. Is this true? To address this question, a measure of trade openness—the freedom of individuals to engage in voluntary exchange across national boundaries—is needed. The international exchange area of the *Economic Freedom of the World* data provides information on the trade openness of 115 countries for 1995–2017. To achieve a high rating on the zero-to-ten scale (with ten representing more trade openness) on this measure, a country had to maintain low tariff rates, maintain a freely convertible currency (no exchange rate controls), and refrain from imposing quotas and other regulations that restrict its residents from trading with foreigners.[6]

Exhibit 11 shows the countries with the ten highest and ten lowest trade openness ratings. The ratings reflect the average degree of openness for the entire 1995–2017 period.

EXHIBIT 11

Trade Openness, Income, and Growth

	Average Trade Openness Score (1995-2017) (0 to 10 Scale)	GDP Per Capita (2011 dollars)	Average Annual Rate (1995 to 2017)
Ten Most Open Economies			
Hong Kong	9.49	$56,088	2.5%
Singapore	9.41	$87,760	3.0%
Ireland	8.88	$66,132	4.0%
United Kingdom	8.81	$39,862	1.5%
Netherlands	8.77	$48,809	1.5%
New Zealand	8.74	$36,046	1.6%
Estonia	8.71	$29,916	4.4%
Denmark	8.66	$47,270	1.1%
Luxembourg	8.63	$93,102	1.6%
Sweden	8.52	$46,681	1.8%
Average	**8.86**	**$55,167**	**2.3%**
Ten Least Open Economies			
Nigeria	5.12	$5,351	2.6%
Niger	5.04	$921	0.7%
Congo, Rep. Of	4.99	$5,103	0.3%
Central African Republic	4.86	$754	–0.8%
Venezuela	4.77	$15,219	–0.2%
Iran	4.76	$19,098	2.0%
Burundi	4.48	$671	–0.9%
Algeria	4.32	$13,876	1.8%
Zimbabwe	4.29	$2,568	–0.3%
Myanmar	3.38	$5,610	8.3%
Average	**4.60**	**$6,917**	**1.4%**

Source: Derived from *Economic Freedom of the World* 2018 Dataset and World Bank, *World Development Indicators*. The purchasing power parity method was used to convert the per capita GDP figures into 2011 international dollars.

[6]The measure of trade openness used here follows the methodology developed by Charles Skipton, *The Measurement of Trade Openness* (PhD diss., Florida State University, 2003).

This is important because the gains from increased openness can only be realized over time. Expanding the openness of trade is a long-term growth strategy, not a short-term "quick fix." Hong Kong, Singapore, Ireland, United Kingdom, and the Netherlands headed the list of the ten most open economies during 1995–2017. At the other end of the spectrum, the trade openness measure indicates Myanmar, Zimbabwe, Algeria, and Burundi were the least open economies during the period. Note that all of the ten most open economies have openness ratings of 8.52 or above, whereas the ratings of the ten least open economies are all 5.12 or lower.

As Exhibit 11 shows, the 2017 average GDP per person of $55,167 for the ten most open economies was nearly eight times the $6,917 figure for the ten least open economies. Moreover, the more open economies also grew more rapidly. During 1995–2017, real GDP per person in the ten most open economies expanded at an annual rate of 2.3 percent, compared with 1.4 percent in the ten least open economies. Of course, the data of Exhibit 11 do not take into account other cross-country differences that theory indicates will influence growth. However, more detailed statistical analysis indicates that even after the differences in other factors such as legal system, geography, climate, inflation, and initial income level are taken into account, trade openness continues to have a strong positive impact on both per capita GDP and growth rates.[7]

18-7 TRADE BARRIERS AND POPULAR TRADE FALLACIES

Fallacies abound in the area of international trade. Why? Failure to consider the secondary effects of international trade is part of the answer. Key elements of international trade are closely linked; you cannot change one element without changing the other. For example, you cannot reduce imports without simultaneously reducing the demand for exports. The political incentive structure is also a contributing factor. As business, labor, and political leaders seek to gain from trade restrictions, they will often use half-truths and wrong-headed ideas to achieve their political objectives. Two of the most popular trade fallacies involve the effects of imports on employment and the impact of trade with low-wage countries. Let's take a closer look at both.

18-7a TRADE FALLACY 1: TRADE RESTRICTIONS THAT LIMIT IMPORTS SAVE JOBS AND EXPAND EMPLOYMENT

Like most fallacies, this one has just enough truth to give it some credibility. When tariffs, quotas, and other trade barriers limit imports, they are likely to foster employment in the industries shielded from competition. But this is only half of the story: Simultaneously, jobs in other domestic sectors will be destroyed. Here's how: When trade barriers reduce the amount of goods Americans buy from foreigners, sales to foreigners will also fall. This is because our imports provide foreigners with the dollars they need to buy our exports. Because foreigners cut back on the items they would normally buy from us, other U.S. sectors will suffer job losses because they're selling less.

In addition, the trade barriers will mean higher prices for domestic consumers. Because the domestic consumers are spending more on the "protected goods," they will have less to spend on other things. This, too, will reduce domestic employment.

Furthermore, when trade restrictions are imposed on a resource domestic producers use as an input, they will increase the cost of domestic firms, reduce their sales, and make

---

[7]For additional information on the relationship between international trade and economic growth, see Jeffrey A. Frankel and David Romer, "Does Trade Cause Growth?" *American Economic Review* (June 1999): 379–99; and Jeffrey D. Sachs and Andrew Warner, "Economic Reform and the Process of Global Integration," *Brookings Papers on Economic Activity*, no. 1 (1995): 1–95.

APPLICATIONS IN ECONOMICS

A Bizarre Tale of Differential Tariffs

The United States imposes a tariff of 2.5 percent on passenger vehicles, but 25 percent on light trucks for the transport of goods. As a result, sometimes importers modify the vehicle so that it will qualify for the lower tariff rate. For example, Subaru added carpeting, two seats, and seat belts to the bed of its small two-seat pickup, the Brat, turning it into a passenger vehicle so that it qualified for the lower tariff rate. Upon taking delivery, many owners simply removed the extra seats.

The Ford Transit Connect, which was produced in Turkey, provides another example of importers making modifications to avoid the higher tariff rates imposed on light trucks. All Transit Connects were imported with rear windows and rear seats with seat belts, making them passenger vehicles. Once they cleared U.S. customs, however, Ford ripped out and recycled the windows, seats, and rear seat belts and blocked the rear windows with solid panels. Doing this transformed them into light trucks. Actions such as these result in waste and inefficiency over and above those highlighted by the economic

analysis of tariffs. Furthermore, they reduce the competitiveness in the market for light trucks.[6]

Car Collection/Alamy Stock Photo

Source: This application is based on Michael Hammock, "Bizarre Tales of Tariffs," http://www.econlib.org/library/Columns/y2016/Hammock-tariffs.html.

it more difficult for them to compete in international markets. The 2018 steel and aluminum tariff increases imposed by the Trump administration under a seldom used 1962 national security law illustrate this point. These tariffs increased the costs of a Missouri nail manufacturer and resulted in a 50 percent decline in sales. An Indiana cookware manufacturer experienced a similar reduction in sales as the result of the higher steel and aluminum prices. Similarly, import quotas that pushed the domestic price of sugar to approximately twice the world level have led to employment reductions in the domestic candy manufacturing industry. Several large candy makers relocated abroad so that they could buy sugar at the lower world price. Again, the jobs lost in U.S. industries using sugar were an offset to any employment gains of the domestic sugar producers.

Sometimes the results of trade restrictions are ironic and almost comical. When the Trump administration imposed tariffs of 20 percent and up on washing machines in January of 2018, the American manufacturer Whirlpool applauded the action. But five months later when the administration imposed tariffs on steel and aluminum, Whirlpool charged that the actions were unfair. While the tariffs on washing machines increased the demand for their product, the steel and aluminum tariffs increased their cost, partially if not entirely eliminating their gains from the initial trade restrictions.

Once the secondary "jobs lost" as the result of the restrictions are considered, on balance, there is no reason to expect that the trade barriers will either create or destroy jobs. Instead, they will reshuffle them. More Americans will be employed producing things we do poorly and fewer will be employed producing things we do well. As a result, our overall income level will be lower than it would have been otherwise.

18-7b TRADE FALLACY 2: FREE TRADE WITH LOW-WAGE COUNTRIES LIKE MEXICO AND CHINA WILL REDUCE THE WAGES OF AMERICANS

Many Americans believe that without trade restrictions, their wages will fall to the wage levels of workers in poor countries. How can Americans compete with workers in countries like Mexico and China who are willing to work for $1 or less per hour? This fallacy stems from a misunderstanding of both the source of high wages and the law of comparative advantage. Workers in the United States generally are well educated, possess high skill levels, and work with large amounts of capital equipment. These factors contribute to their high productivity, which is the source of their high wages. Similarly, in countries like Mexico and China, wages are low precisely because productivity is low. Workers are generally less skilled in these countries, and there is less capital equipment to make them more productive.

The key thing to remember, though, is that gains from trade emanate from comparative advantage, not absolute advantage (see Exhibits 3, 4, and 5). The United States cannot produce *everything* more cheaply than Mexico or China merely because U.S. employees are more productive and work with more capital. Neither can Mexico and China produce *everything* more cheaply merely because their wage rates are low compared with the United Sates.

As long as there are differences between countries when it comes to their comparative advantages, gains from trade will be possible, no matter what the wages of the employees in the two countries are. Trade reflects relative advantage, not wage levels. We can illustrate this point using trade between individuals. No one argues that trade between doctors and lawn service workers, for example, will cause the wages of doctors to fall. Because of their different skills and costs of providing alternative goods, both high-wage doctors and low-wage lawn-care workers can gain from trade. The same is also true for trade between rich and poor nations.

If foreigners have a comparative advantage and can sell us a product for less than we ourselves can produce it, we can gain by buying it. This will give us more resources to invest in and produce other things. Perhaps an extreme example will illustrate this point. Suppose a foreign producer is willing to supply us automobiles free of charge (perhaps because its employees were willing to work for nothing). Would it make sense to impose tariffs or quotas to keep the automobiles from coming into the country? Of course not. Resources that were previously used to produce automobiles would then be freed up to produce other goods, and the real income and availability of goods would expand. It makes no more sense to erect trade barriers to keep out cheap foreign goods than it would to keep out the free autos.

18-8 INSTITUTIONS AND THE CHANGING NATURE OF GLOBAL TRADE

General Agreement on Tariffs and Trade (GATT) An organization formed after World War II to set the rules for the conduct of international trade and reduce trade barriers among nations.

World Trade Organization (WTO) The new name given to GATT in 1994; the WTO is currently responsible for monitoring and enforcing multilateral trade agreements among its 164 member countries.

Since World War II, liberalized trade policies and lower transportation and communication costs have propelled the growth of international trade. The growth of trade has also resulted in a changing institutional environment. In the aftermath of World War II, the major industrial nations of the world established the **General Agreement on Tariffs and Trade (GATT)**. For almost five decades, GATT played a central role in reducing tariffs and relaxing quotas. The average tariff rates of GATT members fell from approximately 40 percent in 1947 to about 3.0 percent in 2010, for example.

Following 1993, GATT was given a new name: the **World Trade Organization (WTO)**. This organization of 164 countries is now responsible for monitoring and enforcing the trade agreements developed through GATT. The WTO gives member nations a forum for development of trade rules and the settlement of disputes among members.

Many countries have also entered into special trade agreements, particularly with regional neighbors. The 1994 North American Free Trade Agreement (NAFTA) established by the United States, Canada, and Mexico is an example. As a result of NAFTA, the tariffs of most goods moving among the three countries have been eliminated. As **Exhibit 12** shows, U.S. trade with both Mexico and Canada grew rapidly following the adoption of NAFTA. Measured as a share of GDP, trade with Mexico jumped from 1.2 percent in 1990 to 3.2 percent in 2019. During the same period, trade with Canada remained at 3.4 percent of GDP.

However, this growth of trade, particularly with Mexico, has not been without controversy. Even though growth of both output and employment in the United States was strong following the NAFTA agreement, many nonetheless argued that American firms and employee groups were disadvantaged by the agreement. In 2018, the Trump administration renegotiated a new treaty, called the United States–Mexico–Canada Agreement. Most of the provisions of the original NAFTA agreement were left intact. The modifications were mixed: some reduced trade barriers while others increased them. The major modifications will affect the auto and dairy industries. The domestic content requirements for automobiles were tightened. In order to avoid a 2.5 percent tariff on autos produced in one of the three countries, but sold in another, the North American content requirement was increased from 62 percent to 75 percent as a share of auto value. Moreover, by 2020, 30 percent (increasing to 40 percent by 2023) of auto production must be done by workers earning an average wage of at least $16 per hour. The agreement also eased Canadian restrictions on imports of American dairy products. These changes are expected to increase the cost of automobiles by at least $500 per vehicle and expand the potential U.S. share of the Canadian dairy market to 3.5 percent. On balance, the changes will exert little, if any, positive impact on the total trade among the three countries.

Since the end of World War II, the United States and most other high-income countries have been leaders among those pursuing and promoting more liberal trade policies. In contrast, India, China, and most of the less-developed economies of Africa and Latin America imposed sizable trade restraints that they were reluctant to relax. However, this pattern has changed during the past three decades. Observing the success of open economies like Hong Kong and Singapore, many less-developed countries (LDCs) unilaterally reduced many of their trade restrictions. On average, the tariff rates of LDCs are now less than half their levels of the early 1980s. Recognizing that trade is an important source of higher income levels, many leaders of LDCs are now among the leading advocates of trade liberalization.

EXHIBIT 12

U.S. Trade with Canada and Mexico, 1980–2018

Measured as a share of GDP, U.S. trade with both Canada and Mexico has increased following the passage of NAFTA.

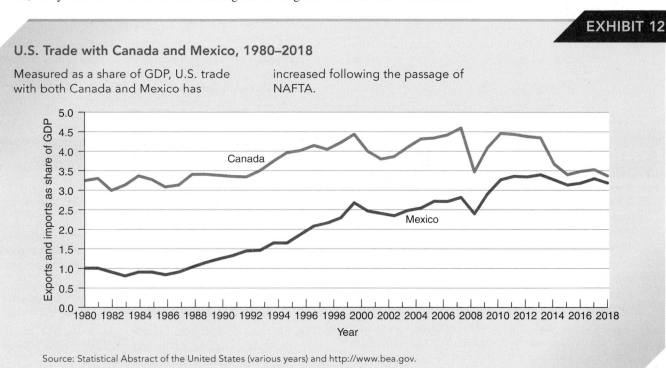

Source: Statistical Abstract of the United States (various years) and http://www.bea.gov.

By contrast, the United States, Japan, and the European Union nations have agricultural price support and subsidy programs that are difficult to maintain in a free trade environment. These programs are now major stumbling blocks that reduce support for trade liberalization. Furthermore, protectionist proponents—particularly those in high-income countries like the United States—have successfully lobbied to impose labor and environmental regulations that block trade liberalization.

During the worldwide COVID-19 pandemic in 2020, the United States and several other nations imposed restrictions prohibiting domestic firms from selling medical products abroad. Moreover, several powerful political leaders called for mandates requiring that various pharmaceutical products be produced domestically. Nations throughout the world also imposed travel restrictions designed to limit the spread of the COVID-19 virus. The pandemic appears to have strengthened the political forces seeking to restrain international trade. At the same time, the internet and other technological changes continue to reduce transport and communications costs and thereby encourage the movement of goods, ideas, and people across national boundaries. This combination of forces is sure to enliven the debate on trade issues in the years immediately ahead.

KEY POINTS

- The volume of international trade has grown rapidly in recent decades. In the United States, international trade (imports plus exports) summed to 26 percent of GDP in 2019, compared with 20 percent in 1980 and 9 percent in 1960.

- Comparative advantage rather than absolute advantage is the source of gains from trade. As long as relative production costs of goods differ, trading partners will be able to gain from trade. Specialization and trade make it possible for trading partners to produce a larger joint output and expand their consumption possibilities.

- Imports increase the domestic supply and lead to lower prices for consumers. Exports reduce the domestic supply and push prices upward, but this means the exporters can sell their products at higher prices. The net effect of international trade is an expansion in total output and higher income levels for both trading partners.

- Import restrictions, such as tariffs and quotas, reduce the supply of foreign goods to domestic markets. This results in higher prices. Essentially, the restrictions are a subsidy to producers (and workers) in protected industries at the expense of (1) consumers and (2) producers (and workers) in export industries. Jobs protected by import restrictions are offset by jobs destroyed in export-related industries.

- Trade restrictions generally provide concentrated benefits to the producers in industries they're designed to protect. The costs are spread thinly among consumers in the form of higher prices. Even though the impact of trade restrictions on the economy as a whole is harmful, they generate benefits for interest groups that politicians can then tap for campaign contributions and other side payments.

- Persistently open economies have grown more rapidly and have achieved higher per capita income levels than economies more closed to international trade.

CRITICAL ANALYSIS QUESTIONS

1. Why do American households and businesses buy things from foreigners? What are the characteristics of the items we buy from foreigners? What are the characteristics of the things we sell to foreigners?

2. *"Trade restrictions limiting the sale of cheap foreign goods in the United States are necessary to protect the prosperity of Americans." Evaluate this statement made by an American political leader.

3. Suppose as the result of the Civil War that the United States had been divided into two countries and that, through the years, high trade barriers had grown up between the two. How might the standard of living in the "divided" United States have been affected? Explain.

4. *Can both of the following statements be true? Why or why not?

    a. "Tariffs and import quotas promote economic inefficiency and reduce the real income of a nation. Economic analysis suggests that nations can gain by eliminating trade restrictions."

    b. "Economic analysis suggests that there is good reason to expect that trade restrictions will exist in the real world."

5. "Imports destroy jobs; exports create them. The average American is hurt by imports and helped by exports." Do you agree or disagree with this statement? Explain.

6. *"An increased scarcity of a product benefits producers and harms consumers. In effect, tariffs and other trade restrictions increase the domestic scarcity of products by reducing the supply from abroad. Such policies benefit domestic producers of the restricted product at the expense of domestic consumers." Evaluate this statement.

7. In 2018, the Trump administration imposed a 25 percent tariff on steel. What is the expected impact on employment in the U.S. auto industry? (*Hint:* Think about how higher steel prices will impact the cost of producing automobiles.)

8. "Getting more Americans to realize that it pays to make things in the United States is the heart of the competitiveness issue." (This is a quote from an American business magazine.)

    a. Would Americans be better off if more of them paid higher prices in order to "buy American" rather than purchase from foreigners? Would U.S. employment be higher? Explain.

    b. Would Californians be better off if they bought goods produced only in California? Would the employment in California be higher? Explain.

9. How do tariffs and quotas differ? Can you think of any reason why foreign producers might prefer a quota rather than a tariff? Explain your answer.

10. *It is often alleged that Japanese producers receive subsidies from their government permitting them to sell their products at a low price in the U.S. market. Do you think we should erect trade barriers to keep out cheap Japanese goods if the source of their low price is a government subsidy? Why or why not?

11. The European Union has virtually eliminated trade restrictions among its members, and most members now use a common currency. What impact have these changes had on European economies?

12. *Does international trade cost Americans jobs? Does interstate trade cost your state jobs? What is the major effect of international and interstate trade?

13. "The United States is suffering from an excess of imports. Cheap foreign products are driving American firms out of business and leaving the U.S. economy in shambles." Evaluate this view.

14. The United States uses an import quota to maintain the domestic price of sugar well above the world price. Analyze the impact of the quota. Use supply and demand analysis to illustrate your answer. To whom do the gains and losses of this policy accrue? How does the quota affect the efficiency of resource allocation in the United States? Why do you think Congress is supportive of this policy?

15. As U.S. trade with low-wage countries like Mexico increases, will wages in the United States be pushed down? Why or why not? Are low-wage workers in the United States hurt when there is more trade with Mexico? Discuss.

16. *"Tariffs not only reduce the volume of imports, they also reduce the volume of exports." Is this statement true or false? Explain your answer.

17. "Physical obstacles like bad roads and stormy weather increase transaction costs and thereby reduce the volume of trade. Tariffs, quotas, exchange rate controls, and other human-made trade restrictions have similar effects." Evaluate this statement. Is it true? Why or why not?

*Asterisk denotes questions for which answers are given in Appendix B.

CHAPTER 19

International Finance and the Foreign Exchange Market

Currencies, like tomatoes and football tickets, have a price at which they are bought and sold. An exchange rate is the price of one currency in terms of another. —**Gary Smith**[1]

Trade across national boundaries is complicated by the fact that nations generally use different currencies to buy and sell goods in their respective domestic markets. The British use pounds; the Japanese, yen; the Mexicans, pesos; nineteen European countries, the euro; and so on. Therefore, when a good or service is purchased from a seller in another country, it is generally necessary for someone to convert one currency to another.

As we previously discussed, the forces of supply and demand will determine the exchange rate value of currencies in the absence of government intervention. This chapter focuses more directly on the foreign exchange market. We will consider how exchange rates both exert an impact on and are influenced by the flow of trade and the flow of capital across national boundaries. We will also analyze alternative exchange rate regimes and consider

some of the recent changes in the structure of currency markets around the world.

As you read this chapter, look for answers to the following questions:

- What determines the exchange rate value of the dollar relative to other currencies?

- Why do exchange rates change?

- What are the alternative types of exchange rate systems? Which types work well and which will lead to financial problems?

- What information is included in the balance-of-payments accounts of a nation? Will the balance-of-payments accounts of a country always be in balance?

- Is a balance-of-trade deficit bad?

---

[1]Gary Smith, *Macro Economics* (New York: W. H. Freeman, 1985), 514.

19-1 FOREIGN EXCHANGE MARKET

When trading parties live in different countries, an exchange will often involve a currency transaction. Currency transactions take place in the **foreign exchange market**, the market where currencies of different countries are bought and sold. Suppose that you own a sporting goods shop in the United States and are preparing to place an order for athletic shoes. You can purchase them from either a domestic or a foreign manufacturer. If you decide to purchase the shoes from a British firm, either you will have to change dollars into pounds at a bank and send them to the British producer or the British manufacturer will have to go to a bank and change your dollar check into pounds. In either case, purchasing the British shoes will involve an exchange of dollars for pounds.

Suppose the British producer has offered to supply the shoes for 30 pounds per pair. How can you determine whether this price is high or low? To compare the price of the British-supplied shoes with the price of those produced domestically, you must know the **exchange rate** between the dollar and the pound. *The exchange rate is one of the most important prices because it enables consumers in one country to translate the prices of foreign goods into units of their own currency. Specifically, the dollar price of a foreign good is determined by multiplying the foreign product price by the exchange rate (the dollar price per unit of the foreign currency).* For example, if it takes $1.50 to obtain 1 pound, then the British shoes priced at 30 pounds would cost $45 (30 times the $1.50 price of the pound).

Suppose the exchange rate is $1.50 = 1 pound and that you decide to buy 200 pairs of athletic shoes from the British manufacturer at 30 pounds ($45) per pair. You will need 6,000 pounds in order to pay the British manufacturer. If you contact an American bank that handles foreign exchange transactions and write the bank a check for $9,000 (the $1.50 exchange rate multiplied by 6,000), it will supply the 6,000 pounds. The bank will typically charge a small fee for handling the transaction.

Where does the American bank get the pounds? The bank obtains the pounds from British importers who want dollars to buy things from Americans. Note that the U.S. demand for foreign currencies (such as the pound) is generated by the demand of Americans for things purchased from foreigners. In contrast, the supply of foreign currencies in exchange for dollars reflects the demand of foreigners for things bought from Americans.

Exhibit 1 presents data on the exchange rate—the cents required to purchase a European euro, Japanese yen, British pound, and Canadian dollar—from 2000 to 2019. Under the flexible rate system present in most industrial countries, the exchange rate between currencies changes from day to day and even from hour to hour. The exchange rate figures are the average for the year.

When a **depreciation** in the value of a nation's currency occurs, more units of the domestic currency will be required to purchase one unit of a foreign currency. For example, as Exhibit 1 shows, it took 200.20 cents to purchase a British pound in 2007, up from 143.96 in 2001. Thus, the dollar depreciated against the pound during this period. As the result of this depreciation, goods purchased from British suppliers became more expensive to Americans.[2] At the same time, the prices of American goods to British consumers moved in the opposite direction. A depreciation of the U.S. dollar relative to the British pound is the same as an appreciation in the British pound relative to the dollar.

When an **appreciation** occurs, it will take fewer units of the domestic currency to purchase a unit of foreign currency. During 2014–2019, the dollar appreciated against the British pound. In 2014, it took 164.84 cents to purchase a British pound, but by 2019, a British pound could be obtained for only 127.68 cents.

Exhibit 1 also provides an index of the foreign exchange value of the dollar against 26 major currencies. This broad index provides evidence of what is happening to the

Foreign exchange market
The market in which the currencies of different countries are bought and sold.

Exchange rate
The domestic price of one unit of foreign currency. For example, if it takes $1.80 to purchase one English pound, the dollar–pound exchange rate is 1.80.

Depreciation
A reduction in the value of the domestic currency relative to foreign currencies. A depreciation makes foreign goods more expensive for domestic residents.

Appreciation
An increase in the value of the domestic currency relative to foreign currencies. An appreciation makes foreign goods cheaper for domestic residents.

---

[2]Because a depreciation means a higher price of foreign currencies, some may think it looks like an appreciation. Just remember that a higher price of the foreign currency means that one's domestic currency will buy fewer units of the foreign currency and thus fewer goods and services from foreigners.

EXHIBIT 1

Foreign Exchange Rates, 2000–2019

Year	Euro	Japanese Yen	British Pound	Canadian Dollar	Index of Exchange Rate Value of the Dollar (26 Currencies)
2000	92.3	0.928	151.56	67.3	119.6
2001	89.5	0.823	143.96	64.6	126.1
2002	94.5	0.799	150.25	63.7	126.8
2003	113.2	0.863	163.47	71.4	119.3
2004	124.4	0.925	183.30	76.8	113.8
2005	124.5	0.908	182.04	82.5	110.8
2006	125.6	0.860	184.34	88.2	108.7
2007	137.1	0.849	200.20	93.2	103.6
2008	147.3	0.967	185.45	93.8	99.9
2009	139.4	1.067	156.61	87.6	105.7
2010	132.6	1.139	154.52	97.1	101.8
2011	139.3	1.255	160.43	101.1	97.2
2012	128.6	1.253	158.53	100.1	99.8
2013	132.8	1.025	156.42	97.1	101.0
2014	133.0	0.946	164.84	90.6	104.1
2015	111.0	0.826	152.84	78.2	117.3
2016	110.7	0.920	135.55	75.5	122.4
2017	113.0	0.892	128.90	77.0	122.1
2018	118.2	0.906	133.63	77.2	122.9
2019	111.9	0.917	127.68	75.4	128.6

Source: http://research.stlouisfed.org/fred2/

Flexible exchange rates
Exchange rates that are determined by the market forces of supply and demand. They are sometimes called floating exchange rates.

dollar's general exchange rate value.[3] An increase in the index implies an appreciation in the dollar, whereas a decline is indicative of a depreciation. Between 2002 and 2011, the dollar depreciated by approximately 25 percent against these twenty-six currencies. In contrast, between 2011 and 2019, the index increased from 97.2 to 128.6, an appreciation of approximately 32 percent relative to this broad bundle of currencies. Frequently, people will use the terms "*strong*" and "*weak*" when referring to the exchange rate value of a currency. A currency is said to be strong when it has been appreciating in value, whereas a weak currency is one that has been depreciating on the foreign exchange market.

A pure **flexible exchange rate** system is one in which market forces alone determine the foreign exchange value of the currency. The exchange rate system in effect since 1973 might best be described as a managed flexible rate regime. It is flexible because all the major industrial countries allow the exchange rate value of their currencies to float. But the system is also "managed" because the major industrial nations have from time to time attempted to alter supply and demand in the foreign exchange market by buying and selling various currencies. Compared with the total size of this market, however, these transactions have generally been small. Thus, the exchange rate value of major currencies like the U.S. dollar, British pound, Japanese yen, and the European euro is determined primarily by market forces. Several countries link their currency to major currencies like the U.S. dollar or European euro. As we proceed, we will investigate alternative methods of linking currencies and analyze the operation of different regimes.

---

[3]In the construction of this index, the exchange rate of each currency relative to the dollar is weighted according to the proportion of U.S. trade with the country. For example, the index weights the U.S. dollar–Japanese yen exchange rate more heavily than the U.S. dollar–Swiss franc exchange rate because the volume of U.S. trade with Japan exceeds the volume of trade with Switzerland.

19-2 DETERMINANTS OF THE EXCHANGE RATE

To simplify our explanation of how the exchange rate is determined, let's assume that the United States and Great Britain are the only two countries in the world. When Americans buy and sell with each other, they use dollars. Therefore, American sellers will want to be paid in dollars. Similarly, when the British buy and sell with each other, they use pounds. As a result, British sellers will want to be paid in pounds.

In our two-country world, the demand for pounds in the exchange rate market originates from the purchases by Americans of British goods, services, and assets (both real and financial). For example, when U.S. residents purchase men's suits from a British manufacturer, travel in the United Kingdom, or purchase the stocks, bonds, or physical assets of British business firms, they demand pounds from (and supply dollars to) the foreign exchange market to pay for these items.

Correspondingly, the supply of foreign exchange (pounds in our two-country case) originates from sales by Americans to foreigners. When Americans sell goods, services, or assets to the British, for example, the British buyers will supply pounds (and demand dollars) in the exchange rate market in order to acquire the dollars to pay for the items purchased from Americans.[4]

Exhibit 2 illustrates the supply and demand curves of Americans for foreign exchange—British pounds in our two-country case. The demand for pounds is downward sloping because a lower dollar price of the pound—meaning a dollar will buy more pounds—makes British goods cheaper for American importers. The goods produced by one country are generally good substitutes for the goods of another country. This means that when foreign (British) goods become cheaper, Americans will increase their expenditures on imports (and therefore the quantity of pounds demanded will increase). Thus, as the dollar price of the pound declines, Americans will both buy more of the lower-priced (in dollars) British goods and demand more pounds, which are required for the purchases.

Similarly, the supply curve for pounds is dependent upon the sales by Americans to the British (i.e., the purchase of American goods by the British). An increase in the dollar price of the pound means that a pound will purchase more dollars and more goods priced in dollars. Thus, the price (in pounds) of American goods, services, and assets to British purchasers declines as the dollar price of the pound increases. As this happens, the British will purchase more from Americans and therefore supply more pounds to the foreign exchange market. Thus, the supply curve for pounds will slope upward to the right.

As Exhibit 2 shows, equilibrium is present at the dollar price of the pound that brings the quantity demanded and quantity supplied of pounds into balance, $1.50 in this case. *The market-clearing price of $1.50 per pound not only equalizes demand and supply in the foreign exchange market but also equalizes (1) the value of U.S. purchases of items supplied by the British with (2) the value of items sold by U.S. residents to the British.* Demand and supply in the currency market are simply the mirror images of these two factors.

What would happen if the price of the pound were above equilibrium—$1.80 = 1 pound, for example? At the higher dollar price of the pound, British goods would be more expensive for Americans. Americans would cut back on their purchases of shoes, glassware, textile products, financial assets, and other items supplied by the British, and the quantity of pounds demanded by Americans would therefore decline. Simultaneously, the higher dollar price of the pound would make U.S. exports cheaper for the British. For example, an $27,000 American automobile would cost British consumers

---

[4]We analyze the foreign exchange market in terms of the demand for and supply of foreign currencies. Alternatively, this analysis could be done in terms of the supply of and demand for dollars. Because one currency is traded for another, the same actions that generate a demand for foreign exchange simultaneously generate a supply of dollars. Correspondingly, the same exchanges that create a supply of foreign currencies simultaneously generate a demand for dollars in the foreign exchange market.

EXHIBIT 4

Inflation with Flexible Exchange Rates

If prices were stable in Britain while the price level increased 50 percent in the United States, the U.S. demand for British products (and pounds) would increase, whereas U.S. exports to Britain would decline, causing the supply of pounds to fall. These forces would cause the dollar to depreciate relative to the pound.

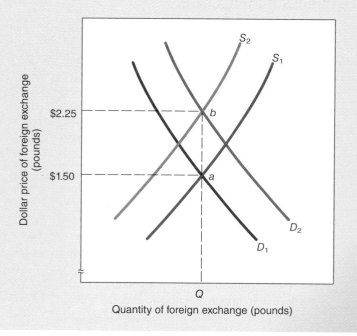

Exchange rate adjustments permit nations with even high rates of inflation to engage in trade with countries experiencing relatively stable prices.[5] A depreciation in a nation's currency in the foreign exchange market compensates for the nation's inflation rate. For example, if inflation increases the price level in the United States by 50 percent and the value of the dollar in exchange for the pound depreciates (such that the value of the foreign currency increases 50 percent), then the prices of American goods measured in pounds are unchanged to British consumers. Thus, when the exchange rate value of the dollar changes from $1.50 = 1 pound to $2.25 = 1 pound, the depreciation in the dollar restores the original prices of U.S. goods to British consumers even though the price level in the United States has increased by 50 percent.

On the one hand, when domestic prices are increasing more rapidly than those of one's trading partners, the value of the domestic currency will tend to depreciate in the foreign exchange market. On the other hand, if a nation's inflation rate is lower than that of its trading partners, then its currency will tend to appreciate.

19-3c CHANGES IN INTEREST RATES

Financial investments will be quite sensitive to changes in real interest rates—that is, interest rates adjusted for the expected rate of inflation. International loanable funds will tend to move toward areas where the expected real rate of return (after compensation for differences in risk) is highest. *Thus, increases in real interest rates relative to a nation's trading partners will tend to cause that nation's currency to appreciate.* For example, if real interest rates rise in the United States relative to Britain, British citizens will demand dollars (and supply their currency, pounds) in the foreign exchange market to purchase the high-yield American assets. The increase in demand for the dollar and supply of pounds will then cause the dollar to appreciate relative to the British pound.

In contrast, when real interest rates in other countries increase relative to rates in the United States, short-term financial investors will move to take advantage of the higher

---

[5]However, high rates of inflation are likely to cause greater variability in the foreign exchange value of a currency across time periods. In turn, this increased variability of the exchange rate will generate uncertainty and reduce the volume of international trade—particularly transactions involving a time dimension. Thus, exchange rate instability is generally harmful to the health of an economy.

American consumer purchases a TV from a Japanese manufacturer.

American vacationer rents a hotel room in Paris.

Foreign student pays tuition to Harvard.

Foreign investor purchases a bond from a U.S. corporation.

How will each of these transactions influence the demand for and supply of foreign currencies in exchange for the dollar?

yields abroad. As investment funds move from the United States to other countries, there will be an increase in the demand for foreign currencies and an increase in the supply of dollars in the foreign exchange market. A depreciation in the dollar relative to the currencies of the countries with the higher real interest rates will be the result.

19-3d CHANGES IN THE BUSINESS AND INVESTMENT CLIMATE

The inflow and outflow of capital will also be influenced by the quality of the business and investment environment. The monetary, legal, regulatory, and tax climates are particularly important here. Countries that follow a monetary policy consistent with price stability, protect property rights, keep taxes low, and treat people impartially will tend to attract capital. In turn, the inflow of capital will strengthen the demand for the domestic currency and thereby cause it to appreciate. In contrast, when investors are concerned about the

Thumbnail Sketch

What Factors Cause a Nation's Currency to Appreciate or Depreciate?

These Factors Will Cause a Nation's Currency to Appreciate:

1. Slow growth of income (relative to one's trading partners) that causes imports to lag behind exports

2. A rate of inflation that is lower than that of one's trading partners

3. Domestic real interest rates that are higher than real interest rates abroad

4. A shift toward sound policies that attract an inflow of capital

These Factors Will Cause a Nation's Currency to Depreciate:

1. Rapid growth of income (relative to one's trading partners) that stimulates imports relative to exports

2. A rate of inflation that is higher than that of one's trading partners

3. Domestic real interest rates that are lower than real interest rates abroad

4. Movement toward unsound policies that cause an outflow of capital

stability of the monetary climate, fairness of the legal system, high taxes, and excessive regulation, many will choose to do business elsewhere. As they do so, an outflow of capital and depreciation in the foreign exchange value of the domestic currency will result. Thus, other things constant, the foreign exchange value of a nation's currency will tend to appreciate when its policy environment is improving, while it will tend to depreciate if investors believe that the policy climate is deteriorating.

The accompanying **Thumbnail Sketch** summarizes the major forces that cause a nation's currency to appreciate or depreciate when exchange rates are determined by market forces.

19-4 INTERNATIONAL FINANCE AND ALTERNATIVE EXCHANGE RATE REGIMES

There are three major types of exchange rate regimes: (1) flexible rates; (2) fixed rate, unified currency; and (3) pegged exchange rates. So far, we have focused on the operation of a flexible rate regime. We now consider the other two.

19-4a FIXED RATE, UNIFIED CURRENCY SYSTEM

Currency board
An entity that (1) issues a currency with a fixed designated value relative to a widely accepted currency (for example, the U.S. dollar), (2) promises to continue to redeem the issued currency at the fixed rate, and (3) maintains bonds and other liquid assets denominated in the other currency that provide 100 percent backing for all currency issued.

Obviously, the 50 states of the United States have a unified currency, the dollar. In addition, the U.S. dollar has been the official currency of Panama for more than a century. Ecuador adopted the U.S. dollar as its official currency in 2000, and El Salvador did so in 2001. The currency of Hong Kong is also closely linked to the U.S. dollar. Hong Kong has a **currency board** that has the power to create currency only in exchange for a specific quantity of U.S. dollars (7.75 HK dollars = 1 U.S. dollar).[6] Countries that adopt the currency board approach do not conduct monetary policy. Instead, they merely accept the monetary policy of the nation to which their currency is tied—the U.S. policy in the case of Hong Kong. Thus, the United States, Panama, Ecuador, El Salvador, and Hong Kong have a unified currency regime.

---

[6]A currency board like that of Hong Kong does two things. First, it issues domestic currency at a fixed rate in exchange for a designated foreign currency. Second, the foreign currency is then invested in bonds denominated in that currency. This means that the money issued by the currency board is backed 100 percent by the foreign currency. Therefore, the holders of the money issued by the currency board know that it will always have sufficient funds to exchange the domestic currency for the foreign one at the fixed rate. In essence, the country with a currency board accepts the monetary policy of the nation to which its currency is tied.

Nineteen countries of the European Union—Austria, Belgium, Cyprus, Estonia, Finland, France, Germany, Greece, Ireland, Italy, Latvia, Lithuania, Luxembourg, Malta, Netherlands, Portugal, Slovakia, Slovenia, and Spain—have also established a unified currency regime. The official currency in each of these countries is the euro. Several other European countries, including Bulgaria, Bosnia, and Herzegovina use a currency board to link their domestic currency to the euro. Thus, the euro is a unified currency in all of these countries. In turn, the foreign exchange value of the euro relative to other currencies, such as the dollar, the British pound, and the Japanese yen, is determined by market forces (flexible exchange rates).

The distinguishing characteristic of a fixed rate, unified currency regime is the presence of only one central bank with the power to expand and contract the supply of money. For the dollar, that central bank is the Federal Reserve System; for the euro, it is the European Central Bank. Those linking their currency at a fixed rate to the dollar or the euro do not conduct monetary policy; they merely accept the monetary policy of the central bank for their currency. For example, the former central banks of the countries now using the euro no longer have the power to create money. In essence, they are now branches of the European Central Bank, much like the regional and district Federal Reserve banks are branches of the Fed. Similarly, currency boards do not create additional currency. They merely agree to exchange their domestic currency for the currency to which it is linked at a fixed rate.

A pure gold standard system, in which each country agrees to exchange units of its domestic currency for gold at a designated price and fully backs its domestic money supply with gold, is also a fixed rate, unified system. In this case, the world supply of gold (rather than a central bank) determines the total supply of money. If a country's purchases from foreigners exceeded its sales to them, its supply of gold would fall, which would reduce the domestic supply of money. This would put downward pressure on the domestic price level and bring the payments to and receipts from foreigners back into balance. Things would change in the opposite direction if a country were selling more to foreigners than it was purchasing from them. In this case, the excess of sales relative to purchases would lead to an inflow of gold, expansion in the domestic money supply, and higher domestic prices. International financial arrangements approximated those of a gold standard during the period between the U.S. Civil War and the establishment of the Federal Reserve System in 1913.

Between 1944 and 1971, most of the world operated under a system of **fixed exchange rates**, where each nation fixed the price of its currency relative to others. In essence, this was a quasi-unified system. It was unified in the sense that the value of one currency was fixed relative to others over lengthy time periods. But it was not a fully unified system because each country continued to exercise control over its monetary policy. Nations maintained reserves with the **International Monetary Fund (IMF)**, which could be drawn on when payments to foreigners exceeded receipts from them. This provided each with some leeway in the conduct of monetary policy. However, countries running persistent payment deficits would eventually deplete their reserves. This constrained the country's monetary independence and provided its policy-makers with an incentive to keep its monetary policy approximately in line with that of its trading partners. Under this fixed exchange rate regime, nations often imposed tariffs, quotas, and other trade barriers in an effort to keep their payments and receipts in balance at the fixed rate. Various restrictions on the convertibility of currencies were also common. These problems eventually led to the demise of the system.

19-4b PEGGED EXCHANGE RATE REGIME

A **pegged exchange rate system** is one in which a country commits itself to the maintenance of a specific exchange rate (or exchange-rate range) relative to another currency (like the U.S. dollar) or a bundle of currencies. In contrast with the currency board approach, however, countries adopting the pegged exchange rate continue to conduct monetary policy. Thus, an excess of purchases from foreigners relative to sales to them does not automatically force the country to reduce its domestic money supply.

Fixed exchange rate
An exchange rate that is set at a determined amount by government policy.

International Monetary Fund (IMF)
An international banking organization, currently with more than 185 member nations, designed to oversee the operation of the international monetary system. Although it does not control the world supply of money, it does hold currency reserves for member nations and makes currency loans to national central banks.

Pegged exchange rate system
A commitment to use monetary and fiscal policy to maintain the exchange rate value of the domestic currency at a fixed rate or within a narrow band relative to another currency (or bundle of currencies).

However, maintaining the pegged rate will restrict the independence of monetary policy. A country can either (1) follow an independent monetary policy and allow its exchange rate to fluctuate or (2) tie its monetary policy to maintain the fixed exchange rate. It cannot, however, maintain the convertibility of its currency at the fixed exchange rate while following a monetary policy more expansionary than the country to which its currency is tied. Attempts to do so will lead to a financial crisis—a situation in which falling foreign currency reserves eventually force the country to forgo the pegged exchange rate.

This is precisely what happened in Mexico during 1989–1994. Mexico promised to exchange the peso for the dollar at a pegged rate, but it also expanded its domestic money supply much more rapidly than the United States. In the early 1990s, this led to a higher rate of inflation in Mexico than in the United States. Responding to the different inflation rates, more and more people shifted away from the Mexican peso and toward the dollar. By December 1994, Mexico's foreign exchange reserves were virtually depleted. As a result, it could no longer maintain the fixed exchange rate with the dollar. Mexico devalued its currency, triggering a crisis that affected several other countries following similar policies.

In 1997–1998, much the same thing happened in Brazil, Thailand, and Indonesia. Like Mexico, these countries sought to maintain fixed exchange rates (or rates within a narrow band), while following monetary and fiscal policies that were inconsistent with the fixed rate. As their reserves declined, they were forced to abandon their exchange rate pegs. This was extremely disruptive to these economies. Imports suddenly became much more expensive and therefore less affordable. Businesses (including banks) that had borrowed money in dollars (or some other foreign currency) were unable to repay their loans as the result of the sharp decline in the exchange rate value of the domestic currency. In turn, these disruptions led to severe economic declines.

Rather than abandoning a pegged rate regime, countries sometimes impose exchange rate controls when they are no longer able to sustain their pegged rate. Exchange rate controls fix the rate at which individuals and businesses can convert the domestic currency to foreign currencies below the market level and prohibit exchange conversions without the authorization of the government. This has been the situation in Venezuela. Venezuelans need foreign currency to purchase goods and services from foreigners, and when they are unable to obtain it because of the controls, they often turn to the black market. Of course, these illegal transactions are risky and the black market exchange rate will be higher, often substantially higher, than the controlled rate. If the conditions in the country continue to deteriorate, the black market rate may change dramatically. This occurred in Venezuela during 2014–2018. In August of 2014, 80 Venezuelan bolivars purchased a U.S. dollar in the black market, but two years later, the black market rate had risen to 1,200 bolivars per dollar, and by August of 2018, it took 3.9 million bolivars to purchase just one U.S. dollar. Like other price controls, exchange rate controls disrupt markets, reduce the gains from trade, and slow economic progress.

Both economic theory and real-world experience indicate that either a purely flexible exchange rate regime or a fixed rate, unified regime with a single central bank will work reasonably well. In contrast, a pegged exchange rate regime is something like a time bomb. Pushed by political considerations, monetary policy makers in most countries are unable to follow a course consistent with the maintenance of pegged rates. Failure to do so, however, eventually leads to abandonment of the peg and a financial crisis.

19-5 BALANCE OF PAYMENTS

Balance of payments
A summary of all economic transactions between a country and all other countries for a specific time period, usually a year. The balance-of-payments account reflects all payments and liabilities to foreigners (debits) and all payments and obligations received from foreigners (credits).

Just as countries calculate their gross domestic product (GDP) so that they have a general idea of their domestic level of production, most countries also calculate their balance of international payments in order to keep track of transactions across national boundaries. The **balance of payments** summarizes the transactions of the country's citizens, businesses, and governments with foreigners. Balance-of-payments accounts are kept according to the principles of basic bookkeeping. Any transaction that creates a demand for foreign currency (and a supply of the domestic currency) in the foreign exchange market is recorded as a debit, or minus, item. Imports are an example of a debit item. Transactions that create a supply of foreign currency (and demand for the domestic currency) on the foreign exchange market are recorded as a credit, or plus, item. Exports are an example of a credit item. *Because the foreign exchange market will bring quantity demanded and quantity supplied into balance, it will also bring the total debits and total credits into balance.*

Exhibit 5 summarizes the balance-of-payments accounts of the United States for 2019. As the exhibit shows, the transactions can be grouped into one of three separate categories: the current account, capital account, or the official reserve account. Let's take a look at each of these major categories.

19-5a CURRENT-ACCOUNT TRANSACTIONS

Current-account transactions involve only current exchanges of goods and services and current income flows (and gifts). They do not involve changes in the ownership of either real or financial assets. **Current-account** transactions are dominated by the trade in goods and services. The export and import of merchandise goods are the largest components in the current account. When U.S. producers export their products, foreigners will supply their currency in exchange for dollars in order to pay for the U.S.-produced goods. Because

Current account
The record of all transactions with foreign nations that involve the exchange of merchandise goods and services, current income derived from investments, and unilateral gifts.

EXHIBIT 5

U.S. Balance of Payments, 2019 (in billions of dollars)

		DEBITS	CREDITS	BALANCE
CURRENT ACCOUNT				
1	U.S. merchandise exports		1652.8	
2	U.S. merchandise imports	−2519.0		
3	Balance of merchandise trade			−866.2
4	U.S. service exports (1 + 2)		845.2	
5	U.S. service imports	−595.4		
6	Balance on service trade (4 + 5)			249.8
7	Balance on goods and services (3 + 6)			−616.4
8	Income receipts of Americans from abroad		1123.1	
9	Income receipts of foreigners in the United States	−866.1		
10	Net income receipts			257.0
11	Net unilateral transfers			−138.9
12	Balance on current account (7 + 10 + 11)			−498.3
CAPITAL ACCOUNT				
13	Foreign investment in the United States (capital inflow)		784.4	
14	U.S. investment abroad (capital outflow)	−422.2		
15	Net other currency transactions[a]		140.8	
16	Balance on capital account (13 + 14 + 15)			503.0
OFFICIAL RESERVE TRANSACTIONS				
17	U.S. official reserve assets			−4.7
18	Total (12 + 16 + 17)			0.0

Source: http://www.bea.gov

[a]Statistical discrepancy is included in this figure.

U.S. exports generate a supply of foreign exchange and demand for dollars in the foreign exchange market, they are a credit (plus) item. In contrast, when Americans import goods, they will demand foreign currencies and supply dollars in the foreign exchange market. Thus, imports are a debit (minus) item.

In 2019, the United States exported $1,652.8 billion of merchandise goods compared with imports of $2,519.0 billion. The difference between the value of a country's merchandise exports and the value of its merchandise imports is known as the **balance of merchandise trade** (or *balance of trade*). If the value of a country's merchandise exports falls short of the value of its merchandise imports, it is said to have a balance-of-trade deficit. In contrast, the situation in which a nation exports more than it imports is referred to as a trade surplus. In 2019, the United States ran a merchandise-trade deficit of $866.2 billion (line 3 of Exhibit 5).

Balance of merchandise trade
The difference between the value of merchandise exports and the value of merchandise imports for a nation. It is also called simply the *balance of trade* or *net exports*. The balance of merchandise trade is only one component of a nation's total balance of payments and its current account.

The export and import of services are also sizable. Service trade involves the exchange of items like insurance, transportation, banking services, and items supplied to foreign tourists. Like the export of merchandise goods, service exports generate a supply of foreign exchange and demand for dollars. For example, a Mexican business that is insured by an American company will supply pesos and demand dollars to pay its premiums for the service. Thus, service exports are recorded as credits in the balance-of-payments accounts of exporting nations. Conversely, the import of services from foreigners generates a demand for foreign currency and a supply of dollars in the exchange market. Therefore, service imports are a debit item.

As Exhibit 5 illustrates, in 2019, U.S. service exports were $845.2 billion, compared with service imports of $595.4 billion. Thus, the United States ran a $249.8 billion surplus on its service trade transactions (line 6 of Exhibit 5). When we add the balance of service exports and imports to the balance of merchandise trade, we obtain the **balance on goods and services**. In 2019, the United States ran a $616.4 billion deficit (the sum of the $866.2 billion merchandise-trade deficit and the $249.8 billion service surplus) in the goods and services account.

Balance on goods and services
The exports of goods (merchandise) and services of a nation minus its imports of goods and services.

Two other relatively small items are also included in current-account transactions: (1) net income from investments and (2) unilateral transfers. Americans have made substantial investments in stocks, bonds, and real assets in other countries. As these investments abroad generate income, dollars will flow from foreigners to Americans. This flow of income to Americans will supply foreign currency (and create a demand for dollars) in the foreign exchange market. Thus, the net income to Americans is entered as a credit in the U.S. current account. Correspondingly, foreigners earn income from their investments in the United States. This net income to foreigners is recorded as a debit in the U.S. current account because the supply of dollars to the foreign exchange market creates a demand for foreign exchange.

As Exhibit 5 shows, in 2019, Americans earned $1,123.1 billion from investments abroad, whereas foreigners earned $866.1 billion from their investments in the United States. On balance, Americans earned $257.0 billion more on their investments abroad than foreigners earned on their investments in the United States. This $257.0 billion net inflow of investment income reduced the size of the deficit on current-account transactions.

Gifts to foreigners, like U.S. aid to a foreign government or private gifts from U.S. residents to their relatives abroad, generate a demand for foreign currencies and supply of dollars in the foreign exchange market. Thus, they are a debit item. Correspondingly, gifts to Americans from foreigners are a credit item. Because the U.S. government and private U.S. citizens gave $138.9 billion more to foreigners than we received from them, this net unilateral transfer was entered as a debit item on the current account in 2019.

19-5b BALANCE ON CURRENT ACCOUNT

The difference between (1) the value of a country's current exports (both goods and services) and earnings from its investments abroad and (2) the value of its current imports (again, both goods and services) and the earnings of foreigners on their domestic assets (plus net unilateral transfers to foreigners) is known as the **balance on current account**. The current-account balance provides a summary of all current-account transactions. As with the balance of trade, when the value of the current-account debit items (import-type transactions) exceeds the value of the credit items (export-type transactions), we say that the country is running a current-account deficit. Alternatively, if the credit items are greater than the debit items, the country is running a current-account surplus. In 2019, the United States ran a current-account deficit of $498.3 billion.

Because trade in goods and services dominates current-account transactions, the trade- and current-account balances are closely related. Countries with large trade deficits (surpluses) almost always run substantial current-account deficits (surpluses).

19-5c CAPITAL-ACCOUNT TRANSACTIONS

In contrast with current-account transactions, **capital-account** transactions focus on changes in the ownership of real and financial assets. These transactions are composed of (1) direct investments by Americans in real assets abroad (or by foreigners in the United States) and (2) loans to and from foreigners. When foreigners make investments in the United States—for example, by purchasing stocks, bonds, or real assets from Americans—their actions will supply foreign currency and generate a demand for dollars in the foreign exchange market. Thus, these capital inflow transactions are a credit.

Conversely, capital outflow transactions are recorded as debits. For example, if a U.S. investor purchases a shoe factory in Mexico, the Mexican seller will want to be paid in pesos. The U.S. investor will supply dollars (and demand pesos) on the foreign exchange market. Because U.S. citizens will demand foreign currency (and supply dollars) when they invest in stocks, bonds, and real assets abroad, these transactions enter into the balance-of-payments accounts as a debit. As we noted earlier, the international exchange rate regime is not a pure flexible rate system. Countries with pegged exchange rates will often engage in reserve transactions in an effort to maintain their pegged rate. Like other capital flows, these transactions are recorded as debits and credits. Even countries with flexible exchange rates may engage in reserve transactions to influence their exchange rate. When a nation's currency is appreciating rapidly, a country may try to slow the appreciation by purchasing foreign financial assets. Conversely, when a currency is depreciating, the country may attempt to halt the depreciation by using some of its foreign currency reserves to purchase the domestic currency in the foreign exchange market. Because of the credibility and widespread use of the U.S. dollar, these transactions often involve assets denominated in dollars, particularly bonds issued by the U.S. Treasury.

When foreign governments and central banks purchase U.S. securities, they will increase the demand for the dollar in the foreign exchange market, causing the foreign exchange value of the dollar to be higher than would otherwise be the case. There is a positive side to these purchases of the dollar. If foreign governments did not have confidence in both the economy and the monetary policy of the United States, they would not want to purchase and hold U.S. financial assets.

In 2019, foreign investments in the United States (capital inflow) summed to $784.4 billion, whereas U.S. investments abroad (capital outflow) totaled $422.2 billion. In 2019, there was also a net capital inflow of $140.8 billion from other currency transactions (including the statistical discrepancy). Because the capital inflow exceeded the outflow, the United States ran a $503.0 billion capital-account surplus in 2019.

19-5d OFFICIAL RESERVE ACCOUNT

When a country follows a flexible exchange rate policy, the transactions of its **official reserve account** will be small relative to the size of the foreign exchange market. This is the case for the United States. In 2019, the net official reserve transactions of the United States were –$4.7 billion.

Balance on current account
The import–export balance of goods and services, plus net investment income earned abroad, plus net private and government transfers. If the value of the nation's export-type items exceeds (is less than) the value of the nation's import-type items plus net unilateral transfers to foreigners, a current-account surplus (deficit) is present.

Capital-account
The record of transactions with foreigners that involve either (1) the exchange of ownership rights to real or financial assets or (2) the extension of loans.

Official reserve account
The record of transactions among central banks.

19-5e THE BALANCE OF PAYMENTS MUST BALANCE

The sum of the debit and credit items of the balance-of-payments accounts must balance. Thus, the following identity must hold:

Current-Account Balance + Capital-Account Balance + Official Reserve-Account Balance = 0

However, the specific components of the accounts need not balance. For example, the debit and credit items of the current account need not be equal. Specific components may run either a surplus or a deficit. Nevertheless, because the balance of payments as a whole must balance, a deficit in one area implies an offsetting surplus in other areas. Similarly, even though market forces will bring about an overall balance, there is no reason to expect that the trade flows between any two countries will be in balance. See the accompanying Applications in Economics box feature on this topic.

If a nation is experiencing a current-account deficit, it must experience an offsetting surplus on the sum of its capital-account and official reserve-account balances. This has been the case for the United States in recent years.

In 2019, the United States ran a $498.3 billion current-account deficit and a $503.0 billion capital-account surplus. The difference between these two figures—a $4.7 billion surplus—was exactly offset by a $4.7 billion deficit in the official reserve account. Thus, the deficits and surpluses of the current-, capital-, and official reserve accounts summed to zero as is shown in Exhibit 5 (line 18).

Under a pure flexible rate system, official reserve transactions would be zero. Under these conditions, a capital-account surplus (inflow of capital) would mean that the current account must have a deficit. Similarly, a capital-account deficit (outflow of capital) would mean that the current account must have a surplus.

With flexible exchange rates, changes in the net inflow of capital will influence the current-account balance. If a nation is experiencing an increase in net foreign investment, perhaps as the result of attractive investment opportunities, this increase in the capital-account surplus (inflow of capital) will enlarge the current-account deficit. In contrast, capital flight (outflow of capital) will move the current account toward a surplus.

19-6 EXCHANGE RATES, CURRENT ACCOUNT BALANCE, AND CAPITAL INFLOW

Exhibit 6 presents data on the foreign exchange value of the dollar, current-account balance, and inflow of capital for the United States since 1978. (*Note:* While the data in the middle frame are for the current-account balance, the trade balance figures would be virtually identical because trade in goods and services is the dominant component of the current account.) The link between the inflow of capital and the current-account deficit is clearly visible. As the middle and lower panels illustrate, the two are mirror images. When the inflow of capital increases, the current-account (trade) balance shifts toward a deficit. Correspondingly, when net capital inflow shrinks, so, too, does the current-account deficit. This is the expected outcome under a flexible rate system. With flexible rates, the overall payments to and receipts from foreigners must balance. Thus, a deficit in one area is not an isolated event. If a nation runs a current-account (trade) deficit, it must also run a capital-account (plus official reserve account) surplus of equal magnitude.

As Exhibit 6 demonstrates, there is a close relationship between an inflow of capital and trade (and current account) deficits. When foreigners are making more "investments" in a country than the residents of the country are making abroad, a capital account surplus will occur. In turn, the capital account surplus generally leads to a trade (and current account) deficit. In essence, trade (and current-account) deficits are the flip side of capital inflows.

Whether an inflow of capital is good or bad depends on the source of the inflow and how the funds are used. When the inflow of capital occurs because the investment

EXHIBIT 6

The Exchange Rate, Current-Account Balance, and Net Foreign Investment

Here, we show the relationship between the exchange rate, the current-account deficit, and net foreign investment (capital inflow). The shaded areas represent recessions.

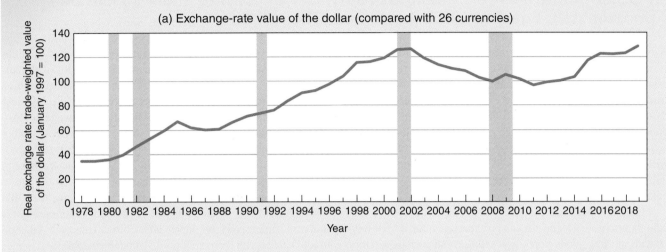

(a) Exchange-rate value of the dollar (compared with 26 currencies)

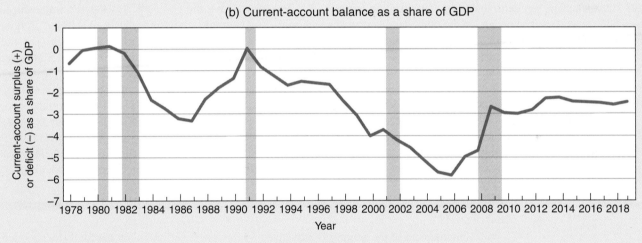

(b) Current-account balance as a share of GDP

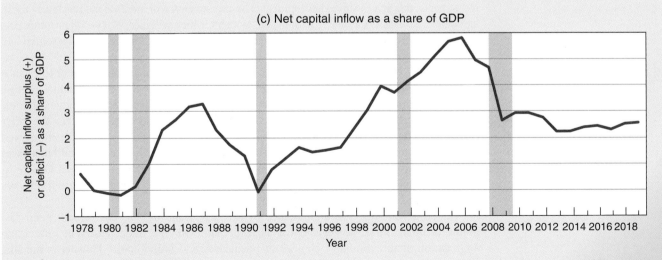

(c) Net capital inflow as a share of GDP

Note: Data are given in billions of dollars.

Source: http://research.stlouisfed.org/fred2/

APPLICATIONS IN ECONOMICS

"If Other Countries Are Treating Us Fairly, Our Exports to Them Should Be Approximately Equal to Our Imports from Them."

American politicians like to bash countries like Japan and China that export much more to us than they import from us. Some have even called for trade restraints to limit imports from these countries until our exports to and imports from them are brought into balance. This view is based on a misconception about bilateral trade balances. Flexible exchange rates will bring total purchases from foreigners into balance with total sales to them. However, there is no reason to expect that imports and exports with any specific country will be in balance.

Consider the trade "deficits" and "surpluses" of a doctor who likes to golf. The doctor can be expected to run a trade deficit with sporting goods stores, golf caddies, and course operators. Why? These suppliers sell items that the golfer–doctor purchases in sizable quantities. The doctor, on the other hand, probably sells few items the sporting goods store purchases. Similarly, the doctor can be expected to run trade surpluses with medical insurers, elderly patients, and those with chronic illnesses. These trading partners are major purchasers of the services provided by the doctor, although the doctor might purchase very little from them.

The same principles are at work across nations. A nation will tend to run trade deficits with countries that are low-cost suppliers of items it imports and trade surpluses with countries that buy a lot of the things it exports. Japan is a major importer of resources like oil and a major exporter of high-tech manufacturing goods. Americans import a lot of the latter, but they export very little of the former. Similarly, China is a low-cost producer of labor-intensive items like toys and textile products, items that are costly for a high-wage country like the United States to produce domestically. On the other hand, the United States is a low-cost producer of high-tech products and grains like wheat and corn that are purchased only in small quantities by poor countries like China. The bottom line is this: Japan and China are low-cost producers of many items that we import, and the United States is not a major exporter of items imported intensively by Japan and China. Thus, our bilateral trade deficits with them are perfectly understandable.

In recent years, the United States has run trade surpluses with, for example, the Netherlands, Australia, Belgium, Luxembourg, Brazil, and the United Kingdom. Do these bilateral trade surpluses indicate that the United States treats these countries unfairly? Of course not. The surpluses merely reflect that these countries import substantial amounts of items supplied economically by U.S. producers and export only small amounts of items imported intensively by Americans. It may be good politics to bash those with whom we run bilateral trade deficits, but the argument is nonetheless based on a fallacious view of trade balances between countries.

environment of the country is attractive and foreigners are providing the funds for productive investments, this is a positive development. The investments will increase the machines, tools, and other capital assets available to domestic workers, which will increase both their future productivity and earnings. Clearly, trade and current account deficits arising from this source will exert a positive impact on both the country's current and future income.

However, if the inflow of capital is used to increase current consumption or to finance unproductive projects, it will reduce future income. In recent years, a substantial portion of the capital inflow to the United States has been used to finance federal budget deficits. This borrowing has made it possible for Americans to consume more today, but the interest expenses will mean less consumption in the future. Further, to the extent the borrowed funds are channeled into counterproductive projects and subsidies for favored businesses and interest groups, they will reduce future income. As the financial troubles of Greece illustrate, when this process is taken to a high level, it can lead to indebtedness to foreigners that will even endanger the creditworthiness of a government.

When considering the significance of the U.S. trade deficit, one should keep two points in mind. First, no legal entity is responsible for the trade deficit. It reflects an aggregation of the voluntary choices of businesses and individuals.[7] Thus, it is not like

---

[7]As the late Herbert Stein, a former chair of the President's Council of Economic Advisers, once put it: "The trade deficit does not belong to any individual or institution. It is a pure-statistical aggregate, like the number of eggs laid in the U.S. or the number of bald-headed men living here." See Herbert Stein, "Leave the Trade Deficit Alone," *The Wall Street Journal* (March 11, 1987).

a business loss or even the budget deficit of a government. Second, to a large degree, the inflow of capital reflects the confidence of investors in both the U.S. economy and the policies of the United States. If either should become less attractive in the future, the situation would change. For example, if the United States continued to run large deficits that push the federal debt to high levels, the confidence of both domestic and foreign investors would diminish. This would lead to a decline in the capital inflow and a reduction in the trade deficit. As the experience of Greece indicates, this is not an attractive way to shift the trade balance toward a surplus.

KEY POINTS

- Because countries generally use different currencies, international trade usually involves the conversion of one currency to another. The currencies of different countries are bought and sold in the foreign exchange market. The exchange rate is the price of one national currency in terms of another.

- The dollar demand for foreign exchange arises from the purchase (import) of goods, services, and assets by Americans from foreigners. The supply of foreign currency in exchange for dollars arises from the sale (export) of goods, services, and assets by Americans to foreigners. The equilibrium exchange rate will bring these two forces into balance.

- With flexible exchange rates, the following will cause a nation's currency to appreciate: (1) rapid growth of income abroad (and/or slow domestic growth), (2) low inflation (relative to one's trading partners), (3) rising domestic real interest rates (and/or falling rates abroad), and (4) improvement in the business and investment environment. The reverse of these conditions will cause a nation's currency to depreciate.

- There are three major types of exchange rate regimes: (1) flexible rates; (2) fixed rate, unified currency; and (3) pegged exchange rates. Both flexible rate and fixed rate, unified currency systems work quite well. Pegged rate systems, however, often lead to problems because they require that the nation follow a monetary policy consistent with maintaining the pegged rate. Political pressure often makes this difficult to do.

- The balance-of-payments accounts provide a summary of transactions with foreigners. There are three major balance-of-payments components: (1) the current account, (2) capital account, and (3) the official reserve account. The balances of these three components must sum to zero, but the individual components of the accounts need not be in balance.

- Under a pure flexible rate system, there will be no official reserve-account transactions. Under these circumstances, the current and capital accounts must sum to zero. This implies that an inflow of capital will shift the current account toward a deficit, while an outflow of capital will move the current account toward a surplus.

- Trade deficits are not necessarily bad. Countries that grow rapidly and follow policies that investors find attractive will tend to experience an inflow of capital and a trade deficit. However, if the inflow of capital is used to finance a higher level of current consumption or channeled into unproductive projects, future income will be adversely affected

- There is no reason to expect that bilateral trade between countries will balance. A country will tend to run a bilateral trade deficit with countries that are low-cost producers of items that it imports in large quantities.

CRITICAL ANALYSIS QUESTIONS

1. If the dollar depreciates relative to the Japanese yen, how will this affect the dollar price of a Japanese camera produced by Nikon, for example? How will this change influence the quantity of Nikon cameras purchased by Americans?

2. How will the purchases of items from foreigners compare with the sales of items to foreigners when the foreign exchange market is in equilibrium? Explain.

3. Will a flexible exchange rate bring the imports of goods and services into balance with the exports of goods and services? Why or why not?

4. *The accompanying chart indicates an actual newspaper quotation of the exchange rate of various currencies. On February 2, did the dollar appreciate or depreciate against the

British pound? How did it fare against the Canadian dollar?

U.S. DOLLAR EQUIVALENT

	FEBRUARY 1	FEBRUARY 2
British pound	1.755	1.746
Canadian dollar	0.6765	0.6775

5. *Suppose the exchange rate between the United States and Mexico freely fluctuates in the open market. Indicate whether each of the following would cause the dollar to appreciate or depreciate relative to the peso.
   a. an increase in the quantity of drilling equipment purchased in the United States by Pemex, the Mexican oil company, as a result of a Mexican oil discovery

b. an increase in the U.S. purchase of crude oil from Mexico as a result of the development of Mexican oil fields

c. higher real interest rates in Mexico, inducing U.S. citizens to move some of their financial investments from U.S. to Mexican banks

d. lower real interest rates in the United States, inducing Mexican investors to borrow dollars and then exchange them for pesos

e. inflation in the United States and stable prices in Mexico

f. an increase in the inflation rate from 2 percent to 10 percent in both the United States and Mexico

g. an economic boom in Mexico, inducing Mexicans to buy more U.S.-made automobiles, trucks, electric appliances, and manufacturing equipment

h. attractive investment opportunities in Mexico, inducing U.S. investors to buy stock in Mexican firms

6. Explain why the current-account balance and capital-account balance must sum to zero under a pure flexible rate system.

7. Rapidly growing strong economies often experience trade deficits, whereas economies with sluggish growth often have trade surpluses. Can you explain this puzzle?

8. *In recent years, a substantial share of the domestic capital formation in the United States has been financed by foreign investors. Is this dependence on foreign capital dangerous? What would happen if the inflow of foreign capital came to a halt?

9. *Suppose that the United States were running a current-account deficit. How would each of the following changes influence the size of the current-account deficit?

a. a recession in the United States

b. a decline in the attractiveness of investment opportunities in the United States

c. an improvement in investment opportunities abroad

10. If taxes imposed on personal and corporate income increased substantially in the United States and the monetary policy of the United States was less stable and more inflationary than other countries, how would these policies affect the trade deficit? Why?

11. If foreigners have confidence in the U.S. economy and therefore move to expand their investments in the United States, how will the U.S. current-account balance be affected? How will the exchange-rate value of the dollar be affected?

12. Is a trade surplus indicative of a strong, healthy economy? Why or why not?

13. *"Changes in exchange rates will automatically direct a country to a current-account balance under a flexible exchange rate system." Is this statement true or false?

14. *Several members of Congress have been highly critical of Japan and China because U.S. imports from these countries have persistently been substantially greater than our exports to them.

a. Under a flexible exchange rate system, is there any reason to expect that the imports from a given country will tend to equal the exports to that country?

b. Can you think of any reason why the United States might persistently run a trade deficit with these countries?

15. *In recent years, the central banks of both Japan and China have purchased large amounts of U.S. Treasury bonds. These purchases increase the exchange rate value of the dollar relative to the Japanese yen and Chinese yuan. Are these purchases harmful to the U.S. economy? Why or why not?

*Asterisk denotes questions for which answers are given in Appendix B.

PART 5

Applying the Basics: Special Topics in Economics

Economics is about how the real world works.

Economics has a lot to say about current issues and real-world events. How are government spending, taxes, and borrowing affecting the future prosperity of Americans? Does the current Social Security system face problems, and what might be done to minimize them? Are stocks a good investment for a young person? What caused the 2020 COVID-19 Recession, the Great Recession of 2008–2009, and the Great Depression of the 1930s, and what are the important lessons we need to learn from these crises? What might be done to improve the quality of health care? Why do the earnings of men and women differ? This section focuses on these topics and several other current issues.

SPECIAL TOPIC 1

Government Spending and Taxation

I'm proud to be paying taxes in the United States. The only thing is—I could be just as proud for half the money. —**Comedian Arthur Godfrey**

In Chapters 5 and 6, we analyzed the economic role of government and the operation of the political process. We learned that whereas the political process and markets are alternative ways of organizing the economy, a sound legal system, secure property rights, and stable monetary regime are vitally important for the efficient operation of markets. We also noted that there may be advantages of using government to provide certain classes of goods that are difficult to supply efficiently through markets. However, as public-choice analysis indicates, the political process is not a corrective device. Even democratic representative government will often lead to the adoption of counterproductive programs. This feature will take a closer look at government in the United States and will provide additional details with regard to its spending, taxing, and borrowing.

As you read this special topic, look for answers to the following questions:

- Historically, how has government spending and its composition changed in the United States?

- Do taxes measure the cost of government?

- Do the rich pay their fair share of taxes? Do they pay a smaller share now than they did a couple of decades ago?

- How has the share of the population paying taxes and receiving various types of transfer benefits changed in recent years? How is this likely to influence the fiscal future of the United States?

ST01-1 GOVERNMENT EXPENDITURES

As we noted in Chapter 6, total government spending (federal, state, and local) sums to approximately 36 percent of the U.S. economy. The size of government has grown substantially over the past century. Measured as a share of GDP, total government spending rose from less than 10 percent in 1930 to roughly 40 percent in 2010. In 2019, government spending had declined to just over 36 percent of the economy, but this will be much higher in coming years due to the government response to the COVID-19 pandemic and associated economic recession. The additional spending in the emergency legislation in May 2020 alone was over $3 trillion.

Approximately three-fifths of the spending by government now takes place at the federal level. Federal expenditures on just four things—(1) income transfers (including Social Security and other income-security programs), (2) health care, (3) national defense, and (4) net interest on the national debt—accounted for 86 percent of federal spending in 2019. (See Chapter 6, Exhibit 2.) This means that expenditures on everything else— the federal courts, national parks, highways, education, job training, agriculture, energy, natural resources, federal law enforcement, and numerous other programs—were less than 14 percent of the federal budget. Major spending categories at the state and local level include education, public welfare and health, transportation and highways, utilities, and law enforcement.

ST01-1a FEDERAL SPENDING PER PERSON, 1792–2019

Article 1, Section 8, of the U.S. Constitution outlined a limited set of functions that the federal government was authorized to perform. These included the authority to raise up an army and navy, establish a system of weights and measures, issue patents and copyrights, operate the post office, and regulate the value of money that it issued. Beyond this, the federal government was not authorized to do much else. The founders of the United States were skeptical of governmental powers, and they sought to limit those powers, particularly those at the federal level.

During the United States' first 125 years, the constitutional limitations worked pretty much as planned; the economic role of the federal government was quite limited, and its expenditures were modest. In the nineteenth century, except during times of war, most government expenditures were undertaken at the state and local level. The federal government spent funds on national defense and transportation (roads and canals) but not much else.

Exhibit 1 presents data on real federal spending per person (measured in terms of the purchasing power of the dollar in 2010). Just before the Civil War, real federal expenditures were $60 per person, not much different than the $50 figure of 1800. Federal spending per person rose sharply during the Civil War, but it soon receded and remained in a range between $125 and $200 throughout the 1870–1916 period. Thus, before World War I, federal expenditures per person were low and the growth of government was modest.

Beginning with the World War I spending of 1917, however, the situation changed dramatically. Federal spending remained well above the prewar levels during the 1920s and rose rapidly during the 1930s. It soared during World War II, and after receding at the end of the war, federal spending continued to grow rapidly throughout the 1950–1990 period. After a brief reduction during the 1990s, per capita real federal spending began to trend upward again, with a spike after the 2008 recession. Whereas per capita federal spending fell by 4.6 percent during the 1990s, it increased by 47 percent during 2000–2019. In 2019, it amounted to $11,767, roughly 83 times the $142 figure of 1916. The additional government expenditures came with a cost. On average, Americans pay more inflation-adjusted federal taxes in one week today than they would have paid during the entire year in 1916. The sizable additional expenditures associated with the COVID-19 pandemic and associated recession will push this even higher in the beginning years of the 2020s.

EXHIBIT 1

Real Federal Expenditure per Capita: 1792–2019

Real federal spending per person (measured in 2010 dollars) was generally less than $50 before the Civil War, and it ranged from $125 to $200 throughout the 1870–1916 period. However, beginning with the spending buildup

for World War I in 1917, real federal spending per person soared, reaching $11,767 in 2019—roughly 83 times the level of 1916.

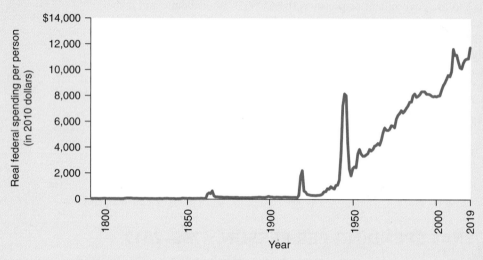

Source: U.S. Census Bureau, *Historical Statistics of the United States* (Washington, DC: U.S. Dept. of Commerce, U.S. Bureau of the Census, 1975); *Economic Report of the President* (Washington, DC: U.S. Government Printing Office, 2020); and Bureau of Labor Statistics.

ST01-1b THE CHANGING COMPOSITION OF FEDERAL SPENDING

Not only has federal spending grown rapidly, but also there has been a dramatic shift in the composition of that spending. Since 1960, spending on defense has fallen as both a share of the budget and as a share of the economy, whereas expenditures on health care, transfer payments, and subsidies have soared.

As **Exhibit 2** illustrates, defense expenditures constituted more than half (52.2 percent) of federal spending in 1960. By 2019, defense spending was only 15 percent of the federal budget. Government expenditures on income transfers (including Social Security and other transfer programs) and health care (primarily Medicare and Medicaid) have soared during the past half century. As Exhibit 2 shows, income transfers and health care expenditures rose from 21.5 percent of the federal budget in 1960 to 62.5 percent in 2019.

Thus, there has been a dramatic change in the composition of federal spending during the last five decades. In contrast with earlier times, national defense is no longer the primary focus of the federal government. In essence, the federal government has become an entity that taxes working-age Americans in order to provide income transfers and health care benefits primarily for senior citizens. Furthermore, spending on the elderly is almost certain to increase as the baby-boomers move into the retirement phase of life during the next two decades.

ST01-2 TAXES AND THE FINANCE OF GOVERNMENT

Government expenditures must be financed through taxes, user charges, or borrowing.[1] Borrowing is simply another name for future taxes that will have to be levied to pay the

---

[1]In addition to user charges, taxes, and borrowing, the operations of government might be financed by printing money. But this is also a type of tax (it is sometimes called an "inflation tax") on those who hold money balances.

EXHIBIT 2

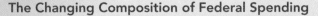

The Changing Composition of Federal Spending

In 2019, national defense expenditures accounted for 15.1 percent of the federal budget, down from 52.2 percent in 1960. In contrast, spending on income transfers and health care rose from 21.5 percent of the federal budget in 1960 to 61.6 percent in 2019.

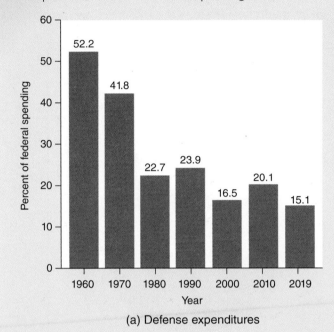

(a) Defense expenditures

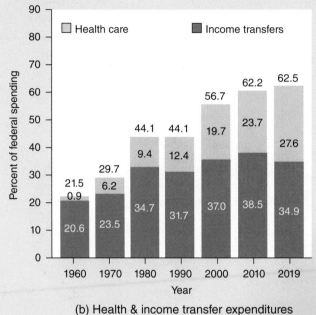

(b) Health & income transfer expenditures

Source: *Economic Report of the President* (Washington, DC: U.S. Government Printing Office, 2020).

interest on the borrowed funds. Thus, it affects the timing but not the level of taxes. In the United States, taxes are by far the largest source of government revenue. The power to tax sets governments apart from private businesses. Of course, a private business can put whatever price tag it wishes on its products, but no private business can force you to buy its goods. With its power to tax, a government can force citizens to pay, whether or not they receive something of value in return. As government expenditures have increased, so, too, have taxes. Taxes now take approximately one-third of the income generated by Americans.

ST01-2a TYPES OF TAXES

Exhibit 3 indicates the major revenue sources for the federal (panel a) and state and local (panel b) levels of government. At the federal level, the personal income tax accounts for more than 49 percent of all revenue. Although income from all sources is covered by the income tax, only earnings derived from wages and salaries are subject to the payroll tax. Payroll taxes on the earnings of employees and self-employed workers finance the Social Security and Medicare programs. The payroll tax accounts for about 36 percent of federal revenue. The remaining sources of revenue, including the corporate income tax, excise taxes, and customs duties, account for a little less than 15 percent of federal revenue.

Both sales and income taxes are important sources of revenue for state governments. A sales tax is levied by 45 of the 50 states (Alaska, Delaware, Montana, New Hampshire, and Oregon are the exceptions). State and local governments derive 14.8 percent of their revenue from this source. Personal income taxes are imposed by 41 states (Alaska, Florida, Nevada, New Hampshire, South Dakota, Tennessee, Texas, Washington, and Wyoming are the exceptions), and they provide approximately 9.8 percent of state and local government

EXHIBIT 3

Sources of Government Revenue

The major sources of government revenue are shown here. Almost half of federal revenues are derived from the personal income tax. The share of federal revenue derived from the payroll tax is only slightly less. The major revenue sources of state and local governments are sales and excise taxes, personal income taxes, user charges, insurance trust (including employee retirement, unemployment compensation, and workers compensation), grants from the federal government, and property taxes.

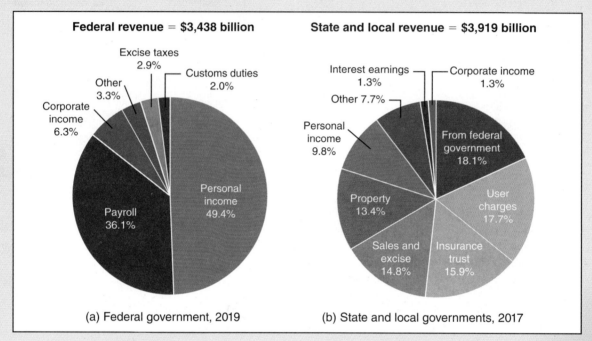

(a) Federal government, 2019   (b) State and local governments, 2017

Source: *Economic Report of the President* (Washington, DC: Government Printing Office, 2020) and U.S. Census Bureau, *State and Local Government Finances*, 2017.

revenue.[2] Property taxes (levied mostly at the local level), insurance trust revenue (including employee retirement contributions, workers' compensation, and unemployment compensation), grants from the federal government, and user charges (prices for government services) also provide substantial revenues for state and local governments.

ST01-3 TAXES AND THE COST OF GOVERNMENT

There are no free lunches. Regardless of how they are financed, activities undertaken by the government are costly. When governments purchase resources and other goods and services to provide missiles, education, highways, health care, and other goods, the resources used by the government will be unavailable to produce goods and services in the private sector. As a result, private-sector output will be lower. This reduction in private-sector output is an opportunity cost of government. Furthermore, this cost will be present whether government activities are financed by taxes or borrowing.

Moreover, a tax dollar extracted from an individual or a business ends up costing the private economy much more than just one dollar. There are two main reasons why this is the case. ***First, the collection of taxes is costly***. The administration, enforcement, and

---

[2]New Hampshire and Tennessee have limited income taxes; they only tax income derived from dividend and interest (so wage income is not subject to the personal income tax).

compliance of tax legislation require a sizable volume of resources, including the labor services of many highly skilled experts. The IRS itself employs more than 75,000 people. In addition, an army of bookkeepers, tax accountants, and lawyers is involved in the collection process. Each year individuals and businesses spend more than 9 billion hours (the equivalent of 4.5 million full-time year-round workers) keeping records, filling out forms, and learning the tax rules and other elements of the tax-compliance process.[3] The estimated compliance costs imposed on individuals and businesses by the IRS amounts to over $400 billion annually. In total, the resources involved amount to between 3 percent and 4 percent of national income (or 12 to 15 percent of the revenues collected). If these resources were not tied up with the tax-collection process, they could be employed producing goods and services for consumption.

Second, taxes impose an additional burden on the economy because they eliminate some productive exchanges (and cause people to undertake some counterproductive activities). As we noted in Chapter 4, economists refer to this as an *excess burden* (or *deadweight loss*) because it imposes a burden over and above the tax revenue transferred to the government. It results because taxes distort incentives. When buyers pay more and sellers receive less due to the payment of a tax, trade and the production of output become less attractive and decline. Individuals will spend less time on productive (but taxed) market activities and more time on tax avoidance and untaxed activities such as leisure. Research indicates that these deadweight losses add between 9 percent and 16 percent to the cost of taxation.[4] This means that $1 in taxes paid to the government imposes a cost of somewhere between $1.20 and $1.30 on the economy. Thus, the cost of a $100-million government program financed with taxes is really somewhere between $120 million and $130 million. As a result, the government's supply of goods and services generally costs the economy a good bit more than either the size of the tax bill or the level of government spending implies.

When considering the cost of taxation, it is also important to recognize that all taxes are paid by people. Politicians often speak of imposing taxes on "business" as if part of the tax burden could be transferred from individuals to a nonperson (business). This is not the case. Business taxes, like all other taxes, are paid by individuals. A corporation or business firm might write the check to the government, but it merely collects the money from someone else—from its customers in the form of higher prices, its employees in the form of lower wages, or its stockholders in the form of lower dividends—and transfers the money to the government.

ST01-4 HOW HAS THE STRUCTURE OF THE PERSONAL INCOME TAX CHANGED?

The personal income tax is the largest single source of revenue for the federal government. The rate structure of the income tax is progressive; taxpayers with larger incomes face higher tax rates. During the past half century, the structure of the rates has been modified several times. In the early 1960s, there were 24 marginal tax brackets ranging from a low of 20 percent to a high of 91 percent. The Kennedy–Johnson tax cut reduced the lowest marginal rate to 14 percent and the top rate to 70 percent. The rate reductions during the Reagan years cut the top marginal rate initially to 50 percent in 1981 and later to approximately 30 percent during the period 1986–1988. During the 1990s, the top rate was increased to 39.6 percent, but the tax reductions during the administration of George W. Bush rolled back the top rate to 35 percent. The top rate was increased back to 39.6 percent in 2013, but was then reduced to 37 percent beginning in 2018.

Thus, since the late 1980s, Americans with the highest incomes have paid sharply lower top marginal tax rates—rates in the 30 to 40 percent range, compared to top rates of

---

[3]Scott A. Hodge, "The Compliance Costs of IRS Regulations," Tax Foundation Fiscal Fact No. 512 (June 2016).
[4]The classic article on this topic is Edgar K. Browning, "The Marginal Cost of Public Funds," *Journal of Political Economy* 84, no. 2 (April 1976): 283–98.

91 percent in the early 1960s and 70 percent before 1981. These reductions in the top rate make it tempting to jump to the conclusion that high-income Americans are now getting a free ride—that they now shoulder a smaller share of the personal income tax burden than in the past. But such a conclusion would be fallacious.

Exhibit 4 presents the Internal Revenue Service data on the share of the personal income tax paid by various classes of high-income taxpayers, as well as those in the bottom half of the income distribution, for the years 1963, 1980, 1990, 2010, and 2017. These data show that the share of the personal income tax paid by high-income Americans has increased substantially since 1963, and the increase has been particularly sharp since 1980. For example, the top 1 percent of earners paid 38.5 percent of the personal income tax in 2017, up from 19.1 percent in 1980 and 18.3 percent in 1963. The top 10 percent of income recipients paid 70.1 percent of the personal income tax in 2017, compared to 49.3 percent in 1980 and 47 percent in 1963. At the same time, the share of the personal income tax paid by the bottom half of the income recipients has fallen from 10.4 percent of the total in 1963 to 7.1 percent in 1980 and 3.1 percent in 2017.

What is going on here? How can one explain the fact that high-income Americans are now paying more of the personal income tax even though their rates are now sharply lower than those in effect before 1981? Two major factors provide the answer. First, when marginal rates are cut by a similar percentage, the "incentive effects" are much greater in the top tax brackets. For example, when the top rate was cut from 91 percent to 70 percent during the Kennedy–Johnson years, high-income taxpayers in this bracket got to keep $30 out of every $100 of additional earnings after the tax cut, compared to only $9 before the rates were reduced. Thus, their incentive to earn additional income increased by a whopping 233 percent (30 minus 9, divided by 9)! Conversely, the rate reduction in the lowest tax bracket from 20 percent to 14 percent meant that the low-income taxpayers in this bracket now got to keep $86 of each additional hundred dollars that they earned compared to $80 before the tax cut. Their incentive to earn increased by a modest 7.5 percent (86 minus 80, divided by 80). Because the rate reductions increased the incentive to earn by much larger amounts in the top tax (and therefore highest-income) brackets, the income base on which high-income Americans were taxed expanded substantially as their rates were reduced. As a result, the tax revenues collected from them declined only modestly. In the very highest brackets, the rate reductions actually increased the revenues collected from

EXHIBIT 4

Share of Federal Income Taxes Paid by Various Groups, 1963–2017

Even though marginal tax rates have been reduced substantially during the past three decades, upper-income Americans pay a much larger share of the federal income tax today than was previously the case. In 2017, the richest 1 percent of Americans paid 38.5 percent of the federal income tax, up from 18.3 percent in 1963 and 19.1 percent in 1980. The 5 percent of Americans with the highest incomes paid almost 60 percent of the personal income tax, whereas the entire bottom half of the income distribution (the bottom 50 percent) paid only 3.1 percent of the total.

INCOME GROUP	SHARE OF TOTAL FEDERAL PERSONAL INCOME TAX PAID				
	1963	1980	1990	2010	2017
Top 1%	18.3%	19.1%	25.1%	37.4%	38.5%
Top 5%	35.6%	36.8%	43.6%	59.0%	59.1%
Top 10%	47.0%	49.3%	55.4%	70.6%	70.1%
Top 25%	68.8%	73.0%	77.0%	87.1%	86.1%
Top 50%	89.6%	93.0%	94.2%	97.6%	96.9%
Bottom 50%	10.4%	7.1%	5.8%	2.4%	3.1%

Source: Internal Revenue Service (also available online from the Tax Foundation).

high-income Americans. (See Laffer curve analysis of Chapter 4.) In contrast, the incentive effects were much weaker in the lower tax brackets and, as a result, rate reductions led to approximately proportional reductions in revenues collected from low- and middle-income taxpayers. This combination of incentive effects shifts the share of taxes paid toward those with higher incomes, the pattern observed in Exhibit 4.

Second, both the standard deduction and personal exemption have been increased substantially during the last couple of decades. This means that Americans are now able to earn more income before they face any tax liability. In 2017, for example, almost 42 percent of those filing an income tax return either had zero tax liability or actually received funds from the IRS as the result of the **Earned Income Tax Credit**. This change in the structure of the personal income tax explains why people in the bottom half of income now pay such a small percentage of the personal income tax: 3.1 percent in 2017 compared to 10.4 percent in 1963.[5]

Earned Income Tax Credit
A provision of the tax code that provides a credit or rebate to people with low earnings (income from work activities). The credit is eventually phased out if the recipient's earnings increase.

ST01-5 INCOME LEVELS AND OVERALL TAX PAYMENTS

In addition to the personal income tax, the federal government also derives sizable revenues from payroll, corporate income, and excise taxes. How is the overall burden of federal taxes allocated among the various income groups? **Exhibit 5** presents Congressional Budget Office estimates for the average amount of federal taxes paid in 2016 according to income. On average, the top quintile (20 percent) of earners are estimated to pay 26.5 percent of their income in federal taxes. The average federal tax rate for the quintile with the next-highest level of income falls to 17.9 percent, and the average tax rate continues to fall as income declines. The average tax rate of the bottom quintile is 1.7 percent, less than one-fifteenth the average rate for the top quintile of earners. Clearly, the federal

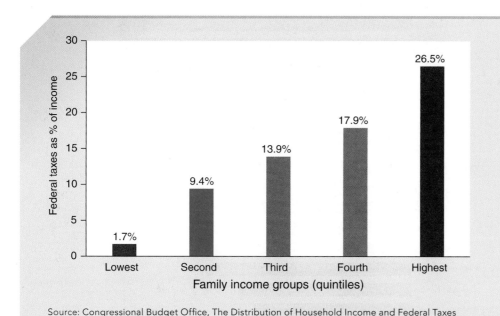

EXHIBIT 5

Total Federal Taxes as a Share of Income, 2016

Federal taxes are highly progressive. In 2016, federal taxes took 26.5 percent of the income generated by the top quintile (20 percent) of earners, compared to 13.9 percent from the middle-income quintile and 1.7 percent from the lowest quintile of earners.

Source: Congressional Budget Office, The Distribution of Household Income and Federal Taxes 2016 (http://www.cbo.gov/publication/55413). Total federal taxes include income, payroll, corporate income, and excise taxes.

---

[5]The data of Exhibit 4 consider only the tax liability of taxpayers. They do not reflect the payments from IRS to taxpayers as the result of the Earned Income Tax Credit, which was established in the mid-1980s. If these payments to taxpayers were taken into consideration, the net taxes paid by the bottom half of income recipients would have been less than 1 percent. Thus, the data of Exhibit 4 actually understate the reduction in the net share of taxes paid by the bottom half of income recipients during the last two decades.

tax system is highly progressive, meaning that it takes a larger share of the income of those with higher incomes than from those with lower income levels.

ST01-6 SIZE OF GOVERNMENT: A CROSS-COUNTRY COMPARISON

There is substantial variation in the size of government across countries. As **Exhibit 6** illustrates, the relative size of government in most other high-income industrial countries is greater than that of the United States. In 2017, government spending summed to more than 50 percent of the economies of France, Belgium, and Denmark, with Italy, Austria, Norway, and Greece not far behind. Government spending as a share of the economy in Japan and Australia was similar to that of the United States, about 36 percent. Interestingly, the size of government was substantially smaller in Singapore, Thailand, and Hong Kong—three Asian nations that have achieved rapid growth and substantial increases in living standards during the last four decades. It will be interesting to see if the size of government grows in Hong Kong now that mainland China has taken control of the island.

EXHIBIT 6

The Size of Governments—An International Comparison, 2017

The size of governments varies substantially across countries. In France, government spending sums to more than 55 percent of the economy, compared to 35.7 percent in the United States and roughly 20 percent or less in Hong Kong, Thailand, and Singapore.

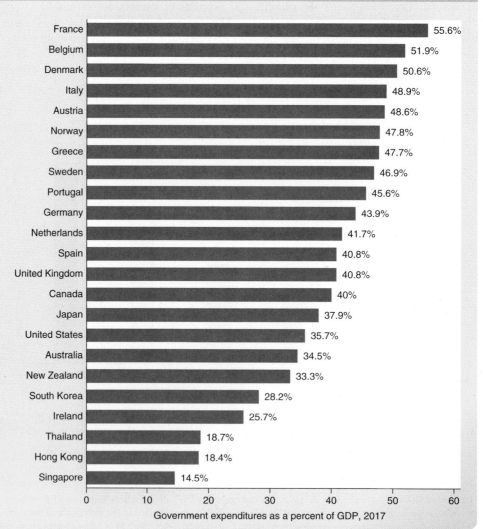

Country	Government expenditures as a percent of GDP, 2017
France	55.6%
Belgium	51.9%
Denmark	50.6%
Italy	48.9%
Austria	48.6%
Norway	47.8%
Greece	47.7%
Sweden	46.9%
Portugal	45.6%
Germany	43.9%
Netherlands	41.7%
Spain	40.8%
United Kingdom	40.8%
Canada	40%
Japan	37.9%
United States	35.7%
Australia	34.5%
New Zealand	33.3%
South Korea	28.2%
Ireland	25.7%
Thailand	18.7%
Hong Kong	18.4%
Singapore	14.5%

Government expenditures as a percent of GDP, 2017

Source: International Monetary Fund, World Economic Outlook Database, Government Finance Statistics series GF2 (2020).

ST01-7 HOW DOES THE SIZE OF GOVERNMENT AFFECT ECONOMIC GROWTH?

Throughout this text, we have analyzed how governments influence the efficiency of resource use and the growth of income. It is clear that a legal environment that protects people and their property and provides for the impartial enforcement of contracts is vitally important. So, too, is a monetary and regulatory environment that provides the foundation for the smooth operation of markets. As we discussed in Chapter 5, there are also a few goods—economists call them *public goods*—that may be difficult to provide through markets. National defense, roads, and flood-control projects provide examples. Because they generate joint benefits and it is difficult to limit their availability to paying customers, sometimes they can be provided more efficiently through government. But public goods are rare, and the market can often devise reasonably efficient methods of dealing with them without any government involvement. If resources are going to be allocated efficiently, government spending on provision of public goods will generally be only a small share of the economy.

As governments expand beyond these core functions, however, the beneficial effects wane and eventually become negative as government moves into areas ill suited for political action and in which the political process works poorly. Thus, expansion of government activities beyond a certain point will eventually exert a negative impact on the economy. Exhibit 7 illustrates the implications with regard to the expected relationship between the size of government and economic growth, *assuming that governments undertake activities based on their rate of return.* As the size of government, measured on the horizontal axis, expands from zero (complete anarchy), initially the growth rate of the economy—measured on the vertical axis—increases. The *A* to *B* range of the curve illustrates this situation. As government continues to grow as a share of the economy, expenditures are channeled into less-productive (and later counterproductive) activities, causing the rate of economic growth to diminish and eventually to decline. The range of the curve beyond *B* illustrates this point.[6] Thus, our analysis indicates that there is a set of activities and size

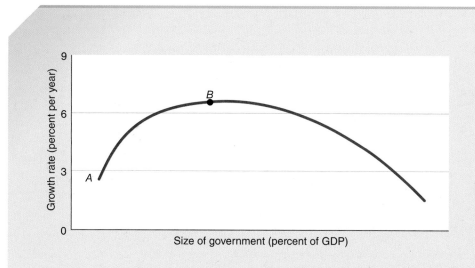

EXHIBIT 7

Economic Growth Curve and Government Size

If a government undertakes activities in the order of their productivity, its expenditures will promote economic growth (the growth rate will move from *A* to *B*). Additional expenditures, however, will eventually retard growth (the growth rate will move along the curve to the right of *B*).

---

[6]In the real world, governments may not undertake activities based on their rate of return and comparative advantage. Many governments that are small relative to the size of the economy fail to focus on the core activities that are likely to enhance economic growth. Thus, one would expect that the relationship between size of government and economic growth will be a loose one.

of government that will maximize economic growth. Expansion of government beyond (and outside of) these functions will retard growth.

How large is the growth-maximizing size of government? Do large governments actually retard economic growth? These are complex questions, but they have been addressed by several researchers. **Exhibit 8** sheds light on these issues. This exhibit presents data on the relationship between size of government (*x*-axis) and economic growth (*y*-axis) for the twenty-three long-standing members of the Organization for Economic Co-operation and Development (OECD). The exhibit contains five dots (observations) for each of the 23 countries—one for each of the five decades during the period 1960–2009. Thus, there are 115 total dots. Each dot represents a country's total government spending as a share of GDP *at the beginning of the decade* and its accompanying growth of real GDP *during that decade*. Government expenditures ranged from a low of about 15 percent of GDP in some countries to a high of more than 60 percent in others. As the plotted line in the exhibit shows, there is an observable negative relationship between size of government and long-term real GDP growth. Countries with higher levels of government spending grew less rapidly. The line drawn through the points of Exhibit 9 indicate that a 10-percentage-point increase in government expenditures as a share of GDP leads to approximately a 1-percentage-point reduction in economic growth.[7]

EXHIBIT 8

Government Spending and Economic Growth Among the Twenty-Three OECD Countries: 1960–2009

Here we show the relationship between size of government and the growth of real GDP for the 23 longtime OECD members during each decade since 1960. The data indicate that a 10 percent increase in government expenditures as a share of GDP reduces the annual rate of growth by approximately 1 percent. The data also imply that the size of government in these countries is beyond the range that maximizes economic growth.

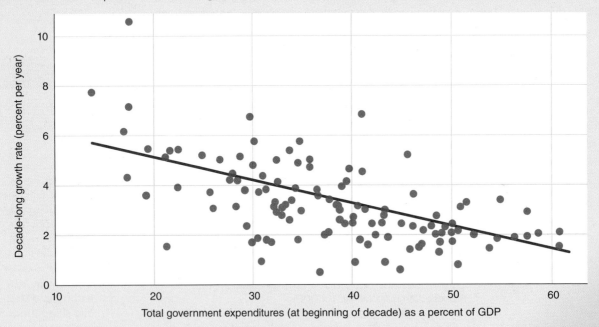

Source: OECD, OECD *Economic Outlook* (various issues), and the World Bank, *World Development Indicators* (various issues).

[7]For additional information on the relationship between size of government and growth, see James Gwartney, Robert Lawson, and Randall Holcombe, "The Scope of Government and the Wealth of Nations," *The Cato Journal* (Fall 1998): 163–90.

Time series data for specific countries have also been used to investigate the link between size of government and growth. Edgar Peden estimates that for the United States, the "maximum productivity growth occurs when government expenditures represent about 20% of GDP." Gerald Scully estimates that the growth-maximizing size of government (combined federal, state, and local) is between 21.5 percent and 22.9 percent of the economy. Although the methodology of these studies differs, they do have one thing in common: They indicate that in the ranges observed, high levels of government spending tend to retard economic growth.[8] They also indicate that the size and scope of most governments around the world are larger than the size that would maximize the income growth of their citizens. Moreover, the estimates imply that the recent expansion in the size of the government sector in the United States is likely to reduce the growth of income in the years immediately ahead.

ST01-8 EXPENDITURES, TAXES, DEBT FINANCE, AND DEMOCRACY

Exhibit 9 presents data on the percent of persons age 18 and older without a personal income tax liability. While roughly one-third of the population paid no income tax in 2000, this had risen sharply to almost half of the population by 2010. While many without an income tax liability are responsible for payroll taxes, the payroll tax is directed toward only two programs: Social Security and Medicare. Thus, payroll taxes do not contribute to the finance of government in other areas.

At the same time as the share of people paying no income tax has risen sharply, the share benefiting from government transfers has also been rising. As Exhibit 10 shows, the percent of families receiving transfers from at least one program has risen from 41.9 percent in 2000 to 52.6 percent in 2018. When income from government employment

---

EXHIBIT 9

Share of Population 18 and Older without a Personal Income Tax Liability, 2000–2017

The percent of the population age 18 and older without a personal income tax liability is shown here. In 2000, the share with no income tax liability was about one-third of the adult population. This rose to about half by 2010. In 2017, 41.8 percent of Americans did not have an income tax liability.

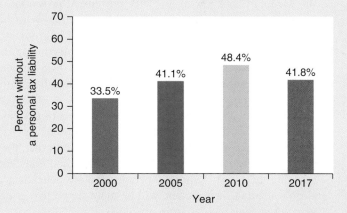

Source: Internal Revenue Service and U.S. Census Bureau. The number of persons without an income tax liability was derived by summing (1) the joint returns without a tax liability times two and (2) the number of individual returns without a tax liability. This figure was then divided by the population age 18 and older to derive the percentage of the 18 and older population without a tax liability.

---

[8]See Edgar Peden, "Productivity in the United States and Its Relationship to Government Activity: An Analysis of 57 Years, 1929–1986," *Public Choice* 69 (1991): 153–73; and Gerald Scully, *What Is the Optimal Size of Government in the United States?* (Dallas, TX: National Center for Policy Analysis, 1994).

EXHIBIT 10

Share of Families Deriving Income from Government, 2000–2018

More than half of American families derive income from transfer programs. The percent of families receiving transfers from at least one program rose from 41.9 percent in 2000 to 52.6 percent in 2018. When income from government employment is also included, 62.7 percent of

American families now derive income from the government, up from 54.5 percent in 2000. When only families with individuals younger than age 62 are included, the percentage receiving transfers is somewhat lower, but the pattern over the past two decades is the same.

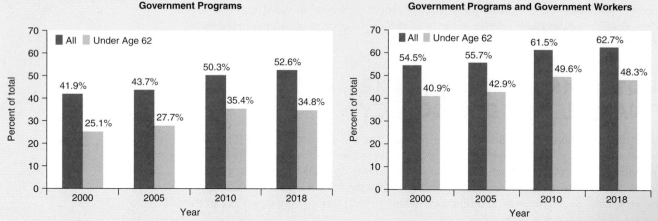

Source: These figures were derived from the Current Population Survey data. The following income transfers were included: Medicare, Medicaid, food stamps, unemployment compensation, school lunch program, Social Security, and welfare.

is included, 62.7 percent of families derived income from either transfer programs or government employment in 2018. If the people employed by businesses with government contracts and those receiving subsidies (for example, housing subsidies, the producers of ethanol, sugar and several other agricultural products, and wind and solar energy) were also included, the share of Americans heavily dependent on government would be even larger.

One might think that the large share of Americans receiving transfers is driven by the Medicare and Social Security retirement programs. In order to shed light on this issue, the share receiving transfers for families with only individuals younger than the age of 62 was derived. The pattern for this group was essentially the same as for all families. The percent of the younger family group that were recipients of transfer payments rose from 25.1 percent in 2000 to 34.8 percent in 2018. When government employees are included, almost half of the families with individuals younger than 62 derived income from the government.

What are the implications of these patterns of tax payments and government spending? People who are not paying taxes have little reason to resist increases in government spending because they are not paying for them. In fact, they have every incentive to pressure politicians for more government services and transfers because someone else will be covering their cost. Similarly, people who are dependent on government spending for a sizable share of their income will be more supportive of government spending than those who derive their income from private-sector activities.

Debt financing is also related to the observed pattern of taxing and spending. Borrowing makes it possible for politicians to provide voters with current benefits without having to impose a parallel visible cost in the form of higher taxes. This enables elected officials to increase the number of people dependent on government spending without having to increase current taxes.

To a large degree, the modern democratic political process has become a game in which politicians seek to use the fiscal powers of government to assemble a political majority. Is this a dangerous trend that may undermine democracy and lead to fiscal collapse? Eighteenth-century Scottish philosopher Alexander Tytler warned of this possibility:

A democracy cannot exist as a permanent form of government. It can only exist until the voters discover that they can vote themselves largesse from the public treasury. From that moment on, the majority always votes for the candidates promising the most benefits from the public treasury with the result that a democracy always collapses over loose fiscal policy.[9]

Is Tytler correct? Are the spending, taxing, and debt financing policies of the United States going to cause a dangerous fiscal crisis? We do not know the answer to this question, but there are troubling signs. Government spending as a share of GDP has increased substantially since 2000. Large budget deficits, even during good times, have pushed the federal debt to more than 100 percent of GDP. The huge expansion in federal debt during the COVID-19 pandemic has resulted in a national debt as a share of the economy that is now well above the level at the conclusion of World War II. Further, the retirement of the baby-boom generation and shortfall of revenues for Social Security and Medicare will continue to push the federal deficit upward in the decade immediately ahead. Interest rates are currently low, but they will rise in the future, and when they do, the burden of debt financing will increase sharply. Other countries, Greece most recently, have been caught in a debt trap. Actions could be taken to avoid a future crisis, but special interest politics and the myopic nature of the political process make them politically unpopular. We are in the midst of an interesting, though unattractive, experiment in political economy as the United States and other Western democracies face troubled fiscal waters in the years immediately ahead.

KEY POINTS

- During the first 125 years of U.S. history, federal expenditures per person were small and grew at a relatively slow rate. But the size and nature of government has changed dramatically during the past 100 years. Today, the real (adjusted for inflation) spending per person of the federal government is roughly 83 times the level of 1916.

- During the last six decades, the composition of federal spending has shifted away from national defense and toward spending on income transfers and health care.

- As the size of government has grown, taxes have increased. Taxes impose a burden on the economy over and above the revenue transferred to the government because of (1) the administration and compliance costs and (2) the deadweight losses that accompany taxation.

- Overall, the federal tax system of the United States is highly progressive. Taxes as a percentage of income are approximately 15 times greater for the top quintile (20 percent) of families than for the bottom quintile.

- The size of government of the United States is smaller than that of the major Western European countries but is larger than for a number of high-growth Asian economies.

- When governments focus on the core activities of providing (1) a legal and enforcement structure that protects people and their property from aggression by others and (2) a limited set of public goods, they promote economic growth. However, when governments grow beyond this size, expanding into activities for which they are ill suited, they deter growth.

- More than half of American families derive benefits from various transfer programs, while the share of the population paying federal income tax has declined substantially during the past two decades. The Social Security and Medicare programs are now running large deficits as the huge baby-boom generation moves into the retirement phase of life. Large budget deficits have already pushed the debt-to-GDP ratio to levels even higher than at the conclusion of World War II. Special interest politics and the shortsighted nature of political decision making make it difficult to control government spending and debt and to take the steps needed to avoid a fiscal crisis.

---

[9]Some attribute this statement to Lord Thomas Macaulay. The author cannot be verified with certainty. For additional information on this topic, see Loren Collins, "The Truth About Tytler" at www.lorencollins.net/tytler.html.

CRITICAL ANALYSIS QUESTIONS

1. *How do taxes influence the efficiency of resource use? How much does it cost for the government to raise an additional dollar (or $1 billion) of tax revenue?

2. During the past six decades, there has been a shift in the composition of the federal budget toward more spending on income transfers and health care and a smaller share for national defense. Does economics indicate that this change will help Americans achieve higher living standards? Discuss.

3. Because the structure of the personal income tax is progressive, a larger share of income is taxed at higher rates as real income increases. Therefore, economic growth automatically results in higher taxes unless offsetting legislative action is taken. Do you think this is an attractive feature of the current tax system? Why or why not?

4. Compared with the situation before 1981, the marginal tax rates imposed on individuals and families with high incomes are now lower. What was the top marginal personal income tax rate in 1980? What is the top rate now? Are you in favor of or opposed to the lower marginal rates? Why?

5. *As the result of changes during the last two decades, the bottom half of income recipients now pay little or no personal income tax. Rather than paying taxes, many of them now receive payments back from the IRS as the result of the Earned Income Tax Credit and Child Tax Credit programs. Do you think the increase in the number of people who pay no taxes will affect the efficiency of the political process? Why or why not?

6. How have the size and functions of government changed during the last two centuries? Did the framers of the U.S. Constitution seek to limit the size of the federal government? If so, how?

7. Can democracy survive if a majority of citizens pay little or nothing in taxes while benefiting directly from a higher level of government spending? Why or why not? Discuss.

*Asterisk denotes questions for which answers are given in Appendix B.

SPECIAL TOPIC 2

The Economics of Social Security

Over the next 30 years, the retirement of the baby-boom generation will pose new challenges for the Social Security program, the federal government, and the U.S. economy. —**Dan Crippen**[1]

The Social Security program in the United States is officially known as Old Age and Survivors Insurance (OASI). It is designed to provide the elderly with a flow of income during retirement.

This feature will examine the finances of Social Security as well as how it affects different types of people.

As you read this chapter, look for answers to the following questions:

- Why will the Social Security program confront problems in the near future?

- Will the Social Security Trust Fund make it easier to pay the promised benefits to future retirees?

- Does Social Security transfer income from the rich to the poor? How does it impact the economic status of blacks, Hispanics, and those with fewer years of life expectancy?

- Does the Social Security system need to be modernized?

[1]Dan Crippen, Statement of Congressional Budget Office Director, before the Special Committee on Aging, United States Senate, December 10, 2001.

ST02-1 THE FINANCING AND DETERMINATION OF BENEFITS OF SOCIAL SECURITY

In spite of its official title, Social Security is not based on principles of insurance. Private insurance and pension programs invest the current payments of customers in buildings, farms, or other real assets. Alternatively, they buy stocks and bonds that finance the development of real assets. These real assets generate income that allows the pension fund (or insurance company) to fulfill its future obligations to its customers.

Social Security does not follow this savings-and-investment model. Instead, it taxes current workers and uses the revenues to finance benefits for existing retirees. There is no buildup of productive assets that the federal government can use to fund the future benefits promised today's workers. When current workers retire, their promised Social Security benefits will have to come from taxes levied on future generations. *In essence, Social Security is an intergenerational income-transfer program.* The system is based on "pay as you go" rather than on the savings-and-investment principle.

The Social Security retirement program is financed by a flat-rate payroll tax of 10.6 percent applicable to employee earnings up to a cutoff level. In 2020, the earnings cutoff was $137,700. Thus, employees earning $137,700 or more paid $14,596 in Social Security taxes to finance the OASI retirement program.[2] The income cutoff is adjusted upward each year by the growth rate of nominal wages. Whereas the payroll tax is divided equally between employee and employer, it is clearly part of the employees' compensation package, and most economists believe that the burden of this tax falls primarily on the employee. The formula used to determine retirement benefits favors those with lower earnings during their working years. However, as we will discuss later, the redistributive effects toward those with lower incomes are more apparent than real.

When the program began in 1935, not many people lived past age 65, and the nation had lots of workers and few eligible retirees. As **Exhibit 1** illustrates, there were

---
[2]Additional payroll taxes are levied for the finance of disability programs (1.8 percent) and Medicare (2.9 percent). (*Note:* The earnings cutoff does not apply to the Medicare portion of the payroll tax.) Further, a Medicare income tax rate of 3.8 percent exists for income above $200,000 for singles and $250,000 for married couples.

EXHIBIT 1

Workers per Social Security Beneficiary

In 1950, there were 16.5 workers per Social Security beneficiary. By 2020, the figure had fallen to just 2.7. By 2035, there will be only 2.3 workers per retiree. As the worker/beneficiary ratio falls under a pay-as-you-go system, either taxes must be increased or benefits reduced (or both).

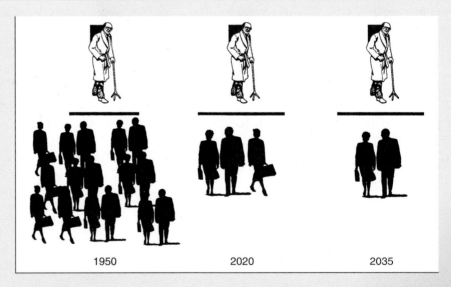

Source: *2019 Annual Report of the Board of Trustees of the Federal Old Age and Survivors Insurance and Disability Insurance Trust Funds* (Washington, DC: Government Printing Office, 2019), p. 60.

16.5 workers for every Social Security beneficiary in 1950. That ratio has declined sharply through the years. As a result, higher and higher taxes per worker have been required just to maintain a constant level of benefits. There are currently 2.7 workers per Social Security retiree. By 2035, however, that figure will decline to only 2.3.

When there were many workers per beneficiary, it was possible to provide retirees with generous benefits while maintaining a relatively low rate of taxation. Many of those who retired in the 1960s and 1970s received real benefits of three or four times the amount they paid into the system, far better than they could have done had they invested the funds privately. The era of high returns, however, is now over. The program has matured, and the number of workers per beneficiary has declined. Payroll taxes have risen greatly over the decades, and still higher taxes will be necessary merely to fund currently promised benefits.

Studies indicate that those now age 40 and younger can expect to earn a real rate of return of about 2 percent on their Social Security tax dollars, substantially less than what they could earn from personal investments. Thus, Social Security has been a good deal for current and past retirees. It is not, however, a very good deal for today's middle-aged and younger workers.

ST02-2 WHY IS SOCIAL SECURITY HEADED FOR PROBLEMS?

The flow of funds into and out of a pay-as-you-go retirement system is sensitive to demographic conditions. The Social Security system enjoyed a period of highly favorable demographics between 1990 and 2010. The U.S. birthrate was low during the Great Depression and World War II. As this relatively small generation moved into the retirement phase of life during 1990–2010, the number of Social Security beneficiaries grew slowly. At the same time, the large baby-boom generation born following World War II was working and pushing the revenues flowing into the system upward. Thus, the payments to Social Security recipients increased at a modest rate, while the tax revenues grew rapidly during the two decades following 1990.

However, as **Exhibit 2** shows, the situation is going to change dramatically in the years immediately ahead. The retirement of the large baby-boom generation, along with rising life expectancies, will lead to a rapid increase in senior citizens during the next fifteen years. The number of people age 65 years and older will soar from 54 million in 2019 to 78 million in 2035. As a result, the number of workers per Social Security retiree will fall from today's 2.7 to only 2.3 in 2035.

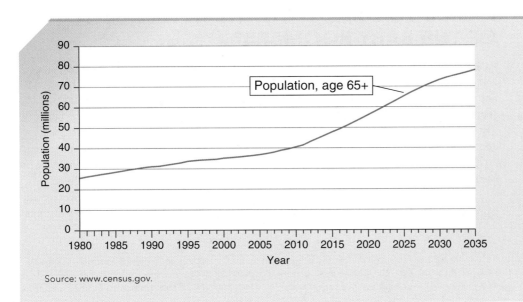

EXHIBIT 2

U.S. Population Age Sixty-Five and Over, 1980–2019, and Projections to 2035

As shown here, the growth rate of the elderly population will continue to accelerate rapidly as the baby-boomers move into the retirement phase of life as they have since 2010. This will place strong pressure on both the Social Security and Medicare programs.

Source: www.census.gov.

EXHIBIT 3

The Deficit between Payroll Tax Revenues and Benefit Expenditures

Given current payroll taxes and retirement benefit levels, the system will run larger and larger deficits in the years ahead.

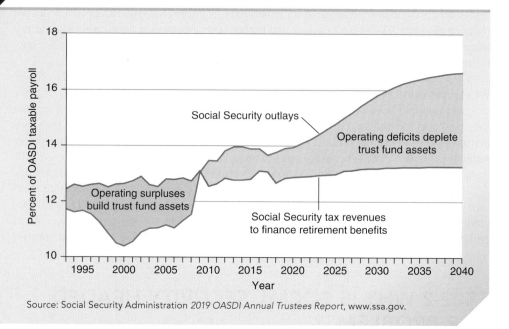

Source: Social Security Administration *2019 OASDI Annual Trustees Report*, www.ssa.gov.

Exhibit 3 illustrates the impact of these demographic changes on the pay-as-you-go Social Security system. Between 1984 and 2009, the funds flowing into the system (pushed up by the large baby-boom generation) exceeded the expenditures on benefits to retirees (pulled down by the small Great Depression/World War II generation). But the retirement of the baby-boomers that began in 2010 will push the future expenditures of the system upward at a rapid rate. The deficit of revenues from the payroll tax relative to retirement benefits will grow larger and larger as the number of beneficiaries relative to workers continues to grow in the decades ahead.

What happened to the 1984–2009 surpluses of Social Security receipts relative to expenditures? Congress spent the surpluses, and the U.S. Treasury issued a special type of IOU, nonmarketable bonds, into the Social Security Trust Fund (SSTF). The future deficits of the system will draw down these bonds and are projected to deplete them by 2035.

ST02-3 WILL THE TRUST FUND MAKE IT EASIER TO DEAL WITH THE RETIREMENT OF THE BABY-BOOMERS?

Perhaps surprising to some, the answer to this question is "No." Unlike the bonds, stocks, and physical assets of a private pension fund or insurance company, the SSTF bonds will not generate a stream of future income for the federal government. Congress has already spent the funds, so there is no "pot of money" set aside for the payment of future benefits. Instead, the trust fund bonds are an IOU from one government agency, the Treasury, to another, the Social Security Administration. The federal government is both the payee and recipient of the interest and principal represented by the SSTF bonds. *No matter how many bonds are in the trust fund, their net asset value to the federal government is zero!*

Thus, the number of IOUs in the trust fund is largely irrelevant.[3] The size of the trust fund could be doubled or tripled, but that would not give the federal government

---

[3]Of course, the SSTF bonds represent funds borrowed by the Treasury from the Social Security system. This increases the legitimacy of claims on these funds by future Social Security recipients. It also indicates that the trust fund is similar to what is called *budget authority*, which provides the legal permission for the government to spend funds on an item.

any additional funds for the payment of benefits. Correspondingly, the trust fund could be abolished and the government would not be relieved of any of its existing obligations or commitments. In order to redeem the bonds and thereby provide the Social Security system with funds to cover future deficits, the federal government will have to raise taxes, cut other expenditures, or borrow from the public. Neither the presence nor the absence of the trust fund will alter these options.

As we indicated in Chapter 6, politicians have an incentive both to spend on programs providing highly visible benefits and conceal the burden of taxes. The Social Security Trust Fund has helped them do this. During the last two decades, the government has spent the entire surplus and even borrowed beyond these amounts. Moreover, as Congress and several presidents were spending the surpluses on current programs, most political leaders projected the view that funds were being set aside for the future retirement of the baby-boomers. Given the structure of political incentives, this art of deception should not be surprising.

ST02-4 THE REAL PROBLEM CREATED BY THE CURRENT SYSTEM

The payroll tax revenues flowing into the Social Security system are now less than the benefits paid out to current retirees, and this deficit will become larger and larger in the future. Under current law, revenues will be sufficient to pay only about four-fifths of promised benefits by 2035, and less in later years. If benefits are reduced, then current beneficiaries and people near retirement will—quite understandably—feel that a commitment made to them has been broken.

There are only four ways to cover future shortfalls: (1) cut benefits, (2) increase taxes, (3) cut spending in other areas, or (4) borrow. None of these options is attractive, and, regardless of how the gap is filled, there is likely to be an adverse impact on the economy. Moreover, not even robust economic growth will eliminate the future shortfall. Retirement benefits are indexed to average growth in nominal wages. If higher productivity enables *real* (inflation-adjusted) wages to rise quickly, so will future Social Security benefits. For example, if inflation is zero and real wages start growing at 2 percent a year instead of their previous level of 1 percent, then the formula used to calculate Social Security benefits will also begin to push those benefits up more rapidly. Higher economic growth may temporarily improve Social Security's finances, but under current law the improvement will not last.[4]

ST02-5 DOES SOCIAL SECURITY HELP THE POOR?

Social Security has gained many supporters because of the belief that it redistributes wealth from the rich to the poor. The system is financed with a flat tax rate up to the cutoff limit, but the formula used to calculate benefits disproportionately favors workers with low lifetime earnings.[5] However, other aspects of the system tend to favor those with higher incomes. First, workers with more education and high earnings tend to live longer than those with

---

[4]See Garth Davis, "Faster Economic Growth Will Not Solve the Social Security Crisis," Heritage Center for Data Analysis (February 3, 2000).

[5]Retirement benefits are based on the best 35 years of earnings from a worker's career. Benefits are calculated by taking 90 percent of the first $11,520 a year of earnings, 32 percent of earnings between $11.520 and $69,420, and just 15 percent of earnings above $69,420 up to the earnings cutoff of $137,700. Therefore, as base earnings rise, benefits fall as a percentage of average earnings (and payroll taxes paid) during one's lifetime. For example, the retirement benefits of people with base annual earnings of $15,000 sum to 77 percent of their average working year earnings. In contrast, the retirement benefits of those with base earnings of $60,000 are only 45 percent of their average pre-retirement earnings. These figures are based on the formula for 2020. The figures are adjusted each year for the growth of nominal wages.

EXHIBIT 4

Mortality Rates by Level of Education

As shown here, the age-adjusted mortality rates are lower for those with more education. Because of the close link between education and income, people with higher incomes tend to live longer and, therefore, draw Social Security benefits for a lengthier time period than those with less education and income.

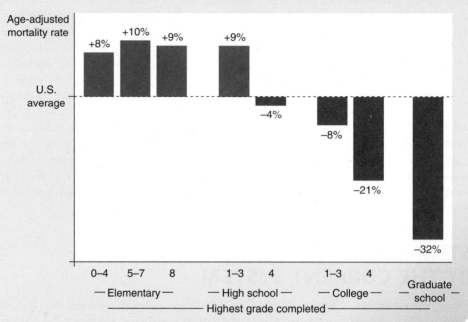

Source: Center for Data Analysis, Heritage Foundation.

less education and lower earnings. As **Exhibit 4** shows, the age-adjusted mortality rate of people with less than a high school education is 8 to 10 percent higher than the average for all Americans. As years of schooling increase, mortality rates fall. The age-adjusted mortality rate of college graduates is 21 percent below the average for all Americans, whereas the rate for people with advanced degrees is 32 percent below the average.[6] Given the strong correlation between education and earnings, the age-adjusted mortality figures indicate that, on average, Americans with higher earnings live longer than their counterparts with less education and lower earnings. As a result, high-wage workers will, on average, draw Social Security benefits for a longer period of time than will low-wage workers. Correspondingly, low-wage workers are far more likely to pay thousands of dollars in Social Security taxes and then die before, or soon after, becoming eligible for retirement benefits.

Second, low-wage workers generally begin full-time work at a younger age. Many work full time and pay Social Security taxes for years, while future high-wage workers are still in college and graduate school. Low-wage workers generally pay more into the system earlier and therefore forgo more interest than do high-wage workers.

Third, labor participation tends to fall as spousal earnings increase. As a result, couples with a high-wage worker are more likely to gain from Social Security's spousal benefit provision, which provides the nonworking spouse with benefits equal to 50 percent of those the working spouse receives.

Two studies taking these and other related factors into consideration suggest that Social Security may actually transfer wealth from low-wage to high-wage workers. A research project using data from the Social Security Administration and the Health and Retirement Study found that when Social Security benefits are assessed for family units rather than for individuals, the progressivity of the system disappears. Another study adjusted for differences in mortality rates, patterns of lifetime income, and other factors. It found that if a 2 percent real interest rate (discount rate) is used to evaluate the pattern

---

[6]An alternative approach is to compare life expectancies across education levels. For men at age 25, high school dropouts are expected to live 44 more years whereas their counterparts with a graduate degree are expected to live 60 extra years. For women at age 25, high school dropouts are expected to live 50 more years whereas those with a graduate degree are expected to live 62 additional years. See Brian L. Rostron et al., "Education Reporting and Classification on Death Certificates in the United States," *Vital and Health Statistics* Series 2, no. 151 (2010), pp. 1–16.

of taxes paid and benefits received, the redistributive effects of Social Security are essentially neutral. However, at a 4 percent real interest rate, Social Security actually favors higher-income households.[7]

ST02-6 SOCIAL SECURITY AND THE TREATMENT OF BLACKS AND WORKING MARRIED WOMEN

When Social Security was established in 1935, the population was growing rapidly, only a few Americans lived to age 65, and the labor-force participation rate of married women was very low. Social Security was designed for this world. But today's world is dramatically different. Several aspects of the system now seem outdated, arbitrary, and in some cases, unfair. Let's consider a couple of these factors.

ST02-6a SOCIAL SECURITY ADVERSELY AFFECTS BLACKS AND OTHER GROUPS WITH BELOW-AVERAGE LIFE EXPECTANCY

Currently, the average retiree reaching age 65 can expect to spend 18 years receiving Social Security benefits, after more than 40 years of paying into the system. But what about those who do not make it into their eighties or even to the normal retirement age of 65? Unlike private financial assets, Social Security benefits cannot be passed on to heirs. Thus, those who die before age 65 or soon thereafter receive little or nothing from their payroll tax payments.

Social Security was not set up to transfer income from some ethnic groups to others, but under its current structure it nonetheless does so. Because of the shorter life expectancy of blacks, the Social Security system adversely affects their economic welfare. Compared with whites and Hispanics, blacks are far more likely to pay a lifetime of payroll taxes and then die without receiving much in the way of benefits. Thus, the system works to their disadvantage. In contrast, Social Security is particularly favorable to Hispanics because of their above-average life expectancy and the progressive nature of the benefit formula. As a result, Hispanics derive a higher return than whites and substantially higher than blacks.[8]

Exhibit 5 presents the expected real returns for those born in 1975, according to gender, marital status, and ethnicity.[9] Single black males born in 1975 can expect to derive a real annual return of negative 1.3 percent on their Social Security tax payments, compared with returns of 0.2 percent for single white males and 1.6 percent for single Hispanic males.

[7]Alan L. Gustman, Thomas L. Steinmeier, and Nahid Tabatabai, "Redistribution Under the Social Security Benefit Formula at the Individual and Household Levels, 1992 and 2004," *Journal of Pension Economics and Finance*, January, 2013: 1–27; and Julia Lynn Coronado, Don Fullerton, and Thomas Glass, "Long Run Effects of Social Security Reform Proposals on Lifetime Progressivity," in Martin Feldstein and Jeffrey B. Liebman, eds., *The Distributional Aspects of Social Security and Social Security Reform* (Chicago: University of Chicago Press, 2002).

[8]For additional details on the redistributive effects of Social Security across ethnic groups, see William W. Beach and Gareth Davis, "More for Your Money: Improving Social Security's Rate of Return," in David C. John, ed., *Improving Retirement Security: A Handbook for Reformers* (Washington, DC: Heritage Foundation, 2000), 25–64; and Martin Feldstein and Jeffrey Liebman, "The Distributional Effects of an Investment-Based Social Security System," in Martin Feldstein and Jeffrey B. Liebman, eds., *The Distributional Aspects of Social Security and Social Security Reform* (Chicago: University of Chicago Press, 2002).

[9]It is common to calculate a rate of return on financial investments by comparing initial investments with the stream of projected future income (or benefits). Social Security is not like a regular financial investment because there is no accumulation of assets and no legal right to benefits. Nonetheless, a rate of return can be calculated by comparing the payroll taxes a worker pays with the future benefits he or she is promised. The rate-of-return figures of Exhibit 5 were derived in this manner. They assume that the current tax level and promised future benefits will be maintained. However, as we noted, projections indicate that current tax rates will cover only about four-fifths of promised benefits by 2035. Thus, higher taxes will be required to maintain the promised benefit levels. In turn, the higher taxes will lower rates of return. Therefore, the figures of Exhibit 5 probably overstate the rates of return for the various groups.

EXHIBIT 5

Rates of Return by Gender, Marital Status, and Ethnicity

The earnings of blacks are lower than whites, but blacks have a shorter life expectancy. The latter effect dominates, and therefore blacks derive a lower rate of return from Social Security than whites. In contrast, Hispanics have both lower earnings and a little longer life expectancy than whites. Thus, their returns from Social Security are higher than whites and substantially higher than blacks.

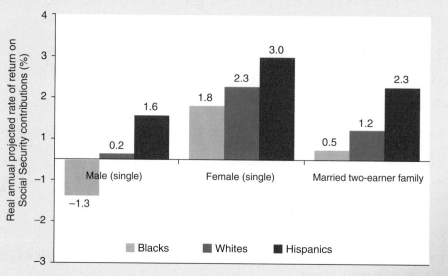

Source: Center for Data Analysis, Heritage Foundation

Similarly, a two-earner black couple born in 1975 can expect a real return of 0.5 percent, compared with returns of 1.2 percent and 2.3 percent for white and Hispanic couples born during the same year. A similar pattern exists when comparisons are made for those born in other years.

The Social Security retirement system also works to the disadvantage of those with life-shortening diseases. People with diabetes, heart disease, AIDS, and other diseases often spend decades paying 10.6 percent of their earnings into the system only to die with loved ones unable to receive benefits from the Social Security taxes they have paid. (People with life-shortening diseases may receive disability insurance, but if they die before retirement they collect nothing from their payments into the retirement system.)

ST02-6b DISCRIMINATION AGAINST MARRIED WOMEN IN THE WORKFORCE

When Social Security was established, relatively few married women worked outside the home. Therefore, individuals were permitted to receive benefits based on either their own earnings or 50 percent of the benefits earned by their spouse, whichever is greater. This provision imposes a heavy penalty on married women in the workforce. In the case of many working married women, the benefits based on the earnings of their spouses are approximately equal to, or in some cases greater than, benefits based on their own earnings. Thus, the payroll tax takes a big chunk of their earnings without providing them with any significant additional benefits.

ST02-7 IS THE STRUCTURE OF SOCIAL SECURITY SUITABLE FOR THE TWENTY-FIRST CENTURY?

When the number of retirees grows more rapidly than the number of workers, pay-as-you-go financing does not work well. The return retirees can expect from their tax payments into the system will be low. As we mentioned, today's typical worker can expect a return of only 2.0 percent from the taxes paid into the Social Security system. By way of comparison,

THE WIZARD OF ID

stock market investments have averaged a real return of approximately 7 percent annually for more than a century. Furthermore, when regular investments are made into a diverse holding of stocks, the variation in the return has been relatively low.[10] Mutual funds now make it feasible for even a small novice investor to invest in a diverse stock portfolio while still keeping administrative costs low. (See Special Topic 3, a feature on the stock market.)

As a result of the changing demographics, the Social Security and Medicare programs now confront huge **unfunded liabilities**, shortfalls between promised future benefits and the revenues that can be expected at current tax rates. The trustees of these two programs project that the unfunded liability of Social Security is $17 trillion, whereas that of Medicare is estimated to be $42 trillion.[11] The sum of these figures is more than three times the current size of the U.S. economy. Predictably, deteriorating financial conditions will lead politicians to look for ways of dealing with this situation. Thus, a combination of factors—low returns from Social Security, a structure that seems outdated, and deteriorating financial conditions—may virtually force Congress to seriously consider modifications in the future.

From an economic viewpoint, the most viable option would be some form of **personal retirement accounts (PRAs)** that would incorporate savings and investment into the financing of retirement. In varying degrees, several countries have already moved in this direction. Beginning in the early 1980s, Chile shifted to a retirement system based on saving and investing through PRAs rather than pay as you go. The Chilean plan was so successful that other Latin American countries, including Mexico, Bolivia, Columbia, and Peru, adopted similar plans in the 1990s. High-income countries have also moved in this direction. In 1986, the United Kingdom began allowing workers to channel 4.6 percentage points of their payroll tax into PRAs in exchange for acceptance of a lower level of benefits from the pay-as-you-go system. The PRA option is currently chosen by nearly three-fourths of British workers. Other countries that now permit at least some substitution of PRAs for payroll taxes and pay-as-you-go benefits include Netherlands, Australia, Sweden, Hungary, Poland, and Germany.

Ownership rights exert a powerful impact on incentives. Personal retirement accounts would provide workers with a property right to the funds contributed into their accounts. The funds paid into a PRA could be passed along to heirs. In contrast with higher taxes, payments into a personally owned investment account that would enhance one's retirement income would not exert a harmful impact on the incentive to work and earn. Furthermore, PRAs would encourage saving and investment, which would help to promote economic growth. They would also reduce the dependency of senior citizens on political officials.

Unfunded liability
A shortfall of tax revenues at current rates relative to promised benefits for a program. Without an increase in tax rates, the promised benefits cannot be funded fully.

Personal retirement account (PRA)
An account that is owned personally by an individual in his or her name. The funds in the account could be passed along to heirs.

---

[10]See Liqun Liu, Andrew J. Rettenmaier, and Zijun Wang, "Social Security and Stock Market Risk" (*NCPA Policy Report No. 244*, National Center for Policy Analysis, July 23, 2001).

[11]See *2019 Annual Report of the Boards of Trustees of the Federal Hospital Insurance and Federal Supplementary Medical Insurance Trust Fund*, https://www.cms.gov/Research-Statistics-Data-and-Systems/Statistics-Trends-and-Reports/ReportsTrustFunds/index.html.

There are numerous ways to structure personal retirement accounts. Several plans have already been put forth, and others may arise in the future.

Political debate about the structure of Social Security and how to plan for retirement will continue in the years ahead. This debate is particularly important for younger people because the way it is handled will exert a major impact on their future tax liability and the quality of their life during retirement.

KEY POINTS

- Social Security does not follow the saving-and-investment model. Most of the taxes paid into the system are used to finance the benefits of current retirees.

- As the baby-boomers began moving into the retirement phase of life in 2010, the Social Security system shifted from a surplus to a deficit. The deficits will persist and become larger and larger in the decades immediately ahead.

- The previous surpluses of the Social Security system were used to cover current expenditures, and the U.S. Treasury provided the Social Security Administration with nonmarketable bonds. Because the federal government is the payee and the recipient of these bonds, their net asset value to the federal government is zero. They will not reduce the level of future taxes needed to cover the Social Security deficits.

- The major problem resulting from the current pay-as-you-go system is that large tax increases, spending cuts, or additional borrowing will be required to cover the Social Security deficits following the retirement of the baby-boom generation.

- While the Social Security benefit formula favors those with lower lifetime earnings, low-wage workers have a lower life expectancy, begin work at a younger age, and gain less from the spousal benefit provisions of the current system. These latter factors largely, if not entirely, offset the egalitarian effects of the benefit formula.

- Because of their shorter life expectancy, blacks derive a lower rate of return from Social Security than whites and a substantially lower return than Hispanics.

- The demographics of the twenty-first century reduce the attractiveness of pay-as-you-go Social Security. Various plans that would place more emphasis on saving and investment are likely to be considered in the future.

CRITICAL ANALYSIS QUESTIONS

1. Is the Social Security system based on the same principles as private insurance? Why or why not?

2. *Why does the Social Security system face a crisis? Are there real assets in the Social Security Trust Fund that can be used to pay future benefits? Will the trust fund help to avert higher future taxes or benefit reductions or both when the baby-boomers retire? Why or why not?

3. Do you think workers should be permitted to invest all or part of their Social Security taxes into a personal retirement account? Why or why not?

4. How does Social Security affect the economic well-being of blacks relative to whites and Hispanics? Explain.

5. Does the current Social Security system promote income equality? Why or why not?

6. The Social Security payroll tax is split equally between the employee and the employer. Would it make any difference if the entire tax were imposed on employees? Would employees be helped if all the tax were imposed on employers? (Hint: You may want to consult the section on tax incidence in Chapter 4.)

*Asterisk denotes questions for which answers are given in Appendix B.

SPECIAL TOPIC 3

The Stock Market: Its Function, Performance, and Potential as an Investment Opportunity

Though the stock market functions as a voting machine in the short run, it acts as a weighing machine in the long run. —**Ben Graham**[1]

The market for corporate shares is called the *stock market*. The stock market makes it possible for investors, including small investors, to share in the profits (and the risks) of large businesses. About one-half of all households now own stock, either directly or indirectly through shares in an equity mutual fund. In recent years, changes in stock prices have often been front-page news. This feature will focus on the economic functions of the stock market and analyze its potential as an investment tool through which people can build their wealth.

As you read this special topic, look for answers to the following questions:

- What is the economic function of the stock market?

- What determines the price of a stock? Can experts forecast the future direction of stock prices?

- Historically, how does the return on stock investments compare with other alternatives? Is it risky to invest in a diverse bundle of stocks over a lengthy time period?

[1]As quoted by Warren Buffett in Carol Loomis, "Warren Buffett on the Stock Market," *Fortune* (December 10, 2001), 80–87.

ST03-1 THE DIFFERENCE BETWEEN STOCKS AND BONDS

Stock
Ownership shares of a corporation. Corporations raise funds by issuing stock ownership shares, which entitle the owners to a proportional share of the firm's profits. The stock owners are not liable for the debts of the corporation beyond their initial investment. However, there is no assurance that the owners will receive either their initial investment or any return in the future.

Bond
A promise to repay the principal (amount borrowed) plus interest at a specified time in the future. Organizations such as corporations and governments issue bonds as a method of borrowing from bondholders.

The two most common financial assets are stocks and bonds. Let's make sure you understand the nature of these two instruments. **Stocks** represent ownership of corporate businesses. Stock owners are entitled to the fraction of the firm's future revenues represented by their ownership shares. If the business generates attractive future revenues, the stockholders will gain. The gains of stockholders typically come in the form of either dividends (regular payments to owners) or appreciation in the value of the stock. But there is no assurance the business will be successful and earn income in the future. If unsuccessful, the value of the firm's stock will decline. Although the stockholders are not liable for the debts of the corporation, they may lose all of the funds used to purchase the stock. (Note: Equity is another term for stock.)

Bonds provide businesses, governments, and other organizations with a convenient way to borrow money. These organizations acquire funds from bond purchasers in exchange for the promise (and legal obligation) to pay interest and repay the entire principal (amount borrowed) at specified times in the future. In contrast with ownership of stock shares, owners of bonds can count on the principal and interest to be repaid as long as the organization issuing the bond is solvent.

ST03-2 THE ECONOMIC FUNCTIONS OF THE STOCK MARKET

The stock market performs several important functions in a modern economy. Let's consider three of the most important.

1. The stock market provides investors, including those who are not interested in participating directly in the operation of the firm, with an opportunity to own a fractional share of the firm's future profits. As a firm earns profits, its shareholders may gain as the result of both dividend payments and increases in the market value of the stock. Ownership of stock is risky. There is no guarantee that any firm will be profitable in the future. But the shareholders' potential losses are limited to the amount of their initial investment. Beyond this point, shareholders are not responsible for the debts of the corporations that they own.

2. New stock issues are often an excellent way for firms to obtain funds for growth and product development. Essentially, there are three ways for a firm to obtain additional financing. It can use retained earnings (profits earned but not paid out to stockholders), it can borrow money, or it can sell stock. When borrowing, the firm promises to repay the lender a specific amount, including principal and interest. Conversely, new stock issues provide the firm with additional financing, and the owner of the stock acquires an ownership right to a fraction of the future revenues generated by the firm.

Primary market
The market in which financial institutions aid in the sale of new securities.

Secondary market
The market in which financial institutions aid in the buying and selling of existing securities.

Newly issued stocks are sold to the public through specialized firms. A firm that issues new stock sells it in the **primary market**. When news reports tell us about how stock prices are changing, they are referring to **secondary markets**, in which previously issued stocks are traded. Secondary markets make it easy to buy and sell listed stock. This is important to the primary market. The initial buyers want to know that their stock will be easy to sell later. Entry is more attractive when exit will be easy. This will help the corporation issuing new stock to sell it for a higher price.

A stock exchange is a secondary market. It is a place where stockbrokers come to arrange trades for buyers and sellers. The largest and best-known stock market is the New York Stock Exchange, in which more than 2,800 stocks are traded. There are other such markets in the United States, as well as in London, Tokyo, Hong Kong, and other trading centers around the world.

3. Stock prices provide information about the quality of business decisions. Changing stock prices reward good decisions and penalize bad ones. It pays for a stockholder, especially a large one, to be alert to whether the firm's decisions are good or bad. Those who spot a corporation's problems early can sell part or all of their stock in that firm before others notice and lower the price by selling their own stock. Similarly, those who first notice decisions that will be profitable can gain by increasing their holdings of the stock. Stockholder alertness benefits the corporation, too. The firm's board of directors can utilize the price changes resulting from investor vigilance to reward good management decisions. They often do so by tying the compensation of the top corporate officers to stock performance. How? Rather than paying these officers entirely in the form of salaries, a board of directors can integrate **stock options** into the compensation package of top executives. On the one hand, when good decisions drive the stock price up, the executives' options will be very valuable. On the other hand, if bad decisions cause the stock price to fall, then the options will have little or no value.

Stock options
The option to buy a specified number of shares of the firm's stock at a designated price. The designated price is generally set so that the options will be quite valuable if the firm's shares increase in price but of little value if their price falls. Thus, when used to compensate top managers, stock options provide a strong incentive to follow policies that will increase the value of the firm.

ST03-3 STOCK MARKET PERFORMANCE: THE HISTORICAL RECORD

Investors in American stocks have done exceedingly well. Furthermore, this has been true over a lengthy period of time. During the last two centuries, after adjustment for inflation, corporate stocks have yielded an average real return of approximately 7 percent per year, compared with a real return of about 3 percent for bonds. The historic returns derived from savings accounts and money market mutual funds are even lower. A 7 percent real return may not sound particularly good, but when it is compounded, it means that the real value of your investment will double every ten years. In contrast, it will take 23 years to double your money at a 3 percent interest return.[2]

The Standard and Poor's 500 Index (S&P 500) is one measure of the performance of the broad stock market. This index factors in the value of dividends as if they were reinvested in the market. Thus, it provides a measure of the rate of return received by investors in the form of both dividends and changes in share prices. **Exhibit 1** presents data on the real rate of return earned by stockholders each year since 1950 as measured by the changes in the S&P 500 during the year. The compound annual nominal rate of return of the S&P 500 was 10.8 percent during the 70-year period. Even after adjustment for inflation, the real compound annual return was 7.4 percent over this lengthy time period. The returns during the 1980s and 1990s were even higher, but the returns since 2000 have been lower than the historic average. During 2008 alone investors experienced a negative 37 percent return.

Exhibit 1 highlights one of the risks that accompanies the ownership of stock: The returns and therefore the value of the stock can be quite volatile. The broad stock market, as measured by the S&P 500, provided double-digit returns during 43 of the 70 years between 1950 and 2019, but the returns were negative during 15 of those years. Stock market investors can never be sure what return they will earn or what the value of their stock holdings will be at a specified time in the future.

But this volatility is a big reason that stocks yield a significantly higher return than savings accounts, money market certificates, and corporate or government bonds, all of which guarantee you a given nominal return in the future. Because most people value the additional certainty in the yields that bonds and savings accounts provide over stocks, the average return on stocks has to be higher to attract investors away from financial assets with more predictable returns.

As large reductions in stock prices like those of 2008 illustrate, stocks are risky. However, historically stock prices have rebounded and yielded attractive returns when held

---

[2]You can approximate the number of years it will take to double your funds at alternative interest rates by simply dividing the yield into 70. This is sometimes referred to as the *rule of 70.*

EXHIBIT 1

Annual Return for Stocks, 1950–2019

During the past 70 years, the broad S&P 500 Index indicates that stock investors earned a 10.8 percent compound annual rate of return. Double-digit returns were earned in 43 of the 70 years, whereas returns were negative during only 15 of the years.

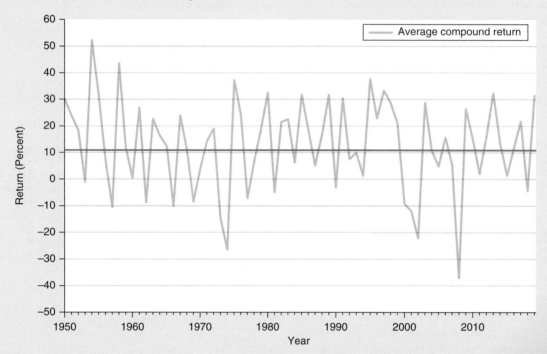

Source: Global Financial Data, http://www.globalfindata.com; and Standard & Poor's, www.standardandpoors.com.

over a lengthy time frame. Even if one would have started a regular monthly investment program at just about the worst possible time in the history of the U.S. stock market—just before the crash of 1929 and the Great Depression of the 1930s in which the value of stocks declined by almost 90 percent—one would still have earned a better return within four years than a person who had invested in U.S. Treasury bills and would have ended up with a 13 percent nominal return (or an 11 percent real return) over the next 30 years.

ST03-4 THE INTEREST RATE, THE VALUE OF FUTURE INCOME, AND STOCK PRICES

The present value of the firm's expected future net earnings (profit) underlies today's price of a firm's stock. What those future profits are worth to an investor today depends on three things: (1) the expected size of future net earnings, (2) when these earnings will be achieved, and (3) how much the investor discounts the future income. The last depends on the interest rate. As we noted in an earlier chapter, the present-value procedure can be used to determine the current value of any future income (or cost) stream. If D represents dividends (and gains from a higher stock price) earned in various years in the future (indicated by the subscripts) and i represents the discount or interest rate, the present value of the future income stream is:

$$PV = \frac{D_1}{(1 + i)} + \frac{D_2}{(1 + i)^2} + \cdots + \frac{D_3}{(1 + i)^3}$$

For a specific annual income stream in perpetuity, the present value is simply equal to R/i, where R is the annual revenue stream and i is the interest rate. Thus, for example, when the interest rate is 12.5 percent, the discounted value of $10 of future income to be received each year in perpetuity is $80 ($10 divided by 0.125), eight times the stream of earnings. But when the interest rate is 5 percent, the discounted value of this same income stream is $200 ($10 divided by 0.05), or 20 times the stream of earnings. Therefore, if the $10 represented the expected future income stream from a share of stock, the present value of the income stream would be higher when the interest rate was lower. Other things being constant, lower interest rates will increase the value of future income and thereby increase the market value of stocks.

As the present value formula indicates, an increase in future net earnings that the asset is expected to generate will increase the current market value of the asset. On the other hand, higher interest rates will reduce the present value of the future income and therefore reduce the market value of the asset generating the income stream. Lower interest rates will exert the opposite impact. Thus, the market value of an asset will be directly related to the expected future net income stream generated by the asset and inversely related to the interest rate.

Exhibit 2 presents data for the nominal interest rates on ten-year U.S. Treasury bonds since 1900. Note that nominal interest rates were particularly high in the late 1970s and early 1980s. On the other hand, interest rates were low—less than 4 percent during 1900–1911, 1925–1958, and 2008–2019. In fact, the nominal interest rate has been less than 3 percent throughout 2012–2019.

How can you determine whether stock prices are high or low? The present value formula indicates that the price of a stock (or group of stocks) will depend on both the interest rate and the expected future earnings of the stock. The price/earnings ratio for a stock

---

EXHIBIT 2

Long-Term Government Bond Rate, 1900–2019

The nominal interest rate on the ten-year Treasury bond is shown here. Note that the rate rose gradually during the two decades following World War II and increased still more rapidly during the 1970s and early 1980s. Since the early 1980s, it has trended downward and declined to less than 3 percent during 2012–2019. What is the expected impact of the recent low interest rates on stock prices? Is the data of Exhibit 1 for 2012–2019 consistent with this view?

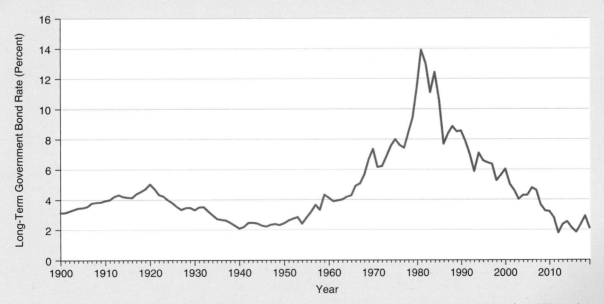

Source: http://www.econ.yale.edu/~shiller/data.htm. The interest rate is the ten-year Treasury bond rate starting in 1953. Before 1953, it is the government bond yield from Sidney Homer and Richard Sylla, *A History of Interest Rates*, 4th Edition (Hoboken, NJ: Wiley, 2005).

provides some information, but the ratio of price to current earnings is often a misleading indicator because of the fluctuations in corporate earnings over the business cycle. Corporate earnings generally fall sharply during a recession, and this will push the price/earnings ratio upward, making it look like stocks are really expensive. In turn, corporate earnings generally increase substantially during an economic boom. This will reduce the price/earnings ratio, making it appear that stocks are cheap. Because of the fluctuations in corporate earnings over the business cycle, the current price/earnings ratio is often misleading. In many cases, it provides investors with precisely the wrong signal. Therefore, instead of focusing on the current price/earnings ratio, it makes sense to focus on the relationship between the stock price and earnings over a more lengthy time frame such as a decade.

This is precisely what Robert Shiller, the 2013 Nobel Prize winner, has done. Shiller's methodology averages the inflation-adjusted earnings figures over a ten-year period to minimize the distortions resulting from both business cycle and inflation effects. **Exhibit 3** presents Shiller's cyclically adjusted price/earnings (CAPE) ratio for the S&P 500 for 1900–2019. This ratio is a weighted average of the current stock price divided by the ten-year average of earnings adjusted for inflation of the 500 stocks in the index. Other things constant, when this ratio is high, it indicates that stocks are relatively expensive. In contrast, when the ratio is low, it signals that stocks are relatively cheap.

As Exhibit 3 shows, the cyclically adjusted price/earnings ratio indicated that stock prices were exceedingly high in the late 1920s, late 1960s, and late 1990s. Interestingly, each of these time intervals was followed by an extended period of declining stock values and poor stock market performance. In contrast, the CAPE ratio indicated that stocks were relatively cheap during 1918–1923, 1932, 1942–1944, and 1978–1984. Each of these periods was followed by a substantial move upward in stock prices.

EXHIBIT 3

Cyclically Adjusted Price/Earnings Ratio, 1900–2019

The cyclically adjusted price/earnings (CAPE) for the S&P 500 is shown here. This ratio is the stock price divided by the ten-year average of earnings adjusted for inflation. It is an indicator of whether stock prices are high or low. Note that the ratio signaled that stock prices were exceedingly high in the late 1920s, late 1960s, and late 1990s. Each of these periods was followed by poor stock market performance. Similarly, the CAPE ratio indicated that stocks were relatively cheap during 1918–1923, 1932, 1942–1944, and 1978–1984. Each of these periods was followed by a substantial upward move in stock prices.

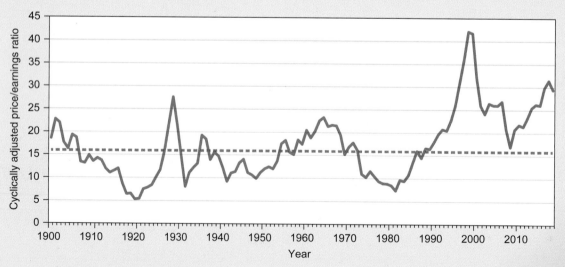

Source: http://www.econ.yale.edu/~shiller/data.htm.

ST03-5 THE RANDOM WALK THEORY OF THE STOCK MARKET

Most economists adhere to the **random walk theory** of stock prices. According to this theory, current stock prices already reflect all available information that is known or can be predicted with any degree of accuracy, including information about the future state of corporate earnings, interest rates, the health of the economy, and other factors that influence stock prices. In other words, current stock prices will already reflect the best information currently available. In the future, the direction of stock prices will be driven by surprise occurrences—things that differ from what people are currently anticipating. By their very nature, these factors are unpredictable. If they were predictable, they would already be reflected in current stock prices.

> **Random walk theory**
> The theory that current stock prices already reflect known information about the future. Therefore, the future movement of stock prices will be determined by surprise occurrences. This will cause them to change in a random fashion.

The random walk theory applies to the price of a specific stock as well as to the market as a whole. The prices of specific stocks will reflect their future earnings prospects. The stock prices of firms with attractive future profit potential will be high relative to their current earnings. Consequently, their current prices will already reflect their attractive future earnings prospects. The opposite will be true for firms with poor future prospects. Although numerous factors affect the future price of any specific stock, changes in the current price will be driven by changes that differ from current expectations. Thus, because the future prices of both specific stocks and the market as a whole are driven by unexpected and unpredictable factors, no one can consistently forecast their future path with any degree of accuracy.

As Exhibit 3 shows, the cyclically adjusted price/earnings ratio for the S&P 500 has been above 30 since mid-year 2017. Compared to historic levels, the CAPE ratio was exceedingly high in early 2020. Does this mean that stock prices will soon plunge to substantially lower levels? Some analysts fear that this will be the case, and the high CAPE ratio provides reason for caution. But, do not forget that low interest rates will result in higher asset prices, including the prices of stocks. During the past decade, the share of population in high-income developed countries age 50 to 75 years has increased relative to the share under age 50. Because the expanding age grouping tends to be savers and the contracting group borrowers, these changes are increasing the supply of loanable funds relative to the demand, thereby placing downward pressure on interest rates.[3] This demographic factor is expected to continue for at least another decade. If the low interest rates continue in the future, stock prices (and the CAPE ratio) may remain high relative to their expected earnings in the future. However, demographics are not the only factor influencing interest rates. If nominal interest rates rise in the future, perhaps as the result of monetary policy, stock prices are likely to fall from their lofty 2020 levels. But no one can be certain about the future direction of interest rates. Therefore, as the random walk theory indicates, no one will be able to forecast the future direction of stock prices with any degree of certainty.

ST03-6 HOW THE ORDINARY INVESTOR CAN BEAT THE EXPERTS

Historically, ordinary Americans have often refrained from investing in the stock market because of the volatility of stock prices. The value of any specific stock can rise or fall by a huge amount within a relatively short time period. But the risk accompanying these movements can be reduced by holding a diverse **portfolio**, a collection of stocks characterized by relatively small holdings of a large number of companies in different markets and industries. **Equity mutual funds** make this possible. They provide the ordinary investor with a low-cost method of owning a diverse bundle of stocks. An equity mutual fund is a corporation

> **Portfolio**
> All the stocks, bonds, or other securities held by an individual or corporation for investment purposes.
>
> **Equity mutual fund**
> A corporation that pools the funds of investors, including small investors, and uses them to purchase a bundle of stocks.

---

[3]For a detailed analysis of the impact of demographic changes on interest rates, see Michael A. Walker, "Why Are Interest Rates So Low? A Framework for Modeling Current Global Financial Developments," Fraser Institute Report, February 2016, https://www.fraserinstitute.org/sites/default/files/why-are-interest-rates-so-low.pdf.

that buys and holds shares of stock in many firms. This diversification puts the law of large numbers to work for you. Whereas some of the investments in a diversified portfolio will do poorly, others will do extremely well. The performance of the latter will offset that of the former, and the rate of return will converge toward the average. Remember, the average real return of equities has been substantially higher than for bonds, savings accounts, and other readily accessible methods of saving.

A second source of risk facing the stock market investor is the possibility that nearly all stocks in the market can rise or fall together when expectations about the entire economy change. This has happened on several occasions. For example, on October 19, 1987, the stocks listed in the Dow Jones Industrial Average lost more than 22 percent of their value in just one trading day. The high-tech stocks listed on the NASDAQ exchange lost about 70 percent of their value during 2000 and 2001; and most recently the S&P 500 lost about 57 percent of its value between October 2007 and March 2009. However, the risks accompanying such short-term movements can be substantially reduced if an investor either continually adds to or holds a diverse portfolio of stocks over a lengthy period of time, say, 30 or 35 years.

Exhibit 4 illustrates this point. This exhibit shows the highest and lowest real returns (the returns adjusted for inflation) earned from stock market investments for periods of varying lengths between the years 1871 and 2019. The exhibit assumes that the investor paid a fixed amount annually into a mutual fund that mirrored the S&P 500, a basket of stocks thought to represent the market as a whole. Clearly, huge swings are possible when stocks are held for only a short time period. During the 1871–2019 period, the single-year returns of the S&P 500 ranged from 47.2 percent to −40.8 percent. Even over a five-year period, the compound annual returns ranged from 29.8 percent to −16.7 percent. Note that the "best returns"

EXHIBIT 4

The Risk of Holding Stocks Is Lower When Held for a Lengthy Time Period

This exhibit shows the best and the worst annualized real performance for each investment period from 1871 to 2019. It shows that there is less risk of a low or negative return when an investment in a portfolio of stocks (S&P 500) is held for a longer period of time.

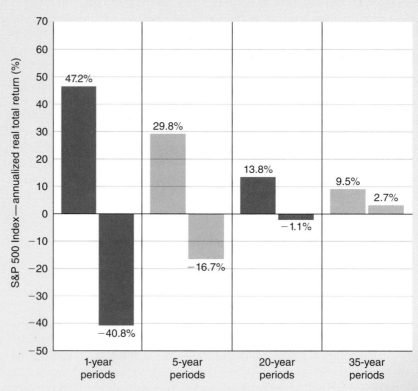

Source: Liqun Liu, Andrew J. Rettenmaier, and Zijun Wang, "Social Security and Market Risk," National Center for Policy Analysis Working Paper Number 244 (July 2001). The returns are based on the assumption that an individual invests a fixed amount for each year in the investment period. Data updated through 2019.

and "worst returns" converged as the length of the investment period increased. When a 35-year period was considered, the compound annual return for the best 35 years between 1871 and 2019 was 9.5 percent, compared with 2.7 percent for the worst 35 years.[4] Thus, the annual real return of stocks during the worst-case scenario was about the same as the real return for bonds. Furthermore, the annual real rate of return from the stock investments during the period was 7 percent—more than twice the comparable rate for bonds.

The bottom line is this: When held over a lengthy period, a diverse portfolio of stocks has yielded a high rate of return, and the variation in that return has been low. Thus, for the long-term investor, such as a person saving for his or her retirement years, a diverse portfolio of stocks is not particularly risky.

Are stocks riskier than bonds? If held for only a short time—five years, for example—stocks are riskier. However, when held over lengthy periods, such as 20 or 30 years, historically the rate of return on stocks has been both higher and less variable than that of bonds. What does this imply for people in their twenties and thirties who are saving for their retirement? Where should they put their funds?

ST03-7 THE ADVANTAGES OF INDEXED MUTUAL FUNDS

When purchasing a mutual fund, the investor can choose either a managed or an indexed fund. A **managed equity mutual fund** is one in which an "expert," generally supported by a research staff, tries to pick and choose the stock holdings of the fund in a manner that will maximize its rate of return. In contrast, an **indexed equity mutual fund** merely holds stocks in the same proportion as they exist in a broad stock market index like the S&P 500 or the Dow Jones Industrials.

In the case of indexed funds, neither comprehensive research nor extensive stock trading is needed because the fund merely seeks to mirror the index and earn the rate of return of the broad market that it represents. Thus, because they do not spend much on either research or stock trading, the operating costs of indexed funds are substantially lower than they are for managed funds. Therefore, they are able to charge lower fees, which means that a larger share of the investor's money flows directly into the purchase of stock.

The average rate of return yielded by a broad indexed fund beats the return of almost all managed mutual funds when comparisons are made over periods of time such as a decade. This is not surprising because, as the random walk theory indicates, not even the experts will be able to forecast consistently the future direction of stock prices with any degree of accuracy. Over the typical ten-year period, the S&P 500 has yielded a higher return than 85 percent of actively managed funds. And over 20-year periods, mutual funds indexed to the S&P 500 have generally outperformed about 98 percent of actively managed funds.[5] Thus, the odds are very low, about 1 in 50, that you or anyone else will be able to select an actively managed fund that will do better than the market average *over the long run*.

ST03-7a SHOULD YOU INVEST IN A FUND BECAUSE OF ITS PAST PERFORMANCE?

People marketing mutual funds often encourage customers to invest in mutual funds that have yielded high rates of return in the past. This sounds like a good strategy, but history

Managed equity mutual fund
An equity mutual fund that has a portfolio manager who decides what stocks will be held in the fund and when they will be bought or sold. A research staff generally provides support for the fund manager.

Indexed equity mutual fund
An equity mutual fund that holds a portfolio of stocks that matches their share (or weight) in a broad stock market index such as the S&P 500. The overhead of these funds is usually quite low because their expenses on stock trading and research are low.

---

[4]Based on Liqun Liu, Andrew J. Rettenmaier, and Zijun Wang, "Social Security and Market Risk" (Working Paper Number 244, National Center for Policy Analysis, Washington, DC, July 2001). Data updated through 2019.

[5]See Jeremy J. Siegel, *Stocks for the Long Run*, 3rd ed. (New York: McGraw-Hill, 2002), 342–43.

indicates that it is not. Mutual funds with outstanding records over a 5- or 10-year period often perform poorly in the future. The top 20 managed equity funds of the 1990s outperformed the S&P 500 by 3.9 percent per year over the course of the decade. But if investors entering the market in 2000 thought they would beat the market by choosing the "hot" funds of the 1990s, they would have been disappointed. The top 20 funds of the 1990s underperformed the S&P 500 by 1.3 percent per year during the 2000s.

Why is past performance such an unreliable indicator? Two factors provide insight on the answer to this question. First, some of the mutual funds with above-average returns during a period were merely lucky. After all, if you flip a coin 100 times, you will not always get 50 heads and 50 tails. Sometimes, the coin will come up heads maybe 60 times out of 100. But this does not mean you can expect 60 heads during the next sequence of 100. So it is with stock market mutual funds. Given that there are a large number of funds, some of them will have above-average performance for a time period. But this does not mean that the above-average performance can be expected in the future.

Second, a strategy that works well in one environment, inflationary conditions, for example, is often disastrous when conditions change. For example, mutual funds with substantial holdings of gold-mining companies did exceedingly well during the inflationary 1970s. But their performance was disastrous during the 1980s and 1990s as the inflation was brought under control. Similarly, some mutual funds that performed well during the bull market of the 1990s were among the worst performers during the bear market that began in 2000.

What is the most important takeaway from this analysis? Virtually none of the experts are able to "beat the market average" consistently over lengthy time periods and changing market conditions. Regular contributions into an indexed equity mutual fund will provide you with attractive returns on long-term investments because broad market indexes such as the S&P 500 will outperform the "expert" stock pickers in the long run. This is valuable information and you are unlikely to hear it from brokerage firms and other experts trying to sell their services to you. But knowing this will make you a smarter investor.

KEY POINTS

- The stock market makes it possible for investors without either specialized business skills or the time to become involved in the operation of a business firm to share in the risks and opportunities that accompany the ownership of corporate businesses.

- During the last two centuries, after adjustment for inflation, corporate stocks have yielded a real return of approximately 7 percent per year, compared with a real return of about 3 percent for bonds and even lower yields for savings accounts and money market mutual funds.

- The present value of an asset such as shares of a stock will reflect the expected future stream of income generated by the asset discounted by the interest rate. As interest rates decline, this discounted value will rise. This explains why stock prices (a) are highly sensitive to a change in the interest rate and (b) generally move in the opposite direction of the interest rate change.

- Most economists adhere to the random walk theory of stock prices. According to this theory, current stock prices already reflect all information about factors influencing stock prices that is known or can be forecast with any degree of accuracy. Thus, the future direction of stock prices will be driven by surprise occurrences and, as a result, no one will be able to forecast future stock prices with any degree of accuracy.

- Buying and selling individual stocks without specialized knowledge for a quick profit is very risky. But regular investment into a diverse portfolio of unrelated stocks over a lengthy period of time greatly reduces the risk of stock ownership.

- An equity mutual fund that is tied to a broad stock market index like the S&P 500 provides an attractive method for long-term investors to obtain relatively high yields with minimal risk. Indexed mutual funds have substantially lower operating costs than managed funds because they engage in less trading and have no need for either a market expert or research staff.

CRITICAL ANALYSIS QUESTIONS

1. *A friend just inherited $50,000. She informs you of her investment plans and asks for your advice. "I want to put it into the stock market and use it for my retirement in 30 years. What do you think is the best plan that will provide high returns at a relatively low risk?" What answer would you give? Explain.

2. Suppose that more expansionary monetary policy leads to inflation and higher nominal interest rates. How is this likely to affect the value of stocks? Explain.

3. *Alphabet (Google) stock rose from $208 at year-end 2005 to $1,337 per share at year-end 2018. Google has made sizable profits but never paid a dividend. Why were people willing to pay such a high price knowing that they might not get dividends for many years?

4. If an investment adviser gives you some hot new stock tip, is it likely to be a "sure thing"? Why or why not? If you have a stockbroker and purchase the stocks promoted by the broker, are you likely to earn a high return on your stock investments? Why or why not?

5. *Nominal interest rates were historically low during 2010–2020, and they trended slightly downward. What impact did the low and declining interest rates have on stock prices during this period? Why?

6. What is an indexed equity mutual fund? What is a managed equity mutual fund? How will the administrative costs of the two differ?

7. What is the random walk theory of stock prices? What does it indicate about the ability of "experts" to forecast accurately the future direction of stock prices?

8. Are stocks a risky investment? How can one reduce the risk accompanying stock market investments?

*Asterisk denotes questions for which answers are given in Appendix B.

Keynes and Hayek: Contrasting Views on Sound Economics and the Role of Government

We've been going back and forth for a century

[Keynes] I want to steer markets,

[Hayek] I want them set free

—Chorus from Keynes–Hayek video[1]

John Maynard Keynes and Friedrich August Hayek are two of the most important economists of the twentieth century. Moreover, their scholarly work represents sharply contrasting theories and ideas about the central issues of our day, including economic instability, central planning, and the operation of the political process. The debate between Keynes and Hayek provides a vivid example of how scholarly writings have consequences.

As you read this special topic, look for answers to the following questions:

- Why are the views of John Maynard Keynes and Friedrich Hayek often compared and contrasted?

- Are market economies inherently unstable, or are counterproductive government policies the primary source of economic instability?

- If we want to allocate resources efficiently and achieve higher income levels, should we rely primarily on markets or political allocation?

---

[1]From the video "Fear the Boom and Bust: Keynes versus Hayek" available at www.youtube.com/watch?v=d0nERTFo-Sk.

ST04-1 KEYNES AND HAYEK: TWO GREAT ECONOMISTS

Even though their views are in many ways polar opposites, Keynes and Hayek both command respect among professional economists. Keynes is widely regarded as the most influential economist of the twentieth century. Hayek was the recipient of the 1974 Nobel Prize in Economics. Interestingly, Keynes and Hayek were contemporaries at Cambridge University and the London School of Economics in the early 1940s. During World War II, they even spent a night together on the roof of the chapel of King's College, Cambridge watching for German bombers.

Keynes's *General Theory* provided a reasonable explanation of what went wrong during the Great Depression and what could be done to prevent such an event from occurring in the future. His ideas inspired a generation of economists that transformed macroeconomic analysis. Hayek was born in Vienna in 1899, and he was a rising star in the 1930s. The London School of Economics lured him from Austria, at least partly to counter the influence of Keynes and the reputation he brought to rival Cambridge University. In his 1944 book *The Road to Serfdom*, Hayek argued that the growth of government was endangering freedom and leading to tyranny in the Western democracies, just as it had done in both Nazi Germany and the Soviet Union.

Keynes and Hayek were polar opposites not only in their economic views but also in their personality characteristics. Keynes was outgoing and dominant. Some charged that he was arrogant, but all recognized that his skills as a persuader were supreme. In contrast, Hayek was quiet and unassuming. While Keynes reveled in policy-making, Hayek was content to remain outside policy circles. Keynes was optimistic, and his message was well suited for the "We're fixing it" mentality of politicians. On the other hand, Hayek's message was not one political officials like to hear: Policy-makers have messed things up, and it will take time for the market to correct their errors.

A popular PBS video series, *Commanding Heights* (Episode One: "The Battle of Ideas"), used the contrasting views of these two economists to illustrate how major trends in economic thinking impacted global economic events during the twentieth century.[2] Following in this tradition, this special topic will use the ideas of Keynes and Hayek to explain and contrast their viewpoints and the alternative theories they represent. Most economists recognize the validity of many of the arguments presented by both sides. Hence, most are eclectic; their views are a mixture of these two polar views.[3]

An entertaining pair of rap videos, "Fear the Boom and Bust: Keynes versus Hayek" and "Fight of the Century: Keynes vs. Hayek Round Two," available on YouTube, contrast the views of these two famous economists.

ST04-2 KEYNES, HAYEK, AND GREAT DEBATES IN ECONOMICS

The contrasting views of Keynes and Hayek can be generalized to help illustrate the most important debates in economics. Much of the disagreement can be attributed to differing views of the effectiveness of markets versus the political process in coordinating economic activity.

Photo of Keynes and Hayek

---

[2]The PBS series was based on the book by Daniel Yergin and Joseph Stanislaw, *The Commanding Heights: The Battle Between Government and the Marketplace That Is Remaking the Modern World* (New York: Simon & Schuster, 1998).

[3]There is some evidence that just prior to his heart attack and untimely death in 1946, Keynes developed a genuine appreciation for the views of Hayek. After reading the *Road to Serfdom*, Keynes wrote the following to Hayek in a personal letter about the book: "Orally and philosophically I find myself in agreement with virtually the whole of it, and not only in agreement with it, but in a deeply moved agreement."

ST04-2a WHAT IS THE CAUSE AND CURE FOR THE BUSINESS CYCLE?

The underlying causes of the business cycle and potential effectiveness of policy responses have been focal points of debate among economists for at least a century. The perspectives of Keynes and Hayek represent alternative viewpoints on this issue.

The Keynesian viewpoint argues that capitalist market economies are inherently unstable. Private investment in particular is fickle and prone to extreme fluctuations driven by changes in business optimism, or what Keynes referred to as "animal spirits." Moreover, the booms and busts will tend to feed on themselves, and therefore, a market economy will swing back and forth between a boom that will lead to inflation and a bust that will generate high rates of unemployment that may persist for long periods of time.

But there is good news in the Keynesian theory. Government can use fiscal and monetary policy to control aggregate demand and thereby promote economic stability. During a recession, government spending should be increased to offset the weak private investment, taxes should be reduced to stimulate consumption, budget deficits should be used to finance these activities, and monetary policy should keep interest rates low. With large multiplier effects, debt-financed government spending can have large impacts on aggregate spending, helping to cure the recessions. Keynesians focus on policies that promote consumption (both private and government) over those that encourage savings. In Keynesian models, spending is the key component driving the economy. In fact, Keynesians refer to "the paradox of thrift" in which if individuals increase their savings, the economy will be harmed because the saving will drain funds away from consumption spending. Keynesians view government spending as more stimulating than tax cuts precisely because individuals will save part of a tax cut, and therefore, the entire amount of the tax cut will not flow into consumption.

In contrast, the Hayekian viewpoint argues that booms and busts are caused by perverse government policy and that the economy would be considerably more stable if political decision-makers followed stable policies and refrained from activist interventions. Several schools of thought in macroeconomics share this view but differ with regard to the explanation. The monetarists, for example, would point to the improper timing of changes in monetary policy, whereas the Austrians (including Hayek) would blame excessive credit expansion by the Fed that pushes interest rates to artificially low levels. At the abnormally low interest rates, businesses are induced to undertake investments that will later prove to be both unprofitable and unsustainable. In the wake of the financial crisis of 2008–2009, the Austrian theory of the business cycle attracted renewed interest because it provided a plausible explanation of what actually occurred, particularly in the housing market.

The core of the Austrian view is that the market interest rate is one of the most important prices in the economy and when the central bank manipulates this rate, it distorts the signals sent to borrowers and lenders. In the Austrian view, the interest rate is a key determinant of the time structure of capital and the length of the production process. When interest rates are low, the time structure of production lengthens as longer-term investments become more profitable. On the other hand, when interest rates are high, the time structure of production shortens as the higher interest rates make longer-term investments less attractive. Undertaking a five-year process of building a new factory, for example, might be profitable at a lower interest rate but not a higher one.

Normally, changes in the market interest rate correspond to changes in the time preferences of consumers. When households cut back on current consumption and save more for their retirement, for example, they are sending a signal to producers that they want fewer goods today in exchange for more goods in the future. The increase in saving (the supply of loanable funds) will result in lower real interest rates. In turn, the lower interest rates will provide entrepreneurs with the incentive to undertake longer-term investments that will expand the supply of consumer goods in the future.

Hayakians believe savings is a key source of growth. Saving provides the necessary funds for bank loans and the funding of business investment for machinery and equipment that increase productivity. When individuals save, this doesn't harm the economy by reducing consumption, it helps the economy by expanding investment, and this investment enhances our ability to produce in the future, leading to economic growth.

Summarizing, Keynesians believe that the economy is inherently unstable and that government should play an active role in offsetting swings in private spending and aggregate demand. In contrast, Hayakians believe that the primary source of economic instability is government intervention and that a more hands-off policy would result in more stability, investment, and long-term growth.

ST04-2b SHOULD AN ECONOMY BE DIRECTED BY GOVERNMENT PLANNING OR DECENTRALIZED INDIVIDUAL PLANNING AND THE INVISIBLE HAND OF MARKET PRICES?

The Keynesian view holds that government intervention is needed not only to keep the macroeconomy on track but also to correct market failures and ensure an equitable distribution of income. Relying on information derived from economists and other experts, Keynesians believe that policy-makers will be able to selectively intervene in ways that will improve market outcomes. In Keynesian models, government is often portrayed as a benevolent social planner that can step in whenever market outcomes are less than ideal and implement an idealized correction.

Keynesian economists are more likely to view potential market failures such as externalities, information problems, public goods, and lack of competition as widespread and damaging to the overall economy. As a result, they are also more likely to favor increased government regulations on the behavior of individuals and businesses as well as controls on prices and wages (including minimum wages). In addition, they view markets and prices as more rigid and not rapidly adjusting to equilibrium.

In contrast, Hayekians argue that government planners do not have sufficient information to direct the economy and their efforts to do so will do more damage than good. According to the Hayekian view, decentralized decision-making, directed by market prices, will be a more reliable method of directing resources into productive projects and away from ones that are counterproductive. Instead of centralized planning, individuals should be left free to make their own plans, relying on information and incentives communicated by market prices, competitive forces, and the profit and loss system. Hayekians believe that a spontaneous order will emerge from the market process and that this order will result in more economic freedom and economic progress. The contrast is not between having planning and not having planning; instead, the contrast is between having a centralized government make plans for everyone versus allowing individuals to make their own plans over the resources they control.

Moreover, dynamic competition provides decision-makers with a strong incentive to discover better ways of doing things, improve technologies, and institute practical innovations that will improve our lives. In this view, the information necessary to guide the economy is not known to anyone in total, but instead is generated through the process of decentralized market interaction. According to Hayekians, the proper role of government is simply to provide the rule of law, enforce contracts, and protect property rights, leaving the rest to market forces.

Put simply, Keynesians believe that markets suffer from widespread problems that result in inefficient allocation of resources and undesirable outcomes, and that interventions by government planners will generally improve the situation. On the other hand, Hayekians believe that the invisible hand of markets will be more likely to direct individuals and businesses toward productive actions and that political decision-makers have neither the incentive nor information to direct resources reliably toward productive projects and away from unproductive projects.

ST04-2c CAN DEMOCRATIC DECISION-MAKING BE COUNTED ON TO ALLOCATE RESOURCES EFFICIENTLY?

As we discussed in Chapter 6, public-choice analysis provides insights on the operation of the political process. It indicates that the incentives confronted by voters, interest groups, politicians, and bureaucrats will sometimes conflict with sound policy and the efficient allocation of resources. Even when decisions are made democratically, the political process will often favor well-organized interest groups and shortsighted policies that generate highly visible gains at the expense of costs that are less visible. Predictably, some inefficient use of resources will arise from these forces. Put another way, there is "government failure" as well as "market failure."

The Keynesian perspective seldom addresses this issue directly. Instead, it is assumed that the job of the economists is to figure out the ideal or optimal solutions, and once these are developed, political decision-makers can be expected to adopt them. Moreover, many Keynesians charge that analysis of how the political process works is outside the scope of economics and therefore that those who address this issue are not really addressing economic issues. Keynes himself had great confidence in his ability to convince policy-makers to adopt his advice. Within the Keynesian framework, it is essentially assumed that political decision-makers will implement policies in a proper manner.

The Hayekian perspective argues that the structure of incentives and institutions exert a major impact on how government works. The government failures described within public-choice theory will be a major problem or barrier to implementing good policy. Thus, it is vitally important to adopt institutions and constitutional rules that bring personal self-interest of policy-makers into harmony with growth and prosperity.

The father of economics, Adam Smith, held a similar view. Smith stated,

> The man of system is apt to be very wise in his own conceit. He seems to imagine that he can arrange the different members of a great society with as much ease as the hand arranges the different pieces upon a chess-board; he does not consider that the pieces upon the chess-board have not another principle of motion besides that which the hand impresses upon them; but that, in the great chess-board of human society, every single piece has a principle of motion of its own, although different from that which the legislature might choose to impress upon it. If those two principles coincide and act in the same direction, the game of human society will go on easily and harmoniously, and is very likely to be happy and successful. If they are opposite or different, the game will go on miserably, and the society must be at all times in the highest degree of disorder.[4]

Whereas some economists view the government as a corrective device that can be counted on to fix problems within the market, others view the potential failures of government to be larger than the potential failures of the market. Public policies are determined by a complex interaction of special-interest groups, voters, elected officials, and government employees who react to the personal incentives they face. The individuals involved in the process of collective decision-making react to incentives in their personal behavior as workers and consumers, and their actions within the political realm are governed by these same incentives. In other words, there is no reason to assume that voters or elected officials behave any differently in their motivations when they step into political roles.

When voters are uninformed about the political process, powerful interest groups will be able to get government policies enacted that favor them at the expense of the general public. The government failures discussed in Chapter 6, including the special-interest effect, the shortsightedness effect, and the lack of incentives for efficiency within

---

[4]Adam Smith, *The Theory of Moral Sentiments*, Glasgow Edition of Oxford University Press (Indianapolis: Liberty Fund, Inc., [1790] 1976): 233–34. Also available at www.econlib.org/library/Smith/smMS6.html#VI.II.42).]

government budgets, create a situation in which one cannot automatically assume government intervention will improve even a problematic area within the market.

Thus, an area of continued debate in economics regards the relative effectiveness of the political process in allocating resources. This debate takes on two dimensions: disagreements about the degree to which markets are efficient and need correction and disagreements about the degree to which government actions are efficient at solving these potential shortcomings.

Keynes and Hayek represent two of the most important strands of economic thinking. Although it is somewhat of an oversimplification to consider it simply a debate of Keynes versus Hayek, it is a general framework for understanding the two main sides of the larger debates within economic theory. In reality, there are many different schools of thought, each with its own explanations for the relative effectiveness of market outcomes and government interventions that generally reflect some elements of both sides. You will see these two contrasting views represented in several of the special topics that follow, including the ones on the Great Recession, the Great Depression, the healthcare debate, use of natural resources, and the environment. As a student in economics, it is useful to understand both of these perspectives and their underlying foundations.

KEY POINTS

- John Maynard Keynes and Friedrich Hayek are giants in the economics profession. Their theories and ideas represent contrasting views on several of the central issues of economics.

- Although there are many different schools of thought in economics, they can be grouped roughly into (1) those that view market outcomes as often problematic and government interventions as effective and (2) those that alternatively view market outcomes as generally efficient and government interventions as suffering from various shortcomings.

- Keynes believed that market economies were inherently unstable and government intervention in the form of fiscal and monetary stimulus could be used effectively to promote economic stability. Hayek believed that economic instability was primarily the result of malinvestment generated by monetary and credit expansion and that government stimulus would slow market adjustments and the recovery process.

- Keynesians stress the role of aggregate demand and spending in the macroeconomy and view savings as a leakage detrimental

to the economy. In contrast, Hayekians have a more favorable view of the role of savings in providing the funds necessary for investment and growth in productivity and output.

- Keynesians believe that government intervention can generally improve market outcomes. Hayekians believe that policymakers simply do not have the information or incentives to plan the economy effectively and that their efforts to do so would be far less efficient than allocation through markets.

- Keynesians believe that the job of the economist is to develop policies that will reduce economic instability and correct market failures. Keynesian analysis largely ignores how economic incentives influence the operation of the political process. Hayekians recognize that the political incentive structure often caters to well-organized interest groups and results in the adoption of shortsighted policies. Thus, they stress the importance of legal and political institutions that will provide both market participants and political decision-makers with incentives to engage in productive rather than counterproductive actions.

CRITICAL ANALYSIS QUESTIONS

1. *According to Keynes, when the economy is in a recession, increased government spending can bring the economy back to full employment. This spending could be on conducting a war with the military or on financing public works projects. Hayekians would alternatively argue that building and dropping bombs only destroys valuable resources. Why would a Keynesian view a war as stimulating?

2. Is savings harmful or beneficial to the economy? Contrast the views of Keynes and Hayek on this issue.

3. Without government intervention, would the economy fluctuate more or less over the business cycle? Contrast the views of Keynes and Hayek on this issue. Be sure to address both the inherent stability of the market economy as well as the impact of government interventions to steer the economy.

4. Can markets generally be counted on to achieve desirable outcomes and adjust quickly and appropriately to changes, or are they rigid and subject to frequent problems that need correction? Discuss the potential problems with the market and how government intervention could potentially solve these problems.

5. Can government intervention generally be counted on to act more like a benevolent social planner, fixing problems with the best interest of citizens as the goal, or will government tend to cater toward special-interest groups at the expense of the general public? Discuss the potential problems with the incentives faced by those involved in collective decision-making.

*Asterisk denotes questions for which answers are given in Appendix B.

SPECIAL TOPIC 5

The 2020 COVID-19 Recession: Cause, Response, and Implications for the Future

In times of crisis, politicians want to look like they're doing something, and don't want to hear about limits on their authority. In times of crisis, people want someone to do something, and don't want to hear about tradeoffs. **—Antony Davies and James R. Harrigan**[1]

The COVID-19 pandemic shattered normality in the United States and throughout the world. There had been previous severe pandemics, most notably the 1918–1919 Spanish flu virus, which claimed the lives of between 20 and 50 million people worldwide, including 675,000 Americans. But that was a long time ago, and surely something like that could not happen today given modern medicine, or so we thought. The lives lost as the result of the COVID-19 pandemic were far less than those of the Spanish flu, but nonetheless it was an earth-shaking event, similar to that of a world war or Great Depression. Even though, in some respects, we are still experiencing the event, let's take a closer look at the accompanying Great Suppression.[2]

As you read this special topic, look for answers to the following questions:

- What caused the 2020 recession, and why was this recession different from the ones that preceded it?

- What was the policy response to the pandemic? Was it effective?

- How will the United States be different after the pandemic is over?

---

[1]Antony Davies and James R. Harrigan, "Coronavirus Shutdowns May be Shortsighted," *The Philadelphia Inquirer*, April 20, 2020, https://www.inquirer.com/opinion/commentary/coronavirus-economic-shutdown-unemployment-pennsylvania-20200420.html.

[2]To the best of our knowledge, the term "Great Suppression" was coined by Gene Epstein in "Anatomy of the Great Suppression," American Institute for Economic Research, April 9, 2020, https://www.aier.org/article/anatomy-of-the-great-suppression/. Like Epstein, we believe the term is descriptive of the recession accompanying the COVID-19 pandemic.

ST05-1 THE COVID-19 PANDEMIC AND ITS IMPACT ON THE ECONOMY

In February 2020, life was good in the United States. The unemployment rate was 3.5 percent, and the economic expansion was already ten and a half years old. Americans were busy with their work, studies, entertainment, and enjoyment of life. The first Sunday in February was Super Bowl Sunday. In the 2020 Super Bowl, the Kansas City Chiefs, just as they had done in their previous playoff games, came from behind to defeat the San Francisco 49ers. As February rolled on, students were planning for spring break, and college basketball teams were getting ready for conference tournaments and March Madness. There were some stories about a mystery virus in China, but the information was sketchy and seemingly of little relevance to Americans. However, on the last day of February, the United States experienced its first reported death from the COVID-19 virus, an elderly resident of a nursing home just outside of Seattle, Washington.

Two months later, the lives of most Americans had been turned upside down by the worldwide COVID-19 pandemic and government actions to combat it. By mid-March, the classes of virtually all students had been shifted from regular in-person classrooms to online distance learning. In most states, government mandates required people to shelter in their homes, ordered the closure of nonessential businesses, and prohibited group gatherings of various sizes. Numerous events were canceled, and a new phrase, "social distancing," became part of our vocabulary.

By April, nearly half of the labor force had shifted to online work. But millions of businesses were forced to close their doors. The number employed fell from 158.8 million in February to 133.4 million in April, and so the unemployment rate soared to levels not seen since the Great Depression of the 1930s. In a matter of a few weeks, the long economic expansion had ended abruptly.

Worldwide, there were 10 million cases and 500 thousand deaths during the first six months of 2020. Even though the COVID-19 virus started in China, both Europe and the United States were hit hard. By mid-July 2020, the number of cases in the United States had risen to approximately 3.5 million, and more than 135 thousand Americans had died from the virus. COVID-19 was particularly deadly for the elderly. In the United States, people age 65 and older accounted for 80 percent of the deaths, and the worldwide figures were similar. Between one-third and one-half of the victims were residents of nursing homes. The danger of COVID-19 was amplified by the fact that many people, particularly the young, tested positive for the virus even though they had no symptoms. Because many of these people were unaware that they had the virus, they continued to circulate in the general public and infect others.

The COVID-19 pandemic and associated policy responses caused an abrupt closure of many businesses and a large shift to online work and education.

ST05-1a THE 2020 RECESSION WAS DIFFERENT

In the past, recessions resulted because of unexpected shifts in aggregate demand or short-run aggregate supply, leading to a temporary equilibrium at an output level

less than the economy's full-employment potential. The shifts in aggregate demand or short-run aggregate supply were generally the result of supply shocks (for example, a sharp increase in oil prices), a miscalculation by business decision-makers, or policy errors (for example, abrupt shifts in monetary or fiscal policy). Typically, the onset of a recession is gradual. Real GDP growth slows and eventually becomes negative. Employment falls as workers are dismissed or laid off, and the unemployment rate rises. A sizeable share of households experience substantial reductions in income. In the eleven recessions since the end of World War II, the unemployment rate reached 10 percent only twice, and it never exceeded 11 percent.

The 2020 recession was different. It was caused by government mandates requiring people to stay in their homes and businesses to close their operations to combat the COVID-19 virus. The effects on output and employment were immediate and massive. In just three months, one in six employed workers lost their jobs. Unemployment soared, real GDP plunged by double digits, and fear dominated the country.

ST05-2 POLICY RESPONSE TO THE PANDEMIC AND RECESSION

Governments throughout the world enacted unprecedented policies in response to the pandemic and its economic effects. Limits on group interactions and travel, stay-at-home orders, restrictions on nonessential medical procedures, and mandated business closures were imposed to reduce the externalities associated with human interactions created by the highly contagious nature of the virus. These government mandates, designed to reduce the spread of the virus and "flatten the curve" to avoid overwhelming the health care system, imposed a huge cost on both individuals and businesses.

At the state and local level, many governments declared states of emergency that automatically imposed restrictions on price increases that caused widespread shortages and resulted in consumer hoarding of hand sanitizer, masks, toilet paper, gloves, and cleaning products. While supply chains and producers were struggling to adapt and readjust to these abrupt changes without the normal flexibility of market price signals, they were also hampered by forced business closures and mandated reductions in the level of social interaction. Operating required generating enough revenue to cover the costly measures of capacity reduction, distancing, barriers, and provision of personal protective equipment to employees and customers.

Painful adjustments were widespread across a multitude of industries, with tourism, entertainment, and food and beverage hit particularly hard. While some restaurants were able to derive revenue from providing take-out service, others were unable to operate. Food producers that normally distributed to restaurants or food service providers were left with excess crops and meat that they had to destroy, while simultaneously, these items were in short supply and unavailable at the consumer level in grocery stores. Many food banks were so overwhelmed by donations from local food producers they stopped accepting items. As at-home baking surged, flour producers who normally sold large wholesale bags of flour to bakeries (that were now shut down) were unable to quickly convert their surplus production and supply chains to provide small bags to grocery stores. Government restrictions to combat the virus had suddenly disrupted the ability of decentralized markets and the price system to coordinate economic activity as efficiently as it had just weeks earlier.

Political decision-makers responded with policies designed to aid or compensate affected workers and business owners. By May of 2020, emergency legislation summing to $3 trillion in additional federal spending had been passed, providing:

a. A paycheck protection provision designed to compensate laid-off and dismissed workers for the harm imposed by the government shutdown. This legislation provided additional federal funding for unemployment compensation and loosened the qualifying requirements for those benefits. In addition, supplementary benefits of $600 per week were temporarily added to the regular unemployment benefit package provided by states.

b. Grants and loans of approximately $650 billion were directed toward small businesses harmed by the government-mandated shutdown. The loans were arranged through local banks, and 75 percent of the funds were allocated for wages, while the remaining 25 percent could be used to pay expenses such as utilities, rent, and mortgage payments. If the business maintained its employees through the end of July 2020, it did not have to repay any of the loan.

c.   Grants and loans were provided to large businesses for harm imposed on their business and their employees. A substantial share of these funds was earmarked for hard-hit industries such as airlines and airplane manufacturing.

d.   Government checks for $1,200 per adult and $500 per child were provided to taxpayers with an adjusted gross income of less than $75,000 for singles ($150,000 for couples).

In addition, the Federal Reserve moved quickly to provide additional liquidity through the banking system. The Fed purchased a broad range of assets amounting to nearly $2 trillion during March and April of 2020. These purchases increased the reserves available to banks and, at least temporarily, expanded the M1 money supply rapidly.

These actions were an imperfect instrument with which to compensate people for the damages imposed by the shutdown to control the COVID-19 virus. The financial position of some people was actually improved as a result of the programs, but the transfers were insufficient to make up for the harm imposed on others. While many were desperate to reopen the economy and return to work, others derived financial and personal benefits from additional delays in the reopening process.

In addition to the fiscal and monetary actions, both federal and state governments suspended a number of regulations in response to the virus. Several states altered their licensing requirements for health care professionals, making it possible for doctors, nurses, and other health care workers licensed in other states to work in their state. The U.S. Department of Health and Human Services issued temporary waivers allowing doctors to provide Medicare and Medicaid patients with **telemedicine** services. Texas adopted reforms that made it possible for doctors to receive the same payment for over-the-phone telemedicine visits that they would for in-person visits for patients on state-regulated insurance plans. Many cities suspended regulations on carry-out food and alcohol sales, repealed plastic bag bans, and enabled establishments to expand operations into their parking lots in order to provide socially distanced outdoor dining. The Transportation Security Administration (TSA) even allowed people with 12-ounce containers of hand sanitizer to travel on airplanes. Perhaps most important, the U.S. Food and Drug Administration (FDA), whose regulatory rules reduced the initial availability of tests to determine if a person has the COVID-19 virus, permitted private firms to also develop and provide these tests. Later, the FDA expedited its safety and efficacy procedures to hasten the development of a vaccine to combat the virus. These actions and similar reforms were intended to both expand the availability of health care services and improve the well-being of those shut in by the government mandates.

Telemedicine
Medical service provided by telephone or video hookup between patient and doctor rather than via patient visit to a doctor's office or clinic.

ST05-2b SWEDEN: AN ALTERNATIVE POLICY STRATEGY

Most European governments followed policies similar to those of the United States. However, Sweden was an interesting exception.[3] Rather than closing schools and requiring people to be locked down in their homes, Sweden relied mostly on the voluntary cooperation of its citizens. People were asked to follow sanitation and social distancing practices. Public gatherings of more than 50 people were prohibited, and high schools and colleges shifted to online distance learning, but elementary schools continued to operate in a classroom setting. There were no generalized mandated business closings. Restaurants and retail businesses continued to operate, although they often voluntarily adopted procedures designed to protect both employees and customers.

The Swedish strategy was designed to reduce the cases to a level that would not overwhelm hospitals and health care facilities. They also sought to provide nursing homes and

[3]For additional details on the approach of Sweden, see Nils Karlson, Charlotta Stern, and Daniel B. Klein, "Sweden's Coronavirus Strategy Will Soon Be the World's: Herd Immunity Is the Only Realistic Option—The Question Is How to Get There Safely," *Foreign Affairs* (May 12, 2020), and Charlotta Stern and Daniel B. Klein, "Give Sweden a B- in Coronavirus 101," American Institute for Economic Research (May 29, 2020), https://www.aier.org/article/give-sweden-a-b-in-coronavirus-101/.

assisted living facilities with special protection. However, elderly people living in nursing homes constituted a large proportion (more than 50 percent) of the Swedish deaths from the virus, indicating this was an area where their efforts fell short.

The Swedish approach also sought to develop herd immunity within the general populace through contagion, particularly among the young and healthy, the groups least likely to suffer complications as they contacted COVID-19. In turn, the more widespread immunity of the population who had recovered would mean fewer cases and deaths from potential future waves. In essence, the Swedish strategy focused on the protection of those with a high risk of death from the virus (the elderly and those with respiratory and related problems) while allowing the healthy to continue producing goods and services so the pandemic would not turn into a Great Depression.

Was the Swedish strategy effective? It resulted in a smaller initial decline in real GDP than both Sweden's Scandinavian neighbors and other European economies. However, during the first half of 2020, both the COVID-19 cases and deaths per capita of Sweden were higher than those of Denmark, Norway, Finland, and Germany, but lower than those of other European countries, including Belgium, France, Italy, Spain, and the United Kingdom. More time is needed for a valid test of the Swedish strategy. How did the COVID-19–related deaths per capita during 2020–2021 in Sweden compare with those of other European countries? How did the Swedish economy perform throughout the 2020–2021 period compared to other economies? Once answers to these questions are available, it will be possible to provide a better assessment of the Swedish strategy.

Further, there will be unforeseen secondary effects of different government policies that will take a while to fully understand and measure. The negative impacts of the various economic shutdowns on human capital accumulation, willingness to obtain preventative (or even necessary) medical procedures and care, domestic abuse and divorce, social networks and interaction, and the many harms associated with increased poverty and reduced employment will only be known with the passage of time and careful study.

ST05-3 HOW WILL THE 2020 COVID-19 RECESSION CHANGE AMERICA?

In the late summer and early fall of 2020, the future duration and full impact of the virus was uncertain. But one thing was for sure: Life in America was not going to be the same after the crisis. Like the Great Depression and World War II, the COVID-19 pandemic will exert an impact for years, perhaps even decades, into the future. No doubt, some of the changes will be surprising. However, there are also some areas where long-term changes are highly likely. What are some of these potential areas of change? Consider the following six possibilities.

1. Changes in the structure of the economy. The virus crisis forced people to do things differently. As a result of these changes, some people will have discovered options and developed skills that will cause them to make different choices in the future. For example, after the widespread use of online meeting technology, some businesses will use this more intensely in the future, expanding work-at-home opportunities and potentially cutting back on travel to meetings. Similarly, some doctors and patients will have discovered that online doctor visits work well compared to office visits. Some educational institutions and students may even find that online education works well and is more economical than traditional in-person education. Some people learned to cook and others discovered how to enhance their own living spaces. These changes will exert a positive impact on some sectors of the economy and an adverse impact on others. There will be a reallocation of productive resources and a potentially higher unemployment rate in the aftermath of the crisis as a result.

2. Substantial increase in government debt. The initial increases in federal expenditures accompanying the virus summed to between $4 trillion and $6 trillion. In addition, the recession reduced federal, state, and local government revenue by at least another trillion dollars. The increased expenditures and reduction in government revenue will be

financed almost exclusively by borrowing. As a result, the federal debt will be pushed to $30 trillion sometime during 2021 or 2022. Measured as a share of GDP, the federal debt will rise to 140 percent, a historically high figure, greater than even the level at the height of World War II. Currently, interest rates are low, which will reduce the cost of servicing this debt. But interest rates will inevitably rise at some time in the future. When this happens, the additional interest cost will have to be covered by either higher taxes or money creation. The former will slow future economic growth, while the latter will be inflationary.

3. Increased risk of monetary policy error as the result of Fed actions to combat the crisis. As the unemployment rate soared in March and April of 2020, the Fed quickly injected initial liquidity into the banking system by purchasing additional assets of $2 trillion. The COVID-19 crisis confronts the Fed with a difficult task. High rates of unemployment and underutilized production capacity place downward pressure on the general level of prices. The Fed will want to follow an expansionary monetary policy to combat this potential deflation. However, monetary policy exerts an impact on both output and the price level with a lag. This makes it more difficult for the Fed to follow a policy consistent with price stability. As a result, the risk of policy error is greater. The Fed may follow a policy that is too expansionary, leading to high rates of inflation. Alternatively, it may follow a policy that is not expansionary enough, and therefore the recovery will be weak. If either of these errors occurs, economic instability and slower future growth will result.

4. Reassessment of several government regulations. As previously discussed, a number of regulations in health care and other areas were suspended during the COVID-19 crisis. Will this result in a serious assessment of the long-term value of many of these regulations? If regulatory reforms facilitating telemedicine and provision of health care and other services across state boundaries and increasing the speed at which life-saving drugs can be brought to the market made sense during the COVID-19 crisis, why not make the reforms permanent? Removal of rules, regulations, licenses, and certifications that merely act as entry barriers, rather than protect public safety, might well both increase the flexibility of the U.S. economy and its resilience to future shocks from pandemics and other sources.

5. Increased restrictions on international trade and travel. The United States and several other countries argue that China covered up the dangers of the COVID-19 virus and even encouraged international travel from China in January and February of 2020, thereby contributing to the worldwide spread of the virus. As a result, leading political figures argue trade restrictions should be imposed on China as punishment. Further, the United States and other countries also imposed restraints on the export of health care equipment such as ventilators and respirators during the virus crisis. Currently, this combination of factors has increased the political support for various types of trade restrictions. Will this lead to an expansion in trade restrictions? Might it even result in a trade war, such as was generated by the 1930 Smoot-Hawley tariff bill? Will restrictions on the travel of individuals between countries persist? Modern living standards are the result of the specialization and interconnected exchanges, including international exchanges, that occur daily. If trade and travel restrictions undermine this process, future output will be lower, and living standards will suffer. Moreover, if politically managed trade replaces market exchange, both rent-seeking and political corruption will expand. In turn, this will reduce the credibility of the political process.

6. A ratchet effect resulting in permanently higher levels of future government expenditures and intervention. Robert Higgs, a noted economic historian, argues that crises such as wars and catastrophic economic events lead to permanently higher levels of government expenditures and other forms of intervention.[4] As Higgs notes, government intervention increases during a crisis, but virtually never subsequently

---

[4]Robert Higgs, *Crisis and Leviathan: Critical Episodes in the Growth of American Government* (New York: Oxford University Press, 1987).

falls back to the pre-crisis level. The higher expenditures during the crisis create interest groups that benefit from the policy, and therefore, it is politically difficult to reduce the spending after the crisis is over. As a result of this ratchet effect, the government becomes more and more involved in the economy. In turn, this replacement of markets with political allocation leads to a less efficient allocation of resources and an increase in political cronyism and corruption. Will the COVID-19 crisis follow this pattern? The crisis certainly led to a substantial increase in government expenditures almost entirely financed by debt. It will be interesting to see if government spending and borrowing after the crisis continue at levels well above those present before the crisis.

With the passage of time, the impact of the 2020 COVID-19 Recession in these six and other areas will become more obvious.

ST05-3a DECENTRALIZED INNOVATION AND ENTREPRENEURSHIP: THE PATH FORWARD

Unless restrained by the political process, entrepreneurship and innovation will play a significant role in the economic recovery and reallocations of productive effort that will unfold in the years ahead. As the flood of conflicting information regarding the virus and the proper preventative procedures illustrated, there is often no right one-size-fits-all solution. Upon economic reopening, some businesses were requiring masks for customers to enter, and some were not, and those wanting to avoid turning away customers were providing masks for free. Simultaneously, some customers were refusing to patronize establishments that followed (or did not follow) certain procedures. Many businesses were innovating "contact-less" delivery, pick up, and payment methods. Decentralized experimentation makes it possible for many potential solutions to compete in the marketplace so we may discover the best way forward.

In the aftermath of the COVID-19 crisis, entrepreneurs will address challenges in different ways. The profit and loss system, based on consumer preferences and demands relative to production costs, will determine which solutions survive and which do not. This experimentation undertaken by entrepreneurs in decentralized markets guided by the profit and loss system will help us to discover which solutions are the most effective in our forever-changed post-pandemic world.

KEY POINTS

- The recession of 2020 was different. It was caused by government mandates forcing people to stay home and businesses to close to control the COVID-19 virus. The impact on the economy was both huge and abrupt. Unemployment soared and output plunged in just a few weeks during March and April of 2020.

- The federal government responded to the crisis by borrowing funds to provide individuals and businesses with payments and loans designed to compensate them for the harm imposed by the government-mandated shutdown. In addition, the Federal Reserve purchased a large quantity of financial assets to inject liquidity into the banking system.

- The crisis exerted a significant impact on the lives of almost all Americans. Given this impact and the magnitude of the policy response, this event is virtually certain to generate long-term changes that will persist even after the crisis has passed. While some of the areas of change are predictable, others are likely to be surprising and will be discovered through innovation and entrepreneurship.

CRITICAL ANALYSIS QUESTIONS

1. *The Paycheck Protection Program provided unemployment recipients with a $600 per week payment in addition to their regular unemployment benefits. If the regular unemployment benefits replaced 50 percent of the employee's previous earnings, how large is the total replacement income (including the supplement) of an employee who was working 40 hours per week at a wage of $15 per hour prior to their layoff? How will the replacement income affect the incentive of the worker to quickly return to his or her previous job?

2. Was the U.S. policy response to the COVID-19 pandemic effective? Did it reduce the harm imposed on individuals and businesses? Did it reduce the length of the crisis? Provide an assessment of the policy response.

3. Has the COVID-19 crisis led to permanent changes in various sectors of the U.S. economy? If so, please provide examples.

4. Assess the response of the Federal Reserve to the COVID-19 crisis. Has monetary policy been too restrictive, too expansionary, or about right? Use data from https://fred.stlouisfed.org/ on employment, inflation, length of the recession, and the recovery process to answer this question.

5. Did the United States adopt additional trade restrictions during and after the COVID-19 crisis? If so, cite evidence.

6. What is the ratchet effect? Is there evidence that the COVID-19 crisis generated a ratchet effect with regard to the expenditures and borrowing levels of the federal government? Explain.

7. How did the response of Sweden to the COVID-19 crisis differ from that of the United States and most European countries? Was the Swedish strategy effective? Cite evidence on both fatalities from the virus and the path of real GDP in Sweden and other countries in your response. Data on real GDP in Sweden and other countries can be accessed from https://fred.stlouisfed.org/, and data on fatalities can be obtained from https://coronavirus.jhu.edu/.

8. *Why did economic output plunge so rapidly during March to May of 2020?

*Asterisk denotes questions for which answers are given in Appendix B.

SPECIAL TOPIC 6

The Great Recession of 2008–2009: Causes and Response

U.S. housing policies are the root cause of the current financial crisis. Other players—"greedy" investment bankers; foolish investors; imprudent bankers; incompetent rating agencies; irresponsible housing speculators; shortsighted homeowners; and predatory mortgage brokers, lenders, and borrowers—all played a part, but they were only following the economic incentives that government policy laid out for them. **—Peter J. Wallison**[1]

The headlines of 2008 were dominated by falling housing prices, rising default and foreclosure rates, failure of large investment banks, and huge bailouts arranged by both the Federal Reserve and the U.S. Treasury. The Great Recession of 2008–2009 substantially reduced the wealth of most Americans and generated widespread concern about the future of the U.S. economy. This crisis is one of the most important macroeconomic events in American history. This special topic will take a closer look at what happened, why things went wrong, and the lessons that need to be learned from the experience.

As you read this special topic, look for answers to the following questions:

- What caused the Great Recession of 2008–2009?

- Why did housing prices rise rapidly during 2002–2005 and then fall in the years immediately following?

- Did government policies undermine credit standards and the operation of the mortgage market?

- Did monetary policy contribute to the housing boom and bust?

---

[1]Peter J. Wallison, "Cause and Effect: Government Policies and the Financial Crisis," AEI Financial ServicesOutlook, www.aei.org/publication29015.

ST06-1 KEY EVENTS LEADING UP TO THE GREAT RECESSION

The housing boom and bust during the first seven years of the 21st century are central to understanding the economic events of 2008. As Exhibit 1 shows, housing prices were relatively stable during the 1990s, but they began to increase rapidly toward the end of the decade. By 2002, housing prices were booming. Between January 2002 and mid-year 2006, housing prices increased by a whopping 87 percent. This translates to an annual growth rate of approximately 13 percent. But the housing boom began to wane in 2006. Housing prices leveled off, and by the end of 2006, they were falling. The boom had turned to a bust, and the housing price decline continued throughout 2007 and 2008. By year-end 2008, housing prices were approximately 30 percent below their 2006 peak.

Exhibit 2 panel (a) presents data on the **mortgage default rate** from 1979 through 2008. (*Note:* The default rate is also known as the serious delinquency rate.) As these figures illustrate, the default rate fluctuated, within a narrow range, around 2 percent prior to 2006. It increased only slightly during the recessions of 1982, 1990, and 2001.

However, even though the economy was relatively strong and unemployment low, the default rate began to increase sharply during the second half of 2006. By the fourth quarter of 2007, it had already risen to 3.6 percent, up from 2.0 percent in the second quarter of 2006. The increase continued and the default rate reached 5.2 percent in 2008.

As Exhibit 2 panel (b) illustrates, the pattern of the housing **foreclosure rate** was similar. It fluctuated between 0.2 and 0.5 during 1978–2005. The recessions of 1980, 1982, 1990, and 2001 exerted little impact on the foreclosure rate. However, like the mortgage default rate, the foreclosure rate started to increase during the second half of 2006, and it tripled over the next two years.

During 2008, housing prices were falling, default rates were increasing, and the confidence of both consumers and investors was deteriorating. These conditions were reinforced

Mortgage default rate
The percentage of home mortgages on which the borrower is late by ninety days or more with the payments on the loan or it is in the foreclosure process. This rate is sometimes referred to as the serious delinquency rate.

Foreclosure rate
The percentage of home mortgages on which the lender has started the process of taking ownership of the property because the borrower has failed to make the monthly payments.

EXHIBIT 1

Annual Change in the Price of Existing Houses, 1987–2008

Housing prices increased slowly during the 1990s, but they began rising more rapidly toward the end of the decade. Between January 2002 and mid-year 2006, housing prices increased by a whopping 87 percent.

But the boom turned to a bust during the second half of 2006, and the housing price decline continued throughout 2007–2008.

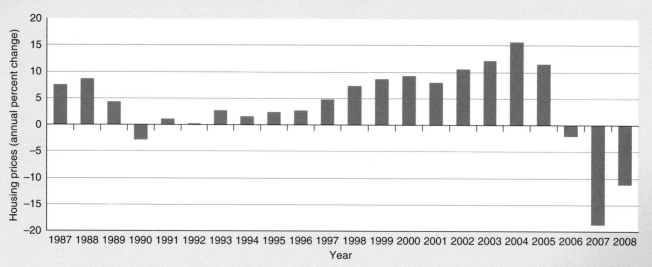

Source: www.standardpoors.com, S&P Case-Shiller Housing Price Index.

EXHIBIT 2

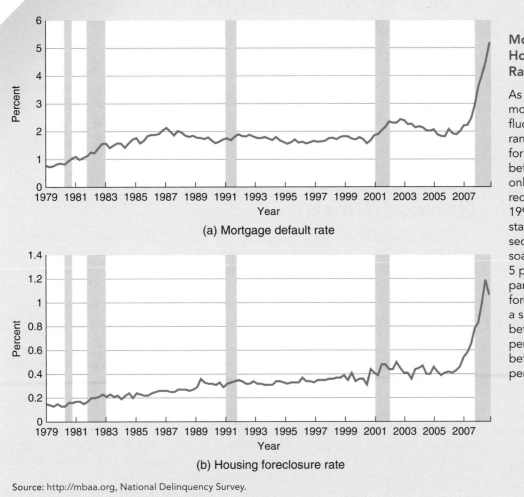

(a) Mortgage default rate

(b) Housing foreclosure rate

Source: http://mbaa.org, National Delinquency Survey.

Mortgage Default and Housing Foreclosure Rates, 1979–2008

As panel (a) shows, the mortgage default rate fluctuated within a narrow range around 2 percent for more than two decades before 2006. It increased only slightly during the recessions of 1980, 1982, 1990, and 2001 but started to increase in the second half of 2006 and soared to more than 5 percent in 2008. As panel (b) shows, the foreclosure rate followed a similar pattern. It ranged between 0.2 and 0.5 percent before 2006, before soaring to 1.2 percent in 2008.

by sharply rising prices of crude oil, which pushed gasoline prices to more than $4 per gallon during the first half of the year. Against this background, the stock market took a huge tumble. As **Exhibit 3** shows, the S&P 500 index of stock prices fell by 55 percent between October 2007 and March 2009. This collapse eroded the wealth and endangered the retirement savings of many Americans.

EXHIBIT 3

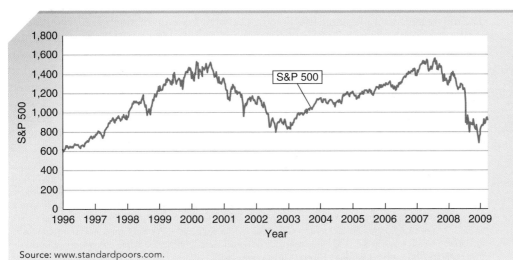

Source: www.standardpoors.com.

Changes in Stock Prices, 1996–2009

Stock prices as measured by the Standard & Poor's 500 are shown here. Note how stock prices fell by approximately 55 percent between October 2007 and March 2009. This collapse eroded the wealth and endangered the retirement savings of many Americans.

ST06-2 WHAT CAUSED THE GREAT RECESSION?

Why did housing prices rise rapidly, then level off, and eventually collapse? Why did the mortgage default and housing foreclosure rates increase rapidly well before the start of the recession, which did not begin until December 2007? Why were the default and foreclosure rates during 2007 so much higher than the rates of earlier years, including those of prior recessions? Why did large, and seemingly strong, investment banks like Bear Stearns and Lehman Brothers run into financial troubles so quickly? Four factors combine to provide the answers to all of these questions.[2]

ST06-2a FACTOR 1: CHANGE IN MORTGAGE LENDING STANDARDS

The lending standards for home mortgage loans changed substantially beginning in the mid-1990s. The looser lending standards did not just happen. They were the result of federal policy designed to promote home ownership among households with incomes below the median. Home ownership is a worthy goal, but it was not pursued directly through transparent budget allocations and subsidies to homebuyers. Instead, the federal government imposed a complex set of regulations and regulatory mandates that forced various lending institutions to extend more loans to low- and moderate-income households. To meet these mandates, lenders had to lower their standards. By the early years of the twenty-first century, it was possible to borrow more (relative to your income) and purchase a house or condo with a lower down payment than was the case a decade earlier.

The Federal National Mortgage Association and Federal Home Loan Mortgage Corporation, commonly known as Fannie Mae and Freddie Mac, played a central role in this relaxation of mortgage lending standards. These two entities were created by Congress to help provide liquidity in secondary mortgage markets. Fannie Mae, established by the federal government in 1938, was spun off as a *government-sponsored enterprise* (GSE) in 1968. Freddie Mac was created in 1970 as another GSE to provide competition for Fannie Mae.

Fannie Mae and Freddie Mac were privately owned (for-profit) businesses, but because of their federal sponsorship, it was widely perceived that the government would back their bonds if they ever ran into financial trouble. As a result, Fannie and Freddie were able to borrow funds at 50 to 75 **basis points** cheaper than private lenders. This gave them a competitive advantage, and they were highly profitable for many years. However, the GSE structure also meant that they were asked to serve two masters: their stockholders, who were interested in profitability, and Congress and federal regulators, who predictably were more interested in political objectives.

As a result of their GSE structure, Fannie Mae and Freddie Mac were highly political. The top management of Fannie and Freddie provided key congressional leaders with large political contributions and often hired away congressional staffers into high-paying jobs lobbying their former bosses. Between the 2000 and 2008 election cycles, high-level managers and other employees of Fannie Mae and Freddie Mac contributed more than $14.6 million to the campaign funds of dozens of senators and representatives, most of whom were on congressional committees important for the protection of their privileged status.

The lobbying activities of Fannie Mae and Freddie Mac were legendary. Between 1998 and 2008, Fannie spent $79.5 million and Freddie spent $94.9 million on

Basis points
One one-hundredth of a percentage point. Thus, 100 basis points are equivalent to one percentage point.

---

[2]For additional details on the Great Recession, see Thomas Sowell, *The Housing Boom and Bust* (New York: Basic Books, 2009); Stan J. Liebowitz, "Anatomy of a Train Wreck: Causes of the Mortgage Meltdown," in *Housing America: Building Out of a Crisis*, ed. Randall G. Holcombe and Benjamin Powell (New Brunswick, NJ: Transaction Publishers, 2009); Peter J. Wallison, "Cause and Effect: Government Policies and the Financial Crisis," *Critical Review: A Journal of Politics and Society,* Issue 2-3 2009, pp. 365–376; and Fernando Ferreira and Joseph Gyourko, "A New Look at the U.S. Foreclosure Crisis: Panel Data Evidence of Prime and Subprime Borrowers from 1997 to 2012," NBER Working Paper 21261, August 2015.

congressional lobbying, placing them among the biggest spenders on these activities. They also set up "partnership offices" in the districts and states of important legislators, often hiring the relatives of these lawmakers to staff these local offices.[3] The politicians, for their part, and the regulators who answered to them fashioned rules that made very high profits possible for the GSEs, at least in the short run. Although it was a relationship that reflected political favoritism (some would say corruption), members of Congress, particularly those involved in banking regulation, were highly supportive of the arrangement.

Fannie Mae and Freddie Mac did not originate mortgages. Instead, they purchased the mortgages originated by banks, mortgage brokers, and other lenders. Propelled by their cheaper access to funds, Fannie Mae and Freddie Mac grew rapidly during the 1990s. As **Exhibit 4** shows, the share of all mortgages held by Fannie Mae and Freddie Mac jumped from 25 percent in 1990 to 45 percent in 2001. Their share fluctuated around 40 percent during 2001–2008. Their dominance of the **secondary mortgage market** was even greater. During the decade prior to their insolvency and takeover by the federal government during the summer of 2008, Fannie Mae and Freddie Mac purchased about 90 percent of the mortgages sold in the secondary market. Because of this dominance, their lending practices permitted them to exert a huge impact on the standards accepted by mortgage originators.

Responding to earlier congressional legislation, the Department of Housing and Urban Development (HUD) imposed regulations designed to make housing more affordable. The HUD mandates, adopted in 1995, required Fannie Mae and Freddie Mac to extend a larger share of their loans to low- and moderate-income households. For example, under the HUD mandates, 40 percent of new loans financed by Fannie Mae and Freddie Mac in 1996 had

Secondary mortgage market
A market in which mortgages originated by a lender are sold to another financial institution. In recent years, the major buyers in this market have been Fannie Mae, Freddie Mac, and large investment banks.

EXHIBIT 4

The Share of Total Outstanding Mortgages Held by Fannie Mae and Freddie Mac, 1990–2008

Fannie Mae and Freddie Mac dominated the mortgage market for many years. Because of their government sponsorship, they were able to obtain funds cheaper than private firms. They held 45 percent of all mortgages in 2001, up from 25 percent in 1990. During 2001–2008, their share fluctuated around 40 percent. Their dominance of the secondary market, where loans are purchased from originators, is even greater. In July 2008, they were declared insolvent and taken over by the U.S. Treasury.

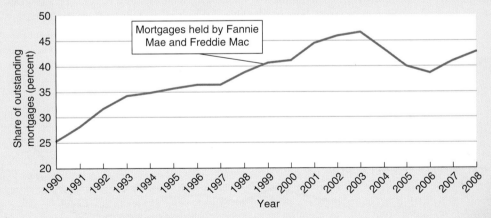

Source: Office of Federal Housing Enterprise Oversight, www.ofheo.gov.

---

[3]For additional details, see Peter J. Wallison and Charles W. Calomiris, "The Destruction of Fannie Mae and Freddie Mac," American Enterprise Institute, online (posted Tuesday, September 30, 2008). Also see Common Cause, "Ask Yourself Why…They Didn't See This Coming" (September 24, 2008), available at http://www.commoncause.org/research-reports/National_092408_Education_Fund_Report_Lending_Industry_in_the_Financial_Crisis.pdf; and Center for Responsive Politics, "Lobbying: Top Spenders" (2008), available at www.opensecrets.org/lobby/top.php?indexType=s.

Subprime loan

A loan made to a borrower with blemished credit or one who provides only limited documentation of income, employment history, and other indicators of creditworthiness.

FICO score

A credit score measuring a borrower's likely ability to repay a loan. A person's FICO score will range between 300 and 850. A score of 700 or more indicates that the borrower's credit standing is good. FICO is an acronym for the Fair Isaac Corporation, the creators of the FICO score.

Alt-A loans

Loans extended with little documentation or verification of the borrowers' income, employment, and other indicators of their ability to repay. Because of this poor documentation, these loans are risky.

to go to borrowers with incomes below the median. This mandated share was steadily increased to 50 percent in 2000 and 56 percent in 2008. Similar increases were mandated for borrowers with incomes of less than 60 percent of the median. Moreover, in 1999, HUD guidelines required Fannie Mae and Freddie Mac to accept smaller down payments and permitted them to extend larger loans relative to income.

The policies of Fannie Mae and Freddie Mac exerted an enormous impact on the actions of banks and other mortgage lenders. Recognizing that riskier loans could be passed on to Fannie and Freddie, mortgage originators had less incentive to scrutinize the creditworthiness of borrowers and more incentive to reduce the required down payment, in order to sell more mortgages. After all, when the mortgages were soon sold to Fannie or Freddie, the risk was transferred to them also. The bottom line: Required down payments were reduced and the accepted credit standards lowered.

As the HUD regulations tightened, the share of loans that were **subprime loans** steadily increased. **Exhibit 5** illustrates this point. Measured as a share of mortgages originated during the year, subprime mortgages rose from 4.5 percent in 1994 to 13.2 percent in 2000 and 20 percent in 2005 and 2006. (*Note:* Bank examiners consider a loan to be subprime if the borrower's **FICO score** is less than 660.) When the **Alt-A loans**, those extended without full documentation, were added to the subprime, a third of the mortgages extended in 2005–2006 were to borrowers with either poor or highly questionable credit records.

As the mortgages extended to those with weak credit soared, so too did the number with little or no down payment. **Exhibit 6** shows both the number of loans issued by Fannie Mae and Freddie Mac and the share extended to borrowers with 5 percent or less down payment. Note how the number of new loans financed by the government sponsored corporations increased from less than one hundred thousand in the late 1990s to more than six hundred thousand in 2007. At the same time, the share of mortgages to borrowers making a down payment of 5 percent or less rose from 4 percent in 1998 to 12 percent in 2003 and 23 percent in 2007. Thus, Fannie Mae and Freddie Mac were flooding the market with low-down-payment loans extended to borrowers with weak credit. Meanwhile, conventional loans for which borrowers were required to make at least a 20 percent down payment fell from two-thirds of the total in the early 1990s to only one-third in 2005–2006.

The shift from conventional loans to "creative finance" and "flexible standards," as the regulators called the new criteria, is highly important because the default and foreclosure rates for subprime loans ranges from seven to ten times the rate for conventional loans to prime borrowers. This differential is even greater in the case of mortgages with

---

EXHIBIT 5

Subprime and Alt-A Mortgages as a Share of the Total, 1994–2007

Both subprime and Alt-A mortgages reflect loans to borrowers with a weak credit history. Note how the share of loans to borrowers in these two categories jumped from roughly 10 percent in 2001–2003 to 33 percent in 2005–2006.

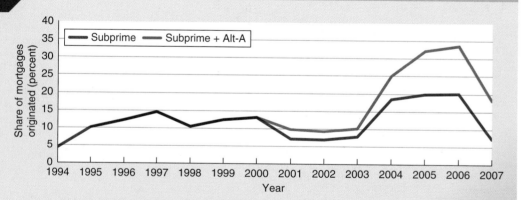

Source: The data for 1994–2000 are from Edward M. Gramlich, Financial Services Roundtable Annual Housing Policy Meeting, Chicago, Illinois (21 May 2004), www.federalreserve.gov/boarddocs/speeches/2004/20040521/default.htm. The data for 2001–2007 are from the Joint Center for Housing Studies of Harvard University, The State of the Nation's Housing 2008, www.jchs.harvard.edu/son/index.htm.

EXHIBIT 6

Growth of Low-down-payment Loans Extended by Fannie Mae and Freddie Mac

Following the 1999 HUD guidelines encouraging Fannie Mae and Freddie Mac to extend more low-down-payment loans, the GSEs both increased the number of their mortgages (left frame) and the share extended with a down payment of 5 percent or less. As the right frame shows, the share of these low down payment mortgages extended by Fannie Mae and Freddie Mac increased from 4 percent in 1998 to 12 percent in 2003 and 23 percent in 2007.

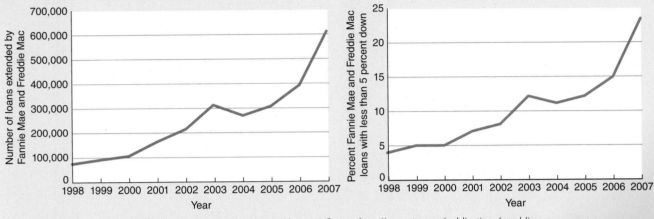

Sources: Russell Robert's, *Gambling With Other Peoples Money*, Mercatus Center, http://mercatus.org/publications/gambling-other-peoples-money.

little or no down payment. Initially, this easy credit policy increased demand and pushed housing prices upward. But, the policy was not sustainable and it was predictable where it would lead. Eventually, the growing share of low-down-payment loans extended to those with weak credit would result in substantially higher default and foreclosure rates. This is precisely what happened.

ST06-2b FACTOR 2: PROLONGED LOW INTEREST RATE POLICY OF THE FED DURING 2002–2004

Following the high and variable inflation rates of the 1970s, Federal Reserve policy focused on keeping the inflation rate low and stable. By the mid-1980s, the inflation rate had been reduced to 3 percent. Throughout 1985–1999, the Fed kept the inflation rate low and avoided abrupt year-to-year changes. In turn, the relative price stability reduced uncertainty and created an environment for both strong growth and economic stability.

However, beginning in 1999, Fed policy became more erratic. Monetary policy was expansionary just before 2000, restrictive prior to the recession of 2001, and then highly expansionary during the recovery from that recession. As Exhibit 7 shows, the Fed kept short-term interest rates at historic lows throughout 2002–2004. These extremely low short-term rates increased the demand for interest-sensitive goods like automobiles and housing.

The Fed's artificially low short-term rates substantially increased the attractiveness of **adjustable rate mortgages (ARMs)** to both borrowers and lenders. As Exhibit 8 shows, adjustable rate mortgages jumped from 10 percent of the total outstanding mortgages in 2000 to 21 percent in 2005. The low initial interest rates on adjustable rate mortgages made it possible for homebuyers to afford the monthly payments for larger, more expensive homes. This easy credit provided fuel for the housing boom. But the low rates and ARM loans also meant that as short-term interest rates increased from their historic low levels, home buyers would face a higher monthly payment two or three years in the future. Unsurprisingly, this is precisely what happened.

Adjustable rate mortgage (ARM)
A home loan in which the interest rate, and thus the monthly payment, is tied to a short-term rate like the one-year Treasury bill rate. Typically, the mortgage interest rate will be two or three percentage points above the related short-term rate. It will be reset at various time intervals (e.g., annually), and thus the interest rate and monthly payment will vary over the life of the loan.

EXHIBIT 7

Fed Policy and Short-Term Interest Rates, 1995–2009

Here we show the federal funds and one-year Treasury bill interest rates. These short-term rates are reflective of monetary policy. Note how the Fed pushed these rates to historic lows (less than 2 percent) throughout 2002–2004 but then increased them substantially during 2005–2006.

The low rates provided fuel for the housing price boom, but the rising rates led to higher interest rates and monthly payments on adjustable rate mortgage (ARM) loans, which helped push the mortgage default and foreclosure rates upward beginning in the second half of 2006.

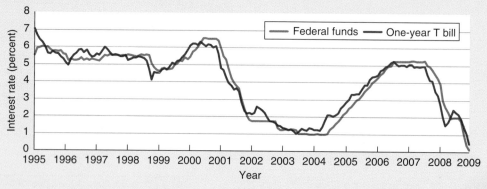

Sources: www.federalreserve.gov and www.economagic.com.

EXHIBIT 8

Adjustable Rate Mortgages (ARMs) as a Share of Total Outstanding Mortgages, 1990–2008

The interest rate and monthly payment on ARMs are tied to a short-term interest rate (e.g., the one-year Treasury bill rate). The Fed's low-interest rate policy of 2002–2004

increased the attractiveness of ARMs. Note how ARM loans increased as a share of total mortgages from 10 percent in 2000 to 21 percent in 2005.

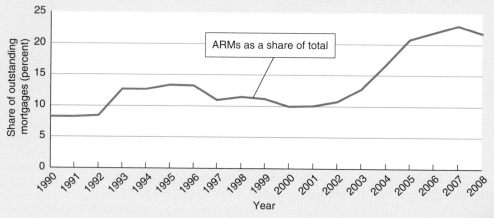

Source: Office of Federal Housing Enterprise Oversight, www.ofheo.gov.

By 2005, the expansionary monetary policy of 2002–2004 was clearly placing upward pressure on the general level of prices. The Fed responded with a shift to a more restrictive monetary policy, which pushed interest rates upward (see Exhibit 7). Many who purchased houses with little or no down payment and adjustable rate loans when interest rates were low during 2002–2004 faced substantially higher monthly payments as interest rates rose and the monthly payments on their ARM loans were reset during 2006 and 2007. These owners had virtually no equity in their homes. Therefore, when housing prices leveled off and began to decline during the second half of 2006, the default and foreclosure rates on these loans began to rise almost immediately (see Exhibits 1 and 2). Some owners with little or no initial equity simply walked away as their outstanding loan exceeded the value of their house.

Essentially, the small down payment and ARMs combination made it possible for homebuyers to gamble with someone else's money. If housing prices rose, buyers could reap a sizable capital gain without risking much of their own investment capital. Based on the rising housing prices of 2000–2005, many of these homebuyers expected to sell the house for a profit and move on in a couple of years. There were even television programs and investment seminars pushing this strategy as the route to riches.

Exhibit 9 shows the foreclosure rates for fixed interest rate and ARM loans for both subprime and prime loans. Compared to their prime borrower counterparts, the foreclosure rate for subprime borrowers was approximately ten times higher for fixed rate mortgages and seven times higher for adjustable rate mortgages. These huge differentials explain why

EXHIBIT 9

The Foreclosure Rate of Fixed and Adjustable Rate Mortgages for Subprime and Prime Borrowers, 1998–2008

The foreclosure rates on fixed and adjustable interest rate mortgages are shown here for both subprime (panel a) and prime (panel b) borrowers. Note how the foreclosure rate was generally seven to ten times higher for subprime loans than for those to prime borrowers. As housing prices leveled off and declined in 2006–2008, the foreclosure rate on fixed interest rate mortgages did not change much. In contrast, the foreclosure rate for ARM loans soared beginning in the second half of 2006, and this was true for ARM loans to both subprime and prime borrowers. Clearly, the increasing share of both subprime and ARM loans during 2000–2005 contributed to the boom and bust of the housing market.

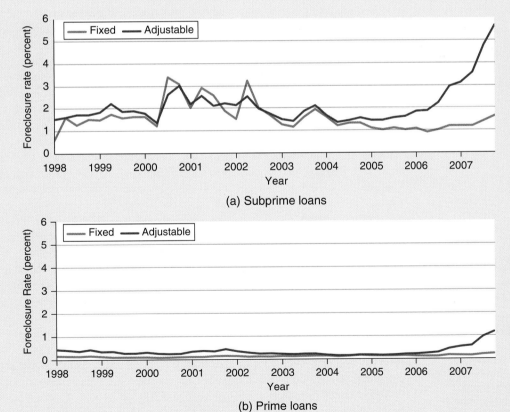

(a) Subprime loans

(b) Prime loans

Source: Stan J. Liebowitz, "Anatomy of a Train Wreck: Causes of the Mortgage Meltdown," Ch. 13 in Randall G. Holcombe and Benjamin Powell, eds, *Housing America: Building Out of a Crisis* (New Brunswick, NJ: Transaction Publishers, 2009). We would like to thank Professor Liebowitz for making this data available to us.

the increasing share of loans to subprime borrowers substantially increased the default and foreclosure rates.

As Exhibit 9 shows, there was no upward trend in the foreclosure rate on fixed interest rate loans for either prime or subprime borrowers during 2000–2008. On the other hand, the foreclosure rate on ARMs soared for both prime and subprime loans during 2006–2008. In fact, the percentage increase in foreclosures on ARM loans was higher for prime than subprime borrowers. This is highly revealing. It illustrates that both prime and subprime borrowers played the low-down-payment, mortgage casino game.

The loan default problem is often referred to as the *subprime mortgage crisis*. This is true, but it is only part of the story. It was also an ARM loan crisis. Fed policy encouraging ARM loans, the increasing proportion of these loans as a share of the total, and their higher default and foreclosure rates also contributed substantially, first to the housing boom and then to the bust. The combination of the mortgage lending regulations and the Fed's artificially low interest rate policies encouraged decision-makers to borrow more money and make unwise and inefficient investments.

ST06-2c FACTOR 3: THE INCREASED DEBT-TO-CAPITAL RATIO OF INVESTMENT BANKS

Investment bank
An institution that acts as an underwriter for securities issued by other corporations or lenders. Unlike traditional banks, investment banks do not accept deposits from, or provide loans to, individuals.

Leverage ratios
The ratio of loans and other investments to the firm's capital assets.

A rule change adopted by the Securities and Exchange Commission (SEC) in April 2004 made it possible for **investment banks** to increase the leverage of their investment capital, which eventually led to their collapse. A firm's **leverage ratio** is simply the ratio of its investment holdings (including loans) relative to its capital. Thus, if a firm had investment funds that were twelve times the size of its equity capital, its leverage ratio would be 12 to 1. Prior to the SEC rule change, this was approximately the leverage ratio of both investment and commercial banks.

Essentially, the SEC applied regulations known as Basel I to investment banking. These regulations, which have been adopted by most of the industrial countries, require banks to maintain at least 8 percent capital against assets like loans to commercial businesses. This implies a leverage ratio of approximately 12 to 1. However, the Basil regulations provide more favorable treatment of residential loans. The capital requirement for residential mortgage loans is only 4 percent, which implies a 25 to 1 leverage ratio. Even more important, the capital requirement for low-risk securities is still lower at 1.6 percent. This means that the permissible leverage ratio for low-risk securities could be as high as 60 to 1.

Key investment banking leaders, including Henry Paulson who was CEO of Goldman Sachs at the time, urged the SEC to apply the higher leverage ratio to investment banks. Ironically, Paulson later became Secretary of the Treasury and was in charge of the federal "bailout" of the banks that got into trouble because of the excessive leveraging of their capital.

Following the rule change, large investment banks, like Lehman Brothers, Goldman Sachs, and Bear Stearns, expanded their mortgage financing activities. They bundled large holdings of mortgages together and issued securities for their finance. Because of the diversity of the mortgage portfolio, investment in the underlying securities was thought to involve minimal risk. If the **security-rating** firms provided the **mortgage-backed securities** with a AAA rating, then the investment banks could leverage them up to 60 to 1 against their capital.

Security rating
A rating indicating the risk of default of the security. A rating of AAA indicates that the risk of default is low.

Mortgage-backed securities
Securities issued for the financing of large pools of mortgages. The promised returns to the security holders are derived from the mortgage interest payments.

The mortgage-backed securities, financed with short-term leveraged lending, were highly lucrative. The large number of mortgages packaged together provided lenders with diversity and protection against abnormally high default rates in specific regions and loan categories. But it did not shield them from an overall increase in mortgage default rates. As default rates increased sharply in 2006 and 2007, it became apparent that the mortgage-backed securities were far more risky than had been previously thought. When the risk of these mortgages became more apparent, the value of the mortgage-backed securities plummeted because it was difficult to know their true value. As the value of the mortgage-backed securities collapsed, the highly leveraged investment banks faced massive short-term debt obligations with little reserves on which to draw. This is why the investment banks collapsed so quickly. In fact, when the Fed financed the acquisition of Bear Stearns by JPMorgan Chase, the leverage ratio of Bear Stearns was an astounding 33 to 1, about two and a half times the historical level associated with prudent banking practices.

Why didn't key Wall Street decision makers see the looming danger? No doubt, they were influenced by the low and relatively stable default rates over the past several decades (see Exhibit 2). Even during serious recessions like those of 1974–1975 and 1982–1983, the mortgage default rates were only a little more than 2 percent, less than half the rates of 2008. But one would still have thought that analysts at investment companies and security-rating firms would have warned that the low historical rates were for periods when down payments were larger, borrowing was more restricted relative to income, and fewer loans were made to subprime borrowers. A few analysts did provide warnings, but their views were ignored by high-level superiors.

However, the incentive structure also helps explain why highly intelligent people failed to see the oncoming danger. The bonuses of most Wall Street executives are closely tied to short-term profitability, and the mortgage-backed securities were highly profitable when housing prices were rising and interest rates were low. If a personal bonus of a million dollars or more is at stake this year, one is likely to be far less sensitive to the long-term dangers.

The incentive structure accompanying the regulation and rating of securities also played an important role. Only three firms—Moody's, Standard & Poors, and Fitch—are legally authorized to rate securities. These rating agencies are paid by the firm requesting the rating. A Triple-A rating was exceedingly important. It made higher leveraging possible, but, even more important, the Triple-A rating made it possible to sell the mortgage-backed securities to institutional investors, retirement plans, and investors around the world looking for relatively safe investments. The rating agencies were paid attractive fees for their ratings, and Triple-A approval would mean more business for the rating agencies as well as the investment banks. Clearly, this incentive structure is not one that encourages careful scrutiny and hard-nosed evaluation of the quality of the underlying mortgage bundle. Paradoxically, the shortsighted and counterproductive incentive structures that characterize some of Wall Street's best-known firms contributed to their collapse.

ST06-2d FACTOR 4: HIGH DEBT/INCOME RATIO OF HOUSEHOLDS

During 1985–2007, household debt grew to unprecedented levels. As **Exhibit 10** shows, household debt as a share of disposable (after-tax) income ranged from 40 percent to 65 percent during 1953–1984. However, since the mid-1980s, the debt-to-income ratio of households climbed at an alarming rate. It reached 135 percent in 2007, more than twice the level of the mid-1980s. Unsurprisingly, more debt means that a larger share of household income is required just to meet the interest payments.

Interest payments on home mortgages and home equity loans are tax deductible, but household interest on other forms of debt is not. This incentive structure encourages households to concentrate their debt into loans against their housing. But a large debt against one's housing will mean that housing will be the hardest hit by unexpected events that force major adjustments. This is precisely what occurred in 2006–2008. The rising interest rates and mere leveling off of housing prices soon led to an increase in mortgage defaults and foreclosures, because households were heavily indebted and a huge share of that indebtedness was in the form of mortgages against their housing. As the economy weakened, of course, this situation quickly worsened. Thus, the high level of household indebtedness also contributed to the Great Recession.

EXHIBIT 10

Household Debt to Disposable Personal Income Ratio, 1953–2008

Between 1953 and 1984, household debt as a share of disposable (after-tax) income ranged from 40 percent to 65 percent. However, the household debt-to-income ratio rose steadily throughout 1985–2007. By 2007, it soared to 135 percent, more than twice the level of the mid-1980s.

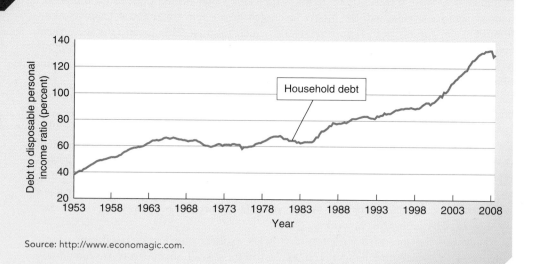

Source: http://www.economagic.com.

ST06-3 THE GREAT RECESSION, PERVERSE INCENTIVES, AND POTENTIAL REFORMS

The combination of the HUD regulations, low-down-payment requirements, and the Fed's low interest policy of 2002–2004 resulted in the rapid growth of both subprime and ARM loans during the first five years of this century. As is often the case with policy changes, the initial effects were positive—strong demand for housing, rising housing prices, and a construction boom. But the long-term effects were disastrous. The increasing share of subprime loans began to push default rates upward. Similarly, the low short-term interest rates that made adjustable rate mortgages attractive during 2004 soon reversed and led to higher monthly payments as the interest rates on ARM loans were reset in the years immediately ahead. As these two factors converged in the latter half of 2006, they generated falling housing prices and soaring mortgage default and foreclosure rates. The housing and lending crisis soon spread to other sectors and economies around the world. Moreover, the Triple-A rated mortgage-backed securities were marketed throughout the world, and, as their value plunged with rising default rates, turmoil was created in global financial markets.

It is important to note that both the mortgage default and foreclosure rates soared well before the recession began in December 2007. This illustrates that the housing crisis was not caused by the recession. Instead, it was the other way around.

Policies that generated perverse incentives and undermined sound lending practices were a central cause of the Great Recession of 2008–2009. Has action been taken to alter the structure of incentives that plague the mortgage loan market? To a large degree, the mortgage loan market has been nationalized. Fannie Mae and Freddie Mac were declared insolvent and taken over by the federal government in 2008. The federal government now dominates the mortgage market. When the mortgage loans of the Federal Housing Administration are added to those of Fannie Mae and Freddie Mac, 90 percent of the new mortgages for housing are currently financed by the federal government. The operating policies of Fannie Mae and Freddie Mac are largely unchanged. Both continue to accept mortgages from borrowers with little or no down payment. Moreover, because of their federal ownership, both continue to have access to funds at 50 to 75 basis points below the funds available to private firms in the lending market.

Further, the tax deductibility of mortgage interest payments continues to encourage Americans to overinvest in housing and concentrate their indebtedness in mortgage loans. High-income recipients are the primary beneficiaries of the deductibility. Even though this policy helped to fuel the housing boom, no action has been taken in this area.

A decade later, most of the perverse incentives that generated the Great Recession remain in place. Constructive reforms would focus on getting the incentives right. Consider the following questions. Would the mortgage market work better if loan originators were held responsible for defaults on loans they originated, even if they sold them to another party? Does it make sense to encourage the purchase of housing with little or no down payment? Does it make sense to encourage people to concentrate their indebtedness in the form of a mortgage loan against their housing, as current tax policy does? Although the precise action is debatable, the Great Recession suggests that review of current policies that generate counterproductive incentives would be wise.

KEY POINTS

- After soaring during the previous five years, housing prices began to decline during the second half of 2006, and mortgage defaults and housing foreclosures started to increase. As the housing bust spread to other sectors, stock prices plunged, major investment banks experienced financial troubles, unemployment increased sharply, and by 2008 the economy was in a severe recession.

- Fannie Mae and Freddie Mac grew rapidly during the 1990s. Their government sponsorship made it possible for them to obtain funds cheaper than private rivals. Because of their dominance of the secondary market, in which mortgages are purchased from originators, their lending standards exerted a huge impact on the mortgage market.

- Beginning in the mid-1990s, mandates imposed on Fannie Mae and Freddie Mac, along with regulations imposed on banks, forced lenders to reduce their lending standards, extend more mortgages to subprime borrowers, and reduce down payment requirements. The share of mortgages extended to subprime borrowers (including Alt-A loans) rose from 10 percent in 2001–2003 to 33 percent in 2005–2006. Correspondingly, the share of low-down-payment loans extended by Fannie Mae and Freddie Mac soared from 4 percent in 1998 to 23 percent in 2007. These changes were highly important because the default and foreclosure rates on subprime and low-down-payment loans are several times higher than for conventional loans to prime borrowers.

- The historically low interest rate policies of the Fed during 2002–2004 increased the demand for housing and the attractiveness of adjustable rate mortgages. This provided fuel for the soaring housing prices. ARM loans increased from 10 percent of total mortgages in 2000 to 21 percent in 2005. Fed policy pushed interest rates up in 2005–2006 and ARM loans were reset, pushing monthly payments higher. As a result, the default and foreclosure rates on these loans soared for prime as well as subprime borrowers.

- As a result of regulations adopted in April 2004, investment banks were allowed to leverage their capital by as much as 60 to 1 when financing mortgages with Triple-A rated securities. The rating agencies provided the Triple-A ratings, and the mortgage-backed securities were sold around the world. As the mortgage default rates rose in 2007–2008, Fannie Mae, Freddie Mac, and the major investment banks holding large quantities of these securities quickly fell into financial troubles, and several collapsed.

- The ratio of household debt to personal income increased steadily during 1985–2007, reaching a historic high at the end of that period.

- Low-down-payment requirements, the growth of subprime and ARM loans, the Fed's easy credit policy, highly leveraged mortgage-backed securities, and heavy borrowing by households fueled the run-up in housing prices. With time, however, this was a disastrous combination that provided the ingredients for the Great Recession.

CRITICAL ANALYSIS QUESTIONS

1. What were the major causes of the Great Recession of 2008–2009?

2. Why did housing prices rise rapidly during 2002–2005? Why did the mortgage default rate increase so sharply during 2006 and 2007 even before the 2008–2009 recession began?

3. *If owners have little or no equity in their houses, how will this influence the likelihood that they will default on their mortgage? Why?

4. What happened to the credit standards (e.g., minimum down payment, mortgage loan relative to the value of the house, and creditworthiness of the borrower) between 1995 and 2005? Why did the credit standards change? How did this influence the 2002–2005 housing price bubble and later the default and foreclosure rates?

5. *When mortgage originators sell mortgages to Fannie Mae, Freddie Mac, and investment banks the originators have no

additional liability for possible default by the borrower. How will this arrangement influence the incentive of the origina- tors to scrutinize the creditworthiness of the borrower? Would the incentive structure be different if the originator planned to hold the mortgage until it was paid off? Why or why not?

6. Some charge that the crisis of 2008 was caused by the "greed" of Wall Street firms and other bankers. Do you agree with this

view? Do you think there was more greed on Wall Street in the first five years of this century than during the 1980s and 1990s? Why or why not?

*Asterisk denotes questions for which answers are given in Appendix B.

Lessons from the Great Depression

We now know, as a few knew then, that the depression was not produced by a failure of private enterprise, but rather by a failure of government in an area in which the government had from the first been assigned responsibility. —**Milton and Rose Friedman**[1]

The Great Depression is perhaps the most catastrophic economic event in American history. It is also one of the most misunderstood. Misconceptions abound with regard to what actually happened. The Great Depression is a tragic story about economic illiteracy and the adverse impact of unsound policies. People who do not learn from the lessons of history are prone to repeat them. If we want to avoid similar experiences in the future, it is vitally important that we understand the factors underlying the tragic events of this era.

As you read this special topic, look for answers to the following questions:

- What caused the Great Depression? Was it the stock market crash of 1929?

- Why was the Great Depression so long and severe?

- Did the New Deal policies end the Great Depression?

- Does the Great Depression reflect a failure of markets or a failure of government?

---

[1]Milton and Rose Friedman, *Free to Choose* (New York: Harcourt Brace Jovanovich, 1980), 71.

ST07-1 THE ECONOMIC RECORD OF THE GREAT DEPRESSION

Exhibit 1 presents data on the change in real GDP and the rate of unemployment during 1929–1940. As panel (a) illustrates, real GDP fell by 8.6 percent in 1930, 6.5 percent in 1931, and a whopping 13.1 percent in 1932. By 1933, real GDP was nearly a third less than that in 1929. There was a temporary rebound during 1934–1936, but growth slowed in 1937 and real GDP fell once again in 1938. In 1939, a full decade after the disastrous downturn started, the real GDP per capita of the United States was about the same as it had been in 1929.

While output was declining during the depression era, unemployment was soaring. As Exhibit 1, panel (b), shows, the rate of unemployment rose from 3.2 percent in 1929 to 8.7 percent in 1930 and 15.9 percent in 1931. During 1932 and 1933, the unemployment rate soared to nearly one-quarter of the labor force. Even though real GDP grew substantially during 1934 and 1935, the unemployment rate remained above 20 percent during both of those years. After declining to 14.3 percent in 1937, the rate of unemployment rose to 19.0 percent during the downturn of 1938, and it was still

EXHIBIT 1

Real GDP and the Rate of Unemployment, 1929–1940

The change in real GDP (panel a) and rate of unemployment (panel b) figures during the Great Depression are shown here. These data illustrate both the severity and length of the economic contraction. For four successive years (1930–1933), real output fell. Unemployment soared to nearly one-quarter of the workforce in 1932 and 1933. Although real output expanded and the rate of unemployment declined during 1934–1937, the economy again fell into the depths of a depression in 1938. In 1939, a decade after the economic plunge started, 17.2 percent of the labor force was still unemployed and real GDP was virtually unchanged from the level of 1929.

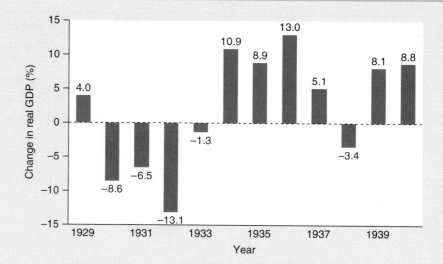

(a) Change in real GDP

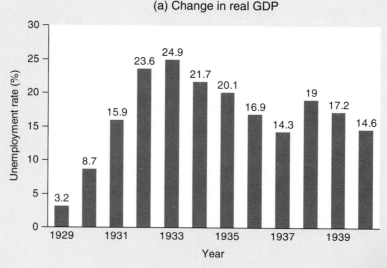

(b) Unemployment rate

Sources: Real GDP growth rates are from www.bea.gov. The unemployment data are from the Bureau or Labor Statistics (BLS) at www.bls.gov.

17.2 percent in 1939, a full decade after the catastrophic era began. The unemployment rate was 14 percent or more throughout the ten years from 1931 through 1940. By way of comparison, the unemployment rate has averaged less than 6 percent during the past quarter of a century, and it has never reached 11 percent during the 80 years from 1940 through 2019. Moreover, the statistics conceal the hardship and suffering accompanying the economic disaster. It was an era of farm foreclosures, bank failures, soup kitchens, unemployment lines, and even a sharply declining birthrate. America would never quite be the same after the 1930s.

ST07-2 WAS THE GREAT DEPRESSION CAUSED BY THE 1929 STOCK MARKET CRASH?

The prices of stock shares rose sharply during the 1920s. But this is not surprising because the 1920s was a remarkable decade of innovation, technological advancement, and economic growth. The production of automobiles increased more than tenfold during the 1920s. Households with electricity, telephones, and indoor plumbing spread rapidly throughout the economy. The first regularly scheduled radio programs were broadcast in the early 1920s, providing an amazing new vehicle for mass communication. Air conditioning received a boost from its use in "movie houses," as theaters were called at the time. There is good reason why the decade was known as the "Roaring Twenties." Perhaps more than any other era, the lives of ordinary Americans were transformed during the 1920s. To a large degree, the stock market was merely registering the remarkable growth and development of the decade.[2]

Generations of students have been told that the Great Depression was caused by the stock market crash of October 1929. Is this really true? Let's take a look at the figures. As Exhibit 2, panel (a), shows, the Dow Jones Industrial Average opened in 1929 at 300, rose to a high of 381 on September 3, 1929, but gradually receded to 327 on Tuesday, October 22. A major sell-off started the following day, and the Dow began to plunge. By October 29, which is known as Black Tuesday, the Dow closed at 230. Thus, in exactly one week, the stock market lost nearly one-third of its value. A couple of weeks later on November 13, the Dow fell to an even lower level, closing at 199.

However, it is interesting to see what happened during the next five months. From mid-November 1929 through mid-April 1930, the Dow Jones Industrial Average increased every month, and by mid-April the index had risen to 294, regaining virtually all of the losses experienced during the late October crash. This raises an interesting question: If the October crash caused the Great Depression, how can one explain that the stock market had regained most of those losses by April 1930?

But from mid-April throughout the rest of 1930, stock prices moved steadily downward and closed the year at 165. Apparently something happened during May–June 1930, which caused the stock market to head downward. We will return to this issue in a moment. Exhibit 2 panel (b) presents data for the Dow Jones Industrials for 1931–1940. The index continued to fall in 1931–1932 and rebounded strongly in 1933 but then fluctuated between 100 and 200 for the remainder of the decade. Note the Dow stood at 131 at year-end 1940, even lower than the closing figure for 1930.

The Great Depression was a prolonged period of falling incomes, high unemployment, and difficult living conditions. The decline in output and high unemployment were the most severe in American history. Why was the economy so weak for so long?

INTERFOTO/Alamy Stock Photo

---

[2]Popular writers often argue that speculators drove the stock market to unsustainable highs in the late 1920s, but this view is an exaggeration. The price/earnings ratio for the Dow was 19 just before the crash. This places it at the upper range of normal but not at an unprecedented high. On October 9, 1929, *The Wall Street Journal* reported that railroad stocks were selling at 11.9 times earnings, which would place their P/E ratio toward the lower range of normal. RCA was the hot "high-tech" company of the era, and it earned $6.15 per share in 1927 and $15.98 per share in 1928. It traded at a high in 1928 of $420. This would imply a P/E ratio of 26, not unreasonable for a growth stock with outstanding future earning prospects.

EXHIBIT 2

The Stock Market (Dow Jones Industrial Average), 1928–1940

The figures for the Dow Jones Industrial Average (DJIA) are shown here. Clearly, stock prices plunged in September–October 1929, but note how they recovered during the five months from mid-November 1929 through mid-April of 1930. However, this recovery reversed as the Smoot–Hawley tariff bill was debated, passed, and eventually signed into law on June 17, 1930. As panel (b) shows, the Dow continued to fall throughout 1931 and 1932 and never reached 200 throughout the remainder of the decade.

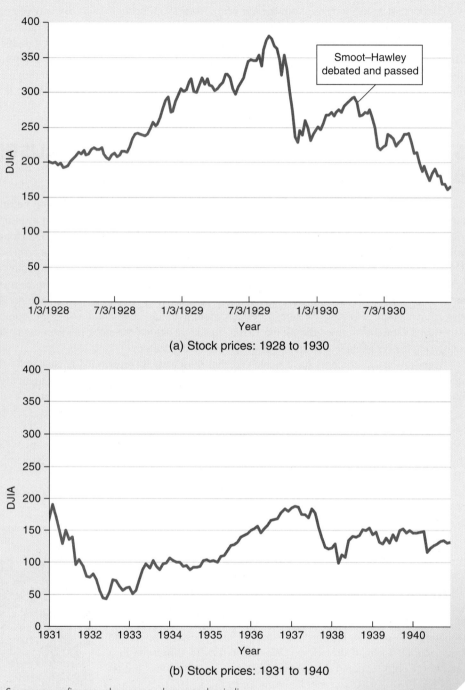

(a) Stock prices: 1928 to 1930

(b) Stock prices: 1931 to 1940

Sources: www.finance.yahoo.com and www.analyzeindices.com.

There have been several downturns in stock prices of the magnitude experienced during 1929, both before and after the Great Depression, and none of them resulted in anything like the prolonged unemployment and lengthy contraction of the 1930s. For example, the stock market price declines immediately before and during the recessions of 1973–1975 and 1982–1983 were as large as those of the 1929 crash, approximately 50 percent. But both of these recessions were over in about 18 months. Moreover, in 1987, the Dow Industrials fell from 2,640 on October 2 to 1,740 on October 19, a decline of 34 percent. Whereas the collapse of stock prices in 1987 was similar to the October 1929 crash, that is where the similarity ends. The 1987 crash did not lead to economic disaster. In fact, it was not even followed by a recession.

11. A public good reflects the characteristics of the good, not the sector in which it is provided. Elementary education is not a public good because it is relatively easy to exclude nonpaying customers and to establish a one-to-one link between payment for and receipt of the good.

CHAPTER 6: THE ECONOMICS OF COLLECTIVE DECISION-MAKING

4. The problem is not so much that the "wrong guys" won the last election as it is the incentive structure confronted by political decision-makers. Even if the "right people" were elected, they would be unlikely to improve the efficiency of government, at least not very much, given the strong incentive to support special-interest and shortsighted policies and the weak incentives for operational efficiency when decisions are made by the political process.

8. It is difficult for the voter to know what a candidate will do once elected, and the rationally ignorant voter is usually unwilling to spend the time and effort required to understand issues because the probability that any single vote will decide the issue is exceedingly small. Special-interest voters, in contrast, will know which candidate has promised them the most on their issue. Also, the candidate who is both competent and prepared to ignore special interests will have a hard time getting these facts to voters without financial support from special-interest groups. Each voter has an incentive to be a "free rider" on the "good government" issue. Interestingly, controlling government on behalf of society as a whole is a public good. As in the case of other public goods, there is a tendency for too little of it to be supplied.

10. No. The government is merely an alternative form of organization. Government organization does not permit us to escape either scarcity or competition. It merely affects the nature of the competition. Political competition (eg, voting, lobbying, political contributions, and politically determined budgets) replaces market competition. Neither is there any reason to believe that government organization modifies the importance of personal self-interest.

12. When the welfare of a special-interest group conflicts with that of a widely dispersed, unorganized majority, the legislative political process can reasonably be expected to work to the benefit of the special interest.

CHAPTER 7: TAKING THE NATION'S ECONOMIC PULSE

1. Choices (a), (c), (f), (g), and (h) will exert no effect on GDP; (b) and (d) will increase GDP by the amount of the expenditure; and (e) will increase GDP by $250 (the commission on the transaction).

3. Because the furniture was produced last year, the sale does not affect GDP this year. It reduces inventory investment by $100,000 and increases consumption by $100,000, leaving GDP unchanged.

7. $8.87.

9. **a.** $1,000; **b.** $600; **c.** $200; **d.** 0; **e.** $20,000.

11. **a.** False. Inventory investment indicates whether the holdings of unsold goods are rising or falling. A negative inventory investment merely indicates that there was a reduction in the size of inventories during the period. **b.** False. If gross investment is less than the depreciation of capital goods during the period, net investment would be negative. Net investment in the United States was negative for several years during the Great Depression of the 1930s. **c.** Not necessarily. Rather, it may be the result of an increase in prices, population, or hours worked.

12. Neither the receipts nor the expenditures on payouts would count toward GDP because they are merely transfers—they do not involve production. However, expenditures on

operations, administration, and government-provided goods and services from lottery proceeds would add to GDP.

16. **a.** $3,267 billion; **b.** 4,946.1 billion; **c.** 42.3; **d.** 5,963.1 billion; **e.** 78.1; **f.** 16,197.0 billion; **g.** 19,080.8 billion

CHAPTER 8: ECONOMIC FLUCTUATIONS, UNEMPLOYMENT, AND INFLATION

2. Job seekers do not know which employers will offer them the more attractive jobs. They find out by searching. Job search is "profitable" and consistent with economic efficiency as long as the marginal gain from search exceeds the marginal cost of searching. The job search process will lead to a better match between the skills of employees and the requirements of the available jobs.

3. Individuals (e) and (f) would be classified as employed; (a), (b), and (c) would be classified as unemployed; (d) is not in the labor force.

6. When the actual unemployment rate is equal to the natural rate of unemployment, cyclical unemployment is absent and potential GDP is at its sustainable rate.

7. **a.** 60 percent; **b.** 8.3 percent; **c.** 55 percent.

8. No. It means that there were no jobs available at wage rates acceptable to the potential workers who were unemployed. Thus, they continued to search for more attractive opportunities.

13. The wages people earn are also prices (prices for labor services) and, like other prices, they usually rise as the general level of prices increases. The statement ignores this factor. It implicitly assumes that money wages are unaffected by inflation—that they would have increased by the same amount (6 percent) even if prices would have been stable. Generally, this will not be the case.

CHAPTER 9: AN INTRODUCTION TO BASIC MACROECONOMIC MARKETS

4. When the price level is higher than anticipated, real wages will decline and employment expands. Profit rates will be higher than normal, and the actual rate of unemployment will fall below the natural rate. The abnormally high rate of output will not be sustainable, because the real wage rates will rise when the long-term contracts expire and are renegotiated.

6. An increase in the real interest rate will make it more attractive for foreigners to purchase bonds and make other investments in the United States. As a result, there will be an increase in the inflow of capital from abroad.

10. They are all equal.

12. $10,000; $20,000.

CHAPTER 10: DYNAMIC CHANGE, ECONOMIC FLUCTUATIONS, AND THE AD–AS MODEL

1. Choice (a) would decrease *AD*; (b), (c), and (d) would increase it; and (e) would leave it unchanged. For the "why" part of the question, see the Factors That Shift Aggregate Demand section at the beginning of the chapter.

2. Choices (a), (b), (c), and (d) will reduce *SRAS*; (e) will increase it.

8. Tightness in resource markets will result in rising resource prices relative to product prices, causing the *SRAS* to shift to the left. Profit margins will decline, output rates will fall, and long-run equilibrium will be restored at a higher price level. The above-normal output cannot be maintained because it reflects input prices that people would not have agreed to and output decisions they would not have chosen if they had

anticipated the current price level (and rate of inflation). Once they have a chance to correct these mistakes, they do so; output returns to the economy's long-run potential.

CHAPTER 11: FISCAL POLICY: THE KEYNESIAN VIEW AND HISTORICAL PERSPECTIVE

3. The multiplier principle is the concept that a change in one of the components of aggregate demand—investment, for example—will lead to a far greater change in the equilibrium level of income. Because the multiplier equals $1/(1 - MPC)$, its size is determined by the marginal propensity to consume. The multiplier makes stabilizing the economy more difficult, because relatively small changes in aggregate demand have a much greater effect on equilibrium income.

6. Either an increase in government expenditures or a reduction in taxes should be employed to shift the budget toward a larger deficit (or smaller surplus).

CHAPTER 12: FISCAL POLICY, INCENTIVES, AND SECONDARY EFFECTS

2. The crowding-out effect is the theory that budget deficits will lead to higher real interest rates, which retard private spending. The crowding-out effect indicates that fiscal policy will not be nearly as potent as the simple Keynesian model implies. The new classical theory indicates that anticipation of higher future taxes (rather than higher interest rates) will reduce private spending when government expenditures are financed by debt.

9. In the Keynesian model, investment is determined by factors other than the interest rate. Thus, budget deficits would not exert much effect on capital formation. In the crowding-out model, capital formation would be reduced because the budget deficits would lead to higher interest rates, which would crowd out private investment. In the new classical model, households will save more, and, as a result, budget deficits could be financed without either an increase in the interest rate or a reduction in capital formation.

12. No. If it takes more workers to generate a specific amount of energy with wind power, this implies that wind power is a more costly method of generating energy than either coal or natural gas. Thus, the implications of the statement are exactly the opposite of what the wind energy proponents imply.

CHAPTER 13: MONEY AND THE BANKING SYSTEM

1. A liquid asset is one that can easily and quickly be transformed into money without experiencing a loss of its market value. Assets such as high-grade bonds and stocks are highly liquid. In contrast, illiquid assets cannot be easily and quickly converted to cash without some loss of their value. Real estate, a family-owned business, business equipment, and artistic works are examples of illiquid assets.

3. Money is valuable because of its scarcity relative to the availability of goods and services. The use of money facilitates (reduces the cost of) exchange transactions. Money also serves as a store of value and a unit of account. Doubling the supply of money while holding output constant would simply cause its purchasing power to fall without enhancing the services that it performs. In fact, fluctuations in the money supply generally create uncertainty about the future value of money and thereby reduce its ability to serve as a reliable store of value, accurate unit of account, and medium of exchange for time-dimension contracting.

6. **a.** There is no change; currency held by the public increases, but checking deposits decrease by an equal amount. **b.** Bank reserves decrease by $100. **c.** Excess reserves decrease by $100, minus $100 multiplied by the required reserve ratio.

8. Answers (b), (e), and (f) will reduce the money supply; (a) and (c) will increase it. If the Treasury's deposits (or the deposits of people who receive portions of the Treasury's spending) are considered part of the money supply, then (d) will leave the money supply unchanged.

10. Fed holdings of U. S. government securities and other financial assets have increased by a huge amount since 2009. The Feds purchase and increased holdings of these assets make it easier for the federal government to finance its budget deficits.

11. Since 2008, the Fed has used interest payments to banks as the means of controlling bank reserves. Throughout this era, the bank reserves relative to deposits have been much higher than when the level of reserves were controlled via reserve requirements. Under these circumstances, lowering reserve requirements would exert little or no impact on the reserves held by banks. Thus, the Fed eliminated, at least temporarily, required reserves in March 2020. Even prior to 2008, changes in reserve requirements were seldom used to control the money supply because they were often disruptive of banking operations and the magnitude of their impact on the money supply was less precise than for open market operations.

15. **a.** Money supply increases by $100,000; **b.** $80,000; **c.** $500,000; **d.** no; there will be some leakage in the form of additional currency holdings by the public and additional excess reserve holdings by banks.

CHAPTER 14: MODERN MACROECONOMICS AND MONETARY POLICY

2. Choices (a) and (c) would increase your incentive to hold money deposits; (b) would reduce your incentive to hold money.

3. **a.** The cost of obtaining the house is $100,000. **b.** The cost of holding it is the interest forgone on the $100,000 sales value of the house. **c.** The cost of obtaining $1,000 is the amount of goods one must give up in order to acquire the $1,000. For example, if a pound of sugar sells for 50 cents, the cost of obtaining $1,000 in terms of sugar is 2,000 pounds. **d.** As in the case of the house, the cost of holding $1,000 is the interest forgone.

10. If the time lag is long and variable (rather than short and highly predictable), it is less likely that policy makers will be able to time changes in monetary policy so that they will exert a countercyclical effect on the economy. The policy makers will be more likely to make mistakes and thereby exert a destabilizing influence.

11. Association does not reveal causation. Decision-makers, including borrowers and lenders, will eventually anticipate a high rate of inflation and adjust their choices accordingly. As the expected rate of inflation increases, the demand for loanable funds will increase and the supply will decrease. This will lead to higher nominal interest rates. Thus, economic theory indicates that the causation tends to run the opposite direction from that indicated by the statement.

CHAPTER 15: STABILIZATION POLICY, OUTPUT, AND EMPLOYMENT

2. Compared with earlier periods, the United States has experienced less economic instability since 1960. This has been particularly true during the past twenty-five years. An increase in the stability of monetary policy deserves much of the credit for the more stable economic conditions of recent decades.

5. For (a) and (b), the actual and natural rates of unemployment will be equal. For (c), the actual rate will be less than the natural rate. For (d), the actual rate will exceed the natural rate.

11. **a.** Keep the inflation rate at a low and highly predictable level; **b.** No; **c.** Both nominal interest rates and the general level of prices will rise.

CHAPTER 16: CREATING AN ENVIRONMENT FOR GROWTH AND PROSPERITY

3. The three major sources of economic growth are gains from trade, entrepreneurship, and capital formation. Trade permits the realization of larger outputs because of division of labor, specialization in areas of comparative advantage, and adoption of mass production processes. Entrepreneurial discovery results in new products that are valued highly relative to cost and lower cost production methods. Capital formation provides machines, structures, and human knowledge that make larger future outputs possible.

8. Measurement of the quality of institutions over a lengthy time frame is important because credibility is important. When evaluating the quality of institutions, business decision-makers will want to know if they can count on the current degree of institutional quality in the future. Persistence will enhance their confidence this will be the case. Similarly, it is important to measure the performance of an economy over a lengthy time frame in order to minimize measurement error because of business cycle-related factors.

10. When considering the answer to this question, think about the following: Is there an opportunity cost of the capital used by government firms? Do government firms have a strong incentive to keep costs low? Are government firms innovative?

12. Regulations such as price ceilings, price floors, and mandated product characteristics will generally reduce the volume of gains from trade. Simultaneously, they will encourage rent-seeking activities, which will increase the contributions available to political officials. Policies of this type will reduce economic growth because they will increase the incentive to engage in wasteful rent-seeking activities and reduce the incentive to discover and undertake production of goods and services that are highly valued relative to cost.

CHAPTER 17: THE ECONOMICS OF DEVELOPMENT

8. It is hard to see how the less-developed economies could have grown so rapidly without borrowing technologies and ideas from the high-income countries. The high-income countries also provided both investment capital and markets for the sale of products for the LDCs. Historical growth records buttress this view. The per capita incomes of several economies including Hong Kong, Singapore, South Korea, and China have grown at annual rates of 5 percent or more over periods of twenty-five years or more. Prior to 1960, no country was able to achieve long-term growth anywhere near such a rate. By way of comparison, per capita income in the United Kingdom and the United States grew at an annual rate of approximately 1 percent during the nineteenth century when countries with significantly higher incomes were absent.

10. A country does not have to be democratic in order to be economically free. Hong Kong illustrates this point. Neither does democracy guarantee economic freedom. India was democratic, but it was one of the world's least free economies prior to 1990.

13. Poor economic institutions and policies provide the primary reason.

CHAPTER 18: GAINING FROM INTERNATIONAL TRADE

2. Availability of goods and services, not jobs, is the source of economic prosperity. When a good can be purchased cheaper abroad than it can be produced at home, a nation can expand the quantity of goods and services available for consumption by specializing in the production of those goods for which it is a low-cost producer and

trading them for the cheap (relative to domestic costs) foreign goods. Trade restrictions limiting the ability of Americans to purchase low-cost goods from foreigners stifle this process and thereby reduce the living standard of Americans.

4. Statements (a) and (b) are not in conflict. Because trade restrictions are typically a special-interest issue, political entrepreneurs can often gain by supporting them even when they promote economic inefficiency.

6. True. The primary effect of trade restrictions is an increase in domestic scarcity. This has distributional consequences, but it is clear that, as a whole, a nation will be harmed by the increased domestic scarcity that accompanies the trade restraints.

10. In thinking about this issue, consider the following points. Suppose that the Japanese were willing to give products such as automobiles, electronic goods, and clothing to us free of charge. Would we be worse off if we accepted the gifts? Should we try to keep the free goods out? What is the source of real income—jobs or goods and services? If the gifts make us better off, doesn't it follow that partial gifts would also make us better off?

12. Although trade reduces employment in import-competing industries, it expands employment in export industries. On balance, there is no reason to believe that trade either promotes or destroys jobs. The major effect of trade is to permit individuals, states, regions, and nations to generate a larger output by specializing in the things they do well and trading for those things that they would produce only at a high cost. A higher real income is the result.

16. True. If country A imposes a tariff, other countries will sell less to A and therefore acquire less purchasing power in terms of A's currency. Thus, they will have to reduce their purchases of A's export goods.

CHAPTER 19: INTERNATIONAL FINANCE AND THE FOREIGN EXCHANGE MARKET

4. On February 2, the dollar appreciated against the British pound and depreciated against the Canadian dollar.

5. Scenarios (a) and (g) would cause the dollar to appreciate; (b), (c), (d), (e), and (h) would cause the dollar to depreciate; (f) would leave the exchange rate unchanged.

8. Some people fear that foreign investment makes the United States vulnerable because foreigners might decide to sell their assets and leave suddenly. When you consider this argument, it is important to recognize that foreign and domestic investors are influenced by pretty much the same considerations. Anything that would cause foreigners to withdraw funds would also cause domestic investors to do likewise. In fact, the vulnerability runs the other way. If foreign investors were to leave, the assets financed by their funds would remain. Thus, they would be in a weak position to impose harm on the U.S. economy.

9. Each of the changes would reduce the size of the current-account deficit.

13. False. Flexible exchange rates bring the sum of the current and capital accounts into balance, but they do not necessarily lead to balance for either component.

14. **a.** No. The exchange rate will bring the overall purchases and sales into balance, but there is no reason to expect the imports and exports to any given country to be in balance. **b.** The United States imports large quantities of goods Japan and China produce at a low cost (for example, electronic products, and labor intensive goods like toys and textiles), but it is not a major exporter of goods purchased intensively by these countries (natural resources, building materials, and inexpensive consumer items).

15. These purchases increase the foreign exchange value of the dollar, which makes imports cheaper relative to exports and thereby enlarges the trade deficit. Politicians often charge that this reduces output and employment. However, the bond purchases

are an inflow of capital that will also result in lower U.S. interest rates, which will tend to stimulate output and employment. Thus, there is little reason to believe that the net effect will be either substantial or harmful.

SPECIAL TOPIC 1: GOVERNMENT SPENDING AND TAXATION

1. Taxes reduce economic efficiency because they eliminate some exchanges and thereby reduce the gains from these transactions. Because of (a) the deadweight losses accompanying the elimination of exchanges and (b) the cost of collecting taxes, the costs of additional tax revenue will be greater than the revenue transferred to the government. Studies indicate that it costs between $1.20 and $1.30 for each dollar of tax revenue raised by the government.

5. As we discussed in Chapter 6, the political process works better when there is a close relationship between who pays for and who benefits from government programs. An increase in the number of people who pay no income taxes is likely to weaken this relationship. Whereas those with low incomes pay payroll taxes, the revenues from this tax are earmarked for the finance of the Social Security and Medicare programs. Thus, expansions in government are financed primarily by the personal income tax. In the future, exemption of large numbers of people from this tax is likely to make it more difficult to control the growth of government. If you do not have to help pay for more government spending, why would you oppose it?

SPECIAL TOPIC 2: THE ECONOMICS OF SOCIAL SECURITY

2. The pay-as-you-go Social Security system is facing a crisis because the inflow of tax revenue is insufficient to cover the promised benefits. Although the Social Security Trust Fund has bonds, they are merely an IOU from the Treasury to the Social Security Administration. To redeem these bonds and provide additional funds to finance Social Security benefits, the federal government will have to raise taxes (or pay the interest on additional Treasury bonds it sells), or cut other expenditures, or both. Thus, the presence of the SSTF bonds does not do much to alleviate the crisis.

SPECIAL TOPIC 3: THE STOCK MARKET: ITS FUNCTION, PERFORMANCE, AND POTENTIAL AS AN INVESTMENT OPPORTUNITY

1. History shows that in the U.S. stock market, fairly high returns can be gained at a relatively low risk by people who hold a diverse portfolio of stocks in unrelated industries for a period of twenty years or more. An indexed equity mutual fund is an option that would allow a person to purchase a diverse portfolio while keeping commission costs low.

3. The expectation of high profits in the future drove up the price of the stock, despite the lack of a dividend payment in the early years of the firm. Investors are equally happy with high dividends or the equivalent in rising stock value due to the firm's retaining its profits for further investment.

5. The low and declining interest rates increase the present value of future income generated by stocks, which tends to push stock prices upward. The empirical evidence is consistent with this view. The S&P 500 rose from 1,115 at year end 2009 to 3,231 at year end 2019, an annual rate of increase of 11 percent.

SPECIAL TOPIC 4: KEYNES AND HAYEK: CONTRASTING VIEWS ON SOUND ECONOMICS AND THE ROLE OF GOVERNMENT

1. Keynes is arguing that it does not matter much how the government spends stimulus funds. According to the Keynesian view, the key consideration is to spend the funds so they will generate income for those undertaking the project, and as those funds are spent, a multiple expansion in income and aggregate demand will result.

SPECIAL TOPIC 5: THE 2020 COVID-19 RECESSION: CAUSE, RESPONSE, AND IMPLICATIONS FOR THE FUTURE

1. Individuals working 40 hours per week at $15 per hour would have weekly earnings of $600. If they were living in a state where the unemployment benefits replaced 50 percent of prior earnings, they would receive $300 per week from this source. The $600 per week supplement would increase their replacement income to $900 per week, or $300 more than their prior earnings. Because their replacement income is greater than their earnings from work, their incentive to return to their prior job would be weakened.

8. Output plunged because in an effort to reduce the impact of the COVID-19 virus, governments mandated that people stay at home and banned meetings of more than ten people. This eliminated a huge amount of trade: mutually advantageous exchanges between employees and employers, consumers and businesses, and self-employed contractors and potential customers. Exchange makes larger outputs possible as the result of specialization, division of labor, innovation, and adoption of mass production processes. When exchange is restricted, the gains from these sources are eliminated and output plunges. The sharp reduction in output highlights the importance of gains from trade.

SPECIAL TOPIC 6: THE GREAT RECESSION OF 2008–2009: CAUSES AND RESPONSE

3. The less equity the owner has in his or her house, the more likely he or she will default. This is particularly true in the United States because most home mortgages here are nonrecourse loans: The owner is not responsible for the debt beyond turning the property over to the lender in case of default. The lender has no legal claim on assets of the borrower beyond the asset that was mortgaged. Thus, when the value of a house falls below the outstanding loan, the borrower will often gain by simply abandoning the property. This is precisely what many have done in recent years.

5. The incentive to evaluate the borrower's creditworthiness carefully is reduced. If the mortgage originator had to keep the loan until it was repaid, there would be greater incentive for the lender to evaluate the creditworthiness of the borrower more diligently.

SPECIAL TOPIC 7: LESSONS FROM THE GREAT DEPRESSION

5. The statement reflects a failure to recognize the secondary effects of limiting imports. If we buy less from foreigners, they will have fewer dollars that are required for the purchase of our exports. Therefore, a reduction in imports will also reduce exports and there is no reason to expect any net increase in employment. Instead, trade restraints lead to less output and lower incomes.

GLOSSARY

A

Absolute advantage A situation in which a nation, as the result of its previous experience and/or natural endowments, can produce more of a good (with the same amount of resources) than another nation can.

Activists Economists who believe that discretionary changes in monetary and fiscal policy can reduce the degree of instability in output and employment.

Adaptive-expectations hypothesis The hypothesis that economic decision-makers base their future expectations on actual outcomes observed during recent periods. For example, according to this view, the rate of inflation actually experienced during the past two or three years would be the major determinant of the rate of inflation expected for the next year.

Adjustable rate mortgage (ARM) A home loan in which the interest rate, and thus the monthly payment, is tied to a short-term rate like the one-year Treasury bill rate. Typically, the mortgage interest rate will be two or three percentage points above the related short-term rate. It will be reset at various time intervals (e.g., annually), and thus the interest rate and monthly payment will vary over the life of the loan.

Administrative lag The time period after the need for a policy change is recognized but before the policy is actually implemented.

Aggregate demand curve A downward-sloping curve showing the relationship between the price level and the quantity of domestically produced goods and services all households, business firms, governments, and foreigners (net exports) are willing to purchase.

Aggregate supply curve The curve showing the relationship between a nation's price level and the quantity of goods supplied by its producers. In the short run, it is an upward-sloping curve, but in the long run the aggregate supply curve is vertical.

Alt-A loans Loans extended with little documentation or verification of the borrowers' income, employment, and other indicators of their ability to repay. Because of this poor documentation, these loans are risky.

Anticipated change A change that is foreseen by decision-makers in time for them to make adjustments.

Anticipated inflation An increase in the general level of prices that was expected by most decision-makers.

Appreciation An increase in the value of a currency relative to foreign currencies. An appreciation increases the purchasing power of the currency over foreign goods.

Automatic stabilizers Built-in features that tend automatically to promote a budget deficit during a recession and a budget surplus during an inflationary boom, even without a change in policy.

Average tax rate (ATR) Tax liability divided by taxable income. It is the percentage of income paid in taxes.

B

Balance of merchandise trade The difference between the value of merchandise exports and the value of merchandise imports for a nation. It is also called simply the *balance of trade* or *net exports*. The balance of merchandise trade is only one component of a nation's total balance of payments and its current account.

Balance of payments A summary of all economic transactions between a country and all other countries for a specific time period, usually a year. The balance-of-payments account reflects all payments and liabilities to foreigners (debits) and all payments and obligations received from foreigners (credits).

Balance on current account The import–export balance of goods and services, plus net investment income earned abroad, plus net private and government transfers. If the value of the nation's export-type items exceeds (is less than) the value of the nation's import-type items plus net unilateral transfers to foreigners, a current-account surplus (deficit) is present.

Balance on goods and services The exports of goods (merchandise) and services of a nation minus its imports of goods and services.

Balanced budget A situation in which current government revenue from taxes, fees, and other sources is just equal to current government expenditures.

Bank reserves Vault cash plus deposits of banks with Federal Reserve banks.

Basis points One one-hundredth of a percentage point. Thus, 100 basis points are equivalent to one percentage point.

Black market A market that operates outside the legal system in which either illegal goods or services are sold, or legal ones are sold at illegal prices or terms.

Bond A promise to repay the principal (amount borrowed) plus interest at a specified time in the future. Organizations such as corporations and governments issue bonds as a method of borrowing from bondholders.

Budget deficit A situation in which total government spending exceeds total government revenue during a specific time period, usually one year.

Budget surplus A situation in which total government spending is less than total government revenue during a time period, usually a year.

Business cycle Fluctuations in the general level of economic activity as measured by variables such as the rate of unemployment and changes in real GDP.

C

Capital Human-made resources (such as tools, equipment, and structures) used to produce other goods and services. They enhance our ability to produce in the future.

Capital inflows Sales of real and financial assets to foreigners. This includes real investments such as real estate and factories, and financial or portfolio investments such as stocks and bonds.

Capital outflows Purchases of real and financial assets from foreigners. This includes real investments such as real estate and factories, and financial or portfolio investments such as stocks and bonds.

Capital-account The record of transactions with foreigners that involve either (1) the exchange of ownership rights to real or financial assets or (2) the extension of loans.

Capitalism An economic system in which productive resources are owned privately and goods and resources are allocated through market prices.

Cartel An organization of sellers designed to coordinate supply and price decisions so that the joint profits of the members will be maximized. A cartel will seek to create a monopoly in the market for its product.

Central bank An institution that regulates the banking system and controls the money supply.

Ceteris paribus A Latin term meaning "other things constant" that is used when the effect of one change is being described, recognizing that if other things changed, they also could affect the result. Economists often describe the effects of one change, knowing that in the real world, other things might change and also exert an effect.

Chained consumer price index A measure of the consumer price index that accounts for changes in the market basket of goods bought on a monthly basis rather than on a lagged basis as done with the traditional consumer price index. This change typically reduces the annual inflation rate by 0.2 to 0.3 percentage points.

Choice The act of selecting among alternatives.

Civilian labor force The number of people 16 years of age and older who are either employed or unemployed. To be classified as unemployed, a person must be looking for a job.

Collective decision-making The use of the political process (voting, taxes, government spending, regulation, political bargaining, lobbying, and so on) to make decisions and allocate resources. In a democratic setting, the votes of citizens and their representatives will determine the actions undertaken.

Commercial banks Financial institutions that offer a wide range of services (for example, checking accounts, savings accounts, and loans) to their customers. Commercial banks are owned by stockholders and seek to operate at a profit.

Comparative advantage The ability to produce a good at a lower opportunity cost than others can produce it. Relative costs determine comparative advantage.

Complements Products that are usually consumed jointly (for example, bread and butter, hot dogs and hot dog buns). A decrease in the price of one will cause an increase in demand for the other.

Consumer price index (CPI) An indicator of the general level of prices. It attempts to compare the cost of purchas-ing the market basket bought by a typical consumer during a specific period with the cost of purchasing the same market basket during an earlier period.

Consumer sentiment index A measure of the optimism of consumers based on their responses to a set of questions about their current and expected future personal economic situation.

Conducted by the University of Michigan, it is based on a representative sample of U.S. households.

Consumer surplus The difference between the maximum price consumers are willing to pay and the price they actually pay. It is the net gain derived by the buyers of the good.

Countercyclical policy A policy that tends to move the economy in an opposite direction from the forces of the business cycle. Such a policy would stimulate demand during the contraction phase of the business cycle and restrain demand during the expansion phase.

Creative destruction The replacement of old products and production methods by innovative new ones that consumers judge to be superior. The process generates economic growth and higher living standards.

Credit Funds acquired by borrowing.

Credit unions Financial cooperative organizations of individuals with a common affiliation (such as an employer or a labor union). They accept deposits, including checkable deposits, pay interest (or dividends) on them out of earnings, and lend funds primarily to members.

Crony capitalism A situation where the institutions of markets are maintained, but to a large degree the allocation of resources, and the profit and loss of businesses, are determined by political decision-making rather than consumer purchases and market forces. Many of the business firms will use contributions and other forms of political support to compete for government favors.

Crowding-out effect A reduction in private spending as a result of higher interest rates generated by budget deficits that are financed by borrowing in the private loanable funds market.

Currency Medium of exchange made of metal or paper.

Currency board An entity that (1) issues a currency with a fixed designated value relative to a widely accepted currency (for example, the U.S. dollar), (2) promises to continue to redeem the issued currency at the fixed rate, and (3) maintains bonds and other liquid assets denominated in the other currency that provide 100 percent backing for all currency issued.

Current account The record of all transactions with foreign nations that involve the exchange of merchandise goods and services, current income derived from investments, and unilateral gifts.

Cyclical unemployment Unemployment due to recessionary business conditions and inadequate labor demand.

D

Deadweight loss The loss of gains from trade to buyers and sellers that occurs when a tax is imposed. The deadweight loss imposes a burden on both buyers and sellers over and above the actual payment of the tax.

Demand deposits Non–interest-earning checking deposits that can be either withdrawn or made payable on demand to a third party. Like currency, these deposits are widely used as a means of payment.

Demand for money A curve that indicates the relationship between the interest rate and the quantity of money people want to hold. Because higher interest rates increase the opportunity cost of holding money, the quantity of money demanded will be inversely related to the interest rate.

Democracy A form of political organization in which adult citizens are free to participate in the political process (vote, lobby, and choose among candidates), elections are free and open, and majority voting, either directly or by elected representatives, decides outcomes.

Deposit expansion multiplier The multiple by which an increase in reserves will increase the money supply. It will be larger when banks loan out a larger share of the newly created reserves.

Depository institutions Businesses that accept checking and savings deposits and use a portion of them to extend loans and make investments. Banks, savings and loan associations, and credit unions are examples.

Depreciation (Macro) A reduction in the value of a currency relative to foreign currencies. A depreciation reduces the purchasing power of the currency over foreign goods.

Depreciation (Micro) The estimated amount of physical capital (for example, machines and buildings) that is worn out or used up producing goods during a period.

Depression A prolonged and very severe recession.

Developing countries Countries with stagnating levels of GDP per capita that lagged behind the high-income countries of Western Europe, North America, Oceania, and Japan during the decades following the Industrial Revolution. They are sometimes referred to as less-developed countries.

Discount rate The interest rate the Federal Reserve charges banking institutions for short-term loans.

Discretionary fiscal policy A change, in laws or appropriation levels, that alters government revenues and/or expenditures.

Division of labor A method that breaks down the production of a product into a series of specific tasks, each performed by a different worker.

Dumping Selling a good in a foreign country at a lower price than what it cost to produce, or at a lower price than it's sold for in the domestic market.

E

Earned Income Tax Credit A provision of the tax code that provides a credit or rebate to people with low earnings (income from work activities). The credit is eventually phased out if the recipient's earnings increase.

Economic efficiency A situation in which all of the potential gains from trade have been realized. An action is efficient only if it creates more benefit than cost. With well-defined property rights and competition, market equilibrium is efficient.

Economic freedom Method of organizing economic activity characterized by (1) personal choice, (2) voluntary exchange coordinated by markets, (3) freedom to enter and compete in markets, and (4) protection of people and their property from aggression by others.

Economic theory A set of definitions, postulates, and principles assembled in a manner that makes clear the "cause-and-effect" relationships.

Economizing behavior Choosing the option that offers the greatest benefit at the least possible cost.

Employment/population ratio The number of employed civilians 16 years of age and over divided by the total civilian population 16 years of age and older. The ratio is expressed as a percentage.

Entrepreneur A person who decides what resources will be used, how they will be combined, and what goods and services they will be utilized to produce. Typically, entrepreneurs will undertake these activities within a business enterprise. A successful entrepreneur's actions will increase the value of resources and expand the size of the economic pie.

Equation of exchange $MV = PY$, where M is the money supply, V is the velocity of money, P is the price level, and Y is the output of goods and services produced in an economy.

Equilibrium A state in which the conflicting forces of demand and supply are in balance. When a market is in equilibrium, the decisions of consumers and producers are brought into harmony with one another, and the quantity demanded will equal the quantity supplied.

Equity mutual fund A corporation that pools the funds of investors, including small investors, and uses them to purchase a bundle of stocks.

Excess burden of taxation Another term for deadweight loss. It reflects losses that occur when beneficial activities are forgone because they are taxed.

Excess reserves Actual reserves that exceed the legal requirement.

Exchange rate The price of one unit of foreign currency in terms of the domestic currency. For example, if it takes $1.50 to purchase an English pound, the dollar–pound exchange rate is 1.50.

Expansionary fiscal policy An increase in government expenditures and/or a reduction in tax rates, such that the expected size of the budget deficit expands.

Expansionary monetary policy A shift in monetary policy designed to stimulate aggregate demand. Injection of additional bank reserves, lower short-term interest rates, and acceleration in the growth rate of the money supply are indicators of a more expansionary monetary policy.

Expenditure multiplier The ratio of the change in equilibrium output to the independent change in investment, consumption, or government spending that brings about the change. Numerically, the multiplier is equal to 1 *divided by* (1 − MPC) when the price level is constant.

Exports Goods and services produced domestically but sold to foreigners.

External benefit Spillover effects that generate benefits for nonconsenting parties.

External cost Spillover effects that reduce the well-being of nonconsenting parties.

Externalities Spillover effects of an activity that influence the well-being of nonconsenting parties.

Extreme poverty rate Share of the population with income less than $1.90 per day, measured in 2011 purchasing power parity dollars.

F

Fallacy of composition Erroneous view that what is true for the individual (or the part) will also be true for the group (or the whole).

Federal Deposit Insurance Corporation (FDIC) A federally chartered corporation that insures the deposits held by commercial banks, savings and loans, and credit unions.

Federal Open Market Committee (FOMC) A committee of the Federal Reserve system that establishes Fed policy with regard to the buying and selling of government securities—the primary mechanism used to control the money supply. It is composed of the seven members of the Board of Governors and the twelve district bank presidents of the Fed.

Federal Reserve System The central bank of the United States; it carries out banking regulatory policies and is responsible for the conduct of monetary policy.

Fiat money Money that has neither intrinsic value nor the backing of a commodity with intrinsic value; paper currency is an example.

FICO score A credit score measuring a borrower's likely ability to repay a loan. A person's FICO score will range between 300 and 850. A score of 700 or more indicates that the borrower's credit standing is good. FICO is an acronym for the Fair Isaac Corporation, the creators of the FICO score.

Final market goods and services Goods and services purchased by their ultimate user.

Fiscal policy The use of government taxation and expenditure policies for the purpose of achieving macroeconomic goals.

Fixed exchange rate An exchange rate that is set at a determined amount by government policy.

Flexible exchange rates Exchange rates that are determined by the market forces of supply and demand. They are sometimes called floating exchange rates.

Foreclosure rate The percentage of home mortgages on which the lender has started the process of taking ownership of the property because the borrower has failed to make the monthly payments.

Foreign exchange market The market in which the currencies of different countries are bought and sold.

Fractional reserve banking A system that permits banks to hold reserves of less than 100 percent against their deposits.

Franchise A right or license granted to an individual to market a company's goods or services or use its brand name. The individual firms are independently owned but must meet certain conditions to continue to use the name.

Free riders People who receive the benefit of a good without paying for it. Because it is often virtually impossible to restrict the consumption of public goods to those who pay, these goods are subject to free-rider problems.

Frictional unemployment Unemployment due to constant changes in the economy that prevent qualified unemployed workers from being immediately matched up with existing job openings. It results from imperfect information and search activities related to suitably matching employees with employers.

Full employment The level of employment that results from the efficient use of the labor force taking into account the normal (natural) rate of unemployment due to information costs, dynamic changes, and the structural conditions of the economy. For the United States, full employment is thought to exist when approximately 95 percent of the labor force is employed.

G

GDP deflator A price index that reveals the cost during the current period of purchasing the items included in GDP relative to the cost during a base year (currently 2012). Unlike the consumer price index (CPI), the GDP deflator also measures the prices of capital goods and other goods and services purchased by businesses and governments.

General Agreement on Tariffs and Trade (GATT) An organization formed after World War II to set the rules for the conduct of international trade and reduce trade barriers among nations.

Goods and services market A highly aggregated market encompassing the flow of all final-user goods and services. The market counts all items that enter into GDP. Thus, real output in this market is equal to real GDP.

Government failure A situation in which the structure of incentives is such that the political process, including democratic political decision-making, will encourage individuals to undertake actions that conflict with economic efficiency.

Gross domestic product (GDP) The market value of all final goods and services produced within a country during a specific period.

Gross national product (GNP) The total market value of all final goods and services produced by the citizens of a country. It is equal to GDP minus the net income of foreigners.

I

Impact lag The time period after a policy change is implemented but before the change begins to exert its primary effects.

Import quota A specific limit or maximum quantity (or value) of a good permitted to be imported into a country during a given period.

Imports Goods and services produced by foreigners but purchased by domestic consumers, businesses, and governments.

Index of leading indicators An index of economic variables that historically has tended to turn down prior to the beginning of a recession and turn up prior to the beginning of a business expansion.

Indexed equity mutual fund An equity mutual fund that holds a portfolio of stocks that matches their share (or weight) in a broad stock market index such as the S&P 500. The overhead of these funds is usually quite low because their expenses on stock trading and research are low.

Indirect business taxes Taxes that increase a business firm's costs of production and, therefore, the prices charged to consumers. Examples are sales, excise, and property taxes.

Industrial Revolution Development of machines and improvements in technology beginning around 1800 that propelled increases in output and rising income levels.

Inflation An increase in the general level of prices of goods and services. The purchasing power of the monetary unit, such as the dollar, declines when inflation is present.

Inflationary premium A component of the money interest rate that reflects compensation to the lender for the expected decrease, due to inflation, in the purchasing power of the principal and interest during the course of the loan. It is determined by the expected rate of future inflation.

Innovation The successful introduction and adoption of a new product or process; the economic application of inventions and marketing techniques.

Institutions The legal, regulatory, and social constraints that affect the security of property rights and enforcement of contracts. They exert a major impact on the incentive to engage in productive activities, innovate, and realize gains from trade, particularly when the trading partners do not know each other.

Intermediate goods Goods purchased for resale or for use in producing another good or service.

International Monetary Fund (IMF) An international banking organization, currently with more than 185 member nations, designed to oversee the operation of the international monetary system. Although it does not control the world supply of money, it does hold currency reserves for member nations and makes currency loans to national central banks.

Invention The creation of a new product or process, often facilitated by the knowledge of engineering and science.

Inventory investment Changes in the stock of unsold goods and raw materials held during a period.

Investment The purchase, construction, or development of resources, including physical assets, such as plants and machinery, and human assets, such as better education. Investment expands an economy's resources. The process of investment is sometimes called capital formation.

Investment bank An institution that acts as an underwriter for securities issued by other corporations or lenders. Unlike traditional banks, investment banks do not accept deposits from, or provide loans to, individuals.

Invisible hand principle The tendency of market prices to direct individuals pursuing their own interests to engage in activities promoting the economic well-being of society.

L

Labor force participation rate The number of people in the civilian labor force 16 years of age or older who are either employed or actively seeking employment as a percentage of the total civilian population 16 years of age and over.

Laffer curve A curve illustrating the relationship between the tax rate and tax revenues. Tax revenues will be low at both very high and very low tax rates. When tax rates are quite high, lowering them can increase tax revenue.

Law of comparative advantage A principle that states that individuals, firms, regions, or nations can gain by specializing in the production of goods that they produce cheaply (at a low opportunity cost) and exchanging them for goods they cannot produce cheaply (at a high opportunity cost).

Law of demand A principle that states there is an inverse relationship between the price of a good and the quantity of it buyers are willing to purchase. As the price of a good increases, consumers will wish to purchase less of it. As the price decreases, consumers will wish to purchase more of it.

Law of supply A principle that states there is a direct relationship between the price of a good and the quantity of it producers are willing to supply. As the price of a good increases, producers will wish to supply more of it. As the price decreases, producers will wish to supply less.

Less-developed countries Countries with low per capita incomes, low levels of education, widespread illiteracy, and widespread use of production methods that are largely obsolete in high-income countries. They are sometimes referred to as developing countries.

Leverage ratios The ratio of loans and other investments to the firm's capital assets.

Liquid asset An asset that can be easily and quickly converted to money without loss of value.

Loanable funds market A general term used to describe the market that coordinates the borrowing and lending decisions of business firms and households. Commercial banks, savings and loan associations, the stock and bond markets, and insurance companies are important financial institutions in this market.

Logrolling The exchange between politicians of political support on one issue for political support on another.

Loss A deficit of sales revenue relative to the opportunity cost of production. Losses are a penalty imposed on those who produce goods even though they are valued less than the resources required for their production.

M

M1 (money supply) The sum of (1) currency in circulation (including coins), and (2) checkable deposits maintained in depository institutions.

M2 (money supply) Equal to M1 plus (1) savings deposits, (2) time deposits (accounts of less than $100,000) held in depository institutions, and (3) money market mutual fund shares.

Macroeconomics The branch of economics that focuses on how human behavior affects outcomes in highly aggregated markets, such as the markets for labor or consumer products.

Malthusian trap Theory that income per person can never rise much above subsistence level, because if it does, population will grow rapidly and soon drive the income per person back to the subsistence level.

Managed equity mutual fund An equity mutual fund that has a portfolio manager who decides what stocks will be held in the fund and when they will be bought or sold. A research staff generally provides support for the fund manager.

Marginal Term used to describe the effects of a change in the current situation. For example, a producer's marginal cost is the cost of producing an additional unit of a product, given the producer's current facility and production rate.

Marginal propensity to consume (MPC) Additional current consumption divided by additional current disposable income.

Marginal tax rate (MTR) The additional tax liability a person faces divided by his or her additional taxable income. It is the percentage of an extra dollar of income earned that must be paid in taxes. It is the marginal tax rate that is relevant in personal decision-making.

Market An abstract concept encompassing the forces of demand and supply and the interaction of buyers and sellers with the potential for exchange to occur.

Market failure A situation in which the structure of incentives is such that markets will encourage individuals to undertake activities that are inconsistent with economic efficiency.

Market organization A method of organization in which private parties make their own plans and decisions with the guidance of unregulated market prices. The basic economic questions of consumption, production, and distribution are answered through these decentralized decisions.

Medium of exchange An asset that is used to buy and sell goods or services.

Microeconomics The branch of economics that focuses on how human behavior affects the conduct of affairs within narrowly defined units, such as individual households or business firms.

Middlemen People who buy and sell goods or services or arrange trades. A middleman reduces transaction costs.

Minimum wage Legislation requiring that workers be paid at least the stated minimum hourly rate of pay.

Moderate poverty rate Share of the population with income less than $3.20 per day, measured in 2011 purchasing power parity dollars.

Monetary base The sum of currency in circulation plus bank reserves (vault cash and reserves with the Fed). It reflects the purchases of financial assets and extension of loans by the Fed.

Monetary policy The deliberate control of the money supply, and, in some cases, credit conditions, for the purpose of achieving macroeconomic goals.

Money interest rate The percentage of the amount borrowed that must be paid to the lender in addition to the repayment of the principal. The money interest rate overstates the real cost of borrowing during an inflationary period. When inflation is anticipated, an inflationary premium will be incorporated into this rate. The money interest rate is often called the nominal interest rate.

Money market mutual funds Interest-earning accounts that pool depositors' funds and invest them in highly liquid short-term securities. Because these securities can be quickly converted to cash, depositors are permitted to write checks (which reduce their share holdings) against their accounts.

Money supply The supply of currency, checking account funds, and traveler's checks. These items are counted as money because they are used as the means of payment for purchases.

Mortgage default rate The percentage of home mortgages on which the borrower is late by ninety days or more with the payments on the loan or it is in the foreclosure process. This rate is sometimes referred to as the serious delinquency rate.

Mortgage-backed securities Securities issued for the financing of large pools of mortgages. The promised returns to the security holders are derived from the mortgage interest payments.

Multiplier principle The concept that an increase in spending on a project will generate income for the resource suppliers, who will then increase their consumption spending. In turn, their additional consumption will generate income for others and lead to still more consumption. As this process goes through successive rounds, total income will expand by a multiple of the initial increase in spending.

N

National debt The sum of the indebtedness of the federal government in the form of outstanding interest-earning bonds. It reflects the cumulative impact of budget deficits and surpluses.

National income The total income earned by a country's nationals (citizens) during a period. It is the sum of employee compensation, self-employment income, rents, interest, and corporate profits.

Natural rate of unemployment The "normal" unemployment rate due to frictional and structural conditions in labor markets. It is the unemployment rate that occurs when the economy is operating at a sustainable rate of output. The current natural rate of unemployment in the United States is thought to be approximately 5 percent.

Net exports Exports minus imports.

Net income of foreigners The income that foreigners earn by contributing labor and capital resources to the production of goods within the borders of a country minus the income the nationals of the country earn abroad.

New classical economists Economists who believe that there are strong forces pushing a market economy toward full-employment equilibrium and that macroeconomic policy is an ineffective tool with which to reduce economic instability.

Nominal GDP GDP expressed at current prices. It is often called money GDP.

Nominal values Values expressed in current dollars.

Nonactivists Economists who believe that discretionary macro policy adjustments in response to cyclical conditions are likely to increase, rather than reduce, instability. Nonactivists favor steady and predictable policies regardless of business conditions.

Normative economics Judgments about "what ought to be" in economic matters. Normative economic views cannot be proved false because they are based on value judgments.

O

Objective A fact based on observable phenomena that is not influenced by differences in personal opinion.

Official reserve account The record of transactions among central banks.

Open market operations The buying and selling of U.S. government securities and other financial assets in the open market by the Federal Reserve.

Opportunity cost The highest valued alternative that must be sacrificed as a result of choosing an option.

Opportunity cost of production The total economic cost of producing a good or service. The cost component includes the opportunity cost of all resources, including those owned by the firm. The opportunity cost is equal to the value of the production of other goods sacrificed as the result of producing the good.

Other checkable deposits Interest-earning deposits that are also available for checking.

P

Paradox of thrift The idea that when many households simultaneously try to increase their saving, actual saving may fail to increase because the reduction in consumption and aggregate demand will reduce income and employment.

Pegged exchange rate system A commitment to use monetary and fiscal policy to maintain the exchange rate value of the domestic currency at a fixed rate or within a narrow band relative to another currency (or bundle of currencies).

Per capita GDP Income per person. Increases in income per person are vital for the achievement of higher living standards.

Personal consumption Household spending on consumer goods and services during the current period. Consumption is a flow concept.

Personal retirement account (PRA) An account that is owned personally by an individual in his or her name. The funds in the account could be passed along to heirs.

Phillips curve A curve that illustrates the relationship between the rate of inflation and the rate of unemployment.

Pork-barrel legislation A package of spending projects bundled into a single bill. It is often used as a device to obtain funding for a group of projects intensely desired by regional or interest groups that would be unlikely to pass if voted on separately.

Portfolio All the stocks, bonds, or other securities held by an individual or corporation for investment purposes.

Positive economics The scientific study of "what is" among economic relationships.

Potential deposit expansion multiplier The maximum potential increase in the money supply as a ratio of the new reserves injected into the banking system. If the newly created reserves are all held as bank deposits rather than currency and banks loan out all of their excess reserves, it will be equal to the inverse of the required reserve ratio.

Potential output The level of output that can be achieved and sustained in the future, given the size of the labor force, its expected productivity, and the natural rate of unemployment consistent with the efficient operation of the labor market. Actual output can differ from the economy's potential output.

Price ceiling A legally established maximum price sellers can charge for a good or resource.

Price controls Government-mandated prices that are generally imposed in the form of maximum or minimum legal prices.

Price floor A legally established minimum price buyers must pay for a good or resource.

Primary market The market in which financial institutions aid in the sale of new securities.

Private investment The flow of private-sector expenditures on durable assets (fixed investment) plus the addition to inventories (inventory investment) during a period. These expenditures enhance our ability to provide consumer benefits in the future.

Private property rights Property rights that are exclusively held by an owner and protected against invasion by others. Private property can be transferred, sold, leased, or mortgaged at the owner's discretion.

Privately held government debt The portion of the national debt owed to domestic and foreign investors. It does not include bonds held by agencies of the federal government or the Federal Reserve.

Producer surplus The difference between the price that suppliers actually receive and the minimum price they would be willing to accept. It measures the net gains to producers and resource suppliers from market exchange. It is not the same as profit.

Production possibilities curve A curve that outlines all possible combinations of total output that could be produced, assuming (1) a fixed amount of productive resources, (2) a given amount of technical knowledge, and (3) full and efficient use of those resources. The slope of the curve indicates the amount of one product that must be given up to produce more of the other.

Productivity The average output produced per worker during a specific time period. It is usually measured in terms of output per hour worked.

Profit An excess of sales revenue relative to the opportunity cost of production. The cost component includes the opportunity cost of all resources, including those owned by the firm. Therefore, profit accrues only when the value of the good produced is greater than the value of the resources used for its production.

Progressive tax A tax in which the average tax rate rises with income. People with higher incomes will pay a higher percentage of their income in taxes.

Property rights The rights to use, control, and obtain the benefits from a good or resource.

Proportional tax A tax in which the average tax rate is the same at all income levels. Everyone pays the same percentage of income in taxes.

Public goods Goods for which rivalry among consumers is absent and exclusion of nonpaying customers is difficult.

Public-choice analysis The study of decision-making as it affects the formation and operation of collective organizations, like governments. In general, the principles and methodology of economics are applied to political science topics.

Purchasing power parity (PPP) method Method in which the relative purchasing power of each currency is determined by comparing the amount of each currency required to purchase a common bundle of goods and services in the domestic market. This information is then used to convert the GDP of each nation to a common monetary unit like the U.S. dollar.

Q

Quantity theory of money A theory that hypothesizes that a change in the money supply will cause a proportional change in the price level because velocity and real output are unaffected by the quantity of money.

Quartile A quarter (25 percent) of a group. The quartiles are often arrayed on the basis of an indicator like income or degree of economic freedom.

R

Random walk theory The theory that current stock prices already reflect known information about the future. Therefore, the future movement of stock prices will be determined by surprise occurrences. This will cause them to change in a random fashion.

Rational ignorance effect Because it is highly unlikely that an individual vote will decide the outcome of an election, a rational individual has little or no incentive to search for and acquire the information needed to cast an informed vote.

Rational-expectations hypothesis The hypothesis that economic decision-makers weigh all available evidence, including information concerning the probable effects of current and future economic policy, when they form their expectations about future economic events (such as the probable future inflation rate).

Rationing Allocating a limited supply of a good or resource among people who would like to have more of it. When price performs the rationing function, the good or resource is allocated to those willing to give up the most "other things" in order to get it.

Real GDP GDP adjusted for changes in the price level.

Real interest rate The interest rate adjusted for expected inflation: It indicates the real cost to the borrower (and yield to the lender) in terms of goods and services.

Real values Values that have been adjusted for the effects of inflation.

Recession A downturn in economic activity characterized by declining real GDP and rising unemployment. In an effort to be more precise, many economists define a recession as two consecutive quarters in which there is a decline in real GDP.

Recognition lag The time period after a policy change is needed from a stabilization standpoint but before the need is recognized by policy-makers.

Regressive tax A tax in which the average tax rate falls with income. People with higher incomes will pay a lower percentage of their income in taxes.

Rent-seeking Actions by individuals and groups designed to restructure public policy in a manner that will either directly or indirectly redistribute more income to themselves or the projects they promote.

Repeat-purchase items An item purchased often by the same buyer.

Required reserves The minimum amount of reserves that a bank is required by law to keep on hand to back up its deposits. If reserve requirements were 15 percent, banks would be required to keep $150,000 in reserves against each $1 million of deposits.

Required reserve ratio The ratio of reserves relative to a specified liability category (for example, checkable deposits) that banks are required to maintain.

Resource An input used to produce economic goods. Land, labor, skills, natural resources, and human-made tools and equipment provide examples. Throughout history, people have struggled to transform available, but limited, resources into things they would like to have—economic goods.

Restrictive fiscal policy A reduction in government expenditures and/or an increase in tax rates such that the expected size of the budget deficit declines (or the budget surplus increases).

Restrictive monetary policy A shift in monetary policy designed to reduce aggregate demand and put downward pressure on the general level of prices (or the rate of inflation). A reduction in bank reserves, higher short-term interest rates, and a reduction in the growth rate of the money supply are indicators of a more restrictive monetary policy.

Ricardian equivalence The view that a tax reduction financed with government debt will exert no effect on current consumption and aggregate demand because people will fully recognize the higher future taxes implied by the additional debt.

Rule of 70 If a variable grows at a rate of x percent per year, $70/x$ will approximate the number of years required for the variable to double.

S

Saving (Macro) The portion of after-tax income that is not spent on consumption. Saving is a "flow" concept.

Savings and loan institutions Financial institutions that accept deposits in exchange for shares that pay dividends. Historically, these funds were channeled into residential mortgage loans, but today they offer essentially the same services as a commercial bank.

Scarcity Fundamental concept of economics that indicates that there is less of a good freely available than people would like.

Scientific thinking Developing a theory from basic principles and testing it against events in the real world. Good theories are consistent with and help explain real-world events. Theories that are inconsistent with the real world are invalid and must be rejected.

Secondary effects The indirect impact of an event or policy that may not be easily and immediately observable. In the area of policy, these effects are often both unintended and overlooked.

Secondary market The market in which financial institutions aid in the buying and selling of existing securities.

Secondary mortgage market A market in which mortgages originated by a lender are sold to another financial institution. In recent years, the major buyers in this market have been Fannie Mae, Freddie Mac, and large investment banks.

Security rating A rating indicating the risk of default of the security. A rating of AAA indicates that the risk of default is low.

Shortage A condition in which the amount of a good offered for sale by producers is less than the amount demanded by buyers at the existing price. An increase in price would eliminate the shortage.

Shortsightedness effect The misallocation of resources that results because public-sector action is biased (1) in favor of proposals yielding clearly defined current benefits in exchange for difficult-to-identify future costs and (2) against proposals with clearly identifiable current costs that yield less concrete and less obvious future benefits.

Socialism A system of economic organization in which (1) the ownership and control of the basic means of production rest with the state and (2) resource allocation is determined by centralized planning rather than by market forces.

Special-interest issue An issue that generates substantial individual benefits to a small minority while imposing a small individual cost on many other citizens. In total, the net cost to the majority might either exceed or fall short of the net benefits to the special-interest group.

Stock options The option to buy a specified number of shares of the firm's stock at a designated price. The designated price is generally set so that the options will be quite valuable if the firm's shares increase in price but of little value if their price falls. Thus, when used to compensate top managers, stock options provide a strong incentive to follow policies that will increase the value of the firm.

Stock Ownership shares of a corporation. Corporations raise funds by issuing stock ownership shares, which entitle the owners to a proportional share of the firm's profits. The stock owners are not liable for the debts of the corporation beyond their initial investment. However, there is no assurance that the owners will receive either their initial investment or any return in the future.

Store of value An asset that will allow people to transfer purchasing power from one period to the next.

Structural unemployment Unemployment due to the structural characteristics of the economy that make it difficult for job seekers to find employment and for employers to hire workers. Although job openings are available, they generally require skills many unemployed workers do not have.

Subjective An opinion based on personal preferences and value judgments.

Subprime loan A loan made to a borrower with blemished credit or one who provides only limited documentation of income, employment history, and other indicators of creditworthiness.

Subsidy A payment the government makes to either the buyer or the seller, usually on a per-unit basis, when a good or service is purchased or sold.

Substitutes Products that serve similar purposes. An increase in the price of one will cause an increase in demand for the other (examples are hamburgers and tacos, butter and margarine, Chevrolets and Fords).

Supply shock An unexpected event that temporarily increases or decreases aggregate supply.

Supply-side economists Economists who believe that changes in marginal tax rates exert important effects on aggregate supply.

Surplus A condition in which the amount of a good offered for sale by producers is greater than the amount that buyers will purchase at the existing price. A decline in price would eliminate the surplus.

T

Tariff A tax levied on goods imported into a country.

Tax base The level or quantity of an economic activity that is taxed. Higher tax rates reduce the level of the tax base because they make the activity less attractive.

Tax incidence The way the burden of a tax is distributed among economic units (consumers, producers, employees, employers, and so on). The actual tax burden does not always fall on those who are statutorily assigned to pay the tax.

Tax rate The per-unit amount of the tax or the percentage rate at which the economic activity is taxed.

Technological advancement The introduction of new techniques or methods that increase output per unit of input.

Technology The technological knowledge available in an economy at any given time. The level of technology determines the amount of output we can generate with our limited resources.

Telemedicine Medical service provided by telephone or video hookup between patient and doctor rather than via patient visit to a doctor's office or clinic.

Trade deficit The situation when a country's imports of goods and services are greater than its exports.

Trade openness Situation where the residents of a country are permitted to trade freely with foreigners. Trade restrictions such as tariffs, quotas, restrictions on the convertibility of currency, and other political roadblocks limiting international trade are largely absent.

Trade surplus The situation when a country's exports of goods and services are greater than its imports.

Transaction costs The time, effort, and other resources needed to search out, negotiate, and complete an exchange.

Transfer payments Payments to individuals or institutions that are not linked to the current supply of a good or service by the recipient.

Transportation-Communication Revolution Large reductions in transportation and communication costs that propelled higher growth rates of GDP per capita beginning around 1970. The acceleration of economic growth in developing countries was particularly strong.

U

Unanticipated change A change that decision-makers could not reasonably foresee. The choices they made prior to the change did not take it into account.

Unanticipated inflation An increase in the general level of prices that was not expected by most decision-makers.

Underground economy Unreported barter and cash transactions that take place outside recorded market channels. Some are otherwise legal activities undertaken to evade taxes. Others involve illegal activities, such as trafficking drugs and prostitution.

Unemployed The term used to describe a person not currently employed who is either (1) actively seeking employment or (2) waiting to begin or return to a job.

Unemployment rate The percentage of unemployed people in the labor force. Mathematically, it is equal to the number of people unemployed divided by the number of people in the labor force.

Unfunded liability A shortfall of tax revenues at current rates relative to promised benefits for a program. Without an increase in tax rates, the promised benefits cannot be funded fully.

Unit of account A unit of measurement used by people to post prices and keep track of revenues and costs.

User charges Payments users (consumers) are required to make if they want to receive certain services provided by the government.

Utility The subjective benefit or satisfaction a person expects from a choice or course of action.

V

Velocity of money The average number of times a dollar is used to purchase final goods and services during a year. It is equal to GDP divided by the stock of money.

Virtuous cycle of development The reduction in the birth rate, slower population growth, and increase in the share of population in the prime working-age categories that generally provide a boost to productivity and economic growth once per capita GDP begins to grow. This pattern is nearly always observed soon after a country begins the growth process.

W

World Trade Organization (WTO) The new name given to GATT in 1994; the WTO is currently responsible for monitoring and enforcing multilateral trade agreements among its 164 member countries.

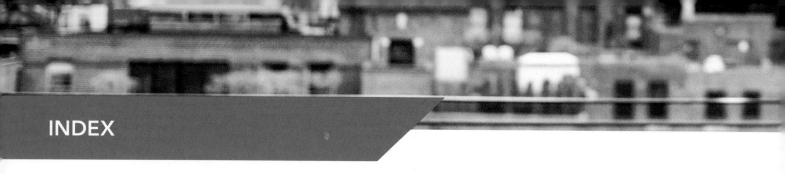

INDEX

Note: Page numbers followed by "*n*" indicate notes and "e" indicate exhibit.